The American School:

A GLOBAL CONTEXT FROM THE PURITANS TO THE OBAMA ERA

EIGHTH EDITION

Joel Spring
Queens College
City University of New York

Mc Graw Hill
Connect
Learn
Succeed™

KH

THE AMERICAN SCHOOL: A GLOBAL CONTEXT FROM THE PURITANS TO THE OBAMA ERA, EIGHTH EDITION

Published by McGraw-Hill, a business unit of The McGraw-Hill Companies, Inc., 1221 Avenue of the Americas, New York, NY 10020. Copyright © 2011 by The McGraw-Hill Companies, Inc. All rights reserved. Previous editions © 2008, 2005, and 2001. No part of this publication may be reproduced or distributed in any form or by any means, or stored in a database or retrieval system, without the prior written consent of The McGraw-Hill Companies, Inc., including, but not limited to, in any network or other electronic storage or transmission, or broadcast for distance learning.

Some ancillaries, including electronic and print components, may not be available to customers outside the United States.

This book is printed on acid-free paper.

1 2 3 4 5 6 7 8 9 0 DOC/DOC 1 0 9 8 7 6 5 4 3 2 1 0

ISBN 978-0-07-809784-3
MHID 0-07-809784-3

Vice President & Editor-in-Chief: *Michael Ryan*
Vice President EDP/Central Publishing Services: *Kimberly Meriwether David*
Publisher: *David Patterson*
Sponsoring Editor: *Allison McNamara*
Managing Editor: *Meghan Campbell*
Executive Marketing Manager: *Pamela S. Cooper*
Project Manager: *Erin Melloy*
Buyer: *Kara Kudronowicz*
Design Coordinator: *Margarite Reynolds*
Manager, Photo Research: *Brian Pecko*
Cover Credit: Left to right: © *Bettmann/CORBIS; Library of Congress Prints and Photographs Division; AFP/Getty Images*
Media Project Manager: *Sridevi Palani*
Compositor: *Laserwords Private Limited*
Typeface: *10/12 Times Roman*
Printer: *R. R. Donnelley*

All credits appearing on page or at the end of the book are considered to be an extension of the copyright page.

Library of Congress Cataloging-in-Publication Data

Spring, Joel H.
    The American school : a global context from the puritans to the Obama era/Joel Spring.—8th ed.
        p. cm.
    Includes bibliographical references and index.
    ISBN 978-0-07-809784-3 (alk. paper)
        1. Education—United States—History. 2. Education—Social aspects—United States—History. 3. United States—Politics and government—21st century. I. Title.
    LA205.S64 2010
    370.973—dc22

                                          2010010898

www.mhhe.com

2/28/12

ABOUT THE AUTHOR

JOEL SPRING received his Ph.D. in educational policy studies from the University of Wisconsin. He is currently a professor at Queens College of the City University of New York. His major research interests are the history of education, multicultural education, Native American culture, the politics of education, global education, and human rights education. He is the author of many books. The most recent are *How Educational Ideologies Are Shaping Global Society; Education and the Rise of the Global Economy; The Universal Right to Education: Justification, Definition, and Guidelines; Globalization and Educational Rights; Educating the Consumer Citizen: A History of the Marriage of Schools, Advertising, and Media; A New Paradigm for Global School Systems: Education for a Long and Happy Life;* and *Globalization of Education: An Introduction.*

CONTENTS

LIST OF TIME LINES

PREFACE

This eighth edition of *The American School* places its development in a global context. Early American colonies were part of a process of globalization of education that started with European voyages of discovery in the fifteenth century. European colonialists with their accompanying missionaries spread around the world their cultures and educational institutions. In North American colonies, the British transplanted their education ideals and tried to use education to change the culture and beliefs of Native Americans.

In the nineteenth century United States and European models of mass public education began to spread around the world. In addition, the increasing pace of global migration ensured the growth of educational credentials that were transnational. Global migration also resulted in issues regarding the education of multicultural populations. By the late twentieth century most of the world's nations had adopted the Western educational ladder of primary, middle, and secondary schools leading to higher education and the American invention of the age-graded classroom. By the twenty-first century most nations of the world, including the United States, had the educational objective of preparing students to work in a global economy. The globalization of similar school systems made it possible for global educational industries to develop such as textbook publishing, testing companies, and educational software and information corporations.[i]

Changes in the eighth edition of *The American School* focus on the process of educational globalization and the development of American schools in a global context. These changes include the following:

- Chapter 1
  - New section discussing the globalization framework.
  - Edited and focused on global context.

- Chapter 2
  - Edited with the colonial period framed as part of the process of globalization initiated by European voyages of discovery.

- Chapter 3
  - Added discussion of world culture theorists who argue that Western-style mass public education became globalized as a result of the spread of constitutional governments similar to that in the United States.

---

[i]For a study of the globalization of education, see Joel Spring, *Globalization of Education: An Introduction* (New York: Routledge, 2009).

- Chapters 4 and 5
  - Edited for clarity.

- Chapter 6
  - New focus on the features of nineteenth-century American schools that were globalized.

- Chapter 8
  - New focus on educational globalization.
  - Edited for clarity.

- Chapter 9
  - New focus on the globalization of human capital ideas developed in the United States in the late nineteenth and early twentieth centuries.

- Chapter 10
  - New focus on the development of scientific management of schools in the early twentieth century as a prelude to the Obama era.

- Chapters 11 and 12
  - Edited for clarity.

- Chapter 13
  - New focus and addition of material on educational globalization.
  - New title reflecting global focus: "American Schools and Global Politics: The Cold War and Poverty."

- Chapter 15
  - New chapter: "Globalizing the American School: From Nixon to Obama."

1

Thinking Critically about History

My goal in this book is to provide varied views of educational history as a means of sparking critical thinking about history and schools. Consequently I provide throughout the text a variety of interpretations of American school history ranging from conservative to leftist. Like historians who weave together the drama of the past, consumers of history have their own political and social opinions that they impose on historical events. Readers should ask themselves how their personal beliefs determine their interpretations of historical events.

This chapter discusses

- Interpreting school history—from the right to the left.
- Purposes of educational history and its effect on public images and emotions regarding schools.
- Themes in American educational history.
- A globalization framework.
- The effect of cultural and religious differences on schools.
- Schools as managers of public ideas.
- Racial and ethnic conflict as a theme in school history.
- The role in educational history of equality of opportunity and human capital.
- Consumer and environmental education.

INTERPRETING SCHOOL HISTORY: FROM THE RIGHT TO THE LEFT

Is there a correct interpretation of historical events? A correct and precise historical interpretation is often difficult to arrive at because of the wide range of lives and events during any particular period. For instance, we know there was an eighteenth-century American Revolution against England, which had a profound effect on the development of schools. But why was there a revolution? What did people in the colonies think about the revolution? What were the concerns of European settlers, Native Americans, and enslaved Africans concerning the Revolutionary War? What was the effect of American independence on educational development? These and a host of other questions are debated among historians, with answers often reflecting the political and social opinions of particular historians.

Many readers of history assume there is a correct interpretation of history. This attitude often reflects the study of a single standardized American history text in elementary and high school. History is often presented to young students within a single interpretative framework with little suggestion of the existence of alternative historical interpretations.

Consider the debate, which I discuss in Chapters 4 and 5, over why public schools were created in the 1830s and 1840s. Historians might agree on dates and personalities involved in historical events, but they might not agree about motives. Were public schools established to ensure that all citizens would be able to protect their political and economic rights? Were public schools established to protect the power of an elite by controlling the economic and political ideas taught to students? Were public schools established to ensure the dominance of Protestant Anglo-American culture over Native American, Irish American, and African American cultures? Were public schools necessary to ensure the education of the whole population? These questions, which have been asked at the creation and expansion of public schools, raise issues that are debated in the writing of history.

Historical debates about schools continue in current educational concerns. Today a concern, as in the nineteenth century, is about whether schools can end poverty. Many other debates from the nineteenth century are reflected in today's struggles over educational policy. Should public school curricula attempt to promote a single national culture or a multicultural society? What social and political values should be taught in public schools? Should public schools supplant parental power, or should parents be given a wide variety of choices such as home schooling and alternative institutions? Will education produce any answers to global economic competition? Should public schools teach values that might conflict with home values? What knowledge is most worth teaching? Through intellectual dialogue about historical interpretations, readers should be able to clarify their opinions about educational institutions and about the relationship of education to other institutions and to social events.

PURPOSES OF EDUCATIONAL HISTORY AND ITS EFFECT ON PUBLIC IMAGES AND EMOTIONS REGARDING SCHOOLS

History can serve multiple purposes. It can be read and taught to establish or strengthen a person's identification with a nation, community, family, ethnic group, religion, or other social group. Or it can serve a moral purpose by condemning or praising certain historical events. History can be approached analytically, wherein the historian or student tries to discern why historical events took place. And finally, history can serve social and political purposes such as creating loyalty to a government or preparing citizens to actively participate in social change. The history of American schools can serve all these purposes.[1]

This book emphasizes an analytical approach with the goal of educating a reader who will have the knowledge to actively participate in improving educational policies. This analytical approach encompasses issues of both identity and moral judgments. Regarding identity, after reading this book, school staff, students, parents, and other citizens should be able to walk through an American school and identify the historical origins of present school practices. Sometimes there is a gasp of recognition by a student of school history: "Oh, that's why the schools do that!" Consequently, readers who have attended or are working in American schools might find their identity with American schools strengthened. "Whenever we hear that history 'tells us who we are,'" write Keith Barton and Linda Levstik in their study of the variety of reasons for teaching history, "we are dealing with some version of the identification stance."[2] In other words, current conditions can be seen as mirroring past events.

There is also a moral element to an analytical approach that can leave readers with mixed feelings about the past. A reader might approve of certain aspects of school history, such as educating the informed voter, providing equal opportunity in the labor market, improving public health practices, or fighting crime. On the other hand, a reader might find other aspects of school history morally offensive, such as the denial of education to enslaved Africans, the attempt to use education to destroy Native American cultures, the Protestant religious bias of early public schools, or racial segregation.

In other words, the history of American schools will cause mixed emotional responses. It is not just a history of heroic and triumphant accomplishments. Yes, some people dedicated themselves to schooling the public for the common good. But others believed schooling could serve their own personal or group interests by educating compliant workers and voters, destroying cultures and languages, and perpetuating their own power.

The answers to historical questions have implications for a person's future choices and actions. The answers shape images and feelings about the past. Many people do not remember the details of history, but they develop images and emotions about past events. For instance, the attitudes and feelings about public schools of a person who concludes that public schools were established to protect the political and economic rights of citizens will be quite different from the attitudes of a person who concludes that public schools were established to protect the political and economic power of an elite. Or if a person concludes that the establishment of public schools was necessary for the education of all children, then that person's attitudes regarding privatization of schools will be quite different from those of someone who concludes the opposite.

Thinking about history involves an intellectual consideration of conflicting interpretations, emotions, and images of public schools. For example, at an early age a person might be taught a history that is designed to foster an emotional attachment, in the form of patriotism, to the political and economic organization of the United States. Later in life this person's emotional feelings about the United States might be challenged if the person reads a critical history.

One's knowledge, images, and emotions regarding the past have an impact on future actions. Individuals often make decisions based on what they believe to be the historical purposes and goals of an institution. The various interpretations presented in this book give readers an opportunity to think about past events in a manner that might influence their future actions. As suggested, these differing interpretations might elicit conflicting feelings of approval, outrage, or disbelief. Readers will probably be supportive of interpretations that support their own social and political values.

THEMES IN AMERICAN EDUCATIONAL HISTORY

Though this book contains a variety of historical interpretations, it is dominated by what *I* consider to be important historical themes. No historian can write about all the events and actions of a population in a given day or century. Historical writers must report events they think are important. Therefore, I have selected certain themes that I consider important in the history of schooling. These themes are my interpretative perspective.

Consequently, I have written thematic chapters rather than a purely sequential account. Because many of the chapters are thematic and cover similar periods, at various places in the book I provide time lines to help the reader understand the sequencing of events. In the remainder of this chapter I will elaborate on the following historical themes:

- *Globalization:* Both the colonization of North America and the development of American schools occurred and continue to occur within the framework of a global society.
- *Conflict:* A major part of the history of U.S. schools involves conflicts over culture and religion. Racial and ethnic conflict are also central issues in U.S. history and in educational history.
- *Ideological management:* Schools are among the many institutions that attempt to manage the distribution of ideas in society.
- *Immigration:* Educating immigrant populations has been a central concern of American schools.
- *Economic goals:* These have been central to the evolution of U.S. schools.
- *Consumerism and environmental education:* These are pressing issues in the evolution of human society.

GLOBALIZATION FRAMEWORK

The development of American education was part of European imperialism, which involved not only the colonization of the Americas but also European expansion into Africa, Asia, and other parts of the world.[3] In their quest for control of foreign lands, the imperial powers attempted to impose their schools, culture, and languages on local populations. Education as a form of cultural imperialism was aided by Christian missionaries who spread European ideas about schooling and culture.

In North American colonies missionaries hoped to use education to convert Native Americans to Christianity, which, it was hoped by some, would aid in the conquest of America's indigenous peoples. After the American Revolution, some American leaders called for a nationalistic education that would define the United States' identity and role in a global system of nations. With the advent of the common school period in the nineteenth century, U.S. educators traveled to Europe to learn about educational systems. Many of the ideas learned abroad were incorporated into the U.S. school system. Today there is a continuing global exchange of educational ideas and policies.

The global movement of people has been central to American school policies from the early colonization of the Americas and the massive immigration of the late nineteenth to early twentieth centuries to today's global movement of people. Schools have been considered central to the assimilation of new populations into American culture. Of course, this has sparked debates about what should be the culture and language of schooling.

Today school policies are framed in the language of global economic competition. Good schools are considered by many to be essential for ensuring American power in a world economic system. Human capital economics now dominates discussions of school reform. The promise of human capital economics is that investment in schools will result in better workers who will ensure economic growth. It is difficult to separate discussions of U.S. schools from those related to global education policies.

THE EFFECT OF CULTURAL AND RELIGIOUS DIFFERENCES ON SCHOOLS

The multicultural nature of the U.S. population has sparked struggles over which cultural and religious values should be taught by public schools. In the early years, public schools functioned to ensure the domination of a Protestant Anglo-American culture in the United States.[4] But as immigration increased from non-Protestant countries and minority cultures struggled for recognition, the schools became a battleground over multicultural education. Should schools support minority languages and cultures? Should schools support only English as the national language and only something called "American culture"? Should immigrants be Americanized in the schools, or should the schools support immigrant cultures and a pluralistic society?

These questions can cause emotional reactions. "They should all become Americans," one person might angrily proclaim about immigrants, while another with equal emotional fervor might glorify the image of an American society that is multilingual and multicultural. Readers of this book will have differing reactions to cultural and language issues.

"Culture wars"—the term originated in the work of Ira Shor—are a distinguishing characteristic of American history.[5] English colonists declared their superiority over Native American cultures and attempted to impose their culture on

Native Americans. Finding English culture to be exploitative and repressive, Native Americans resisted attempts by colonists to transform their cultures. The hope of the leaders of the newly formed U.S. government was to create a national culture that would be unified around Protestant Anglo-American values. One reason for the nineteenth-century development of public schools was to ensure the dominance of Anglo-American values that were being challenged by Irish immigration, Native Americans, and African Americans. Public schools became defenders of Anglo-American values with each new wave of immigrants. In the twentieth century, the culture wars were characterized by Americanization programs, civil rights movements demanding representation of minority cultures in public schools, and the multicultural debate.

The concept of cultural perspective is important for understanding culture wars. For instance, in the late eighteenth and early nineteenth centuries, some Native Americans decided that literacy might be an important tool for protecting their tribal lands and culture. In contrast, many whites considered the education of Native Americans to be a means of acquiring Native American lands and transforming Native American cultures. This difference in perspective resulted both in major misunderstandings and in a cultural war that continues to the present.

The mixture of cultures in the United States has resulted in the necessity of constantly asking, How do other cultures perceive this event? In the nineteenth century, many Irish Catholics believed the public schools were attempting to destroy the Catholic faith. In the twentieth and twenty-first centuries, some religious groups protested the teaching of evolutionary theory and claimed that the secular values of schooling were undermining the morality of the nation. In the twentieth century, many educators thought that the development of separate curriculum tracks in high school served individual differences. In contrast, many African Americans, Mexican Americans, and Native Americans considered separate curriculum tracks to be another means of providing them with an inferior education.

SCHOOLS AS MANAGERS OF PUBLIC THOUGHT

The culture wars are one aspect of what I call *ideological management*. Ideological management involves the creation and distribution of knowledge in a society. Schools play a central role in distributing knowledge to a society. Public schools were established to distribute knowledge to children and youth. Because knowledge is not neutral, a continuing debate exists about the political, social, and economic content of schooling. There is a heated debate over the content and purpose of multicultural education in public schools. How this debate is decided has important implications for shaping a student's perspective on the nature of society and politics in the United States.[6]

Recent historical interpretations stress the importance of the influence of different political and economic groups on the content of knowledge and the cultural values distributed by schools. In the same fashion, political and economic pressures influence the knowledge and cultural values distributed by sources other than educational institutions. Ideological management refers to the effect of these political and economic forces on the ideas disseminated to society.

I include mass media along with public schools as important managers of ideas and cultural values disseminated to children and youth. Consequently, this book includes sections on the development of movies, radio, and television. In the twenty-first century, the media are considered the third educator of children along with schools and the family. Schools and the media compete for influence over children's minds and national culture.

In the framework of ideological management, an important question is this: What should be the culture or cultures of the public school curriculum? Should the population of the United States be united by a single culture, or should the United States be composed of distinct cultural traditions? What would North America be like today if English colonists had adopted the cultural values of Native Americans?

RACIAL AND ETHNIC CONFLICT AS A THEME IN SCHOOL HISTORY

Certainly, a major strand of American history has been the quest for democracy and equality. However, another strand dating from the first arrival of English settlers has been characterized by claims of racial and cultural superiority. The most violent and troubled parts of American history have resulted from the clash between racism and demands for equality, including

- Almost 1 million dead from the U.S. Civil War.
- The Trail of Tears covered by the bodies of European Americans and Native Americans who died as a result of the Indian wars that began with the arrival of the first European settlers and lasted through the nineteenth century.
- The lynching and beating of Chinese Americans in nineteenth-century California.
- The killing and beating of enslaved Africans.
- The lynching and beating of African Americans during Reconstruction and segregation periods in the South.
- Race riots in northern cities in the nineteenth and twentieth centuries.
- The murder and beating of Mexican Americans during the "Zoot Suit" riots in 1943.
- The murders, riots, and church bombings during the civil rights struggles of the 1950s and 1960s.
- The continuing quest in the twenty-first century to reduce the achievement gaps among racial and ethic groups.

Violence and racism are a basic part of American social and school history. From colonial times to today, educators have preached equality of opportunity and good citizenship while engaging in acts of religious intolerance, racial segregation, cultural genocide, and discrimination against immigrants and nonwhites. Schooling has been plagued by scenes of violence, including

- Urban riots between Protestants and Catholics in the nineteenth century.
- The punishment of enslaved African Americans for learning to read.
- Racial clashes over the education of African Americans, Asians, Native Americans, and Mexican Americans.
- Riots and killings over the integration of schools from the 1950s to the 1970s.

From colonial times to the present, racism and ethnic and religious intolerance have been part of the beliefs in republicanism, democracy, and equality held by *some*—I emphasize the word *some*—Americans of European descent. This intertwining of what on the surface appear to be contradictory beliefs has been a major tragedy and a deep flaw, from my perspective, in the unfolding history of the United States and American schools. For some Americans, racism and democracy are not conflicting beliefs but are part of a general system of American values.

Rogers Smith contends in *Civic Ideals,* his massive and award-winning study of U.S. citizenship, that most historians neglect the importance of racist viewpoints in the forming of U.S. laws. As Smith demonstrates, U.S. history has been characterized by a long tradition of discrimination and bigotry. After evaluating the combination of legal restrictions on voting rights and immigration and naturalization laws, Smith concludes that "for over 80 percent of U.S. history, American laws declared most people in the world legally ineligible to become U.S. citizens solely because of their race, original nationality, or gender. For at least two-thirds of American history, the majority of the domestic adult population was also ineligible for full citizenship for the same reasons."[7]

Understanding how republicanism, democracy, and equality are compatible with racism and religious intolerance in some people's minds is key to understanding American violence and the often tragic history of education. However, I want to emphasize that many Americans of European descent have fought against racism and religious bigotry. For those believing in racial equality, the European Americans who were abolitionists and civil rights advocates are the real exemplars of democracy and equality in American history.

THE ROLE IN EDUCATIONAL HISTORY OF EQUALITY OF OPPORTUNITY AND HUMAN CAPITAL

With the founding of common schools in the early nineteenth century, education was hailed as a means of ending poverty, providing equal opportunity, and increasing national wealth. These grandiose claims continued into the twentieth century with a strong emphasis on schools selecting students and preparing them for different segments of the labor market. Standardized tests, ability grouping in elementary school classrooms, and the separation of high school students into differing educational programs ranging from college preparatory to vocational training were considered important components in linking schools to the economy.

In the 1960s, many people believed that the educational components of the federal government's so-called War on Poverty were the key to ending poverty. These War on Poverty programs included Head Start, compensatory programs in reading and math, and the television program *Sesame Street.* In the 1970s, the magic bullet for the economy was "career education." Different from vocational education, career education involved the actual study of jobs. Career education appeared in schools in the form of career education fairs, actual career education courses, career counselors, and classroom literature containing job descriptions. In the 1980s, many corporate and government leaders blamed schools for the declining ability of the United States to compete in the world economy. During the 1980s and 1990s, a major goal of public schools became the education of workers who would increase the ability of U.S. corporations to dominate world markets.

Throughout all these periods debates continued about the purposes of these goals and whether they were attainable. Were some people arguing that schools could eliminate poverty because they did not want to change the economic system? Did the schools become a scapegoat for the continuing existence of poverty? Could public schools actually end poverty? Did attempts to end poverty through schooling ensure economic inequality? Were lower wages, increased profits, and control of workers the real reasons why politicians and corporate leaders wanted schools to educate students to meet the needs of the labor market? How did education for the labor market affect citizenship education? Whose values dominated citizenship education? Should students be educated to help U.S. corporations dominate world markets?

These debates have a central role in shaping the destiny of U.S. schools. Consequently, my framework for interpreting educational history includes—along with cultural domination, ideological management, and racism—a discussion of economic issues. However, the final decision about the meaning of history belongs to the reader.

CONSUMER AND ENVIRONMENTAL EDUCATION

In the 1970s, the consumerist ideology that dominated American education in the twentieth century was criticized because of the environmental damage it was causing. Consumerism, an economic philosophy born in the 1890s, assumes that the ideal economic system is one that continually grows and develops new products. In this framework, the key to economic growth is the endless consumption of new industrial products. Late-nineteenth-century economists worried that industrial efficiency would reduce the time people spent working and that the result would be social decay as people searched for ways of utilizing greater leisure time. The antidote to the potentially decadent world of leisure time was the idea that people should be spurred to work harder to consume more goods. Home economics instruction in public schools played a major role in introducing women to the ideology of a consumer society. In addition, children and particularly high school students were considered an important consumer market. The word *teenager* was created to define these new adolescent consumers.

Environmental educators have called for a shift from an "industrial–consumer" paradigm to a biospheric paradigm. The biospheric paradigm considers the earth and all species of animals and plants as an interrelated and dependent system. Sustainable development and sustainable consumption are now the goals of many environmental educators as they try to limit the damage caused by consumerist ideology. In schools in the twenty-first century there is a struggle between commercial interests that continue to promote consumerism and environmental educators and students who are thinking within the biospheric paradigm.[8]

Notes

1. For a perspective on differing reasons for studying history, see Keith Barton and Linda Levstik, *Teaching History for the Common Good* (Mahwah, NJ: Lawrence Erlbaum, 2004).
2. Ibid., p. 45.
3. For a history of the globalization of education, see Joel Spring, *Pedagogies of Globalization: The Rise of the Educational Security State* (Mahwah, NJ: Lawrence Erlbaum, 2006).
4. My views of multicultural history were influenced by Ronald Takaki's *A Different Mirror: A History of Multicultural America* (Boston: Little, Brown, 1993) and the research I did for my book *The Cultural Transformation of a Native American Family and Its Tribe, 1763–1995: A Basket of Apples* (Mahwah, NJ: Lawrence Erlbaum, 1996).
5. Ira Shore, *Cultural Wars: School and Society in the Conservative Restoration, 1969–1984* (Boston: Routledge & Kegan Paul, 1986).
6. As an example of this debate, see Catherine Cornbleth and Dexter Waugh's *The Great Speckled Bird: Multicultural Politics and Education Policymaking* (Mahwah, NJ: Lawrence Erlbaum Associates, 1995).
7. Rogers Smith, *Civic Ideals: Conflicting Visions of Citizenship in U.S. History* (New Haven, CT: Yale University Press, 1997), p. 15.
8. See Joel Spring, *Educating the Consumer-Citizen: A History of the Marriage of Schools, Advertising, and Media* (Mahwah, NJ: Lawrence Erlbaum, 2003).

2

Globalization and Religion in Colonial Education

The Americas were part of the expanding educational and cultural exchanges during the era of globalization sparked by European voyages of discovery beginning in the fifteenth century. By the twentieth century, Western forms of schooling had spread around the world as European colonies girdled the globe with colonial settlements in Africa, Asia, the Americas, the Middle East, and the South Pacific. Wherever they went, European colonialists assumed the role of cultural imperialists trying to replace what they considered inferior local cultures with European traditions.

Another important factor in the global spread of Western schooling was that European colonialists in Africa, Asia, and the Americas feared a loss of their own cultural traditions. Wherever they settled, Europeans established schools and religious institutions to maintain their cultural traditions. The process of globalization led to a global movement of cultural influences.

By the twenty-first century most nations of the world had organized their school systems along American and European lines, with grades leading from primary to middle to secondary schools to universities and other postsecondary institutions. Most people had accepted the fact of a common global school organization and found nothing peculiar in international organizations reporting school attendance and graduation rates according to the same grade levels.

In the nineteenth century the United States would play a major role in creating a global model of mass schooling as the country developed its public education system. British colonialists in North America set the stage for the development of U.S. public schools as an institution to create a national culture and instill a public morality.

This chapter will examine the cultural and educational impact of British colonialism, including

- Education and culture in colonial society.
- Different historical interpretations of colonial education.
- The role of colonial education in protecting authority and social status.
- Colonial educational policies.
- Issues of language and education in the colonies.
- Colonial education of African and Native Americans.
- Academies and secular education.

- Benjamin Franklin and education for social mobility.
- The colonial families and children.

EDUCATION AND CULTURE
IN COLONIAL SOCIETY

Colonialists believed that Native Americans would benefit from having their cultures and religions supplanted by British culture and Christianity. "Come over and help us," a Native American was depicted as saying while standing as the central figure on the seal of the Governor and Company of Massachusetts Bay, 1629. This figure held an arrow in one hand and a bow in the other; a band of leaves covered his midsection.[1] Undoubtedly, English colonists sincerely believed they were bringing a superior culture to a "heathen" and "uncivilized" people. This seal symbolized the feelings of cultural superiority.

North American colonialists were surprised by Native American resistance. Native Americans did not rush to accept the offer of religious and cultural conversion. Native Americans responded by offering food and aid, which made it possible for the Europeans to survive and expand, while the Native Americans experienced the catastrophic effects of European-introduced diseases. For Native Americans, the primary problem presented by the European invasion was physical and cultural survival. Frequently, this meant warfare or finding a means of protecting cultural traditions while adapting to the social and economic changes brought by Europeans.

For English colonists, the cultural resistance of Native Americans was an affront to the teachings of Christ and a hindrance to colonial expansion. Motivated by sincere religious convictions and a belief in the superiority of English culture, European Americans engaged in an educational crusade to turn "heathen" and "uncivilized" Indians into models of Protestant and English culture.

It is my hypothesis that the educational crusade for the religious and cultural conversion of Native Americans contributed to the nineteenth-century vision of the public school as the primary means for ending crime, poverty, and social and political conflict. As I will argue in later chapters, there was little difference in the minds of nineteenth-century Protestant public school advocates between "savage" Indians, unrepentant criminals, the rebellious poor, and the "heathen" Irish Catholic immigrants. In fact, the English and Protestant sense of cultural and moral superiority originally developed during the twelfth-century English invasion of Ireland. Many English colonialists likened the "savage" Indian to the "savage" Irish.[2]

The 1629 seal of the Governor and Company of Massachusetts Bay also symbolizes to many historians the colonial dedication to education and the establishment of schools. Traditionally, the educational policies of the Massachusetts Bay Colony have been considered the precursors to the development of public schooling in the United States and to the belief that public schools could end crime, eliminate poverty, provide equal opportunity, improve the economy, train workers, and create social and political stability. This belief in the power of schooling set the agenda for educational discussions throughout the twentieth century.

Therefore, I am beginning the story of the American school by focusing on the educational policies of the New England colonies. This discussion will provide a necessary background for understanding the development of public schools.

THE ROLE OF EDUCATION
IN COLONIAL SOCIETY

Colonial education illustrates some important social functions of education. In the seventeenth and eighteenth centuries, education in colonial New England was used to maintain the authority of the government and religion. People were taught to read and write so they could obey the laws of the state and religion. A just society was to result from inculcating religious commandments and teaching obedience to civil law.

In addition, education in the colonies helped maintain social distinctions. For many, learning Latin and Greek in grammar schools or with tutors and attendance at a college was a means of maintaining or gaining elite status. For others, attending an academy was the key to social mobility. From the seventeenth century to present times, there has been a continuous debate over the role of schools in creating social classes and providing social mobility.

Also, education was increasingly considered a means of improving the material prosperity of society. In the seventeenth and eighteenth centuries, some colonialists and Europeans believed that scientific research would improve the quality of life for all people. They believed that the key to scientific research was freedom of thought and the freedom to pursue any form of inquiry. In England, the quest for intellectual freedom resulted in the establishment of academies that eventually were transplanted to the American colonies.

The concern about the advancement of science and intellectual freedom raised issues regarding the control of education. As I will discuss in this chapter, some people argued that intellectual freedom could be achieved only by separating schools from religious organizations and the government. It was argued that government-supported church schools primarily taught obedience to God and the state, and consequently limited freedom of thought. Others argued that any control by government over education would result in despotism over the mind and a limitation of free inquiry because government officials would always use education to support their own power. The concern about freedom of thought sparked debates about whether education should be secular and controlled by government. Similar debates about the role of education in providing material benefits to society and the control of schools continue to present times.

Colonial education also illustrates the relationship between education and concepts of the child and family. Throughout the history of education, concepts

TIME LINE OF COLONIAL EDUCATION

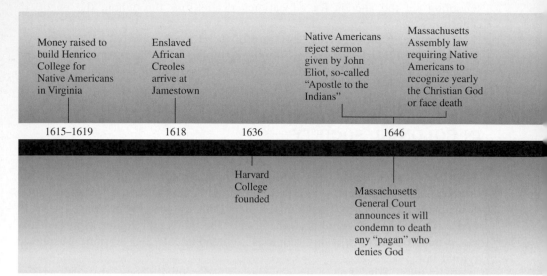

Money raised to build Henrico College for Native Americans in Virginia

Enslaved African Creoles arrive at Jamestown

Native Americans reject sermon given by John Eliot, so-called "Apostle to the Indians"

Massachusetts Assembly law requiring Native Americans to recognize yearly the Christian God or face death

1615–1619   1618   1636   1646

Harvard College founded

Massachusetts General Court announces it will condemn to death any "pagan" who denies God

of childhood and youth have played important roles in determining methods of instruction. A child who is thought of as being born good is treated quite differently from one who is considered to be born evil. The authoritarian quality of colonial education reflected an authoritarian family structure and a belief that the inherent evil of childhood needed to be controlled.

The effort to change Native American cultures was a prelude to future debates about multicultural education. The issue would gain added importance with the seventeenth-century arrival of enslaved Africans. Schools would continue to play a leading role in attempting to unify indigenous and immigrant populations.

In summary, these themes in colonial education continue to the present:

- Education is still considered, by some, to be a means of preparing children to obey government laws.
- Education is still consider a social panacea that will eliminate crime, immorality, and poverty.
- Education is still considered, by some, to be a means of maintaining social class differences.
- Education is still considered a source of social mobility.
- Education still must address cultural differences.

My discussion will begin with education's role in maintaining authority and social differences in colonial New England. This will be followed by an examination of educational policies and efforts to educate Native Americans. Throughout this chapter, I will be relating these themes to different historical interpretations of the colonial period. A goal of this book is to help readers understand the importance of a historian's interpretation of our images of the past. Different

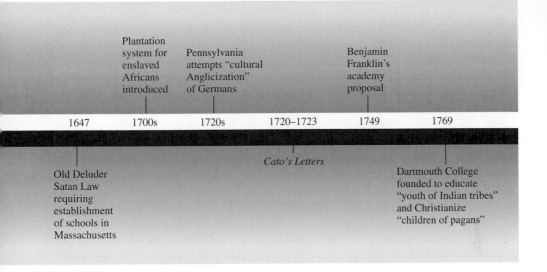

historians have emphasized different themes in interpreting the development of colonial education.

HISTORICAL INTERPRETATIONS OF COLONIAL EDUCATION

Historians have differing interpretations of the importance and meaning of colonial education for the later development of public schools. The importance of religion in New England colonies has led some historians to emphasize the Protestant nature of colonial education and the effect of that legacy on the development of public schools in the nineteenth century. The following paragraphs discuss some of the differing interpretations of the meaning of colonial education for the future.

Historian Carl Kaestle argues that the Protestant–Calvinist nature of colonial education strongly influenced the development of public schools in the nineteenth century.[3] As a result, Catholic groups in the nineteenth century rebelled against the Protestant quality of public schools and established their own school system, and in the nineteenth and twentieth centuries Catholics referred to public schools as Protestant schools. Even recently, after Bible reading and school prayer were banned by the U.S. Supreme Court, many religious groups continued to protest the loss of traditional Christian morality in public schools.

Ellwood Cubberley argues that colonial schools were eventually transformed from instruments of religion to servants of the state.[4] "The first schools in America were clearly the fruits of the Protestant Revolts in Europe," Cubberley wrote. And of all the Protestant groups that settled in colonial America, according to Cubberley, "the Puritans [Calvinists] who settled New England contributed most that was valuable for our future educational development."[5]

In contrast to Cubberley, Rush Welter argues that the religious and authoritarian qualities of New England schools cannot be found in the public schools of the nineteenth and twentieth centuries. He believes there was no continuity of development between colonial schools and public schools in the nineteenth century. He argues that the public school movement of the nineteenth century resulted from a desire to educate citizens for a democratic society. Welter finds little in colonial education that contributes to a democratic theory of education, and he views colonial education as a "false start from which it was necessary to turn away before education could become a key principle of democratic faith."[6] According to Welter, colonial education was oriented toward teaching respect for authority and maintaining the existing social and religious order. This orientation was contrary, in his opinion, to the later educational emphasis on preparing citizens for independent democratic behavior.

Merle Curti, in *The Social Ideas of American Educators,* identifies two distinct schemes of education in the colonies. One served the elite, which included merchants, planters, clergy, and lawyers. The other scheme served the rest of the population. In the southern colonies, he argues, the class system was most in evidence; there the children of the rich were educated by private tutors or attended private schools while other children received only a minimal education. In New England, the class distinctions began in the reading-and-writing schools: The children of the elite attended private dame schools, and the children of the poor attended the town schools. The sharpest distinction was between children in apprenticeship and those attending grammar schools and colleges. The majority of boys were placed into apprenticeship, but the sons of the elite were sent to grammar schools and then to college.[7]

AUTHORITY AND SOCIAL STATUS IN COLONIAL EDUCATION

Although differences in historical interpretations of colonial education exist, no one denies the important role of religion and authority. When the Puritans settled in the Massachusetts Bay Colony in the 1630s, they believed they were creating a model religious community. Early Puritan leader John Winthrop told his fellow colonists in 1630, "We must consider that we shall be as a city upon a hill, the eyes of all people are upon us."[8] Their goal was to create the "good society," which meant a well-ordered religious society that would win God's approval and be used as a model by the rest of the world.

Within the context of the Massachusetts Bay Colony's attempt to create a model religious commonwealth, education was considered essential to maintaining religious piety and social stability. The purpose of teaching reading and writing was to ensure not only that individuals read the Bible and religious tracts, but also that they became good workers and obeyed the laws of the community. These educational goals were explicitly given in the earliest colonial law regarding education, the Massachusetts Law of 1642. This law opens with a general complaint about the neglect of parents and masters in the training of children in learning and labor and calls for the appointment of individuals to investigate the ability of children "to read and understand the principles of religion and the capital laws of this country."[9]

The religious theme received even greater emphasis five years later in the "Old Deluder Satan Law," enacted in 1647 in Massachusetts. This law became famous because it required communities to establish and support schools. Specifically, the law required any community having at least fifty households to appoint a teacher to provide instruction in reading and writing and any community of one hundred or more households to establish a grammar school. The law opens with the famous words, "It being the chief project of old deluder, Satan, to keep men from the knowledge of the Scriptures. . . . It is therefore ordered. . . ."[10]

Several important points about these two laws should be noted. The first is the reference to masters and parents. In both the colonies and England, some children were apprenticed to a master for seven years. During the apprenticeship, the master had the responsibility for ensuring that the apprentice learned to read and write. The shortage of labor in the colonies often led to a shortening of the apprenticeship period and to the neglect by masters and parents of their obligation to provide instruction. Both laws were intended to correct this neglect. Second, both laws made a distinction between instruction in reading-and-writing schools and in grammar schools. Unlike reading-and-writing schools, grammar schools provided primarily instruction that prepared their students for college and for leadership positions.

When historians argue that colonial schools perpetuated the existing social order, what they have in mind are the implications of the distinctions among apprenticeship, reading-and-writing schools, and grammar schools. Merle Curti argues that colonial education as an instrument for preserving existing economic and social arrangements was rooted in European traditions. In England, for instance, the sons of the nobility were educated in the well-endowed public schools, while the well-to-do middle class studied at the local grammar schools. The vast number of children of the poor were apprenticed, and the minimal instruction they received in reading and writing was for the purpose of maintaining religious conformity and the power of existing authority.

In New England as well as in the other colonies, Curti argues, the identity of interests between the dominant religious group and the ruling authorities was even closer than in Europe, which resulted in education protecting the existing authority structure. As was stated earlier, the minimal instruction in reading and writing given to apprentices was solely for the purpose of teaching religious conformity and conveying an understanding of the laws of the colony. In Curti's words, "Apprentices were taught to respect their superiors and the sons of their superiors who were conning Latin verbs and acquiring the other requisites of the culture and polish that characterized the class to which they belonged."[11]

To understand Curti's argument, the history of reading and writing instruction and the development of grammar schools must be examined. The primary content in colonial reading and writing instruction was religious and moral, whereas the grammar schools emphasized Latin and Greek as part of a Renaissance concept of the educated person.

Both reading-and-writing schools and grammar schools were products of an educational revolution that had swept England in the sixteenth century. This revolution embodied the emphasis of the Protestant Reformation on the individual's responsibility to know the word of God and learn proper religious behavior. Reading-and-writing schools, often called petty schools, concentrated on teaching reading, with some teaching of writing and ciphering. This instruction took place in a variety of settings including households, churches, and schools. Instruction was conducted by means of a hornbook—a piece of wood with a thin layer of horn on top bearing the letters of the alphabet and a brief prayer. A majority of these schools were conducted by a single master or mistress.

A popular form of the petty school in the colonies was the dame school for neighborhood children. The dame school was often conducted in the kitchen or living room of the teacher's home. These schools gave instruction primarily in reading and writing, whereas writing schools provided a more advanced level of instruction in writing and also instruction in arithmetic and the simple elements of merchants' accounts. Instruction in these schools became a prerequisite for admission to grammar school.

The content of instruction in the petty schools was primarily religious and authoritarian. The best example of this is *The New England Primer,* which became the most popular text for primary instruction.[12] The content of *The New England Primer* reflects the strong religious and authoritarian nature of colonial education. It opens with the alphabet and a guide to spelling. This section is followed by the short statement, "Now the child being entered in his letters and spelling, let him learn; these and such like sentences by heart, whereby he will be both instructed in his duty and encouraged in his learning." The authoritarian context of the child's duty is presented in the first lines of the following verse, which the student was required to memorize:

> I will fear God, and honour the KING.
> I will honour my Father & Mother.
> I will obey my Superiors.
> I will Submit to my Elders.

After that verse comes "An Alphabet of Lessons for Youth"—an alphabetic listing of statements containing religious and moral maxims that the student was required to memorize:

> A wise son makes a glad Father, but a foolish son is the heaviness of his Mother.
> Better is little with the fear of the Lord, than great treasure and trouble therewith.
> Come unto CHRIST all ye that labour and are heavy laden, and He will give you rest.

That list is followed by the Lord's Prayer, the Creed, the Ten Commandments, a section called "Duty of Children towards Their Parents," a list of the books of the Old and New Testaments, and a list of numbers. Numbers are introduced with the statement, "The numeral letters and figures, which serve for the ready finding of any Chapter, Psalm and Verse in the Bible." After the section on numbers comes a long exhortation given by John Rogers to his nine children in 1554 at the time the entire family was burned at the stake. The *Primer* ends with the Shorter Catechism.

A catechism is a series of questions with a set of correct answers. The child was required to memorize both the questions and the answers. The catechism in *The New England Primer* provided lessons in the basic tenets of Protestant faith. It opens with the question "What is the chief end of Man?" This question was to be answered, "Man's chief end is to glorify God, and to enjoy him forever." The next question is this:

Q: What rule hath God given to direct us how we may glorify and enjoy him?
A: The Word of God, which is contained in the Scriptures of the Old and New
    Testament, is the only Rule to direct us how we may glorify and enjoy him.

The catechism then takes the student through a series of religious lessons to a final question on the meaning of the conclusion of the Lord's Prayer.[13]

After reading *The New England Primer,* it is not difficult to understand why a historian like Rush Welter would consider colonial education a false start on the road to a democratic education. The content of colonial education emphasized not only submission to authority but also a particular method of instruction. Students were required to memorize the entire text. The method used to teach reading and writing was not one that taught individuals to give direction to their own lives, but one by which individuals would learn to submit to the laws of religion and the government. Students were not asked to analyze and give their opinions about religious texts; they were taught to accept official interpretations as correct.

At this point in the history of education, this method of instruction and the content covered were part of a worldview whose adherents believed the good society could be achieved only through obedience to the word of God. In other words, educational practices were consistent with the philosophy and organization of society at that time. It is important to understand the continuity in history. For example, in the nineteenth century the most important schoolbook was Noah Webster's spelling book, which shares many characteristics of *The New England Primer.*

The grammar school provided a strikingly different type of education than the reading-and-writing schools did. The purpose of the grammar school, in contrast to that of the petty school, was to educate the leaders of society. For instance, the typical goal of the grammar school was stated by the Hopkins Grammar School at New Haven in 1684 as "[the education] of hopeful youth in the Latin tongue, and other learned languages so far as to prepare such youths for the college and public service of the country in church and commonwealth."[14]

Historian Lawrence Cremin, in his monumental study *American Education: The Colonial Experience, 1607–1783,* links the development of grammar schools to the Renaissance ideal of the educated public leader. During the Renaissance in the sixteenth century, intellectual leaders began to argue for the proper education of future leaders as a means of creating the just society. Foremost among these thinkers was Desiderius Erasmus, who in the early sixteenth century wrote a treatise titled *The Education of the Christian Prince.* This work calls for the education of a just and wise prince through the study of the Scriptures and the selected works of Plutarch, Seneca, Aristotle, Cicero, and Plato. Of great importance to the development of grammar schools is the emphasis on the study of classical Greek and Roman writers, which would, it was believed, lead to the development of civic character and prepare students for leadership.

Cremin argues that it was a logical step for the middle class in England to see the type of education proposed by Renaissance writers such as Erasmus as a method of enhancing the social status of the middle class. This argument highlights an important distinction between education as a means of conferring status and education as a means of confirming status. In the education of a prince, the status of the prince is confirmed by the type of education he receives. But the same type of education would enhance the social position of the middle class and confer an improved status.[15]

Confirming social status means education is used to maintain the existing status of a person. *Conferring* social status means education improves the social status of the individual.

Therefore, the grammar school became an important institution in England and the colonies for conferring status on the middle class. This represented a great shift in the role of education—one that would have lasting results. First, by conferring status, education assumed the role of providing upward mobility. By the nineteenth century, increasing numbers of individuals began turning to education as a means of enhancing their social status.

The typical grammar school provided a seven-year education with major emphasis on the study of Latin and minor emphasis on Greek and Hebrew. Remember that the purpose of classical education in the grammar school was to provide instruction in the wisdom of the Greeks and Romans as preparation for civic and religious responsibilities and leadership. Another step in this preparation was to receive a college education. After the American Revolution, many leaders, including Thomas Jefferson, began to view American colleges as the source of republican leadership; this idea had roots in sixteenth- and seventeenth-century educational arguments.

In 1636, the Massachusetts Bay Colony established Harvard College. Its founding is described in a pamphlet, *New England's First Fruits,* published in London in 1642: "After God had carried us safe to New England, and we had built our houses, provided necessaries for our livelihood, rear'd convenient places for God's worship, and settled the Civil Government: One of the next things we longed for, and looked after was to advance Learning, and perpetuate it to Posterity."[16] To advance learning, the colonists accepted money and books from John Harvard for the founding of Harvard College.

New England's First Fruits states clearly that the purpose of Harvard College was to ensure an educated ministry for the colony. It was feared that no replacements would be forthcoming for the religious leaders who had led the colonists from England. In the words of *New England's First Fruits,* there was a "dreading to leave an illiterate Ministry to the Churches, when our present Ministers shall lie in the Dust."[17] Thus the goal of Harvard College was to guarantee continuity in the social organization and leadership of the colony.

Studies of the occupations of Harvard graduates in the seventeenth century confirm the role of the college in educating religious and civic leaders. Roughly half, or 180, of the 368 Harvard alumni completing their studies between 1642 and 1689 became clergymen. The next largest group of alumni, 42, became public servants—governors, councilors, judges, and permanent government officials. Twenty-seven of the alumni became physicians, and 13 became schoolmasters and college tutors. Occupations for 68 of the alumni could not be determined, and 27 died young. The remaining alumni were classified as merchants, planters, gentlemen, soldiers, mariners, and miscellaneous.[18]

After reviewing the purposes and history of reading-and-writing schools and grammar schools and the establishment of Harvard College, one can understand historian Merle Curti's argument that the educational system in New England was designed to protect existing authority by providing a class system of education. Reading-and-writing schools, which the majority of the school-going population attended, provided an authoritarian education and taught only the skills necessary to read and understand religious and civil decrees. Grammar schools and Harvard College trained society's future leadership by providing an education in the classics; this latter type of education provided knowledge that was ornamental but not necessarily useful. In other words, education in the classics became a means of conferring and identifying social status.

Education in colonial New England must be understood in the context of a group of people struggling for survival in an unknown wilderness. The colonists faced many problems and experienced labor shortages that blurred social class lines. The different forms of schooling were not a closed system in which all individuals below a certain level of social status were excluded from attendance at a grammar school. Nor was education the chief and only means of improving one's position in society. In fact, when viewing education from the perspective of the twenty-first century, one always faces the problem of attributing too much importance to its past social role. What is described here is only the early beginning of a system that rapidly increased in importance and size during the nineteenth century.

COLONIALISM AND EDUCATIONAL POLICY

In the seventeenth century, marked differences existed among the colonial policies of the various nations with colonies in North and South America. In fact, national policies differed during the various periods of colonization. The differences in colonial policies were reflected in the educational practices of the various North American colonies. The result was sharp variations in educational practices among the different regions of North America in the seventeenth and eighteenth centuries and, in the nineteenth century, differences among the states.

The differences in English colonial policy in different regions can be understood by comparing Virginia with New England. The Virginia companies chartered in 1606 were concerned primarily with establishing plantations that would yield a profit. During the early years of Virginia settlement, education was in the hands of ministers for the purposes of maintaining discipline and order and controlling Native Americans. During these early years Virginia was viewed as a trading post in the wilderness. In 1609 this colonial policy changed when families were transported from England to settle on small plots of land. The colony was governed like a military outpost as opposed to an agricultural community. Education consisted of little more than colonists going to church twice daily. By the 1620s more settlers were brought to Virginia, and an ordered community was established. Several unsuccessful attempts to establish schools occurred between 1618 and 1622.

The regional differences in early colonial policies created different educational traditions in Virginia and New England. As discussed earlier, the Massachusetts Bay Colony was established with a particular religious purpose and as a colony of self-sustaining families. Unlike the colony of Virginia, its major goal was not to provide a profit for English-based companies. Consequently, schooling became important as a means of sustaining a well-ordered religious commonwealth. In Virginia, in contrast, less attention was paid to the education of the average colonist. Reading-and-writing schools were established in Virginia in the seventeenth century, but their numbers were small compared with those in New England. By 1689 Virginia had six reading-and-writing schools and Massachusetts had twenty-three.[19]

Most historians of colonial education have depicted early education in Virginia and the rest of the South as being aristocratic. Only a few pauper schools and apprenticeship training were available for the poor, but for the elite there were private-pay schools and opportunities for education in the mother country. It can be argued that within the context of colonial policy, Virginia best represented the educational policies of England in contrast to the colonies in New England. This was a result of more direct control from the mother country and the emphasis on colonization for profit.

Colonial policy in New Netherland (New York) represented a different and more complex situation. By the time of the English conquest of New Netherland in 1664, it had a population of over five thousand living in a dozen Dutch villages and a few Puritan, Swedish, and Finnish settlements. The Dutch villages had less self-government than the New England towns and less of a sense of educational mission.

Before the English conquest of New Netherland, the Dutch West Indies Company had founded schools in eleven of the twelve Dutch communities. A struggle within the Dutch West Indies Company over schools in New Amsterdam resulted in the company paying the cost of the schoolmaster, the city paying for the schoolhouse and the teacher's dwelling, and the local government administering control. The English continued the practice of letting local officials and the courts hire, remove, and supervise teachers in local schools.

A major result of the more diverse population that settled in New York was the emergence of a variety of educational institutions. New York City (New Amsterdam) developed a system of private schools that dominated the educational scene until the early nineteenth century. These private schools offered a broad range of subjects, including instruction in the practical arts. They also served the particular needs of several religious interests and therefore avoided any major clash among the different religious factions over the content of schooling. This would become a major issue in New York in the nineteenth century, when public support for education was expanded. Therefore, in New York, English colonial policy involved a certain degree of respect for religious and ethnic differences; this allowed the development of more diverse educational institutions.

LANGUAGE AND CULTURAL CONFLICT

A similar development occurred in the settlement of Pennsylvania, but with a major clash between German and English settlers over language use. In many respects, the problems encountered in Pennsylvania foreshadowed conflicts in later centuries over which language should be used in the schools. Pennsylvania is also a good example of how colonial policy viewed education as a means of establishing the superiority of one ethnic group over another. Here the language used in the schools was thought to be the means by which one ethnic group could gain cultural ascendancy.

William Penn, the Quaker founder of Pennsylvania, actively recruited the oppressed from England and continental Europe to settle in the New World. The original settlement of English Quakers and Anglicans was followed by a large German settlement of religious minorities, including Mennonites, Dunkers, and Amish. The Amish and Mennonites would be in conflict with civil authorities over the issue of schooling through the twentieth century. Groups of other religious minorities from Scotland, Ireland, England, and Germany also settled throughout Penn's colony. By 1766 Benjamin Franklin estimated that the colonial population of 160,000 consisted of one-third Quakers, one-third Germans, and one-third religious minorities from a variety of places in Europe.[20]

Major differences existed between English control in New York and in Pennsylvania. In New York, the English attempted to Anglicize the administration of the colony while allowing diversity in cultural and social institutions. In Pennsylvania, the English embarked on a policy of "cultural Anglicization."[21] This policy was directed in particular at the Germans. A letter to John Penn in 1727 warned him about German immigration: "At this rate you will soon have a German colony here, and perhaps such a one as Britain once received from Saxony in the fifth century."[22] Concern was so great that the Pennsylvania Assembly passed a law in 1727 requiring all male German immigrants to swear an oath of allegiance to the British Crown.

The great fear was that the culture and language of the settlers would become German. As a result, proposals began to appear that would prohibit German printing houses, the publication of German government documents, and the importing of German books. Of great importance were the recommendations for the establishment of English-language schools. These were viewed as a means of countering and suppressing the expansion of German culture.

Benjamin Franklin was a major proponent of English-language schools and opponent of the expansion of German culture. He played a significant role in the establishment of charity schools, which were to be used for Anglicization. The schools originated as religious institutions for educating the poor German children of the province. Appeals for school funds spread to London, where in 1753 an enthusiastic supporter of the endeavor, William Smith, proclaimed, "By a common education of English and German youth at the same schools, acquaintances and connections will be formed, and deeply impressed upon them in their cheerful and open moments. The English language and a conformity of manners will be acquired."[23]

In early 1755 the first schools were organized, and a press was purchased from Franklin. Immediately the German community attacked the schools for giving a false picture of German culture. This attack caused the schools to fail. At their peak in 1759 the schools served only 600 to 750 children, of whom two-thirds were German. By 1764 the effort was considered a failure.[24]

This brief history of the attempt to Anglicize the Germans in Pennsylvania illustrates a continuing theme in American educational history: The use of schools as a means of spreading a particular culture has resulted in tensions between organized school systems on one side, and immigrant groups, Native Americans, Mexican Americans, Puerto Ricans, and African Americans on the other. In the nineteenth century many of the religious tensions caused by the Catholic perception of the public school system as Protestant could also be considered a result of cultural differences.

NATIVE AMERICANS: EDUCATION AS CULTURAL IMPERIALISM

Contrary to the Indian portrayed on the seal of the Governor and Company of the Massachusetts Bay as requesting help, Native Americans demonstrated little interest in being educated and converted by the colonists. But the English persisted in their efforts. English colonialists throughout the world tried to use educational methods to impose their culture on others. In North America, these efforts were accompanied by the genocide of the indigenous population. The diseases brought by the invaders destroyed a large proportion of the Indian population.[25] It is estimated that 90 percent of the Native American population on the East Coast was lost during the European invasion. In 1633, Governor John Winthrop of the Massachusetts Bay Colony reported that the colony was surrounded by Indians who prior to the invasion cleared timber for eight to ten miles from the seashore. Obviously, clearing this much timber required a substantial Native American population. English colonists near the Narragansetts estimated their population at 30,000. It is estimated that prior to English colonization the population of lower New England tribes ranged from 72,000 to 90,000.[26] Francis Jennings writes, "Available data for New England, for example, suggest that immigration from Europe in the seventeenth century was required to restore the same level of total population that had existed prior to European colonization."[27]

Attitudes of cultural and racial superiority underpinned plans for the religious and cultural conversion of Native Americans. English colonists brought with them a sense of righteousness about their Protestant beliefs and the superiority of English culture. Colonists branded Native Americans as "heathen savages." These attitudes of superiority would accompany the English around the world as their colonial empire was extended from North America to Africa and India.

For the English, the invasion of Ireland in the twelfth century initiated a colonial expansion based on the supposed superiority of English culture. From Ireland in the twelfth century to India in the nineteenth century, the English were convinced that colonialism was just because it spread Anglo-Saxon culture around the world. According to historian Ronald Takaki, when the English invaded Ireland in the twelfth century, they felt the Irish were inferior savages who could be redeemed only by adopting English culture. Eventually, English opinion was divided between the possibility of civilizing the Irish and a belief in the innate inferiority of the Irish. The latter position became part of a generalized English belief in their racial superiority.[28]

English colonists in North America compared their experiences with Native Americans to their experiences with the Irish. Takaki found many written comparisons during colonial times between the "wild Irish" and the "wild Indians." As with the Irish, English opinion was divided over the possibility of civilizing Native Americans.[29] Extreme racist opinions led to the conclusion that the only solution to the "Indian problem" was genocide. This attitude continued into the nineteenth century and is reflected in General Philip Sheridan's comment in 1867 after defeating the Cheyenne, "The only good Indians I ever saw were dead." This statement was refined by one of Sheridan's officers to the famous saying, "The only good Indian is a dead Indian."[30]

Also, many European Americans envisioned North America as a land that would be inhabited primarily by whites. Benjamin Franklin worried that there were larger numbers of Africans and Asians in the world than European whites. He considered expansion into North America an opportunity to increase the white race. Shortly before the Revolution, as Takaki points out, Franklin argued that the English were the "principle body of white People" that should populate North America. The clearing of the forests, Franklin noted, would serve to make room for more whites. "Why," he asked, "increase the Sons of Africa, by Planting them in America, where we have so fair an opportunity, by excluding all Blacks and Tawnys, of increasing the lovely White . . . ?"[31]

In the British colonial empire, English feelings of cultural superiority and racism were used to justify economic exploitation and the expropriation of lands. For many European Americans, Native Americans were an obstacle to the spread of white Europeans from coast to coast. To make room for the expansion of whites, the options were genocide or containment on small farms and reservations. In Takaki's words, "This social construction of race occurred within the economic context of competition over land."[32]

Some of the things the English hoped to change through education were Native American attitudes about work and sexuality. The Protestant ethic stressed the sacrifice of pleasure for work and wealth. What horrified New England Puritans was that not only did Native Americans seem unconcerned about avoiding personal pleasure, but they also enjoyed sexual pleasure. Because the Christian concept of sin was absent from traditional Native American cultures, tribal members were not driven by a fear of hell to replace personal pleasure with work and accumulation of property. In addition, the lack of a Christian concept of sin regarding sexuality contrasted sharply with the sexual repression evident among many European Americans. James Axtell provides, as an example of differing attitudes regarding sexuality, the laughter by Hurons when Father Le Caron tried to explain the Sixth Commandment regarding adultery. The Hurons simply stated, "It was impossible to keep that one."[33]

English colonists often called Native Americans "filthy." Originally, I was perplexed by this comment because of the English abhorrence of bathing in contrast to the daily plunge by most Native Americans into a river or other body of water. From the sixteenth through the nineteenth centuries, Europeans labeled Native Americans as "filthy" because of their seemingly unrepressed sexuality and not for their inattention to bathing.[34]

Another important cultural difference was in family organization. Most Native American tribes were organized into extended clans. Europeans wanted to replace the clan system with a nuclear family structure that would give power to the father. In the clan system, gender roles were divided by work. Women took care of domestic and agricultural work, and men did the hunting. The major responsibility for child rearing was not with the father but with the mother and her relations within the clan.

Many European American men were offended by the power of women in the clan structure. James Axtell found, however, that many colonial women captured by Native Americans preferred to remain with the tribe because of the higher status of women in Native American society in contrast with colonial society. Captured by Native Americans at the age of fifteen, Mary Jemison described female Native American work as being not so severe or hard as that done by white women. "In the summer season," she wrote, "we planted, tended and harvested our corn, and generally had all our children with us but had no master to oversee or drive us, so that we could work as leisurely as we pleased." Axtell concludes, "Unless Jemison was correct, it would be virtually impossible to understand why so many women and girls chose to become Indians."[35]

Native American women often exercised political power. The Cherokees, in particular, were noted for having female leaders and, frequently, female warriors. White male settlers often spoke despairingly of the "petticoat" government of the Cherokees. Cherokee women decided the fate of captives; they made decisions in Women's Council that were relayed to the general tribe by the War Woman or Pretty Woman. Clan mothers had the right to wage war. War Women, among the Cherokees, were called Beloved Women and had the power to free victims from the punishment prescribed by the general council.[36] Paula Gunn Allen forcefully describes the consequences for Native American women and children of a nuclear family and authoritarian child-rearing practices. Allen describes these changes as "the replacing of a peaceful, nonpunitive, nonauthoritarian social system wherein women wield power by making social life easy and gentle with one based on child terrorization, male dominance, and submission of women to male authority."[37]

Early Native American Educational Programs

In the early seventeenth century, the meager efforts of the Virginia Company to educate Native Americans in colonial homes and to establish Henrico College for the education of Native Americans were doomed to failure because, as Margaret Szasz writes, "the powerful Powhatan Algonquian saw their culture as superior to the colonial culture. As a result, Virginians encountered overwhelming difficulty in attempting to . . . educate their children."[38]

Francis Jennings argues that early claims by the Virginia Company and Massachusetts Bay Company to be interested in the education of Native Americans were, in his words, a "missionary racket." The companies would collect money for missionary work and divert the money to other purposes. In 1615 and in 1617, the Church of England collected money in all of its parishes in England for the establishment of a college for Native Americans at Henrico, Virginia. But the Virginia Company kept diverting the collected funds to other projects. Beginning in 1619, the college fund was used to pay the cost of the supply ship from England. Consequently, the college was never built.[39]

In the 1640s, criticism from England about the failure to convert Native Americans forced colonists into action. Leading these missionary efforts was John Eliot, who became known as "the Apostle to the Indians." Eliot quickly discovered that Native Americans were not receptive to his preaching. Having learned to speak Native American languages, Eliot first preached on July 5, 1646, to a gathering of Native Americans at Dorchester Mill. Eliot's account of the experience is a clear indication of Native American attitudes toward colonial culture. "They gave no heed unto it," he recorded, "but were weary, and rather despised what I said."[40]

Setting the tone of religious intolerance that would characterize European American educational efforts into the twentieth century, the Massachusetts General Court declared in 1646, after Eliot's sermon, that any "Christian or pagan [obviously referring to Indians] . . . wittingly and willingly . . . deniing [sic] the true God, or his creation or government of the world . . . shalbe [sic] put to death." And to ensure compliance by Native Americans, the General Court enacted a law requiring that once a year Indians be informed of their possible execution for denying the validity of the Christian God.[41]

These early New England efforts set the pattern of linking religious conversion with cultural conversion. From the seventeenth to the twentieth centuries, most educators and Protestant ministers believed that Native Americans had to become "civilized" to become Christian. John Eliot argued that converted Native Americans, called "praying Indians," should be separated from their villages and placed in small reservations called "praying towns." Kept from contact with the "uncivilized" life of typical Native American villages, praying Indians, according to Eliot, could become civilized. Eliot believed that helping praying Indians to live a true Christian life required punishment for such things as long hair and the killing of lice with teeth.[42]

The founding of Dartmouth College in 1769 and the work of Eleazar Wheelock and Samson Occom represent the most famous colonial efforts at Native American education and the initiation of the tradition of using boarding schools to civilize Native Americans. Foreshadowing later plans of the U.S. government, Wheelock advocated removing Indian children from contact with the tribal traditions of their families and placing them in boarding schools for cultural conversion. Also foreshadowing later arguments, Wheelock claimed that education was cheaper than war. If Native Americans were educated to live like the colonists, Wheelock believed, there would be no more Indian wars.

In the 1740s, Wheelock's first educational success was Samson Occom, a Mohegan, who later went to England to raise money for the founding of Dartmouth. After that success, Wheelock in 1754 established Moor's Charity School, which provided instruction in religion and classical training in Latin and Greek. In addition, boys received instruction in farming and girls in household tasks. This vocational training was designed to prepare Native American students to live in a manner similar to white New England farmers.[43]

One of the outstanding features of Wheelock's school was the decision to educate women. The first women enrolled in the school in 1761. Later educational efforts would also include the education of girls and women because their education was considered essential for the complete "civilization" of Native Americans. Conversion to the way of life that colonial New England required, in the opinion of ministers and educators, called for the creation of a nuclear household with the husband in charge and the wife doing domestic chores. Reacting as they had done to previous educational efforts, Native Americans did not rush to receive instruction at Wheelock's school. For instance, only sixteen women attended between 1761 and 1769.

Even the founding of Dartmouth in Hanover, New Hampshire, indicates resistance among colonists to major efforts at religious and cultural conversion. The Dartmouth charter reads, "for the education and instruction of youth of the Indian Tribes . . . and christianizing Children of Pagans . . . and also of English youth and others." Despite this charter, Wheelock used the money to create a college that served primarily white youth.[44] After the American Revolution these rather faint efforts by colonists to "civilize" Native Americans were replaced by a major effort of the U.S. government to use civilization policies as a means of gaining Native American lands. In turn, Native Americans became aware that they would have to become literate to deal with this new government.

ENSLAVED AFRICANS: ATLANTIC CREOLES

Contributing to the multicultural mix of the colonies was the arrival of the first enslaved Africans at Jamestown in 1618. These enslaved Africans spoke European languages, had Hispanic and English names, and in some cases, had both African and European ancestry. The enslaved Africans who arrived before the development of the eighteenth-century plantation system came from trading areas established by Europeans along the west coast of Africa. The word *Creole* refers to a person of mixed European and black descent. At these African trading posts, Europeans took African wives and mistresses. The result was the growth of a substantial Creole population. These Creoles found themselves in cultural conflict with both the European and African populations. When they adopted African traditions, Europeans declared them outcasts. Europeans also resented Creoles when they wore European clothing and adopted European manners. In addition, the Creoles were scorned by Africans, who denied them the right to marry, inherit property, and own land.[45]

Enslaved and shipped to the Americas, Creoles arrived partially assimilated to the world of their owners. Their ability to speak European languages and their understanding of European culture were welcomed by their purchasers. They were bought in small lots and found themselves working side by side with white indentured servants. They were considered part of the same social class as indentured servants. The major difference between the two groups was that white indentured servants were free after working a set number of years, and enslaved Creoles had to purchase their freedom. For instance, Anthony Johnson was sold as a slave to the Bennett family in the Chesapeake Bay area in 1621. The Bennetts allowed Johnson to marry and baptize his children. Eventually Johnson earned his freedom and owned a 250-acre farm, and his son received a patent for a 550-acre farm. In turn, Johnson bought slaves to help operate their farms.[46]

Many Atlantic Creoles purchased in northern colonies also assimilated into Anglo-American culture and bought their freedom. In the seventeenth and eighteenth centuries, large numbers of enslaved Africans congregated in New York City, Philadelphia, Newport, and Boston. In the first decade of the eighteenth century, one-sixth of the population of Philadelphia was composed of enslaved Africans. During this period, New York had the largest number of freed slaves. In the northern colonies, enslaved Africans did various types of labor ranging from shipping to farmwork.

ENSLAVED AFRICANS: THE PLANTATION SYSTEM

In the eighteenth century, the plantation system began to spread through the tobacco-growing regions of the Chesapeake area to the rice-growing regions of the Carolinas and eventually to the cotton fields of the Deep South. The plantation system originated in the sugar-growing areas of the Mediterranean in the twelfth century, where owners used both white and black slaves. The model was transplanted to the sugar, tobacco, rice, and cotton areas of the Americas, making its appearance in Brazil in the sixteenth century. All of these crops could be grown by small farmers. In contrast to the small farmer, the plantation system involved the cultivation of vast areas of land by an army of regimented workers. A great plantation house surrounded by workshops, barns, sheds, and slave quarters was the center of this factory-like system. The plantation owner issued orders to the overseers, who commanded a regimented labor force in the workshops and fields. Discipline and order were the keys to making the hierarchical system work.

Unlike slave owners in the North, plantation owners used the lash and other brutal punishments to control enslaved Africans. Southern courts did not prosecute plantation owners if their punishments resulted in the death of a slave. Plantation owners lived in constant fear that their slaves would either run away or revolt against their masters. Brutality, they believed, was the key to control.

Deculturalization was also considered key to making enslaved Africans dependent on their owners. As mentioned previously, the demand for slaves caused slave traders to exploit the interior regions of Africa, ripping people away from villages and families. One of the first things planters did after purchasing an enslaved African was to take away his or her identity by giving the person a new name. Most newly purchased slaves from interior Africa did not speak English, so the plantation owner and overseers made it a practice to frequently repeat the name until the enslaved African realized that it represented his or her new identity.

The deculturalization process continued with the housing of newly purchased slaves in barrack-like structures. Living in these conditions, the recent arrivals on a plantation experienced linguistic isolation. They could not communicate with their owners because they could not speak English. Often they could not speak to other slaves because they did not share a common language. The combination of the psychological trauma of capture and transportation to the Americas along with renaming and linguistic isolation separated newly purchased slaves from their former identities, villages, clans, and families.

Plantation owners made little effort to provide organized instruction in English. Consequently, enslaved Africans on plantations had to create a language of communication that would be understood by owners and overseers and by their fellow slaves. Also, enslaved Africans had to create new modes of interaction because they came from a variety of African cultures and had been separated from traditional cultural patterns related to marriage, family relations, property, child rearing, friendships, and social status.

Deculturalization did not result in the assimilation of enslaved plantation workers to European culture. Members of the first generation carried with them all the marks of their African heritage, including hairstyles, scarification, and filed teeth. Discovering the economic value of having slaves reproduce, planters supported the rapid increase of native enslaved Africans. As African Americans, this second generation of plantation slaves abandoned the outward bodily symbols of their African parents and rarely gave African names to their children. Words, gestures, and language forms of their parents were adapted to the new living and working conditions. Rituals involving birth and death incorporated traditional African practices into the requirements of plantation life.

Enslaved Africans developed cultural styles for interacting with an owner who had the power of life and death—an owner who could at any time inflict severe punishment. It was a relationship in which the slave was not protected by any legal institution from the arbitrary brutality of the master and the owner could demand sexual relations with any slave. The owner had the power to break up families and wrench children from their parents by selling them.[47]

The oral tradition that developed among enslaved Africans provided a psychological refuge against the degradation of slavery. Slaves sang while working, during whatever leisure time was available to them, and during religious services. The lyrics of their songs reflect the slaves' effort to create a culture that could cope with inhuman conditions. In *Black Culture and Black Consciousness: Afro-American Folk Thought from Slavery to Freedom,* Lawrence Levine concludes, "The slaves' oral traditions, their music, and their religious outlook . . . constituted a cultural refuge at least potentially capable of protecting their personalities from some of the worst ravages of the slave system."[48]

Ira Berlin describes the result of this deculturalization and cultural transformation as not being "assimilation to a European ideal. Black people kept their African ways as they understood them, worshiping in a manner that white observers condemned as idolatry and superstition. If a new generation of American-born peoples was tempted toward Christianity, an older generation would have nothing of it. Indeed, the distinctive nature of African-American culture led some white observers to conclude there could be no reconciliation of African and European ways."[49]

THE IDEA OF SECULAR EDUCATION: FREEDOM OF THOUGHT AND THE ESTABLISHMENT OF ACADEMIES

As Native and African Americans came under the domination of European colonizers, the idea of secular schooling was becoming popular among the English. The concept of a secular school free from religious control emerged from concerns about political freedom and the scientific revolution. Political freedom was central to the American Revolution. The belief that a republican society requires freedom of thought and beliefs became embodied in American political life in the words of the First Amendment to the Constitution, which prohibits Congress from making any laws that would abridge freedom of speech and the press. Both of these intellectually revolutionary concepts were related to new developments in science and technology that promised to enhance the quality of human existence.

In England, the struggle for intellectual freedom found its outlet in the establishment of dissenting academies. The idea of the academy was brought to the colonies, where it changed to meet the practical needs of the New World. The academy movement provided a clear alternative to the classical education of the grammar schools and colleges of the seventeenth and eighteenth centuries. The academies also provided an early model for the development of the high school.

The curriculum of the academy, with its dissenting tradition and its emphasis on practical skills, made the school something more than an institution for cultivating religious and civic obedience or shaping future leaders. The academy taught ideas and skills directly related to the practical side of life and provided intellectual tools for developing new knowledge about the material world.

The changes in thinking about schooling and freedom of ideas were part of the ideological justification of the American Revolution that appeared in pamphlets and newspapers distributed in England and the colonies during the seventeenth and eighteenth centuries. Historian Bernard Bailyn describes his study of these pamphlets and newspapers:

> It confirmed my belief that intellectual developments in the decade before Independence led to a radical idealization of the previous century and a half of American experience, and that it was this intimate relationship between Revolutionary thought and the circumstances of life in eighteenth-century America that endowed the Revolution with its peculiar force and made it so profoundly a transforming event.[50]

An early work in this revolutionary tradition, and the one most directly related to schools, was Robert Molesworth's *Account of Denmark as It Was in the Year 1692*. Molesworth's book is one of the first criticisms of the use of schooling to create obedient and submissive citizens. The purpose of his study was to find the elements that had been most important in transforming Denmark into a system of hereditary absolutism. A key to explaining this transformation was the gaining of absolute obedience of the people to the state.

Molesworth believed that obedience had been gained by linking religion to the state and making education a function of religion. He argued that religious orders preached and taught a doctrine of submission and obedience to both heavenly and earthly rulers. When religion linked arms with government, religious doctrines were used to justify tyranny; and when education was a function of a state-established religion, religious doctrines were used to justify the power of the state and to mold future citizens into a condition of obedience.

In his study of tyranny in Denmark, Molesworth writes, "Enslaving the Spirits of the People, as preparative to that of their Bodies; . . . those Foreign Princes think it their Interest that Subjects should obey without reserve, and all Priests, who depend upon the Prince, are for their own sakes obliged to promote what he esteems his Interest." After establishing the interrelationships of interests, he goes on to lament, "Tis plain, the Education of Youth, on which is laid the very Foundation Stones of the Public Liberty, has been of late years committed to the sole management of such as make it their business to undermine it."[51]

According to Molesworth, a major service that religion performed for the state through education of youth was "to recommend frequently to them what they call the Queen of all virtues, Viz., Submission to Superiors, and an entire blind Obedience to Authority." Of even greater importance, this educational system caused the people to forget that government was a product of human actions—not divine intervention. By making government appear divine in origin, religiously controlled education could teach obedience to government as if it were obedience to divine authority. Such education taught "that the People ought to pay an

Absolute Obedience to a limited Government; fall down and worship the Work of their own Hands, as if it dropt from Heaven."[52]

A major conclusion of Molesworth's study is that to contribute to liberty and freedom, education must be secular and separated from religion. He called for the professor to replace the priest and for students to learn the content of their classical studies rather than just the grammar. He believed that education must be both free of religious dogma in service to the state and free to lead the learner down the path of reason.

Molesworth's criticisms of education could easily have been applied to the type of education provided in *The New England Primer* and to the reading-and-writing schools of the seventeenth and eighteenth centuries. His study became part of a general discussion with his friends John Trenchard and Thomas Gordon, who provided the broadest defense of freedom of ideas and learning that had so far been offered. Their essays were distributed between 1720 and 1723 as *Cato's Letters* and were reprinted many times during the subsequent twenty-five years. These essays, which are considered a primary source for the justification of the American Revolution, provided topics for endless political discussions on both sides of the Atlantic Ocean.[53]

The essays defend free thought and speech as essential to the economic and social development of a nation. In making the link between social progress and freedom, the *Letters* offer their defense in concrete terms, not merely as an appeal to abstract justice: A country needs freedom because without freedom there can be no growth in human wisdom and invention and, consequently, no progress in economic development. The authors of *Cato's Letters* believed that tyranny and slavery stop social development and improvement in human well-being, whereas freedom and liberty lead people down the road to progress and happiness.[54]

The text of *Cato's Letters* defines freedom of thought and speech as a right that can be abridged only to protect the freedom of others: "Without Freedom, there can be no such Thing as Wisdom; and no such Thing as public liberty, without Freedom of Speech: Which is the Right of every Man, as far as by it he does not hurt and control the Right of another." This one limitation on freedom, they declared, "is the only Check which it ought to suffer, the only Bounds which it ought to know."[55]

In linking freedom of thought to human progress, the authors of *Cato's Letters* argued that humans in their original state of nature contented themselves with "the Spontaneous Productions of Nature," but these "spontaneous" supplies proved insufficient to support increasing numbers of humans. The next step was "to open the bosom of the Earth, and, by proper Application and Culture, to extort her hidden stores." The differing degrees of prosperity that existed among nations were considered largely a product of different levels of advancement in the state of learning, which allowed more advanced nations to enjoy greater productivity. Wisdom and art, the authors argued, promote prosperity, which in turn provides full employment, economic well-being, and a general elevation of people's spirit and culture. If the advancement of wisdom and learning fails to occur, unemployment will result in human misery. In describing the conditions that produce human misery, they write, "People, in most countries, are forced, for want of other Employment, to cut the Throats of one another, or of their neighbors; and to ramble after their Princes in all their mad conquests . . . and all to get, with great Labour, Hazard, and often with great Hunger and slaughter, a poor precarious, and momentary subsistence."[56]

The equation made in *Cato's Letters* between freedom of ideas and the good life is this: Freedom of thought and speech promotes wisdom, which in turn provides the basis for prosperity and the elimination of the crime that grows from hunger and poverty. Within the framework of this argument, tyranny must be avoided because it hinders the growth of wisdom, prosperity, and social happiness. "Ignorance of Arts and Sciences, and of everything that is good, together with Poverty, misery, and desolation, are found for the most part all together, and are all certainly produced by Tyranny."[57]

The arguments in *Cato's Letters* and in Molesworth's writings give an entirely different perspective on the nature of schooling and the role of schooling in society. In the context of their arguments, if education were to take place in an environment free of ideological restraints, particularly those of religion, it would be the source of material benefits for society. These arguments reflect the scientific revolution that emerged in the seventeenth century as the result of work by individuals such as Francis Bacon.

Bacon was one of the first people to see in science hope for the progress of humanity. During his life as a barrister, essayist, and scientist, he envisioned a utopia made possible by the scientific method. In his book *Novum Organum* (1620), he argued that scientific experimentation would unlock the secrets of nature and usher in a golden era. His utopian novel *New Atlantis* describes a society in which the central institution is a College of Six Days Works, devoted to the scientific study of nature.[58]

Bacon's early arguments were accepted by intellectuals such as Molesworth and the authors of *Cato's Letters*. In the eighteenth century these English political thinkers, scientists, inventors, and early industrialists were known as commonwealthmen. The scientists and inventors in the group included Matthew Boulton, James Watt, Erasmus Darwin, Samuel Galton, and Joseph Priestley.[59] These people had contact with other intellectuals in Glasgow and Edinburgh and interacted freely with members of the leading philosophical societies in England.

This group of intellectuals took the argument for freedom of ideas one step further than would their counterparts in North America. They objected to government-provided systems of education as a threat to intellectual freedom. English historian Brian Simon has written about Joseph Priestley and this group of intellectuals: "In common with . . . all other dissenters, Priestley was adamantly opposed to education becoming a function of the state. Should it do so, it would not achieve the object he desired, on the contrary, it would be used to promote uniformity of thought and belief."[60] Joseph Priestley used specific examples to show the negative results of government-controlled education. For instance, he often referred to the attempt at Oxford University to discourage the reading of John Locke's *Essay on Human Understanding*.

Priestley believed that any group that gained control of the educational system could greatly increase its power over the rest of society. He argued that education should encourage free inquiry and inspire the love of truth, and that state-endowed education would be more committed to instilling a particular set of religious, moral, or political principles than to training the mind for the free use of reason.

Historian Caroline Robbins summarizes Priestley's ideas about state-provided education as follows: "The chief glory of human nature, the operation of reason in a variety of ways and with diversified results, would be lost. Every man should educate his children in his own manner to preserve the balance which existed among the several religious and political parties in Great Britain."[61]

In England, the institution through which the advocates of intellectual freedom expressed their beliefs became the dissenting academies established in the latter half of the seventeenth century. These academies served as refuges for nonconformist ministers and others dissenting against the major religious and educational institutions in England. Their growth was a direct result of the closing in 1662 of Oxford and Cambridge to non-Anglicans. The dissenting academies became centers of intellectual and educational innovation as they promoted science and rejected a strictly classical curriculum. In fact, the academies introduced English as the language of instruction.

Although various types of academies served numerous purposes, many academies accepted the idea that science and politics were suitable subjects for the curriculum and that freedom of inquiry should be encouraged. Some academies were run by individuals; others were operated by religious denominations. The variety of schools and the commitment of most of them to intellectual freedom made the academies an important source of educational innovation in the eighteenth century. In England they were considered an alternative to older forms of higher education. When the academy idea was introduced into the colonies, it served as a model both for newly established colleges and, in the nineteenth century, for the development of the high school.

In conclusion, the intellectual revolution that fostered the importance of freedom of ideas had two significant consequences for schooling. First, it led to a different concept of the purposes of education and institutional organization. Within this framework, education was viewed as providing the intellectual tools, scientific knowledge, and inventions required to create a better society. Second, this intellectual revolution attacked the notion that the primary purpose of education was to bring people into obedience to a church or government.

BENJAMIN FRANKLIN AND EDUCATION AS SOCIAL MOBILITY

The academy movement in North America was primarily a result of the desire to provide a more utilitarian education than classical grammar schools provided. The North American academies were modeled after the English dissenting academies;

but unlike those in England, they were not a response to exclusion from other educational institutions, nor did they place as much emphasis on intellectual freedom. In North America these institutions served two needs: They provided a useful education, and at the same time they transmitted the culture required for entrance into the middle class. In other words, they were institutions that could provide social mobility for the average citizen. They were often called people's colleges.

The academy movement spread rapidly in the eighteenth and nineteenth centuries. In 1855 Henry Barnard reported the existence of 6,185 academies in the United States, with a total enrollment of 263,096. As in England, the academies in North America varied in curriculum and organization. In general, a mixture of public and private control and financing was used. Small towns would often provide financial support to local academies under the control of a private board of trustees. The curricula of the academies tended to be flexible and adaptable to the needs of the student, although of course this varied from institution to institution.[62]

One of the earliest and most famous plans for an academy was Benjamin Franklin's *Proposals Relating to the Education of Youth in Pennsylvania* (1749). Ironically, the institution established to carry out his plans, which eventually became the University of Pennsylvania, failed to teach his curriculum; but nonetheless it became a widely discussed model for other academies. Franklin's model academy embodied his life experiences and education. A famous phrase from his academy proposal states, "It would be well if [students] could be taught every Thing that is useful, and every Thing that is ornamental: But Art is long, and their Time is short. It is therefore propos'd that they learn those Things that are likely to be most useful and most ornamental."[63]

Franklin's life was a model for getting ahead in the New World. He was exposed early in life to the major types of educational institutions that existed in the colonies. Benjamin Franklin was born in Boston in 1706, and at the age of eight he was sent by his father to grammar school to prepare to be a minister. His father, who became financially unable to carry through with this plan, later withdrew Franklin from the grammar school. He was sent to a school for writing and arithmetic and was made an apprentice to his brother in the newspaper trade. Eventually he rebelled and left Boston, going to Philadelphia in 1723 to pursue his trade of printer.

Although his life in Philadelphia demonstrated the opportunities available in the New World for upward mobility, Franklin's ability eventually to become an internationally recognized scientist and statesman was dependent on his self-education. The "useful" elements in Franklin's education were the skills he learned in his apprenticeship and through reading. The "ornamental" elements were the knowledge and social skills he learned through reading, writing, and debating, which gave him the culture needed to advance in the world. A main source of his ornamental education was the Junto, a club he organized in Philadelphia. The Junto met every Friday evening, and its members were required to prepare questions dealing with morals, philosophy, and politics. Every three months they had to write an essay and defend it to the other members. As Franklin wrote in his *Autobiography,* the purpose of the club was "mutual improvement."[64]

Mutual improvement and self-education were also Franklin's reasons for founding the first subscription library in America. He recommended to the members of the Junto that they place all their individually owned books into a common library for the benefit of all members. Out of this grew the idea of a subscription library, to which library members would pay a fee for expenses and the purchase of new books. Franklin believed that these libraries improved the general culture of the average citizen:

> These libraries have improved the general conversation of the Americans, made the common tradesmen and farmers as intelligent as most gentlemen from other countries, and perhaps have contributed in some degree to the stand so generally made throughout the Colonies in defense of their privileges.[65]

The academy Franklin proposed was an institutionalized version of both his formal schooling and his self-education. The academy proposal was a model of an educational system that would confirm status in the middle class and confer status on those wanting to enter the middle class in eighteenth-century North America. Certainly Franklin's *Autobiography* can be considered a guide to social mobility in the world as he knew it.

The educational content that Franklin proposed reflects the influence of the radical English writers who did so much to spark the American Revolution. His plan includes the study of English through reading *Cato's Letters* and the writings of the English radical Algernon Sidney. *Cato's Letters* was published only a few decades before the publication of Franklin's proposal, but in his proposal Franklin refers to the work as a classic.

Franklin placed a great deal of emphasis on the teaching of style in both writing and speaking. Proper style, for Franklin, included writing clearly and concisely and "pronouncing properly, distinctly, emphatically, not with an even Tone, which under-does, nor a theatrical, which over-does Nature."[66] Style in writing and speaking would allow an individual to move through the social world with grace.

According to Franklin, the substance behind the style would emerge from the study of history, which in its broadest sense would be the vehicle for learning the "most useful" knowledge. In Franklin's words, "But if History be made a constant Part of their Reading . . . may not almost all Kinds of useful Knowledge be that Way introduc'd to Advantage, and with Pleasure to the Student?"[67] For Franklin, history was a vehicle for teaching morality, oratory, geography, politics, philosophy, human affairs, agriculture, technology, science, and invention. The teaching of history, combined with the teaching of style in writing and speech, would provide the "most useful and most ornamental" in learning.

Franklin's proposal heralded the beginning of the academy movement in North America. Although academies came in many forms and were governed by a variety of public and religious groups, they were all considered to be distinct from the classical grammar school. Unlike the grammar schools, the academies were conceived as institutions to provide a practical education. This is best exemplified in the wording of the constitution of Phillips Academy, founded in 1778. It states that the founding of the academy was "for the purpose of instructing Youth, not only in English and Latin Grammar, Writing, Arithmetic, and those Sciences, wherein they are taught; but more especially to learn them the great end and real business of living."[68]

Over the years the identity of the academies fluctuated: They were sometimes considered to be small colleges, and at other times high schools. By the latter part of the nineteenth century, however, academies had established a primary identity as institutions providing a secondary education. Also by the end of the nineteenth century, they had become identified as institutions for educating the elite. This view of the academy had not yet emerged in the eighteenth and early nineteenth centuries.

A direct contribution by the academy movement to the development of high schools in the United States was made in 1821, when the English Classical School was founded in Boston. At that time most academies were country boarding schools. A group of parents in Boston complained about having to send their children outside the city to attend an academy or—the only alternative—to Boston Latin School, where a traditional grammar school curriculum was taught. The city responded to the complaints by founding the English Classical School, which offered a curriculum typical of academies of the time, including English, geography, arithmetic, algebra, geometry, trigonometry, history, navigation, and surveying. Within a few years the school was renamed English High School and became the first high school in the United States.

The history of dissenting academies in England and academies in North America demonstrates the interrelationship among politics, the organization of society, and education. The dissenting academies, born in the midst of revolutionary talk that quickly spread to the North American continent, were institutions reflecting the new spirit of science and industrial development. Transplanted to the New World, they became institutions for teaching what was considered useful knowledge and for providing social mobility. A real irony of history is that by the late nineteenth century the academies in the United States served primarily to confirm the social status of elite members of society.

THE FAMILY AND THE CHILD

A popular interpretation of historical change in the United States is to view it as a process of institutional expansion and contraction. In this framework, the institution of the family is portrayed as contracting while other institutions assume roles once performed by it. In terms of the history of education, this means the school has assumed tasks previously performed by the family as educational responsibilities have shifted from the parents to the schoolteacher. In addition, changes in commonly held concepts of children and women have fundamentally affected the organization of education. Changes in the concept of childhood provided a basis for the belief that the proper education of children could create the ideal political and social world.

In *American Education,* Cremin interprets educational history mainly as a shifting set of institutional arrangements wherein the family had the basic responsibility for education. Cremin writes, "The household remained the single most fundamental unit of social organization in the eighteenth-century colonies and, for the vast majority of Americans, the decisive agency of deliberate cultural transmission."[69] In frontier areas, he argues, the family often assumed the functions of both church and school, whereas in more settled areas it shared these responsibilities with other institutions.

The importance of the socializing role of the family in colonial life is highlighted in John Demos's study *A Little Commonwealth: Family Life in Plymouth Colony.* Demos ascribes a variety of functions to the colonial family. First, it was a business; work was a natural part of family life, and most households were self-sufficient. Second, it was a school; parents and masters were required by law to attend to the education of their children. Third, it was a vocational institution; it transmitted skills for earning a living. Fourth, it was a church; family worship supplemented the work of formal religious institutions. Fifth, the family was a house of correction in which idle and even criminal persons were sentenced to live as servants. And last, the family was a welfare institution that functioned at various times as a hospital, orphanage, old people's home, and home for the poor.[70]

Within this broad-ranging institution was a strict hierarchy, with the father at the top and the children at the bottom. The colonial family operated on a simple premise: "He for God only, she for God in him." This meant that women were to bow to the God in men, and men were to assume the spiritual care of women. In legal matters, the married woman was at the mercy of her husband; she was without rights to own property, make contracts, or sue for damages.

Although women were dependent on men, they still had to assume responsibility for their own individual salvation, and in order to do so they had to learn how to read. This created an ambivalent situation regarding the education of women. The education of women was undertaken purely for purposes of religious control; but ironically, even though women were considered the weaker sex with regard to intellectual capacities, they not only assumed responsibility for teaching reading within the household but also functioned as neighborhood teachers in the dame schools and, during the summer, the district schools of New England.

In general, the education of women was limited to basic reading, writing, and arithmetic; but their role as teachers in the family and in dame schools foreshadowed their dominant role as teachers in public schools in the late nineteenth and twentieth centuries. This role of teacher opened the door to further education for women and provided a career for them that became an important stepping-stone on the road to greater equality and rights.

Children in the colonial family were in a position of complete subordination to their parents. The requirement to honor one's parents extended even into adulthood. This is best exemplified by a statute of the Plymouth Colony that stated, "If any Childe or Children above sixteen years old, and of competent Understanding, shall curse or Smite their Natural Father or Mother; he or they shall be put to Death, unless it can be sufficiently testified that the Parents have been very Unchristianly negligent in the Education of such Children."[71]

Of major importance to the family was the economic function of the child. In a world where most families were financially self-sufficient, each new pair of helping hands was welcomed. After infancy, the colonial child usually helped with agricultural chores during the summer and attended school in the winter. Between the age of seven and puberty, children were fully integrated into the workforce. Many times, the family would apprentice out to another family boys over the age of seven. The economic value of the child to the family was clearly demonstrated by the requirement that if the boy left home to work he was expected to pay for a substitute for his labor. Often families considered the child's value during the winter to be no more than the cost of providing board, but during the summer months the child's labor was considered essential. It is not surprising that families would resist child labor laws in the nineteenth and twentieth centuries, given the deep roots of this traditional view of the economic worth of the child to the family unit.[72]

The primary responsibility of colonial parents to their children was to raise them to live according to God's commandments. This meant caring for their physical and spiritual needs. Parental strictness was required because of a belief that all children at birth shared in the common sins of humanity. This belief is best exemplified by the alphabet in *The New England Primer,* which begins,

> *A* in Adam's Fall We Sinned All
> *B* Thy Life to Mend This Book Attend.[73]

The "Book" referred to is the Bible, which was presented as the source of correction of the Original Sin in which all children were believed to have been born.

The emphasis in child rearing was to prevent children from leading a life of sin. In other words, parents had an obligation to make sure their children were good. What this meant is expressed in the following verse from *The New England Primer:*

> Good Children Must
> Fear God all Day
> Love Christ Always,

Parents Obey,
In Secret Pray,
No False thing Say,
Mind Little Play,
By no Sin Stray,
Make no delay,
In doing Good.[74]

This attitude toward children can be understood more clearly by contrasting it with other concepts of childhood that began to be popularized in the eighteenth century. For instance, French philosopher Jean-Jacques Rousseau believed that the child is born good and that the greatest danger in childhood is corruption by the outside world. He popularized this concept of childhood in his book *Emile* (1762). *Emile* is Rousseau's plan for the ideal education of a child. To provide Emile, the protagonist, with the best education, Rousseau isolates him from society until the onset of adolescence and places him in a country home under the supervision of a tutor who allows Emile to discover what is necessary and useful for living. The concept of education that permits the child to learn through experience and discovery was a major departure from schooling that emphasized memorization and subordination to authority.[75]

A major contrast exists between colonial ideas about child rearing and Rousseau's theory that moral education should not take place until the child has reached the age of social reasoning—adolescence. Rousseau calls this *negative education,* by which he means that learning is to be a product of experience, not moral and verbal instruction. According to Rousseau, during the early period of their development, human beings are incapable of reasoning about morality and social relations. Thus it is important to avoid placing a child in situations requiring moral choices before she or he is old enough to handle them with her or his own powers of social reasoning. Rousseau felt that books are a great plague in childhood. He meant by this not that children should not be taught how to read, but that learning to read should be attached to experience and necessity. For example, Emile receives invitations to dinners and parties but cannot find anyone to read them to him. These experiences lead Emile to learn how to read out of self-interest and necessity. Rousseau's method of teaching reading avoids moral instruction; it is not based on a sense of duty or on a belief in an abstract good. For Rousseau, learning and knowledge are tools to be used by the individual—not tools enabling society to use the individual.

Emile heralded the beginning of a romantic concept of childhood that would persist into the twenty-first century and influence global educational practices. The book sparked educational trends emphasizing instructional techniques that would allow the free development of the child. In modern times, the major rival to this concept is the idea that the child is born as a blank slate (*tabula rasa*) and is completely molded by the environment. In this theory of childhood, which can be traced to the eighteenth century, can be found the roots of modern behavioral psychology.

The book most closely identified with the origins of the concept of the child as a blank slate is English philosopher John Locke's *Some Thoughts Concerning Education* (1693). For Locke, the adult is primarily a product of his or her education in the world, and this education is a result of rewards and punishments received during childhood. Consequently, Locke argues, the most important factor in education is the development of correct habits, which depends on proper manipulation of rewards and punishments. Locke writes, "I grant, that good and evil, reward and punishment, are the only motives to a rational creature; these are the spur and reins, whereby all mankind are set on work and guided, and therefore they are to be made use of to children too."[76]

According to Locke, the most powerful reward for children is esteem, and the most powerful punishment is disgrace (as opposed to corporal punishment). In a sense, Locke calls for the manipulation of parental love as a means of shaping the character of the child. He also expresses concern about children learning bad habits from other children, and he warns parents that sending their offspring to school might lead to such contagion.

Locke's solution to the influence that children exert on one another in school is to have teachers who are able both to teach subject matter and to shape proper habits. He advises parents to keep their children out of school until they find a school "wherein it is possible for the master to look after the manners of his scholars, and . . . show as great effects of his care of forming their minds to virtue, and their carriage to good breeding, as of forming their tongues to the learned languages."[77] In one sense, this echoes the traditional view that the teacher is responsible for the virtue of students. In another sense, however, Locke envisioned what we might call the modern concept of the teacher—a teacher who is given responsibility not only for imparting subject matter but also for consciously shaping character. Locke viewed the child not as being either good or evil but as a person to be molded for the future.

Locke's concept of childhood, like Rousseau's, led to the rejection of traditional methods of instruction. Locke criticized what he called the ordinary method of instruction, which fills the mind with rules and precepts that are not understood and are quickly forgotten, and he considered memorization to be the poorest method of instruction. Locke advocated instead that the child learn through performance until the object of the lesson is mastered: "By repeating the same action, till it be grown habitual in them, the performance will not depend on memory, or reflection, the concomitant of prudence and age, and not of childhood; but will be natural in them."[78]

Locke's concept of childhood greatly influenced the development of public schools in the nineteenth and twentieth centuries. The concept of the child as a blank slate allowed educational leaders to believe they could create the good society through the proper molding of children. Nineteenth-century common school reformers such as Horace Mann specifically rejected the Calvinist view of the child born in sin for a concept of the child as a lump of clay that can be shaped for the future. This new concept allowed school reformers to dream of creating the perfect school—one that would produce the perfect political citizen, the perfect moral person, the perfect worker.

These concepts of childhood have never been so distinct in real life as they are in a historian's conceptualization, but they provide a basis for understanding the effects of different concepts of childhood on the organization of education. The colonial view of childhood created an environment that was controlling and authoritarian. Major changes in education occurred with the rejection of the idea that the child is born in a state of sin and therefore must be controlled and made submissive. The viewpoint that the child is neither good nor evil and is a product of the environment allowed educators to view the school as a panacea for social, economic, and political problems.

CONCLUSION

What distinguishes education in pre-Revolutionary America from that in post-Revolutionary America is the concept of service to the broader needs of government and society. After the American Revolution, many Americans began to believe that a public system of education was needed to build nationalism, to shape good citizens, and to reform society. In other words, education in the post-Revolutionary period was brought into the service of public policy.

Before the Revolution, education served mainly to prepare an individual to live a godly life and to confirm and confer status. The major goal of education was to ensure that the public knew how to read the Bible, religious tracts, and laws. Status was confirmed by the classical education of the grammar school and college through the teaching of a particular cultural style and body of knowledge.

Although the colonists thought education was important, they did not believe the creation of an extensive and well-organized system of education was necessary. Not until education was viewed as a government function, as opposed to a family function, did organized systems of schooling appear. This occurred when government leaders began to see education as a useful tool for governing society. The closest any of the colonies came to creating a system of education was in the town schools in New England. However, even though these schools were established according to law, they were never organized into an educational system. The middle colonies contained a diversity of religious and private schools, and the southern colonies for the most part neglected the education of the general public.

The forces behind the changes that took place after the Revolution were in evidence in the pre-Revolutionary colonies. The academy movement stimulated thinking about education serving the practical needs of humanity as well as religious needs. Changing concepts of childhood made it possible for educators to dream of schools as institutions for creating the perfect society. And more important, the general population began to realize the value of learning as a tool for gaining independence, not just for instilling subservience. For instance, Benjamin Franklin believed the rebellious spirit of the population was a result of the wide availability of libraries. In fact, the political tracts read by the colonists were instrumental in setting the stage for the American Revolution. As the history of schooling in the colonial period demonstrates, education can be brought into the service of either authority or independence.

And of course the educational efforts to change the language and culture of non-Europeans would extend into the future. The attempt to change languages and cultures would eventually include not just Native and African Americans but also Mexican, Asian, and Puerto Rican Americans.

Notes

1. Francis Jennings, *The Invasion of America: Indians, Colonialism, and the Cant of Conquest* (New York: Norton, 1976), p. 229.
2. See ibid., pp. 45–46, and Ronald Takaki, *A Different Mirror: A History of Multicultural America* (Boston: Little, Brown, 1993), pp. 26–29, 139–166.
3. Carl F. Kaestle, *Pillars of the Republic: Common Schools and American Society, 1780–1860* (New York: Hill and Wang, 1983).
4. Lawrence Cremin, *The Wonderful World of Ellwood Patterson Cubberley* (New York: Teachers College Press, 1965).
5. Ellwood Cubberley, *Public Education in the United States: A Study and Interpretation of American Educational History* (Boston: Houghton Mifflin, 1934), p. 14.
6. Rush Welter, *Popular Education and Democratic Thought in America* (New York: Columbia University Press, 1962), p. 9.
7. Merle Curti, *The Social Ideas of American Educators* (Paterson, NJ: Pageant Books, 1959).
8. Quoted in Lawrence Cremin, *American Education: The Colonial Experience, 1607–1783* (New York: Harper & Row, 1970), p. 15.
9. Reprinted in Ellwood Cubberley, ed., *Readings in Public Education in the United States: A Collection of Sources and Readings to Illustrate the History of Educational Practice and Progress in the United States* (Cambridge, MA: Riverside Press, 1934), p. 16.
10. Ibid., pp. 18–19.
11. Curti, *The Social Ideas*, pp. 23–24.
12. Paul Leicester Ford, ed., *The New England Primer* (New York: Teachers College Press, 1962).
13. All the quotes from *The New England Primer* are from the edition reprinted in ibid.
14. Quoted in Cremin, *American Education*, p. 186.
15. Ibid., pp. 58–79.
16. Reprinted in Cubberley, *Readings in Public Education*, p. 13.
17. Ibid.
18. Cremin, *American Education*, pp. 220–221.
19. Ibid., p. 183.
20. Ibid., p. 259.
21. Ibid.
22. Quoted in ibid., p. 260.
23. Quoted in ibid., p. 261.
24. Ibid., p. 262.
25. Jennings, *The Invasion of America*, pp. 15–31.
26. Ibid., pp. 28–29.
27. Ibid., p. 30.

28. Takaki, *A Different Mirror,* p. 28.
29. Ibid., pp. 28–29.
30. Dee Brown, *Bury My Heart at Wounded Knee: An Indian History of the American West* (New York: Holt, 1970), pp. 171–172.
31. Takaki, *A Different Mirror,* p. 79.
32. Ibid., p. 39.
33. James Axtell, *The Invasion Within: The Contest of Cultures in Colonial North America* (New York: Oxford University Press, 1985), p. 123.
34. Jennings, *The Invasion of America,* pp. 49–50.
35. Axtell, *The Invasion Within,* p. 324.
36. Paula Gunn Allen, *The Sacred Hoop: Recovering the Feminine in American Indian Traditions* (Boston: Beacon Press, 1992), pp. 36–37.
37. Ibid., pp. 40–41.
38. Margaret Szasz, *Indian Education in the American Colonies, 1607–1783* (Albuquerque: University of New Mexico Press, 1988), p. 259.
39. Jennings, *The Invasion of America,* pp. 53–54.
40. Ibid., p. 239.
41. Ibid., p. 241.
42. Ibid., pp. 249–251.
43. Szasz, *Indian Education,* pp. 191–258.
45. Jon Reyhner and Jeanne Eder, *A History of Indian Education* (Billings: Eastern Montana College, 1989), pp. 20–22.
45. See Ira Berlin, *Many Thousands Gone: The First Two Centuries of Slavery in North America* (Cambridge, MA: Harvard University Press, 1998), pp. 29–46.
46. Ibid., pp. 29–30.
47. Toni Morrison captures the full psychological impact of this system in her Pulitzer Prize–winning novel *Beloved* (New York: Penguin Books, 1988).
48. Lawrence W. Levine, *Black Culture and Black Consciousness: Afro-American Folk Thought from Slavery to Freedom* (New York: Oxford University Press, 1977), p. 54.
49. Berlin, *Many Thousands Gone,* p. 128.
50. Bernard Bailyn, *The Ideological Origins of the American Revolution* (Cambridge, MA: Harvard University Press, 1967), pp. vi–vii.
51. Robert Molesworth, *An Account of Denmark as It Was in the Year 1692* (Copenhagen: Rosenkilde and Bagger, 1976). No pages of the preface are numbered; all quotations are taken from the preface.
52. Ibid.
53. *Cato's Letters: Unabridged Reproduction of 6th Edition, 1755,* vols. 1 and 2, ed. Leonard W. Levy (New York: Da Capo Press, 1971).
54. Ibid.
55. Ibid., vol. 1, p. 96.
56. Ibid., vol. 2, pp. 306–309.
57. Ibid., p. 312.
58. Cremin, *American Education,* pp. 94–96.
59. Caroline Robbins, *The Eighteenth-Century Commonwealthman* (Cambridge, MA: Harvard University Press, 1959).
60. Brian Simon, *Studies in the History of Education, 1780–1870* (London: Lawrence & Wishart, 1960), pp. 34–35.
61. Robbins, *Eighteenth-Century Commonwealthman,* p. 350.
62. Theodore Sizer, ed., *The Age of the Academies* (New York: Teachers College Press, 1964), pp. 1–48.

63. Quoted in ibid., pp. 70–71.
64. L. Jesse Lemisch, ed., *Benjamin Franklin: The Autobiography and Other Writings* (New York: New American Library, Signet Classics, 1961), p. 72.
65. Ibid., p. 82.
66. Quoted in Sizer, *The Age of the Academies,* p. 71.
67. Quoted in ibid.
68. Quoted in ibid., pp. 77–78.
69. Cremin, *American Education,* p. 480.
70. John Demos, *A Little Commonwealth: Family Life in Plymouth Colony* (New York: Oxford University Press, 1970), pp. 183–186.
71. Reprinted in ibid., p. 100.
72. Joseph F. Kett, *Rites of Passage: Adolescence in America, 1790 to the Present* (New York: Basic Books, 1977), pp. 1–38.
73. Ford, *The New England Primer.* Pages are unnumbered in the reproduction of the original work contained herein.
74. Ibid.
75. Jean-Jacques Rousseau, *Emile* (1762, reprint, New York: Dutton, 1911).
76. Peter Gay, ed., *John Locke on Education* (New York: Teachers College Press, 1964), p. 36.
77. Ibid., p. 48.
78. Ibid., p. 50.

3

Nationalism, Multiculturalism, and Moral Reform in the New Republic

Educational developments after the Revolutionary War set the stage for the formation of the common or, as it is now called, public school. It is argued by World Culture theorists that the American experience of linking mass schooling with creation of the modern state would be a process replicated around the world. American revolutionary leaders worried about stabilizing the political system and maintaining the loyalty of European Americans. Obviously citizens needed to be taught about the workings of the newly created government. In addition, former English colonists, particularly those who remained loyal to England during the Revolution, had to be persuaded to shift their allegiance from the English government.

This chapter will consider the important debates and institutional changes that foreshadowed the development of the common school system and the modern system of higher education. In summary, the major educational concerns during the post-Revolutionary period were

- Turning a multicultural society into a single-culture society.
- Creating nationalism and loyalty to the new government.
- Regulating freedom through citizenship and moral education.
- Determining the best method for educating future citizens.
- Using moral education to eliminate crime and poverty.

I will discuss these issues by focusing in this chapter on

- The argument of world culture theorists that Western schooling spread around the globe with new ideas about government.
- The issue of schooling and cultural diversity in the new republic.
- Noah Webster and education for a new American language and culture.
- Thomas Jefferson and the education of American leaders.
- Education as a source of moral reform.

- Childhood in the new republic.
- The development of charity schools.
- The growth of the American college.

WORLD CULTURE THEORISTS

The development of American common or public schools, according to a group of sociologists called world culture theorists, was part of a global process involving the development of what is called the nation-state. In the phrase *nation-state, nation* refers to the culture, image, and geography of a country, and *state* refers to its government. To achieve a nation-state such as the United States, citizens develop common allegiance to the nation. It is argued that mass education is necessary for creating a sense of nation among the citizenry. Also, schools are necessary for teaching about the workings of government and obedience to the law.

Globally, most nations now have a common school and curricular organization. This has resulted, according to the authors of *School Knowledge for the Masses,* from the worldwide spread of the Western concept of the nation-state, which included a belief in educating citizens to love their nation and to ensure political stability and economic growth. The authors of *School Knowledge for the Masses* argue that "the gradual rationalization of the Western polity, the modern curricular structure became a taken-for-granted 'model' by the turn of the twentieth century."[1] As the Western concept of the nation-state spread, "the standard model of the curriculum has also diffused throughout the world, creating a worldwide homogeneity in the overall categorical [curriculum categories] system."[2] Regarding curricula, the authors of *School Knowledge for the Masses* found a significant worldwide similarity in organization and course labels for primary education. They concluded from an examination of national curricular outlines that there was "more homogeneity and standardization among the curricula prescribed by nation-states, than might have been expected . . . The labels, at least, of mass curricula are so closely tied to great and standardized worldwide visions of social and educational progress, they tend to be patterned in quite consistent ways around the world."[3]

The United States pioneered this relationship between the nation-state and mass schooling. As I will discuss, common or public schools were to create a common culture and allegiance to a concept of the nation. They were also considered key to creating citizens who understood the workings of government and who were obedient to laws.

As I discuss in the next section, the diversity of the American population set for post-Revolutionary leaders a monumental task of creating a sense of nation based on common culture and language. Also, post-Revolutionary leaders worried that the new republic would not survive unless there was a moral and lawful citizenry.

THE PROBLEM OF CULTURAL DIVERSITY

The diverse backgrounds of European Americans—including Anglo-Americans, French Americans, German Americans, and Dutch Americans—and the presence of Native Americans and African Americans created a major crisis for post-Revolutionary leaders. Could the United States survive as a multicultural society? Did the survival of the new nation depend on the creation of a single unified culture?

Those living in the twenty-first century might not consider the 1790 origins of the U.S. population shown in Table 3.1 as representing a diverse white population. However, most Europeans in the 1790s lived rather insular lives, and cultural differences were well defined. In addition, religious differences were extremely important, particularly between Protestants and Catholics. Missing from the table are statistics for the Native American population, which was not included in the first census. Enslaved Africans were counted, but their national or regional identities were not noted.

An important thing to note in Table 3.1 is that the majority (60.9 percent) of those classified as "white" were of English ancestry. The other English-speaking groups were Scottish (8.3 percent) and Irish (including Ulster and Free State, 9.7 percent). This meant that almost 80 percent of the free white population in 1790 arrived in North America speaking English. Of course, this English-speaking statistic of 80 percent would be reduced if we had accurate statistics for languages originally spoken by enslaved Africans. Also distorting the picture is the lack of statistics on the populations of Native American tribes.

The overwhelming Protestant nature of the population is also highlighted by Table 3.1. Irish people from Ulster were primarily Protestant and in the United States were called Scottish-Irish to distinguish them from Irish Catholics. Many immigrants from Germany, Holland, France, and Sweden were also Protestant. Therefore, Protestants made up more than 75 percent of the population.

Another picture of the national and linguistic stock of the United States emerges when slaves are included. According to the 1790 U.S. Census, as shown in Table 3.2, slaves made up 16 percent of the total population of the United States, not counting Native Americans. As shown in Table 3.2, there were large variations between states in slave populations, with Massachusetts and Rhode Island having no slaves and Vermont having .002 percent, in contrast to Virginia

TABLE 3.1 National and Linguistic Stocks in the United States (Whites Only)

English	Scottish	Irish Ulster	Irish Free State	German	Dutch	French	Swedish	Unassigned
60.9%	8.3%	6.0%	3.7%	8.7%	3.4%	1.7%	0.7%	6.6%

Source: Adapted from Table 4.1 in Roger Daniels, *Coming to America: A History of Immigration and Ethnicity in American Life, Second Edition* (New York: Perennial, 2002), p. 68.

TABLE 3.2 1790 Census: Slaves as a Percentage of Total Population by Nation and District

Locality	Slaves as a Percentage of Total Population
Nation	16%
Vermont	0.002
New Hampshire	0.11
Maine	None
Massachusetts	None
Rhode Island	1.3
Connecticut	1.1
New York	6
New Jersey	6
Pennsylvania	0.9
Delaware	15
Maryland	32
Virginia	39
Kentucky	16.8
North Carolina	26
Georgia	35

Source: Calculations in table based on statistics in *A Schedule of the Whole Number of Persons within the Several Districts of the United States,* taken according to "An Act Providing for the Enumeration of the Inhabitants of the United States," passed March 1, 1790, *Return of the Whole Number of Persons within the Several Districts of the United States* (Philadelphia: J. Phillips, GeorgeBYard, Lombard Street, 1793), p. 3.

(39 percent), Georgia (35 percent), and Maryland (32 percent). New York and New Jersey are frequently overlooked as slave-holding states, but according to the 1790 census, 6 percent of the populations of both states was enslaved.

Therefore, in the 1790s the overwhelming percentage of the U.S. population came from English-speaking, Protestant stock, with 16 percent of the population being denied any political rights because of enslavement. The largest percentage was Anglo-Saxon Protestants. Most post-Revolutionary leaders rejected the idea of a multicultural society and advocated the creation of a unified American culture formed around Protestant Anglo-Saxon traditions. In addition, Anglo-American culture (I will be using the term *Anglo-American culture* to refer to the American culture) had to be distinguished from the culture of England. Leading the efforts to create a dominant Protestant Anglo-American culture was Noah Webster, often called the "Schoolmaster of America."

Creating a dominant Protestant Anglo-American culture meant winning the loyalty of citizens. An important source of loyalty is patriotism, or "love of your country." This form of patriotism involves an emotional attachment to symbols of the country.

The use of education during the post-Revolutionary period to promote feelings of patriotism was not unique to the United States. Leaders of many European countries, particularly Prussia, had realized the importance of encouraging feelings of patriotism as a means of unifying the citizenry and building military strength. The ultimate end of patriotism was to strengthen emotional ties to the country so that common citizens would be willing to die in military service to the government.

Methods of teaching patriotism included studying national literature and language, singing nationalistic songs, honoring the flag, and participating in patriotic exercises. In the United States, Noah Webster combined his effort to create a dominant national culture with the promotion of patriotism. Webster's spelling book, with its nationalistic themes, replaced *The New England Primer* as the major school text in the post-Revolutionary period.

NOAH WEBSTER: NATIONALISM AND THE CREATION OF A DOMINANT CULTURE

Noah Webster worked hard to create a dominant Anglo-American culture. A prolific writer, he constantly combined efforts to create a dominant culture and build nationalism. His legacy includes a standardized American dictionary of the English language, an American version of the Bible, and his famous spelling book. The wide use of Webster's speller and dictionary throughout the United States created a lasting mold for the American language.

Webster also contributed politically to the development of the American common school system. Between 1815 and 1819 he served in the Massachusetts legislature and worked actively for a state school fund. One of his speeches to the legislature captures what he believed would be the result of a system of common schools:

> I should rejoice to see a system adopted that should lay a foundation for a permanent fund for public schools, and to have more pains taken to discipline our youth in early life to sound maxims of moral, political, and religious duties. I believe more than is commonly believed may be done in this way towards correcting the vices and disorders of society.[4]

One historian claims that Webster's activities in the state legislature initiated the movement for common schools that culminated in Horace Mann's work in the 1830s.[5]

Born in Connecticut in 1758, Webster began his early career as a country schoolmaster. While teaching in 1779, he conceived the idea of developing a new system of instruction. In 1783 he completed one spelling book, the first of three volumes in a series titled *A Grammatical Institute of the English Language*. In 1784 he completed a grammar book, the second volume in the series, and a reader, which was the third. In 1785 he packed his bags and rode through the country as an itinerant lecturer, selling his instructional system.

Both his salesmanship and the content of his textbooks proved successful. One-and-a-half million copies of the speller had been sold by 1801, 20 million

TIME LINE: MULTICULTURALISM, NATIONALISM, SOCIAL REFORM, AND THE COMMON SCHOOL

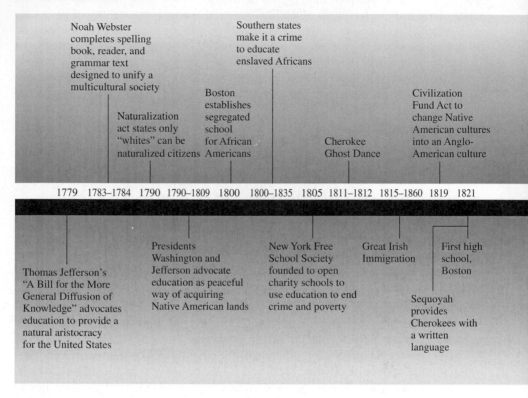

Noah Webster completes spelling book, reader, and grammar text designed to unify a multicultural society

Southern states make it a crime to educate enslaved Africans

Naturalization act states only "whites" can be naturalized citizens

Boston establishes segregated school for African Americans

Cherokee Ghost Dance

Civilization Fund Act to change Native American cultures into an Anglo-American culture

1779 1783–1784 1790 1790–1809 1800 1800–1835 1805 1811–1812 1815–1860 1819 1821

Thomas Jefferson's "A Bill for the More General Diffusion of Knowledge" advocates education to provide a natural aristocracy for the United States

Presidents Washington and Jefferson advocate education as peaceful way of acquiring Native American lands

New York Free School Society founded to open charity schools to use education to end crime and poverty

Great Irish Immigration

First high school, Boston

Sequoyah provides Cherokees with a written language

by 1829, and 75 million by 1875. The speller became a model used by other spelling book authors. Its popularity was demonstrated by the publication in 1863 of a Civil War edition in the South that was adapted "to the youth of the Southern Confederacy."[6]

Webster believed that in addition to teaching reading and writing, his texts should produce good and patriotic Americans, develop an American language, and create a unified national spirit. As his biographer Harry Warfel states, "This unified series of textbooks effactually shaped the destiny of American education for a century. Imitators sprang up by the dozen, and each echoed Websterian nationalism. The word 'American' became indispensable in all textbook titles; all vied in patriotic eloquence."[7]

Webster believed that moral and political values had to be imposed on the child: "Good republicans . . . are formed by a singular machinery in the body politic, which takes the child as soon as he can speak, checks his natural independence and passions, makes him subordinate to superior age, to the laws of the state, to town and parochial institutions."[8]

One method used to instill proper political values was the Federal Catechism, which appeared in the early versions of Webster's spelling book. The inclusion

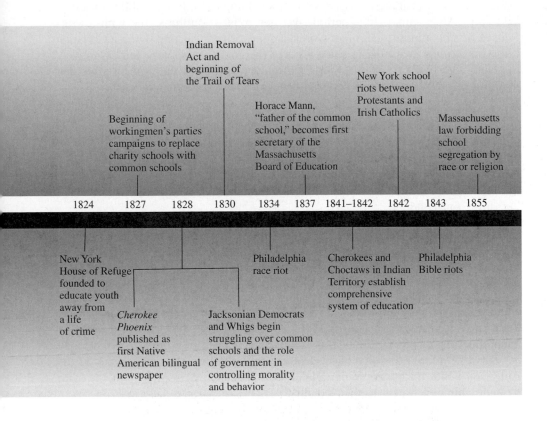

of a catechism in a spelling book was not an original idea. *The New England Primer* contained one, but it was mainly religious in content. However, a catechism with political content was probably Webster's original idea. The use of a catechism required children to memorize questions and answers, which perpetuated an authoritarian method of instruction.

The content of Webster's Federal Catechism reflected his own concern that the new republican government should remain primarily a representative institution and not become democratic. For example, the Federal Catechism contains the following question and answer to be memorized by the reader:

Q: What are the defects of democracy?

A: In democracy, where the people all meet for the purpose of making laws, there are commonly tumults and disorders. A small city may sometimes be governed in this manner; but if the citizens are numerous, their assemblies make a crowd or mob, where debates cannot be carried on with coolness and candor, nor can arguments be heard: Therefore a pure democracy is generally a very bad government. It is often the most tyrannical government on earth; for a multitude is often rash, and will not hear reason.[9]

Webster's spelling books also contained a Moral Catechism to teach the moral values Webster considered necessary for maintaining order in a republican society. Like most Americans of this period, Webster equated public virtue with a Protestant Christian morality. In other words, a good citizen was one living a Christian life. This attitude is similar in some ways to the goals of the early settlers in New England. The first part of the Moral Catechism illustrates the type of Christian morality people like Webster believed necessary in a republican society:

Q: What is moral virtue?

A: It is an honest upright conduct in all our dealings with men.

Q: Can we always determine what is honest and just?

A: Perhaps not in every instance, but in general it is not difficult.

Q: What rules have we to direct us?

A: God's word contained in the Bible has furnished all necessary rules to direct our conduct.

Q: In what part of the Bible are these rules to be found?

A: In almost every part; but the most important duties between men are summed up in the beginning of Matthew, in Christ's Sermon on the Mount.[10]

One aspect of Webster's concern with nationalism and virtue was the building of an emotional feeling of patriotism. In an essay titled "On the Education of Youth in America," published in 1790, Webster writes, "It is an object of vast magnitude that systems of education should be adopted and pursued which may not only diffuse a knowledge of the sciences but may implant in the minds of the American youth the principle of virtue and of liberty and inspire them . . . with an inviolable attachment to their country."[11]

What he meant by an "inviolable attachment" is an emotional bond between citizen and government: Webster believed that "every class of people should know and love the laws" and that attachment to the law "may be formed by early impressions upon the mind." This emotional bond was to be forged by the creation of a national language and by the wide dissemination of the patriotic content of his textbooks. The following statement about Webster's method of selecting material for his readers illustrates his patriotic objectives: "In the choice of pieces, I have not been inattentive to the political interests of America. Several of those masterly addresses of Congress, written at the commencement of the late revolution, contain such noble, just and independent sentiments of liberty and patriotism, that I cannot help wishing to transfuse them into the breasts of the rising generation."[12]

Illustrative of his patriotic themes was the cover of his 1787 reader, which contained the words "Begin with the infant in the cradle; let the first word he lisps be Washington."[13] His readers contained Washington's Farewell Orders to the Army, patriotic poems, and (for the first time in a schoolbook) a history of the Revolutionary War.

For Webster, patriotism, nationalism, and virtue were the foci of educating the republican citizen. These educational values clearly emphasized representative, as opposed to democratic, government. Noah Webster's importance in the history of American education is twofold: He represented widely held opinions of his time, and he had a major effect on the education of children in the United States in the late eighteenth and nineteenth centuries.

Webster's work symbolizes the rejection by Revolutionary leaders of a multicultural society. Webster's creation of an American language and his spelling books helped to form a dominant English-speaking, Protestant, Anglo-American culture. In the late twentieth century, this dominant culture of U.S. schools would be seriously challenged by Native Americans, Latinos, and African Americans.

THOMAS JEFFERSON: A NATURAL ARISTOCRACY

Thomas Jefferson's opinions on education in the new republic were quite different from those of his contemporaries and of later leaders of the common school movement. Unlike Noah Webster and Benjamin Rush (discussed in the next section), Jefferson did not believe schooling should impose political values or mold the virtuous republican citizen. Rather, he believed education should provide the average citizen with the tools of reading and writing and that political beliefs would be formed through the exercise of reason. For Jefferson, the most important means of political education was the reading of history and newspapers. In one of his more famous statements, he argues, "The basis of our government being the opinion of the people, the very first object should be to keep that right; and were it left to me to decide whether we should have a government without newspapers, or newspapers without a government, I should not hesitate a moment to prefer the latter."[14]

Jefferson was concerned with the education of future republican leadership. He believed the new republic needed to identify its future leaders in the early years of their schooling and provide them with an education through college. This educated leadership would form a natural aristocracy.

Jefferson was born in 1743 in Shadwell, near Charlottesville, Virginia. His father was a Virginia magistrate and surveyor, and his mother was a member of one of the most prominent families in the colony. After graduating from the College of William and Mary, Jefferson was admitted to the Virginia bar in 1767. Between 1769 and 1775 he served as a member of the Virginia legislative assembly; in 1776, as a member of the Continental Congress, Jefferson helped draft the Declaration of Independence. As a strong proponent of individualistic democracy, he championed legislative proposals and constitutional amendments protecting freedom of speech and religion. In 1800 he was elected president of the United States.

One reason for Jefferson's opinion that democracy is possible was his belief in the existence of an inborn moral sense, which he referred to as "common sense." For this reason, his educational writings do not emphasize shaping and controlling students' moral behavior as a preparation for citizenship. Jefferson wrote to his friend Peter Carr in 1787 that the individual is "endowed with a sense of right and wrong. . . . This sense is as much a part of his nature as the sense of hearing, seeing, feeling; it is the true foundation of morality." Jefferson argued that this innate sense of right and wrong can be improved through exercise, like any other part of the body, and can be guided by reason. He warned that the study of moral rules can interfere with the proper functioning of this innate sense of morality. He wrote, for example, "State a moral case to a ploughman and a professor. The former will decide it as well, and often better than the latter, because he has not been led astray by artificial rules."[15]

Jefferson's belief in reason and a moral sense did not cause him to reject the importance of knowledge and learning. In a letter to John Adams in 1814 he commented on his disgust with his recent reading of Plato's *Republic*. In simple terms, Plato argues that individuals are born with the world's knowledge and that the role of education is to reveal that inner knowledge to the individual. Jefferson complained in his letter that post-Revolutionary youths seemed to have a similar idea that they had acquired "all learning in their mother's womb and bring it into the world ready made." He went on to attack the shallow education provided at academies, which committed "pupils to the theatre of the world, with just taste enough of learning to be alienated from industrious pursuits, and not enough to do service in the ranks of science." Jefferson then described his dream for the establishment of a university that would teach every branch of science to its "highest degree."[16]

Jefferson's ideas on the role of education and knowledge in society reflect a belief in the possibility of improving the human condition: Individuals are born with reason and a moral sense, and education can improve the workings of these faculties and contribute to the increase of human knowledge. In his 1818 "Report of the Commissioners Appointed to Fix the Site of the University of Virginia," Jefferson likens this process to that of creating a new and better tree by grafting a cultivated tree onto a wild and uncultivated one. "Education, in like manner, engrafts a new man on the native stock, and improves what in his nature was vicious and perverse into qualities of virtue and social worth." In addition, he argues, each generation adds to the store of human knowledge, and this "constant accumulation must advance the knowledge and well-being of mankind, not infinitely, as some have said, but indefinitely, and to a term which no one can fix and foresee."[17]

Jefferson's belief that education can provide the tools and knowledge for the improvement of the exercise of morality and reason is evident in his most famous educational proposal, "A Bill for the More General Diffusion of Knowledge," made to the Virginia legislature in 1779. This bill proposed that schools be established to provide tuition-free education for three years for all male and female children. In these schools, children were to be taught "reading, writing, and common arithmetick [sic], and the books which shall be used therein for instructing the children to read shall be such as will at the same time make them acquainted with Grecian, Roman, English and American history."[18] This was to be the basic education of the citizens of the new republic.

Jefferson elaborated on the reasons for the content of this education in "Notes on the State of Virginia." He rejected the teaching of the Bible in reading instruction, stating, "Instead, therefore, of putting the Bible and Testament into the hands of the children at an age when their judgments are not sufficiently matured for religious inquiries, their memories may here be stored with the most useful facts from Grecian, Roman, European, and American history." The development of morality, he argued, should be postponed until reason matures. The first elements of moral instruction should be for the purpose of teaching children "how to work out their own greatest happiness, by shewing [sic] them that it does not depend on the condition of life in which chance has placed them, but is always the result of a good conscience, good health, occupation, and freedom in all just pursuits."[19]

The most important part of moral instruction, according to Jefferson, is the study of history, which guides reason by providing the individual with knowledge about human actions. "History, by apprising them of the past, will enable them to judge of the future; it will avail them of the experience of other times and other nations; it will qualify them as judges of the actions and designs of men."[20]

For Jefferson, education would contribute to the balance between freedom and order by providing all citizens with the basic tools of learning, a knowledge of history, and the ability to work out their own happiness and morality. He believed that knowledge, reason, and a developed moral sense would result in a natural order in a free society.

"A Bill for the More General Diffusion of Knowledge" also contained a plan for the selection and education of a natural aristocracy. The bill proposed the establishment of grammar schools in every county. An overseer of the reading-and-writing schools would choose "the boy of best genius in the school, of those whose parents are too poor to give them further education, and . . . send him forward to one of the grammar schools." After every one or two years in the Latin school, the best student of the group would be selected and given six more years of education. "By this means," Jefferson wrote in "Notes on the State of Virginia," "twenty of the best geniuses will be raked from the rubbish annually, and instructed, at the public expence [sic], so far as grammar schools go." Out of the selected group of grammar school graduates, half of the best would be sent at public expense for three years to the College of William and Mary.[21]

The talent selected through this three-tier system of education was to provide the leadership for the republic. According to Jefferson, the purpose of higher education is to "form statesmen, legislators and judges, on whom public prosperity and individual happiness are so much to depend." In addition, higher education should teach the principles and structure of government, promote the interests of agriculture and business, and advance the sciences.[22]

Jefferson's educational plan combined two ideas: preparing the citizen and preparing the political leader. Of the two goals, Jefferson believed the instruction of the citizen was the more important: "But of all the views of this law none is more important, none more legitimate, than that of rendering the people the safe, as they are the ultimate, guardians of their own liberty."[23]

From Jefferson's educational writings emerges the following portrait of the ideal citizen. Guided by a knowledge of history and the reading of newspapers, the individual would exercise reason and moral common sense to make political decisions. One of the most important decisions would be the selection of republican leadership. Ideally, the choice would be among members of the natural aristocracy who had been selected by the school system and given a university education. In the end, Jefferson compromised his belief in the free exercise of individual reason by proposing the censorship of political texts in the university training of the natural aristocracy. In this regard, Jefferson succumbed to the temptation of using education to teach what he believed were correct political doctrines. Even the major defender of the role of reason in a democratic society could not resist shaping the political education of future leaders. But even with this qualification of Jefferson's belief in the free exercise of reason, his doctrines provide a sharp contrast to those who believed that public schooling should educate "republican machines."

MORAL REFORM AND FACULTY PSYCHOLOGY

Some Americans in the early nineteenth century were taken with the idea that institutions could perfect the good person and create the good society. This pattern of thinking made it possible for educational leaders to envision a system of common schooling that would lead to a moral and political reformation of society. The belief that institutional structures could be used to develop the good society was reflected in the expansion of charity schools in the early part of the nineteenth century and in the establishment of special institutions for delinquent youth.

Charity schools were the first to be based on the Lancasterian system of school organization and instruction, which revolutionized the concept of schooling. Before the introduction of the Lancasterian method, the main purpose of education was to develop the moral character of the child through memorization and recitation of didactic readings. *The New England Primer* is a good example of this type of instruction.

What was new about the institutional changes in the early part of the nineteenth century, and the Lancasterian system of instruction, was the idea that institutional arrangements were important to developing moral character. A belief developed that moral character could be shaped by the way students interacted in the school as well as through the learning of didactic material. In later years this would be referred to as "the process of socialization."

In the early nineteenth century the belief in the importance of institutional arrangements in shaping moral character contributed to the already developing idea that schooling of the entire population was necessary for social and political order. As discussed earlier in this chapter, post-Revolutionary leaders viewed education as important for promoting nationalism and balancing freedom and order. These ideas, combined with a belief in the necessity of particular institutional arrangements, easily led to the conclusion that all children of the republic should be educated in a single common school system.

The acceptance of the notion of malleability of character provided the basis in the early nineteenth century for the belief that the good society could be created through schooling and other institutional changes. Of primary importance was the widespread belief in some form of faculty psychology. Behavioral and romantic concepts of childhood began to develop in the eighteenth century. The behavioral concept of human psychology stressed the importance of the environment in shaping character, whereas the romantic concept stressed the unfolding of the inner nature of the individual.

Faculty psychology contained elements of both behaviorism and romanticism. The human mind was said to be divided into several different parts, such as intelligence and morality. These different faculties were natural components of the individual and could be influenced by the environment. For instance, Benjamin Rush, the leading American physician of the post-Revolutionary period and often called the "father of American psychiatry," argued in 1786 that a moral faculty is a natural part of the human mind. Rush believed that the moral faculty had the function of "distinguishing and choosing good and evil." From this perspective, moral actions were dependent on the degree of development of the moral faculty. Rush argued that the moral faculties of some individuals were developed out of proportion to other faculties. He referred to these individuals as "benevolent idiots" and gave as an example an individual who "spent several hours of every day in devotion, in which he was so careful to be private that he was once found in the most improbable place in the world for that purpose, vz. in an oven." Rush also described individuals in whom all faculties except the moral faculty were highly developed. For instance, he cited the Duke of Sully, who was very learned, creative, and athletic but who "died in the flower of his age, in a common brothel, perfectly corrupted by his debaucheries, and expired with the glass in his hand, cursing and denying God."[24]

People adhered to many different forms of faculty psychology during the early part of the nineteenth century. For instance, Horace Mann, often called the "father of the common school," was a phrenologist, and his educational writings often refer to the different faculties of the mind. In a report to the Massachusetts State Board of Education in 1848, for example, he likened an uneducated republic to an obscene giant "whose brain has been developed only in the region of the appetites and passions, and not in the organs of reason and conscience."[25]

One common characteristic of all varieties of faculty psychology was a belief that the virtuous functioning of the moral faculty is dependent on how it is cultivated. For instance, the prescription given by Rush for a well-functioning moral faculty included sunshine, a plain diet, water, and cleanliness. Rush also included with these physical remedies "mechanical means of promoting virtue," such as odors, eloquence from the pulpit, music, and solitude.[26]

Also, discipline and exercise of the various faculties of the mind were considered necessary for their proper development. This type of reasoning would often appear in educational reports. Yale College's famous report of 1828, which will be discussed in more detail later in this chapter, states, "In laying the foundation of a thorough education, it is necessary that all the important mental faculties be brought into exercise. . . . If the student exercises his reasoning powers only, he will be deficient in imagination and taste, in fervid and impressive eloquence."[27]

Faculty psychology in all its various forms reflected the growing belief in the perfectibility of the human being. This belief provided the intellectual basis for reform movements in the early part of the nineteenth century that produced modern systems of education and other institutions designed to improve human character. Of major importance was the idea of controlling the institutional environment affecting the individual as a means of achieving perfection.

CONCEPTS OF CHILDHOOD: PROTECTED, WORKING, POOR, RURAL, AND ENSLAVED

Besides nationalism and worries about political leadership, changing concepts and social conditions of childhood contributed to the desire to create public schools. In *Huck's Raft: A History of American Childhood,* Steven Mintz provides a synthesis of historical research about changing concepts of American childhood.[28] He argues that the historical images of childhood are filled with misconceptions. First, he debunks the myth that American children in the nineteenth and early twentieth centuries had a carefree childhood. This, he argues, became a reality for most children only in the second half of the twentieth century. In prior years, including the period covered by this chapter, most children experienced the death of a sibling or one or both parents. Rampant childhood diseases left many children dead or seriously debilitated. Most children began working at an early age. A high percentage of children, because of the death of a parent, lived in single-parent homes; it has been calculated that at the end of the nineteenth century fully a third of all children lived at one time in single-parent homes.[29] Consequently, Mintz argues that despite worries in the late twentieth and early twenty-first centuries that childhood was in decline and disappearing in a flood of commercialism and media, the condition of childhood has actually been progressing since the first half of the twentieth century.

After the American Revolution, urban families wealthy enough not to need income from working children could provide a "protected childhood." These urban families believed that it was their responsibility to protect their children from corruption from the outside world. Believing children were born innocent, these families considered childhood as something to be enjoyed and prolonged. Adopting the viewpoint of faculty psychology, they believed childhood was a stage of life where character could be shaped to make the virtuous adult. Schools were seen as logical institutions for the extension of childhood that would protect and mold children.[30]

The charity school movement discussed in the next section was a result of concerns about urban street children who plagued city dwellers with constant begging and theft. Infanticide was rampant among the urban poor, with reports that as late as the middle of the nineteenth century over fifty bodies of infants were found each month in New York City.[31] Those who survived infanticide and childhood diseases were often condemned to homelessness and a street life of stealing, panhandling, and prostitution. Mintz cites many incidents of children being arrested for picking pockets and stealing. Besides helping her mother sell stolen goods, one 12-year-old girl claimed that she had "learnt the trick of getting money from men, with the promise that she would go with them, and afterwards run away."[32]

Many urban families depended on their children's wages. Rural families needed children for farmwork; or if they proved a burden on the family, children were apprenticed to city dwellers and villagers. Later many were sent to work in factories. In the 1830s, at the time of the development of the common school, surplus farm children were often sent to work in New England textile mills. Children in textile factories worked from 5 a.m. to 7 p.m. six days a week, with only a half hour off for breakfast and dinner, in factories described as "the windows nailed shut, the dim light, the dust and fabric fibers that fill the air."[33] Throughout the nineteenth century, reformers wanted to extend "protected childhood" to working children with child labor and compulsory education laws. However, a social class of laboring children continued into the twentieth century.[34]

What about enslaved African American children? Early family breakup along with forced labor were the most characteristic features of life among enslaved children. It is estimated that half of all enslaved children grew up separated from their fathers because of death or living on separate plantations, or because their fathers were white and refused to admit to having enslaved children. Laws in slave states made it illegal to educate enslaved children. Slave children were the targets of abuse and violence by their owners. There was a particular harshness shown toward children of free white fathers and enslaved African mothers, as illustrated by a statement by an enslaved African: "There are no slaves that are so badly abused as those that are related to some of the [white] women, or the children of their own husband; it seems as though they never could hate these quite bad enough."[35]

After the American Revolution, it was the elite who worried about street children and wanted to extend to them some form of protected childhood by providing institutional care in charity schools or schools for delinquent children. With the advent of charity schools to keep the kids off the streets and to keep them from stealing from the wealthy, labor leaders by the 1830s began to demand schools for working children that would provide them with a protected childhood. The combination of families who could provide their children with a protected childhood, elites wanting to end the problem of street children, and labor leaders seeking a protected childhood for working children contributed to the eventual development of public schools in the 1830s.

CHARITY SCHOOLS, THE LANCASTERIAN SYSTEM, AND PRISONS

Charity schools and juvenile reformatories developed in the United States in the early part of the nineteenth century as part of a general attempt to reduce crime and poverty and end the problem of urban street children. The charity school movement was the first major attempt to use schooling as a means of socializing children into the world of work. Common school reformers of the 1830s and 1840s would use the same arguments for the ameliorating power of education as charity schools did. In addition, in some places charity schools provided the basic institutional structure for the development of common schools.

In general, charity schools and juvenile reformatories in the early nineteenth century sought to create good moral character by replacing a weak family structure and destroying criminal associations. An individual, it was believed, became a potential criminal when the family failed to provide adequate moral training and was eventually led astray through contact with a criminal community.

For instance, the failure of the family structure is emphasized in the petition for incorporation in 1805 of the organization that became the major promoter of the Lancasterian system—the New York Free School Society. The incorporation statement declares that the condition of the children of the poor "is deplorable indeed; reared up by parents who . . . become either indifferent to the best interests of their offspring, or, through intemperate lives, are rendered unable to defray the expense of their instruction." The petition goes on to argue that the neglect of education had resulted in "ignorance and vice, and all those manifold evils resulting from every species of immorality."[36] This society, which was organized to provide education for the poor, within a short time dominated charity schooling in New York City. By the 1840s the schools of the New York Free School Society came under public control and became the core of the early system of public schools in New York City.

Like those involved with charity schools, reformers involved with juvenile reformatories linked waywardness with the failure of the family. The first reformatories, called houses of refuge, were founded in New York in 1824, in Boston in 1826, and in Philadelphia in 1828. The organization responsible for opening the New York House of Refuge was the New York Society for the Prevention of Pauperism, founded in 1815. In 1823 this organization changed its name to the Society for the Reformation of Juvenile Delinquents. Its report for 1822 states that children become wayward because no "moral standard of conduct has been placed before their eyes. No faithful parent has watched over them and restrained their vicious propensities."[37]

Arguing in the same manner, the Boston House of Refuge went so far as to advocate the use of its institution by any child who was considered to have an improper family life. Its 1829 report to the city of Boston argues that to avoid the evils arising from the neglect of family government, the city's laws should be extended so that any "parents, or guardians, or friends of children, who are unable to exercise any moral government, might place them in this institution."[38]

Thus the purpose of charity schools and reformatories was to correct the problems caused by the failure of parental government. In addition, they were to keep children and youth from exposure to immoral education by isolating them from criminal contacts. Members of the New York Free School Society believed that criminal associations were one of the major problems of raising children in a city. DeWitt Clinton, president of the New York Free School Society, issued this warning in 1809: "Great cities are, at all times, the nurseries and hotbeds of crimes . . . and the dreadful examples of vice which are presented to youth, and the alluring forms in which it is arrayed . . . cannot fail of augmenting the mass of moral depravity."[39]

The preceding arguments provided the rationale for the charity schools. In essence, they were supposed to eliminate crime and poverty by replacing the failed government of the family with the government of the school and by keeping children off the streets and out of contact with potential criminal associates. The argument that an important function of schooling is to keep children off the streets continued into the twentieth century.

Reformers involved in charity schools and juvenile reformatories believed the solution to crime and poverty to be education and provision of the proper institutional environment. Education was supposed to provide the tools by which an individual could function in a social role, and the institutional environment was supposed to teach an individual how to use these tools in a moral manner.

The charity school movement spread rapidly in the 1790s and the early 1800s. These schools, which provided the basic framework for the later development of public schools, were organized mainly by private associations such as the New York Free School Society. The existence of charity schools created a division between social classes: The poor attended charity schools, and the better-off attended other private and public institutions.

Although the stated intention of charity schools was to save the children of the poor from a life of crime and poverty, their creation also had important effects on existing private schools and, later, on the development of public schools. The best history of the early effects of the development of charity schools is Carl Kaestle's *Evolution of an Urban School System: New York City, 1750–1850.* Kaestle examined the registers of the private schools in New York City in the 1790s and found that they were not exclusive or limited to the education of the children of the wealthy. In fact, he argues, the private schools were common in several respects. First, they were the most common or prevalent system of education. Second, they all provided what was called a common system of education. And third, they were attended in common by children from a wide range of families with differing incomes and occupations.[40]

As Kaestle indicates, this last point is most important because school reformers would later argue for the necessity of common public schools as a means of mixing the children of the rich and poor in the same classroom in order to eliminate social class divisions in education: "This third fact is the most important, for it is this sense of the word that was central to the ideology of the 'common school' reformers of the nineteenth century. The data . . . suggest that their reform, whether they knew it or not, was an attempt to restore the social mixing that had existed, at least in New York, before the creation of the free schools."[41] Private schools were attended by a variety of children from different social classes because tuition was adjusted according to the income of the parents. Furthermore, Kaestle found little difference between the percentage of children annually attending school in the 1790s and the percentage attending free public schools in the middle 1800s.

Kaestle also found that attempts in the 1790s to systematize the private schools in New York City failed and that these schools were unable to accommodate the influx of immigrants, particularly from Ireland and France. The result was that in the early nineteenth century private schools became, in Kaestle's words, "restricted more and more to the wealthy minority. Meanwhile, the city's public school system arose from the charity schools, which had played a traditional but numerically slight role in the colonial period."[42]

In addition to laying the foundation for later public schooling, charity schools provided the first organized educational opportunities for the increasing number of freed slaves settling in the North. Kaestle details these developments in *Pillars of the Republic: Common Schools and American Society, 1780–1860.* He states that schools for freed black slaves were opened in Philadelphia in 1770, in New York in 1787, and in Baltimore in 1792.[43]

The Lancasterian system, introduced into charity schools in the United States and England in the early nineteenth century, was revolutionary in its emphasis on the process of schooling as a means of developing moral character. It was considered ideally suited to charity schools because it was inexpensive and provided training in character development.

The New York Free School Society was mainly responsible for introducing and spreading the fame of the Lancasterian system in the United States. Most of DeWitt Clinton's dedicatory speech for the new Free School Society building in 1809 was devoted to praising the new instructional system. He was so enraptured with its potential that he stated, "I consider his [Joseph Lancaster's] system as creating a new era in education, as a blessing sent down from heaven to redeem the poor."[44] The system spread rapidly throughout the country, and its adoption was not limited to charity schools. Ellwood Cubberley found that the system was in use in the early nineteenth century from Massachusetts to Georgia and as far west as Detroit, Cincinnati, and Louisville. In 1822 the Pennsylvania state legislature, in an act reorganizing the second school district, required the use of the Lancasterian system.[45]

The popularity of the system in the United States eventually caused its English developer, Joseph Lancaster, to make his home here. He died in 1838 when he was run over by a horse and carriage after inspecting a New York Lancasterian school. At the time of his death, he had plans to push his system to a new height of educational efficiency. He had contracted with the New York Free School Society to run an experiment in which a system of instruction would be used that was supposed to teach forty children to read and spell accurately in four to six weeks.

Claims were made that civilization owed Joseph Lancaster a debt for coining the pregnant mottoes "A place for everything and everything in its place" and "Let every child at every moment have something to do and a motive for doing it."[46] These were the mottoes of a system designed to handle large numbers of pupils in an efficient, inexpensive manner. The system could supposedly handle as many as a thousand students at a time. Under the Lancasterian system, pupils were seated in rows and received their instruction from monitors, who received their instruction from the master, who sat at the end of the room. Monitors were selected from among the better students in the class, and they wore badges indicating their rank.

The discipline and orderliness required by the Lancasterian system were meant to provide moral training. An engraving of a Lancasterian schoolroom in Pennsylvania illustrates how training in orderliness was inherent in the classroom management system. This particular room was designed to accommodate 450 students. The teacher sat at the head of the room on a raised platform. Beneath and in front of the teacher were three rows of monitors' desks placed directly in front of the pupils' desks. The pupils' desks were divided into three sections, each of which was divided into two parts, and each section was in line with one of the rows of monitors' desks. Arrows on the engraving indicate that a group of pupils would march to the front of the room and stand around the monitors' desks, where they would receive instruction from the monitors. When they finished, they would march to the rear part of their section and recite or receive further instruction from another monitor. While this group was marching to the rear, another group would be marching up to the front to take their places around the monitors. When finished, these pupils would march to the rear, and the group in the rear would move forward to the second part of their section to receive instruction from yet another monitor. Because each of the three sections had a group in front, one in the rear, and one in the middle working on different things, a total of nine different recitations could be carried on at one time.

Educators of the period made an analogy between the Lancasterian system and a factory. An unidentified French writer was quoted as saying, "It is a masterpiece which must produce a revolution in popular education. . . . It may be styled a manufactory of knowledge."[47] DeWitt Clinton described it as "a system which is, in education, what the neat finished machines for abridging labor and expense are in the mechanic arts."[48] Undoubtedly the greatest selling point of the system was its cheapness. It provided a system for educating poor children inexpensively. Those promoting the system also believed it provided character training for the child.

A student's submission to this factory system of education was supposed to lead to a sense of orderliness and obedience. The periodic movement of pupils and materials required order and discipline. Each student had an assigned place in the educational machine, and the machine was kept well oiled by a distribution of awards and punishments. Virtue was rewarded by a system of badges, the highest being the Order of Merit. Virtue and ability led to appointment to the rank of monitor. Lancaster developed a unique system of punishments. Children who talked frequently or were idle were punished by having wooden logs placed around their necks. Extreme offenders were placed in a sack or basket suspended from the roof of the school in full view of the rest of the pupils.

The constant activity, regimentation, and lockstep marching were supposed to imprint the virtues of orderliness and obedience indelibly on the student's mind. Clinton hailed Lancaster as the benefactor of the human race: "I contemplate the habits of order which it [the Lancasterian system] forms, the spirit of emulation which it excites, the rapid improvement which it produces, the purity of morals which it inculcates—when I behold the extraordinary union of celerity in instruction and economy of expense."[49]

The virtues of submission, order, and industriousness were considered necessary for functioning in the world of business. The Boston School Committee investigated the New York Lancasterian schools in 1828 and reported that the system kept students attentive and interested by permitting no moments of idleness. The committee praised the method and declared that "its effects on the habits, character, and intelligence of youth are highly beneficial; disposing their minds to industry, to readiness of attention, and to subordination, thereby creating in early life a love of order, preparation for business."[50]

The Lancasterian system was supposed to help the pauper child escape poverty and crime by imparting formal knowledge and instilling the virtues needed in the world of work. Within this framework of reasoning, the qualities of submission, order, and industriousness made the child moral by making him or her useful to and functional in society. In addition, the very act of attending school kept pupils off the streets and away from the kind of learning believed to occur through contact with criminals.

Concern about the evil influence of the criminal community on the molding of human character was the basis for establishing houses of refuge for juvenile delinquents. At first the New York Society for the Reformation of Juvenile Delinquents wanted only separate buildings within prisons for youthful offenders; but in 1824, after deciding this did not provide complete enough separation, it founded the New York House of Refuge.

Just as charity school reformers viewed cities as colleges of vice, promoters of juvenile reformatories viewed prisons as systems of criminal education. This attitude is clearly stated in the 1828 report of the New York House of Refuge, which called prisons "so many schools of vice . . . so many seminaries to impart lessons and maxims, calculated to banish legal restraints, moral consideration, pride of character, and self-regard."[51]

Like the charity schools, the juvenile reformatories sought to provide an institutional replacement for what was believed to be a failed family structure. The Lancasterian system was used in an attempt to create an ideal family structure within the institutional setting of the reformatory. The ideal family government would separate the juvenile from evil and teach the habits of order and discipline. The Boston Prison Discipline Society's report in 1832 claims, "How much may parents, and all who have the care of youth, learn from the Houses of Refuge for Juvenile Delinquents." What could be learned, according to this report, was the morally rewarding effect on youth of "regular hours for solitude and sleep; regular hours for promoting cleanliness; regular hours for exercise and recreation; regular hours for obtaining knowledge human and divine; and regular hours for manual labor." The report goes on to state that the significance of the houses of refuge was their "unspeakably important lessons of instruction to the world, on these every day duties of parents and others."[52]

The houses of refuge emphasized regimentation and order. The New York House of Refuge instituted a rigorous schedule of Lancasterian instruction and labor. The first two hours of the morning were devoted to classroom instruction, and then there were four hours of labor in workshops. Then came lunch and a "little time . . . [for] recreation." In the afternoon, four hours were devoted to labor. Then came supper, followed by two more hours of Lancasterian instruction. Religious exercises were given in the early morning and before retirement at night.[53]

The New York and Philadelphia houses of refuge followed similar schedules. In both systems, each child was placed in a separate cell at night. During the day, the children were not allowed to communicate while receiving instruction or performing work. Conversation was allowed only during free time.

In this manner, the juvenile offender was to be isolated from evil and trained in the habits of order, obedience, and industriousness. The 1833 annual report of the New York House of Refuge states that "obedience and industry are necessary to make good boys good men and useful citizens." The report goes on to hail its own success at being able "to implant principles of virtue and habits of industry, where the vilest and wickedest associations have pre-occupied the mind."[54] The education and training received by the inmates were intended to prepare them to fit into the social structure. Basic occupational skills were to be learned in the classrooms and workshops. The virtues instilled by the system were considered necessary in the world of work.

The development of charity schools, the Lancasterian system, and the houses of refuge reflected growing faith in the power of schooling to solve the problems of society. They all contained, in varying degrees, institutional procedures that provided the individual with moral examples, habituated the student to moral conduct, and disassociated the pupil from evil influences. What is most important about these institutions is that they embodied the belief that education could end poverty and crime in society.

This belief in the ameliorating power of schooling became an essential part of the common school movement of the 1830s and 1840s. Charity schools provided a working model and, in some places, the basic institutional structure for the establishment of a common school system. In addition, they became a target of attack by some common school reformers who believed the existence of charity schools separated the children of the rich and the poor. This, it was believed, reinforced social class differences. The hope of the common school was to overcome the problems of social class by mixing together all children in the same schoolhouse. A major result of this argument was the extension of the moral training provided in the charity schools to the children of all social classes.

INSTITUTIONAL CHANGE AND THE AMERICAN COLLEGE

Although the charity schools and houses of refuge served a different social stratum than did the colleges, similar arguments were given in support of a traditional collegiate life. *The Yale Report* of 1828, regarded as the standard for the maintenance of colleges in the nineteenth century, argued that it was necessary for the residential college to provide a family form of control over students, and it used faculty psychology to defend a traditional liberal arts curriculum against pleas for more practical studies and electives.

In the early nineteenth century, American colleges were established at an incredible rate in response to denominational rivalries, local boosterism, and public demand. Concerns about the nature of the college curriculum and the differences between public and private institutions were sparked by this growth. The resolution of these institutional issues was to have an important effect on the history of the college in the nineteenth century.

Nine colleges had been established in the colonies before the Revolutionary War. Between the Revolutionary War and the Civil War, approximately 250 colleges were established, and 182 of these survived into the twentieth century. The growth of the American college was highlighted in a striking comparison made in 1880 between American and British institutions of higher learning. It pointed out that England had four universities to serve a population of 23 million, while Ohio had thirty-seven institutions of higher learning to serve a population of 3 million.[55]

The rapid expansion of American colleges created many institutional problems. A major issue was the nature of the college curriculum. In the early part of the nineteenth century, public demand for higher education placed pressure on colleges to achieve a balance between what Benjamin Franklin had referred to as the useful and the ornamental in learning. The traditional classical curriculum of Latin and Greek was still considered an ideal for the education of gentlemen. But the usefulness of the study of science and modern languages, along with a demand for education in practical subjects, created conflict over the nature of the college curriculum.

The increased number of institutions of higher education led to the inevitable problem of separating public and private control. Colonial colleges developed during a period when few distinctions were made between public and private schools. Public and private financing combined with public and private control to blur the status of colleges in relationship to government. This issue was finally resolved in *Dartmouth College v. Woodward* (1819), which affected not only the later history of colleges but also the development of American corporations.

The curriculum issues faced by colleges in the early nineteenth century reflected a general concern about the role of higher education in society and the proper education of the individual. Higher education during the early colonial period was concerned primarily with the education of ministers and public leaders. The classical curriculum of Latin and Greek was considered appropriate to serve these two social functions. The study of Latin was the traditional education for the ministry, and the study of Greek was part of the Renaissance ideal for the education of the gentleman ruler.

During their early years, all the colonial colleges reflected these social goals and educational ideas. This was certainly true of the early years of Harvard and was true also of the College of William and Mary, established by royal charter in 1693 in Virginia to ensure a steady supply of Anglican clergymen. Yale and Princeton were established to serve religious purposes, but in a spirit of denominational rivalry. Yale was established in 1701 in reaction to what was believed to be the more liberal theological orientation of Harvard. In 1746 Princeton was established through support given by one branch of the Presbyterian church that had been affected by the religious Great Awakening of the eighteenth century. Baptists established the College of Rhode Island (later Brown University) in 1764; the Dutch Reformed church established Queen's College (later Rutgers University) in 1766; the Congregationalists founded Dartmouth in 1769; and King George III appealed for funds for the founding of what would later become the University of Pennsylvania and Columbia University.

The curriculum of colonial colleges did not remain static. Both science and the emphasis of the Enlightenment on reason found their way into the curriculum under the general label "natural philosophy." The works of Locke and Newton and Copernican theory began to appear in the readings at Yale in the eighteenth century. In 1734 Yale imported a telescope, a microscope, and a barometer. The growth in the influence of science is reflected in the curriculum changes made at Yale: In 1726 mathematics was required only in the fourth year, but by 1745 arithmetic was made an entrance requirement and mathematics was required in the second, third, and fourth years. At King's College (later Columbia University) in New York an attempt was made in 1754 to introduce a course of study in navigation, surveying, geography, and natural history that would teach "the knowledge . . . of every Thing useful for the Comfort, the Convenience and Elegance of Life . . . and everything that can contribute to . . . true Happiness."[56] These are only a few examples of the changes that began to take place in the college curriculum of the eighteenth century.

Richard Hofstadter argues in *Academic Freedom in the Age of the College* that the college boom of the early nineteenth century caused a major regression in the college curriculum and academic freedom. In the academy movement, freedom of thought was considered an essential element in the development of science and the progress of society. Hofstadter writes, "During the last three or four decades of the eighteenth century the American colleges had achieved a notable degree of freedom, vitality, and public usefulness and seemed to have set their feet firmly on the path to further progress."[57] He describes the opening decades of the nineteenth century as the great retrogression in collegiate education and academic freedom. Hofstadter argues that this retrogression occurred because colleges came to serve narrow religious interests. In the eighteenth century, the small number of colleges in existence had begun to move away from serving narrow sectarian interests, but the multiplication of colleges in the nineteenth century reflected particular denominational concerns. Added to these religious concerns was local boosterism, which resulted, according to Hofstadter, in an intense denominational rivalry "to supply every locality with a cheap and indigenous institution that would make it possible for local boys who desired degrees to get them easily."[58]

In addition to the problems caused by the creation of a large number of colleges serving narrow sectarian interests, there was the problem of quality. Many of these institutions employed a limited number of faculty members, who were required to teach a maximum number of courses. Quality declined as, for example, the teaching of the classics was reduced to the teaching of grammar, so that the culture of antiquity was no longer conveyed.

Colleges started in the spirit of local boosterism often made little attempt to plan academic quality. Historian Frederick Rudolph describes the college-building mania: "Often when a college had a building, it had no students. If it had students, frequently it had no building. If it had either, then perhaps it had no money, perhaps no professors; if professors, then no president, if a president, then no professors." Rudolph portrays college building during this period as an activity that was undertaken with the same zeal as "canal-building, cotton-ginning, farming, and gold-mining."[59]

In the midst of the college boom, a search for a guiding standard was in progress. For many colleges, this standard came in the form of *The Yale Report* of 1828, which used faculty psychology to defend a traditional curriculum. In part, *The Yale Report* was a reaction to other proposed reforms in the college curriculum. Theodore Crane writes, "For decades after 1828 *The Yale Report* sustained traditionalists. Its assumptions seemed to reflect a realistic appraisal of the role played by American colleges and of the expectations of the public."[60] Rudolph argues that *The Yale Report* satisfied the established elites because it withstood demands for reforms that would have given American colleges a more practical and popular curriculum: "The religious, the very pious, the privileged—were the people who ran the colleges, people who also knew that the American college was running on a shoestring and that the old course of study, while the best, was also the cheapest."[61]

The Yale Report, like the charity schools and other reforms of the period, placed a great deal of importance on maintaining a family structure within an institutional setting. In defining the appropriate goal of a college, the report states its goal is "to lay the foundation of a superior education: and this is to be done, at a period of life when a substitute must be provided for parental superintendence." The report argues that students, when removed from the family, need to be protected against "untried scenes of temptation," and this protection would result from providing a substitute for parental control. These regulations "should approach as near to the character of parental control as the circumstances of the case will admit."[62]

To achieve this form of parental control, the report argues strongly for the necessity of a residential college: "The parental character of college government, requires that the students should be so collected together, as to constitute one family, that the intercourse between them and their instructors may be frequent and familiar."[63] To accomplish this objective, the report calls for the establishment of residence halls on college campuses.

Discussion took place during this period about the need to arrange the institutional environment of residence halls at colleges and academies. For example, in 1829 the Boston Prison Discipline Society gave full support to the dormitory plans of an unnamed "important school in Massachusetts." These plans called for three stories of galleries along which individual rooms would face a large open space in the middle. Each room was to have a glass window. The master of the school could stand in the middle of the building and observe all the rooms. In this building, the society reported, the student would have time to read and reflect in his own room, and, more important, "the idle, profane and vicious youth is effectually prevented from corrupting his fellows, during those hours of darkness, in which there is the greatest danger."[64]

Within the residential environment of college life, students were to develop an intellectual culture—referred to in *The Yale Report* as "the discipline and the furniture of the mind"—through study of a general curriculum. *The Yale Report* rejects the idea of colleges providing practical and professional studies: "The great object of a collegiate education, preparatory to the study of a profession, is to give that expansion and balance of the mental powers, those liberal comprehensive views, and those fine proportions of character, which are not to be found in him whose ideas are always confined to one particular channel."[65]

Within the framework of the preceding statement, collegiate education was to provide a general background of knowledge and an exercise of mental powers so that the individual would be able to participate in a wide range of intellectual activities. In the words of the report, "Wherever he [the college graduate] goes, into whatever company he falls, he has those general views, on every topic of interest, which will enable him to understand, to digest, and to form a correct opinion, on the statements and discussions he hears."[66]

In addition to knowledge, a collegiate education was supposed to provide a balanced exercise of the different mental faculties. *The Yale Report* uses faculty psychology to explain the processes involved in achieving the goal of balanced mental training: "In laying the foundation of a thorough education, it is necessary that all the important mental faculties be brought into exercise." The report goes on to argue that if exercising any particular mental faculty were neglected, the mind would not reach full perfection. Full perfection was to be achieved through bringing each mental faculty to "the fair proportions which nature designed."[67]

The reasoning used in the report was that balanced mental faculties would result in a balanced character. The general studies offered by the college were to provide the exercise necessary for achieving a balance of mental faculties and character. As stated in the report, "In the course of instruction in this college, it has been an object to maintain such proportion between the different branches of literature and science, as to form in the student a proper balance of character."[68] Each subject matter area would contribute to the exercise of a different part of the mind. For instance, the report claims that mathematics would teach demonstrative reasoning, physical sciences would teach inductive reasoning, ancient literature would provide finished models of taste, English reading would teach speaking and writing, philosophy would teach thinking, and rhetoric and oratory would teach the art of speaking.

The Yale Report has often been viewed as a conservative response to reforms proposed during the 1820s for electives and specialization in the college curriculum. Its attraction might have been the promise it offered of providing a general education that would confirm or confer a social status. Implicit in the idea of education as developing a balanced character that could fit into any intellectual conversation or gathering was the assumption of easy movement between social classes. Receiving a general collegiate education might not have guaranteed access to any particular occupation, but it did promise to inculcate the culture and manners that might be useful in achieving any social advancement.

The Yale Report seems to have reflected general sentiments about the type of education required for the development of moral character. Similar arguments for parental government and for the training of mental faculties could be found in the charity school movement. Charity schools sought moral development through classroom management and instruction that replicated family government and exercised mental faculties; *The Yale Report* extolled the use of residential colleges and a general curriculum to achieve a similar purpose. The difference, of course, was that charity schools wanted to uplift the children of the poor from a life of poverty and crime and the colleges wanted to confer or confirm social status. In either case, however, education was used to shape the moral character of the individual for social purposes.

The Yale Report is important because it set the tone for collegiate education in the nineteenth century. The importance of the *Dartmouth College* case of 1819 lies in the fact that it began to define the lines between private and public education. In the seventeenth and eighteenth centuries, colleges, academies, reading-and-writing schools, and grammar schools were often established with little concern for distinctions between public and private education. As mentioned previously, most of these institutions received a combination of public and private money and were governed through a mixture of public and private control. Even a charity school organization—the New York Free School Society—received both public and private funds and was controlled by a private board of trustees, though eventually the schools established by this society came under complete public control.

The *Dartmouth College* case was the result of a dispute between Dartmouth president John Wheelock (son of Dartmouth's founder, Eleazor Wheelock) and an absentee board of trustees. To protect his power against the board of trustees, John Wheelock asked the New Hampshire state legislature to investigate the college. The board of trustees fired Wheelock, who immediately won the support of the state Republican Party. The Republican governor charged the board of trustees with being a self-perpetuating group of aristocrats and worked with the state legislature to pass a bill that would change the name of the institution from Dartmouth College to Dartmouth University and, more important, bring the institution under state control.

The board of trustees immediately went to the Superior Court of New Hampshire to contest the state's action. Part of the state of New Hampshire's case rested on the fact that it had originally chartered the college. The question that quickly emerged in this case was whether Dartmouth was a public or a private corporation. On November 6, 1817, the Superior Court ruled that Dartmouth was a public corporation and subject to legislative control. On March 10, 1819, the case was heard before the U.S. Supreme Court.

The lawyer for the board of trustees was Dartmouth graduate Daniel Webster (class of 1801), who argued his case for five continuous hours. His eloquence, it was reported, brought Chief Justice John Marshall to tears. Webster presented his case in the form of an argument that asked, "Shall our state legislature be allowed to take that which is not their own, to turn it from its original use, and apply it to such ends or purposes as they, in their discretion shall see fit?"[69] Embodied in this question is the fundamental issue of the extent to which government power should be allowed to operate in the management of institutions. This question reaches beyond a consideration of educational institutions alone to encompass all institutions, including corporations.

PUBLIC VERSUS PRIVATE SCHOOLS

Certainly in colonial times there would have been little debate over the right of government to intervene in the affairs of institutions serving the public. Society was viewed as an integrated whole in which government had the responsibility to ensure correct actions by all its parts. However, the early nineteenth century was still influenced by the Revolutionary War, which had sought to limit the power of government, and by a rising capitalistic ideology that sought to eliminate all government involvement in the economic system. In fact, the major conflicts about expansion of the common school system in the 1830s and 1840s centered on the political issue of the extent to which government should be involved in the educational system. The significance of the *Dartmouth College* case was in delineating the line between government-controlled and private institutions.

Webster's famous statement before the Supreme Court—"It is, sir, as I have said, a small college, and yet there are those that love it"—may have influenced the Court's decision in favor of the board of trustees. The Supreme Court ruled that the charter granted by the New Hampshire legislature was a contract protected by the federal Constitution against alteration by the state.

The decision, written by Chief Justice Marshall, made a sharp distinction between private and public educational institutions. Recognition was given to the importance of education as a national concern and to the notion that this concern could be reflected in "an institution founded by government, and placed entirely under its immediate control, the officers of which would be public officers, amenable exclusively to government."[70] But, the argument continued, did this mean that all education should be entirely in the hands of government and every teacher a public employee? Did it mean that all donations for education became public property?

The Court's response to these questions was given in the form of a description of a corporation. Marshall's decision described a corporation chartered by a state as having immortality and individuality. These properties, given to a perpetual succession of persons or boards of trustees that acted as a single person, allowed a corporation to hold property and manage its own affairs. "It is chiefly for the purpose of clothing bodies of men, in succession," Marshall wrote, "with these qualities and capacities, that corporations were invented, and are in use."[71] Furthermore, the chief justice argued, a corporation did not participate in civil government unless that was the reason for its creation.

Therefore, according to the Court's decision, a corporation "is no more a state instrument than a natural person exercising the same powers would be."[72] This meant that a college chartered by the state had the same rights against government interference as did an individual. It also meant that if a state wished to promote education to serve its own purposes, it would need to create its own institutions and hire its own faculty. The same argument, of course, would apply to institutions for elementary and secondary education. Thus a sharp distinction was drawn between private and public institutions as a result of the *Dartmouth College* case, and a precedent was set that privately created educational institutions could not be forced to serve the purposes of government; this could be done only through institutions owned and operated by the government. Although court decisions in the twentieth century would allow state regulation of private schools, the *Dartmouth College* case clearly drew the line between private and public schooling.

The college boom of the early nineteenth century was characterized by an emphasis on shaping individual character through a system of private, residential colleges. In the middle nineteenth century, reform movements began to expand public colleges to serve public purposes. The most important factor in this reform movement was the Morrill Federal Land Grant Act of 1862.

CONCLUSION: CONTINUING ISSUES IN AMERICAN EDUCATION

The debates about nationalism and civic education, the developing faith that education can solve social problems, the expansion of urban charity schools, and the growing distinctions between private and public institutions set the stage for the common school movement of the 1830s and 1840s. In addition, the educational issues of the post-Revolutionary period continue to exist today.

One important issue is the degree to which political education should attempt to control the future actions of citizens. As noted in this chapter, there is a major difference between the imposition of political values as advocated by Noah Webster and the forming of political values by the reading of newspapers as argued by Thomas Jefferson. This same argument is relevant to issues of nationalism and patriotism. Should the schools build emotional attachments to symbols of the state through activities such as saluting the flag and singing nationalistic songs? Or should patriotism be the expression of beliefs freely arrived at by the exercise of reason?

These questions are reflected in the differing interpretations of post-Revolutionary history by twentieth-century historians such as Rush Welter, Carl Kaestle, and Merle Curti, as summarized in the following paragraphs:

Rush Welter: Writing in the 1960s, when there was a concern about expanding democratic rights to a broader range of citizens, Rush Welter argues that the democratic orientation of the Founding Fathers was lost in the debates over schooling. Welter notes that these early writings have a "tendency to stress the conservative role of educational institutions in overcoming an excess of popular liberty."[73]

Carl Kaestle: The same interpretation of the period is given by Carl Kaestle in *Pillars of the Republic.* Writing during the politically peaceful times of the late 1970s and early 1980s, Kaestle found that the main concern of the post-Revolutionary period was to balance freedom and order: "Political theorists and policy makers were therefore concerned not only with protecting liberty, for which the Revolution had been fought, but also with maintaining order, without which all might be lost."[74] The purpose of education, according to Kaestle, was to maintain the balance between order and freedom by producing virtuous, well-behaved citizens.

Kaestle places his interpretation in the broader framework of republicanism. According to him, during the post-Revolutionary period, republicanism meant combining the concepts of virtue, balanced government, and liberty. By virtue, "republican essayists meant discipline, sacrifice, simplicity, and intelligence." Many of the early leaders believed in the natural virtue of the landed yeoman— virtue that did not depend on deliberate instruction. However, the problem for these leaders was the increasing population of citizens who did not belong to the class of landed yeomen. For this group, natural virtue could not be assumed and deliberate instruction was needed.[75]

Kaestle indicates that educational proposals were motivated by factors other than fear of the disorder that would result from liberty. He argues that Revolutionary leaders were also captured by the idea of the perfectibility of humans and human institutions. They wanted to create a society that would be an alternative to the corrupt society of Europe, and they believed that education, by perfecting virtue, would contribute to achieving this utopian goal.

Merle Curti: Kaestle does not draw a clear distinction between Jefferson's belief in individual reason and virtue and the more authoritarian ideas of leaders such as Benjamin Rush and Noah Webster. In *The Social Ideas of American Educators,* Curti considers educational leaders like Webster to represent a clearly conservative viewpoint on the organization of society. Writing in the radical economic and political climate of the 1930s, Curti states that Webster's spelling book contains a social philosophy "appropriate to a system which attached great value to acquiescence on the part of the poor in their poverty and at the same time promised ultimate success to those who would practice the virtues of frugality, industry, and submissiveness to moral teachings and to God's will."[76]

Curti concludes from his review of the moral maxims in Webster's speller that they were designed primarily to protect the property of the wealthy and that "other half-truths, equally fitting to a society in which some had more and others less, were read and re-read by American youth who learned their letters from the old 'blue-back.'"[77] In general, Curti finds that most post-Revolutionary educational practices and proposals continued, with only minor changes, the colonial class system of education.

Curti does think that Thomas Jefferson's ideas on education contrast sharply with others of the period. Curti argues that Jefferson displayed little sympathy for authoritarianism in education and that the ideas he advanced were hostile to the class character of existing educational practice. According to Curti, Jefferson's educational plan was a major step in the direction of breaking down class barriers in education. Specifically, Curti contends that Jefferson's proposal to select leaders from the masses through his three-tier system of education was the beginning of more democratic thinking about education: "Jefferson's quest for genius among the poor was far more democratic than anything that existed then, or was for a long time to exist."[78]

Nonetheless, Curti argues that Jeffersonian thought was limited by aristocratic pretensions. Without taking into account Jefferson's beliefs regarding the exercise of virtue and the role of history, Curti criticizes Jefferson for proposing a mainly literary education for the low and middle schools. Curti argues that education of this type would be of little benefit "to common folk struggling on the less fertile soils and to frontiersmen with their peculiar problems."[79] He also criticizes Jefferson for displaying more interest in the organization of university studies than of schools for the common folk. Despite these reservations, Curti hails Jefferson as the first American "to emphasize public education as an instrument for the realization of democracy and for the furthering of social reform."[80]

In summary, major tension in post-Revolutionary education debates existed between those who believed schooling should mold the virtuous citizen and those who believed schooling should provide the tools for the exercise of freedom. From the nineteenth century until the present, some have argued that a democratic society needs a school system that imposes morality, emphasizes patriotism, teaches respect for authority, and inculcates certain basic political values. At the same time, others have argued that schooling in a democratic society should provide the intellectual tools to all people that will enable them to select their own moral and political values.

Notes

1. John Meyer, David Kamens and Aaron Benavot, *School Knowledge for the Masses: World Models and National Primary Curricular Categories in the Twentieth Century* (Bristol, Pennsylvania: Falmer Press, 1992), p. 72.
2. Ibid., p. 72.
3. Ibid., p. 72.
4. Quoted in Harry Warfel, *Noah Webster: Schoolmaster to America* (New York: Macmillan, 1936), p. 335.
5. Ibid., pp. 335–336.
6. Ibid., pp. 71–75.
7. Ibid., p. 93.
8. Quoted in ibid., p. 21.
9. "Noah Webster's Federal Catechism (1798)," in *Education in the United States: A Documentary History,* ed. Sol Cohen (New York: Random House, 1974), pp. 769–770.
10. "Noah Webster's Moral Catechism," ibid., p. 771.
11. Noah Webster, "On the Education of Youth in America," in *Essays on Education in the Early Republic,* ed. Frederick Rudolph (Cambridge, MA: Harvard University Press, 1965).
12. Quoted in Warfel, *Noah Webster,* p. 86.
13. Quoted in ibid., p. 90.
14. Thomas Jefferson, "To Edward Carrington," in *Crusade against Ignorance: Thomas Jefferson on Education,* ed. Gordon Lee (New York: Teachers College Press, 1961), p. 102.
15. Thomas Jefferson, "To Peter Carr, with Enclosure," ibid., pp. 145–146.
16. Thomas Jefferson, "To John Adams," ibid., pp. 109–112.
17. Thomas Jefferson, "Report of the Commissioners Appointed to Fix the Site of the University of Virginia, &c.," ibid., p. 119.
18. Thomas Jefferson, "A Bill for the More General Diffusion of Knowledge," ibid., pp. 83–92.
19. Thomas Jefferson, "Notes on the State of Virginia," ibid., p. 95.
20. Ibid., p. 96.
21. Ibid., p. 94.
22. Jefferson, "Report of the Commissioners," pp. 117–118.
23. Jefferson, "Notes on the State of Virginia," p. 96.
24. Benjamin Rush, "The Influence of Physical Causes upon the Moral Faculty," in *Selected Writings of Benjamin Rush,* ed. Dagobert D. Runes (New York: Philosophical Library, 1947), p. 186.

25. Horace Mann, "Twelfth Annual Report," in *The Republic and the School: Horace Mann on the Education of Free Men,* ed. Lawrence Cremin (New York: Teachers College Press, 1957), p. 92.
26. Rush, "Influence of Physical Causes," pp. 198–202.
27. "The Yale Report (1828)," in *The Colleges and the Public, 1787–1862,* ed. Theodore Crane (New York: Teachers College Press, 1963), p. 86.
28. Steven Mintz, *Huck's Raft: A History of American Childhood* (Cambridge: Harvard University Press, 2004).
29. Ibid., p. 2.
30. Ibid., pp. 75–93.
31. Ibid., pp. 155.
32. Ibid., pp. 154–155.
33. Ibid., p. 133.
34. Ibid., pp.133–153.
35. Ibid., p. 97.
36. "Incorporation Statement of the New York Free School Society," in William O. Bourne, *History of the Public School Society of the City of New York* (New York: Wood, 1870), p. 3.
37. "1828 Report of the New York Society for the Prevention of Pauperism," in *Report of the Prison Discipline Society, Boston, 1828* (Boston: Press of T. R. Marvin, 1855), p. 174.
38. "1829 Boston House of Refuge Report to the City of Boston," in *Report of the Prison Discipline Society, Boston, 1829,* p. 246.
39. Quoted in Bourne, *History of the Public School Society,* p. 17.
40. Carl F. Kaestle, *The Evolution of an Urban School System: New York City, 1750–1850* (Cambridge, MA: Harvard University Press, 1973).
41. Ibid., p. 42.
42. Ibid., p. 187.
43. Carl F. Kaestle, *Pillars of the Republic: Common Schools and American Society, 1780–1860* (New York: Hill and Wang, 1983).
44. Quoted in Bourne, *History of the Public School Society,* p. 19.
45. Ellwood Cubberley, *Public Education in the United States: A Study and Interpretation of American Educational History* (Boston: Houghton Mifflin, 1934), p. 129.
46. David Salmon, *Joseph Lancaster* (London: McKay, 1904), p. 9.
47. Quoted in George H. Martin, *The Evolution of the Massachusetts Public School System* (Englewood Cliffs, NJ: Prentice Hall, 1901), p. 138.
48. Quoted in Bourne, *History of the Public School Society,* p. 38.
49. Ibid., p. 19.
50. "Report on Monitorial Instruction to the Boston School Committee; Boston, 1828," in *Readings in Public Education in the United States: A Collection of Sources and Readings to Illustrate the History of Educational Practice and Progress in the United States,* ed. Ellwood Cubberley (Cambridge, MA: Riverside Press, 1934), p. 137.
51. "1828 Report of the New York House of Refuge," in *Report of the Prison Discipline Society, Boston, 1828,* p. 174.
52. *Report of the Prison Discipline Society, Boston, 1832,* p. 570.
53. Ibid.
54. "1833 Report of the New York House of Refuge," in *Report of the Prison Discipline Society, Boston, 1833,* p. 694.
55. See Frederick Rudolph, *The American College and University* (New York: Knopf, 1962), pp. 48–49.

56. Quoted in ibid., pp. 31–32.
57. Richard Hofstadter, *Academic Freedom in the Age of the College* (New York: Columbia University Press, 1955), p. 209.
58. Ibid, p. 214.
59. Rudolph, *American College,* pp. 47–48.
60. Crane, *Colleges and the Public,* pp. 17–18.
61. Rudolph, *American College,* p. 135.
62. "The Yale Report (1828)," p. 88.
63. Ibid.
64. *Report of the Prison Discipline Society, Boston, 1829,* p. 290.
65. "The Yale Report (1828)," p. 90.
66. Ibid., p. 89.
67. Ibid., p. 86.
68. Ibid.
69. Quoted in Rudolph, *American College,* p. 209.
70. *Dartmouth College v. Woodward* (1819), quoted in Crane, *Colleges and the Public,* p. 70.
71. Ibid., p. 71.
72. Ibid.
73. Rush Welter, *Popular Education and Democratic Thought in America* (New York: Columbia University Press, 1962), p. 27.
74. Kaestle, *Pillars of the Republic,* p. 5.
75. Ibid.
76. Merle Curti, *The Social Ideas of American Educators* (Paterson, NJ: Pageant Books, 1959), p. 32.
77. Ibid., p. 34.
78. Ibid., p. 41.
79. Ibid., p. 43.
80. Ibid., p. 44.

4

The Ideology and Politics of the Common School

During the 1830s and 1840s, the common or public school movement put into practice many of the educational ideas of previous generations. As part of the growing globalization of education, common school advocates traveled to Prussia to study that country's attempts to create mass schooling. Common school reformers believed that education could be used to ensure the dominance of Protestant Anglo-American culture, reduce tensions between social classes, eliminate crime and poverty, stabilize the political system, and form patriotic citizens. For common school advocates, education would be the key to creating the good society. The major difference between schools before and after the common school movement was their goals. The common school was to be administered by state and local governments for the purpose of achieving public goals, such as remedying social, political, and economic problems.

It is important to understand that children went to school *before* the lofty dreams of social reform were actualized by common school reformers. Before the common school period, a variety of public and private school organizations existed. Massachusetts had laws requiring the provision of education and established the first system of urban education in Boston in the 1790s. Many states, such as New York and Pennsylvania, supported charity schools, although a majority of children in those states attended private schools. Newer states had passed laws allowing for the development of schools but had not actively created organized systems of education. For instance, Ohio, after its admission to the Union in 1802, passed legislation in 1806 and 1816 allowing for the organization of schools supported by tuition and rents from lands . Beginning in 1821, Ohio law permitted the taxation of all property in a district for the support of schools. The state created a permanent school fund in 1827.

These educational developments occurred before the common school movement. Then, according to Carl Kaestle and Maris Vinovskis, between 1840 and 1880—after the common school movement—the percentage of people under twenty years of age attending school in Massachusetts actually declined. In addition, the amount of money spent per $1,000 of state valuation increased only slightly during this period. Nevertheless, the average child in the same period received more days of instruction, and the length of the average school year in Massachusetts increased from 150 days in 1840 to 192 in 1880. Kaestle and

Vinovskis found that one of the primary effects of the common school reform was a shift of student population from private to public schools.[1]

The common school reform brought education into the service of the public goals of the government and created new forms of school organization. It established and standardized state systems of education designed to achieve specific public policies. As discussed next, three distinctive aspects of the common school movement made it different from past educational developments.

THREE DISTINCTIVE FEATURES OF THE COMMON SCHOOL MOVEMENT

The first distinctive feature of the common school movement was educating all children in a common schoolhouse to create a common culture and reduce social class conflict. Common school advocates argued that if children from a variety of religious, social class, and ethnic backgrounds were educated in common, there would be a decline in hostility and friction among social groups. In addition, if children educated in common were taught a common social and political ideology, political conflict and social problems would decrease. Obviously this aspect of the common school movement can be traced to late eighteenth-century and early nineteenth-century educational advocates who wanted to teach nationalism as a means of promoting national unity and to supporters of charity schools who wanted education to eliminate poverty and crime. The idea of using education to solve social problems and build a political community became an essential concept in the common school movement. The term "common school" came to have a specific meaning: a school that was attended in common by all children and in which a common political and social ideology was taught.

The second important aspect of the common school movement was the use of schools to improve public morality, end crime and poverty, and provide equal opportunity. Certainly this aspect of education had existed in the past. Colonial schools were established to train a population that would understand and obey secular and religious laws. Writers after the Revolution advocated systems of schools to provide leaders and a responsible citizenry. What was different about the common school movement was the acceptance of the idea of a direct link between government educational policies and the solving and control of social, economic, and political problems. In this concept, the common school was to be a panacea for society's problems.

The third distinctive feature of the common school movement was the creation of state agencies to control local schools. In part, this was necessary if schools were to carry out government, social, political, and economic policies. Earlier some states, like Massachusetts, had passed laws requiring the establishment of schools in local communities or, in the cases of New York and Pennsylvania, had established state school funds for charity schools. In these situations, an official position had not been established to oversee the state educational system. In 1812 New York became the first American state to create the position of state superintendent of schools; in the 1820s some other states followed New York's lead, but it was during the 1830s that state supervision and organization of schools became a major educational reform. In part, this was the work of the "father of the common school," Horace Mann, who in 1837 became the first secretary of the Massachusetts board of education.

These three distinct features of the common school movement reflected beliefs about the social and political role of education—beliefs that had been gaining increasing support during the early nineteenth century. Probably the most important of these ideas was the belief that human nature can be formed, shaped, and given direction by training within formally organized institutions. This thinking was embodied in faculty psychology and in the charity schools. It was a logical step for common school reformers to apply this reasoning to the entire society and to argue that government-operated schools could create the perfect society. Also, various groups, such as advocates of Lancasterian schools and charity schools, believed that schooling could be a means of economic and social improvement. They began to demand common schools, but often for reasons quite different from those given by full-time common school reformers. Although these differences existed within the common school movement, the outcome of the movement's reforms was the beginning of the modern American school system.

No other period in American educational history has stimulated as extensive a debate about the meaning and goals of education. In part, this debate reflects the importance of the common school movement to the American educational system. This chapter begins with a discussion of the various social and political groups that supported the common school movement, including the full-time educational reformers who devoted their lives to the common school ideal. Political, economic, and religious groups that opposed the establishment of the common school are considered next. Last, I will discuss the meaning of the common school movement for the later development of the American school.

This time line, from Chapter 3, is intended to illustrate the intersection of multicultural concerns and social reform impulses with the development of the common school. As indicated, the removal of the southern tribes to Indian Territory was occurring at the same time that Horace Mann was advocating the creation of a common Anglo-American culture by the common school. Also, before and after Mann initiated his campaign, there were disputes about the education of freed African Americans, and confrontations between Protestants and Irish Catholics over religion in the schools. Illustrated in the time line are the importance of multiculturalism, nationalism, and social reform during the common school period.

The Ideology of the Common School Movement

The ideology of the common school movement established the basic framework, from the nineteenth century to the present, for popular and official discussions about the goals and purposes of public schooling in American life. Within these early arguments for common schools can be found most of the hopes and aspirations that many Americans have had for the public schools. These early justifications for public schooling not only claimed that schools could solve the major social, economic, and political problems of society but also argued that common schools were necessary for society's survival.

For the purpose of understanding the basic ideology of these full-time common school reformers, this section concentrates on the life and ideas of Horace Mann. The popularly stated common school ideology did not necessarily reflect the reality of the changes taking place in American education or positions held by all supporters of the common school. For instance, as will be discussed in a later section, the workingmen's parties supported the establishment of common schools for reasons different from those given in the more popular rhetoric of the common school movement.

The life and writings of Horace Mann can be characterized as a constant search for a means of social salvation. During his life he rejected Calvinism and adopted law as the means of social redemption; and after finding little hope in saving society through the establishment of proper laws, he turned to education. Mann was born in 1796 into a harsh Calvinistic environment in Franklin, Massachusetts. He claimed throughout his life that he abandoned Calvinism when, at the funeral of his twelve-year-old brother, who had drowned, the family's Calvinist minister used the occasion to warn other young people of the dangers of dying unconverted. Mann described this minister as one who expounded all the doctrines of total depravity, election, and reprobation and not only the eternity, but the extremity, of hell torments, unflinchingly and in their most terrible significance, while he rarely if ever discussed the joys of heaven and or the essential and necessary happiness of a virtuous life.[2]

For Mann, phrenology and the common school became substitutes for his youthful experience with Calvinism. Calvinism had created for him a living hell that "spread a pall of blackness . . . beyond [which] . . . I could see the bottomless and seething lake filled with torments, and hear the wailing and agony of its victims."[3] In a series of letters to his sister in 1836, one year before becoming secretary of the Massachusetts board of education, he describes his rejection of this haunting vision of hell for a belief in good works in the present life. "My nature revolts at the idea of belonging to a universe in which there is to be never-ending anguish . . . while we are on earth, the burden of our duties is toward man."[4]

Mann entered the practice of law with the same fervor that would later characterize his involvement in common school reform. He was educated at Brown University and in 1823 was admitted to the bar and practice of law at Dedham, Massachusetts. Between 1827 and 1833, he served in the Massachusetts state legislature, where concerns with reforming society made him instrumental in enacting laws limiting the sale of alcohol and lottery tickets, establishing hospitals for the insane, and creating the Massachusetts state board of education.

While serving in the state legislature, he was surrounded by political and social events that affected his belief in the importance of common school reform and helped to shape his justification of the movement. A good way of understanding the social context of his decision to accept common school reform as the answer to society's problems is to read his description in his journal of events between the time he was asked to serve as secretary of the board of education and his acceptance of that position.

On May 18, 1837, Mann received a letter proposing his nomination to the newly created state board of education and urging him to lead the board as secretary. He wrote in his journal on that date that, could a person be successful in that office, "what a diffusion, what intensity, what perpetuity of blessings he would confer! How would his beneficial influence upon mankind widen and deepen as it descended forever!"[5] He did not communicate his acceptance of that position until the end of June. During that time, according to his journal entry for May 25, he read *Combe on the Constitution of Man.* This was his basic text in phrenology, which provided him with the scientific hope that the mental faculties could be developed and shaped to create a moral and good individual and, consequently, a moral and just society. His continued involvement in general social reform was reflected by his attendance at meetings of the Massachusetts Temperance Society. This society believed that the ending of alcohol consumption would contribute to the elimination of poverty and crime and add stability to the family. Mann noted on May 25, after attending a meeting of the society, "The faith [temperance] is now in a forward state of realization; and what a triumph it will be! not like a Roman triumph that made hearts bleed, and nations weep, and reduced armies to captivity, but one that heals hearts, and wipes tears from a nation's eyes, and sets captivity free."[6]

Mann's fear of growing social disorder in the United States was heightened when, on May 30, someone tried to start a fire next to his hotel room. He says about the event, "Fortunately it was discovered early, and extinguished. A gang of incendiaries infests the city. What a state of morals it reveals." Mann wondered how a group or individual could be driven to such an act. In the closing line of his description of the event, he touched on an important theme in the common school movement: The hope for eliminating this type of crime, as he argued in his later writings on education, was the training of the young child. Or as he asks in his closing line, "When will society, like a mother, take care of all her children?"[7]

His fear of social disorder and religious conflict was further intensified when on Sunday, June 11, a riot took place between Catholics and Protestants in Boston. Tension between the two religious groups had been increasing in the United States with the immigration of large numbers of Irish. Irish Catholics generally were widely discriminated against in housing and employment; a popular song of the time was "No Irish Need Apply." In his description of the riot, Mann writes, "As I sit down to write, martial music is playing in the streets. A riot of almost unheard-of atrocity has raged for several hours this afternoon between the Irish population . . . and the enginemen and those who rallied to their assistance. . . . It is said lives are lost: it is certain that great bodily injury has been inflicted."[8] Mann goes on to reflect that the real problem was public opinion, which played a major role in the power of American government. The key to eliminating this type of riot, he felt, would be the proper education of public opinion.

Three days after the riot, Mann worried in his journal over whether to accept the leadership of the board of education. Finally, on June 30, after having reflected on phrenology, attended temperance meetings, experienced a firebombing, and observed a religious riot, he accepted the position. His journal for the date contains a statement of his belief in the ameliorating power of the school. With almost a religious passion, he states, "Henceforth, so long as I hold this office, I devote myself to the supremest welfare of mankind upon earth. . . . I have faith in the improvability of the race."[9]

Horace Mann believed that he was moving from the profession of law, which he felt had failed to save society, to a field of endeavor that promised universal salvation. A month after his acceptance he wrote to a friend that he had abandoned the practice of law for a higher calling. He explained that laws failed because they dealt with adults, whose character was already shaped, and that the real hope was in molding the child: "Having found the present generation composed of materials almost unmalleable, I am about transferring my efforts to the next. Men are cast-iron; but children are wax. Strength expended upon the latter may be effectual, which would make no impression upon the former."[10]

Mann's hopes and dreams for the common school unfolded in the pages of the reports he wrote as secretary of the Massachusetts state board of education. The most important was the Twelfth Annual Report, written in 1848 after Mann resigned his educational post for a seat in the U.S. Congress. This report contained a summary of his ideas on the purposes of the common school.

In the Twelfth Annual Report, Mann returned to the reasoning he had used eleven years earlier when abandoning law for education. Again he argued that the hope for ridding society of evil actions was not in the law but in moral education. The increasing complexity of society, he felt, continually expanded the possibilities for moral transgression. He even dismissed as futile his earlier involvement in the passage of laws against the sale of alcohol because "the government sees the evils that come from the use of intoxicating drinks, and prohibits their sale; but unprincipled men pander to depraved appetites, and gather a harvest of dishonest profits."[11]

The answer to this steady expansion of crime, he maintained, was to educate the child. In language reflecting his ardent belief in the moral power of the school, he stated that there was one experiment society had not tried in its attempt to control crime: "It is an experiment which, even before its inception, offers the highest authority for its ultimate success. Its formula is intelligible to all; and it is as legible as though written in starry letters on an azure sky." This formula, and the key to the good society, he stated, was "best expressed in these few and simple words:—'*Train up a child in the way he should go, and when he is old he will not depart from it.*'"[12] Mann claimed that all attempts to reform humanity had failed to realize the possibilities for shaping the character of children and youth.

In a broader sense, Mann put his hope in the schoolteacher, who, by educating children so that they would not transgress the law, would replace the police. This concept made schools the central institution for the control and maintenance of social order. Also, it opened the door to the explosive political issue of whose morality would be taught in the public schools.

Mann walked a delicate tightrope in his advocacy of moral education in the schools. Given the temper of the times, moral education, which for most people meant a religious education, was considered an essential part of overall education.

On one hand, this meant that if Mann did not advocate a moral education with religious foundations, he faced the possibility of being called irreligious and of having the common school condemned as a secular institution without religious foundations. For most people during this period, the education of character had to be linked to religious doctrines; otherwise it could be accused of being antireligious. On the other hand, if he did link moral education to religion, he had to make a choice about the religious tenets to which moral education should be linked. Given the fierce denominational rivalries of the time, any choice he made would create the possibility that the common school might be destroyed by competing religious groups.

Mann defended his position on this issue in the Twelfth Annual Report by arguing that the presence and use of the Bible in the schools provided instruction in the fundamental doctrines of Christianity without reference to denominational differences, and this provided the basis for all creeds: "Is it not, indeed, too plain, to require the formality of a syllogism, that if any man's creed is to be found in the Bible, and the Bible is in the schools, then that man's creed is in the schools? . . . If a certain system, called Christianity, were contained in . . . the Bible, then wherever the Bible might go, there the system of Christianity must be."[13]

In addition to the use of the Bible in the schools, Mann claimed that the laws of Massachusetts required teaching the basic moral doctrines of Christianity, which he listed as instruction in piety, justice, love of country, benevolence, sobriety, industry, frugality, chastity, moderation, and temperance. "Are not these virtues and graces," asked Mann, "part and parcel of Christianity?"[14] Within the framework of this reasoning, religious education in the common schools was to be based on nonsectarian use of the Bible with the teaching of broad religious principles common to all Christian denominations.

Mann envisioned four destructive alternatives to this form of nonsectarian moral education. The first was to exclude all religious instruction from the schools. This, he argued, would make the schools "un-Christian," and the schools would receive no support from the general population. The second alternative was for the law to define and prescribe a system of religion for the schools, which, according to Mann, would involve the government in the establishment of religion and force a particular religion on all children. The third alternative was to give each religious sect with a majority in a community the power to define the religion of the schools. Mann strongly felt that this would destroy the common school by the heat of religious rivalries as all denominations fought for the inclusion of their doctrines. The last alternative was for the government to abandon all interference in the education of the young. As an advocate of the common school system, Mann quickly rejected this last possibility.

In the context of these arguments, the term *common* took on added meaning. Children in the common school were to receive a common moral education based on the general principles of the Bible and on common virtues, and such education was to eliminate crime and corruption in society.

Mann used the same type of reasoning in defining his goals for political education in the common schools. Like religious instruction, political instruction opened the door for groups with differing political ideas to fight over the content of political instruction. Mann stated in his Twelfth Annual Report, "It is obvious . . . that if the tempest of political strife were to be let loose upon our Common Schools, they would be overwhelmed with sudden ruin." His answer was to have schools teach only those articles of republican faith that were approved by "all sensible and judicious men, all patriots, and all genuine republicans." This political education, he proclaimed, would contain "articles in the creed of republicanism, which are accepted by all, believed in by all, and which form the common basis of our political faith."[15]

To avoid political controversy in the schoolroom, Mann proposed that the teacher avoid any discussion of or comment that touched on political disputes. However, "when the teacher, in the course of his lessons or lectures on the fundamental law, arrives at a controverted text, he is either to read it without comment or remark; or, at most, he is only to say that the passage is the subject of disputation, and that the schoolroom is neither the tribunal to adjudicate, nor the forum to discuss it."[16]

In this manner, Mann hoped to provide instruction in the fundamentals of politics without destroying the common school in the fury of political controversy.

Within the context of political education, the "common" in "common school" meant the teaching of a common political creed. The combination of moral and political instruction meant that the student leaving the common school would share with fellow students a set of moral and political beliefs; the result would be the creation of a society with a consensus of political and moral values.

For Mann, the inculcation of a common set of political beliefs would reduce the level of political violence in society as a whole. He hoped that a common school education would lead to political discussions based on a shared set of political beliefs. Thus, even though some disputes over political issues might arise, these disputes would take place in the context of a common political faith. Mann envisioned that political violence would be avoided because of the adherence to common articles of republican faith.

According to Mann, it was necessary to teach the importance of using the vote, as opposed to revolution and violence, to bring about political change. This was a particularly important issue during Mann's time because the extension of universal male suffrage had taken place in the 1820s. Before that time, the vote had been restricted by property requirements. In reference to the vote replacing political violence, Mann stated, "Had the obligations of the future citizen been sedulously inculcated upon all children of this Republic, would the patriot have had to mourn over so many instances, where the voter, not being able to accomplish his purpose by voting, has proceeded to accomplish it by violence."[17]

Mann wished to avoid not only political violence but also violence between social classes. Like Karl Marx in Europe, Mann was concerned with the creation of divisions between social classes caused by the growth of modern industry. *The Communist Manifesto* by Karl Marx and Friedrich Engels was published in 1848, the same year that Mann wrote his Twelfth Annual Report for the Massachusetts state board of education. Unlike Marx and Engels, Mann believed that the answer to social class conflict was a common school education—not revolution by the working class.

Like Marx and Engels, however, Mann recognized that modern industrial development had created a major split between capital and labor and thus the intensification of class consciousness. Writing in the Twelfth Annual Report about industrial development in Massachusetts, he poses a warning question: "Are we not in danger of . . . those hideous evils which are always engendered between Capital and Labor, when all the capital is in the hands of one class and all the labor is thrown upon another?" He goes on to argue that if one class possesses all the wealth and education, and the other is poor and ignorant, then the latter will be "servile dependents and subjects of the former."[18]

"Now, surely," Mann writes with a great deal of conviction about the social power of the common school, "nothing but Universal Education can counter-work this tendency to the domination of capital and servility of labor." He believed that two alternatives existed through which common schooling could eliminate the problems between capital and labor. The first was to eliminate the friction caused by class consciousness. Mann admits that "a fellow-feeling for one's class or caste is the common instinct of hearts not wholly sunk in selfish regards for person, or for family." For Mann, the problem was not the elimination of class consciousness but its expansion across social boundaries. Mann hoped that a common school education would spread feelings of class consciousness among all members of society: "The spread of education, by enlarging the cultivated class or caste, will open a wider area over which the social feelings will expand; and, if this education should be universal and complete, it would do more than all things else to obliterate factitious distinctions in society." In Mann's words, the expansion of class consciousness would "disarm the poor of their hostility towards the rich."[19]

The second way common schooling would eliminate the conflict between capital and labor was by increasing the general wealth of society. Mann felt that common schooling, by improving the general wealth of society, would be the answer to those reformers who were calling for a redistribution of property from the rich to the poor. His argument is one of the earliest considerations of schooling as capital investment and of teaching as the development of human capital. Within his framework of reasoning, education would produce wealth by training intelligence to develop new technology and methods of production. Investment in education is a form of capital investment because it leads to the production of new wealth, and teaching is a means of developing human capital because it provides the individual with the intellectual tools for improved labor.

In other words, according to Mann, common schooling would eliminate the problems of the unequal distribution of property by increasing the general wealth of society and, consequently, improving the economic conditions of the poor. It would prevent poverty by giving individuals the tools for enhancing their economic position in society. Therefore, as Mann stated in one of his more famous passages in the Twelfth Annual Report, "Education, then, beyond all other devices of human origin, is the great equalizer of the conditions of men—the balance-wheel of the social machinery."[20]

Mann's arguments regarding the conflict between labor and capital added another meaning to the word *common*. Common schooling was to create a common social class by extending a common class consciousness among all members of society. Mixing the rich and poor within the same schoolhouse would cause social class conflict to give way to a feeling of membership in a common social class and would thus provide society with a common set of political and moral values.

Mann used arguments about education as capital investment to justify public financial support of the common school. One of the questions asked during the period was why those without children, or those who sent their children to private schools, should pay for the education of other people's children. Mann's answer was that the value of property is dependent on the work of previous generations and on the general level of prosperity of the community. He argued that property is held in trust by each generation, which through its labors increases its value. In other words, even a family without any children benefits from common schooling because common schooling increases the wealth of the entire community, which in turn increases the value of the family's property. Therefore, all members of society benefit economically from common schooling, whether or not they make any direct use of the schools.

With minor variations, Mann's stated goals and purposes of common schooling in his reports to the Massachusetts board of education were shared by the leading educational reformers of the time. This does not mean they were shared by all members of society. In a sense, Mann's reports represented the official justification for the creation of a common system of education. Involved in this justification was the hope that all the social, economic, and political problems of society would be solved by putting together in a common school the children of all members of society and by teaching them a common set of political and moral beliefs.

But this utopian vision of the good society created by a system of common schooling has, and had then, certain inherent problems. First was the real problem of agreement on a common set of political and moral values to be taught in the classroom. Such agreement concerning religious values never occurred, and as a result, a private parochial system of education developed side by side with the common school. In the simplest terms, the common school never became common to all students. In addition, no proof existed that education would eliminate crime. In fact, one could argue that increased education simply meant improving the educational level of the criminal. Nor was there any real proof that a common school education could eliminate social, political, and economic unrest. It is possible, for instance, that social unrest is rooted in real economic and political problems that cannot be solved without dealing directly with the problems themselves. In this sense, the official ideology of the common school might be considered essentially conservative because it did not call for any basic changes in the economic and political structure of society but placed its hope for social improvement on the education of the individual. In fact, the official ideology of the common school accepted the existing political and economic organization of society and held that any problems were the result of individual deviance or failure. Therefore, it was argued by common school reformers, the common school could create a utopian world by educating the individual to conform to the needs of existing political, social, and economic organizations.

Although there were obvious flaws in the reasoning of common school reformers, their faith in the power of the school continued into the twentieth century. The ideology of the common school became a standard part of the beliefs held by most Americans. Since the mid-1800s, the school has continually been seen as a means of eliminating poverty, crime, and social problems. In addition, the idea of education as capital investment and as a means of developing human capital became one of the major justifications for schooling in the twentieth century. Horace Mann and other common school reformers made a lasting contribution to the ongoing debate about the relationship between school and society.

WORKINGMEN AND THE STRUGGLE FOR A REPUBLICAN EDUCATION

The educational demands made by the workingmen's parties between 1827 and 1835 provide an example of how support of similar ideas and institutions by different groups and for different reasons can contribute to social change. Clearly, workingmen's parties wanted common schools, but for reasons different from those given by common school reformers. Nonetheless, the combined efforts of the workingmen's parties and the common school reformers gave the appearance of a popular struggle for the establishment of a common school system.

Although the political impact and social composition of workingmen's parties between 1827 and 1835 have been debated, there has been no dispute about the importance of education in the political campaigns of the workingmen's parties. Their educational arguments shared many characteristics of the ideology of common school reformers, particularly a general demand for free common public schooling to serve political and economic purposes. But the reasons given by workingmen's parties for the establishment of common schools were distinctly different from those given by Horace Mann and other common school reformers. The reformers stressed the necessity of teaching a common moral and political creed as a means of eliminating crime, poverty, and social unrest and providing equal economic opportunity, whereas the workingmen's parties argued for the necessity of education as a means by which workers could protect themselves from economic and political exploitation. Common school reformers emphasized education as a mechanism of social control, whereas the workingmen's parties emphasized education as a mechanism for gaining political and economic power. Both groups agreed that a common education was necessary to eliminate distinctions between the rich and the poor and to promote equal economic opportunity.

The workingmen's political movement began in Philadelphia in 1827 with a demand by the Mechanics Union of Trade Associations for worker influence on legislative action. In the spring of 1828, the Philadelphia Workingmen's Party nominated and campaigned for candidates to the state legislature. The organization of labor parties quickly spread through Pennsylvania, Delaware, Massachusetts, and New York. For most of these workingmen's parties, education became a central theme of their political campaigns.

Representative of the workingmen's parties' concern about education was the establishment in 1829 by the Philadelphia Mechanics Union of Trade Associations of a committee to investigate educational conditions in the city and state. In all areas of the state except Philadelphia, Lancaster, and Pittsburgh, the committee found little support for public instruction. The committee also attacked the existence of charity schools. First, there was a concern that private individuals were using government money to provide education of questionable quality for the poor. In his excellent study "Education and the Working Class: The Expansion of Public Education during the Transition to Capitalism," historian William Russell quotes the committee as claiming that a large number of charity schools were "irresponsible institutions, established by individuals, from mere motives of private speculation or gain, who are destitute of character, and frequently, of the requisite attainments and abilities." In addition, the schools suffered from "ignorance, inattention and immorality." Criticisms were also raised that charity schools offered a limited curriculum and led to a loss of pride among parents.[21]

In general, the committee believed that government monies were being used primarily to support colleges and universities—a situation it argued was "exclusively for the benefit of the wealthy, who [were] thereby enabled to procure a liberal education for their children, upon lower terms than it could otherwise be afforded them." If this condition persisted, the committee reported, knowledge would be mostly in the hands of the privileged few and would "[consign] the multitude to comparative ignorance, and [secure] the balance of knowledge on the side of the rich and the rulers."[22] The answer to this situation was to make equal knowledge a common property of all groups in society.

In New York, a similar complaint was voiced about the private control of charity schools by the New York School Society (originally the New York Free School Society). The New York Workingmen's Party believed that the existence of charity schools and inadequate school funding were increasing social class differences. The lack of education among workingmen, it was argued, kept them ignorant of their rights and allowed for exploitation by the privileged.

One of the most important points made in the arguments of the New York Workingmen's Party was that, in an industrial society, knowledge was power. Thus keeping knowledge from the masses was considered one method of assuring the upper classes a monopoly on power. Russell explains the general view of the workingmen's parties: "Kept in ignorance, workers could be deprived of their rights, cheated in their daily business, and 'gulled and deceived' by 'designing schemers,' 'parasitic politicians,' 'greedy bank directors,' and 'heartless manufacturers.'"[23] In summary, workingmen's parties believed that the lack of a common school system was an attempt to deny them their rights and their share of economic and political power.

Workingmen's groups believed that common schooling was essential to protect their rights—that knowledge was necessary for the equal exercise of power in a democratic system of government. This argument is best expressed in an 1830 statement in the *Workingmen's Advocate*: "*The right of self government implies a right to a knowledge necessary to the exercise of the right of self government.*

If all have an equal right to the first, all must consequently have an equal right to the second; therefore, all are entitled to equal education."[24]

In addition, access to knowledge meant protection of rights against what was considered the tyranny of the upper class. One statement in the *Workingmen's Advocate* in 1831 stresses that education was the only sure "defense against not only an infringement, but a total usurpation of the native rights of the people, by the monopolizing demagogues of the land."[25] An editorial in 1830 in the *Sentinel,* a workingmen's newspaper, wishfully claims that if the previous generation had been properly educated, it would not have been cheated and blinded by those currently wielding political and economic power.

Differences and similarities existed between the workingmen's parties' arguments for the necessity of education in a republic and those of the common school reformers like Horace Mann. Both groups agreed that education was necessary to maintain a republican and democratic form of government, but the common school reformers emphasized political education as a means of making individuals worthy of democratic rights and as necessary for maintaining political harmony, whereas workingmen's groups emphasized the necessity of education for the equal sharing of power and the protection of rights. These differences suggest a different content in the political instruction to be offered in the schools. As a means of achieving his objectives, Mann wanted the basic principles of government and a common republican creed to be taught, whereas workingmen's groups called for the teaching of how to exercise power in the political system, the nature of political rights, and the protection of those rights as the means of achieving their goals.

With regard to crime and poverty, workingmen's groups and common school reformers shared an equal faith in the power of the school. In fact, in response to the issue of why a person without children should pay for the education of other people's children, workingmen's groups often advanced the argument that education increased the security of all people from criminal activities.

Common school reformers and workingmen's groups also shared a belief that equal education for all was necessary to reduce distinctions among economic classes, but again their reasons were different. The reason common school reformers wanted a common education was to reduce friction between capital and labor. Workingmen's groups wanted equal education as a means of ensuring that capital did not maintain a monopoly over knowledge and as a means of protecting their economic interests. As an editorial in the *Workingmen's Advocate* of 1834 states that education would provide workers with "a correct knowledge of their value as producers . . . [and of their] general interest as productive laborers." This knowledge, it was hoped, would destroy the causes of the dependence of workers on owners and the unjust accumulation of capital.[26]

Because knowledge was viewed as power and as a means by which capital maintained its grip over labor, it was logical for workingmen's groups to support equal education as a means of providing equal economic opportunity. The relationship between equality of educational opportunity and equality of economic opportunity was stressed throughout the nineteenth and twentieth centuries.

The most extreme, but logical, link between equal education and equal economic opportunity was made by the New York Workingmen's Party in its state guardianship plan. The basic argument behind this plan was that equal educational opportunity could not be achieved if one child went from school to an impoverished home life and another child went home to a life that was rich and offered many advantages. To achieve true equality of educational opportunity, the state guardianship plan argued, all children must be taken from their families and placed in state boarding schools, where they would receive equal treatment, equal clothes, equal food, and an equal education. Although the radicalism of this proposal split the party, it did highlight the extreme importance workingmen's groups gave to the connection between equal educational opportunity and equal economic opportunity.[27]

It remains unclear whether workingmen, as represented by these early labor parties, gained the type of education they wanted through the establishment of a common school system. Tension existed in the nineteenth and twentieth centuries between organized labor and the public school system over the content of instruction. Labor often claimed that public school instruction was conservative and taught principles opposed to the organization of workers into unions. Whether or not this was the case does not detract from the important effect workingmen's parties had on spreading ideas favoring common school education and on winning support for the establishment of common schools. In fact, when one considers the dates of the activities of the workingmen's parties and the common school reformers, it is clear that the workingmen's parties paved the way for reformers such as Barnard (discussed later) and Mann.

The differences between the common school reformers and the workingmen's parties highlight the differences in meaning that can exist over commonly used words. One cannot assume that if all people say they favor education, they all favor the same thing. The word *education* has meant different things to different people. This is particularly true of the way the word was used in the different arguments given in support of the establishment of common schools.

HOW MUCH GOVERNMENT INVOLVEMENT IN SCHOOLS? THE WHIGS AND THE DEMOCRATS

Since the founding of public schools there has been a debate about the degree of government control of schools. The common school movement was born during a period of intense political change and rivalry. Of primary political importance in the 1820s was the ending of property qualifications for voting and the establishment of universal male suffrage. In addition, modern political parties were born in 1828, when the Jacksonian Democrats competed against the National Republican Party (which died in the early 1830s and was replaced by the Whigs). The Whigs and the Democrats had almost equal shares of the nation's voters.

These political changes were related to the common school movement in several ways. First, universal suffrage created a concern with the education of the future voter. Many supporters of the common school movement stressed the importance of education in ensuring the maintenance of political order as democratic rights were extended. Second, political affiliation was the most important difference between groups advocating different forms of school organization. Most leaders of the common school movement were Whigs, who believed that government should intervene to maintain social order through a centrally managed school system designed to educate moral and responsible citizens. In contrast, members of the Democratic Party believed that social order would occur naturally, and therefore they believed in minimal government intervention and local control of the schools.

In their analysis of voting patterns in six states, Herbert Ershkowitz and William Shade found that between 1833 and 1843 the voting patterns of the members of each party were clearly different. By 1840, 80 to 100 percent of both Whigs and Democrats adhered to the point of view of their party. With regard to educational legislation, in most cases there were significant differences in party voting patterns.[28]

The differences between the parties' political philosophies highlight important aspects of the common school and the continuing controversy over the political structure of schooling. Both political groups believed that education was a necessity but differed over the goals and structure of the educational system. In general, Whigs were concerned with morality, duty, and the reduction of social conflict and thus wanted an educational system that would shape moral character, teach social and political duties, and reduce conflict among social classes and political groups. Whigs believed these goals could best be achieved through centralized supervision by state governments. Democrats resisted the trend toward centralization of government control and talked mainly about rights and a society of conflicting interests.

In *The Concept of Jacksonian Democracy: New York as a Test Case,* Lee Benson describes the differences between these two political groups as positive versus negative liberalism. Within this framework, Whigs advocated a positive liberalism that called for government intervention to assure the workings of a free-market economy. Therefore, Whigs believed government should provide money for education and for internal improvements to guarantee the establishment and functioning of institutions and economic organizations essential to the development of the country. For instance, Whigs argued that because private capital was not available for the development of canals and railroads essential for economic growth, the government should supply the needed capital. Benson quotes New York Governor William Seward's 1839 message as a summary of the Whig position on internal improvements and education. Seward argued that government action and spending were necessary "to enlarge . . . national prosperity, while we equalize its enjoyments and direct it to the universal diffusion of knowledge."[29]

The Democrats represented negative liberalism and argued that government governed too much. They believed the economy should function without any state intervention and that state monies should not be used to support a common school system. Benson states that John Bigelow, a leading writer for the Democrats in New York, "believed that the common school fund should be applied to the present crippling state debt and that thereafter the state should cease to propagate any science, art, trade, or religion among any class of people."[30]

In *The Political Culture of the American Whigs,* Daniel Howe argues that faculty psychology had the strongest influence on the moral philosophy of the Whigs, who believed that the balancing and regulating of the moral faculties were essential to the maintenance of social order. From this perspective, schools were necessary for ensuring harmony within the individual. Whigs believed that if moral faculties were left to themselves, the lower powers would escape control and wreak havoc. An unregulated faculty—whether pride, licentiousness, or some other appetite or emotion—was called a "passion." The good life entailed continual self-discipline as one sought to "suppress his passions" or "cultivate and improve his virtues."[31]

As Howe indicates, this philosophical perspective ruled out the idea of a laissez-faire society completely free of some form of regulation and "implied an active, purposeful central government, 'administering the affairs of the nation according to its best judgment for the good of the whole, and all parts of the whole.'"[32] According to this political ideology, the government should play an active role in maintaining the economy, regulating morality, and ensuring political and social order. Consequently, Whigs supported not only government funding of internal improvements (such as canals) but also the passage of laws to regulate morality. For instance, the temperance movement received strong support from Whigs.

For Whigs, schooling was the key to an ordered society. Howe summarizes the Whig political campaigns as being part of "a cultural struggle to impose on the United States the standards of morality we usually term Victorian. They were standards of self-control and restraint, which dovetailed well with the economic program of the party, for they emphasized thrift, sobriety, and public responsibility."[33] Whigs believed these values were necessary to bring discipline to voters.

The Whig idea that society requires a consciously arranged order and the Democratic free-market ideas reflected two different concepts of freedom. In turn, these differing concepts of freedom were reflected in attitudes about the political and social role of the school. For Whigs, true freedom occurred only when the balance of mental faculties within an individual ensured that passion did not reign over reason. In addition, Whigs contended, social conditions must be organized so that the individual was not tempted into activity that would disrupt the harmony of the mind. In other words, the Whig position was that true freedom was possible only if individuals received a proper education and social temptations were removed. This explains why many common school reformers were active in the temperance movement while working for greater centralization and uniformity in the school system.[34] Democrats, in contrast, believed that true freedom was possible only in a society in which there was a minimum of government interference in the social order. Democrats viewed government attempts to order society as attempts to promote and protect the special privileges of the upper class.

Not all members of American society in the 1830s and 1840s complacently accepted the moral reform efforts of the Whigs. For example, Howe reports that many thought the Whig assumption of moral responsibility for others meddlesome. He tells the story of the burning of the church of Lyman Beecher, who was a Whig, temperance advocate, and minister. When Lyman Beecher's church on

Hanover Street in Boston burned down, the volunteer fire companies, who hated his temperance crusading, refused to fight the flames. Instead, it is reported, they watched and sang, "While Beecher's church holds out to burn/The vilest sinner may return"—a parody of a hymn.[35]

The best study of the differences in educational philosophy between the Democrats and the Whigs was conducted by Carl Kaestle and Maris Vinovskis for their book *Education and Social Change in Nineteenth-Century Massachusetts*.[36] They studied the attempt in 1840 to abolish the Massachusetts state board of education and, of course, Horace Mann's position as its secretary. This action was considered a direct attack on the common school movement. Kaestle and Vinovskis report that in the year preceding the attempt to abolish the board, a leading Massachusetts Democrat, Orestes Brownson, attacked the board for trying to "Prussianize" education by centralizing control over the schools. Brownson contended that the board was a vehicle for Whig ideas about education and maintained that control should remain at the local level.

In 1840 a legislative committee composed of three Whigs and two Democrats was established to investigate the work of the board of education. Surprisingly, given the majority of Whigs on the committee, its report attacked the board as an unnecessary expense and, to quote Kaestle and Vinovskis, as "a danger to political and religious freedoms." The committee report argues, "District schools, in a republican government need no police regulations, no systems of state censorship, no checks of moral, religious, or political conservatism, to preserve either the morals, the religion, or the politics of the state. 'Let them ever be kept free and pure.'"[37] Obviously this reasoning was almost the exact opposite of that given by Mann for establishing a common school system.

The committee's report provoked a series of other investigations that eventually led to a vote by the members of the state legislature on the abolition of the board. The attempt to abolish the board failed by a vote of 182 to 245. The legislative vote gave Kaestle and Vinovskis data by which they could analyze the nature of the supporters and opponents of the common school system in Massachusetts.

Kaestle and Vinovskis classified the legislature members according to religion, occupation, the geographical area they represented, and party affiliation. They hoped to determine which factors were most important in determining support or nonsupport of the board. The assumption was made that a legislator's position on this issue reflected that individual's support or nonsupport of the common school movement. After analyzing the data, Kaestle and Vinovskis concluded that party affiliation was the most important factor in determining a legislator's support or nonsupport of the board. They also found that religion was not an important factor in legislative action. Of course the legislature did not include a large Catholic faction, so the rift between Catholics and Protestants was not represented in their findings. They did find that legislators from manufacturing areas tended to support the board, unlike those from rural areas.

The fact that party affiliation was the most important factor does not mean that all Whigs supported the existence of the board and that all Democrats stood in opposition. One-fifth of Whigs and one-third of Democrats did not follow the general voting pattern of their respective parties. But even with these defections from the positions of both political parties, political ideology was the most important factor in differentiating between supporters and nonsupporters of the board of education.

The differences between the political parties in Massachusetts reflected more general differences between the two political groups throughout the nation. According to Kaestle and Vinovskis, "the Whigs argued that positive government intervention was a necessary and useful means of improving the quality of public schools throughout the commonwealth." Democrats, however, felt "that any increased state interference in local educational matters created the potential, if not the reality, of a centralized state school system that would dictate how children were to be educated."[38]

The struggle between Whigs and Democrats over the common school reflected a more general concern about how schools should be controlled and whose values should be taught in a school's curriculum. This debate, which has continued into the twenty-first century, reflects in varying degrees the tension between those wanting popular control of the schools and little government intervention and those believing that government should work actively to ensure that the schools serve general social, political, and economic goals.

THE BIRTH OF THE HIGH SCHOOL

In 1821 the Boston town meeting approved the opening of the first high school. Despite its early beginnings, the high school did not become a mass institution until the 1920s and 1930s. In the most authoritative source for the early history of the high school, *The Origins of the American High School,* William Reese argues that there was no clear definition of the meaning of *high school* in the 1820s and 1830s.[39] Reflecting this uncertainty, school activist Henry Barnard provided in 1838 a vague and almost meaningless definition that a "Public or Common High School, is intended . . . [to be] a public or common school for the older and more advanced scholars of the community . . . [with] a course of instruction adapted to their age, and intellectual and moral wants and, to some extent, to their future pursuits in life."[40] These are nice words without any meaningful specificity about goals or content.

Regardless of the confusion about their exact definition, high schools were justified with arguments similar to those given in support of common schools. According to Reese, arguments supporting the establishment of high schools included the following:

- Like common school reformers, high school advocates argued that well-educated people would be taught to believe that equal opportunity through schooling justified the existence of social differences based on income and wealth.
- High schools would promote the idea that achievement depends on individual responsibility.
- A high school education would lead to obedience to the law.

- A high school education would undercut the potential for political revolution by instilling basic republican values.
- High schools would contribute to reduction of crime by instilling basic moral values.[41]

Reese found that from the 1820s through the 1880s, those arguments were presented to local communities as reasons for building a high school.

Many early high schools were architectural masterpieces and could be described, according to Reese, as "cathedrals of learning." Within the walls of these cathedrals of learning was a continuing debate about whether the emphasis should be on practical preparation for life and occupations or on formal instruction to form a well-disciplined mind and wisdom to ponder the larger questions about the meaning of life and happiness. In the end, the high school curriculum centered on the teaching of advanced sciences, mathematics, English studies, history, and political economy. The actual content of these courses was most often determined by available textbooks, which determined the content of instruction. Reese asserts, "Textbooks thus served many crucial functions in the nineteenth century. They set common academic expectations for advanced pupils . . . [and] helped create a common curriculum."[42]

As the high school became a universal institution in the twentieth century, the concerns with formal learning for the discipline of the mind would be displaced by concerns for preparation for occupations. A dramatic shift in the curriculum would occur as a result of this emphasis on a practical education for life and jobs.

THE CONTINUING DEBATE ABOUT THE COMMON SCHOOL IDEAL

Differing historical interpretations reflect the conflicts of the common school period. Also, these differences in interpretation reflect modern concerns about the role of education in American society. On one hand, some historians see the common school period as a battle between liberals and conservatives for the establishment of a school system that would be of great benefit to all members of society. On the other hand, some argue that common schools were established to protect the dominant economic and cultural elites. These broad differences in historical interpretation contain elements of the debate that continues to this day about whose interests are served by the public schools. Therefore, understanding the differences in historical interpretation of the common school period is important to understanding both the common school reforms and current debates about schooling. The following paragraphs represent the major interpretations of the common school movement.

Ellwood Cubberley: Cubberley portrayed the common school as a battle between liberals and conservatives. In his 1919 publication, *Public Education in the United States: A Study and Interpretation of American Educational History,*[43] Cubberley describes liberals as good people who struggle for education for all people against avarice-minded conservatives.

Cubberley created a list of differing reasons for the support or nonsupport of common schools. The arguments he lists as being given in support of the common school movement include prevention and reduction of poverty and crime, increased workforce productivity, elimination of "wrong ideas as to the distribution of wealth," reduction of tensions among social classes, elimination of charity schools because they stigmatized a certain class in society, assimilation of immigrants, and preparation of the citizenry for voting. Of course these became the traditional arguments for the support of public schooling in the United States.

Cubberley also lists arguments for the expansion of state control over education. In one sense, these arguments can be viewed as part of the continuing debate about the rights of parents versus the rights of the state over the education of children. In Cubberley's words, the major arguments were as follows: "That a State which has the right to hang has the right to educate"; that "the taking over of education by the State is not based on considerations of economy, but is the exercise of the State's inherent right to self-preservation and improvement"; and finally, as a reflection of the common school emphasis on education serving government policies, "that only a system of state-controlled schools can be free to teach whatever the welfare of the State may demand."[44] Cubberley's list of the arguments favoring state control of education describes the actual political divisions that occurred during the 1830s and 1840s over the degree of government intervention in social and economic issues.

He lists the following as arguments given in opposition to the expansion of state power: "That taxes would be so increased that no state could long meet such a lavish drain" and "that there was a priestcraft in the scheme, the purpose being first to establish a State School, and then a State Church." Cubberley's list greatly oversimplifies the political debate about the extension of state control.[45]

Cubberley lists the arguments of those opposed to the social and economic reform arguments for the common school, which, according to his interpretations, centered around aristocratic ideas of social class: fear that common schools would destroy desirable social class differences and educate people out of their proper place in society; fear that the industrious would be taxed to pay for the education of the indolent; fear that people without children would be forced to pay for the education of other people's children; fear that native-language instruction of non-English-speaking students would supplant English-language instruction in the schools; concerns of religious groups that the common school would hinder their advancement; and fear that private schools would be forced to close.

In general, Cubberley's interpretation depicts the common school movement as the correct historical route to the development of an educational system that would benefit the majority of people by solving economic, political, and social problems. This vision of the common school movement received added support in Merle Curti's *Social Ideas of American Educators,* first published in 1935. Curti's history of education was written during the Depression, when there was a great deal of concern over the historical struggle between the haves and have-nots.

Merle Curti: For Curti, the common school movement was a major democratic movement designed to extend social benefits to lower social classes. His description of the period is given mainly in chapters devoted to Horace Mann. He portrays

Horace Mann as a great egalitarian and reformer. For Curti, Mann's primary motivation was a desire to ensure that all classes of society had equal access to knowledge. Curti states, "[Mann's] social vision remained undimmed to the end, and all his work in the educational field was an effort to introduce into that field a more humane and democratic spirit."[46] But unlike Cubberley, Curti is highly critical of the conservative economic and social ideas held by Mann—an attitude that puts a critical edge on Curti's praise of the common school movement.

Michael Katz: Katz's 1968 book, *The Irony of Early School Reform,* dealt with the 1860 decision by voters in Beverly, Massachusetts, to abolish the local high school.[47] Katz used his discovery of resistance to the establishment of a high school in Beverly as a vehicle for providing a new interpretation of common school reforms. In the opening statement of his introductory chapter, "Educational Reform: The Cloud of Sentiment and Historiography," he states, "For the most part historians have helped to perpetuate this essentially noble story, which portrays a rational, enlightened working class, led by idealistic and humanitarian intellectuals, triumphantly wresting free public education from . . . selfish, wealthy elite and from the bigoted proponents of orthodox religions."[48] This, of course, is the interpretation given to the period by Ellwood Cubberley.

But, Katz argues, one should immediately begin to question this historical interpretation when one considers that by the end of the nineteenth century most urban schools were "cold, rigid, and somewhat sterile bureaucracies." He goes on to ask, "Could a truly humanitarian urge to help realize widely diffused aspirations have turned so quickly into the dispassionate ethos of red tape and drill?"[49] In answering this question, Katz paints an entirely different picture of the evolution of the common school.

For Katz, the most important factors in explaining the common school movement are the social and economic changes associated with the building of factories, the increase in immigration, and the growth of cities. Within the context of these events, upper-class reformers were seeking to ensure that they would benefit from these changes by imposing a common school system that would train workers for the new factories, educate immigrants to accept values that supported the ruling elite, and provide order and stability among the expanding populations of the cities.

From this perspective, the rigid, bureaucratic schools that Katz claims existed by the end of the nineteenth century were not accidental but were the logical result of a school system designed to discipline a population to serve the needs of an urban industrial society. The emphasis on attendance, disciplined study, and order was designed to socialize the student, particularly the immigrant child, to the requirements of the new factory systems. Learning to behave in school was a preparation for learning to work in the factory. Also, Katz argues, the bureaucratic structure of education, which evolved from common school reforms, was designed to ensure upper-class control of schooling. In his conclusion, Katz states that the common school movement was "a coalition of the social leaders, status-anxious parents, and status-hungry educators to impose educational innovation, each for their own reasons, upon a reluctant community."[50]

Katz's interpretation does not change the identity of the leaders of the common school movement, but it does change their motivations. According to Katz, their actions were not the result of disinterested humanitarian impulses but were caused by a desire to protect their social positions and to provide the new industrial system with disciplined workers.

What became the most controversial aspect of this interpretation is the argument that common school reforms were imposed on an unwilling working class—an argument that posed an important challenge to traditional ways of viewing American schools. This interpretation suggests that the vast majority of people in the nineteenth century did not want the type of school organization that became standard in the nineteenth and twentieth centuries. This attitude did not reflect a general opposition among the populace to education and schooling but represented a rejection of common school reforms that sought to organize schools under central state control for the purposes of serving the social, political, and economic goals of government.

Katz's interpretation challenges not only Cubberley's benign view of the reformers but also interpretations that emphasize the importance of working-class support of the common school movement. Traditional labor history, beginning with the work of John R. Commons at the University of Wisconsin in 1918, stresses the key role of workingmen's parties in the late 1820s and 1830s in fighting for common school reforms. This interpretation places the American worker at the forefront of the battle for common schools. Of particular importance in this interpretation is the opposition of workers to the existence of charity schools, which they felt reinforced social class distinctions. According to Commons's interpretation, members of the workingmen's parties supported common schools because they provided the children of the poor with equal educational opportunity by mixing the rich and poor. Equal educational opportunity, it was believed, would give children of the poor and the working class equal opportunities to compete with children of the more affluent classes.

Rush Welter: Welter emphasizes the role of workingmen's parties in *Popular Education and Democratic Thought in America* (1962), but his discussion minimizes their contribution to common school reform and stresses their contribution to later thinking about the democratic role of education. Welter, discussing the organized workingmen of the late 1820s and early 1830s, states, "Their numbers were few and their direct political influence was slight, but they first spelled out the educational perspective in which several generations of American democrats would see their society and their politics."[51]

A more complicated picture of common school reform emerges from Welter's interpretation of the workingmen's contribution to democratic educational theory: Although the workingmen's parties accepted the common school ideal of eliminating social class distinctions and providing equal opportunity, they also supported public schooling as a means of providing the working class with knowledge to protect itself against the interests and power of the privileged in society. This concept of political education in the common school, according to Welter, was different from the concept of education as a means of maintaining order in a free society. On the contrary, the workingmen's parties saw political education as a means of arming the working class against the authority and power of the upper class. In Welter's words, "In their [workingmen's] eyes political knowledge was useful, not because it supported the exercise of governmental authority, but because it provided an intellectual resource against authority."[52]

The importance of Welter's interpretation is his emphasis on the working-men's support of school reform and his argument that the workingmen supported the common school for reasons different from those of other members of society. Within Welter's framework, the common school did not arise from a consensus of values about what the common school should accomplish but arose from the ideas of different social groups, each hoping that the common school would fulfill particular educational goals.

Carl Kaestle: In *Pillars of the Republic,*[53] Kaestle emphasizes the role of the common school in ensuring the dominance of Protestant Anglo-American culture over other cultures in the United States. From Kaestle's point of view, common school reformers were primarily concerned that the United States did not become a multicultural society. Kaestle identifies ten major tenets of Protestant Anglo-American culture that the common school was designed to protect. These ten principles can be divided into four groups. The first group includes the belief in the fragility of the republican form of government, the importance of developing individual character to achieve social morality, and the role of personal effort in defining merit. This group of beliefs can be traced back to the early proponents of republican education, who believed that order could be maintained in a free republican society only through the education of responsible citizens. Kaestle argues that by the 1830s a certain confidence had developed that the experiment in republican government would survive, but there was still concern that action had to be taken to ensure its survival. In the common school movement, stress was placed on protecting the fragile republican form of government by providing a political education that taught a common set of political beliefs, emphasized the exercise of intelligence, and promoted respect for laws. Or as Kaestle states, the implication of native Protestant ideology was that "schooling should stress unity, obedience, restraint, self-sacrifice, and the careful exercise of intelligence."[54]

The belief that social morality was achieved through improving the quality of individual morality was a central theme of the charity school movement. As part of Protestant ideology and the common school movement, Kaestle argues, it resulted in a belief that a good moral education would produce a moral society. In addition, this aspect of Protestant ideology stressed that poverty could be eliminated if the children of the poor were taught that they could advance in society through their own individual effort.

The second group of factors in Kaestle's discussion is the role of women in society and the importance of the family and social environment in building character. According to Kaestle, Protestant ideology defined three central roles for women in middle-class families: to provide a sanctuary for the hardworking husband, to manage the household intelligently, and to nurture children. Of crucial importance was the role of women in child rearing because this role involved education for the political and moral well-being of the nation. The arguments given for the importance of this social role for women provided a justification for recruiting women as teachers in common schools—an important aspect of common school reforms—because of their supposed skills in nurturing and developing morality. Another important factor is the fact that women were cheaper to employ as teachers than men were.

In the third group of themes characterizing Protestant ideology, Kaestle includes a belief in the virtue of property and the availability of economic opportunity in the United States. Both Protestant ideology and the common school ideology contain the belief, according to Kaestle, that "property was to be respected because it taught virtue. Everyone should be taught to desire property and to respect property."[55] Related to this belief was a vision of America as the land of economic opportunity: The availability of property and education would make it possible for all people to achieve economic success.

The last group of themes Kaestle identifies includes a belief in the superiority of American Protestant culture, in the manifest destiny of American society, and in the necessity of unifying America's population. In the context of these beliefs, American Protestants believed their religious values were the core of the American experiment with republicanism. Educational writers after the Revolutionary War, such as Noah Webster, equated Protestant Christian values with republican values. Kaestle argues that this same theme appears in the Protestant ideology associated with the common school movement. Kaestle also argues that the belief in the superiority of Protestantism merged with a belief in America's unique destiny to "suggest to Americans that their nation was destined to reach the peak of human civilization."[56] The assumption of the superiority of Protestantism logically led to the belief that all people should be united by being educated into a Protestant culture.

These different interpretations highlight the complex factors involved in the common school movement. No single interpretation provides an adequate explanation. Rather, the common school appears to have been a result of a complicated set of often conflicting social and economic factors that included a humanitarian impulse to create the good society, a desire of the working class to enhance its political and economic position in society, a desire of manufacturers to have a disciplined and well-trained workforce, a desire of the upper classes to protect their economic and social privileges, and a desire of a Protestant majority to maintain an American Protestant culture.

CONCLUSION

The common school movement provided the basic ideology and structure of the modern American school system. No single set of reasons or social forces brought the common school movement into existence. Rather, the movement was a product of a combination of political, economic, and social concerns that existed in the early part of the nineteenth century.

The success of the common school movement represents the victory of one political philosophy over another. Most individuals who supported and worked for a common school system believed that government should play an active role in ensuring the success of the economic and social system and that this was best achieved by centralizing and standardizing governmental processes. Many who opposed the development of the common school system believed that the government that governed best governed least, that the success of the economic and social system depended on the absence of government intervention, and that the free actions of the marketplace guaranteed the most equitable distribution of economic benefits. They opposed the centralizing tendencies of government and hoped to maximize popular control of the political process by maintaining local control.

In the 1830s, these differences in political philosophy separated the Whigs from the Democrats: Most Whigs favored the centralization of control over education and the intervention of government, whereas most Democrats resisted the expansion of government power and fought to retain democratic localism. The tension and struggle between these two different political philosophies have continued into the twenty-first century under different political labels and represent a major area of disagreement in American political thought. By the middle of the twentieth century, conflict over this issue was expressed as a concern with centralization of educational control at the federal level. The Democratic Party supported this trend because of the promise it held for a more just and equitable school system, whereas the Republican Party resisted continued federal intervention and argued for local control and the benefits of the free marketplace. Throughout the history of the modern American school, differences in political philosophies have had a major impact on the development and organization of education.

Culturally, the common school movement attempted to ensure that Protestant Anglo-American culture would remain dominant as large groups of immigrants with differing religious and cultural values entered American life. During the early period of common school reforms, this primarily meant protecting a Protestant ideology against an influx of Irish Catholics, African Americans, and Native Americans. In the late nineteenth and early twentieth centuries, Americanization programs for immigrants in the public schools served the same function.

The protection of a particular set of cultural and religious values was made possible by the way in which control of the school system was organized. The growth of centralized and bureaucratic control, as opposed to democratic localism, ensured that the dominant values of the school system would be Protestant and middle-class. Beginning in the nineteenth century and continuing into the twentieth, the shifting patterns of control usually reflected the desire of one or more groups in society to ensure that the schools served particular political, social, and economic interests.

The development of the common school also reflected changing economic conditions. The early growth of industrialism placed a premium on education as preparation for work. From the standpoint of employers, common schooling could serve the useful function of socializing and training workers for the factory. From the workers' perspective, as reflected in the workingmen's parties, common schooling was a means of ensuring that employers did not maintain a monopoly over knowledge. Knowledge was power in the evolving modern industrial setting, and workers did not want to be kept from that source of power.

Also, the promise of American life was improved economic opportunity for all people. In fact, one could argue that the concept of equal economic opportunity is a theme that has united all American people. For the worker, equal economic opportunity was a means of improving one's personal economic condition. For the school reformer, such as Horace Mann, equal economic opportunity was a means of reducing friction among social classes. For the employer, equal economic opportunity was a means of ensuring a supply of the best possible workers by creating competition among workers in the labor market. For most members of society, the common school became the hope for providing and maintaining a society based on equality of economic opportunity.

Most social groups believed the common school was the best means of controlling crime, social unrest, and political disruptions. In the early nineteenth century, workingmen, Protestants, Catholics, reformers, urban dwellers, and others shared a belief that the school was the key to social control and social stability. This belief became a standard fixture in the rhetoric surrounding the American school in the nineteenth and twentieth centuries.

In summary, by the middle of the nineteenth century most of the major themes of the modern American school had emerged. Persistent political divisions over schooling would occur, and dissent would continue in certain areas. Also, hope would continue that common schooling would bring forth the good society by improving economic conditions, providing equal opportunity, eliminating crime, maintaining political and social order, and protecting the domination of Protestant Anglo-American culture.

Notes

1. Carl F. Kaestle and Maris Vinovskis, *Education and Social Change in Nineteenth-Century Massachusetts* (New York: Cambridge University Press, 1980), pp. 9–46.
2. Mary Peabody Mann, ed., *Life of Horace Mann* (Washington, DC: National Education Association, 1907), p. 13; Horace Mann's edited letters and journal are reprinted in this book.
3. Ibid., p. 14.
4. Ibid., pp. 49–50.
5. Ibid., p. 71.
6. Ibid., pp. 71–72.
7. Ibid., pp. 72–73.
8. Ibid., pp. 74–75.
9. Ibid., pp. 80–81.
10. Ibid., p. 83.
11. Edited copies of Horace Mann's reports can be found in Lawrence Cremin, ed., *The Republic and the School: Horace Mann on the Education of Free Men* (New York: Teachers College Press, 1958), p. 98.
12. Ibid., p. 100; italics in original.
13. Ibid., p. 106.
14. Ibid.
15. Ibid., pp. 94–97.
16. Ibid., p. 97.
17. Ibid., p. 93.
18. Ibid., p. 86.
19. Ibid., p. 87.
20. Ibid.
21. Quoted in William Russell, "Education and the Working Class: The Expansion of Public Education during the Transition to Capitalism" (Ph.D. dissertation, University of Cincinnati, 1981), pp. 274–275.

22. Quoted in ibid., pp. 276–277.
23. Ibid., p. 291.
24. Quoted in ibid., p. 294; italics in original.
25. Quoted in ibid., p. 295.
26. Quoted in ibid., p. 300.
27. Rush Welter, *Popular Education and Democratic Thought in America* (New York: Columbia University Press, 1962), pp. 51–52.
28. Herbert Ershkowitz and William G. Shade, "Consensus or Conflict? Political Behavior in the State Legislatures during the Jacksonian Era," in *The Many-Faceted Jacksonian Era: New Interpretations,* ed. Edward Pessen (Westport, CT: Greenwood Press, 1977), pp. 212–231.
29. Quoted in Lee Benson, *The Concept of Jacksonian Democracy: New York as a Test Case* (New York: Atheneum, 1966), p. 107.
30. Ibid.
31. Daniel Walker Howe, *The Political Culture of the American Whigs* (Chicago: University of Chicago Press, 1979), p. 29.
32. Ibid., pp. 29–30.
33. Ibid., p. 33.
34. Major L. Wilson, "What Whigs and Jacksonian Democrats Meant by Freedom," in Pessen, *Many-Faceted Jacksonian Era,* pp. 192–212; Howe, *Political Culture,* pp. 23–43.
35. Howe, ibid., pp. 34–35.
36. Kaestle and Vinovskis, *Education and Social Change* (see note 1).
37. Quoted in ibid., p. 215.
38. Ibid., p. 230.
39. William Reese, *The Origins of the American High School* (New Haven: Yale University Press, 1995).
40. Quoted in ibid., p. 35.
41. Ibid., pp. 38–58.
42. Ibid., p. 121.
43. Ellwood Cubberley, *Public Education in the United States: A Study and Interpretation of American Educational History* (Boston: Houghton Mifflin, 1934), pp. 164–165.
44. Ibid., pp. 165–166.
45. Ibid., p. 166.
46. Merle Curti, *The Social Ideas of American Educators* (Paterson, NJ: Pageant Books, 1959), p. 138.
47. Michael B. Katz, *The Irony of Early School Reform* (Cambridge, MA: Harvard University Press, 1968).
48. Ibid., p. 1.
49. Ibid., p. 2.
50. Ibid., p. 218.
51. Welter, *Popular Education,* p. 45.
52. Ibid., p. 48.
53. Carl F. Kaestle, *Pillars of the Republic: Common Schools and American Society, 1780–1860* (New York: Hill and Wang, 1983), p. 103.
54. Ibid., p. 81.
55. Ibid., p. 90.
56. Ibid., p. 94.

5

The Common School and the Threat of Cultural Pluralism

In the 1830s, the desire to establish public schools as a means of creating a common culture was heightened by increased immigration, particularly by the immigration of Irish Catholics. Discriminated against by the English, Irish Catholics threatened Protestant domination of American culture. The growth of public schools paralleled the growth of the immigrant and enslaved populations.

The common school movement of the 1830s and 1840s was, in part, an attempt to halt the drift toward a multicultural society. Self-proclaimed protectors of Protestant Anglo-American culture worried about the Irish immigrants streaming ashore, the growing numbers of enslaved Africans, and the racial violence occurring in northern cities between freed Africans and whites. Also during the 1830s, President Andrew Jackson implemented his final solution for acquiring the lands of the southern Native Americans by forcing the tribes off their lands and removing them to an area west of the Mississippi. The Native American removal was called the "Trail of Tears." Upon completion of this forced removal, the government was to "civilize" the southern tribes through a system of segregated schools. In addition to concern about the risk posed to Anglo-American culture, there was hysterical fear among European Americans during the common school period that Africans and Native Americans would "contaminate" white blood. This fear resulted in a demand by some whites for laws forbidding interracial marriages.

Many New Englanders hoped common schools would eradicate these "savage" cultures. The sensuous and emotional rhythms of African and Native American drums and the incense and ritual of the Irish Catholic Church offered a stark contrast to the stiff, repressed, and self-righteous way of life of white New Englanders. With the possibility of a multicultural society existing in North America, many European Americans hoped the common school would ensure that the United States was dominated by a unified Protestant Anglo-Saxon culture.

As Carl Kaestle argues in *Pillars of the Republic: Common Schools and American Society, 1780–1860,* the common school movement was primarily designed to protect the ideology of an American Protestant culture. Most of the common school reformers, Kaestle documents, were native-born Anglo-American Protestants, and their public philosophy "called for government action to provide schooling that would be more common, more equal, more dedicated to public policy, and therefore more effective in creating cultural and political values centering on Protestantism, republicanism, and capitalism."[1]

This chapter will discuss the following issues regarding multicultural education after the founding of public schools:

- The increasing multicultural population of the United States.
- Catholic and Protestant struggles over public schooling.
- Freed slaves and public schools.
- The education of Native Americans.

THE INCREASING MULTICULTURAL POPULATION OF THE UNITED STATES

The following tables show the increasing diversity of the U.S. population during the development and expansion of public schools from the 1830s to the 1850s. It is possible, but not necessarily provable, that public schools expanded in order to create a common culture and language. In 1830, six years before Horace Mann became secretary of the Massachusetts board of education, immigration expanded from Ireland and Germany as indicated in Table 5.1. The reader will recall from Chapter 3 that in 1790 60.9 percent of free whites were of English ancestry, 80 percent had English-speaking ancestry, and about 75 percent were Protestant. The reader can see from Table 5.1 that immigration almost quadrupled between the decades 1820–1830 (151,824 immigrants) and 1831–1840 (599,125 immigrants). During the 1820–1830 period the majority of immigrants still came from England (about 59 percent). But this dramatically changed between 1831 and 1840 with the increase in German immigration to 25.4 percent of the total immigration, reducing the number of immigrants from England to about 39 percent. The percentage of immigrants who did not come from England, as indicated in Table 5.2, rose to 72 percent by 1850.

The domination of immigrants by Irish and Germans during the early common school period of 1830–1840 threatened the Protestant majority among free whites. Almost all Irish during this period were Catholic, while Germans were a mixture of Jews, Catholics, and Protestants. Also, the increased German immigration increased the number of free whites whose first language was not English.

Adding to the possible anxiety about multiculturalism among free whites were the growing numbers of the nonwhite population. As indicated in Tables 5.3 and 5.4, the number of enslaved African Americans increased from 2,009,050 in 1830 to 3,953,760 in 1860, while the number of free African Americans increased from 319,576 in 1830 to 488,070 in 1860. And as I discuss in more detail in Chapter 7, an Asian population began to develop as the result of the California gold rush. Not included in these tables or in the U.S. census for these decades was a growing Mexican American population as a result of the Mexican American War. I discuss this Mexican American population and their educational experiences in more detail in Chapter 7.

TABLE 5.1 Immigration to the United States from Countries Other Than England by National Origin, 1820–1860

Total and National Origin by Decade	Numbers of Immigrants	Percentage of Total Immigration
Total Number of Immigrants		
1820–1830	151,824	100%
1831–1840	599,125	100
1841–1850	1,713,251	100
1851–1860	2,598,214	100
Ireland		
1820–1830	54,338	35.7
1831–1840	207,381	34.6
1841–1850	780,719	45.5
1851–1860	914,119	35.1
Germany		
1820–1830	7,729	5.0
1831–1840	152,454	25.4
1841–1850	434,626	25.3
1851–1860	951,667	36.6
Scandinavia (Sweden, Norway, Denmark)		
1820–1830	283	0.18
1831–1840	2,264	0.37
1841–1850	14,442	0.25
1851–1860	24,680	0.94
Italy		
1820–1830	439	0.28
1831–1840	2,253	0.37
1841–1850	1,870	0.10
1851–1860	9,231	0.35
Greece and Turkey		
1820–1830	41	0.02
1831–1840	56	0.009
1841–1850	75	0.004
1851–1860	114	0.004

Source: Calculated and compiled from tables provided in Roger Daniels, *Coming to America: A History of Immigration and Ethnicity in American Life, Second Edition* (New York: Perennial, 2002), pp. 124, 129, 146, 165, 189, and 202.

TABLE 5.2 Approximate Percentage of Non-English Immigrants to the United States, 1820–1860

Decade	Approximate Percentage of Non-English Immigrants to the United States
1820–1830	41.2%
1831–1840	60.7
1841–1850	72.05
1851–1860	72.9

Source: Calculations based on Table 5.1, Immigration to the United States from Countries Other Than England by National Origin, 1820–1860.

TABLE 5.3 Free and Slave Population of the United States by Race, 1830 Census

Status and Race	Population	Percentage of Total Population
Total population	12,858,670	100%
Free white	10,530,044	81.9
Free black	319,576	2.5
Slaves	2,009,050	15.6

Source: Abstract of the Returns of the Fifth Census, Showing the Number of Free People, The Number of Slaves (Washington, DC: Duff Green, 1832), p. 47.

TABLE 5.4 Free, Slave, Native American, and Asian Population of the United States, 1860

Status and Race	Population	Percentage of Total Population
Total population	31,443,321	100%
Free white	26,922,537	85.6
Free black	488,070	1.6
Slaves	3,953,760	12.6
Native Americans	44,021	0.1
Asian	34,933	0.1

Source: Campbell Gibson and Kay Jung, *Historical Census Statistics on Population Totals by Race, 1790 to 1990, and by Hispanic Origin, 1970 to 1990, for the United States, Regions, Divisions, and States* (Washington, DC: U.S. Census Bureau, 2002), Table F-1.

IRISH CATHOLICS: A THREAT TO ANGLO-AMERICAN SCHOOLS AND CULTURE

"No Irish Need Apply," a famous folk song of the common school period, referred to rental and employment signs telling Irish Americans they were not welcome as residents or workers. English colonists in North America stereotyped the Irish as "savages" and "slaves of their passions." These stereotypes developed during the long English domination of Ireland, which by 1700 left the Irish owning only 14 percent of Ireland.[2]

By the time of the great Irish immigration to the United States, English exploitation of Irish workers had reduced the average Irish family to a life of misery and famine. Living in one-room mud huts with straw roofs with only a hole cut through the straw for a chimney, the typical Irish family ate little more than a daily ration of potatoes. By 1845, a million Irish people had immigrated to the United States. When the smell of decay from the potato blight crossed the land in 1845, another one and a half million Irish people set sail to escape starvation. For those who stayed behind, the choice was often a deadly one. By 1855, the potato famine had killed a million people.[3]

As the Irish arrived at the great port cities, such as Boston and New York, they were greeted with open hostility. Competing with freed Africans for jobs, the Irish found employment building roads and railroads, working in mines, and digging canals. Irish workers were thought of by other European Americans as "dogs" and "dray horses" to be worked like other animals in the building of the new nation.[4]

Protestant Anglo-Saxons feared that the "drunken Irish," acting mainly out of "passion" rather than reason, might destroy the American dream. The Reverend Theodore Parker warned his congregation of "The Dangerous Classes," who were "inferior in nature, some perhaps only behind us in development . . . a lower form . . . [consisting of] negroes, Indians, Mexicans, Irish, and the like."[5]

The Catholicism of the Irish also bothered Protestants. By the nineteenth century, many Protestants feared that the Catholic Church was the church of Satan, and they worried that the pope had sent an army of Irish Catholics to undermine Protestant churches. Ironically, it was the English who had forced the Irish to become Christian, and after the Church of England became Protestant, most Irish remained Catholic. The majority of Irish immigrating to the United States in the nineteenth century were Catholic.[6]

The hostility between Catholics and Protestants resulted in the common school never truly being "common" to all children in the nineteenth century. The common or public schools in the United States in the nineteenth century were dominated by Protestant religious values. This resulted in disputes over the use of state educational funds for the support of public schools. In large part, this conflict resulted from strong anti-Catholic feelings in the Protestant community. In the end, Catholics felt excluded from the common schools and found it necessary to establish their own system of independent parochial schools.

In the 1830s and 1840s, New York City was the scene of religious conflicts when Catholics demanded a share of the state educational funds that were being monopolized by the Public School Society (originally the New York Free School Society). Until this time, Catholics had been operating their own schools in an attempt to provide children of Catholic parents with an alternative to the Protestant-dominated schools of the Public School Society. Catholics objected to the use of the Protestant version of the Bible and textbooks containing anti-Catholic statements.

The smoldering conflict between Catholics and Protestants in New York City erupted during the 1838 election of Governor William Seward. Governor Seward was a strong advocate of government-sponsored internal improvements and increased state support of education. Although he believed a centrally controlled and expanded system of education was necessary for the health of society, he also believed state money for the support of Catholic schools was necessary to achieve this goal.

One of Seward's major concerns was the education of Catholic immigrants, particularly the Irish, for citizenship. Attacking the strong anti-Irish feeling existing in the 1830s and 1840s, he denounced American hatred of "foreigners."[7] While visiting New York City in 1840, Seward concluded that large numbers of New York's Catholic children were not attending public schools because of their anti-Catholic atmosphere. His concern was that immigrant children, particularly the Irish, might grow up to be adult illiterates who would become public burdens and never enter the mainstream of American life. In 1840 he proposed to the state legislature that Catholic schools become part of the state school system while retaining their private charters and religious affiliation. As historian Vincent Lannie writes, "Seward urged the establishment of schools that would be acceptable to this minority group and staffed with teachers who spoke the same language and professed the same religious faith as their pupils. Such schools would be administered by Catholic officials but supported with public funds."[8]

Many Protestants were outraged by Seward's proposal and demanded that no money go to support Catholic schools. In a letter to a friend in 1840, Seward reasoned that it was necessary for the state to provide a moral and religious education to all children in order to maintain social stability, and "if it cannot be otherwise conferred, may rightly be conferred by the employment for the purpose of teachers professing the same language and religious creed."[9]

Accepting Seward's proposal, New York's Catholic community petitioned the Board of Aldermen of New York City for a portion of the common school fund. The petition enumerated Catholic complaints about Protestant dominance of the public schools. First, the Catholic petitioners attacked the supposed nonsectarianism of the schools operated by the Public School Society. The petition cited a number of instances in which the reports of the Public School Society either called for religious instruction or demonstrated the existence of religious instruction in the schools. This religious instruction included reading and study of the Bible, which the petition claimed made the school sectarian. The petitioners argued, "Even the reading of the Scriptures in those schools your petitioners cannot regard otherwise than as sectarian; because Protestants would certainly consider as such the introduction of the Catholic Scriptures, which are different from theirs, and the Catholics have the same ground of objection when the Protestant version is made use of."[10]

In addition, the petitioners complained about anti-Catholic statements in selections used for elementary reading lessons. They argued that historical and religious portions of the reading lessons were selected from Protestant writers who were prejudiced against Catholics. The petition stated, "The term 'Popery' is repeatedly found in them. This term is known and employed as one of insult and contempt towards the Catholic religion, and it passes into the minds of children with the feeling of which it is the outward expression."[11]

The Catholic petition acknowledged that the members of the Public School Society were trying to remove anti-Catholic sentiments from textbooks. According to the petitioners, this effort was failing because Protestants were unable to clearly discern anti-Catholic statements. As an example, the petition quoted the following passage from a textbook approved by the Public School Society:

> Huss, John, a zealous reformer from Popery, who lived in Bohemia, towards the close of the fourteenth, and the beginning of the fifteenth centuries. He was bold and persevering; but at length, trusting himself to the deceitful Catholics, he was by them brought to trial, condemned as a heretic, and burnt at the stake.[12]

The anti-Catholic atmosphere of common schools, according to the Catholic petitioners, forced them to open their own Catholic schools. This situation, they argued, resulted in double taxation whereby they were taxed to support the schools operated by the Public School Society and to support an alternative school system. In the words of the petition, "The expense necessary for this [establishment of Catholic schools], was a second taxation, required not by the laws of the land, but by the no less imperious demands of their conscience."[13] Catholics' claims that they had to assume the burden of double taxation for the maintenance of public and Catholic schools continued into the twentieth century.

The Catholic petitioners recognized that public money should not be used to support of religion. They were willing to remove all religious instruction from their schools during school hours. To ensure that money was not used for religious instruction, they recommended that the organization of their schools and the control of the disbursement of money "shall be conducted, and made, by persons unconnected with the religion of your petitioners, even the Public School Society. . . . The public may then be assured that the money will not be applied to the support of the Catholic religion."[14]

Both Governor Seward's proposal and the Catholic petition brought a storm of protest from the Protestant community. The "great debate" began within a month of the presentation of the petition before the Board of Aldermen in the city's Common Council chambers. The Protestant community responded to the Catholic petition with the argument that if Catholics were willing to postpone religious instruction until after school hours, they should be willing to instruct the children attending the Public School Society schools after school hours. The Reverend Mr. Knox of the Dutch Reformed Church claimed that the public schools were not "adverse to feelings of reverence for Catholic peculiarities." The Reverend Mr. Bangs of the Methodist Church argued that all poor and wayward children should be forced to attend public schools. Bangs argued, in the words of Vincent Lannie, "This coercive action of the state would really be an act of compassion,

© *The Granger Collection, New York*

since these vagrants would be snatched from the streets and their concomitant vices, and taught to become Christian gentlemen and competent citizens." The strong anti-Catholic feelings of Protestants were evident in Presbyterian minister Gardner Spring's statement that he viewed the Catholic petition "with more alarm on account of the source from which it comes . . . if there was no alternative between infidelity and the dogmas of the Catholic Church, I would choose, sir . . . , to be an infidel tomorrow."[15]

By 1842 the school issue inflamed public feelings to the point of causing a riot between anti-Catholics and Irish Catholics. Beginning in front of the city prison, the riot quickly spread to attacks on unsuspecting Catholic individuals and homes. Some Catholics took refuge in a hotel that was then stormed by anti-Catholic mobs. Rioters even attacked the residence of Bishop Hughes behind the major symbol of Irish Catholicism, St. Patrick's Cathedral.

New York City was not the only place where riots erupted between Catholics and Protestants. In 1843 the Philadelphia public school board ruled that Catholic children could read their own version of the Bible in public schools and that they could be excused from other religious instruction. Protestants claimed that this was an attempt by Catholics to exclude the Bible from the schools. The result of this conflict was the Philadelphia Bible riots, in which thirteen people died and a Catholic church was burned to the ground. Other conflicts of this type, though not of this intensity, occurred around the country.[16]

In the end, Catholics found it necessary to establish their own system of schooling, the organization of which emerged from the work of plenary councils held in Baltimore in 1852, 1866, and 1884. A major theme of these councils was that religious instruction should not be separated from other forms of instruction. At the First Plenary Council, church leaders told parents they had a responsibility to "watch over the purity of their [children's] faith and morals with jealous vigilance." To avoid neglecting their children's upbringing, Catholic parents were urged to give their children a Christian education "based on religious principles, accompanied by religious practices and always subordinate to religious influence." The council urged that all possible sacrifices be made for the establishment of Catholic schools.[17]

In 1866 the Second Plenary Council emphasized the principle "that religious teaching and religious training should form part of every system of school education." In addition, concern was expressed about the large number of delinquent Catholic youths who were being sent to Protestant reformatories. The council admitted, "It is a melancholy fact, and a very humiliating avowal for us to make, that a very large proportion of the idle and vicious youth of our principal cities are the children of Catholic parents." It recommended the establishment of Catholic industrial schools to care for delinquent Catholic youths.[18]

The Third Plenary Council, in 1884, sent forth decrees for the establishment of a system of Catholic schools. The council warned that the continued trend toward secular education was undermining Christianity and argued that all religious groups were calling for a Christian education in the schools, reflecting a common concern with the preservation of religious faith. The council claimed it was not condemning the state "for not imparting religious instruction in the public schools as they are now organized; because they well know it does not lie within the province of the State to teach religion." In fact, it considered the creation of Catholic schools as beneficial to the state because such schools would create better citizens by educating better Christians. It declared, "Two objects therefore, dear brethren, we have in view, to multiply our schools, and to perfect them."[19]

To achieve the objective of ensuring a Catholic education, the council decreed that every church establish a parish school and that all Catholic parents send their children to Catholic schools. The following decrees of the Third Plenary Council established the ideals of Catholic education in the United States:

> I. That near every church a parish school, where one does not yet exist, is to be built and maintained in perpetuum within two years of the promulgation of this council, unless the bishop should decide that because of serious difficulties a delay may be granted. . . .
> IV. That all Catholic parents are bound to send their children to the parish school, unless it is evident that a sufficient training in religion is given either in their own homes, or in other Catholic schools; or when because of sufficient reason, approved by the Bishop, with all due precautions and safeguards, it is licit to send them to other schools. What constitutes a Catholic school is left to the decision of the Bishop.[20]

The origins of the Catholic school system can be found in the centuries-old struggle between Irish and Anglo-Saxon cultures. Transported to the United States, the cultural conflict threatened Protestant Anglo-American cultural domination. The Catholic rebellion against public school reformers gave proof to the argument that the common school reflected a primarily Protestant ideology. Beginning in the nineteenth century and continuing into the twentieth, many Catholics would refer to public schools as Protestant schools.

SLAVERY AND FREEDOM IN THE NORTH: AFRICAN AMERICANS AND SCHOOLS IN THE NEW REPUBLIC

By the middle of the eighteenth century, there was a dramatic change in the origins of the slave population. The burgeoning northern economy and the development of the southern plantation system augmented the demand for enslaved Africans. Increasingly, slave traders arrived with human cargo who had been enslaved in the interior areas of Africa. Unlike the Atlantic Creoles, these enslaved Africans had been farmers and herders living in small villages. Unlike Atlantic Creoles, they had little or no contact with Europeans before being enslaved and marched to the west coast of Africa, where they were shackled in the disease-infested holds of slave ships. They spoke many different languages and had differing religious traditions. By the time they reached the Americas, if they survived the ocean trip, they were often psychologically devastated by the experience of being wrenched out of their villages, separated from their families, marched to the African coast in shackles, forced into the dark holds of sailing ships, and then sold to some unknown Anglo-American in a country that had little resemblance to their homelands.

By the middle of the eighteenth century, northern slaves were increasingly owned by artisans and tradesmen to help in the rapidly expanding workshops and warehouses of the northern colonies. In New Jersey, the Hudson Valley, and Long Island enslaved Africans played an important role in expanding the agricultural base of the colonies. Ira Berlin reports that by the middle of the eighteenth century, slave men outnumbered free white laborers in many New Jersey counties, such as 262 to 194 in Monmouth County, 281 to 81 in Middlesex County, and 206 to 8 in Bergen County.[21]

As the northern slave population increased, it became more difficult for slaves to gain their freedom. In addition, free blacks found their rights severely restricted by newly enacted laws. Berlin states, "in various northern colonies, free blacks were barred from voting, attending the militia, sitting on juries," and in many places were required to carry "special passes to travel, trade, and keep a gun or a dog."[22]

Unlike the Atlantic Creoles, the newly arrived enslaved Africans resisted the adoption of European culture. Many refused to Europeanize their names. Like Native Americans, they resisted the imposition of Christian religion. In Newport, Rhode Island, local clergy could find only approximately thirty Christians among a black population of a thousand. It was estimated that only one-tenth of New York City's black population was Christian. In the middle of the eighteenth century, Americans of African ancestry established festivals that celebrated African traditions. An observer at a festival in Rhode Island wrote, "All the various languages of Africa, mixed with broken and ludicrous English, filled the air, accompanied with the music of the fiddle, tambourine, banjo, [and] drum."[23]

Inevitably, free and enslaved Africans learned to speak English. In most cases, language instruction did not take place in any systematic way. It was documented

AFRICAN AMERICAN CITIZENSHIP TIME LINE

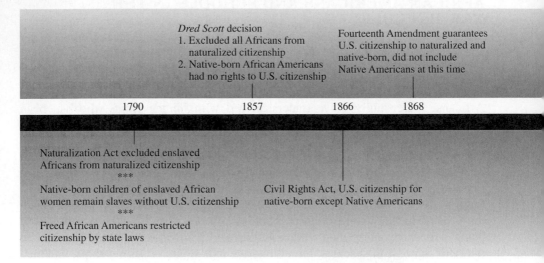

that in fugitive slave notices appearing in New York City's presses between 1771 and 1805, a quarter or more either did not speak English or spoke it poorly.[24] However, some enslaved Africans learned to read and write English well enough to petition the Massachusetts General Court for their freedom by proclaiming, "We have no Property! We have no Wives! No children! We have no City! No country! In common with all other men we have a natural right to our freedoms."[25]

For many northern state legislators, though not for southern, there was an obvious contradiction between the principles of the American Revolution and support of slavery. However, for freed slaves in the North freedom did not mean equality before the law or equality of treatment. The freeing of enslaved Africans highlighted the difference between freedom and equality in the minds of Anglo-Americans of the Revolutionary generation. Also, the treatment of freed slaves underlined the idea that equality was meant for only a select few.

Petitions for freeing enslaved Africans began appearing during the Revolution. In 1778 the Executive Council of Pennsylvania asked the Assembly to prohibit the further importation of slaves with the goal of eventually abolishing slavery. The Council pointed out that Europeans were "astonished to see a people eager for Liberty holding Negroes in Bondage."[26] During the same year, the governor of New Jersey called on the state legislature to begin the process of gradual abolition of slavery because it was "'odious and disgraceful' for a people professing to idolize liberty."[27] In 1785 the New York legislature passed a bill for the gradual abolition of slavery. In Massachusetts slavery ended through court action. By 1830 there were still 3,586 enslaved Africans in northern states, two-thirds of them in New Jersey.[28]

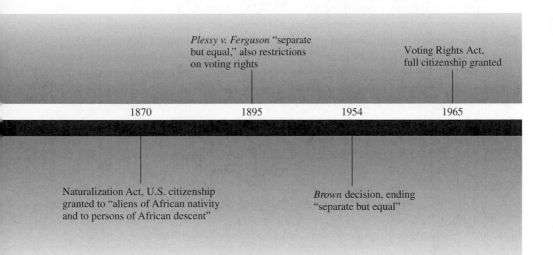

Plessy v. Ferguson "separate but equal," also restrictions on voting rights

Voting Rights Act, full citizenship granted

1870   1895   1954   1965

Naturalization Act, U.S. citizenship granted to "aliens of African nativity and to persons of African descent"

Brown decision, ending "separate but equal"

Also, abolitionist societies sprang up during the Revolutionary years. These societies would play a key role in the education of freed Africans in the North and South after the Civil War. In addition, these abolitionist societies were central to the antislavery movement of the nineteenth century and supported efforts by African Americans to escape bondage in the South. In general, the abolitionist groups had a strong religious orientation that shaped the type of education they provided to freed African Americans. The Pennsylvania Society for the Abolition of Slavery was organized in 1775 and joined with Quakers to ensure the speedy end to slavery in that state. Similar organizations played an active role in other northern states.

Racial Segregation

It was immediately apparent that most Anglo-Americans were not going to accept integrated educational institutions. Racially segregated schools were widely established from the late eighteenth century until the U.S. Supreme Court ruled them unconstitutional in 1954. Segregation meant more than building a racial divide: It also resulted in unequal funding of schools. Educational segregation resulted in unequal educational opportunities.

In 1787 African American leaders in Boston petitioned the legislature for schools because they "now receive no benefit from the free schools."[29] In Pennsylvania and Ohio, school districts were required to build separate educational facilities for African Americans. In Indiana, despite the fact that school laws made no racial distinctions, the white population refused to send their children to schools with African American children. The result was segregated schools. Some Anglo-Americans after the Revolution even protested the provision of any education for African Americans, claiming that it would offend southerners and encourage immigration from Africa.

Resistance to educational integration also extended to higher education. When African American leader Charles Ray tried to enter Wesleyan College in 1832, student protests forced him to leave. In Canaan, New Hampshire, the Noyes Academy in 1835 admitted twenty-eight whites and fourteen African Americans. The school received support from African American communities and abolitionist societies in Massachusetts and New York. However, when the school year began, four-fifths of the residents of Canaan registered a protest against the integrated school. A mob attacked the school but was eventually restrained by local officials.

The residents of Canaan mixed patriotism with racism in protesting the Noyes Academy. For some Americans, racism would always be cloaked in the mantle of patriotism. The protesters in Canaan condemned abolitionism and praised the Constitution and Revolutionary patriots as they removed the school building from its foundations and dragged it by oxen to a new site. Stories of this sort were typical of efforts of African Americans and abolitionist societies to establish integrated schools.

Discrimination and segregation affected other parts of the lives of African Americans in northern states. Attempts to prohibit interracial marriages occurred in New York, Pennsylvania, Indiana, Wisconsin, and Illinois. In Philadelphia, African Americans were allowed to ride only on the front platforms of horse-drawn streetcars, and in New York City blacks rode on "colored-only" vehicles. Race riots broke out in Philadelphia and Cincinnati. In 1834 rioting whites in Philadelphia forced blacks to flee, and in 1841 whites in Cincinnati used a cannon against blacks defending their homes.[30]

Boston and the Struggle for Equal Educational Opportunity

An important example of the early struggle for equal educational opportunity occurred in Boston. Boston organized the first comprehensive system of urban schools after the passage of the Massachusetts Education Act of 1789. This

AFRICAN AMERICAN PRE-CIVIL RIGHTS EDUCATION TIME LINE

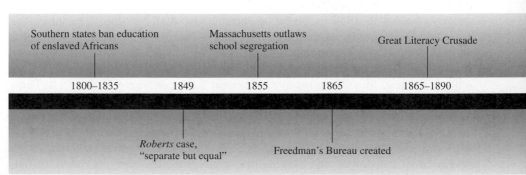

legislation required towns to provide elementary schools for six months of the year and grammar schools in communities with more than 200 families. In 1790 the black population in Boston was 766 in a total population of 18,038. At the beginning of the nineteenth century, no law or tradition excluded black children from the public schools. Some were enrolled in public schools, while others attended private ones.[31]

However, few black children actually attended school. The low attendance rate was a result of the poor economic conditions of the black population and the hostile reception given black children in the public schools. To protect their children from the prejudice of white children, a committee of African Americans in 1798 asked for a separate system of schools for their children. The Boston school committee rejected this request, reasoning that if it provided separate schools for blacks it would also need to provide separate schools for other groups. Receiving aid from white philanthropists, the parents opened a school that survived for only a few months. In 1800 a group of thirty-six African Americans again asked the Boston school committee to establish a separate school for their children. Again the answer was no. Two years later the black community opened another separate private school.[32]

In 1806 the school committee reversed its position and opened a segregated school with a combination of public funds and contributions from white philanthropists. In 1812 the school committee voted for permanent funds for the school and established direct control over it.[33]

The Boston school committee's decision created a complex situation. First, the committee supported and controlled a segregated school, although no law existed requiring segregation. In theory at least, black children were free to attend public schools other than the one established for them. Second, the African American community supported the segregated school as an alternative to the prejudice existing in the white-dominated schools. And last, the school was supported by a combination of private and public money. Private contributions to the school became a major factor when Abiel Smith died in 1815 and left the entire income from his shares in New England turnpikes and bridges and from the U.S. bonds he had owned to the support of black schools. The school committee assumed

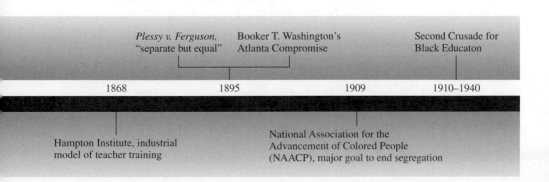

	Plessy v. Ferguson, "separate but equal"	Booker T. Washington's Atlanta Compromise		Second Crusade for Black Educaton
1868	1895	1909		1910–1940

Hampton Institute, industrial model of teacher training

National Association for the Advancement of Colored People (NAACP), major goal to end segregation

trusteeship of the estate, which meant it controlled both the school and the major-ity of private funds supporting the school.[34]

By the 1820s, the African American community realized that segregated edu-cation was resulting in an inferior education for their children. The school com-mittee was appointing inferior teachers to the all-black school and was not maintaining the school building. In 1833 a subcommittee issued a report on the conditions of the schools. The major conclusion of this report was that black schools were inferior to other schools in the quality of education and physical conditions. The report argued that "a classroom better than a basement room in the African Church could be found. After all, Black parents paid taxes which helped to support white schools. They deserved a more equal return on their share of the city's income."[35]

The most important conclusion of the report was that segregated education was not benefiting either race. The Boston school committee responded to the report by focusing efforts on building a new segregated school. The school com-mittee accepted the idea of segregated education and argued that the real problem was ensuring that separate schools for black children were equal to those of whites.

Local black abolitionist David Walker answered this question with a resound-ing "No!" Walker was representative of an increasingly militant and literate Afri-can American community in the northern states. Walker was born in North Carolina in 1779 of a free mother and a slave. According to North Carolina law, Walker was thus born free. He moved to Boston in the early 1820s and became a contributor to and local agent for the nation's first black newspaper, *Freedom's Journal,* published in New York.

In the newspaper and in his other writings, Walker argued that four principal factors were responsible for the poor situation of blacks in the nation: slavery; the use of religion to justify slavery and prejudice; the African colonization move-ment, designed to send free blacks back to Africa; and the lack of educational opportunity. White Americans, he argued, were keeping black Americans from receiving any significant amount of education. As proof, he cited laws in the South that made it illegal to educate slaves. In the North, according to Walker, the infe-rior education blacks received in schools was designed to keep them at a low level of education.[36]

After studying the conditions in Boston schools, Walker reached the conclu-sion that segregated education in the city was a conspiracy by whites to keep blacks in a state of ignorance. Walker's arguments added fuel to the fire. Demands by the black community for integrated education intensified, and for almost two decades the black community struggled with the school committee to end segre-gated education. Part of the issue was the loss of control of black schools by the black community. Originally the black community exercised control over its early private educational endeavors. Over the years, however, the school committee had gained complete control, so that any complaints the black community had about its schools had to be resolved by the committee.

In 1849 the protests over segregated schools finally reached the Massachusetts Supreme Judicial Court when Benjamin Roberts sued the city for excluding his five-year-old daughter from the schools. In this particular case, his daughter passed five white primary schools before reaching the black school. Consequently, Roberts decided to enroll her in one of the closer white schools. He lost the case on a decision by the court that the school system had provided equal schools for black children. This was one of the first separate-but-equal rulings in American judicial history.

The issue of segregation in Massachusetts schools was finally resolved in 1855, when the governor signed into law a requirement that no child be denied admission to a public school on the basis of race or religious opinions. In September of that year the Boston public schools were integrated without any violent hostilities.

This early history of segregated education illustrates the ambivalent attitudes of whites about the education of African Americans. On the one hand, whites might feel that containing the threat of African culture to the dominant Protestant culture of the United States required "civilizing" African Americans in the same manner as Native Americans. This meant providing schools. On the other hand, whites who considered Africans a threat to their racial purity and culture, and who believed Africans were "inferior," wanted the "civilizing" or education of African Americans to occur in segregated schools. As a result of the latter beliefs, public education for African Americans in the United States remained primarily segregated in the nineteenth and twentieth centuries.

Learning in the Plantation System

Literacy was a punishable crime for enslaved Africans in the South. However, by the outbreak of the Civil War in 1860, it is estimated that 5 percent of slaves had learned how to read, sometimes at the risk of life or limb. Individual slaves would sneak books and teach themselves while hiding from their masters. Sometimes self-taught slaves would pass on their skills and knowledge to other slaves. James Anderson quotes a former slave, Ferebe Rogers, about her husband's educational work prior to the Civil War: "On his dyin' bed he said he been de death o' many a nigger 'cause he taught so many to read and write."[37]

It was easier for slaves to learn to read if they worked in cities such as Charleston and Savannah. For enslaved Africans in these communities, as opposed to plantation slaves, there was a chance to earn money to purchase freedom. Also, there was greater assimilation into Anglo-American life. Nevertheless, plantation life sometimes provided the opportunity for clandestine learning.

In *Been in the Storm So Long: The Aftermath of Slavery,* Leon Litwack relates a number of examples of how literacy spread the word of Southern defeats during the Civil War. In one case, discussions of the Civil War by the plantation owners were usually punctuated with the spelling of words so that house slaves could not understand. However, one maid memorized the letters and spelled them out later to an uncle who could read. In Forsyth, Georgia, Edward Glenn, after going to town to get the newspaper, would give it to the local black minister to read before taking it to the plantation house. Litwack writes, "On the day Glenn would never forget, the preacher threw the newspaper on the ground after reading it, hollered,

'I'm free as a frog!' and ran away. The slave dutifully took the paper to his mistress who read it and began to cry. 'I didn't say no more,' Glenn recalled."[38] In another situation, a Florida slave kept his literacy secret from his owner. One day the owner unexpectedly walked in while he was reading the newspaper and demanded to know what he was doing. "Equal to the moment," Litwack states, "[he] immediately turned the newspaper upside down and declared, 'Confederates done won the war.' The master laughed and left the room, and once again a slave had used the 'darky act' to extricate himself from a precarious situation."[39]

NATIVE AMERICANS

U.S. political leaders considered education a method for gaining Native American land. A major problem facing the U.S. government after the Revolution was acquiring the lands of Native Americans to the south and west of the lands already controlled by white settlers. Of particular concern were the tribes occupying southern lands in what is now North and South Carolina, Georgia, Florida, Alabama, Mississippi, and Tennessee. President George Washington and Secretary of War Henry Knox warned the Senate in 1789, "To conciliate the powerful tribes of Indians in the southern District [which included the so-called Five Civilized Tribes—Choctaw, Cherokee, Chickasaw, Creek, and Seminole] amounting probably to fourteen thousand fighting Men, and to attach them firmly to the United States, may be regarded as highly worthy of the serious attention of government."[40]

Having fought a long and costly war with the British, the U.S. government did not have the resources to immediately embark upon a military campaign against the southern tribes. The easiest route to acquiring their lands was to purchase them through treaties. The U.S. government treated the purchase of Native American lands as though it was the same thing as bringing the land under the control of the laws of the American government. In contrast, the traditional practice in Europe was that if an English citizen bought land in France, French laws would continue to govern the land. In North America, Europeans assumed that the purchase of Native American lands resulted in governance by European American laws. If traditional European practices had been followed, then Cherokee land purchased by the U.S. government would have remained under the governance of the Cherokee tribe rather than being placed under the control of U.S. laws.

Therefore, purchase of Native American lands was the same as conquest, and it was cheaper than a military campaign. Washington proposed this approach in a 1783 letter to James Duane, who served as head of a select committee on Native American affairs in the Continental Congress. Washington urged the purchase of Native American lands instead of expropriation. "In a word," Washington wrote, "there is nothing to be obtained by an Indian War but the Soil they live on and this can be had by purchase at less expense, and without bloodshed."[41] The famous Northwest Ordinance of 1787 held out the same promise of peace and negotiation for Native American lands: "The utmost good faith shall always be observed towards the Indians, their lands and property shall never be taken from them without their consent; and in their property, rights and liberty, they never shall be invaded or disturbed."[42]

U.S. government leaders decided that the best methods of convincing the southern tribes to sell their lands were civilization programs. And in what would later be used by Thomas Jefferson as a means of civilizing Native Americans, Washington proposed the establishment of official U.S. government trading houses on tribal lands as a means of "render[ing] tranquility with the savages permanent by creating ties of interest."[43]

When Thomas Jefferson became president in 1801, he also hoped trading houses would be the means for civilizing Native Americans and gaining their lands. The major flaw in these policies was the assumption that Native Americans would be willing to sell their lands. As Jefferson noted in a message to Congress in 1803, "the policy has long been gaining strength with them [Native Americans] of refusing absolutely all further sale on any conditions."[44] In the face of this resistance, Jefferson's problem was developing a plan that would cause tribes to sell their lands.

Jefferson was convinced that the cultural transformation of Native Americans was the key to acquiring tribal lands. For Jefferson, the solution to breaking down resistance to selling land involved transforming Native Americans into yeoman farmers who, living on farms and no longer dependent on hunting, would not need vast tracts of wilderness. In his first annual message to Congress in 1801, he informed the members that "efforts to introduce among them [Indians] the implements and practice of husbandry, and of the household arts" were successful. "They are becoming more and more sensible," he stated, "of the superiority of this dependence for clothing and subsistence over the precarious resources of hunting and fishing." He was pleased to report that as a result of learning European American methods of husbandry and agriculture, tribes "begin to experience an increase of population."[45]

As did many other European Americans, Jefferson believed it was important to teach Native Americans a desire for the accumulation of property and to extinguish the cultural practice of sharing. Like other advocates of "civilizing" the Native Americans, Jefferson linked the creation of the nuclear family with a desire to acquire property and the establishment of a formal government. Writing to the chiefs of the Cherokee Nation in 1806, he congratulated the tribe for beginning a transition from hunting to husbandry and farming. The nuclear family structure resulting from farming, he argued, would create a desire to accumulate and pass on property. "When a man has enclosed and improved his farm," Jefferson wrote, "builds a good house on it and raised plentiful stocks of animals, he will wish when he dies that *these things shall go to his wife and children, who he loves more than he does his other relations, and for whom he will work with pleasure during his life* [emphasis added]."[46]

The accumulation of property, Jefferson warned the Cherokees, requires the establishment of laws and courts. "When a man has property," Jefferson wrote, "earned by his own labor, he will not like to see another come and take it from him because he happens to be stronger, or else to defend it by spilling blood. You will find it necessary then to appoint good men, as judges, to decide rules you shall establish."[47]

By creating in Native Americans a desire for the accumulation of wealth and the purchase of manufactured goods on display at government trading houses, Jefferson believed, European Americans would be able to persuade Native Americans to sell their lands to gain cash. In this manner, Native Americans would become part of a cash economy and would become dependent on manufactured goods.

In a special message to Congress urging the continuation of trading houses, Jefferson wrote that to counteract tribal resistance to selling land "and to provide an extension of territory which *the rapid increase of our numbers will call for* [emphasis added], two measures are deemed expedient." The first, he argued, was to encourage Native Americans to abandon hunting for agriculture and husbandry. "The extensive forests necessary in the hunting life," he told Congress, "will then become useless, and they will see advantage in exchanging them for the means of improving their farms and of increasing their domestic comfort." Second, he argued, the trading houses will make them aware of what they can purchase with the money earned from the sale of lands. Consequently, Jefferson asked Congress "to multiply trading houses among them, and place within their reach those things *which will contribute more to their domestic comfort than the possession of extensive but uncultivated wilds* [emphasis added]."[48]

Jefferson wanted to change Native American values regarding the economy, government, family relations, and property, and to manipulate desires regarding consumption of goods. Civilizing Native Americans, in this case, meant completely wedding them to an economy of increasing production and demand for new goods. "In leading them thus to agriculture, to manufacture, and civilization," Jefferson told Congress, "in bringing together their and our sentiments, and in preparing them ultimately to participate in the benefits of our Government, I trust and believe we are acting for their greatest good."[49]

U.S. government agents were the principal means for instituting Jefferson's civilization policies. Among the Cherokees, government agents were instructed to establish schools to teach women how to spin and sew and to teach men the use of farm implements and methods of husbandry. Agents acted as teachers and advertisers of manufactured goods. They were to begin the cultural transformation of Native Americans that would change Native American ideas about farming, families, government, and economic relations. At the end of his term, according to Francis Prucha, Jefferson felt vindicated by his policies of civilization. "The southern tribes, especially," Prucha writes, "were far ahead of the others in agriculture and the household arts and in proportion to this advancement identified their views with those of the United States."[50]

Native Americans had ambivalent attitudes toward the educational efforts of the government and missionaries. Some Native Americans concluded that education was necessary for protecting their interests against the continual attempts by the U.S. government to expand its territorial control. Consequently, Native American educational goals were quite different from the efforts by the U.S. government to "civilize" Native Americans by sending missionary educators into their lands.

NATIVE AMERICAN CITIZENSHIP TIME LINE

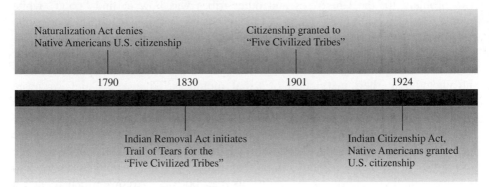

This ambivalence was exemplified by the Cherokee Ghost Dance movement of 1811–1812. Similar to other Ghost Dances that spread through tribes in the nineteenth century, the Cherokee Ghost Dance represented a desire to restore tribal lands to their conditions prior to the invasion of Europeans. The Great Spirit's message for the Cherokees included an educational plan to help the tribe adapt to the reality of European conquest.[51]

The Ghost Dance: The Educational Dilemma for Native Americans

In January 1811 a vision of night riders in the sky appeared to a Cherokee woman and two men who stopped at a deserted cabin on a lonely mountain in northwest Georgia. Pounding on their drums, the ghostly band descended from the sky and encircled the three Cherokees. They announced that the Great Spirit was angry because the Cherokee Nation was allowing bad white people to enter tribal lands and the Cherokees were adopting white people's methods of using large millstones to grind corn. This anger was causing the Mother of the Cherokee Nation to allow game to disappear from the Nation's lands. Reflecting the racial attitudes of many Native Americans, the messengers of the Great Spirit announced that white people and Native Americans were different types of humans. White people were made from white sand and Native Americans from red clay. The message was clear. The game would be restored to the Cherokee forests if the tribe returned to traditional ways and drove bad white people off tribal lands.[52] Suddenly, the ghost riders turned and pointed to a bright light descending from the dark sky. Inside the beam of light were four white houses. The white houses were to be built, the three Cherokees were told, for good white people "who could be useful to them with writing."[53]

By the late eighteenth and early nineteenth centuries, many Cherokees, like other Native American tribes that still survived in the northern and southeastern parts of the United States, had concluded that learning to read and write was essential for trade and the negotiation of treaties with the U.S. government. Avoiding the loss of all lands to white people, these Native Americans believed, required literacy. The problem for the Cherokees and other tribes was how to find "good" white people who would limit their teaching to reading and writing—in other words, white teachers who would not attempt to change traditional tribal values and customs.

Native Americans knew that European Americans harbored a belief in their own cultural superiority. They did not want this sense of cultural superiority to be introjected into their instruction of tribal members. Cherokee Chief Arcowee expressed this sentiment in 1798 to Moravian missionaries who were asking to enter Cherokee lands as teachers. Arcowee told a creation legend that developed after the European invasion. At creation, the Great Spirit offered a Bible to the Native Americans, but they could not read from it. When white people saw the book, they immediately began reading. Consequently, white people, Arcowee told the missionaries, were given the ability to read books.[54] Arcowee then related a vision in which his father told him it was time for Native Americans to learn to read. The problem, Arcowee said, was that white people refused to share the knowledge of reading given to them by the Great Spirit. Indeed, whites failed to recognize that the Great Spirit expected them to treat Native Americans as equals. The Christian missionaries, he stated, should understand that whites had previously failed to share knowledge given to them as a gift by the Great Spirit. Missionaries did not understand the invitation and quickly angered the Cherokees by focusing their efforts on changing social habits before teaching reading and writing.[55]

The Civilization Act

After the Ghost Dance movement, U.S. political leaders made another attempt to acquire Native American lands with the passage of the Civilization Act of 1819. The passage of this legislation was guided by Superintendent of Indian Trade Thomas L. McKenney. He was born into a Quaker family on March 21, 1785. McKenney's religious values were reflected in policies stressing peace and Christianity during the fourteen years of his service as superintendent of Indian trade and, after the office was abolished in 1823, as head of the newly created Office of Indian Affairs from 1824 to 1830.[56]

Thomas McKenney's belief in the power of schooling to culturally transform Native Americans reflected the growing conviction among many European Americans that education was the key to social control and improvement of society. A decade before the common school movement, McKenney's ideas on the power of schooling were enacted by Congress in the Civilization Act of 1819. In the 1820s, McKenney advanced the argument that the creation of tribal school systems operated by white missionary teachers would culturally transform Native Americans in one generation. This extreme belief in the power of the school to change and control societies was later reflected in the thinking of common school reformers in the 1830s and the rise of public schools.

Conceptualizing Native Americans as children, McKenney believed the key to civilizing them was schooling. Consequently, shortly after he was appointed superintendent of Indian trade in 1816, his interests shifted from trade as a means of cultural transformation to the use of schools. By 1819 McKenney was able to convince Congress to pass the Civilization Fund Act to provide money for the support of schools among Native American tribes. Reflecting on his effort to gain approval of the legislation, McKenney wrote, "I did not doubt then, nor do I now, the capacity of the Indian for the highest attainments in civilization, in the arts and religion, but I was satisfied that no adequate plan had ever been adopted for this great reformation."[57]

Just prior to the adoption of the Civilization Fund Act, McKenney recounts, it appeared "to me to be propitious for the making of the experiment."[58] It is important to emphasize that McKenney considered the introduction of schools into Native American tribes as an "experiment" in what I call ideological management. Could schools "civilize" Native Americans? Could schools bring about a cultural transformation? At the time, McKenney didn't consider the possibility that some tribal members might resent and resist this attempt at cultural transformation. He believed the time was right for the experiment because of relative peace with the tribes; and besides, "there were now several missionary stations already in operation, though on a small scale, all of them furnishing proof that a plan commensurate to the object, would reform and save, and bless this long neglected, and downtrodden people."[59]

The Civilization Fund Act of 1819 authorized the president to "employ capable persons of good moral character, to instruct them [Indians] in the mode of agriculture suited to their situation; and for teaching their children in reading, writing, and arithmetic." The legislation provided an annual sum of ten thousand dollars to be used by the president to fund the establishment of schools. The legislation specifically indicated that the funds were to be used with tribes "adjoining the frontier settlements of the United States." In practice, a large percentage of the money funded missionaries to set up schools among the Choctaws and Cherokees.[60]

Native Americans, Education, and Social Class

Surprisingly, the Civilization Fund Act of 1819 contributed to the development of social classes among Native American tribes and to a lasting division between "progressives" and "traditionalists." From the nineteenth century to the present, tribal progressives have argued for acculturation of Native Americans to the dominant social and economic system of the United States. In contrast, traditionalists have tried to maintain Native American customs and ways of living, and they have often rejected European forms of schooling. Progressives adopted European American values regarding the accumulation of wealth and therefore tended to become the wealthiest members of a tribe. Scorning acquisitive values, traditionalists remained the poorest members of the tribe. Note that the idea of social classes and the existence of extreme differences in wealth had origins in European and not Native American societies.

The funds authorized under the Civilization Fund Act were used primarily to send missionary educators to the southern tribes. One reason for the focus on southern tribes was the desirability of their lands for cotton growing. For instance, cotton grown on lands vacated by the Choctaws in the 1830s made Mississippi the leading producer of cotton.[61]

NATIVE AMERICAN PRE-CIVIL RIGHTS EDUCATION TIME LINE

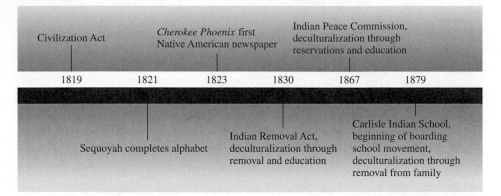

In the southern tribes, missionary educators were primarily welcomed by progressive and wealthy "mixed-blood" members of the tribe. The term *mixed blood* referred to Native Americans who had both Native American and European ancestry. Their fathers were, in most cases, whites who decided to join Native American tribes. Prior to the Civilization Fund Act, some Cherokees were influenced by Jefferson's civilization policies and began growing cotton and raising livestock. By 1809 certain Cherokee families were already accumulating large numbers of slaves and livestock. In 1809 it was reported that Joseph Vann, a mixed blood and at the time the wealthiest Cherokee, owned 115 slaves, 1,000 head of cattle, and 250 horses.[62]

The major political and economic leaders of the Cherokees in the early nineteenth century were members of the McDonald, Ross, Ridge, and Vann families. William McLoughlin estimates that by the 1820s wealth was concentrated in mixed families who made up 25 percent of the population of the tribe. Only 6 percent of the tribe owned one or more slaves, and fewer than 1 percent owned more than ten slaves. Because land was held in common by the tribe, wealth was measured according to the amounts of slaves, wagons, plows, looms, and land under cultivation. The vast majority of Cherokees owned no slaves or wagons and cultivated fewer than forty acres. In the 1820s, McLoughlin concludes, "Over three-quarters of the Cherokees were full bloods who spoke no English. They preferred the steady routine of life and the extended kinship system of their clans."[63]

The mixed-blood Vann, McDonald, Ridge, and Ross families helped missionary educators build their schools. For instance, in 1816 Presbyterian missionary Cyrus Kingsbury bought twenty-five acres of McDonald land to build the Brainerd mission. The U.S. government provided five hundred dollars for the land and furnished the school with farm equipment.[64] On this site, Kingsbury built four log cabins for boarding students and a schoolhouse designed to teach one hundred students.[65]

In the Choctaw tribe, the Folsoms, the Pitchlynns, and the Leflores were the leading families in wealth, political power, and education. Nathaniel Folsom, John

Pitchlynn, and Louis Leflore were the founders of these Choctaw families. Nathaniel Folsom's son, David Folsom, and John Pitchlynn—the two Choctaws who played a leading role in establishing the first school in the Choctaw Nation— were a mixed blood and a white, respectively. The descendants of these three families were active in the government and educational system in Mississippi Territory and, after removal, in Indian Territory.

An 1819 letter written by Choctaw David Folsom underscores the role of progressives and wealthy mixed bloods in the introduction of schooling. The letter was written shortly after the opening of the first school in the Choctaw Nation financed by the Civilization Fund Act. The letter opened with Folsom apologizing for his poor English and his limited school attendance of six months. Then he declared that education was now vital to the tribe because of the decline in hunting. He wrote, "I have been talking to my people, and have advised them for the best, turn their attention to industry and farming, and lay our hunting aside. And here is one point of great work, is just come [sic] to hand, before us which is the establishment of a school; and the Choctaws appear to be well pleased."[66]

These wealthy mixed bloods primarily wanted schools to provide their children with an education that would aid in the further accumulation of wealth and protection of property. The educated children of the mixed-blood families assumed major political positions with the tribe by creating constitutional governments and written laws that made literacy essential for political power. Serving mainly the mixed-blood families, the Civilization Act helped to cement the political power of the wealthy mixed-blood progressives and reduce the political power of traditionalists.[67]

It was the leading mixed bloods in the Cherokee and Choctaw tribes who signed treaties giving up all traditional lands to the U.S. government. From the perspective of traditionalists, mixed-blood progressives and European American schools destroyed the Native American nations.[68]

The Missionary Educators

There was no objection to the U.S. government subsidizing Protestant missionary educators under the provisions of the Civilization Fund Act. From the perspective of the early twenty-first century, government support of missionaries might be considered a violation of the First Amendment prohibition against government support of religion. But for most European Americans in the early nineteenth century, public education and Protestantism went hand in hand. Throughout the nineteenth century, most educators did not think it was strange to begin the public school day with a prayer and a reading from a Protestant Bible. In fact, in the minds of most white Protestants in the early nineteenth century, it probably appeared logical and correct to use missionary educators to "civilize" Native Americans because "civilizing" included conversion to Christianity.

In the United States, Protestant churches organized to civilize Native Americans and to convert the entire non-Christian world. In the early nineteenth century, missionary educators took the message of Protestantism to Asia, Africa, and the South Pacific. In 1810 the Presbyterian and Congregationalist churches founded the American Board of Commissioners for Foreign Missions (ABCFM). The ABCFM had a global mission and began sending missionaries abroad and to Native American tribes in 1812. In the minds of missionaries, Native Americans were foreign "heathens."[69]

Presbyterian missionaries sponsored by the ABCFM and later the Board of Foreign Missionaries believed that missionary work involved the manifest destiny of Anglo-Saxon culture to be spread around the world. And of course the concept of manifest destiny included a belief that it was God's will that the U.S. government extend its power across the continent and over all Native American tribes. The Board of Foreign Missions believed it was proper for the U.S. commissioner of Indian affairs to aid missionary efforts because its members believed the spread of republican government to Native American nations required the spread of Protestantism and Anglo-Saxon culture.[70]

An example of the combining of the civilization of Native Americans with the spread of Anglo-Saxon culture was the Reverend James Ramsey's speech at a Choctaw school in 1846. Ramsey described his initial lecture to students and trustees in the following words: "I showed them [on a map] that the people who speak the English language, and who occupied so small a part of the world, and possessed the greatest part of its wisdom and knowledge; that knowledge they could thus see for themselves was power; and that power was to be obtained by Christianity alone."[71] Then he told them that the key to their success would be to continue the practice of establishing religious schools. In this way, they could share in the glory of Anglo-Saxon culture and Christianity.

The Presbyterian missionaries sent by the ABCFM had more influence on the leadership of Native American tribes than other missionary educators. Presbyterians believed conversion of the tribal leadership would result in Christianity and civilization trickling down to other tribal members. In contrast, Baptists and Methodists believed that their work should begin with conversion of the common full-blood Native American.[72]

All three religious dominations emphasized the importance of changing traditional customs of Native Americans while teaching reading and writing. For instance, the Presbyterian missionary Cyrus Kingsbury, known as the "Apostle to the Choctaws," wrote,

> It is our intention to embrace in their [Native American] education, that practical industry, and that literary, moral and religious instruction, which may qualify them for useful members of society; and for the exercise of those moral principles, and that genuine piety, which form the basis of true happiness.[73]

In the words of historian Michael Coleman, "These Presbyterians could accept nothing less than the total rejection of the tribal past, and the total transformation of each individual Indian, a cultural destruction and regeneration to be brought about by the Gospel of Jesus Christ."[74]

Similar to the Presbyterians, the Missionary Society of the Methodist Episcopal Church, the Kentucky Baptist Society for Propagating the Gospel among the Heathen, and other Protestant missionary organizations defined as their goal the replacement of Native American culture with the culture of white Anglo-Saxon

Protestantism. Many Native Americans had simply asked for literacy, but they received an education designed to bring about their cultural and religious conversion.

Language and Native American Cultures

The relationship between language and culture is clearly evident in the differences between missionary efforts to develop written Native American languages and the creation of a written Cherokee language by Sequoyah. Missionaries wanted to develop written Native American languages so they could translate religious tracts. Missionaries did not want to use a written Native American language as a means of preserving Native American history and religions. For missionaries, a written Native American language was another means of teaching Protestant Anglo-American culture. The teaching of English was also considered a means of cultural transformation. Moravian educator John Gambold wrote, "It is indispensably necessary for their [Cherokee] preservation that they should learn our *Language* and adopt our Laws and Holy Religion."[75]

In contrast, Sequoyah developed a written Cherokee language for the purpose of preserving Cherokee culture. Missionaries reacted negatively to Sequoyah's invention because it threatened their efforts. The Reverend John Gambold wrote, regarding Sequoyah's invention, "The study of their language would in a great measure prove but time and labor lost. . . . It seems desirable that their Language, Customs, Manner of Thinking should be forgotten."[76]

In 1821 Sequoyah, a mixed-blood Cherokee whose English name was George Guess, returned to the Cherokee Nation from Arkansas with a Cherokee alphabet using eighty-six characters of his invention. Sequoyah was born in a small Cherokee village in Tennessee, served in the War of 1812, and joined a group of Cherokees in 1819 who migrated to Arkansas. He worked twelve years on the development of his alphabet. An important thing to note about Sequoyah's work is that he was illiterate and did not speak English. Consequently, his approach to developing a written language was different from that of a literate missionary using English or another European language to render the Cherokee language into a written form. Although he probably got the idea of having a written language from Europeans, Sequoyah's invention was based on his creation of characters to represent different sounds in the Cherokee language.[77]

The genius of Sequoyah's alphabet was that since each of the eighty-six characters matched a particular sound in the Cherokee language, it was possible for a Cherokee to quickly become literate in Cherokee. With diligence, a person speaking Cherokee could learn the alphabet in one day and learn to read Cherokee in one week. A Moravian missionary described the following changes resulting from Sequoyah's invention:

> The alphabet was soon recognized as an invaluable invention . . . in little over a year, thousands of hitherto illiterate Cherokees were able to read and write their own language, teaching each other in cabins or by the roadside. The whole nation became an academy for the study of the system. Letters were written back and forth between the Cherokees in the east and those who had emigrated to the lands in Arkansas.[78]

SE-QUO-YAH
Inventor of the Cherokee Alphabet

Courtesy Bureau of American Ethnology, Smithsonian Institution

"By cloud-capped summits in the boundless West,
Or mighty river rolling to the sea,
Where'er thy footsteps led thee on thy quest
Unknown, rest thee, illustrious Cherokee."

The future editor of the first Native American newspaper, Elias Boudinot, recognized the importance of Sequoyah's invention and decided to publish a newspaper in English and Cherokee. While requesting funds in 1826 for his newspaper, Boudinot told the congregation at the First Presbyterian Church in Philadelphia that one of the most important things to happen to the tribe was the "invention of letters." He pleaded for funds for a printing press "with the types . . . to be composed of English letters and Cherokee characters. Those characters," he informed the congregation, "have now become extensively used in the nation; their religious songs are written in them; there is an astonishing eagerness in people of all classes and ages to acquire a knowledge of them."[79]

After his address in Philadelphia, Boudinot headed to Boston to collect the newly cast type in Sequoyah's symbols. He returned to the Cherokee Nation, and on February 21, 1828, he published the first Native American newspaper, the *Cherokee Phoenix,* with columns written in English and Cherokee. Of primary importance for full bloods, the newspaper published Cherokee laws in both English and Cherokee.

Despite the fact that missionaries had struggled for years to create a written Cherokee language, they were not receptive to Sequoyah's invention. One important reason for their reluctance to embrace the new alphabet was that it required a knowledge of spoken Cherokee. None of the missionary educators had been able to learn Cherokee, so Sequoyah's symbols were of little use to them. In addition, many missionaries feared that if Cherokees learned to read and write in their own language, they would never learn English. For most missionaries, learning English was essential for the purpose of destroying traditional Cherokee culture. Therefore, while Sequoyah's invention proved a uniting force among full-blood Cherokees, it did not become a language of the missionary schools established on Cherokee lands in the East.

Education and the Trail of Tears

The supposed failure of the Civilization Act to clear Native Americans off southern lands resulted in a painful episode in American history referred to as the "Trail of Tears." During the 1820s, Thomas McKenney reiterated his position that the solution for gaining the lands of the southern Native Americans was "to give them a country, and to secure it to them by the most ample and solemn sanctions . . . in exchange for theirs."[80] Once they were moved to new lands, according to McKenney, schools and churches could be established to enlighten the next generation.

By the time of his election to the presidency and his First Annual Message to Congress in December of 1829, Andrew Jackson had concluded that civilization policies originating with Presidents Washington and Jefferson, and extended by the Civilization Act of 1819, had failed to educate southern tribes to the point where they would want to sell their lands. In his First Annual Message to Congress, Jackson devoted considerable space to outlining his arguments for Native American removal to lands west of the Mississippi.[81] A crucial part of Jackson's argument was the right of white settlers to Native American lands. President Washington had argued that Native American lands should be acquired by treaties and purchases.

Now President Jackson proposed a combination of treaties and exchange of tribal lands for land west of the Mississippi. In addition, Jackson maintained that white settlers had rights to Native American lands that were not cultivated. In other words, he recognized as legitimate land claims by Native Americans only those claims for land on which they had made improvements. Claims could not be made for land, in Jackson's words, "on which they have neither dwelt nor made improvements, merely because they have seen them from the mountain or passed them in the chase."[82]

In proposing to set aside land west of the Mississippi for the relocation of Native Americans, Jackson promised to give each tribe control over the land and the right to establish any form of government. The only role of the U.S. government, Jackson argued, would be to preserve peace among the tribes and on the frontier. In this territory, Jackson declared, the "benevolent may endeavor to teach them the arts of civilization, and, by promoting union and harmony among them, to raise up an interesting commonwealth, destined to perpetuate the race and to attest the humanity and justice of this Government."[83] The key to fulfilling the humanitarian goals of removal would be education. In its final version, the Indian Removal Act of May 28, 1830, authorized the president to set aside lands west of the Mississippi for the exchange of Native American lands east of the Mississippi. In addition, the president was authorized to provide assistance to the tribes for their removal and resettlement on new lands.

In one of the most infamous acts in human history, entire nations of people were forced from their lands. On the Trail of Tears, Native Americans died of cholera, exposure, contaminated food, and exhaustion. Witnessing the removal of the Choctaws from Mississippi, the missionary William Goode wrote, "Melancholy and dejected with their compulsory removal, years elapsed without much effort for improvement." He told the story of the drunken Choctaw who threw himself into the last boat leaving for Indian Territory shouting, "Farewell white man! Steal my Land!"[84] Near his home in 1832, Horatio Cushman recalled the sounds from the encampment of Choctaws waiting for removal: "there came, borne upon the morn and evening breeze from every point of the vast encampment, faintly, yet distinctly, the plaintive sound of weeping."[85] After visiting the encampment, Cushman recorded this bleak portrait:

> The venerable old men . . . expressed the majesty of silent grief; yet there came now and then a sound that here and there swelled from a feeble moan to a deep, sustained groan—rising and falling till it died away just as it began . . . while the women and children, seated upon the ground, heads covered with shawls and blankets and bodies swinging forward and backward . . . [sent] sad tones of woe echoing far back from the surrounding but otherwise silent forests; while the young and middle-aged warriors, now subdued and standing around in silence profound, gazed into space . . . here and there was heard an inarticulate moan seeking expression in some snatch of song, which announced its leaving a broken heart.[86]

The Cherokees faced the horror of actual physical roundup by the U.S. Army. By 1838 only 2,000 of 17,000 Cherokees had made the trip west. The remaining 15,000 did not seem to believe that they would be driven out of their country.[87]

In 1838 General Winfield Scott with a combined military force of 7,000 was placed in charge of the removal process. General Scott issued a proclamation that within a month every Cherokee man, woman, and child should be headed west. Scott's troops moved through the countryside, surrounding houses, removing the occupants, looting and burning the houses, and forcing the families into stockades. Men and women were run down in the fields and forests as the troops viciously pursued their prey. Sometimes the troops found children at play by the side of the road and simply herded them into stockades without the knowledge of their parents. Besides stealing directly from the Cherokees, the troops and white out-laws drove off cattle and other livestock. The Cherokees placed in stockades were left destitute. A volunteer from Georgia, who later served as a colonel in the Confederate Army, wrote, "I fought through the Civil War and have seen men shot to pieces and slaughtered by thousands, but the Cherokee removal was the cruelest work I ever knew."[88]

The removal of tribes to Indian Territory raised the issue of the legal status of tribal governments and, as part of the operation of government, tribal school systems. This issue was clarified in a U.S. Supreme Court ruling in 1831 involving the extension of the laws of the state of Georgia over the Cherokee Nation. The Cherokees argued that this extension was illegal because they were a foreign nation. The question, as posed in the decision of the Court, was this: "Is the Cherokee nation a foreign state in the sense in which that term is used in the Constitution?"[89] The Court argued that the section of the Constitution dealing with the regulation of commerce made a distinction between foreign nations, states, and Native American tribes. Consequently, Native American tribes were not for-eign countries but political entities distinct from states. In the words of the Court, Native American tribes are "domestic dependent nations . . . they are in a state of pupilage. Their relation to the United States resembles that of a ward to his guardian."[90]

Once settled in Indian Territory, the tribes quickly engaged in the business of organizing governments and establishing school systems. Because of their segre-gation in Indian Territory, the tribal school systems were only for tribal children. One example of a successful Native American school system was the system cre-ated by the Choctaws, who sent their best graduates to the East to attend college. In 1842 the ruling council of the Choctaw Nation established a comprehensive system of schools. A compulsory attendance law was enacted by the Choctaw Nation in 1889. The Choctaw schools were developed in cooperation with the missionaries. In this regard, Superintendent of Indian Affairs Thomas McKenney's dream of establishing schools in Indian Territory became a reality. The Spencer Academy (this author's uncle, Pat Spring, died in the fire that burned down the academy in 1896) was opened in 1844 and the Armstrong Academy in 1846. By 1848 the Choctaws had nine boarding schools paid for by tribal funds. In addition, a system of day or neighborhood schools was organized, and by 1860 these schools enrolled five hundred students. After the Civil War, the Choctaws estab-lished a system of segregated schools for the children of freed slaves.[91]

In addition, missionaries developed an adult literacy program through a sys-tem of Saturday and Sunday schools. Whole families would camp near a school or church to receive instruction in arithmetic, reading, and writing. Instruction was bilingual in both Choctaw and English. Although there were not many texts in Choctaw, missionaries translated into Choctaw many portions of the Bible, hymn books, moral lectures, and other religious tracts.[92]

Many teachers were Choctaws educated in tribal schools. The teachers were examined in the common school subjects and the Choctaw constitution. Teachers followed a course of study modeled on that of neighboring states and taught in English, using the *Choctaw Definer* to help children translate from Choctaw into English.

The Spencer Academy for boys and the New Hope Academy for girls were the leading schools. The children who attended these schools were selected by district trustees until 1890 and after that by county judges. Selection was based on "promptness in attendance and their capacity to learn fast."[93] Only one student could be selected from each family.

In 1885 the tribal council removed the two academies from missionary management and placed them under the control of a board of trustees. In 1890 a school law was enacted that required male teachers at the Spencer Academy to be college graduates and to have the ability to teach Greek, Latin, French, and German, and female teachers at the New Hope Academy to have graduated from a college or normal school and to be able to teach two modern languages besides English. The faculty of both schools included both white and Choctaw instructors.

The success of the Choctaw educational system was paralleled by that of the Cherokee Nation. The Cherokees were given land north of the Choctaw Nation. In 1841, after removal, the Cherokee National Council organized a national system of schools with eleven schools in eight districts, and in 1851 it opened academies for males and females. By the 1850s the majority of teachers in these schools were Cherokee. Reyhner and Eder write, "By 1852 the Cherokee Nation had a better common school system than the neighboring states of Arkansas and Missouri."[94]

The success of the Choctaw and Cherokee school systems was highlighted in a congressional report released in 1969. The report noted, "In the 1800s, for example, the Choctaw Indians of Mississippi and Oklahoma [Indian Territory] operated about 200 schools and academies and sent numerous graduates to eastern colleges."[95] The report went on to praise the Cherokee schools: "Using bilingual teachers and Cherokee texts, the Cherokees, during the same period, controlled a school system which produced a tribe almost *100% literate* [emphasis added]."[96] The report concluded, "Anthropologists have determined that as a result of this school system, the literacy level in English of western Oklahoma Cherokees was higher than the white populations of either Texas or Arkansas."[97]

CONCLUSION

There were many reasons for the establishment of a common or public school system in the United States, including educating students for good citizenship, ending poverty and crime, and stimulating national economic growth. The perception by many whites that Irish Americans, African Americans, and Native Americans were a threat to the dominance of white Protestant Anglo-American culture in the United States resulted in the segregation of Native Americans and most African Americans, and the establishment of a competing parochial school system. As a result, the common school was never common to all children, and the struggle over cultural dominance continued through the end of the twentieth century.

Notes

1. Carl F. Kaestle, *Pillars of the Republic: Common Schools and American Society, 1780–1860* (New York: Hill and Wang, 1983), p. 103.
2. See Ronald Takaki, *A Different Mirror: A History of Multicultural America* (Boston: Little, Brown, 1993), pp. 139–166.
3. Ibid., pp. 141–143.
4. Ibid., pp. 146–147.
5. Ibid., p. 149.
6. Ibid., p. 141.
7. Quoted in Vincent Lannie, *Public Money and Parochial Education: Bishop Hughes, Governor Seward, and the New York School Controversy* (Cleveland: Press of Case Western Reserve University, 1968), p. 16.
8. Ibid., p. 21.
9. Quoted in ibid., p. 24.
10. "To the Honorable Board of Aldermen of the City of New York," in *Catholic Education in America: A Documentary History,* ed. Neil McCluskey (New York: Teachers College Press, 1964), pp. 70–71.
11. Ibid., p. 71.
12. Ibid., p. 72.
13. Ibid., p. 73.
14. Ibid., p. 76.
15. Quoted in Lannie, *Public Money,* pp. 85–87.
16. Carl F. Kaestle, *Pillars of the Republic,* pp. 167–172.
17. "First Plenary Council (1852)," in McCluskey, *Catholic Education in America,* pp. 78–81.
18. "Second Plenary Council (1866)," ibid., pp. 82–85.
19. "Third Plenary Council (1884)," ibid., pp. 86–92.
20. Ibid., p. 94.
21. Ira Berlin, *Many Thousands Gone: The First Two Centuries of Slavery in North America* (Cambridge, MA: Harvard University Press, 1998), p. 181.
22. Ibid., p. 187.
23. Quoted in ibid., p. 191.
24. Ibid., p. 184.
25. Quoted in ibid., p. 193.
26. Quoted by Leon F. Litwack, *North of Slavery: The Negro in the Free States, 1790–1860* (Chicago: University of Chicago Press, 1961), p. 7.
27. Ibid., p. 7.
28. Ibid., p. 14.
29. Ibid., p. 114.
30. Takaki, *A Different Mirror,* pp. 106–138.

31. Stanley Schultz, *The Culture Factory: Boston Public Schools, 1789–1860* (New York: Oxford University Press, 1973).
32. Ibid.
33. Ibid.
34. Ibid.
35. Ibid., p. 16.
36. Quoted in ibid., p. 173.
37. James Anderson, *The Education of Blacks in the South, 1860–1935* (Chapel Hill: University of North Carolina Press, 1988), p. 17.
38. Leon F. Litwack, *Been in the Storm So Long: The Aftermath of Slavery* (New York: Vintage Books, 1980), p. 22.
39. Ibid., p. 23.
40. Quoted in Francis Paul Prucha, *The Great Father: The United States Government and the American Indians* (Lincoln: University of Nebraska Press, 1984), p. 53.
41. "George Washington to James Duane, September 7, 1783," in *Documents of United States Indian Policy,* 2nd ed., ed. Francis Paul Prucha (Lincoln: University of Nebraska Press, 1990), pp. 1–2.
42. "Northwest Ordinance, July 13, 1787," ibid., pp. 9–10.
43. "President Washington on Government Trading Houses, December 3, 1793," ibid., p. 16.
44. "President Jefferson on Indian Trading Houses," ibid., p. 21.
45. "First Annual Message, December 8, 1801," in *The Life and Selected Writings of Thomas Jefferson,* ed. Adrienne Koch and William Peden (New York: Modern Library, 1944), p. 324.
46. "To the Chiefs of the Cherokee Nation, Washington, January 10, 1806," ibid., p. 578.
47. Ibid., p. 579.
48. "President Jefferson on Indian Trading Houses, January 18, 1803," in Prucha, *Documents,* pp. 21–22.
49. Ibid., p. 22.
50. Prucha, *The Great Father,* p. 143.
51. For information about the Cherokee Ghost Dance movement, see William G. McLoughlin, *Cherokee Renascence in the New Republic* (Princeton: University of Princeton Press, 1986), pp. 168–185. For a description of the Ghost Dances in the late nineteenth century, see Dee Brown, *Bury My Heart at Wounded Knee: An Indian History of the American West* (New York: Holt, 1970), pp. 416–445.
52. McLoughlin, *Cherokee Renascence,* pp. 179–180.
53. Quoted by McLoughlin, ibid., from a diary kept by Moravian missionaries at Springplace, Cherokee Nation, February 11, 1811.
54. William G. McLoughlin, *Cherokees and Missionaries 1789–1839* (New Haven: Yale University Press, 1984), pp. 39–40.
55. Ibid., p. 40.
56. Herman J. Viola, "Introduction," *Thomas L. McKenney: Memoirs, Official and Personal,* ed. Herman J. Viola (Lincoln: University of Nebraska Press, 1973), pp. vii–xxvii.
57. Viola, *Memoirs,* p. 34.
58. Ibid., p. 34.
59. Ibid., p. 35.
60. "Civilization Fund Act, March 3, 1819," in Prucha, *Documents,* p. 33.
61. John Hebron Moore, *The Emergence of the Cotton Kingdom in the Old Southwest: Mississippi, 1770–1860* (Baton Rouge: Louisiana State University Press, 1988), pp. 16–17.

62. "Table 5: Schools and Pupils in the Cherokee Nation, 1809" and "Table 6: Prosperous Cherokees in 1809," in McLoughlin, *Cherokee Renascence,* p. 174.

63. McLoughlin, ibid., pp. 328–329.

64. Gary E. Moulton, *John Ross: Cherokee Chief* (Athens: University of Georgia Press, 1978), p. 7.

65. Thurman Wilkins, *Cherokee Tragedy: The Ridge Family and the Decimation of a People,* 2nd ed., rev. (Norman: University of Oklahoma Press, 1986), p. 98.

66. Angie Debo, *The Rise and Fall of the Choctaw Republic* (Norman: University of Oklahoma Press, 1961), p. 42.

67. See Joel Spring, *The Cultural Transformation of a Native American Family and Its Tribe* (Mahwah, NJ: Lawrence Erlbaum Associates, 1996), chs. 3–5.

68. See Wilkins, *Cherokee Tragedy,* and Samuel Wells, "The Role of Mixed-Bloods in Mississippi Choctaw History," in *After Removal: The Choctaws in Mississippi,* ed. Samuel J. Wells and Roseanna Tubby (Jackson: University of Mississippi Press, 1986).

69. See Michael C. Coleman, *Presbyterian Missionary Attitudes toward American Indians, 1837–1893* (Jackson: University of Mississippi Press, 1985).

70. Ibid., pp. 38–42.

71. Ibid., p. 42.

72. McLoughlin, *Cherokees and Missionaries,* pp. 135–151.

73. Quoted in Horatio Bardwell Cushman, *History of the Choctaw, Chickasaw, and Natchez Indians,* ed. Angie Debo (New York: Russell & Russell, 1972), p. 99. Cushman's book, originally published in 1899, is an important primary source of the history and cultural traditions of the Choctaws in the nineteenth century. Cushman was born at the Mayhew missionary station in the Choctaw Nation, where his parents had been sent in 1820 by the American Board of Commissioners for Foreign Missions. Cushman's book is full of fond memories of growing up at Mayhew and participating in Choctaw life. He personally knew the Folsom, Pitchlynn, and Leflore families. See Angie Debo's foreword to the book.

74. Coleman, *Presbyterian Missionary Attitudes,* pp. 5–6.

75. McLoughlin, *Cherokee Renascence,* p. 354.

76. Ibid.

77. See Grant Foreman, *Sequoyah* (Norman: University of Oklahoma Press, 1938).

78. Ibid., p. 11.

79. Boudinot's speech is reprinted in Ralph Henry Gabriel, *Elias Boudinot Cherokee and His America* (Norman: University of Oklahoma Press, 1941), pp. 108–109.

80. "Thomas McKenney to J. Evarts," in *Documents and Proceedings Relating to the Formation and Progress of a Board in the City of New York for the Emigration, Preservation, and Improvement of the Aborigines of America, July 22, 1829* (New York: Vanderpool & Cole, Printers, 1829), p. 41.

81. "President Jackson on Indian Removal, December 8, 1829," in Prucha, *Documents,* pp. 47–48.

82. Ibid., p. 48.

83. Ibid.

84. William H. Goode, *Outposts of Zion, with Limnings of Mission Life* (Cincinnati: Poe & Hitchcock, 1864), p. 51.

85. Quoted in Cushman, *History of the Choctaw,* pp. 99, 114.

86. Ibid., p. 115.

87. See Grant Foreman, *Indian Removal* (Norman: University of Oklahoma Press, 1972), pp. 251–315, for an account of the removal process.

88. Quoted in ibid., p. 287.
89. *"Cherokee Nation v. Georgia 1831,"* in Prucha, *Documents,* p. 58.
90. Ibid., p. 59.
91. Debo, *Rise and Fall,* pp. 60–61, 101–109.
92. Ibid., p. 62.
93. Ibid., p. 238.
94. Jon Reyhner and Jeanne Eder, *A History of Indian Education* (Billings: Eastern Montana College, 1989), p. 34.
95. Senate Committee on Labor and Public Welfare, *Indian Education: A National Tragedy—A National Challenge,* 91st Cong., 1st sess., 1969 (Washington, DC: U.S. Government Printing Office, 1969), p. 25.
96. Ibid.
97. Ibid.

6

Organizing the American School: Teachers and Bureaucracy

Globalization of education includes countries adopting the model of the age-graded classroom, using a standardized curriculum and textbooks, promotion up an educational ladder leading to higher education, and providing professional teacher training. In addition, the global educational community is debating the value of similar theories of instruction.[1] Many of these educational features originated in the United States and were adapted to local educational circumstances.

This chapter will discuss

- The growth of professional teacher training and a teaching corps.
- New methods of instruction.
- The growth of an educational bureaucracy, including the role of school principals.
- The major textbook series of the nineteenth century: McGuffey's Readers.

THE AMERICAN TEACHER

The development of a professional teaching corps for the common schools was directly related to changes in the status of women in the United States. In addition, women were welcomed into the teaching ranks by local school boards because women could be hired at lower wages than men. As a result, by the end of the Civil War women dominated the ranks of teaching, and teacher education centered on the education of women.

Traditional histories of education identify the Reverend Samuel Hall's private school, established in 1823 in Concord, Vermont, as the first teacher training institution. However, a good argument can be made that the first teacher training institution in the United States was the Troy Female Seminary, officially opened by Emma Willard in 1821 but with earlier beginnings in 1814. Willard opened the seminary for the specific purpose of educating women for responsible motherhood and teaching. Her thoughts on the education of women can be traced to the American Revolution, when new ideas about the public role of women opened the door to new educational opportunities. These ideas gave women the necessary leverage for increasing both their level of formal education and their opportunities as teachers, and they also provided later common school reformers with a justification for the increased utilization of women as teachers.

One effect of the American Revolution was to link the domestic responsibilities of women with broader public purposes. During colonial times, little consideration was given to the relationship between the domestic role of women and their role in the public sphere. Personal salvation and service to other family members were the major purposes of education for women during this period. As Mary Beth Norton states in *Liberty's Daughters: The Revolutionary Experience of American Women, 1750–1800,*

> Prior to the Revolution, when the private realm of the household was seen as having little connection with the public world of politics and economics, women's secular role was viewed solely in its domestic setting. . . . [N]o one, male or female, wrote or thought about the possibility that women might affect the wider secular society through their individual or collective behavior.[2]

During and immediately after the Revolution, male and female writers began to link the domestic role of women with the development of republican citizens. Women, as mothers, were seen as having the responsibility for shaping the character of their sons as future republicans. This perception of the role of mothers logically led to the conclusion that women needed to be educated to assume the role of republican motherhood. In Norton's words,

> And so citizens of the republic set out to discover and define woman's public role. They found it not in the notion that women should directly participate in politics. . . . Rather, they located woman's public role in her domestic responsibilities, in her obligation to create a supportive home life for her husband, and particularly in her duty to raise republican sons who would love their country and preserve its virtuous character.[3]

The acceptance of the concept of republican motherhood allowed greater educational opportunities for women. Before the Revolution, the education of women was limited to reading and writing and, for some young girls, education at "adventure schools," which taught music, dancing, drawing, needlework, and handicrafts. After the Revolution, some academies began to open their doors to women, and schools began to be established for the specific purpose of educating young girls. These new educational opportunities for women included academic instruction in subjects such as geography, history, philosophy, and astronomy, which in the past had been taught only to boys. In addition, charity schools for girls were started during this period, and urban school systems—like Boston's—began admitting girls.

One result of the expanding educational opportunities for women was that charity schools began to seek female graduates as teachers. This was different from colonial times, when women without any particular qualifications operated "dame schools." After the Revolution, school authorities began to recruit young female academy graduates. In turn, educated women began to realize that teaching offered career possibilities. "Teaching," Norton argues, "was the first profession

ORGANIZING THE AMERICAN SCHOOL TIME LINE

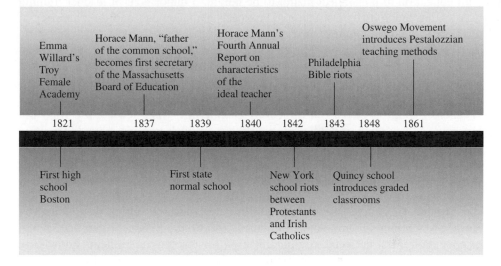

opened to women on a regular basis, and as such it attracted, albeit for only a few years of their lives, a large number of intellectually aware young women, many of them products of the republican academies."[4]

It was against this background that Emma Willard opened the Troy Female Seminary. In an address to the New York legislature in 1819, she declared the hopes of republican motherhood: "Who knows how great and good a race of men may yet arise from the forming hands of mothers, enlightened by the bounty of that beloved country—to defend her liberties, to plan her future improvements and to raise her to unparalleled glory?"[5] In all her public statements, she supported the existence of a patriarchal family. She argued that women needed to be educated to be teachers both because of a shortage of male schoolmasters and in order to function as responsible mothers.

According to Anne Scott, as an encouragement for women to be self-supporting and educated, Willard provided "'instruction on credit' for any woman who would agree to become a teacher, the debt to be repaid from her later earnings." To facilitate this process, Willard maintained a teacher placement agency, which had difficulty meeting the demand for teachers. In Scott's words, "Someone commented that Emma Willard's signature on a letter of recommendation was the first form of teacher certification in this country."[6]

As Paul Mattingly demonstrates, the overriding concern of those interested in the reform of teaching in the 1830s and 1840s was the development of moral character.[7] As women began to be educated in larger numbers, schools began to seek them out as teachers because of the belief in the inherent moral character of females. The teacher was to be a paragon of moral virtue whose influence would be felt and imitated by the students in the common school. If the schools were to reform and morally uplift society, it was reasoned, it was of fundamental importance that the teacher function as a model of morality. Consequently, along with education in the subject matter to be taught, a major goal of teacher training was to link methods of instruction, classroom management, and the character of teachers to the development of students' moral character.

The emphasis on moral character had a lasting effect on the teaching profession. Through the nineteenth century and into the twentieth, teachers were expected to live exemplary lives, with their social activities constantly under public scrutiny. This is still true in some places. According to Willard Elsbree in *The American Teacher: Evolution of a Profession in a Democracy,* "The teacher's private life has always been open to public scrutiny like a goldfish in a glass bowl. Tradition has given teachers a place in society comparable to that accorded to ministers and the restrictions placed upon their conduct have been many and varied."[8] This control of the social life of teachers contributed to the low status of teaching as a profession.

The ideal characteristics of teachers for the common school were stated by Horace Mann in his Fourth Annual Report (1840) to the Massachusetts state board of education. First he listed as a qualification for teaching a "perfect" knowledge of the subjects to be taught in the common schools. He complained that the major defect in existing schools' instruction was the teacher's lack of knowledge of the subject matter. The second qualification he listed was an aptitude for teaching, which he believed could be learned. He feared that inadequate or erroneous methods of teaching could destroy the moral character of students. As an example, he described the custom in surveying land in feudal Scotland of tying boys to landmarks and whipping them so they would retain a knowledge of the boundaries of the land and could be used as witnesses in any litigation. He states, "Though this might give them a vivid recollection of localities, yet it would hardly improve their ideas of justice. . . . But do not those, who have no aptness to teach, sometimes accomplish their objects by a kindred method?" A third essential qualification listed by Mann was the ability to manage and govern a schoolroom and to mold moral character. Mann believed that the primary source of moral instruction in the classroom was the moral character of the teacher.

He listed "Good Behavior" and "Morals" as the fourth and fifth characteristics of a good teacher. With regard to good behavior, he stated, "If, then, the manners of the teacher are to be imitated by his pupils—if he is the glass, at which they 'do dress themselves,' how strong is the necessity, that he should understand those nameless and innumerable practices, in regard to deportment, dress, conversation, and all personal habits, that constitute the difference between a gentleman and a clown." Mann goes on to argue that one could accept eccentricities in a friend, "but it becomes quite a different thing, when the oddity, or eccentricity, is to be a pattern or model, from which fifty or a hundred children are to form their manners." In other words, a major requirement of a schoolteacher was to conform to accepted social customs.[9]

Under "Morals," Mann emphasized the importance of having teachers "of pure tastes, of good manners, [and] of exemplary morals." He gave the responsibility for ensuring the morality of teachers to local school committees or school boards. He wrote, "The school committee are sentinels stationed at the door of every schoolhouse in the State, to see that no teacher ever crosses its threshold, who is not clothed, from the crown of his head to the sole of his foot, in garments of virtue."[10]

The nineteenth-century schoolmarm was to fulfill the requirements of high morality and social conformity demanded by common school reformers. The reason women were recruited into teaching was candidly stated by the Boston board in 1841. Its annual report noted that within the previous year the number of male teachers in the system had declined by 33 while the number of female teachers had increased by 103. The report gave three reasons for supporting this trend. The first was a belief that women are better teachers of young children because of their natural child-rearing talents: "They [women] are endowed by nature with stronger parental impulses, and this makes the society of children delightful, and turns duty into pleasure." Second, the report argued that because female minds are less distracted by worldly forces and because women have no other possibilities of employment, they can more easily concentrate on teaching:

> As a class, they never look forward, as young men almost invariably do, to a period of legal emancipation from parental control, when they are to break away from the domestic circle and go abroad into the world, to build up a fortune for themselves; and hence, the sphere of hope and of effort is narrower, and the whole forces of the mind are more readily concentrated upon present duties.

As statistics show, a major concern of the times was that men remained in teaching for only a short period. It was hoped that the narrow range of opportunities for women would keep them in teaching and thus provide a stabilizing influence.

The third reason for favoring women, the report argued, was that "they are also of purer morals." The report went on to argue, "In the most notorious vices of the age, profanity, intemperance, fraud, &c., there are twenty men to one woman . . . on this account, therefore, females are infinitely more fit than males to be guides and exemplars of young children."[11]

Another reason for employing women was the lack of stability in the male teaching force. In the early nineteenth century, the typical pattern was for young men to enter teaching for a few years before continuing on to some other career. Consequently, the teaching force was young and inexperienced and had a high turnover rate, which made selection of teachers and control of their moral character difficult. Although the number of female teachers did increase (by the end of the Civil War they dominated the ranks of teaching because the men had been called to military action), their teaching careers tended to be as short as those of men, in part because of continued low salaries.

Before the Civil War, the increase in the number of women in teaching varied from state to state. In some states, females became a majority in the teaching force. In Connecticut 56 percent of the total teaching force was female by 1846, and the percentage increased to 71 in 1857. In 1862 the state superintendent in New Jersey reported that in 1852 there had been twice as many male teachers as female, but within ten years female teachers had come to outnumber male teachers. In Vermont 70 percent of the teaching force was female by 1850, and in

Pennsylvania the proportion of female teachers increased from 28 percent in 1834 to 36 percent in 1856. The dramatic effect of the Civil War was felt in states such as Indiana, where the percentage of male teachers dropped from 80 percent in 1859 to 58 percent in 1864, and Ohio, where the number of male teachers declined from 52 percent in 1862 to 41 percent in 1864. New York reported a loss of 1,119 male teachers between 1862 and 1863, and in 1862 Iowa reported that the number of female teachers had exceeded the number of male teachers for the first time.[12]

Although the increased number of female teachers did not seem to fulfill the common school reformers' hopes of creating an experienced, stable teaching force, there was ample evidence that female teachers made education less expensive. In fact, from a look at the differences in salaries between male and female teachers in the nineteenth century, one could argue that the primary reason for the acceptance of women into the ranks of teaching was that they were inexpensive to employ. Table 1 in *The American Teacher,* originally compiled in 1920 by Warren Burgess, indicates not only the differences between the salaries of men and women but also the differences between the salaries of rural and urban teachers. The figures give some indication of the economic position of teachers during this period. In his compilation, Burgess estimated that the weekly wage of a common laborer was $4.86 in 1841 and $7.98 in 1864, while artisans earned an average of $8.28 in 1841 and $12.66 in 1864. This means that male urban teachers earned more during this period than either common laborers or artisans. In contrast, urban and rural female teachers and rural male teachers earned less than common laborers.

Burgess's statistics were supported by a survey that Horace Mann conducted for the *Common School Journal* in 1843. Mann claims to have ascertained the wages of "journeymen, shoemakers, carpenters, blacksmiths, painters, carriage-makers, wheelwrights, harness-makers, cabinet and piano-forte makers and some others," and he reports that all these occupations paid more than teaching and that the salaries of some were 50 to 100 percent higher than the average salary of teachers.[13]

In addition to the utilization of women in teaching, common school reformers hoped to improve teaching through the establishment of teacher institutes and normal schools, both of which introduced the novel idea that methods of instruction could be taught and learned. In a broader sense, this marked the beginning of the study of pedagogy and the investigation of various methods of instruction. Also, normal schools opened a new arena for the education of women. Female students dominated the classes in normal schools, and in turn normal schools contributed to the increase in the number of female teachers.

These early attempts to create a professional corps of teachers in the United States linked the educational concerns of common school reformers with the desires of women for further education and for careers. Women, as republican mothers and vessels of virtue, were considered the ideal teachers for a system of schooling that emphasized moral development. However, the second-class citizenship of women and the low salaries in teaching contributed to the generally low status of teaching as a profession in the nineteenth and early twentieth centuries. Indeed, even the earliest professional teacher training, with its limited preparation for elementary school instruction, its mainly female student population, and its emphasis on moral exhortation, further contributed to the low-status professional image of teaching.

REVOLUTION IN TEACHING METHODS: OBJECT LEARNING

Given the attitudes about morality and women in the early and middle nineteenth century, it is not surprising that the first widespread theory of instruction was based on the concepts of maternal love and the cultivation of the moral faculty. Like the belief in the importance of the role of republican motherhood, the educational theories of Johann Pestalozzi gave to the mother and the household the main responsibility for the salvation of society. Pestalozzi's concept of maternal instruction in the home became his model for instruction in the school.

Any discussion of educational ideas must recognize the difference between theory and practice. Usually there is a time lag between the development of a theory and its impact on practice. For instance, Barbara Finkelstein, in her study of elementary school classrooms in the nineteenth century, found that the majority of teachers had students recite, work at their desks, or listen to verbal instruction by the teacher: "North and south, east and west, in rural schools as well as urban schools, teachers assigned lessons, asked questions and created standards of achievement designed to compel students to assimilate knowledge and practice in a particular fashion." Finkelstein argues that teachers during this period were of two major types: the "intellectual overseer," who stressed memorization and punished failures in assignments, and the "drillmaster," who had the students repeat material in unison.[14]

Many common school reformers hoped those types of classroom practices would be replaced by what they considered the more humane educational methods of Pestalozzi. The major impact of Pestalozzian theory was its emphasis on relating instruction in the early years to objects in the real world, on learning by doing, and on the importance of activity, as opposed to sitting at a desk. By the end of the nineteenth century, these Pestalozzian practices had become an important part of progressive instructional theory, and by the twentieth century they were an important part of elementary classroom practice.

Johann Pestalozzi (1746–1827) was born in Zurich, Switzerland, and in 1781, after dabbling in journalism and education, he wrote his classic, popular description of domestic education, *Leonard and Gertrude.* His ideas on education quickly spread throughout the Western world. Many American visitors to Prussia in the early nineteenth century were impressed by the use of Pestalozzian methods in the schools. The English Home and Colonial Institution, organized in 1836, became a forum for the dissemination of Pestalozzian ideas in England, the United States, and Canada. This organization had developed from the work of Charles Mayo, who, beginning in 1818, adapted Pestalozzian ideas to English infant schools.

Pestalozzi's theories of maternal education paralleled in time and content the development of concepts of republican motherhood in the United States. *Leonard and Gertrude* is the story of the moral and social reform that occurs as a result of the extension of maternal influence and education from the home to the public sphere. The story is set in the small village of Bonnal. The main characters are Leonard, an alcoholic husband, and Gertrude, a brave and pious wife. It is a tale of moral struggle between the forces of evil and idleness and the forces of maternal love and nurturing. The opening lines of the tale describe the social conditions that could be remedied if education were based on maternal values. The reader is told that "his [Leonard's] trade would have enabled him to support his family of a wife and seven children, if he could have resisted the temptation to frequent the tavern, where there were always idle loafers to entice him in, and induce the good-natured, easygoing man to squander his earnings in drink and gambling."[15]

The struggle by women to redeem their men from the pitfalls of "demon rum" and gambling became a classic tale by the end of the nineteenth century. In Pestalozzi's story, Leonard and the village are redeemed because domestic relationships are maintained by Gertrude's becoming a public model. To symbolize the connection between the domestic role of women and the public sphere, Pestalozzi has three male leaders of the village visit Gertrude's home and study her system of household management. Their analysis of Gertrude's actions provides the basis for the development of a pedagogical theory.

In the story, the visit by the three village leaders occurs just as the family is completing breakfast. After the children wash the dishes, they immediately engage in a variety of tasks, including spinning and gardening. What is most impressive for the visitors is Gertrude's ability to integrate instruction into the activities of the household. A trademark of the Pestalozzian method is the use of common objects in instruction and the development of the child's powers of observation, as opposed to abstract teaching that has little connection to the realities of life. For instance, *The New England Primer* taught numbers without any reference to real objects, whereas Gertrude gave instruction in arithmetic by having her children count the number of steps from one end of the room to the other; and two of the rows of five panes each, in one of the windows, gave her an opportunity to unfold the decimal relations of numbers. She also made the children count their threads while spinning, as well as the number of turns on the reel when they wound the yarn into skeins.[16]

Shortly after departing from Gertrude's home, one of the visitors dashes back and proclaims that he will be the schoolmaster of Bonnal. The next day, after returning to observe Gertrude's family further, the village leaders ask Gertrude to help the newly self-appointed schoolmaster. "Then they explained to her that they regarded the proper education of the youthful population as the only means of elevating the condition of the corrupt village; and full of emotion, Gertrude promised them she would do anything in her power to forward the good cause."[17]

Pestalozzi later declared that "maternal love is the first agent in education."[18] In *How Gertrude Teaches Her Children,* written between 1799 and 1804 while Pestalozzi was a schoolmaster, he draws a direct connection between maternal love and individual moral development. He argues that people must love and trust other people before they are able to love and trust God and that the germ of love and trust is developed in the mother's nurturing of the child. The mother's lack of response to the irregular desires of the infant teaches the first lessons in obedience; in addition, the infant learns to be grateful for the mother's actions. The combination of trust, gratitude, love, and obedience forms the early beginnings of a conscience.

According to Pestalozzi, the development of conscience and moral feelings that is learned from interaction with the mother depends on the art of instruction. He argues that society does not provide the child with moral instruction because such instruction is a distortion of nature. It is the responsibility of the teacher to arrange the world encountered by the child so that the early beginnings of moral ideas will be developed.

Like all aspects of Pestalozzian instruction, the development of morality depends on the education of the senses: "The first instruction of the child should never be the business of the head or of reason; it should always be the business of the senses, or the heart, of the mother." What he declares as the second law of instruction is to move slowly from the exercise of the senses to the exercise of reason. In accord with the general attitudes of the time, he associates the senses, or heart, with women and reason with men. "It is for a long time the business of the heart," Pestalozzi states with regard to instruction, "before it is the business of the reason. It is for a long time the business of the woman before it begins to be the business of the man."[19]

Pestalozzi always declared that he was trying to psychologize the education of humanity, by which he meant adapting methods of instruction to human development and the laws of the mind. He was greatly influenced by Jean-Jacques Rousseau's *Emile,* which stresses the inability of children to reason until the age of adolescence. Before that time, Rousseau argues, the child should not be given verbal instruction but should learn from experience and nature. Pestalozzi emphasizes that the young child should receive no verbal instruction and that learning should be a result of experience. In addition, he accentuates the importance of educating the senses. From the education of the senses, one is to move to an understanding of ideas and eventually to a knowledge of God and morality.

The concentration on the education of the senses, the use of objects in instruction, and the replacement of corporal discipline with control through love revolutionized methods of instruction. Certainly a major contrast exists between the type of instruction of young children provided by recitation of *The New England Primer* and Pestalozzi's statement that the best general methods of instruction "are speech, the arts of drawing, writing, reckoning and measuring."[20]

Americans returning from visits to Europe in the early nineteenth century helped to acquaint fellow Americans with Pestalozzian methods of instruction. One of the earliest visitors was John Griscom, who was active in social and educational reform in New York. His visit to Europe in 1818 included tours of hospitals, schools, prisons, and charitable institutions. *A Year in Europe,* the story of his trip, includes glowing reports of Lancasterian schools in England and Pestalozzian schools in Prussia. After the publication of this book, Griscom became actively involved in social and educational reform by serving, among other positions, as chairman of the committee that established the New York House of Refuge and as a leader in the establishment of a monitorial high school in New York in 1825.

On his trip, Griscom visited Pestalozzi at the educational institution he had established at Yverdun in 1805. Griscom was warmly greeted by Pestalozzi and was given a tour of the school, which at that time had ninety boys from a variety of European countries. In the classroom visited by Griscom, the teacher did not use books but relied solely on the use of objects. Griscom claimed that the constant interaction between students and the instructor made it too difficult to write a detailed account of the type of instruction provided in the classroom. His more general description states:

> We saw the exercises of arithmetic, writing, drawing, mathematics, lessons in music. . . .
> To teach a school, in the way practiced here, without book, almost entirely by verbal
> instructions, is extremely laborious. The teacher must be constantly with the child, always
> talking, questioning, explaining, and repeating. The pupils, however, by this process, are
> brought into very close intimacy with the instructor.[21]

In general, Griscom was most impressed by the moral aspects of the Pestalozzian methods: "But the greatest recommendation of the Pestalozzian . . . plan of education, is the moral charm which is diffused throughout all its operations."[22] He felt that children educated under this method would become more moral and intelligent members of society.

Many Americans learned about Pestalozzian methods of instruction while visiting schools in Prussia, where Pestalozzi became very popular in the nineteenth century. Another visitor was Calvin Stowe, whose widely circulated "Report on Elementary Public Instruction in Europe" is discussed in the previous section. Stowe included in his report a description of a classroom in a Berlin school using Pestalozzian methods. Like Griscom, Stowe was struck by the amount of verbal exchange between the teacher and the students. The use of objects for instruction and the education of the senses are very evident in Stowe's description:

> He [the teacher] first directs their [students'] attention to the different objects in
> the school-room, their position, form, color, size, materials of which they are made
> of, &c., and requires precise and accurate descriptions. He then requires them
> to notice the various objects that meet their eye on the way to their respective
> homes; and a description of these objects and the circumstances under which they
> saw them, will form the subject of the next morning's lesson. Then the house in
> which they live; the shop in which their father works; the garden in which they
> walk, &c., will be the subject of the successive lessons; and in this way for six
> months or a year, the children are taught to study things, to use their own power
> of observation, and speak with readiness and accuracy, before books are put into
> their hands at all.[23]

After giving a detailed description of the structure of Prussian schools, Stowe strongly recommends the system as moral and practical. He argues that it educates all faculties of the mind and demonstrates to the student the practical value of knowledge. In addition, he claims it elevates the moral condition of all children.

The model of mother as teacher had a profound impact on textbooks, classroom equipment, and methods of teaching. Just as Gertrude used the objects of her household for instruction, by the late nineteenth century textbooks and teachers began to use real objects to illustrate lessons. For example, map work became important in the study of history and geography, the counting of objects became a method of learning arithmetic, and the study of nature became a source of scientific understanding for young children. In *How Teachers Taught: Constancy and Change in American Classrooms, 1890–1980,* Larry Cuban includes a set of three photographs depicting elementary school classrooms in Washington, DC, in 1900. In two of the photographs, students are shown working alone at individual desks. In the third, students are gathered around a table at the head of the classroom examining, with the teacher, models of parts of the body. On the blackboard is a drawing of the heart, and leaning against the wall is a full-size drawing of the human body with its inner parts illustrated. Although a direct connection cannot be made between the work of Pestalozzi and the student activity depicted in this classroom, Pestalozzi's work and the spread of his ideas must be given some credit for the illustrations, objects, and teaching activities shown in that photograph.[24]

THE EVOLUTION OF BUREAUCRACY: A GLOBAL MODEL

By the late twentieth century, most of the world's nations had adopted an educational organization very similar to that of the United States. By the late nineteenth century, the following elements made up the bureaucratic organization of the typical American school system:

- A hierarchy with a superintendent at the top and orders flowing from the top to the bottom of the organization.
- Clearly defined differences in roles of superintendent, principals, assistant principals, and teachers.
- Graded schools in which students progressively moved from one grade to another.
- A graded course of study for the entire school system to assure uniformity in teaching in all grades in the system.
- An emphasis on rational planning, order, regularity, and punctuality.

David Tyack, in *The One Best System: A History of Urban Education,* cites a number of other causes for the adoption of a bureaucratic organization. He argues that "the pressure of numbers was a main reason for the bureaucratization that gradually replaced the older decentralized village pattern of schooling."[25] According to Tyack, this pressure forced school leaders to seek efficiency in school systems that had grown up haphazardly. In addition, many nineteenth-century school leaders believed that bureaucratic organization taught students values necessary for functioning in an industrial society. Tyack quotes a statement made in 1871 by William T. Harris, a superintendent of schools and U.S. commissioner of education: "The first requisite of the school is Order: each pupil must be taught first and foremost to conform his behavior to a general standard." Harris claimed that modern industrial society required "conformity to the time of the train, to the starting of work in the manufactory," and therefore "the pupil must have his lessons ready at the appointed time, must rise at the tap of the bell, move to the line, return; in short, go through all the evolutions with equal precision."[26]

Just as regular attendance and punctuality became important for factories, these behaviors were considered important by school people for the management of educational systems and as values to be taught to schoolchildren in preparing them to function in society. Nothing more clearly demonstrates this relationship between the requirements of organization and the desire to teach organizational values than the mania that developed among nineteenth-century educators over student attendance and punctuality. Because of the need for organization and the desire to teach industrial values, tardiness to class became a major student offense.

THE AGE-GRADED CLASSROOM

The age-graded classroom has become a central global model. One of the major organizational changes in the schools in the nineteenth century, considered important for introducing efficiency and uniformity of instruction, was the division of students into separate classrooms by age. Before this development, students had been taught in ungraded classrooms in which teachers were responsible for simultaneously teaching a variety of subjects to students at different levels of knowledge. For example, Ellwood Cubberley includes in *Public Education in the United States* a sketch of a Providence, Rhode Island, grammar school in 1840, where each floor seated 228 students in a single room and was conducted as a single school.[27] A master teacher and assistant teachers combined their efforts to teach the entire group within this large, ungraded classroom. In 1823 Boston schools were being built with rooms that seated 300 pupils, on the premise that three large groups would be taught by one master teacher and two assistant teachers. And of course monitorial schools were conducted in large, ungraded groups.

The major inspiration for the creation of graded schools came from accounts of visitors to Prussia concerning school organization in that country. After visiting Prussia in 1843, Horace Mann wrote in his Seventh Annual Report that "the first element of superiority in a Prussian school, and one whose influence extends throughout the whole subsequent course of instruction, consists in the proper classification of the scholars." Mann went on to describe how schoolhouses were constructed so that each group of students, divided by age and attainment, could be housed in a single classroom. The ungraded large classroom, Mann argues, created the difficulty for the teacher of trying to teach a variety of subjects at one time. All these difficulties, he says, "are at once avoided by a suitable classification, by such a classification as enables the teacher to address his instructions at the same time to all children who are before him, and to accompany them to the playground at recess or intermission without leaving any behind who might be disposed to take advantage of his absence."[28]

© *Hulton Archive/Getty Images*

When the first school based on the Prussian method of classification was built in the United States, it incorporated not only graded classrooms but also what Tyack refers to as the "pedagogical harem" of a male principal and female teachers. The establishment of the first graded school, the Quincy School, is credited to John Philbrick, who became its first principal. Philbrick had worked hard to convince the Boston school board of the wisdom of applying Horace Mann's ideas on pupil classification.

When the Quincy School was opened in 1848, its radical design attracted national attention. Rather than the usual school construction of the period—large rooms accommodating hundreds of students—the Quincy School contained a greater number of schoolrooms, each of which could hold fifty-six students. What was considered its greatest improvement was the provision of a separate room for each teacher and a desk for each student. The Boston school committee adopted specific requirements that each classroom be twenty-eight square feet. By 1855 the committee had every building in the city divided into small classrooms. By 1866 the Quincy plan became a model for school construction in San Francisco, New Orleans, Cincinnati, New Haven, and Louisville. The Quincy plan tended to be more popular in urban areas. Many rural areas retained one-room schoolhouses, and in 1920 there were still 200,000 of them.[29]

As this pattern of graded elementary schools spread into other American cities, the grade system became more clearly defined. Once the general category of elementary students was established, it was necessary to determine how many levels of classification should exist in a school. The average duration of common school education when the Quincy School was built was seven to nine years. A survey of forty-five cities conducted by the U.S. commissioner of education in 1870 indicated that, by that time, the majority of elementary schools classified students into eight separate grades. The eight-year elementary school remained the standard until the junior high school was developed in the early twentieth century.[30]

The graded school, the uniform course of study, and an expanding educational administration—the district system—were all elements in the early development of a hierarchical, bureaucratic organization for the administration of American education. In the twentieth century the bureaucratic organization of the schools became more clearly defined as the professionalization of school administration developed. Many factors contributed to the development of this type of organization, including the real problems created by the increased size of schools and school districts, the common school ideal of a uniform curriculum for all children, the desire of the middle class and native groups to protect their values and power, and the need for socialization of students for an industrial workplace. The creation of a hierarchy was facilitated by the use of female teachers. In Lotus Coffman's 1911 study of teachers, he argues that the increasing number of women in the teaching force was "due in part to the changed character of the management of the public schools, to the specialization of labor within the school, to the narrowing of the intellectual range or versatility required of teachers, and to the willingness of women to work for less than men. . . . [A]ll of the graded school positions have been preempted by women; men still survive in public school work as 'managing' or executive officers."[31]

McGUFFEY'S READERS AND THE SPIRIT OF CAPITALISM

The popularity and importance of William McGuffey's Readers in the latter half of the nineteenth century can be compared to the role of *The New England Primer* during colonial times and Noah Webster's spelling book in the first half of the nineteenth century. *The New England Primer* prepared readers for submission to the authority of the family, the Bible, and the government, and Webster's spelling book taught republican values designed to maintain order in a free society. McGuffey's Readers contained numerous moral lessons designed to teach appropriate behavior in a developing industrial society with increasing concentrations of wealth and expanding social divisions between the rich and the poor. Within this context, the readers provide an example of the actual meaning given to attempts to reduce social class tensions by mixing the rich and the poor in the common school.

The growth in popularity of McGuffey's Readers paralleled the development of the common school. Ironically, even as the nineteenth-century schoolmarm took over the schoolroom, girls occupied little space in the new reading series. Females are seldom discussed characters in these moral tales dealing with social behavior in a developing industrial society. If the McGuffey Readers were our sole source for understanding human conduct in the latter half of the nineteenth century, we would have the impression that the only role for women in the development of a capitalistic and industrial society was to serve as models of charity. The concept of charity is important because it justifies the concentration of wealth by making the rich the stewards of wealth for the poor. Even in their role as models of charity, however, girls were less frequently portrayed than boys were. As depicted in the moral tales in McGuffey's Readers, girls were almost invisible in the school relationships of developing capitalism.

The McGuffey Readers were written in the heart of what was considered the West in the 1830s. William Holmes McGuffey was born in 1800 near Washington, Pennsylvania, and was raised on a homestead in Trumbell County, Ohio. In 1825, after a period of education and teaching in the schools of the frontier, McGuffey accepted a teaching post at Miami University in Oxford, Ohio, near the booming city of Cincinnati. Through his work as an educator, McGuffey became an active member of the Western Literary Institute and College of Professional Teachers and a friend of Calvin and Harriet Beecher Stowe at the Lane Seminary in Cincinnati. As a result of his educational contacts in Cincinnati, in 1834 or early 1835 McGuffey was asked by the Cincinnati publishing firm of Truman and Smith to write a series of textbooks.

The McGuffey Readers were prepared specifically for use in the developing common school systems. The series, first published between 1836 and 1838, contained a primer, a speller, and four readers. A fifth reader was added in 1844. The series was revised between 1841 and 1849 and again in 1853, 1857, and 1879. The changes in 1857 and 1879 were primarily in gradation of material and in binding. Sales figures for the series show its use and popularity. Between 1836 and 1920, approximately 122 million copies were sold. The strongest sales, as indicated by the following figures, occurred between 1870 and 1890:[32]

1836–1850	7,000,000
1850–1870	40,000,000
1870–1890	60,000,000
1890–1920	15,000,000

The content of the McGuffey Readers varies in length and difficulty, from short and simple stories in the first, second, and third readers to selected literary writings by a variety of authors in the fourth and fifth readers. Each story and poem in the less advanced readers is preceded by a spelling list and by definitions of words appearing in the selection and is followed by several related questions. The goal of the stories in the readers is to teach reading and, like the general goal of the common school, to impart moral lessons. An analysis of the content of the stories in the 1843 edition of *McGuffey's Newly Revised Eclectic Second Reader* reveals the range of moral values, the importance given to certain moral themes, and the different expectations for boys and for girls in dealing with moral issues.[33]

McGuffey's Newly Revised Eclectic Second Reader contains 104 readings of one to three pages. Some of the readings are religious selections such as the Lord's Prayer, the Story of Joseph, and the Child's Prayer. There are also a number of historical sketches, poems, and tales about animals and birds. Some stories, like "Story of the Coat" and "Store of Buttons," are designed to convey information about objects. Of course, many of these writings about history, nature, and objects are designed to teach particular moral lessons.

The largest group of writings in the second reader, about 35 percent of the 104 selections, deals directly with problems of moral character. Given the primacy of moral education in the common school movement, this emphasis is not surprising. Of these didactic stories, twenty-nine center on the character of boys and only eight on the character of girls.

There are several ways to explain the neglect of girls in these didactic tales. One could assume that it reflects the subordinate, secondary role of women in society. In other words, McGuffey's attitude toward females reflects the more general vision men had of women's place in society. Another explanation could be that the female character was considered to have few moral defects. This explanation is supported by one of the major reasons given for recruiting women into teaching—namely the purity of their moral character. In fact, in the stories in the second reader, the range of moral problems for girls is very narrow compared with that for boys. In two of the stories dealing with girls, "Mary and Her Father" and "The Little Letter Writer," the theme is learning and the value of education. In another story, "The Greedy Girl," the moral problem is gluttony, which is illustrated by a little girl who eats so much that she constantly gets sick. Untidiness is the central theme in "A Place for Every Thing," a story about a girl who constantly loses things and learns from another girl to put everything in its proper place.

One could conclude from these stories that in the nineteenth century the central problems in the character of girls were considered to be overeating, a lack of appreciation for learning, and untidiness. The other four stories dealing with girls present not problems of character but models of charity. In "The Kind Little Girl," the central female character shares with animals and hungry people; in "A Dialogue on Dress," a girl refuses new clothes so that she can save to buy clothes for the poor; in "The Two White Doves," a girl and boy give their doves to a sick child; and in "The Last Two Apples," a girl gives the last apples to her siblings. Thus in half the stories about female character, girls are presented as acting charitably in certain situations.

The theme of charity is also important in the stories about boys. As mentioned previously, this was an important theme in the developing social relationships of capitalism. The range of character problems exhibited by boys in the McGuffey Readers is much greater than that associated with girls. In the twenty-nine stories about boys, the themes include relationship to nature, value of learning, gluttony, mercy, pranks, charity, industriousness, honesty, courage, envy, alcoholism, insolence, and thrift.

Interestingly, the most frequent theme in *McGuffey's Newly Revised Eclectic Second Reader,* one that appears in six of the stories, is a boy's relationship to nature. This probably reflects the importance of the expanding West and the role of nature in nineteenth-century life. In the second story of the reader (the first story deals with the importance of reading), a boy is depicted reflecting on the loveliness of the sun and the goodness of God. In contrast to the boys who love nature are the boys in "The Bird Set Free," who rob birds' nests. The second most frequent theme, which appears in five of the stories about male character, is charity, and the third most frequent theme is the value of education.

To understand the importance of charity, we must consider the general social and political messages in all the McGuffey Readers. This analysis is done by Richard Mosier in *Making the American Mind: Social and Moral Ideas in the McGuffey Readers.* As the title suggests, Mosier approaches his analysis from the perspective that the wide use of the McGuffey Readers had a profound impact on average Americans by shaping their attitudes toward political, social, and economic institutions. In general, Mosier argues that the political messages found in the pages of the McGuffey Readers are conservative and express a distrust of popular participation in government. Within this conservative framework, the primary purpose of government is the protection of property. Mosier contends that most of the political ideas in the readers express the values of the Whig Party as opposed to the Democratic Party of the early nineteenth century. This, of course, means that the books agree with the political values of the leadership of the common school movement.

The fear of spreading democracy, or suffrage, is expressed in the McGuffey Readers' support of the common school system. In Mosier's words, "The antidote for these new forms of demagoguery and radicalism [Jacksonian democracy] was religion and education, the fire engines of Church and State, to which conservatives turned in their darkest hours." He argues that the purpose of education, as reflected in the readers and in conservative political thought, was

> for education . . . [to] be linked particularly with a call to return to the stern moral code of the Puritan fathers . . . [when] the objects of education were considered largely in terms of religious and moral culture. . . . [T]he McGuffey readers voiced their fear for the corrupting influences of the new age that had come upon them, and hinted that in the metaphysical subtleties of the great New England theologians lay the appropriate foundations for state, school, church, and society.[34]

The treatment of economic issues in the McGuffey Readers, Mosier maintains, is premised on the Calvinistic concept that wealth is an outward sign of inner salvation. This economic argument allowed acceptance of a society that was experiencing increasing concentrations of wealth and an expanding social distance between the rich and the poor. Wealth was a sign of God's blessing, and poverty was a sign of God's disapproval. Within this economic argument, the poor had to be godly and industrious to gain wealth, and the rich had to use their wealth in a godly fashion to continue receiving the blessings of God. Therefore, charity was a means for the rich to remain worthy of their wealth in the eyes of God and a justification for a concentration of wealth in their hands. Mosier states about the contents of the McGuffey Readers, "Those who are wealthy are reminded that they are so by the grace of God, and that this grace and concession implies a responsibility toward the poor. . . . Many are the lessons that praise the charitable activities of the merchant, and many are those that show the kindness of the rich to the poor."[35] This conceptual framework gave the wealthy a stewardship over the riches of the earth and the destiny of the poor.

Within the context of this gospel of wealth, the poor were placed in a paradoxical situation. On the one hand, the existence of the poor was considered inevitable and therefore an acceptable part of the social order. On the other hand, some argued that poverty existed because the poor did not have the virtues of the rich and that the poor could escape poverty by being industrious, thrifty, and moral. Mosier summarizes the dominant attitude in the McGuffey Readers: "It was argued that the poor would always be with us, that the best for them was charity and benevolence, but that no one need be poor. There are, argued the apostles of acquisition, numerous avenues to success that stand open for the sober, the frugal, the thrifty, and the energetic."[36]

The best examples of this gospel of wealth are two successive stories in the 1843 edition of *McGuffey's Newly Revised Eclectic Second Reader,* having the descriptive titles "The Rich Boy" and "The Poor Boy." The reader is informed in the first story that the rich boy knows "that God gives a great deal of money to some persons, in order that they may assist those who are poor." In keeping with the idea that the rich are elected by God, the rich boy is portrayed as being humble, kind to servants, and "careful not to make a noise in the house, or break anything, or put it out of its place, or tear his clothes." The reader is also told that this model of virtue "likes to go with his parents to visit poor people, in their cottages, and gives them all the money he can spare. He often says, 'If I were a man, and had plenty of money, I think no person who lived near me should be very poor.'" The story ends with the rich boy dreaming of how he would use his future wealth:

> I would build a great many pretty cottages for poor people to live in, and every cottage should have a garden and a field, in order that the people might have vegetables, and might keep a cow, and a pig, and some chickens; they should not pay me much rent. I would give clothes to the boys and girls who had not money to buy clothes with, and they should all learn to read and write, and be very good.[37]

Certainly a child reading "The Rich Boy" would easily conclude that God is just and that the rich boy deserves to inherit his parents' wealth.

In a similar fashion, the reader of "The Poor Boy" might conclude that poverty is good because of its effects on moral character. The poor boy is portrayed as industrious, helpful, moral, and eager to learn. The story opens, "The good boy whose parents are poor, rises early in the morning; and all day long, does as much as he can, to help his father and mother." It goes on to explain that the poor boy studies hard so that when he grows up, he can read the Bible and find gainful employment. The story makes a clear distinction between the poor boy who is good and poor boys who are bad. In the story, the poor boy hurries home from his lessons to help his parents. On the way, the reader is told, "he often sees naughty boys in the streets, who fight, and steal, and do many bad things; and he hears them swear, and call names, and tell lies; but he does not like to be with them, for fear they should make him as bad as they are; and lest any body who sees him with them, should think that he too is naughty." Unlike the rich boy wanting to help the poor, he dreams of earning his own living. The poor boy likes his food of bread and bacon and does not envy the rich little boys and girls "riding on pretty horses, or in coaches." At the end of the story, the poor boy states his acceptance of his social position:

> I have often been told, and I have read, that it is God who makes some poor, and others rich—that the rich have many troubles which we know nothing of; and that the poor, if they are but good, may be very happy: indeed, I think that when I am good, nobody can be happier than I am.[38]

In summary, the two stories provide a justification for economic inequality and a rationale for accepting one's position in life. After reading the stories, poor boys might have been pleased to learn that they could be happy if they were good and that they were free of the burdens and responsibilities of the wealthy. Rich boys might have been pleased to learn that their good fortune was a blessing from God that required them only to adopt paternalistic attitudes toward the poor.

The economic arguments embodied in the McGuffey Readers provide another means of understanding the goals of the common school. One of the basic reasons given for the establishment of a common school system was that it would reduce antagonisms between the rich and the poor. In addition, consciousness of one's particular social class was to be changed into a consciousness of belonging to the more general social class of humanity.

Because McGuffey's Readers were written for the common schools and were among the most popular texts while the common school system was growing, it can be assumed that they offer an important perspective on how the reduction of tension between the rich and the poor would take place. In other words, the readers provided part of the real content of the more general educational rhetoric. From this perspective, one might conclude that the common school was supposed to solve the problem of social class tension by educating children to accept their positions in society and the existing economic arrangements. The poor were educated to accept the existence of the rich—to learn that the rich would take care of them and that they were free of the responsibilities that accompanied wealth. Indeed, the poor were taught that their happiness depended on behaving in a manner that would not antagonize the wealthy. For their own good and obviously for the good of the wealthy, the poor were taught to be free of envy and to be thrifty, industrious, and moral.

From the standpoint of the rich, social class tensions would be reduced by learning humility and charity toward the poor. The rich were not to disdain the poor but were to learn to love them. Therefore, educating the rich in the common school was meant to reduce social class antagonisms in two ways: first, by disarming the rich of negative feelings about the poor, and second, by teaching the rich to perform acts of charity as a means of disarming the poor of hostility.

The McGuffey Readers' concerns with mortality and with developing virtuous character made them an ideal companion for the growth of the common school and the industrial society. In the readers, the concept of republican motherhood is enlarged to include behaviors considered important in a society of increasing economic and social tensions. In the early nineteenth century, men and women considered the traits of motherhood to be ideal as methods for educating good republicans. In the latter half of the century, it was easy to extend the nurturing qualities of motherhood to include acts of charity. Furthermore, charity, as discussed earlier, was an essential concept for justifying inequalities in the distribution of wealth. Therefore, women, and particularly female teachers, became symbols of the virtues needed to maintain order in a republican society and of the kindness and acts of charity required to maintain order in a capitalistic society.

CONCLUSION

The organization of the common school in the middle of the nineteenth century established certain patterns of development that would begin to change and take on new direction by the late nineteenth and early twentieth centuries, when women began to rebel against their subservient status in the educational hierarchy and to seek a greater voice in educational policy through unionization and participation in school administration. These changes occurred as schools modeled themselves on industry and became more bureaucratic.

The schools developed an expanded economic role in the increasingly urban and industrial society of the late nineteenth century, and as this happened, the high school joined the elementary school as an institution at which attendance was considered essential for all people. Pedagogy—the science of education—changed during this period to meet the needs of the corporate model of the school and the new economic role of schooling. But even with all these changes, the schoolmarm remained the backbone of the educational system. As models of republican motherhood and as symbols of charity, women continued to toil in the factories of education.

Notes

1. See Joel Spring, *Globalization of Education: An Introduction* (New York: Routledge, 2009).
2. Mary Beth Norton, *Liberty's Daughters: The Revolutionary Experience of American Women, 1750–1800* (Boston: Little, Brown, 1980) p. 297.
3. Ibid., pp. 297–298.
4. Ibid., p. 293.
5. Quoted in Anne Firor Scott, "The Ever Widening Circle: The Diffusion of Feminist Values from the Troy Female Seminary, 1822–1872," *History of Education Quarterly* 19, no. 1 (Spring 1979), p. 7.
6. Ibid., p. 8.
7. Paul H. Mattingly, *The Classless Profession: American Schoolmen in the Nineteenth Century* (New York: New York University Press, 1975).
8. Willard Elsbree, *The American Teacher: Evolution of a Profession in a Democracy* (New York: American Book Company, 1939), p. 296.

9. Horace Mann, "Fourth Annual Report (1840)," in *The Republic and the School: Horace Mann on the Education of Free Men,* ed. Lawrence Cremin (New York: Teachers College Press, 1958), p. 47.

10. Ibid., pp. 50–52.

11. Quoted in Elsbree, *American Teacher,* p. 201.

12. Elsbree, *American Teacher,* pp. 202–208.

13. Quoted in ibid., pp. 280–281.

14. Quoted in Larry Cuban, *How Teachers Taught: Constancy and Change in American Classrooms, 1890–1980* (White Plains, NY: Longman, 1984), p. 15.

15. Johann Pestalozzi, *Leonard and Gertrude,* trans. Eva Channing (Lexington, MA: Heath, 1901), p. 11.

16. Ibid., pp. 130–131.

17. Ibid., p. 135.

18. Johann Pestalozzi, "How a Child Is Led to God through Maternal Love," in *Pestalozzi's Educational Writings,* ed. J. A. Green (London: Edward Arnold, 1916), p. 266.

19. Johann Pestalozzi, *How Gertrude Teaches Her Children: An Attempt to Help Mothers to Teach Their Own Children and an Account of the Method,* trans. Lucy Holland and Francis Turner (Syracuse, NY: Bardeen, 1898), p. 294.

20. Ibid., p. 317.

21. John Griscom, "A Year in Europe," *Reports on European Education,* ed. Edgar Knight (New York: McGraw-Hill, 1930), p. 60.

22. Ibid., p. 55.

23. Stowe, "Report on Elementary Public Instruction," in Knight, *Reports,* p. 277.

24. Cuban, *How Teachers Taught,* pp. 20–21.

25. David Tyack, *The One Best System: A History of American Urban Education* (Cambridge, MA: Harvard University Press, 1974), pp. 38–39.

26. Quoted in ibid., p. 43.

27. Ellwood Cubberley, *Public Education in the United States: A Study and Interpretation of American Educational History* (Boston: Houghton Mifflin, 1934), p. 308.

28. Horace Mann, "Seventh Annual Report to the Massachusetts State Board of Education, 1843," in *Readings in Public Education in the United States: A Collection of Sources and Readings to Illustrate the History of Educational Practice and Progress in the United States,* ed. Ellwood Cubberley (Boston: Houghton Mifflin, 1934), pp. 287–288.

29. William Cutler, "Cathedral of Culture: The Schoolhouse in American Educational Thought and Practice since 1820," *History of Education Quarterly* 29, no. 1 (Spring 1989), pp. 1–40.

30. Tyack, *One Best System,* p. 61.

31. Quoted in ibid., p. 61.

32. Richard Mosier, *Making the American Mind: Social and Moral Ideas in the McGuffey Readers* (New York: Russell & Russell, 1965), pp. 167–170; Harvey C. Minnich, *William Holmes McGuffey and His Readers* (New York: American Book Company, 1936), pp. 30–89.

33. William H. McGuffey, *McGuffey's Newly Revised Eclectic Second Reader* (Cincinnati: Winthrop B. Smith, 1843).

34. Mosier, *Making the American Mind,* p. 31.

35. Ibid., p. 161.

36. Ibid., p. 162.

37. McGuffey, *McGuffey's,* pp. 47–48.

38. Ibid., pp. 48–50.

7

Multiculturalism and the Failure of the Common School Ideal

The common school ideal of creating a united culture and common educational experience failed to be achieved because of segregation and discrimination. In the latter half of the nineteenth century, the educational treatment of Mexican, Asian, Native, African, and Puerto Rican Americans ran counter to the common school ideal of uniting all children in the same schoolhouse. Issues of racial segregation, language policies, and attempts to destroy cultures clouded efforts to provide equal educational opportunity for all children. Entangled in the educational issues was the problem of citizenship. The Naturalization Act of 1790 provided naturalized citizenship only for those classified as "white."

This chapter will discuss educational segregation and discrimination regarding

- Mexican Americans.
- Asian Americans.
- Native Americans.
- African Americans.
- Puerto Ricans.

HISPANIC/LATINO CITIZENSHIP TIME LINE

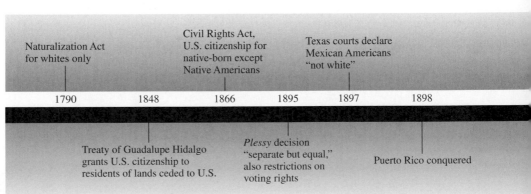

Naturalization Act for whites only — 1790

Treaty of Guadalupe Hidalgo grants U.S. citizenship to residents of lands ceded to U.S. — 1848

Civil Rights Act, U.S. citizenship for native-born except Native Americans — 1866

Plessy decision "separate but equal," also restrictions on voting rights — 1895

Texas courts declare Mexican Americans "not white" — 1897

Puerto Rico conquered — 1898

MEXICAN AMERICANS: RACE AND CITIZENSHIP

The educational treatment of Mexican Americans reflected the racial attitudes of Anglo-Americans toward Mexican Americans, who generally were of Native American and Spanish ancestry. Popular Anglo-American writers in the nineteenth century argued that the mixture of Spanish conquerors and Native Americans resulted in "wretched hybrids and mongrels [who were] in many respects actually inferior to the inferior race itself."[1] At the time, Anglo-Americans did not consider the Spanish to be "white" and therefore believed they were an inferior race. Representative William Brown envisioned "the Anglo-Saxon race, like a mighty flood [spreading over] all Mexico."[2] This flood of Anglo-Saxons, Brown hoped, would eventually cover all of Central and South America, creating republics whose "destinies will be guided by Anglo-Saxon hands."[3]

At the time of the U.S. invasion of Mexico in the 1840s, Secretary of State James Buchanan and Secretary of the Treasury Robert Walker expressed their views that northern Europeans, whom they identified as Anglo-Saxon, were the superior racial group. Within the racial ideology of these American leaders, Mexican mestizos were a substandard racial mixture because they were descended from an inferior European race and Native Americans. The Mexican-American War was, among other things, a race war.

The struggle over inclusion of Mexican Americans and other Hispanic Americans as full citizens of the United States became a serious issue in 1848 with the ending of the Mexican-American War and the ratification of the Treaty of Guadalupe Hidalgo. During treaty negotiations, the Mexican government demanded that Mexicans remaining in the territory that Mexico lost become U.S. citizens. This demand created a dilemma for U.S. leaders.

Today few U.S. citizens are aware of the importance of this war for the territorial expansion of the United States and the disaster for Mexico of losing almost half of its total territory. At the war's conclusion, the United States added territory that included major parts of the future states of California, Colorado, New Mexico, Nevada, Arizona, Utah, and Texas. Although many U.S. citizens fail to remember these territorial gains, Mexicans are constantly reminded of their loss by the huge

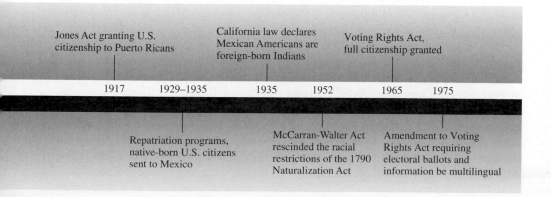

Jones Act granting U.S. citizenship to Puerto Ricans

California law declares Mexican Americans are foreign-born Indians

Voting Rights Act, full citizenship granted

1917   1929–1935   1935   1952   1965   1975

Repatriation programs, native-born U.S. citizens sent to Mexico

McCarran-Walter Act rescinded the racial restrictions of the 1790 Naturalization Act

Amendment to Voting Rights Act requiring electoral ballots and information be multilingual

monument standing at the entrance to Chapultepec Park in Mexico City commemorating the young Mexican boys who died trying to defend the spot against the invading U.S. military.

The events leading to the Mexican-American War occurred during the period of the racial and cultural genocide of the Five Civilized Tribes as they were removed from the Southeast to Indian Territory. In the area that is now Texas, U.S. settlers had been waging a war that culminated in 1837 with the Mexican government accepting the loss of part of its land and recognizing Texas as an independent nation. While the Five Civilized Tribes located on land just north of Texas and organized their governments, the U.S. settlers controlling the nation of Texas formed a government and debated whether they should remain independent or allow themselves to be annexed by the United States.

In the minds of some Anglo-Americans, the United States was destined to rule the continent because of its Protestant culture and republican form of government. In the minds of many U.S. citizens, Mexico stood for Catholicism and feudalism. After the Texas government agreed in 1845 to be annexed to the United States, President James Polk sent a small army to the Rio Grande. Under the leadership of General Zachary Taylor, the army was to protect the Texas border. Taylor's presence sparked a military reaction by Mexico that resulted in the U.S. Congress declaring war on May 13, 1846. Later in the century, former president Ulysses S. Grant wrote about the declaration of war and the subsequent military campaigns as "the most unjust war ever waged by a stronger against a weaker nation . . . an instance of a republic following the bad example of European monarchies."[4]

The United States did not confine its military actions to Texas. Within one month after the congressional declaration of war, President Polk ordered a war party under the command of Colonel Stephen Kearny to travel from Fort Leavenworth, Kansas, and occupy the Mexican city of Santa Fe, New Mexico. After entering Mexican territory, Kearny issued a proclamation saying, "The undersigned enters New Mexico with a large military force for the purpose of seeking union with, and ameliorating the condition of the inhabitants."[5] Kearny promised, without authorization from President Polk, that all Mexican citizens in New Mexico would be given U.S. citizenship, and he convinced many local officials to take an oath of allegiance to the U.S. government. The Mexican governor fled Santa Fe, and Kearny entered the city on August 17, 1846, without encountering any significant resistance.

One month later, on September 25, 1846, Kearny left Santa Fe for the Mexican province of California. A year before Kearny's departure from Santa Fe, a small military force under the command of Captain John C. Frémont had arrived at Fort Sutter, California. Aided by the presence of Frémont's force, a group of American settlers declared that California was the Bear Flag Republic. Their action was similar to that in Texas on July 4, 1846. The leaders of the new nation created a flag featuring a single star and a crude grizzly. At the celebration for the new republic, Frémont announced that he planned to conquer all of California. Military historian General John Eisenhower writes regarding Frémont's proclamation, "This pronouncement was remarkable because it was made at a time when

Frémont had no knowledge of whether or not Mexico and the United States were at war."[6] On December 12, 1846, Kearny arrived in San Diego to complete the final conquest of California.

Eventually, the expanding war led to the occupation of Mexico City by U.S. military forces on September 14, 1847. The war ended on May 30, 1848, when the Mexican congress ratified the Treaty of Guadalupe Hidalgo, which ceded to the United States Mexican territory from Texas to California. Besides creating lasting resentment toward and suspicion of the U.S. government by the Mexican government, the acquisition of Mexican lands presented the problem of what to do with the conquered Mexican citizens. During negotiations regarding the Treaty of Guadalupe Hidalgo, Mexican leaders were concerned about the racial attitudes of U.S. leaders and demanded that Mexicans living in ceded territory be given full citizenship rights in the United States. However, when the treaty was discussed in the U.S. Senate, the majority of senators did not believe that Mexicans were ready for "equal union" with other U.S. citizens. Consequently, the final treaty postponed granting U.S. citizenship to the conquered Mexican population. Article IX of the treaty stated that Mexicans in the ceded territory "shall be incorporated into the Union of the United States, and be admitted, at the proper time (to be judged by the Congress of the United States), to the enjoyment of all rights of citizens of the United States."[7]

Despite the treaty's provisions for citizenship, citizenship rights were abridged throughout the Southwest by limitations placed on voting rights and segregation in public accommodations and schooling. As with cases involving Asian Americans (discussed later in this chapter), courts wrestled with the issue of racial classification. In 1897 Texas courts ruled that Mexican Americans were not "white." In California, Mexican Americans were classified as Caucasian until 1930, when California's Attorney General Webb categorized them as Indians; he argued that "the greater portion of the population of Mexico are Indians." Therefore, Mexican Americans were segregated in accordance with a provision of the California school code that gave school districts the "power to establish separate schools for Indian children, excepting children of Indians . . . who are the descendants of the original American Indians of the U.S." Though classified as Indians, Mexican Americans were not considered "the original American Indians of the U.S."[8]

Segregation, Language, and Mexican American Education

The attitude of racial, religious, and cultural superiority provided motivation for the United States to take over Mexican land, fueled hostilities between the two countries throughout the nineteenth and early twentieth centuries, and was reflected in the treatment of Mexicans who remained in California and the Southwest after the U.S. conquest and of later Mexican immigrants. Segregated schools, housing, and discrimination in employment became the Mexican American heritage. Reflecting the attitude of the Mexican government toward the anti-Mexican feelings in the United States, the president of Mexico, General Porfirio Díaz, was reported to have remarked in the latter part of the nineteenth century, "Poor Mexico! So far from God and so close to the United States."[9]

HISPANIC/LATINO EDUCATION TIME LINE PRIOR TO CIVIL RIGHTS MOVEMENT

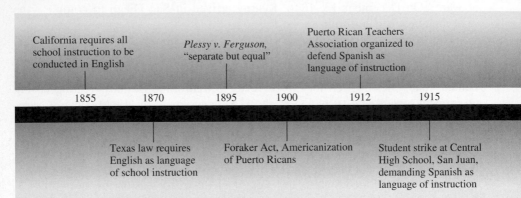

The evolution of discriminatory attitudes and practices toward Mexican Americans occurred in two stages. The first stage involved the treatment of the Mexicans who remained after conquest. The second stage occurred in the late nineteenth and early twentieth centuries, when U.S. farmers encouraged the immigration of farm laborers from Mexico and political and economic conditions in Mexico caused many Mexicans to seek residence in the United States.

In *Anglos and Mexicans in the Making of Texas, 1836–1986,* David Montejano argues that a victor has the choice of either eradicating the conquered population or assimilating them into its own culture.[10] Montejano identifies two patterns in the treatment of the Mexican Americans in Texas in the nineteenth century. The pattern of extermination and ejection occurred in central and southeastern Texas with the uprooting of entire communities. Mexican Americans were physically driven out of Austin in 1853 and 1855 and out of the counties of Matagorda and Colorado in 1856. A large part of the Mexican population of San Antonio was driven out by 1856.[11]

The ejection of the Mexican population was justified by racist attitudes. Frederick Law Olmsted recorded many of these attitudes while traveling through Texas in 1855 and 1856 as a reporter for *The New York Times.* Olmsted overheard newly arrived settlers complaining that Mexicans "think themselves as good as white men" and that they were "vermin to be exterminated."[12] He found a general feeling among Anglo settlers that "white folks and Mexicans" were never meant to live together. He quoted a newspaper article published in Matagorda County that began, "The people of Matagorda County have held a meeting and ordered every Mexican to leave the county."[13] The article went on to justify the expulsion by calling the Mexicans in the area "lower class" and contending that the Mexicans were likely to take black women as wives and to steal horses.

One of the important consequences of this negative action against Mexicans was to make it easier for American settlers to gain land in the area. In this case, racism served as a justification for economic exploitation. Although the Mexican population declined in these areas after the war, it rose again during the early twentieth century.

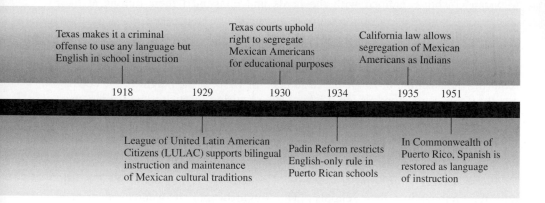

Texas makes it a criminal offense to use any language but English in school instruction

Texas courts uphold right to segregate Mexican Americans for educational purposes

California law allows segregation of Mexican Americans as Indians

1918   1929   1930   1934   1935   1951

League of United Latin American Citizens (LULAC) supports bilingual instruction and maintenance of Mexican cultural traditions

Padin Reform restricts English-only rule in Puerto Rican schools

In Commonwealth of Puerto Rico, Spanish is restored as language of instruction

The same racist arguments were then used to justify paying Mexican farmworkers lower wages and establishing a segregated system of schooling.

In the southern part of Texas, a different pattern developed for the treatment of the conquered Mexican population. Montejano calls this pattern a "peace structure" with two major components. One component involved bringing the Mexicans under the authority of Anglos in political matters; the other involved an accommodation between the Mexican and Anglo elites.[14] This accommodation served as a basis for the creation of large cattle ranches. Anglo cattle raisers gained access to large tracts of land either by marrying into elite Mexican families or through direct purchase. In this accommodation, Anglos made a distinction between what they identified as the "Castilian elite," who controlled vast amounts of land, and the average Mexican, who was identified as a "peon." In the minds of Anglos, this division involved a racial distinction. Peons were considered racially inferior to the Castilian elite because they were mestizos. The Castilian elite were accepted because of their supposed lack of Indian heritage and their Spanish ancestry. In other words, Anglos held the same racist attitudes toward peons as they did toward Indians.[15]

These racist attitudes permeated the life of the cattle ranches established in southern Texas during what is referred to as the "cowboy era" in Texas history. By the 1860s, the railroad was extended to Kansas. This made it possible to raise cattle in Texas, drive them on foot to Kansas, and then ship them east. Between 1866 and 1880, more than four million cattle were marched north out of Texas. The term *cowboy* was coined to describe the workers who took the herds north. The cattle drives would follow either the Chisholm Trail or the Western Trail north from southern Texas through Indian Territory to Kansas.[16] The taxes levied on the drives by the Choctaws in Indian Territory helped to support their school system.

On the cattle ranches of the cowboy era, the authority structure created a division between Mexican and Anglo cowboys. The Anglo cowboys, of course, exercised authority over the Mexican ones. In addition, facilities were segregated.

Anglo cowboys ate in the ranch dining room and refused to eat with the Mexicans; Mexican cowboys camped with the herds and consumed their rations at their campsites.[17] This segregation established a pattern for later forms of segregation.

As with Native Americans, a major concern of the conquered Mexican population was the mandate that English was to be spoken in the schools. In 1856, two years after the Texas legislature established public schools, a law was passed requiring the teaching of English as a subject. In 1870, at the height of the cowboy era, the Texas legislature passed a school law requiring English to be the language of instruction in all public schools.[18] The same attempt to eradicate the Spanish language in the United States occurred in the conquered territory of California. The California Bureau of Instruction mandated in 1855 that all school classes be conducted in English. In *The Decline of the Californios: A Social History of the Spanish-Speaking California, 1846–1890,* Leonard Pitt writes about the English-only requirement in public schools: "This linguistic purism went hand in hand with the nativist sentiments expressed in that year's legislature, including the suspension of the publication of state laws in Spanish."[19]

In general, Mexican Americans in the last half of the nineteenth century tried to escape the anti-Mexican attitudes of public school authorities by attending either Catholic schools or nonsectarian private schools. In California, some members of the Mexican community were interested in providing a bilingual education for their children. They wanted their children to improve their ability to read and write Spanish and become acquainted with the cultural traditions of Mexico and Spain, while at the same time learning to speak English. In some places, such as Santa Barbara, California, local Mexican leaders were able to bypass the state requirement on teaching in English and maintain a bilingual public school. But in most places, bilingual instruction could be had only through schools operated by the Catholic Church.[20]

In Texas, bilingual education could be obtained in parochial schools, and in south Texas, private schools established by the Mexican community offered bilingual education while trying to maintain both the Spanish language and Mexican culture. The three major purposes of these Mexican schools were to impart Mexican ideals, to teach Mexican traditions and history, and to maintain racial pride among the students.[21] Because of the language issue, Mexican American students were discouraged by local school authorities from attending the first public school opened in El Paso in 1883. Consequently, Mexican Americans opened their own Mexican Preparatory School in 1887. As in California, some Texas communities did not enforce the English-only rule. The first public school that opened in Brownsville, Texas, in 1875 was attended primarily by Mexican American children. Because most of these children did not speak or understand English, the English-only rule was not enforced until the fourth grade.[22] The patterns of discrimination and segregation established in the nineteenth century were accentuated during the great immigration of Mexicans into the United States in the early twentieth century. Between 1900 and 1909, some 23,991 Mexicans immigrated to the United States. Between 1910 and 1919, this figure increased dramatically—to 173,663; and between 1920 and 1929, the number rose to 487,775.[23]

One key to understanding the continuing patterns of racism and segregation is the fact that the immigration of Mexicans was encouraged by U.S. farmers because Mexicans were an inexpensive source of labor in the booming agricultural regions of Texas and California. By the 1890s, the era of the cowboy was drawing to a close. Railroads had penetrated Texas, making the cattle drives across Indian Territory unnecessary. In addition, because of a variety of economic changes, the cattle industry itself was in decline. Consequently, many Texans turned to farming. As the twentieth century unfolded, railroad expansion made it possible to ship agricultural goods from California to the East. Like Texans, California farmers needed cheap labor. For some farmers, Mexicans were ideal laborers. As one Texas cotton grower put it, "They are docile and law-abiding. They are the sweetest people in this position that I ever saw."[24]

Anglo attitudes about the education of the children of immigrant Mexicans involved two conflicting positions. On the one hand, farmers did not want Mexican children to go to school because school attendance meant they were not available for farmwork. On the other hand, many public officials wanted Mexican children in school so they could be "Americanized." In addition, many Mexican families were reluctant to send their children to school because of the loss of the children's contribution to family income.

These conflicting positions represent the two methods by which education can be used as a method of social control. The cheapest and easiest was to deny a population the knowledge necessary to protect its political and economic rights and to economically advance in society. Farmers wanted to keep Mexican laborers ignorant as a means of assuring a continued inexpensive source of labor. As one Texas farmer stated, "Educating the Mexicans is educating them away from the job, away from the dirt." Reflecting the values of the farmers in his district, one Texas school superintendent explained, "You have doubtless heard that ignorance is bliss; it seems that is so when one has to transplant onions. . . . So you see it is up to the white population to keep the Mexican on his knees in an onion patch or in new ground. This does not mix very well with education."[25] A school principal in Colorado stated, "Never try to enforce compulsory attendance laws on the Mexicans. . . . The banks and the company will swear that the labor is needed and that the families need the money."[26]

ASIAN AMERICANS: EXCLUSION AND SEGREGATION

The hostility of Anglo-Americans was a rude surprise to Asian immigrants. Like other immigrants, they hoped to make their fortune in the United States and either return to their homelands or build a home in their new country. The first Chinese migrants arrived in California in the 1850s to join the gold rush. In search of the "Golden Mountain," these first arrivals were free laborers who paid their own transportation to the goldfields of California. By 1852 there were about 20,000 Chinese immigrants in California. By the 1860s approximately 16,000 Chinese immigrants were working in the California goldfields. But as mining profits decreased, the Chinese immigrants found themselves without enough money to return to their homeland. Searching for work, these Chinese immigrants were hired to build the transcontinental railroad at wages that were about one-third less than would have been paid to a white worker. In addition, Chinese workers filled low-wage jobs and built the agricultural industry in California.[27] Racial hostility was highlighted in 1871 with the lynching of twenty-two Chinese men by Los Angeles mobs.[28]

Japanese immigrated later because a 1639 Japanese law forbade travel to foreign countries. Circumstances began to change in 1868 when Hawaiian planters were able to recruit 148 Japanese contract laborers and when, in 1869, 100 laborers were signed up for work in the California silk industry. By 1884 the Japanese government allowed open recruitment by Hawaiian planters. Between 1885 and 1920, 200,000 Japanese immigrated to Hawaii and 180,000 to the U.S. mainland. Adding to the Asian American population were 8,000 Koreans who immigrated, primarily to Hawaii, between 1903 and 1920. Between 1907 and 1917, when immigration from India was restricted, 6,400 Asian Indians came to the United States. In 1907 Filipinos, who were citizens of the U.S.-captured Philippine Islands, were recruited as laborers. By 1930, 110,000 Filipinos had settled in Hawaii and 40,000 on the mainland.[29]

As indicated by Table 7.1, Asian Americans represented a small percentage of the total foreign-born population between 1850 and 1930, and their numbers were low compared to the foreign-born population from Europe. As also indicated in the table, the foreign-born population from Asia ranged from less than 1 percent of the total foreign-born population in 1850 to 1.9 percent, whereas the European foreign-born population for the same period ranged from 90.5 percent to 82.9. As

ASIAN AMERICAN CITIZENSHIP TIME LINE

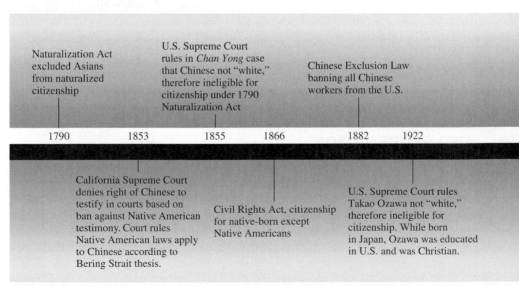

Naturalization Act excluded Asians from naturalized citizenship

U.S. Supreme Court rules in *Chan Yong* case that Chinese not "white," therefore ineligible for citizenship under 1790 Naturalization Act

Chinese Exclusion Law banning all Chinese workers from the U.S.

1790   1853   1855   1866   1882   1922

California Supreme Court denies right of Chinese to testify in courts based on ban against Native American testimony. Court rules Native American laws apply to Chinese according to Bering Strait thesis.

Civil Rights Act, citizenship for native-born except Native Americans

U.S. Supreme Court rules Takao Ozawa not "white," therefore ineligible for citizenship. While born in Japan, Ozawa was educated in U.S. and was Christian.

TABLE 7.1 Region of Birth of the Foreign-Born Population, 1850–1930

Year	Total Foreign-Born in United States	Total Foreign-Born from Europe	Total Foreign-Born from Asia	Percentage of Total Foreign-Born from Europe	Percentage of Total Foreign-Born from Asia
1850	2,244,60	22,031,867	1,135	90.5%	0.0005%
1870	5,567,229	4,941,049	64,565	88.7	1.1
1890	9,249,547	8,030,347	113,383	86.8	1.2
1910	13,515,886	11,810,115	191,484	87.3	1.4
1930	14,204,149	11,784,010	275,665	82.9	1.9

Source: Adapted from Campbell Gibson and Emily Lennon, A Historical Census Statistics on the Foreign-Born Population of the United States: 1850–1990. Table 2, Region of Birth of the Foreign-Born Population: 1850 to 1930 and 1960 to 1990, U.S. Census Bureau, Internet Release Date March 9, 1999, www.census.gov (August 26, 1999).

indicated by these figures, the majority of immigrants for this period, as in earlier periods, came from Europe.

Asian American Citizenship

Nineteenth- and twentieth-century court rulings specifically denied Asian American immigrants the right to be naturalized U.S. citizens. However, unlike most Native Americans until 1924, Asian Americans born in the United States were considered native-born citizens after the passage of the 1866 Civil Rights Act. A legal issue was the racial classification applied to immigrants from northern and

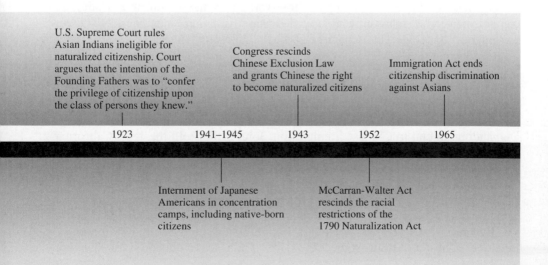

U.S. Supreme Court rules Asian Indians ineligible for naturalized citizenship. Court argues that the intention of the Founding Fathers was to "confer the privilege of citizenship upon the class of persons they knew."

Congress rescinds Chinese Exclusion Law and grants Chinese the right to become naturalized citizens

Immigration Act ends citizenship discrimination against Asians

1923   1941–1945   1943   1952   1965

Internment of Japanese Americans in concentration camps, including native-born citizens

McCarran-Walter Act rescinds the racial restrictions of the 1790 Naturalization Act

southern Asia, southeast Asia, and India. In the nineteenth century, California laws simply classified immigrants from all these areas as "Mongolian." Later, despite the wide-ranging cultural and language differences among these regions, European Americans used the term "Asian" in reference to immigrants from these areas. "Asian American" is now commonly used in the United States, but that term too tends to conceal the differences among people and countries, such as Korea, Japan, China, Cambodia, Indonesia, and India.

Confusion over the legal racial category of Asians began in 1853 with a California court case involving the testimony of Chinese immigrant witnesses regarding the murder of another Chinese immigrant by one George Hall. The California Supreme Court overturned the murder conviction of George Hall by applying a state law that disallowed court testimony from African Americans, mulattoes, and Native Americans. The state law reflected the racist undertones of the state government of California. California's chief justice ruled that the law barring the testimony of Native Americans applied to all "Asiatics" since, according to theory, Native Americans were originally Asians who crossed into North America over the Bering Strait. Therefore, the chief justice argued, the ban on court testimony from Native Americans applied to "the whole of the Mongolian race."[30]

U.S. Supreme Court interpretations of the Naturalization Act of 1790 made it clear that race was defined primarily according to skin color. In denying citizenship to Chan Yong in 1855, a federal district court in California ruled that under the 1790 Naturalization Act citizenship was restricted to whites only, and consequently, immigrant Chinese were not eligible for U.S. citizenship.[31] In addition, the Naturalization Law of 1870 extended U.S. citizenship to "aliens of African nativity and to persons of African descent" while retaining the word *white,* which meant the continued exclusion of Asian immigrants and Native Americans from citizenship.

After the Chan Yong decision, California continued to be a hotbed of anti-Chinese and anti-Japanese sentiment. Race riots accompanied laws designed to deny Asian Americans full citizenship rights. However, despite the sentiments of California congressman James Johnson, who labeled Asians "barbarians" and considered them an "inferior" race, the U.S. Congress in 1864 ratified the Burlingame Treaty with China, allowing unrestricted immigration of Chinese nationals to the United States but continuing to deny them U.S. citizenship.[32] Then in 1875 Congress limited unrestricted immigration with the passage of the Page Law, which forbade entry into the United States of Chinese, Japanese, and "Mongolian" contract labor.[33]

Many California Anglo-Americans objected to the Burlingame Treaty. Demanding an end to Chinese immigration, John Miller told the 1878 California constitutional convention, "Were the Chinese to amalgamate at all with our people, it would be the lowest, most vile and degraded of our race, and the result of that amalgamation would be a hybrid of the most despicable, a mongrel of the most detestable that has ever afflicted the earth."[34] Announcing that the "experiment of blending [the] habits and mutual race idiosyncrasies [of Chinese and European Americans was] unwise, impolitic, and injurious to both nations," President Chester Arthur signed the 1882 Chinese Exclusion Law denying entrance into the United States of all Chinese laborers for ten years while allow-ing merchants, students, teachers, and diplomats.[35] The legislation specifically banned the naturalization of immigrant Chinese. In addition, it required all Chinese residing in the United States to obtain certificates of registration. The Chinese Exclusion Act was one of three immigration acts passed in 1882 that gave major control over immigration to the federal government (as opposed to state governments).

Massachusetts Senator George Hoar led opposition to the Chinese Exclusion Act. He argued that the principles of republican government, the Declaration of Independence, and Christianity required racial equality in the United States and in immigration laws, and he rejected the "doctrine that free institutions are a monopoly of favored races."[36] Tennessee Senator William Moore opposed the law because the United States, as "the recognized champion of human rights," should be "the land where all men, of all climes, all colors, all conditions, all nationali-ties, are welcome to come and go at will."[37] Those who won the day, however, were proponents of the idea that a republican or democratic government could survive only with a population limited to "whites." Vermont Senator George Edmonds and Wisconsin Representative George Hazelton declared that the sur-vival of republican institutions required "a homogenous population."[38] Survival of the U.S. government would not be possible, according to Ohio Representative Alden McLure, with an "ethnological animal show."[39] California Senator John Miller referred to the Chinese as a degraded race unfit for citizenship when com-pared to the higher "Anglo-Saxon." California Representative Romualdo Pacheco argued that the "Chinaman [is] a lithe, sinewy creature, with muscles like iron, and almost devoid of nerves and sensibilities. His ancestors have also bequested to him the most hideous immoralities. They are as natural to him as the yellow hue of his skin, and are so shocking and horrible that their character cannot even be hinted."[40]

While Chinese were specifically excluded from citizenship by the 1882 Chinese Exclusion Act and the 1790 Naturalization Law, a Japanese immigrant in 1894 was denied citizenship by a U.S. circuit court in Massachusetts with the argument that Japanese were not eligible because they were "Mongolians." In 1909 a person with an English father and a half-Chinese and half-Japanese mother was denied citizenship for not being sufficiently "white."[41]

Education of the Coolie and Deviant

The educational experiences of Asian Americans have paralleled their public image in the United States. By *public image* I mean the representation of Asian Americans that appears in the popular press and in media dominated by European Americans. In his study of the portrayal of Asian Americans in U.S. popular culture, Robert Lee identified five major images of Asians—"the coolie, the devi-ant, the yellow peril, the model minority, and the gook."[42] As he points out, each image, including that of "the model minority," has presented some threat to "the American national family."

ASIAN AMERICAN EDUCATION TIME LINE

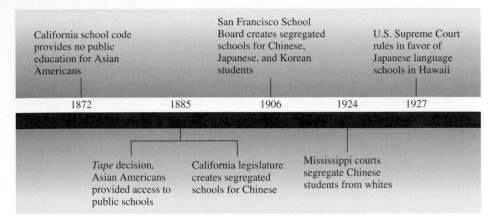

Prior to World War II, educational discrimination and segregation were results of the images held by many European Americans of Asian Americans as "coolies," "deviants," and the "yellow peril." The coolie image was that of the servile Asian worker willing to work endless hours at low wages and accept substandard living conditions; this image was considered a threat to the standard of living of the white working-class family. The deviant image was that of the Chinese opium den and Asian sexual freedom; this image was considered a threat to the morality of the white family. The yellow peril image was that of Asian immigrants overrunning the United States.

Before World War II, the negative images of Asians in European American minds were one reason for Asian Americans' continual struggle for equal educational opportunity. For instance, the California school code of 1872 stated, "Every school, unless otherwise provided by special statute, must be opened for the admission of *all white children* [the emphasis is mine] between five and twenty-one years residing in a district."[43] In other words, the 1872 code made *no* provisions for the education of Asian Americans, Mexican Americans, African Americans, and Native Americans. California state leaders deliberately denied these populations access to public schools.

This denial of equal educational opportunity was challenged in 1884, when the Imperial Chinese Consulate complained to San Francisco School Superintendent Andrew Moulder about the refusal of the school district to admit Mamie Tape. Mamie Tape was a Chinese American born in the United States and therefore had U.S. citizenship. The San Francisco school board swiftly reacted to the complaint by adopting a resolution "That each and every principal of each and every public school [is] hereby absolutely prohibited from admitting any Mongolian child of schoolable age, or otherwise, either male or female, into such school or class."[44]

Reflecting the strong anti-Chinese feelings of white residents, the San Francisco board of supervisors responded to Mamie Tape's request, using the images of "yellow peril" and "deviant." The official statement of the board declared their intentions:

> Guard well the doors of our public schools that they [the Chinese] do not enter. For however stern it might sound, it is but the enforcement of the law of self-preservation, the inculcation of the doctrine of true humanity and an integral part of the iron rule of right by which we hope presently to prove that we can justly and practically defend ourselves from this invasion of Mongolian barbarism.[45]

On January 9, 1885, U.S. Superior Court Judge Maguire ruled in favor of Mamie Tape. Arguing that the Fourteenth Amendment to the Constitution guaranteed equal protection, including equal access to public schooling, Judge Maguire stated, "It would, moreover, be unjust to levy a forced tax upon Chinese residents to help maintain our schools, and yet prohibit their children born here from education in those schools."[46]

Obviously prepared for Maguire's decision, the California legislature on January 23, 1885, only two weeks after the decision, revised the California school code to provide education for Chinese children in "segregated" schools. The revised code gave local school boards the power "to establish separate schools for children of Mongolian or Chinese descent. When such separate schools are established Chinese or Mongolian children must not be admitted into any other school."[47] On April 13, 1885, the segregated Chinese Primary School was opened at Jackson and Powell Streets in San Francisco. Sacramento followed San Francisco's example and established a segregated school for Chinese in 1893. The rigid policy of segregation broke down by 1905, when the San Francisco board of education was forced to let Chinese youths attend the regular city high school.

In Mississippi, Chinese immigrants found themselves caught between their own racist feelings and southern racial politics. In the early twentieth century, several hundred Chinese had settled in Mississippi. State authorities required that Chinese send their children to segregated black schools. Highlighting their own racial prejudice, Chinese families objected to their attending school with African American children. The issue finally reached the courts in 1924 when the school superintendent of Rosedale, Mississippi, informed a local Chinese merchant that his daughter would not be allowed to attend the white school. Hired by the Chinese merchant, a group of white lawyers argued successfully before the U.S. Circuit Court that since no school had been provided for Chinese students, the girl was being denied equal education. The school district appealed the ruling to the Mississippi Supreme Court, which ruled that since Chinese were not "white" they must be "colored" and should attend schools for "colored" children.[48]

While Chinese in Mississippi were required to attend "colored" schools, the children of Asian Indians in California were required to attend segregated schools for Mexican American children. As a result of the lack of immigration of Asian Indian women, Asian Indian male immigrants married primarily Mexican Americans. The result was that California classified the children of these couples as Mexican American.[49]

The establishment of segregated schools for Japanese children in California caused an international incident. Japanese immigrants did not enter California in large numbers until the early twentieth century. Although California employers saw Japan as a cheap source of Asian labor, anti-Asian hysteria greeted the Japanese, as it had the Chinese. While native whites worried about job competition and the resulting low wages, Japanese entered the country with expectations of becoming permanent citizens and with high educational standards. The Japanese, like the Chinese, were caught between American companies wanting to use cheap Asian labor and American workers who did not want the competition. In either case, arguments of racial inferiority and "yellow peril" were used to justify either exclusion from the United States or economic exploitation. The San Francisco school district justified segregation with the public statement, "not only for the purpose of relieving the congestion at present prevailing in our schools, but also for the higher end that our children should not be placed in any position where their youthful impression may be affected by association with pupils of the 'Mongolian race.'"

In 1906 the San Francisco board of education established a separate school for Chinese, Japanese, and Korean children. A majority of the Japanese parents boycotted the school, and the Japanese community then tried to win public opinion in Japan as a means of forcing favorable action from the U.S. government. Editorials began to appear in Tokyo newspapers claiming that segregation was an insult to the nation, and in October 1906 the American ambassador to Japan warned the U.S. government of the developing international situation. The result was that President Theodore Roosevelt threatened the San Francisco school system with federal action if segregation did not end. However, the involvement of the federal government did not end segregation for the Japanese in other areas; they continued to face various exclusionary laws and legal actions through World War II.[50]

NATIVE AMERICAN CITIZENSHIP

The Naturalization Act of 1790 excluded Native Americans from U.S. citizenship. This was in keeping with the belief that the survival of the country depended on a homogeneous citizenry of "whites." At the time, Native Americans were classified as "domestic foreigners." Consequently, because of the 1790 legislation, they could not seek naturalized citizenship because they were not "white."[51] In 1867 Congress created the Indian Peace Commission, which effectively made the requirement for U.S. citizenship for Native Americans, in the words of historian Rogers Smith, the "repudiation of native religions and ways of life, and acceptance of middle-class American Christianity with its attended customs."[52] By the end of the nineteenth century, attitudes began to change as some Native American nations were deculturalized and adopted European culture. The so-called Five Civilized Tribes were among the first Native Americans to be granted citizenship, in 1901.[53] The granting of citizenship to all Native Americans did not occur until 1924, when Congress passed the Indian Citizenship Act. The legislation authorized "the Secretary of the Interior to issue certificates of citizenship to Indians."[54] After winning the Indian wars and confiscating most Native American lands, the U.S. Congress magnanimously declared, "That all non-citizen Indians born within the territorial limits of the United States be, and they are hereby, declared to be citizens of the United States."[55] Therefore, in 1924 Native Americans gained citizenship while immigrant Asians were still being denied naturalized citizenship.

EDUCATIONAL RACISM AND DECULTURALIZATION

Another indication of racism is the attempt by a dominant social group to destroy the culture of another group and replace it with the dominant group's own culture. "Be like us," this form of racism asserts, "and we might accept you." I call this practice *deculturalization*. Deculturalization is one aspect of the strange mixture of democratic thought and intolerance that exists in some minds. The concept of deculturalization demonstrates how cultural prejudice and religious bigotry can be intertwined with democratic beliefs. It combines education for democracy and political equality with cultural genocide—the attempt to destroy cultures.

Deculturalization is an educational process that aims to destroy a people's culture and replace it with a new culture. Schools in the United States have used varying forms of deculturalization in attempts to eradicate the cultures of Native Americans, African Americans, Mexican Americans, Puerto Ricans, and immigrants from Ireland, Southern and Eastern Europe, and Asia. For example, believing that Anglo-American culture—the culture of the descendants of British colonists and immigrants—was a superior culture and the only culture that would support republican and democratic institutions, educators forbade the speaking of non-English languages, particularly Spanish and Native American tongues, and forced students to learn an Anglo-American-centered curriculum. The Great Spirit's warning to the Cherokees to maintain their traditional culture was in direct conflict with the U.S. government's civilization and removal policies in the early nineteenth century. Sensing that Native American resistance would lead to the failure of civilization and removal policies, U.S. government leaders after the 1850s desperately wanted to develop more effective policies as white settlers streamed into lands west of the Mississippi. Consequently, the civilization policies developed for the western tribes in the second half of the nineteenth century involved a more extreme approach to deculturalization: settling tribes on controlled reservations and placing their children in boarding schools.

Manifest destiny—the idea that a certain future event is inevitable and just—provided a rationalization for deculturalization. The expansion of its borders to the Pacific Ocean was felt to be the manifest (obvious) destiny of the United States. Manifest destiny rested on a belief in the superiority of Protestant Anglo-American culture and U.S. political institutions. Whites considered conquered Native American tribes to be culturally and morally inferior. Consequently, educational programs established by the federal government were designed to deculturalize the tribes and then "civilize" them. Deculturalization included attempts to destroy Native American cultures, languages, and religion. Because federal leaders were concerned with winning the loyalty of these conquered people, deculturalization was accompanied by Americanization programs. Conquered Native Americans were exposed to educational programs emphasizing patriotism and loyalty to the U.S. government. As tribal governments fell, Native American schools raised the U.S. flag and forced students to pledge their loyalty to the conquering nation. Forced allegiance to the flag was accompanied by patriotic exercises and celebrations of U.S. national holidays and heroes.

In a broader framework, deculturalization and Americanization could be considered logical educational policies for any conquering nation. Any country interested in controlling another would want to gain the allegiance of the conquered peoples. Indeed, the conquerors would want the conquered to feel emotional ties to the conquerors' government and society. In addition, conquerors would want the conquered to emulate the conquerors' culture. In the United States, federal and state officials attempted to gain emulation by using textbooks that reflected the dominant white culture and that contained no reference to Hispanic or Native American cultures. If conquered peoples could be forced to emulate the dominant culture of the United States, it was believed, they would rush to embrace their conquerors rather than resist subjugation.

I will examine the process of deculturalization and Americanization by tracing the history of Native American education in the United States from the early nineteenth century to the middle of the twentieth century.

© *Corbis*

Native Americans: Reservations and Boarding Schools

As white settlers moved into western lands in the latter part of the nineteenth century, leaders in the U.S. government were forced to reconsider their relationships to tribes and their attempts to "civilize" Native Americans. First there was the problem of land on which to settle displaced tribes. Unlike in the 1820s and 1830s, there was now a realization that white settlement would eventually cover most of the continent. In 1858 Commissioner of Indian Affairs Charles E. Mix, in his annual report, declared that the U.S. government had made several serious errors in dealing with the southeastern tribes, including "the assignment to them of too great an extent of country, to be held in common."[56] Holding large tracts of land in common, according to Commissioner Mix, limited attempts to civilize Native Americans because it prevented them from learning the value of separate and independent property.

Reservations and allotment programs were the responses to the land issue. The reservation system combined with education was considered by the U.S. government as the best method of dealing with what Commissioner of Indian Affairs Luke Lea called the "wilder tribes."[57] In the *Annual Report of the Commissioner of Indian Affairs* in 1850, Commissioner Lea argued that certain Indian tribes, specifically the Sioux and Chippewa, had an "insatiable passion for war" and that it was "necessary that they be placed in positions where they can be controlled."[58] Once concentrated in reservations where they could be controlled, the tribes would be compelled to remain there until they proved themselves to be civilized. Under this system, the federal government was to supply agricultural implements to aid in this process of civilization.

Provisions for manual labor schools on reservations were specified in Commissioner Mix's report of 1858. Mix argued that reservation sites should be selected that would minimize contact with whites and provide opportunities for Indians to learn agricultural skills. To aid in the process of preparing Indians for agriculture, manual labor schools were to be established that would teach basic skills in reading, writing, and arithmetic, along with agricultural skills. Of particular importance, according to Commissioner Mix, was the role of manual labor schools in molding the character of future generations of Native Americans in what he called "habits of industry." To carry out this enterprise, Commissioner Mix recommended that a military force should remain in the vicinity of the reservations "to aid in controlling the Indians."[59]

Adding to the problem for government officials, western Native Americans displayed a great deal of resistance to white incursions onto their lands. This resulted in Native American wars across the plains of the West during the latter half of the nineteenth century. In 1867 Congress created an Indian Peace Commission to deal with the warring tribes. The Indian Peace Commission advocated different methods for the education and civilization of Native Americans. The Peace Commission placed emphasis on the role of education in converting Native Americans to civilization. Nathaniel Taylor, chairman of the Peace Commission, told the Crow Indians at Fort Laramie, "Upon the reservations you select, we . . . will send you teachers for your children."[60] According to Jon Reyhner and

Jeanne Eder, this promise was embodied in the Treaty of Fort Laramie with the Sioux and their allies.[61]

The members of the Peace Commission were not entirely satisfied with the traditional attempts to educate Native Americans, particularly with regard to language. The Indian Peace Commission report of 1868 states that differences in language were a major source of the continuing friction between whites and Native Americans. Therefore, according to the report, an emphasis on the teaching of English would be a major step in reducing hostilities and civilizing Native Americans. In the words of the report, "Through sameness of language is produced sameness of sentiment and thought; customs and habits are moulded [sic] and assimilated in the same way, and thus in process of time the differences producing trouble [will be] gradually obliterated."[62]

Replacing the use of native languages with English, destroying Native American customs, and teaching allegiance to the U.S. government became the major educational policies of the U.S. government toward Native Americans during the latter part of the nineteenth century. The boarding school was an important part of these educational policies. It was designed to remove children from their families at an early age and thereby isolate them from the language and customs of their parents and tribes. These boarding schools were quite different from those operated by the Choctaws in Indian Territory, which were somewhat elite institutions within the Choctaw educational system and were not designed to destroy Native American customs and languages.

In *A History of Indian Education,* Jon Reyhner and Jeanne Eder demonstrate the connections between the establishment of boarding schools for Native Americans and the history of African American education in the South. The first off-reservation boarding school was the Carlisle Indian School, established in Carlisle, Pennsylvania, in 1879. The founder of the school, Richard Pratt, had commanded an African American cavalry in Indian Territory between 1867 and 1875. According to Reyhner and Eder, Pratt's interest in founding a boarding school was sparked when he took seventeen adult Native American prisoners of war to Hampton Institute in Virginia.[63] Hampton played an important role in the development of African American education in the South. Booker T. Washington was educated at Hampton and used it as a model when he established Tuskegee Normal and Industrial Institute in Alabama in 1881. The primary purpose of Hampton Institute was to prepare freed slaves to be teachers who could instill work values in other freed slaves. In the words of historian James Anderson, "The primary aim [of Hampton] was to work the prospective teachers long and hard so that they would embody, accept, and preach an ethic of hard toil or the 'dignity of labor.'"[64]

Pratt not only wanted to instill the work ethic in Native American children but also, as he told a Baptist group, immerse "Indians in our civilization and when we get them under, [hold] them there until they are thoroughly soaked."[65] The slogan for the Carlisle Indian School reflected the emphasis on changing the cultural patterns of Native Americans: "To civilize the Indian, get him into civilization. To keep him civilized, let him stay."[66]

Pratt's educational philosophy embodied the principles behind the allotment movement of the latter part of the nineteenth century. The allotment program, which was applied to the Five Civilized Tribes with the breakup of Indian Territory, was designed to distribute commonly held tribal property to individual Native Americans. It was assumed that individual ownership would instill the capitalistic values of white civilization in Native Americans. Tribal ownership was viewed as a form of socialism that was antithetical to the values of white American society. Also, the allotment program was another method of dealing with the Native American land problem. In the *Annual Report of the Commissioner of Indian Affairs* in 1881, Commissioner of Indian Affairs Hiram Price criticized previous attempts to civilize Native Americans because those attempts did not teach the necessity of labor. This could be accomplished, Price argued, only when individual Native Americans were made responsible for their own economic welfare. This could be done, he contended, by allotting Native Americans "a certain number of acres of land which they may call their own."[67]

Pratt attacked the tribal way of life as socialistic and contrary to the values of "civilization." Reflecting the values of economic individualism, Pratt complained about missionary groups who did not "advocate the disintegration of the tribes and the giving to individual Indians rights and opportunities among civilized people."[68] He wrote to the commissioner of Indian affairs in 1890, "Pandering to the tribe and its socialism as most of our Government and mission plans do is the principal reason why the Indians have not advanced more and are not advancing as rapidly as they ought."[69]

Between the 1879 founding of the Carlisle Indian School and 1905, twenty-five nonreservation boarding schools were opened throughout the country.[70] The nonreservation location of the boarding schools was important because of the educational philosophy that Native American children should be removed from family and tribal influences. At these schools, as well as at the reservation schools, teaching English was an important issue. As discussed previously, many white educators in the latter part of the nineteenth century felt that replacing tribal languages with English would lead to the absorption and practice of white values by Native Americans. In the *Annual Report of the Commissioner of Indian Affairs* in 1887, Commissioner J. D. C. Atkins ordered the exclusive use of English at all Native American schools. Atkins pointed out that this policy was consistent with the requirement that only English be taught in public schools in territories acquired by the United States from Mexico, Spain, and Russia. And comparing the conquest of Native Americans to the German occupation of the French provinces of Alsace and Lorraine, where it was required that German rather than French be used in the schools, Atkins declared, "No unity or community of feeling can be established among different peoples unless they are brought to speak the same language, and thus become imbued with like ideas of duty."[71]

Also, in an attempt to build a sense of community with the white population, it was hoped that Native American children would transfer their allegiance from their tribal governments to the federal government. Consequently, in 1889 Commissioner of Indian Affairs Thomas J. Morgan issued "instructions to Indian Agents in Regard to Inculcation of Patriotism in Indian Schools," which required that an American flag be flown in front of every Native American school. The instructions state, "The 'Stars and Stripes' should be a familiar object, and students should be taught to reverence the flag as a symbol of their nation's power and protection."[72] In addition, the instructions required the teaching of American history and the principles of the U.S. government. There was no suggestion in the instructions that the history of Native Americans and their governments be taught in the schools. Also, the instructions called for the teaching of patriotic songs and the public recitation of "patriotic selections."[73]

In one of the more interesting uses of celebrating national holidays as a method of building support for government policies, Commissioner Morgan's instructions required that schools inculcate in students allegiance to government policies designed to break up tribal lands. After a sentence requiring the celebration of Washington's birthday, Decoration Day, the Fourth of July, Thanksgiving, and Christmas, the instructions state, "It will also be well to observe the anniversary of the day upon which the 'Dawes bill' for giving to Indians allotments of land in severalty become a law, viz, February 8, 1887, and to use that occasion to impress upon Indian youth the enlarged scope and opportunity given them by this law and the new obligations which it imposes."[74]

In 1889 Commissioner Morgan wrote a bulletin on "Indian Education" that outlined the goals and policies of Native American schools. The bulletin was distributed by the U.S. Bureau of Education with an introduction written by Commissioner of Education William T. Harris. Harris praised what he called "the new education for our American Indians," particularly the effort "to obtain control of the Indian at an early age, and to seclude him as much as possible from the tribal influences."[75] Harris singled out the boarding school as an important step in changing the character of Native Americans. He argued that it was necessary to save the Native American; but he wrote, "We cannot save him and his patriarchal or tribal institution both together. To save him we must take him up into our civilization."[76]

Commissioner Morgan opened the bulletin with a statement of general principles of education for what he identified as a Native American population of 250,000 with a school population of 50,000. These general principles called for systematizing Native American education, increasing its availability to Native American children, and making it compulsory for all Native American children to attend school. In addition, Native American education was to place special stress on vocational training for jobs and on teaching English. With regard to instruction in English, the bulletin states, "Only English should be allowed to be spoken, and only English-speaking teachers should be employed in schools supported wholly or in part by the Government."[77] Also, the general principles stressed the importance of teaching allegiance to the U.S. government. As an added note, Morgan stressed the importance of bringing together the members of many different tribes in boarding schools as a means of reducing antagonisms between them.

After outlining the general principles of Native American education, Morgan turned to the issue of the high school. Morgan noted that the government at that time was not supporting high schools for Native Americans but only nonreservation boarding schools, reservation boarding schools, and day schools. Morgan favored the introduction of high schools for Native Americans as a means of breaking "the shackles of . . . tribal provincialism."[78] In advocating high schools, Morgan stressed the character-training qualities of a secondary education. He states, "The whole course of training [high school] should be fairly saturated with moral ideas, fear of God, and respect for the rights of others; love of truth and fidelity to duty; personal purity, philanthropy, and patriotism."[79]

Similarly, Morgan argued that grammar schools should stress systematic habits, "fervent patriotism," and the duties of citizens. He emphasized the character-training aspects of grammar schools, which he felt would develop the economically independent person as compared to one who was dependent on communal tribal living. Reflecting the reality of how Native American schools were conducted, Morgan states that in grammar school, "No pains should be spared to teach them that their future must depend chiefly upon their own exertions, character, and endeavors. . . . In the sweat of their faces must they eat bread."[80] Morgan also advocated early childhood education as a method of counteracting the influence of the Native American home. Like the boarding school, early childhood education would help to strip away the influences of Native American culture and language. Morgan states, "Children should be taken at as early an age as possible, before camp life has made an indelible stamp upon them."[81]

The reservation and boarding school system is a major historical example of attempting to use segregation and education to culturally transform an entire group of people. These were acts of cultural and linguistic genocide. However, resistance among tribal members ensured the ultimate failure of this form of cultural imperialism.

CITIZENSHIP FOR AFRICAN AMERICANS

Prior to the Civil War, the debates about citizenship for free African Americans highlighted the belief of some that only "whites" should have full U.S. citizenship. As previously discussed, the Naturalization Act of 1790 allowed citizenship to be granted only to immigrant whites; African immigrants were denied the right to become U.S. citizens. Granting citizenship to enslaved Africans was rejected by national political leaders. But what about native-born free African Americans? Should free Americans of African descent be considered full citizens? For those believing that the U.S. republic could survive only with a white homogeneous population, the answer was "No!"

In southern states, the citizenship rights of freed slaves were severely restricted. After the American Revolution, southern states passed laws making it difficult for enslaved Africans to achieve freedom. In addition, state laws explicitly denied the vote to free African Americans. The upper tier of southern states adopted the North Carolina system requiring that free African Americans register with state and local governments and wear shoulder patches reading "free." Free blacks were denied the rights to jury trials, to obtain legal counsel, and to testify in court. Although the American Revolution promised political equality and liberty to "free whites," it resulted in greater restrictions being placed on free blacks in southern states.[82] In northern states, free African Americans were denied the right to vote except in Massachusetts, New Hampshire, Vermont, and Maine. Despite the work of James

Forten, an African American and Revolutionary War veteran, to gain equal rights under the protection of the U.S. Constitution, most northern states denied blacks equal protection in the court system and created segregated public institutions.[83]

Blacks were specifically denied U.S. citizenship and the political rights recognized in the Declaration of Independence and the Constitution by the U.S. Supreme Court in the 1857 Dred Scott decision. As a result of a complicated set of events, Dred Scott, an African American, sued to win recognition as a free person, a citizen of the state of Missouri, and a U.S. citizen. Writing for the majority, Chief Justice Roger Taney argued that the Declaration of Independence and the U.S. Constitution were not intended to protect the political rights of blacks. In addition, U.S. citizenship could be achieved only through naturalization, birth on U.S. soil, or birth to an American father. Blacks were specifically excluded from naturalized citizenship by the 1790 Naturalization Act. Also, Taney argued that citizenship resulting from native birth or birth to an American father included only those born into a class that qualified for rights under the Constitution. Blacks, Taney maintained, were not born into a class that qualified for these rights; and therefore even if they were native-born, they still did not qualify for U.S. citizenship.[84]

What about allegiance to state and federal governments? Taney added another link in the chain of denial of black rights. He argued that native-born blacks owed allegiance to state and federal governments even though they could not be U.S. citizens. In other words, blacks had to obey the government but could not exercise the political rights that accompanied full citizenship.[85]

After the Civil War, citizenship for former enslaved Africans became a heated topic. Under the 1790 Naturalization Act, freed slaves not born in the United States were denied citizenship because they were not "white." The Civil Rights Act of 1866 declared that all "persons born in the United States . . . [are] declared to be citizens of the United States." Those excluded from native-born citizenship by this legislation were "Indians not taxed." Most Native Americans had to wait until the 1920s to qualify as native-born U.S. citizens.[86]

During the so-called radical reconstruction period following the Civil War, the Naturalization Act of 1870 was passed; it would have been unimaginable to previous generations of "white" Americans. The Naturalization Act of 1870 extended U.S. citizenship to "aliens of African nativity and to persons of African descent." Senator Charles Sumner wanted the word *white* to be removed from naturalization laws and racial equality to be instituted for citizenship, but other radical Republicans were not willing to go that far. Therefore, Africans and African Americans gained the right to U.S. citizenship, but immigrant Asians and Native Americans were still excluded.[87]

The Fourteenth Amendment: Citizenship and Education

Ratified in 1868, the Fourteenth Amendment with its clause providing equal protection under the laws has had an enormous impact on public schools. Equal educational opportunity is a right provided by the equal protection clause. The interpretation of the Fourteenth Amendment, like many other aspects of the Constitution, has undergone many twists and turns, including first allowing school segregation and then later declaring segregation unconstitutional. Section 1 of the Fourteenth Amendment provides constitutional acknowledgment for the granting of U.S. citizenship to native-born blacks according to the 1866 Civil Rights Act and the later granting of naturalized citizenship according to the 1870 Naturalization Act. In addition, section 1 protects all U.S. citizens from the abridgment of their rights by state governments:

> Section 1. *All persons born or naturalized in the United States, and subject to jurisdiction thereof, are citizens of the United States and the State wherein they reside.* No State shall make or enforce any law which shall abridge the privileges or immunities of citizens of the United States; nor shall any State deprive any person of life, liberty, or property, without due process of law; nor deny to any person within its jurisdiction the equal protection of the laws.[88]

In 1896 the protection provided under the Fourteenth Amendment was severely restricted by a U.S. Supreme Court decision that declared segregation of blacks from whites, including segregation of schools, constitutional. The 1896 decision involved Homer Plessy, who was one-eighth black and seven-eighths white and had been arrested for refusing to ride in the "colored" coach of a train, as required by Louisiana law. At issue was the last clause of the first section of the Fourteenth Amendment, which guarantees that no state government shall "deny to any person within its jurisdiction the equal protection of the laws."

Do segregated public facilities, including segregated schools, deny "equal protection of the laws"? In the 1896 *Plessy* decision, the Supreme Court ruled that segregation did not create a badge of inferiority if segregated and "white" facilities were equal and the law was reasonable. In establishing the "separate but equal doctrine," the Supreme Court failed to clearly define what constitutes equal facilities and what is reasonable. Concurrent with the "separate but equal ruling," the citizenship rights of African Americans in the 1880s and 1890s swiftly disappeared in southern states as state laws curtailed the right of black citizens to vote, created segregated public institutions, and restricted judicial rights. Full citizenship for African Americans was not achieved until the 1950s and 1960s, when federal voting rights and civil rights acts made it possible for black Americans to experience political equality and the right to vote like other U.S. citizens.

The Great Crusade for Literacy

Despite school segregation and harassment from the white population, the African American population of the United States made one of the greatest educational advancements in the history of education. Denied an education by law in slave states and facing unequal educational opportunities in free states, only 7 percent of the African American population was literate in 1863. Within a ninety-year period, the literacy rate jumped to 90 percent.

After the Civil War, former slaves struggled to establish schools, and in many cases they were assisted by African American and missionary teachers from the North. In Reconstruction conventions following the Civil War, blacks fought for the establishment of state school systems. In the words of W. E. B. Du Bois, "Public education for all at public expense was, in the South, a Negro idea."[89] In the early 1870s, black children were enrolled in school systems at percentages higher than those for whites, but by the 1880s this began to change as whites exerted greater control over the state political systems and passed discriminatory laws. By the 1890s, as a consequence of sharecropping and other forms of economic exploitation and discriminatory laws, many blacks found themselves living in conditions that were close to slavery.

During and immediately after the Civil War, former slaves took the initiative in establishing schools. The first of these efforts was made by a black teacher, Mary Peake, who organized a school in 1861 at Fortress Monroe, Virginia.[90] The role of freed slaves in establishing schools was recorded by the first national superintendent of schools for the Freedman's Bureau, John W. Alvord. Based on his travels through the South in 1865, Alvord's first general report for the Freedman's Bureau in 1866 described former slaves' efforts at self-education. Everywhere in the South, he found ex-slaves studying elementary textbooks. He described a school in North Carolina organized by two freed slaves with 150 students in attendance. An illustration in *Harper's Weekly* in 1866 showed a large classroom full of freed slaves and a black teacher in the Zion School in Charleston, South Carolina. The administrators and teachers of the school were African Americans, and the average daily attendance was 720 students.[91]

By the middle of the 1870s, differing ideas about education were struggling for dominance in the South. Because of their need for children as farm laborers, planters resisted most attempts to expand educational opportunities for black children. Nevertheless, former slaves were struggling for an education that would improve their economic and political positions in southern society. Often former slaves wanted practical knowledge that would help them deal with contracts and with weights and measurements. Missionaries from the North wanted to provide an education that emphasized morality. There were groups of white southerners who believed that the expansion of education was necessary for the industrialization of the South. These white southerners supported schooling for African Americans as a means of teaching them industrial habits and keeping them on the lowest rungs of southern society. For southerners who supported industrialization, blacks represented a potential source of cheap labor who, unlike northern workers, would not form unions.[92]

Within the black community in the 1890s, divisions developed over how to pursue the struggle for education. This division is most often associated with two major black leaders—Booker T. Washington and W. E. B. Du Bois. Washington accepted compromise with white demands and the establishment of segregated industrial education. Du Bois maintained that no compromise with white demands should be made and that black education should be concerned with educating the future leaders of the black community. To a certain extent, however, the preceding statements oversimplify their positions. Their hopes for schooling were interwoven with their hopes for their race, the realities of southern society, and their political strategies. In the history of schooling, Washington is most often associated with the establishment of segregated schools, whereas Du Bois was instrumental in the 1909 founding of the National Association for the Advancement of Colored People (NAACP), which has led the successful struggle against school segregation in the United States.

The speech that most clearly outlined the southern compromise and the role of blacks in the developing industrial order was given by Washington at the International Exposition in Atlanta in 1895. Washington tried to convince his all-white audience of the economic value of African Americans to the new industrial South by beginning his speech with a story about a ship lost at sea whose crew was dying of thirst. The ship encountered a friendly vessel, which signaled for the crew to cast down their buckets in the surrounding water. After receiving the signal four times, the captain finally cast down his bucket to find fresh water from the mouth of the Amazon River. This, Washington told his audience, was what the South needed to do to build its industrial might: cast down its buckets and use black workers. Washington continued his speech by outlining the advantages of black workers for the South. Of primary importance was that the South would not need to rely on foreign workers. "To those of the white race," Washington exclaimed, "who look to the incoming of those of foreign birth and strange tongue and habits for the prosperity of the South, were I permitted I would repeat what I say to my own race, 'Cast down your bucket where you are.'"[93] Washington continued by extolling the virtues of black workers and their faithfulness during the years of slavery. He claimed that blacks could show a devotion that no foreign workers would ever display and called for an interlacing of the interests of black and white southerners.

Then, in one sentence that would become famous in both the South and North, Washington presented the compromise he saw as necessary for winning white southerners to his argument: "In all things that are purely social we can be as separate as the fingers, yet one as the hand in all things essential to mutual progress." Here was the great compromise—acceptance by blacks of social segregation for the opportunity to participate in the new industrial order of the South. As Washington explained in the conclusion of his speech, he believed that once the economic value of blacks had been established, social acceptance would follow. "No race," he argued, "that has anything to contribute to the markets of the world is long in any degree ostracized." In Washington's mind, "the opportunity to earn a dollar in a factory just now is worth infinitely more than the opportunity to spend a dollar in an opera-house."[94]

Washington believed that African Americans would be able to prove themselves economically by receiving the right form of education. Before that speech, Washington had received recognition throughout the South for his establishment of the Tuskegee Institute. The Tuskegee idea originated in Washington's educational experiences at the Hampton Institute. Washington had been born into slavery and after the Civil War attended Hampton, which had been established by General Samuel Armstrong, whose missionary parents had organized an industrial school for natives in Hawaii.

Washington was strongly influenced by General Armstrong's vision of the role of education in adjusting former slaves to their new place in the southern social order. Armstrong believed that the purpose of education was to adjust African Americans to a subordinate position in southern society. He also believed that blacks should be denied the right to vote and that they should be segregated— in short, that they should not be granted the same civil equality as whites.[95]

As part of the process of adjusting African Americans to permanent subordination in society, Armstrong argued that the primary purpose of educating African Americans was the development of "proper" work habits and moral behavior. This argument was based on a belief that "savages" were mentally capable but lacked a developed morality. Historian James Anderson quotes Armstrong: "Most savage people are not like 'dumb driven cattle'; yet their life is little better than that of brutes because the moral nature is dormant."[96]

As Armstrong envisioned the process, Hampton graduates would become teachers who would educate the rest of the African American population in the moral and work habits taught at Hampton. Taking its cue from attitudes regarding the education of Native Americans, Hampton was to be the agent for civilizing freed slaves. With Hampton teachers spread across the South, Armstrong believed, African Americans would be "civilized" and brought to accept their subordinate place in society.

The key to the civilizing process advocated by Armstrong and incorporated into Hampton's educational program was hard work. Armstrong believed that hard work was the first principle of civilized life. Through hard work, according to Armstrong, people learned the right moral habits. He believed that African Americans needed to be educated in the value of hard work if they were to assume their proper place in southern society. Consequently, the curriculum at Hampton emphasized hard manual labor as part of teacher training. In addition, Armstrong believed that classical studies developed only vanity in black students and should not be part of the teacher training curriculum for black students. Therefore, rather than studying the traditional liberal arts, Hampton male students worked in a sawmill, on the school farm, as dishwashers and busboys in the kitchen, as waiters in the dining room, and as houseboys in the living quarters. Hampton female students sewed, cooked, scrubbed, and plowed fields on the school's farm.[97] According to many southern whites, the type of work that Hampton students performed was the type of work African Americans should perform. In the context of Armstrong's larger philosophy, the occupational training at Hampton reflected the subordinated roles African Americans would play in the new economic order. By learning the habits and moral values associated with doing these tasks, Hampton graduates, Armstrong believed, would teach other African Americans the habits and values required to make these tasks lifelong occupations.

Therefore, when General Armstrong and Booker T. Washington used the term "industrial education," they meant primarily the development of good work and moral habits as opposed to learning a particular vocational skill. Historian James Anderson in his history of black education reproduces photographs of prospective female teachers at Hampton plowing and tilling a farm field. These future teachers were not being educated to be farmers; they were learning the work habits that Armstrong wanted his graduates to pass on to their students.

Armstrong's philosophy of education guided Washington in the establishment of Tuskegee. Washington scorned the traditional forms of education brought south by northern teachers. He felt that traditional education was useless and left the student with false promises for a better life. In his autobiography, *Up from Slavery,* he tells the story of mothers who taught their daughters the skill of laundering. "Later," Washington says, "these girls entered the public schools and remained there perhaps six or eight years. When the public-school course was finally finished, they wanted more costly dresses, more costly hats and shoes." Washington summarizes the effects of a traditional public school education: "In a word, while their wants had been increased, their ability to supply their wants had not been increased in the same degree. On the other hand, their six or eight years of book education had weaned them away from the occupation of their mothers." In another situation, Washington criticizes a young man fresh out of high school who, "sitting down in a one-room cabin, with grease on his clothing, filth all round him, and weeds in the yard and garden, engaged in studying French grammar."[98] Washington's message was heard throughout the North and South. It was particularly welcomed by those trying to organize the southern school system. The idea of segregated industrial education that stressed proper moral and work habits also received support from major educational conferences and private foundations. This support made segregated education a permanent fixture in southern states until the 1950s and 1960s. In Henry Allen Bullock's words,

> The industrial curriculum to which many Negro children were exposed, supposedly designed to meet their needs, reflected the life that accompanied their status at that time. They had always farmed. The curriculum aimed to make them better farmers. Negro women had a virtual monopoly on laundering, and Negro men had [worked] largely as mechanics. The industrial curriculum was designed to change this only in so far that Negroes were trained to perform these services better.[99]

As James Anderson tells the story, segregated industrial education as the model for black southern education received support from southern industrialists and northern philanthropists. For instance, steel magnate and philanthropist Andrew Carnegie gave the first major endowment to Tuskegee because he believed that educating black workers was necessary to maintain the United States' position in the world economy. Carnegie stressed the importance of maintaining proper work habits among the black southern population. In comparing the black workforce in South Africa to that in the United States, Carnegie wrote, "We should be in the position in which South Africa is today but for the faithful, placable, peaceful, industrious, lovable colored man; for industriousness and peaceful he is compared with any other body of colored men on the earth."[100]

Indeed, southern industrialists welcomed the idea of segregated industrial education because it promised cheap labor and the avoidance of labor unions. One of the things Washington argued in his Atlanta speech was that the industrialists in the South had to choose between immigrant labor and black labor, and that the problem with immigrant laborers was that they formed labor unions. For instance, southern railroad magnate and Tuskegee supporter William H. Baldwin Jr. argued that for the South to compete in international markets, it would have to reject the high wages demanded by white labor unions and rely on the labor of African Americans.[101]

Despite some southern industrialists and educational leaders supporting segregated industrial education for blacks, government financial support declined rapidly after the 1870s. In his classic study *The Education of the Negro in the American Social Order,* Horace Mann Bond collected information on school expenditures from a variety of southern states. For instance, a table illustrating spending in Alabama shows that from 1875 to 1876, expenditure per capita was higher for blacks than for whites. This relationship existed until the 1880s. By 1900 the situation had so far reversed that the per capita expenditure for whites was four to five times higher than that for blacks. Bond found similar statistics throughout the South.[102]

Therefore, by 1900, African Americans in the South faced a segregated public school system that made few expenditures for the education of their children. The major resistance to increased school expenditures for black students came from planters, who considered education a direct threat to their use of black children as agricultural laborers. The concerns of southern planters were similar to those expressed by farmers in Texas and California regarding the education of the children of Mexican American farmworkers. Southern planters foresaw the possibility that schooling would cause African Americans either to leave menial agricultural work or to demand higher wages. In addition, planters depended on the use of child labor and consequently opposed compulsory education laws. Some planters forced schools to begin their school year in December, after the harvest. In addition, they fought efforts to increase state financing of schools.[103]

By 1875, according to James Anderson, the planters' efforts halted the expansion of schools for African Americans in the South. Between 1880 and 1900, Anderson writes, "the number of black children of school age increased 25 percent, but the proportion attending public school fell."[104] Consequently, by 1900 the dream of education for African Americans in the South was shattered as the majority of public expenditures went to support white segregated schools, and large numbers of black children were kept working in the fields. In 1900, 49.3 percent of African American boys between the ages of ten and fifteen were working, while 30.6 percent of African American girls in the same age category were employed. The majority of these children, 404,225 out of 516,276, were employed as unskilled farm labor.[105] In the end, the segregation of public schools denied education to large numbers of black children.

ISSUES REGARDING PUERTO RICAN CITIZENSHIP

Puerto Rico became a colony of the United States in 1898 at the conclusion of the Spanish-American War. The war represented the final demise of the Spanish empire in the Americas. The events leading up to the Spanish-American War were primarily centered in Cuba, where, prior to the outbreak of the war, a liberation army composed of Cuban rebels revolted against Spanish rule and economic domination by foreign sugar and tobacco industries. The liberation army marched through the countryside torching plantations and plunging Cuba into economic chaos. The Spanish response was brutal: 200,000 Spanish troops were sent to Cuba to stop the liberation army, and the infamous concentration camp order was issued. The concentration camp order moved women, children, and men from villages into garrison towns as a method of cutting off all support to the rebel army. Citizens were executed or their property was confiscated if they were found traveling outside garrison towns without a passport.

The U.S. government was interested in the rebellion from several perspectives. First, there was an interest in reducing Spanish influence in the Americas. Within this context, the government was sympathetic to the liberation army's goal of ousting the Spanish. Second, the government was interested in protecting American-owned sugar and tobacco plantations. For this purpose, the U.S. government wanted to establish a stable democratic government that would protect the property interests of foreign investors. As a result of this concern, the U.S. government was not interested in the liberation army's ruling Cuba at the conclusion of the war. Third, the U.S. government was interested in establishing military bases in the Caribbean. But because of the politics surrounding U.S. entry into the war, Puerto Rico (rather than Cuba) became a colony of the United States. Consequently, for military purposes, Guantánamo Bay, Cuba, was retained by the United States, and military bases were established in Puerto Rico.

The event that sparked a congressional declaration of war was the sinking of the battleship *Maine* in the Havana harbor on February 15, 1898. The immediate reaction was to claim that the sinking had been caused by the Spanish, but a later investigation found that a coal fire on the ship had caused a powder magazine to explode. Even though the Spanish might not have been responsible for the sinking, "Remember the *Maine*" became the rallying call for the war.

As a result of the rebel war and the sinking of the *Maine,* President William McKinley asked Congress for a joint resolution authorizing intervention in Cuba. The resolution that Congress passed called on the Spanish to abandon all claims to governing Cuba and to remove all Spanish forces from the island. An important part of the resolution stated that the United States had no intention of exercising sovereignty over Cuba. Spain considered the resolution a declaration of war. The war then quickly escalated to global proportions. On one side of the world, the U.S. Navy sailed into Manila in the Philippines. On the other side of the world, American troops joined the liberation army to oust the Spanish from Cuba. On October 18, 1898, U.S. forces, which had invaded Puerto Rico less than three months previously, raised the U.S. flag in San Juan and declared the end of Spanish rule and the beginning of U.S. dominion.

Although events in Cuba were the main cause for the United States initiating the conflict, the final treaty focused on other Spanish territorial possessions. The U.S. Congress had already declared its intention not to rule Cuba; consequently, the United States demanded that Spain secede Puerto Rico, the island of Guam in the central Pacific, and the Philippines. With the signing of the treaty on December 10, 1898, the U.S. military gained strategic bases in the Caribbean, the

Pacific, and the Far East. In 1901, before relinquishing Cuba, the U.S. Congress passed legislation dictating that Cuba sell or lease lands for naval stations to the United States. This paved the way for the United States to establish a naval base at Guantánamo Bay.[106]

As a conquered people, Puerto Rican Americans have been divided over the issues of independence and U.S. citizenship. In 1915 a debate over citizenship was sparked by the introduction of legislation into the U.S. Congress to grant citizenship to Puerto Rican Americans. Speaking before the House of Representatives in 1916, Puerto Rican leader Muñoz Rivera requested that Congress let the Puerto Rican people vote on whether they wanted U.S. citizenship. Ignoring this plea, Congress passed the Jones Act, which was signed into law by President Woodrow Wilson in 1917.[107] The Jones Act granted U.S. citizenship to Puerto Ricans and obligated Puerto Rican Americans to serve in the U.S. military, but it denied them the right to vote in national elections. Like Native Americans in Indian Territory who were granted citizenship in 1901 as part of the process of abolishing tribal governments, many Puerto Rican Americans did not welcome this grant of citizenship.

Puerto Rican American Educational Issues

Educational policy in Puerto Rico followed a pattern similar to that of Native Americans and Mexican Americans. The policy was based on a desire to win the loyalty of a conquered people and stabilize control of Puerto Rico as part of a broader strategy for maintaining U.S. influence in the Caribbean and Central America. Puerto Rico; Guantánamo Bay, Cuba; and the Panama Canal Zone were the linchpins of this strategy.[108] The use of education as part of the colonization of Puerto Rico was explicitly stated in 1902 in the annual report of the second commissioner of education, Samuel Lindsay: "Colonization carried forward by the armies of war is vastly more costly than that carried forward by the armies of peace, whose outpost and garrisons are the public schools of the advancing nation."[109]

Consequently, U.S. educational policy in Puerto Rico emphasized building loyalty to the U.S. flag and institutions, as well as deculturalization. The patriotic emphasis was similar to the Americanization programs directed at Native Americans. As U.S. and state educational policies attempted to strip Native Americans of their languages and cultures, U.S. educational policy in Puerto Rico attempted to replace Spanish with English as the majority language and introduce children to the dominant U.S. culture.

When considering U.S. educational policy in Puerto Rico, it is important to understand that the citizens of Puerto Rico did not ask to become part of the United States. The goal of the independence movement in Puerto Rico throughout the nineteenth century was independence from Spain, not cession to the United States. As it had done in Cuba, Spain attempted to crush any attempts to gain liberation from its rule. Typical of the independence movement was the Puerto Rican Revolutionary Committee, which in 1863 marched under the banner "Liberty or Death. Long Live Free Puerto Rico." In addition, in 1897, the year before the outbreak of the Spanish-American War, Spain declared Puerto Rico an autonomous state. The residents of the former colony of Spain quickly established a constitutional republican form of government; however, Spain still appointed the governor, who had limited power. The newly independent government assumed power in July 1898, just before the landing of U.S. troops. Therefore, after their long struggle for independence, which the invading U.S. military quickly snatched away, Puerto Rican citizens did not welcome subjugation by the U.S. government. Anger among Puerto Rican Americans was heightened when the United States immediately placed them under the control of a military government operated by the War Department. Within less than a year, Puerto Rico went from being an autonomous state to being ruled by a military dictatorship. Puerto Rican resistance to U.S. control, while not so strong as it was in the early twentieth century, continues today.

The strong Puerto Rican independence movement contributed to a wave of resistance to the educational policies designed for Americanization and deculturalization. A list of these policies was compiled by Aida Negron De Montilla in her book *Americanization in Puerto Rico and the Public School System, 1900–1930*. Here is a summary of the list, followed by an explanation of how these policies evolved. In examining the list, consider the items in the broad context of how a nation can use schools to impose its will on a conquered people. This is a case study in an attempt to dominate through education and in resistance to that domination. Some of the items in the list are presented as "attempts" because of the high level of resistance to these plans by the Puerto Rican people:

Summary of Americanization Policies in Public Schools in Puerto Rico

- Required celebration of U.S. patriotic holidays, such as the Fourth of July, which had not been celebrated prior to conquest.
- Patriotic exercises designed to create allegiance to the United States, such as pledging allegiance to the U.S. flag and studying important historical figures of U.S. history.
- Replacing local textbooks and curricula with ones reflecting the way of life in the United States.
- Attempts to expel teachers and students who engaged in anti–United States activities.
- Attempts to use teachers from the United States instead of local teachers.
- Introduction of organizations, such as the Boy Scouts of America, to promote allegiance to the United States.
- Attempts to replace Spanish with English as the language of instruction.[110]

The first U.S. commissioner of education in Puerto Rico, Martin Grove Brumbaugh, captured the general thrust of these policies when he wrote in a preface to a history book, "President McKinley declared to the writer that it was his desire 'to put the conscience of the American people in the islands of the sea.'"[111] Brumbaugh was appointed in 1900, when military rule was replaced with a colonial government established by Congress under the Foraker Act. With the passage of the Foraker Act, in effect between 1900 and 1917, the president was given the power to appoint a commissioner of education for Puerto Rico. Although the military was in control, the educational system was organized along the lines of a U.S. model. In addition, the War Department created a commission to recommend educational policies for the island. The commission's report became a guide for Brumbaugh and the next six commissioners of education. The report outlined the basic methods of Americanization. It recommended that Puerto Rico have "the same system of education and the same character of books" as the United States, that teachers be "Americans," and that students be instructed in the English language.[112] The commission's attitude about the power of education was similar to the attitude of those who believed that Native Americans could be Americanized in one generation. At times the language of the report gives the school an almost mystical power: "Put an American schoolhouse in every valley and upon every hilltop in Porto [sic] Rico," the report states, "and in these places . . . American schoolteachers, and the cloud of ignorance will disappear as the fog flies before the morning sun."[113]

Although the report stressed Americanization, it cannot be considered simply a cynical statement by a conquering power. The commission found that only 10 percent of the population was literate. The commission's report and the later actions by the commissioners of education were undertaken in the spirit of trying to help the Puerto Rican people. The problem was the assumption that U.S. institutions, customs, and beliefs were the best in the world and that they should be imposed. The attempt to help was accompanied by an attitude of moral and cultural superiority.

During his short tenure (1900–1901), Brumbaugh began the process of Americanization. In a letter to school supervisors, he stated, "No school has done its duty unless it has impressed devout patriotism upon the hearts and minds of all the children."[114] He recruited teachers from the United States; most of them spoke only English, which meant their instruction was not bilingual. Every school on the island was given an American flag; most of the flags were donated by the Lafayette Post, Army of the Republic, New York City. Raising the U.S. flag was used to signal the commencement of classes. Patriotic exercises were organized in the school; children were taught U.S. national songs such as "America," "Hail, Columbia," and "The Star-Spangled Banner."[115]

Within only four years of Puerto Rico's being an autonomous nation, Puerto Rican children were being educated to shift their allegiance from Puerto Rico to another country. The introduction of George Washington's birthday as a school holiday was part of this process. Schools were told to impress on students Washington's "noble traits and broad statesmanship." Exercises were organized that consisted of singing U.S. patriotic songs and reading Washington's speeches. In San Juan, twenty-five thousand students were involved in the celebration. In Brumbaugh's words, "These exercises have done much to Americanize the island, much more than any other single agency."[116]

Letters were sent to teachers instructing them to celebrate on June 14, 1901, the creation of the U.S. flag. Teachers were instructed to engage students in a celebration of the flag beginning with a flag salute followed by singing the U.S.

national anthem. After this opening exercise, teachers were instructed to have students give speeches, recitations, and patriotic readings and to sing patriotic songs and march to band music.

Learning English was considered an important part of the Americanization process. In any language are embedded the customs and values of a particular culture. Like Native Americans, Puerto Rican Americans were taught English to build patriotism. In his annual report, Brumbaugh states, "The first English many of them knew was that of our national songs."[117] Although many teachers from the United States were not capable of conducting bilingual instruction, Brumbaugh believed Spanish should be taught along with English. But Brumbaugh also believed teachers from the United States should be placed in kindergarten and elementary schools to begin English instruction as early as possible. During Brumbaugh's tenure, Puerto Rican resistance to U.S. educational policies began to appear in the magazine *La Educación Moderna* in a 1900 article, "English in the Schools." The article attacked "the spirit of . . . supremacy with which the English language is being imposed."[118]

The second commissioner of education, Samuel Lindsay (1902–1904), introduced more policies designed to educate Puerto Rican children into the U.S. way of life. An important part of his program was sending Puerto Rican teachers and students to the United States to learn the English language and U.S. culture. These trips were designed to prepare Puerto Rican teachers to teach about the United States when they returned to the classroom.[119] Combined with the patriotic celebrations initiated during Brumbaugh's tenure, the program of study abroad was intended to inculcate the values of the dominant society in the United States.

Lindsay also began to tighten policies regarding the teaching of English. First he included an examination in English as part of the general examination for gaining a teacher's certificate.[120] Consider the impact of this requirement in the context of your own country. Imagine that you are a teacher and suddenly, within four years of conquest, you are being examined for your knowledge of the language of the conquering country!

The language issue was taken one step further by Lindsay's successor, Roland Falkner. Falkner's impact on language policies extended far beyond his term (1904–1907). Falkner ordered that instruction past the first grade be conducted in English. The major problem he encountered was that most Puerto Rican teachers did not know enough English to conduct instruction in that language. Consequently, as an incentive to improve their English skills, Falkner ordered that teachers be classified according to their scores on the English examination. In addition, the government provided English instruction for Puerto Rican teachers. It was impossible to convert an entire school system from one language to another in a short time, so the results of the language policy were spotty. The magazine *La Educación Moderna* launched an attack on the language policies. One Puerto Rican teacher complained in the magazine that the instruction given by American teachers and that given by Puerto Rican teachers in English was having a disastrous effect on the students. The newspaper *La Democracia* editorialized that nothing could be done about the situation until the Department of Education was controlled by Puerto Rican Americans.[121]

While the language issue continued as a source of friction between Puerto Rican teachers and U.S. authorities, the next commissioner of education, Edwin Dexter (1907–1912), tried to increase the significance of patriotic celebrations in the schools. Although the Fourth of July did not fall within the school calendar, Dexter dressed a group of schoolchildren in red, white, and blue and marched them through the streets of San Juan under a large patriotic banner. Also, Dexter considered the celebration of Washington's and Lincoln's birthdays and Memorial Day to be an important means of teaching English because all events were conducted in that language. Adding to these activities, Dexter introduced military drill into the schools.[122] All of these efforts followed the typical nineteenth-century pattern of using education as a form of cultural imperialism.

CONCLUSION: SETTING THE STAGE
FOR THE GREAT CIVIL RIGHTS MOVEMENT

Issues of segregation and language would continue to haunt American education into the twenty-first century. Eventually the civil rights movement of the 1950s and 1960s would target the problem of segregated schools. However, multiculturalism and language policies would continue as unresolved issues in efforts to interpret the common school ideal.

Notes

1. Quoted in Rogers Smith, *Civic Ideals: Conflicting Visions of Citizenship in U.S. History* (New Haven: Yale University Press, 1997), p. 205.
2. Ibid.
3. Ibid.
4. John S. D. Eisenhower, *So Far from God: The U.S. War with Mexico 1846–1848* (New York: Anchor Books, 1989), p. xvii.
5. Ibid., p. 208.
6. Ibid., p. 214.
7. David Montejano, *Anglos and Mexicans in the Making of Texas, 1836–1986* (Austin: University of Texas Press, 1987), p. 311.
8. See Ruben Donato, *The Other Struggle for Equal Schools: Mexican Americans during the Civil Rights Era* (Albany: State University of New York, 1997), p. 15.
9. Eisenhower, *So Far from God,* p. xv.
10. Montejano, *Anglos and Mexicans,* p. 25.
11. Ibid., pp. 28–29.
12. Quoted in ibid., p. 29.
13. Quoted in ibid., p. 28.
14. Ibid., p. 34.
15. Ibid., p. 84.
16. Ibid., pp. 53–56.
17. Ibid., pp. 83–84.
18. Guadalupe San Miguel Jr., *"Let All of Them Take Heed": Mexican Americans and the Campaign for Educational Equality in Texas, 1910–1981* (Austin: University of Texas Press, 1987), pp. 6–7.

19. Leonard Pitt, *The Decline of the Californios: A Social History of the Spanish-Speaking California, 1846–1890* (Berkeley: University of California Press, 1968), p. 226.
20. Ibid., pp. 225–226.
21. San Miguel, *"Let All of Them Take Heed,"* p. 10.
22. Ibid., p. 11.
23. Montejano, *Anglos and Mexicans,* p. 180.
24. Quoted in ibid., p. 188.
25. Quoted in ibid., p. 193.
26. Gilbert Gonzalez, *Chicano Education in the Era of Segregation* (Philadelphia: Balch Institute Press, 1990), p. 108.
27. Ronald Takaki, *A Different Mirror: A History of Multicultural America* (Boston: Little, Brown, 1993), pp. 191–225.
28. Smith, *Civic Ideals,* p. 317.
29. Ronald Takaki, *Strangers from a Different Shore: A History of Asian Americans* (New York: Penguin Books, 1989), pp. 21–79.
30. See Sucheng Chan, *Asian Americans: An Interpretative History* (New York: Twayne Publishers, 1993), p. 48.
31. Takaki, *A Different Mirror,* p. 207.
32. Smith, *Civic Ideals,* p. 312.
33. Chan, *Asian Americans,* p. 54.
34. Quoted in Takaki, *Strangers from a Different Shore,* p. 205.
35. Smith, *Civic Ideals,* p. 359.
36. Quoted in ibid., p. 359.
37. Quoted in ibid., p. 360.
38. Quoted in ibid., p. 363.
39. Quoted in ibid., p. 362.
40. Quoted in ibid., pp. 360–361.
41. Chan, *Asian Americans,* pp. 93–94.
42. Robert G. Lee, *Orientals: Asian Americans in Popular Culture* (Philadelphia: Temple University Press, 1999), p. 8.
43. Victor Low, *The Unimpressible Race: A Century of Educational Struggle by the Chinese in San Francisco* (San Francisco: East/West Publishing, 1982), p. 48.
44. Ibid., p. 61.
45. Ibid., p. 62.
46. Ibid., p. 67.
47. Charles M. Wollenberg, *All Deliberate Speed: Segregation and Exclusion in California Schools, 1855–1975* (Berkeley: University of California Press, 1976), p. 53.
48. Chan, *Asian Americans,* p. 58.
49. Ibid., p. 59.
50. Wollenberg, *All Deliberate Speed,* pp. 53–60.
51. Takaki, *A Different Mirror,* p. 80.
52. Smith, *Civic Ideals,* pp. 318–319.
53. "Citizenship for Indians in Indian Territory, March 3, 1901," in *Documents of United States Indian Policy,* 2nd ed., ed. Francis Paul Prucha (Lincoln: University of Nebraska Press, 1990), p. 199.
54. "Indian Citizenship Act, June 2, 1924," ibid., p. 218.
55. Ibid.
56. "Indian Commissioner Mix on Reservation Policy," ibid., p. 92.
57. "Indian Commissioner Lea on Reservation Policy," ibid., p. 82.
58. Ibid.

59. "Indian Commissioner Mix," p. 95.
60. Jon Reyhner and Jeanne Eder, *A History of Indian Education* (Billings: Eastern Montana College, 1989), p. 38.
61. Ibid., p. 39.
62. "Report of the Indian Peace Commission, January 7, 1868," in Prucha, *Documents of United States Indian Policy,* p. 107.
63. Reyhner and Eder, *History of Indian Education,* pp. 79–80.
64. James D. Anderson, *The Education of Blacks in the South, 1860–1935* (Chapel Hill: University of North Carolina Press, 1988), p. 34.
65. Quoted in Reyhner and Eder, *History of Indian Education,* p. 80.
66. Ibid.
67. "Indian Commissioner Price on Civilizing Indians, October 24, 1881," in Prucha, *Documents of United States Indian Policy,* p. 155.
68. Quoted in Reyhner and Eder, *History of Indian Education,* p. 81.
69. Ibid.
70. Ibid., p. 86.
71. "Use of English in the Indian Schools, September 21, 1887," in Prucha, *Documents of United States Indian Policy,* p. 175.
72. "Inculcation of Patriotism in Indian Schools, December 10, 1889," ibid., p. 181.
73. Ibid., pp. 180–181.
74. Ibid., p. 181.
75. General T. J. Morgan, "Indian Education," *Bureau of Education, Bulletin No. 1, 1889* (Washington, DC: U.S. Government Printing Office, 1890), p. 4.
76. Ibid., p. 5.
77. Ibid., p. 9.
78. Ibid., p. 12.
79. Ibid.
80. Ibid., p. 16.
81. Ibid., p. 17.
82. Smith, *Civic Ideals,* p. 179.
83. Ibid., p. 179.
84. Ibid., pp. 263–271.
85. Ibid., p. 267.
86. Ibid., p. 306.
87. Ibid., pp. 286–312, and Chan, *Asian Americans,* p. 92.
88. "Constitution of the United States," *Microsoft® Encarta® 98 Encyclopedia.* © 1993–1997 Microsoft Corporation. All rights reserved.
89. Anderson, *Education of Blacks,* p. 6.
90. Ibid., p. 7.
91. Ibid., pp. 6–8.
92. See Leon F. Litwack, *Been in the Storm So Long: The Aftermath of Slavery* (New York: Vintage Books, 1980), pp. 450–501.
93. Booker T. Washington, "Up from Slavery," in *Three Negro Classics,* ed. John Hope Franklin (New York: Avon Books, 1965), p. 147.
94. Ibid., p. 149.
95. Ibid., p. 36.
96. Anderson, *Education of Blacks,* p. 40.
97. Ibid., p. 55.
98. Washington, "Up from Slavery," pp. 77, 94.

99. Henry Allen Bullock, *A History of Negro Education in the South, from 1619 to the Present* (New York: Praeger, 1970), p. 88.
100. Quoted in Anderson, *Education of Blacks,* p. 91.
101. Ibid., pp. 90–91.
102. Horace Mann Bond, *The Education of the Negro in the American Social Order* (New York: Octagon Books, 1966), p. 153.
103. Anderson, *Education of Blacks,* pp. 22–23.
104. Ibid., p. 23.
105. Ibid., p. 149.
106. Aida Negron De Montilla, *Americanization in Puerto Rico and the Public School System, 1900–1930* (Rio Piedras: Editorial Edil, 1971), pp. 6–79.
107. Ibid., p. 163.
108. Ivan Musicant, *The Banana Wars: A History of the United States Military Intervention in Latin America from the Spanish-American War to the Invasion of Panama* (New York: Macmillan, 1990), p. 2.
109. De Montilla, *Americanization in Puerto Rico,* p. 62.
110. Ibid., pp. xi–xii.
111. Ibid., p. 37.
112. Ibid., pp. 35–36.
113. Ibid., p. 36.
114. Ibid., p. 51.
115. Ibid., pp. 47–48.
116. Ibid., p. 49.
117. Ibid., p. 48.
118. Ibid., p. 58.
119. Ibid., pp. 63–64.
120. Ibid., p. 71.
121. Ibid., pp. 105–106.
122. Ibid., pp. 121–123.

8

Global Migration and the Growth of the Welfare Function of Schools

By the late nineteenth century, the process of globalization would be characterized by the global migration of peoples. This global migration would continue to affect American schools into the twenty-first century.[1] In the late nineteenth century, the United States began to receive large numbers of immigrants from Southern and Eastern Europe. This immigration would occur during a major period of industrialization and urban expansion. Global migration, urbanization, and industrialization would transform the social function of American schools.

In addition to these transformative social changes was growing resistance by African Americans, Native Americans, and Mexican Americans to segregation and discrimination. Combined with concerns about the influx of immigrants, the era was characterized by continuation of the culture wars that had plagued public schools. The culture wars in schools would continue in varying forms into the twenty-first century.

John Dewey, the great educational philosopher of the period, explained the new social functions of the school resulting from global migration, industrialization, and urbanization. Speaking to educators who gathered in 1902 for the annual convention of the National Education Association, he argued that education must provide a "means for bringing people and their ideas and beliefs together, in such ways as will lessen friction and instability, and introduce deeper sympathy and wider understanding." Using the schools as social centers, he argued, would morally uplift the quality of urban living. More important, he considered the school to be a potential clearinghouse of ideas that would interpret to the new urban industrial worker and immigrant the meaning of his or her place in the modern world. The school as social center, Dewey told his audience, "must interpret to [the worker] the intellectual and social meaning of the work in which he is engaged: that is, must reveal its relations to the life and work of the world." For Dewey, therefore, the new role of the school was to serve as an agency providing social services and a community center for immigrants, industrial workers, and urban dwellers.[2]

This chapter will discuss the following educational changes resulting from global migration, industrialization, urbanization, and the resistance to school segregation and discrimination:

- Kindergartens.
- Home economics.
- School cafeterias.
- Playgrounds.
- Summer school.
- Schools as social centers.
- The culture wars.
- Resistance to school segregation and discrimination.

IMMIGRATION FROM SOUTHERN AND EASTERN EUROPE

Until the late 1880s, immigration from Europe was primarily from England, Ireland, and Germany. The Irish and German immigration brought Catholics who sometimes were in conflict with the Protestant majority. Between the late 1880s and 1930s immigration from Southern and Eastern Europe increased the Catholic population and brought larger numbers of Greek and Russian Orthodox and Jews. In addition, the number of spoken languages increased. By 1930 laws restricted the flow of immigrants. The slowdown in immigration continued until the 1960s, when new laws ushered in the most recent period of large-scale immigration.

As shown in Table 8.1, immigration from Southern and Eastern Europe steadily increased from the 1890s to 1930. The statistics for 1910 indicate which countries contributed the most immigrants. In 1910, according to Table 8.1, the Austro-Hungarian empire (after 1920 it was divided into Hungary, Czechoslovakia, Austria, and Yugoslavia) provided the largest number of immigrants (258,737), with Italy being second (215,537) and Russia third (186,792). The numbers for 1930 dramatically show the effect of immigration laws, with the numbers for Hungary, Czechoslovakia, Austria, and Yugoslavia declining to 9,184, Italian immigration declining to 6,203, and Russian immigration to 2,772.

Although there were some immigrants from Asia between the 1880s and 1930s, as indicated in Table 8.2, the numbers from this area did not significantly increase until after the 1960s. Also, the number of immigrants, as indicated in Table 8.3, from the Caribbean and Central and South America remained low between the 1880s and 1930s but increased after the 1960s. The majority of immigrants from other parts of the Americas were from Canada and Mexico. As indicated in Table 8.3, there were few immigrants during this period from Central and South America—for instance, only 3,044 in 1910. There was a steady stream of immigrants from the Caribbean islands with 11,240 in 1910 and 13,800 in 1920.

Therefore, public school Americanization programs between the 1880s and 1930s focused on Southern and Eastern European immigrants. After the upsurge of immigrants resulting from changes in immigration laws in the 1960s, public school programs related to immigration and language began to focus on immigrants from Asia and Central and South America.

DEVELOPING WELFARE FUNCTIONS OF SCHOOLING AND DISCRIMINATION TIME LINE

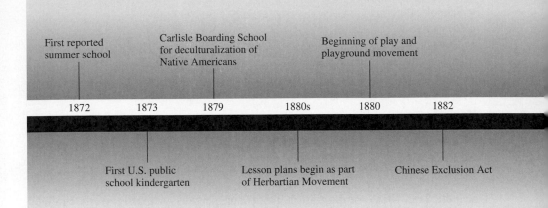

TABLE 8.1 Number of Immigrants from Southern and Eastern Europe by Country and Selected Dates: 1880–1930

Country	1880	1890	1900	1910	1920	1930
Italy	12,354	52,003	100,135	215,537	95,145	6,203
Spain, Portugal, and Greece	1,631	3,960	8,360	37,740	48,009	4,647
Poland		2,177	11,073	Between 1899 and 1919 included with Austria/ Hungary	Between 1899 and 1919 included with Austria/ Hungary	95,089 in 1921	9,231
Russia/ USSR	5,014	35,598	90,787	186,792	1,751	2,772
Romania, Bulgaria, and Turkey in Europe	35	723	6,852	25,287	3,913	2,159
Hungary, Austria, Czechoslovakia (since 1920), Yugoslavia (since 1920)	17,267	56,199	114,847	258,737	5,666	9,184

Source: Compiled from statistics provided in *Historical Statistics of the United States Colonial Times to 1970 Part I* (Washington, DC: U.S. Bureau of the Census, 1975), pp. 105–106.

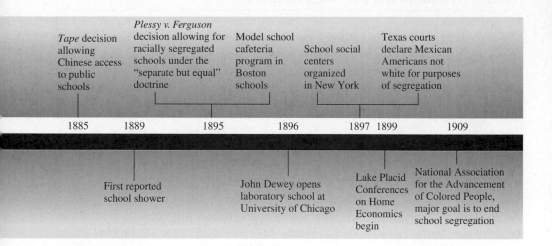

TABLE 8.2 Number of Immigrants from Asia by Country and Selected Dates:1880–1930

Country	1880	1890	1900	1910	1920	1930
China	5,802	1,716	1,240	1,960	2,330	1,589
India	21	43	9	1,696	300	110
Japan	4	691	12,635	2,720	9,432	831
Korea	No record of immigration until 1948	No record of immigration until 1948	No record of immigration until 1948	No record of immigration until 1948	No record of immigration until 1948	No record of immigration until 1948
Turkey in Asia	4	1,126	3,962	15,212	5,033	118

Source: Compiled from statistics provided in *Historical Statistics of the United States Colonial Times to 1970 Part I* (Washington, DC: U.S. Bureau of the Census, 1975), pp. 107–108.

TABLE 8.3 Number of Immigrants from Americas by Country, Region, and Selected Dates:1880–1930

Region	1880	1890	1900	1910	1920	1930
Mexico	492	No records	23	2,680	52,360	12,703
Caribbean Islands	1,851	3,070	4,650	11,240	13,800	5,225
Canada	99,174	183	396	56,555	90,025	65,254
Other America	105	580	166	3,044	6,472	4,922

Source: Compiled from statistics provided in *Historical Statistics of the United States Colonial Times to 1970 Part I* (Washington, DC: U.S. Bureau of the Census, 1975), pp. 108–109.

THE KINDERGARTEN MOVEMENT

The introduction of public kindergartens was supposed to improve the quality of urban living. Kindergartens originally served upper-class families, but by the 1880s and 1890s they were considered a primary educational method of dealing with urban poverty. In a broader context, one could argue that early childhood education, as represented by the kindergarten movement, originated in concerns with urbanization.

As originally introduced in the United States in the 1860s and 1870s by Carl Schurz and Elizabeth Peabody, the kindergarten centered on a romantic vision of childhood and nature. The original kindergarten was opened in Germany in 1840 by Friedrich Froebel (1782–1852) as a method of early childhood education that was to lead the child from a world concentrated on self to a society of children. As its name implies, the *kindergarten* was conceived as a garden of children to be cultivated in the same manner as plants. Like Johann Pestalozzi, Froebel advocated a model maternal teacher whose method "should be passive and protective, not directive and interfering." Froebel believed that the divine spirit existed in all humans and that it was the key to social harmony. By cultivating the garden of children, the kindergarten teacher was to bring forth their divine spirits and create a sense of unity among all humans.[3]

The first public school kindergarten in the United States was opened in St. Louis, Missouri, in 1873, for the specific purpose of dealing with urban poverty. In his excellent history of the St. Louis school system, *The Public and the Schools: Shaping the St. Louis System, 1838–1920,* Selwyn Troen describes how that system's famous Superintendent William Torrey Harris analyzed the distribution of children in the city according to the locality of "haunts of vice and iniquity" and decided that the only way of saving slum children from corruption was to get them into school at an early age. Harris first requested that the school board lower the minimum age of school attendance. After being refused by the school board, he recommended the establishment of kindergartens as a permanent part of the school system. Harris claimed that kindergartens were necessary because traditional socializing agencies such as the family, church, and community had collapsed:

> Living in narrow, filthy alleys, poorly clad and without habits of cleanliness, "the divine sense of shame," which Plato makes to be the foundation of civilization, is very little developed. Self respect is the basis of character and virtue; cleanliness of person and clothing is a sine qua non for its growth in the child. The child who passes his years in the misery of the crowded tenement house or alley, becomes early familiar with all manner of corruption and immorality.[4]

Within this context, the kindergarten was to substitute for the habits of living and moral training formerly taught by the family organization that supposedly had been lost in the slums of the new urban areas.

The first director of Boston's kindergartens, Laura Fisher, wrote in 1904, "The mere fact that the children of the slums were kept off the streets, and that they were made clean and happy by kind and motherly young women; that the child thus being cared for enabled the mother to go about her work in or outside the home—all this appealed to the heart of America, and America gave freely to make these kindergartens possible."[5]

A major goal of the early kindergarten movement was to teach children habits that would reform the home. In other words, the early kindergarten was viewed as a means of educating the parents, particularly the mother. An early example of this thinking can be seen in Lucy Wheelock's tale "A Lily's Mission," in which two slum children bring a flower home to their dingy apartment. The mother has failed to keep the house clean; the father is out drinking. Overjoyed at seeing the flower, the mother places it on a windowsill, only to discover that dirt prevents any sunlight from shining through the window to the flower. With the window clean, the sunlight reveals the filth of the apartment, which is then quickly cleaned. The mother washes and dresses, and the father, overcome by his new environment upon his return home, vows to give up the bottle.[6]

The concept of parental education introduced by the kindergarten movement extended the role of the school in a new direction that gave the kindergarten a social role far beyond anything originally intended by Froebel. As a new educational institution, the kindergarten was to compensate for the supposed loss of socialization within the slum family, to protect the young child from the influences of the street, to provide preparation for entrance into regular elementary school classes, and to educate the parents. These extended social goals resulted in the kindergarten losing its original emphasis on creative play and self-expression. In place of these activities, the kindergarten stressed creating order and discipline in the child's life as compensation for family life and as preparation for school. Lazerson found that as the kindergarten evolved in Massachusetts in the twentieth century, it became less involved in parental education and that, in the end, discipline, order, and protection from the urban environment became its primary objectives.

HOME ECONOMICS: EDUCATION OF THE NEW CONSUMER WOMAN

Another extension of the school into the household was home economics courses. Home economists hoped to educate "the new woman," who through the application of domestic sciences would be freed from household drudgery to pursue further education and participate in urban reform projects. The new woman was to be primarily a consumer rather than a producer of household products. Wishing to professionalize the role of the housewife, home economist experts characterized the new woman as a household manager who was mainly responsible for maintaining household budgets and buying goods for the home. After receiving home economics education in public schools, experts believed, future housewives would have increased time available to pursue an education and engage in social reform movements. Also, home economists hoped that domestic science would protect the family unit against the worst aspects of urbanization and industrialization. The

1909 announcement of the founding of the American Home Economics Association gave as its goal "the improvement of living conditions in the home, the institutional household, and the community."[7]

As a profession, home economics evolved from an annual series of conferences held at Lake Placid, New York, beginning in 1899 under the leadership of Ellen Richards. Richards, the founder of the American Home Economics Association and the first woman to receive a degree from the Massachusetts Institute of Technology (MIT), brought together a faith in the ability of science to improve human existence, a desire to improve women's education, and a belief that the home was the central institution for reforming society. Reflecting these concerns, Richards, after graduating from MIT in 1873, convinced the institution to establish a Woman's Laboratory in 1876. In 1883 Ellen Richards became the first female instructor at MIT as the separate women's laboratory was torn down and women joined men as students at the institution. Richards taught courses on sanitation and household chemistry that focused on cooking and cleaning.[8] In 1887 Richards conducted a study of municipal sewage treatment systems and developed the first water purity standards.[9]

Placing the society's ills at the doorstep of the home, domestic scientists saw a cure through nutritional food, sanitary cooking, budgeting, and household cleanliness. Nutritionally balanced food, it was believed, would provide the energy for hard work and resistance to the temptations of the tavern. Wholesome food served in the home and school cafeteria would stimulate students to study and protect them from illness. Hospital patients would recover more quickly as a result of scientifically planned menus and food. Sanitary cooking and household cleanliness would protect everyone from sickness. Protected from illness and energized by nutritional foods, it was believed, workers would be less likely to miss work and more likely to retain their jobs. According to the calculations of home economists, these circumstances would reduce unemployment, crime, and alcoholism. For the same reasons, students would complete their studies and find good jobs. Also, proper household budget management would keep families from falling into poverty. Workers would be less likely to strike if their wives could make existing wages satisfactory through proper budgeting.

Believing that home economics would improve society, Marion Talbot at the fourth annual meeting of the 1902 Lake Placid Conference on Home Economics stated, "The obligations of home life are not by any means limited to its own four walls, that home economics must always be regarded in light of its relation to the general social system, that men and women are alike concerned in understanding the processes, activities, obligations and opportunities which make the home and family effective parts of the social fabric."[10]

Along with saving society, home economics was to liberate women from household drudgery and make them active participants in shaping society. Ellen Richards worried that "the industrial world is ruled by science and that all the things with which we surround ourselves are now manufactured upon scientific principles, and, alas! women are ignorant of those principles."[11] The study of science and home economics would, Richards hoped, make housekeeping into a profession. A 1890 editorial in the *New England Kitchen Magazine* proclaimed,

"We need to exalt the profession of home making to see that it is as dignified and requires as much intelligence as other professions."[12] Science and technology would be the key to eliminating household drudgery. As Ellen Richards explained, "The woman who boils potatoes year after year, with no thought of the how or why, is a drudge, but the cook who can compute the calories of heat which a potato of given weight will yield, is no drudge."[13]

The so-called philosopher of home economics, Caroline Hunt, clearly delineated the new role of women as consumers. Her interests in science and social reform paralleled those of Ellen Richards. Born in Chicago in 1865, Hunt entered Northwestern University in 1881 and, after interrupting her studies to teach high school, graduated in 1888. After teaching high school for several more years, she returned to Northwestern University to study chemistry. While at Northwestern, she lived with Jane Addams at Hull House and studied newly arrived immigrants, including *The Italians in Chicago: A Social and Economic Study* (1897) and *Dietary Studies in Chicago* (1898). In 1896 she was hired to teach Domestic Economy and operate the cafeteria at Chicago's Lewis Institute. Then in 1903 she was hired by the University of Wisconsin to organize and head a School of Domestic Science.[14]

While at Lewis Institute, Hunt equated women's freedom with a change in household roles from producer to consumer. Women would have more free time for education, she argued, if they bought factory-made products rather than producing them in the home. For instance, a housewife could be a producer of soap or a consumer of factory-made soap. "The woman who today makes her own soap instead of taking advantage of machinery for its production," she wrote, "enslaves herself to ignorance by limiting her time for study. The woman who shall insist upon carrying the home-making methods of today into tomorrow will fail to lay hold of the possible quota of freedom which the future has in store for her."[15]

Throughout her writings, Caroline Hunt highlights the importance of the transition of household tasks from production to consumption. For Hunt, this transition was part of a larger process of industrialization and job specialization. Comparing the past to existing conditions in a paper that she read at the 1904 Lake Placid Conference on Home Economics, Hunt argued, "The home has delegated to the school not only the technical but also the general education of the child; to the factory the manufacture of clothing, of furniture, and of house furnishings."[16]

Hunt envisioned college-educated women finding time for engaging in social reform movements by consuming rather than producing household goods. In other words, women would be freed to engage in "municipal housekeeping." Released from household chores, women could apply their education, particularly from home economics, to protecting the household from deleterious industrial and social practices. She called this "Woman's Public Work for the Home."[17] At the 1907 Lake Placid Conference she argued that when women are "forced by their responsibility for the family welfare into a fight for a public milk supply of assured purity, and are unsuccessful in the fight, we may take this as an indication that young women now in college should be taught to seek and to overcome the difficulties which lie in the way of the present accomplishment of this much needed reform."[18]

© Corbis

Ellen Richards and Caroline Hunt's hopes seemed to be realized with the rapid spread of home economics courses in public schools and colleges. According to Barbara Ehrenreich and Deirdre English, 20 percent of high schools offered courses by 1916–1917, and the number of college students enrolled in courses increased from 213 in 1905 to 17,778 in 1916. Most of those enrolled in college courses were preparing to be home economics teachers.[19] The Smith-Hughes Act of 1917 ensured the spread of home economics courses to public schools and universities. This federal legislation provided support for home economics teachers in public schools to prepare girls for the occupation of homemaker. In turn, this required hiring home economics instructors on college campuses to train teachers. These college and university instructors also trained cooks for hospitals, school cafeterias, and other institutional settings. Home economists also expanded their careers by becoming researchers in food technology at private companies and universities, and consultants to private industry for product development and sales. The vocational emphasis of the Smith-Hughes Act tended to compromise the role of home economists as scientists. Historian Rima Apple concluded, "In the early twentieth century, women who wanted to pursue careers in scientific research were frequently counseled to study home economics. . . . As home economics units became increasingly involved with teacher training for public school instruction . . . [this] lessened the perceived significance of the scientific aspects of home economics."[20]

SCHOOL CAFETERIAS, THE AMERICAN CUISINE, AND PROCESSED FOODS

A major accomplishment of home economics was the creation of an American cuisine in school cafeterias and hospitals, and an emphasis on a diet based on processed foods. Working in school cafeterias and hospital kitchens, home economists hoped to Americanize the diet of immigrants. For example, an early-twentieth-century study found that Italian immigrants in Chicago were staying away from hospitals because of hospital food. Horrified, home economists tried to adjust their menus by making a "few harmless concessions" to immigrant tastes during the initial parts of the hospital stay. Later, food planners hoped, immigrants could be weaned from their traditional foods to the solid and healthful fare of the hospital kitchen. It was suggested, "Perhaps the treatment of an Italian during this period of change should be studied much as the treatment of an inebriate being won from his strong drink is studied."[21] A similar attempt to change the eating habits of immigrant children occurred in school cafeterias.

In *Perfection Salad: Women and Cooking at the Turn of the Century,* Laura Shapiro credits home economists with the development of a distinctive American cuisine. She argues that during the latter part of the nineteenth century home economists "made American cooking American, transforming a nation of honest appetites into an obedient market for instant mashed potatoes."[22] Reflecting on the puritanical quality of the teachings and writings of early home economists, Shapiro wrote, "But to enjoy food, to develop a sense for flavors, or to acknowledge that eating could be a pleasure in itself had virtually no part in any course, lecture, or magazine article."[23]

Home economists helped develop and sell the new American diet of prepackaged foods. In public school and college classes, they taught how to prepare the new American diet. As researchers, they did pioneer work in food technology that resulted in the development of new food products and made possible the proliferation of fast-food chains. They helped manufacturers develop and sell new gadgetry for the home, such as refrigerators, vacuum cleaners, and washing machines.[24] And they helped to make school and hospital cafeteria food healthful, inexpensive, and bland.[25] Through the school cafeteria, they hoped to persuade immigrant children to abandon the diet of their parents for the new American cuisine.

The new American diet resulted, in part, from Ellen Richards's research at MIT and her work with the New England Kitchen and the Boston School of Housekeeping. Richards was not alone at the New England Kitchen and the Boston School of Housekeeping in promoting the belief that improper diet and household management were undermining society. "Is it not pitiful, this army of incompetent wives," declared domestic scientist M. V. Shailer in an 1898 issue of *New England Kitchen Magazine,* "whose lack of all knowledge of domestic science is directly and indirectly the means of filling our prisons, asylums, reformatories and saloons."[26] This feeling echoed earlier claims by Juliet Corson, the superintendent of the New York Cooking School. In 1877 Corson wrote a booklet titled *Fifteen Cent Dinners for Workingmen's Families.* Corson claimed, "The laborer who leaves home in the early morning, after an ill-cooked breakfast, and carries in his basket soggy bread and tough meat for his luncheon, is apt to return at night tired and cross, not unfrequently he tries, *en route,* to cure his discomfort at a neighboring saloon."[27]

Portending the future marketing of packaged and frozen dinners, Ellen Richards helped found the New England Kitchen in 1890. The founders hoped to improve the lives of working and poor people by providing already prepared sanitary and economical food that would have consistent flavor and texture. Richards envisioned a neighborhood establishment that would prepare and sell food. The establishment would be educational because buyers could observe the sanitary conditions and cooking methods. Also, buyers would learn to expect the food, cooked under scientific conditions, to always taste the same.

Richards's dream included the standardization of American eating habits. This standardization was made possible by the work of Fannie Farmer and the Boston Cooking School. The Boston Cooking School was opened in 1879 and by the 1890s became a training ground for public school cooks with a curriculum that included psychology; physiology and hygiene; bacteriology; foods; laundry work; the chemistry of soap, bluing, and starch; and cookery applied to public school work. Fannie Farmer joined the Boston Cooking School in 1888. Legend has it that standardized measurements were born when Marcia Shaw asked Fannie Farmer what it meant to measure out "butter the size of an egg" and "a pinch of salt."[28] In 1896 Fannie Farmer's cookbook, *The Boston Cooking-School Cook Book,* appeared and quickly became a national best seller. A major innovation in Farmer's book was the use of leveled measurements, gaining her the epithet "Mother of Level Measurements." Farmer wrote, "A cupful is measured level. A tablespoonful is measured level. A teaspoonful is measured level."[29]

Ellen Richards's dreams of prepackaged and standardized meals spread across the country. Jane Addams sent a settlement worker from Chicago to learn Richards's methods and created a similar kitchen at Hull House. Another kitchen opened in Providence, and Richards was invited to create a New England Kitchen at the 1893 Chicago World's Fair. The exhibit was lined with food charts, menus, diagrams, and consumerist mottoes, such as "Wherefore do you spend money for that which is not bread, and your labor for that which satisfieth not?"[30]

After the World's Fair, the New England Kitchen focused its efforts on selling prepared foods to Boston's nine public high schools and to office workers. In 1895 Richards helped to create in the Boston school system a model program for public school cafeterias. Prior to 1895, janitors in Boston schools were responsible for the lunch program. Using new theories of nutrition, sanitation, and food preparation, Richards and her cooking colleagues introduced the new American diet to Boston schoolchildren.[31] These efforts set the stage for trained domestic scientists to take over school cafeterias to ensure that students received healthful and sanitary foods. The other focus was on hospital food. Richards declared that "no better school of diet could be found than an intelligently managed hospital."[32]

In both schools and hospitals, cafeterias were to serve the double function of supplying nutritious food and changing people's diets. Of primary concern to reformers was changing what they believed was the harmful diet of immigrants from Southern and Eastern Europe. Home economists believed that immigrants were harmed by foods that required long periods of digestion. These scientific cooks were guided by a timetable created in the 1820s by an American army surgeon who studied a young man with a hole in his stomach caused by a hunting accident. The surgeon suspended food on a string in the man's stomach to determine the speed of digestion. According to this experiment, pork turned out to be the most difficult to digest and clear broth and rice were the easiest.[33]

Concern about rates of digestion had a limiting effect on the role of spices in cooking. In *The Chemistry of Cooking and Cleaning,* Ellen Richards argued that spices did have a role in stimulating digestive juices but warned against heavy seasonings because they might wear out the digestive tract. In her words, spices should be "just enough to accomplish the purpose."[34] Based on concerns about digestion, menus were created that balanced the digestive aspects of one food against another. For instance, it was proposed that first servings should include easily digestible items, such as oysters and white fish, that would prepare the gastric juices for the more difficult meat dishes. The result of concerns about digestion were recipes and menus that were noted for their blandness and lack of sensitivity to taste.

The development of this new American diet was directly linked to the image of the new woman. As home economists invaded school and hospital cafeterias with their gospel of scientific cookery, they saw the possibility of freeing the American woman from home cooking and making it possible for her to extend her education. Ellen Richards believed that prepared foods, like those served by the New England Kitchen, would increase women's freedom.

In addition, the new American diet was associated with the so-called democratization of domesticity. Home economics leaders believed that the school cafeteria and public school courses would unite students from differing social class backgrounds under a single standard of domesticity. In the school cafeteria and in food preparation instruction in home economics classes, students were to develop similar tastes. Girls from lower-class backgrounds were to be brought up to the same standard of cooking and cleaning as upper-class girls, while, in turn, upper-class girls were to learn the arts normally practiced by their household help.

The statement of a supervisor of cooking in the New York public schools exemplifies this democratic leveling. The female student, the supervisor observed, "is wonderfully interested in the bacteria of the dishcloth, and the ice box, and the garbage pail, and when she becomes mistress of a home these things will receive her attention as well as the parlor, library, and music room."[35] Home economists hoped that standardized cooking and shared attitudes about housework and sanitation would open the door to a more democratic society.

Prepared food, it was believed, would mean freedom from cooking and liberation of women along with supplying the family with a sanitary, nutritious, and balanced diet. In choosing the path of prepared food, the housewife shifted her emphasis from producer to consumer. Ellen Richards projected this liberating role for prepared food in a 1900 article titled "Housekeeping in the Twentieth Century." In her dream home, where the purchase of cheap mass-produced furniture allowed more money for "intellectual pleasures," the pantry was filled with a large stock of prepared foods—mainly canned foods and bakery products. Richards's dream pantry was based on the reality of a growing industry for canned foods. As early as the 1820s, William Underwood sold meats packed in bottles, and in 1856 Gail Borden patented a method for condensing milk and preserving it with sugar. By the 1870s the technology for canning meats was perfected. In the 1870s H. J. Heinz sold crocked pickles, horseradish, and sauerkraut, and a decade later the company expanded its product list to include cooked macaroni products and vegetables. In the 1880s the Franco-American Company began to distribute canned meals. And in 1897 Campbell's introduced canned soups after the development of a method for condensing the product. According to Ruth Schwartz Cowan, "By the turn of the century [nineteenth to twentieth], canned goods were a standard feature of the American diet . . . [including] processed foods of all kinds—packed dry cereals, pancake mixes, crackers and cookies machine-wrapped in paper containers, canned hams, and bottled corned beef."[36]

In Richards's imaginary description, a pneumatic tube connected to the pantry was to speed canned and packaged food to the kitchen, where the wife simply heated up the meal. In addition, the meal would be accompanied by store-bought bread. Home economists believed that homemade bread and other bakery goods, besides being unsanitary, required an inordinate amount of preparation time and that therefore there should be greater reliance on factory-produced bread products. Ellen Richards dismissed the issue of taste with the comment, "I grant that each family has a weakness for the flavor produced by its own kitchen bacteria, but that is a prejudice due to lack of education."[37] People would stop worrying about taste, she argued, when they fully realized the benefits of the superior cleanliness and consistency of factory kitchens and bakeries. In a 1900 book, *The Cost of Living as Modified by Sanitary Science,* Ellen Richards provided another version of her vision of the commodification of housework. "Housekeeping," she explained, "no longer means washing dishes, scrubbing floors, making soap and candles; it means spending a given amount of money for a great variety of ready-prepared articles and so using commodities as to produce the greatest satisfaction and the best possible mental, moral, and physical results."[38]

THE PLAY MOVEMENT

As home economists were extending the schools' reach into the household and family diet, other educators were attempting to regulate children's play in efforts to promote healthful living and reduce juvenile crime. This approach to curing urban social problems began in the 1880s with the development of small sandlots for children, and it reached a high point with the establishment of the Chicago park system in 1904. Between 1885 and 1895, sandlots were constructed in congested areas of Boston, Chicago, Philadelphia, and New York City. These play areas were designed for children under twelve years of age and usually included a kindergarten program. One student of the movement reports that the dominant motive for establishing sandlots was "to keep children off the street and out of mischief and vice."[39]

A major result of the play movement was that the school became responsible for the after-school play of urban children. For instance, in 1895 the chairman of the Advisory Committee on Small Parks of New York City asked the police to indicate on a map the areas of high rates of juvenile crime. After the committee found that all areas with newly founded parks had a decreasing crime rate, it attempted to speed the development of parks by having the city adopt the following law: "Hereafter no schoolhouse shall be constructed in the City of New York without an open-air playground attached to or used in connection with the same."

In addition to protecting children from bad influences in the streets, play was to protect individuals from the nervous strain of urban living. In 1917 Henry S. Curtis, an organizer of the Playground and Recreation Association and former supervisor of the playgrounds of the District of Columbia, summarized the reasons for the widespread movement to establish playgrounds and parks in the United States. In urban areas, children confined to schools and adults trapped in factories and businesses needed fresh air and the opportunity to exercise their bodies in order to avoid "the rapid increase of insanity and the growing instability of the nervous system." But according to Curtis, "it has not been these reasons that have weighed most strongly with the people that have promoted the movement." Rather, he stated, the dominant motive and major concern of the leaders of the play movement were the fact that there was "little for the children to do in the cities, and that in this time of idleness the devil has found much for idle hands to do. . . . The home seems to be disappearing, and crime, despite an increasingly effective police and probation system, is increasing everywhere."[40]

Like the kindergarten, the playground was to replace the socializing influence of family life supposedly lost in the growth of urban America. In addition to providing recreation and physical activity, the playground was to teach good habits, such as cleanliness, and contribute to the general health of the community. The development of small parks included the construction of elaborate recreational and bathing facilities. For example, in 1898 Boston created a bath department as part of its city administration. This department had control of the city beaches, the floating baths, and the municipal bathhouses. The floating baths were platforms supporting a row of dressing rooms around an open area of water. In 1899 Boston had fourteen floating baths, two swimming pools, and seven shower baths. In New York, floating baths were started in 1876, and by 1899 a total of fifteen had been built. A campaign was waged in New York in the 1890s to increase the number of shower baths available because they were more usable during the winter than the floating baths were.

It was logical that this aspect of the playground movement would also become a school activity. The first reported school bath was a shower opened in a Boston school in 1889. Lawrence Cremin reports in *Transformation of the School* that "the teachers of New York, for example, found themselves giving hundreds of baths each week. The syllabi said nothing about baths, and teachers themselves wondered whether bathing was their charge. But there were the children and there were the lice."[41] The addition of the shower room to the public school symbolized the expansion of the school as a social agency.

The playground movement was more than just an attempt to reduce urban crime and supplement the socializing influence of the family. The leaders of the movement believed that directed play was necessary for producing the types of adults required by corporate industry. An important concept in this argument is that of directed play as opposed to free play. The early leaders of the play movement did not want to establish playgrounds and parks where adults and children would come to play without guidance; rather, they believed the state should direct play toward social ends. Play movement leaders like Joseph Lee and Henry Curtis wanted organized play to produce future workers who would be good cooperative citizens. Therefore, playground games and activities were organized to produce a sense of team spirit, habits of cooperation, and a willingness to play by the rules. In other words, play was viewed as another method of social control.[42]

SUMMER SCHOOL

The establishment of summer, or vacation, school was another means of extending the influence of the school over children's lives. Cambridge, Massachusetts, was one of the first cities to propose a vacation school, or summer school. In 1872 its school committee reported the need for a vacation school because summer was "a time of idleness, often of crime, with many who are left to roam the streets, with no friendly hand to guide them, save that of the police." The superintendent of the same school district was still asking for a summer school as an inexpensive form of police control when he wrote in his school report in 1897, "The value of these schools consists not so much in what shall be learned during the few weeks they are in session, as in the fact that no boy or girl shall be left with unoccupied time. Idleness is an opportunity for evil-doing. . . . These schools will cost money. Reform schools also cost money."[43]

Summer schools were established in rapid succession in urban areas. Boston established them in 1885, New York in 1894, Cleveland in 1897, and Chicago in 1898. The Chicago vacation schools were considered models. They were opened in the most densely populated parts of the city, and enrollment was limited to a first-come, first-served basis. The principal of the system reported that they were received with such enthusiasm that "at one of the schools it was found necessary to call in the police to remove the parents who crowded the halls of the building, insisting that their children must be accepted. In another area, fifty children were held up on their way to school, and their cards of admission were taken from them."[44]

The school as an expanding social agency also became involved in providing school nurses and lunch programs. Much of this work was the result of the settlement house movement, which sought to reform conditions among the poor. Workers in the settlement house movement campaigned for a broader view of the social functions of the school and were responsible in the late nineteenth and early twentieth centuries for the first citywide lunch program in New York schools, the first school physician (in 1897), and the first experiments in providing school nurses in Chicago.[45]

Kindergartens, playgrounds, showers, lunches, and nurses were recognized as giving broader social meaning and uses to the public school. Clarence Arthur Perry begins his *Wider Use of the School Plant* (1910) by noting, "The children who went to school back in the eighties skipped out of the school house door at half past three and scampered down the street shouting with glee. . . . Within a couple of decades all this has changed." He found that in 1910 public school buildings were "open not only days but evenings. . . . Children go to them Saturdays as well as Mondays, and in some places the school rooms are not left unvisited even on Sundays."[46]

SOCIAL CENTERS

Another important factor in the wider use of the school was concern about the loss of community. Using the school as a social center was viewed as one means of reestablishing within an urban context a sense of community that had been lost with the passing of rural and small-town life. It was believed that the neighborhood school could be a means of organizing urban populations into a corporate body of specialized tasks and lifestyles cemented together by common allegiances. An example of this attitude is provided by J. K. Paulding, a New York writer who argued in 1898 that democracy could function only with the existence of a spirit of democratic fraternalism resulting from the unification of individual aspirations into a common way of life. He argued that the school, by opening its doors a little wider and becoming a social center, could bring in neighborhood life and create the necessary spirit of democratic fraternalism. An article by H. E. Scudder in the *Atlantic Monthly* in 1896 suggested that the school could attract more people by improving the beauty of its buildings, attaching a public library, organizing a museum and conservatory, and using its walls as a public art gallery. The author states, "The common school-house is in reality the most obvious center of national unity."[47]

During the 1890s, social centers developed rapidly throughout the country. New York organized its after-school recreational activities into social centers in

© *Hulton Archive/Getty Images*

1897. The University Settlement in New York organized clubs in twenty-one school buildings for the specific purposes of reducing individual selfishness and promoting a spirit of social cooperation. In Chicago social centers were established in the field houses of the park system, and neighborhood groups engaged in a variety of activities, including community orchestras and choral clubs. A local women's club in Milwaukee persuaded that city in 1907 to open school buildings for local evening meetings. When the Russell Sage Foundation surveyed the social center movement in 1913, it found that 330 of the 788 school superintendents contacted around the country reported the use of their schools as social centers. By 1920 the movement had spread to 667 school districts.[48]

Changes in school architecture reflected the growing commitment to the concept of the school as social center. One school superintendent complained to his colleagues in 1897 that it was difficult to open schools to adults because in most buildings access to assembly rooms was "gained only by climbing flights of stairs, always with embarrassment and often with risk of accident from fire or other causes." His suggestion, which was incorporated into later school plans, was to construct assembly rooms on the ground floor, with easy access from the street.[49]

Classroom furniture also had to be changed to meet the multiple needs of the school and the adult social center. Demands were made to replace school desks bolted to the floor with flat-top desks that could be rearranged for use in club and recreational activities. By 1910 schools such as Washington Irving High School in New York were being designed specifically to function as social centers. The lobby of the school contained a neighborhood art gallery, and the auditorium provided facilities for neighborhood drama groups. Office space was set aside in the school to accommodate the staffs of local clubs and associations.

One leader of the social center movement, Edward J. Ward, believed schools could be a means of reforming urban politics by reducing political tensions. Ward advocated the establishment of social centers in schoolhouses as centers for political discussion. He envisioned the day when voting districts would be the same as school districts and the ballot box would be placed in the schoolhouse. When this occurs, he wrote, "the schoolhouse . . . becomes, for all its possible wider uses, the real social center; and the way is clear and the means are at hand for supplying the fundamental and supreme lack in the machinery of democracy." The social center, he believed, was the key to developing political cooperation.[50]

As the school social center idea spread throughout the United States, it took on a variety of forms. In Chicago the park field houses served the function of bringing the community together on a social basis, and schoolhouses were used to promote political cooperation. In 1914 the Russell Sage Foundation reported that 142 political meetings had been held in Chicago school buildings during a municipal election. The civic clubs of Los Angeles fought to have polling booths and political meetings in school buildings instead of in "livery stables and small, dingy, out-of-the-way and hard-to-find places." They believed that locating the polling booth in the school would protect it from tampering by corrupt political forces.[51]

The social center was also seen as a means of helping immigrants adjust to urban living. For instance, the Women's Municipal League of Boston worked for the opening of social centers in the local schools as part of its more general civic work to improve the lives of immigrants. The president of the league wrote in 1912 that social centers were opened because "it is our endeavor to make our city a true home for the people, it is not enough that we should merely make it a house. . . . We must also ensure that there shall be within it recreation, enjoyment, and happiness for all."[52]

THE NEW CULTURE WARS

In one sense kindergartens, social centers, playgrounds, and the wider use of the school plant were part of the new culture wars. These new functions of the public schools were intended to handle problems created by immigrants from Southern and Eastern Europe. They were part of an effort to "Americanize" immigrants. At the time, the terms *Americanize* and *Americanization* referred to a process of deculturalization where immigrant languages and cultures were replaced by English and Anglo-American culture. Reflecting this process of deculturalization, many schools, in a manner similar to the treatment of Native Americans, actually changed immigrant names so they "sounded American."

In addition to trying to "Americanize" immigrant children, public schools faced real problems in classroom space and instruction. Investigators for the U.S. Senate Immigration Commission in 1908 found that there were more than sixty nationalities in thirty-seven cities and that 58 percent of all students had foreign-born parents. For particular cities, the percentages of students with foreign-born parents were as follows: New York, 72 percent; Chicago, 67 percent; Boston, 64 percent; Cleveland, 60 percent; and San Francisco, 58 percent.[53]

One response of schools to the immigrant population was to offer adult night-school classes in English, government, and naturalization. By offering this activity, the schools were serving a direct need, not trying to compensate for the supposed failure of another institution. Adult night-school classes further opened the door of the schoolhouse to the community and contributed to the claim that the school was becoming the social center of urban America.

In both the adult courses and the accommodation of immigrant children during regular school hours, a tension existed between the wish to protect immigrant culture and the push for Americanization. There is little doubt that most immigrant groups flocked to the schools, but on arrival there they often found a great deal of hostility toward their language and customs. Immigrant children found their names being Anglicized and were frequently told not to speak the language of their parents and to forget their native customs. In these situations, Americanization meant cultural imperialism and the building of a national spirit that was suspicious of foreign countries and ways of living.

One important aspect of Americanization was a fear of radical political ideas. Many national leaders argued that ideas about socialism and communism were being brought to this country by immigrant groups. "One hundred percent Americanism" came to mean opposition to radical economic and political ideologies. For example, in 1917 Cleveland's superintendent of schools, according to historian David Tyack, recommended the firing of "any teacher 'whose sympathies are proved to be with our country's enemies' (it was not necessary, he said, to express disloyalty in words, since teachers influenced pupils merely by the convictions and fundamental desires of the . . . heart)."[54]

Therefore, Americanization continued the traditions of the common school by insisting on the creation of a unified Anglo-American culture. Also, the concept of Americanization changed the political goals of the school to include teaching against radical ideas, particularly socialism and communism. As the social center of the new urban America, the school became a bastion of Anglo-American culture and antiradicalism.

One suspects that when educators talked about the collapse of the family and community, they meant either that the style of family and community life was not to their liking or that they wanted the school to take over the social functions of those institutions. Certainly many immigrant groups maintained strong family structures and community life in urban America, but for those Americans who believed that immigrants were threatening the traditional American way of life, immigrant families and communities were considered to be deviant and in need of change.

Within the context of the preceding argument, the movement to expand the school as a social agency could have had several meanings. It could have meant that traditional institutions were indeed collapsing and the social order of the school needed to expand to replace those institutions. Or it could have meant that immigrant forms of family and community were unacceptable and the school needed to destroy those forms by taking over their functions. The expanded social role of the school could also have been the result of a desire to exert more rational control over the social order by having government institutions assume a greater number of social functions.

Whatever the reason, by the early twentieth century the school had in fact expanded its functions into areas undreamed of in the early part of the previous century. Kindergartens, playgrounds, school showers, nurses, social centers, and Americanization programs turned the school into a central social agency of urban America. The one theme that ran through all these new school programs was the desire to maintain discipline and order in urban life. Within this framework, the school became a major agency for social control and ensuring the domination of Anglo-American culture.

RESISTING SEGREGATION: AFRICAN AMERICANS

While immigrants were being Americanized, African, Mexican, Native, Asian, and Puerto Rican Americans were increasingly segregated or denied language and cultural rights in public schools. Among African Americans the major resistance to school segregation came from the National Association for the Advancement of Colored People (NAACP). W. E. B. Du Bois, a founder of the NAACP and editor of the magazine *Crisis,* became the leading opponent of Booker T. Washington's southern compromise. Du Bois was born in Great Barrington, Massachusetts, earned a Ph.D. at Harvard, studied in Europe, and became one of America's leading sociologists. However, like most blacks in the late nineteenth and early twentieth centuries, he had difficulty finding a university teaching position. Some of his most famous studies were done while he taught at Atlanta University; *The Philadelphia Negro: A Social Study* was written with the support of the University of Pennsylvania but without an appointment to its faculty. One of his major public statements attacking the arguments of Booker T. Washington is *The Souls of Black Folk,* published in 1903.

In *The Souls of Black Folk,* Du Bois claims that Washington's compromise resulted in disaster for black people in the South: "Mr. Washington distinctly asks that black people give up, at least for the present, three things—First, political power, Second, insistence on civil rights, Third, higher education of Negro youth—and concentrate all their energies on industrial education, the accumulation of wealth, and the conciliation of the South." The result, Du Bois argues, would be the "disfranchisement of the Negro," the "legal creation of a distinct status of civil inferiority for the Negro," and the "steady withdrawal of aid from institutions for the higher education of the Negro."[55]

Du Bois envisioned a different type of education for blacks, one that would provide leaders to protect the social and political rights of the black community and make the black population aware of the necessity for constant struggle. He also wanted to develop an Afro-American culture that would blend the African background of former slaves with American culture. In part, this was to be accomplished by the education of black leaders.

What Du Bois hoped to accomplish through education is well described in his study of John. In the story, a southern black community raises money to send John to the North for an education. The community's hope is that he will return to teach in the local black school. After receiving his education in the North, John does return to teach. He goes to the house of the local white judge and, after making the mistake of knocking at the front door instead of the rear door, is ushered into the judge's dining room. The judge greets John with his philosophy of education: "In this country the Negro must remain subordinate, and can never expect to be [the] equal of white men." The judge describes two different ways in which blacks might be educated in the South. The first, which the judge favors, is to "teach the darkies to be faithful servants and laborers as your fathers were." The second way, the one supported by Du Bois and most feared by white southerners, is described by the judge as putting "fool ideas of rising and equality into these folks' heads, and . . . [making] them discontent and unhappy."[56]

What was most important for Du Bois was to educate blacks to be discontented with their social position in the South. Unhappiness—not happiness—was his goal. Du Bois describes John, before his meeting with the judge, standing on a bluff with his younger sister and looking out over an expanse of water:

> Long they stood together, peering over the gray unsettled water.
> "John," she said, "does it make everyone unhappy when they study and learn lots of things?"
> He paused and smiled. "I am afraid it does," he said.
> "And, John, are you glad you studied?"
> "Yes," came the answer, slowly and positively.
> She watched the flickering lights upon the sea, and said thoughtfully, "I wish I was unhappy—and—and," putting both arms about his neck, "I think I am, a little, John."[57]

Du Bois's ideal of an educated black citizenry struggling against oppression became a reality even within a segregated society and educational system. Certainly the combination of segregated education and the lack of funding of schools serving African Americans hindered the social and economic advancement of blacks. It took more than a half century for the NAACP to win its battle against segregated education in the South. During that period of legal struggle, segregated schooling was a major factor in condemning blacks to an inferior status in society.

The Second Crusade for Black Education

The first crusade for black education in the South had taken place during and after the Civil War. The second crusade occurred from 1910 to the 1930s. The second crusade involved the expansion of segregated schools for African American children paid for by a combination of personal donations of time and money by black citizens, donations by private foundations, and government money. By the 1930s, through these efforts, common schools were finally established for black children. In the second crusade black southern citizens had to pay directly from their own income to build schools for their children while, at the same time, they paid local and state taxes, which went primarily to support white segregated schools.

One important private foundation supporting the second crusade was the Anna T. Jeanes Fund. The Jeanes Fund paid up to 84 percent of the salaries for teacher supervisors and elementary industrial education. The Jeanes teachers, as they were called, spent the majority of their time in raising money for the construction of schoolhouses and the purchase of equipment. According to James Anderson, between 1913 and 1928, Jeanes teachers raised approximately $5 million. In this respect, Jeanes teachers played an important role in helping African Americans raise the money for black education that was being denied them by state and local governments dominated by white citizens.

The Julius Rosenwald Fund, named after its founder—Julius Rosenwald, the president of Sears, Roebuck and Company—led the campaign in building schools for black children. The first Rosenwald school was completed in 1914 in Lee County, Alabama. The construction of this one-teacher schoolhouse cost $942. Indicative of how the costs were being shared, impoverished local black residents donated $282 in cash and free labor. Local white citizens gave $360. The Rosenwald Fund gave $300.[58]

Between the building of the first Rosenwald school in 1914 and 1932, 4,977 rural black schools were constructed that could accommodate 663,615 students. The total expenditure for building these schools in 883 counties in fifteen southern states was $28,408,520. James Anderson provides the following breakdown for the financial sources of this massive building program: Rosenwald Fund—15.36 percent; rural black people—16.64 percent; white donations—4.27 percent; and public tax funds—63.73 percent.[59] According to Anderson, the public tax funds used to build the Rosenwald schools came primarily from black citizens. He argues that the majority of school taxes collected from black citizens supported schools for white children. Anderson writes, "During the period 1900 to 1920, every southern state sharply increased its tax appropriations for building schoolhouses, but virtually none of this money went for black schools."[60] Booker T. Washington complained, "The money [taxes] is actually being taken from the colored people and given to white schools."[61]

In reality, because of the source of funding, many of these public black schools were owned by local black citizens. One analysis of school expenditures in the South concluded that blacks owned 43.9 percent, or 1,816, of a total of 4,137 schools. Many of the schools identified as being in the public domain were paid for through the voluntary contributions of black citizens.[62] Therefore, the second crusade for black education in the South involved a great deal of self-help from the black community. It was through the struggles and sacrifices of the black community that by the 1930s African American children in the South had a viable system of education. The major drawbacks to this system were segregation and unequal financial support by state and local governments.

Despite the lack of financial equality between segregated schools, many schools serving black students provided an excellent education. In her study of segregated schools in Caswell County, North Carolina, Vanessa Siddle Walker documents that despite the limited resources resulting from unequal funding, the local African American public school provided an excellent education. Part of the reason was the sense of community created by parental participation in the financial support of the school. In addition, teachers and administers in the school cared about the success of their students and worked to ensure their academic success. Walker concludes, "Caring adults gave individual concern, personal time, and so forth to help ensure a learning environment in which African American children would succeed. Despite the difficulties they faced and the poverty with which they had to work, it must be said that they experienced no poverty of spirit."[63] Walker cites other studies that found positive academic outcomes from segregated black schools because teachers and parents shared a common commitment to the success of their students.

Of course, Walker's conclusions raise the same issues that African American parents faced in Boston in the early nineteenth century. Segregated schools meant unequal funding and poor facilities but included teachers interested in the success of their students. Integrated schools meant equal funding and facilities but also raised the possibility that white teachers might not be dedicated to ensuring the success of their black students.

RESISTING SEGREGATION: MEXICAN AMERICANS

The League of United Latin American Citizens (LULAC) led the resistance of Mexican Americans to the increasing segregation of their children. According to Guadalupe San Miguel Jr. in *"Let All of Them Take Heed": Mexican Americans and the Campaign for Educational Equality in Texas, 1910–1981,* one of the most discriminatory acts against the children of Mexicans was the nonenforcement of compulsory school laws.[64] A survey of one Texas county in 1921 found only 30.7 percent of Mexican school-age children in school. In another Texas county in the 1920s, school authorities admitted that they enforced school attendance on Anglo children but not on Mexican children. San Miguel quotes one school authority from this period: "The whites come all right except one whose parents don't appreciate education. We don't enforce the attendance on the whites because we would have to on the Mexicans."[65] One school superintendent explained that he always asked the local school board if they wanted the Mexican children in school. Any enforcement of the compulsory education law against the wishes of the school board, he admitted, would probably cost him his job.[66]

Mexican children who attended school faced segregation and an education designed, in a manner similar to the programs applied to Native Americans, to rid them of their native language and customs. School segregation for Mexican children spread rapidly throughout Texas and California. The typical pattern was for a community with a large Mexican school population to erect a separate school for Mexican children. For instance, in 1891 the Corpus Christi, Texas, school board denied admission of Mexican children to their "Anglo schools" and built a separate school.

In *Chicano Education in the Era of Segregation,* Gilbert Gonzalez finds that the typical attitude in California schools was reflected in the April 1921 minutes of the Ontario, California, board of education: "Mr. Hill made the recommendation that the board select two new school sites: one in the southeastern part of the town for a Mexican school; the other near the Central School."[67] Gonzalez reports that a survey conducted in the mid-1930s found that 85 percent of the districts investigated in the Southwest were segregated.[68] In *All Deliberate Speed: Segregation and Exclusion in California Schools, 1855–1975,* Charles Wollenberg quotes a California educator writing in 1920: "One of the first demands made from a community in which there is a large Mexican population is for a separate school."[69] A Los Angeles school official admitted that pressure from white citizens resulted in certain neighborhood schools being built to contain the majority of Mexican students.[70]

Rationalized by outright racist attitudes toward Mexican Americans, school segregation was justified by the same argument used to justify isolating southeastern Native Americans in Indian Territory. Educators argued that the segregation of Mexican children would provide the opportunity to, in Gonzalez's words, "Americanize the child in a controlled linguistic and cultural environment, and . . . to train Mexicans for occupations considered open to, and appropriate for, them."[71]

Segregation also served the purpose, according to David Montejano, of maintaining white supremacy. Anglo and Mexican children knew that segregation was intended to separate the superior from the inferior. In addition, Mexican schools were in poorer physical condition, Mexican children used books discarded by Anglo schools, and Mexican teams could not participate in Anglo athletic leagues. The sense of inferiority that children learned in the segregated educational system was reinforced in adult life by the refusal of Anglo restaurants to serve Mexicans and by segregated housing.[72]

Mexican children attending segregated schools were put through a deculturalization program similar to the one for the Native Americans isolated in Indian Territory and in boarding schools. The program was designed to strip away Mexican values and culture and replace the use of Spanish with English. The term most frequently used in the early twentieth century for the process of deculturalization was *Americanization.* The Americanization process for Mexicans should not be confused with the Americanization programs that children of European immigrants encountered in schools. As Gilbert Gonzalez argues, the Americanization of Mexicans, as opposed to Europeans, took place in segregated school systems. In addition, the assimilation of Mexicans was made difficult by the rural economy, which locked Mexicans into segregated farmwork. Anglos also showed greater disdain for Mexican culture than they did for European cultures.[73]

An important element in the Americanization of Mexican schoolchildren, as it was for Native Americans, was eliminating the speaking of their native language. Educators argued that learning English was essential to assimilation and the creation of a unified nation. In addition, language was considered related to values and culture. Changing languages, it was assumed, would cause a cultural revolution among Mexican Americans. Typical of this attitude was a Texas school superintendent quoted by Gonzalez as saying that "a Mexican child 'is foreign in his thinking and attitudes' until he learns to 'think and talk in English.'"[74]

In 1918 Texas passed legislation with stricter requirements for the use of English in public schools. The legislation made it a criminal offense to use any language but English in the schools. In addition, the legislation required that school personnel, including teachers, principals, custodians, and school board members, use only English when conducting school business.[75]

Many Anglos believed that Mexican culture and values (like Native American culture and values) discouraged the exercise of economic entrepreneurship and cooperation required in an advanced corporate society (as I discussed in the previous chapter, many whites believed that the communal lifestyle of Native Americans hindered their advancement in U.S. society). Mexicans were criticized as having a fatalistic acceptance of the human condition, being self-pitying, and being unable to work with others in large organizations. Also, many Anglos felt that Mexicans were overly attached to their families and to small organizations such as local clubs.[76]

The attempted deculturalization of Mexicans did not always extend to food, music, and dance. Advocates of cultural democracy felt that such superficial aspects of culture could be maintained while attempts were made to socialize Mexican children into an entrepreneurial spirit, or what was called an "achievement concept."[77]

Most Mexican children did not encounter these deculturalization programs because of a combination of lack of enforcement of compulsory education laws and the necessity for children to help support their families. In addition, there were reports of Mexican children dropping out of school because of the anti-Mexican bias of the curriculum—particularly in Texas, where in history instruction stressed the Texas defeat of Mexico.[78] In addition, many children of migrant farmworkers received little opportunity to attend school. In some areas of California, state laws on school attendance were routinely violated by local school boards to ensure the availability of children for farmwork. In 1928, with support from the state, the Fresno County, California, superintendent of schools opened a special migratory school. Children attended between 7:30 a.m. and 12:30 p.m. and then joined their parents in the fields. This five-hour school day violated state law on the number of hours of attendance, but the California government never enforced this requirement on the migratory schools, and the five-hour day became typical for schools serving migrant children. In some parts of California, migrant children were completely denied an education. In the 1930s, public schools in Ventura County, California, displayed signs reading "No Migratory Children Wanted Here."[79]

The League of United Latin American Citizens (LULAC)

Many in the Mexican American community protested the denial of education to their children, the existence of school segregation, and the attempts at deculturalization. In 1929 representatives from a variety of Mexican American organizations met in Corpus Christi, Texas, to form LULAC. This organization was composed primarily of middle-class Mexican Americans, as opposed to Mexican farm laborers and migratory workers. Membership was restricted to U.S. citizens.[80]

LULAC adopted a code that reflected the desire of middle-class Mexican Americans to integrate the culture of Mexico with that of the United States. The code attempted to balance respect for U.S. citizenship with maintenance of cultural traditions. On one hand, the code asked members to "Respect your citizenship, converse it; honor your country, maintain its traditions in the minds of your children, incorporate yourself in the culture and civilization." On the other hand, the code told members to "Love the men of your race, take pride in your origins and keep it immaculate; respect your glorious past and help to vindicate your people."[81] Clearly LULAC was committed to a vision of the United States that was multicultural and multilingual. In contrast to the public schools, which were trying to eradicate Mexican culture and the use of Spanish, LULAC favored bilingualism and instruction in the cultural traditions of the United States and Mexico. The LULAC code called on members to "Study the past of your people, or the country to which you owe your citizenship; learn to handle with purity the two most essential languages, English and Spanish."[82]

As an organization, LULAC was dedicated to fighting discrimination against Mexican Americans, particularly in the form of school segregation. One founder of LULAC, J. Luz Saenz, argued that discrimination and the lack of equal educational opportunities were hindering integration of Mexicans into U.S. society. In summarizing the position of LULAC, Saenz stated, "As long as they do not educate us with all the guarantees and opportunities for free participation in all . . . activities . . . as long as they wish to raise up on high the standard of SUPREMACY OF RACES ON ACCOUNT OF COLOR . . . so much will they put off our conversion . . . [to] full citizens."[83]

LULAC's first challenge to school segregation occurred in 1928 with the filing of a complaint against the Charlotte, Texas, independent school district. In this case, a child of unknown racial background adopted by a Mexican family was refused admission to the local Anglo elementary school and was assigned to the Mexican school. Her father argued that because of her unknown racial background, she should be put into the Anglo school. The state admitted that the local school district did not have the right to segregate Mexican children. Local school officials, however, justified the segregation of Mexican children because they required special instruction in English. After determining that the child spoke fluent English, the state school superintendent ordered the local school district to enroll the student in the Anglo school. Although the ruling had the potential to open the doors of Anglo schools to Mexican children who spoke fluent English, it did little to end segregation.[84]

LULAC's second case involving school segregation occurred in 1930, when the Del Rio, Texas, independent school district proposed a bond election to construct and improve school buildings. Included in the proposal were improvements for the Mexican school. Mexican American parents in the district complained that the proposal continued the practice of segregating their children from other students. The local superintendent defended segregation as necessary because Mexican students had irregular attendance records and special language problems. The court accepted the arguments of local school authorities that segregation was necessary for educational reasons. But the court did state that it was unconstitutional to segregate students on the basis of national origin. This decision presented LULAC with the difficult problem of countering the educational justifications used for segregation. At a special 1931 session, LULAC members called for scientific studies of arguments that segregation is necessary for instruction.[85]

While LULAC focused most of its efforts on school segregation, there was a concern about what was perceived to be the anti-Mexican bias of textbooks. In 1939 the state president of LULAC, Ezequiel Salinas, attacked the racism and distortions of Mexicans in history textbooks. Significant changes in the racial content of textbooks, however, did not occur until the full impact of the civil rights movement hit the publishing industry in the 1960s.[86]

While LULAC was struggling to end segregation in Texas, other Mexican American organizations in California were attacking the same problem. By the 1930s, Mexican children were the most segregated group in the state. The California situation was somewhat different from that of Texas because of a 1935 state law allowing for the segregation of Chinese, Japanese, "Mongolians," and Native Americans. Although Native Americans born in the United States were exempt from this law, the state did allow (as discussed in the previous chapter), segregation of Native Americans who were not "descendants of the original American Indians of the United States." According to Charles Wollenberg, "In this torturous and indirect fashion, the 1935 law seemed to allow for segregation of Mexican 'Indians,' but not of Mexican 'whites.'"[87]

The struggle to end segregation played a major role in the civil rights movement of the post–World War II period. The efforts of the NAACP and LULAC finally resulted in the end of legal segregation of African American and Mexican American students. While the civil rights movement brought the end of segregation, it also opened the door to feelings of racial and cultural pride.

NATIVE AMERICAN BOARDING SCHOOLS

During the 1920s, a variety of investigators of Native American boarding schools were horrified by the conditions they found. At the Rice Boarding School in Arizona, Red Cross investigators found that children were fed "bread, black coffee, and syrup for breakfast; bread and boiled potatoes for dinner; more bread and boiled potatoes for supper."[88] In addition to a poor diet, overcrowded conditions contributed to the spread of tuberculosis and trachoma.

Using a paramilitary form of organization, boarding schools were supported by the labor of the students. As early as the fifth grade, boys and girls attended classes for half the day and worked for the other half. As part of the plan to teach agricultural methods, children raised crops and tended farm animals. The paramilitary organization was reflected in the constant drilling of students. The children were given little time for recreation. They were awakened at 5 a.m. and marched to the dining room, then marched back to the dormitories and classrooms. At the Albuquerque Indian School, students marched in uniforms and carried dummy rifles. For punishment children were flogged with ropes, and some boarding schools contained their own jails. In the 1920s anthropologist Oliver La Farge called the Native American schools "penal institutions—where little children were sentenced to hard labor for a term of years to expiate the crime of being born of their mothers."[89]

The publication of the Meriam Report in 1928 began the process that ended this massive educational effort to change the language and culture of an entire people. The report was based on investigations conducted in 1926 by the Institute for Government Research at Johns Hopkins University at the request of the secretary of interior, Hubert Work. The report was known by the name of the principal investigator, Louis Meriam, and it was published as *The Problem of Indian Administration.*[90] The report stated that the most fundamental need in Native American education was a change in government attitude. The report accurately stated that education in "the past has proceeded largely on the theory that it is necessary to remove the Indian child as far as possible from his home environment."[91] Completely reversing this educational philosophy, the report stated that "the modern point of view in education and social work lays stress on upbringing in the natural setting of home and family life."[92] The report went on to argue that the routine and discipline of Native American schools destroyed initiative and independence. In addition, the report criticized the provision of only half a day of schooling and of working students at heavy labor at a young age. In particular, the report was critical of boarding schools and the isolation of children from their families and communities.[93]

Ironically—from the standpoint of the previous history of Native American education—federal policy after the issuance of the Meriam Report stressed community day schools and the support of native cultures. The report argued that community day schools would serve the purpose of integrating education with reservation life. During the 1930s, Native American education emphasized community schools and the rebuilding of the cultural life of Native Americans. As I will discuss in Chapter 14, these policies changed dramatically in the 1950s and 1960s with attempts to terminate tribes and with Native American participation in the civil rights movement.[94] In the end, the legacy of the allotment program and the educational efforts of the latter part of the nineteenth century was increasing illiteracy among the Five Civilized Tribes of the Indian Territory and the destruction of family life and Native American customs on the reservations. For the rest of the century, Native Americans would attempt to rebuild what the federal government had destroyed.

RESISTING DISCRIMINATION: ASIAN AMERICANS

Asian Americans continued to face discriminatory practices in public schools. For instance, in the territory of Hawaii a complicated issue arose over private Japanese language schools. To maintain Japanese culture and language, local Japanese communities opened private schools that children attended on weekdays after public school and on weekends. In 1914 Japanese educators in Hawaii organized the Japanese Education Association, which helped adapt Japanese educational materials to local Hawaiian conditions. Local white leaders began criticizing the Japanese language schools for hindering the "Americanization" of Japanese American children. This criticism was prompted by the general "100 percent Americanism" campaign that was gripping all schools in the United States and its territories, and the growing militancy of Japanese American workers. A territorial government report in 1919 declared, "All Americans must be taught to read and write and think in one language; this is a primary condition to that growth which all nations expect of us and which we demand of ourselves."[95] In calling for the closing of the Japanese language schools, Territorial Superintendent of Education Henry Kinney stated, "The task of the Department of Public Instruction is to weld the large Japanese factor . . . into an integral part of our American body politic."[96] An attempt to close the schools was made through legislation that would require all teachers in public and private schools to be certified. Those demanding certification wanted teachers in Japanese language schools to possess "ideals of democracy and . . . a knowledge of the English language, American history, and methods of government."[97]

Interestingly, both the Anglo and the Japanese communities were divided over the language school issue. Dependent on Japanese laborers, large plantation owners opposed the closing of the language schools and feared Americanization of the Japanese population because Americanization might give Japanese Americans the knowledge and skills to find other types of work. Some members of the Japanese community wanted the schools closed because they favored Americanization. Other Japanese Americans wanted the schools to remain open because they believed the cultural differences with the white community were so great that Americanization was impossible. Some Japanese community members believed the language schools could be used for the purpose of Americanization.

Eventually the territorial government passed a law in 1923 severely curtailing the operation of the Japanese language schools. Contested by the language schools, the issue was brought before the U.S. Supreme Court in 1927. The Court ruled the law unconstitutional and declared it could find no adequate reason for bringing the language schools under strict government control.

What was the effect of racism on the education of Asian American students? Some answers can be found in a study of Nisei (second-generation Japanese students) by researchers from Stanford University between 1928 and 1933. The study found that, up to the eighth grade, Nisei achieved higher grades than their European American counterparts, but after the eighth grade Nisei school performance declined. This finding might have reflected student educational expectations. The first choice of future occupation by Nisei students was agriculture. Compared to European American students, very few Nisei planned to become engineers, chemists, or lawyers.

Perhaps the decline in Nisei performance after the eighth grade was a function of institutional pressures to continue in the occupations of their parents. These institutional pressures are reflected in the report's recommendations regarding the occupational goals for Nisei college students. The Stanford researchers expressed their concern that the first choice of Nisei college students was business followed by medicine and engineering. Only 9 percent of the Nisei college students in their sample wanted to enter agriculture. The report argued that Nisei college students were following an unrealistic path by selecting white-collar occupations that were not open to them. The report recommended against the pursuit of medicine as a career "until it has been sufficiently demonstrated [they] can secure patients from other racial groups."[98] The report advised against an engineering career because "these occupations necessitate the handling of white common and skilled laborers, who resent Japanese being placed over them."[99]

The educational experiences of Asian Americans paralleled those of Native and African Americans; they either were denied an education or experienced segregation. Also, European Americans grouped people from a wide variety of cultural and linguistic backgrounds under the word *Asian.* The all-encompassing term *Asian* facilitated the rationalization of economic and social exploitation and discrimination.

The Asian American experience, however, was changed by World War II. The Japanese attack on the United States was motivated by imperialist desires. For the first time, the U.S. government became a target of foreign imperialism by an Asian country. One result was for European, African, and Native Americans to quickly differentiate between peoples from Asia. The Chinese became friends and the Japanese were enemies. Also, the Japanese attack brought into question the assumption by European Americans that Asia represented a racially inferior other. The Japanese could hardly be considered inferior after destroying the U.S. fleet at Pearl Harbor.

EDUCATIONAL RESISTANCE IN PUERTO RICO

In 1912 Puerto Rican teachers organized the Teachers Association to resist the policies of the commissioner of education. The teacher's magazine *La Educación Moderna* heralded the event: "Day after day we have worked for the defense of our mother tongue and at last today we see our efforts and publicity crowned with success by the meeting of the Teachers Association."[100]

During the term of Commissioner of Education Edward Bainter (1912–1915), the Teachers Association started to campaign to resume teaching in Spanish. The organization passed a resolution calling for the teaching of arithmetic in Spanish. In 1914 the organization requested that Spanish be used as the language of instruction in the first four years of grammar school and that English be taught as a subject.

In 1915 resistance to the imposition of English sparked a student strike at Central High School in San Juan. The strike occurred when a student, Francisco Grovas, was expelled for collecting signatures to support legislation that would require Spanish to be the language of instruction in the Puerto Rican schools. This caused Commissioner of Education Paul Miller (1915–1921) to proclaim that any student participating in a strike would be suspended from school indefinitely.[101]

The strike at Central High School reflected a rising wave of nationalism and calls for independence. Despite the imposition of citizenship, students and other groups continued to campaign for independence. One dramatic outbreak of nationalism occurred in 1921 during graduation exercises at Central High School when a student orator waved a Puerto Rican flag and cheered for independence. Commissioner Miller responded by ordering the removal of "the enemy flag" from the auditorium. Students responded that if the flag were removed, they would leave the ceremonies.[102]

Tensions increased in the 1920s with the appointment of the first Puerto Rican to the post of commissioner of education. As commissioner from 1921 to 1930, Juan B. Huyke imposed Americanization programs with a vengeance. Appointed because he favored assimilation to the United States in contrast to independence, Huyke called the independence movement unfortunate and stated his belief that it would shortly disappear from the minds of Puerto Rican Americans. He considered Puerto Rico to be "as much a part of the United States as is Ohio or Kentucky."[103] Defining Americanism as patriotism, he said, "He that does not want to be a teacher of Americanism would do well not to follow me in my work."[104]

Committed to Americanization, Huyke resisted attempts to return to Spanish as the language of instruction. Huyke required that high school seniors pass an oral English examination before they could graduate. School newspapers written in Spanish were banned. English became the required language at teachers' meetings, and teachers were asked to use English in informal discussions with students. School rankings were based on students' performance on English examinations. Student clubs were established to promote the speaking of English. Teachers who were unable or unwilling to use English in instruction were asked to resign.[105]

Like his predecessors, Huyke linked the ability to speak English to the learning of patriotism. This connection was exemplified by the creation of a School Society for the Promotion and Study of English Language for all eighth, ninth, and tenth graders in Puerto Rico. Supporting patriotism and English, society members were required to wear small American flags in their buttonholes and speak only English. For the celebration of American Education Week in 1921, Huyke recommended as a topic for a speech "American Patriotism—wear the flag in your heart as well as in your buttonhole."[106] In the monthly publication of the Department of Education of Puerto Rico, *Puerto Rico School Review,* Huyke summarized official attitudes about the role of the school in the colonialization of Puerto Rico: "Our schools are agencies of Americanism. They must implant the spirit of America within the hearts of our children."[107]

Resistance to Huyke's policies came from the Puerto Rican Teachers Association and students. The Teachers Association protested the lack of material on Puerto Rico in the curriculum and the failure to recognize Puerto Rican holidays and celebrations in the school calendar. They complained that out of the seventeen high school principals in Puerto Rico, only five were Puerto Rican. And they protested the English language policies. Protest marches by university students were branded by Huyke as "aggressively anti-American," and students were expelled. Professors were warned to stop their support of the protests or resign their positions.[108]

Increasing protests over school policies eventually resulted in the Padin Reform of 1934, which restricted English language instruction to high school and made content instruction in the upper elementary grades in Spanish. But textbooks remained in English. During the 1930s, President Franklin D. Roosevelt urged a bilingual policy with a stress on the importance of learning English. In Roosevelt's words, "But bilingualism will be achieved . . . only if the teaching of English . . . is entered into at once with vigor, purposefulness, and devotion, and with the understanding that English is the official language of our country."[109]

In 1946 the Teachers Association was able to pressure the Puerto Rican legislature into passing a bill requiring that instruction in public schools be given in Spanish. President Harry Truman vetoed the bill. From the perspective of many Puerto Rican Americans, the language issue could be resolved only by giving the island more political autonomy. On October 30, 1950, President Truman signed the Puerto Rican Commonwealth Bill, which provided for a plebiscite to determine whether Puerto Rico should remain a colony or become a commonwealth. In 1951 Puerto Rican Americans voted for commonwealth status despite protests by those urging Puerto Rican independence. Commonwealth status gave Puerto Rican Americans greater control of their school systems, and consequently Spanish was restored in the schools.[110]

CONCLUSION: PUBLIC SCHOOLING AS AMERICA'S WELFARE INSTITUTION

Why have public schools in the United States become a central welfare agency for attempting to solve problems of poverty, nutrition, health, and a host of other problems? In tracing the expansion of the public school as welfare agency in the early twentieth century, historian Miriam Cohen explains, "American commitment to education not only became important as a means for building political support for the early welfare state, but officials relied on the schools because, unlike European states at the turn of the twentieth century, the United States had few government institutions that could provide social services."[111]

In most other countries there existed an extensive government bureaucracy, often a result of monarchical rule and colonial expansion. Given its relatively recent birth and tradition of local rule, the United States lacked an extensive bureaucratic structure at the federal, state, and local levels. The most extensive government structure that existed in practically every community in the United States was the public school. As Cohen explains, "Although the United States had little tradition of state spending for social welfare, no other country outmatches it for public expenditures on education. Americans have never agreed that citizens have the right to jobs, to health care, or to homes. But even our courts have acted to enforce children's right to schooling."[112]

The expansion of the social functions of schooling was part of the process of globalization, which in this case involved a response to increasing global migration of peoples to other countries and to urban areas. The school as a welfare agency became a global model characterized by providing food and health care to children and reaching out to adults through the school as a social center. By the twenty-first century, the introduction of welfare activities in schools was a model used by the World Bank in attempting to help developing nations.[113]

Notes

1. On the educational issues created in nations by the current pattern of global migration see Joel Spring, *Globalization of Education: An Introduction* (New York: Routledge, 2009), pp. 177–200.
2. John Dewey, "The School as Social Center," *National Education Association Proceedings* (1902), pp. 373–383.
3. Friedrich Froebel, *Pedagogics of the Kindergarten,* trans. Josephine Jarvis (Englewood Cliffs, NJ: Prentice-Hall, 1899), pp. 1–15.
4. Quoted in Selwyn K. Troen, *The Public and the Schools: Shaping the St. Louis System, 1838–1920* (Columbia: University of Missouri Press, 1975), p. 101.
5. Quoted in Marvin Lazerson, *Origins of the Urban School: Public Education in Massachusetts, 1870–1915* (Cambridge, MA: Harvard University Press, 1971), p. 50.
6. Ibid., p. 55.
7. Announcement quoted by Sarah Stage in "Ellen Richards and the Social Significance of the Home Economics Movement," in *Rethinking Home Economics: Women and the History of a Profession,* ed. Sarah Stage and Virginia B. Vincenti (Ithaca: Cornell University Press, 1997), p. 17.
8. Ibid., pp. 21–23.
9. Virginia B. Vincenti, "Chronology of Events and Movements Which Have Defined and Shaped Home Economics," in Stage and Vincenti, *Rethinking Home Economics,* p. 322.
10. Quoted by Stage in "Ellen Richards," p. 28.
11. Quoted in Laura Shapiro, *Perfection Salad: Women and Cooking at the Turn of the Century* (New York: Random House, 2001), p. 38.
12. Ibid., p. 39.
13. Ibid., p. 40.
14. Marjorie East, "The Life of Caroline Hunt, 1865–1927," in *Caroline Hunt: Philosopher for Home Economics,* ed. Marjorie East (University Park: Division of Occupational and Vocational Studies, College of Education, Pennsylvania State University, 2001), pp. 1–33.
15. Caroline Hunt, "Revaluations," in East, ibid., p. 56.
16. Caroline Hunt, "Home Economics at the University of Wisconsin, a Housekeeper Conference, from the Sixth Lake Placid Conference on Home Economics, 1904," ibid., p. 71.
17. Caroline Hunt, "Woman's Public Work for the Home, Ninth Lake Placid Conference on Home Economics, 1907," in East, ibid., pp. 86–92.
18. Ibid., p. 87.
19. Barbara Ehrenreich and Deirdre English, *For Her Own Good: 150 Years of the Experts Advice to Women* (New York: Anchor Books, 1978).
20. Rima D. Apple, "Liberal Arts or Vocational Training? Home Economics Education for Girls," in Stage and Vincenti, *Rethinking Home Economics,* p. 85.
21. Shapiro, *Perfection Salad,* p. 152.
22. Ibid., p. 4.
23. Ibid., p. 68.

24. See Carolyn M. Goldstein, "Part of the Package: Home Economists in the Consumer Product Industries, 1920–1940," pp. 271–291; "'Where Mrs. Homemaker Is Never Forgotten': Lucy Maltby and Home Economics at Corning Glass Works, 1929–1965," pp. 163–181; and "Agents of Modernity: Home Economists and Rural Electrification, 1925–1950," pp. 237–252, in Stage and Vincenti, *Rethinking Home Economics.* Also see James C. Williams, "Getting Housewives the Electric Message: Gender and the Energy Marketing in the Early Twentieth Century," *His and Hers: Gender, Consumption, and Technology,* eds. Roger Horowitz and Arwen Mohun (Charlottesville: University Press of Virginia, 1998), pp. 95–114.

25. See Lynn Nyhart, "Home Economists in the Hospital, 1900–1930," in Stage and Vincenti, *Rethinking Home Economics,* pp. 125–144.

26. Quoted in Shapiro, *Perfection Salad,* p. 34.

27. Ibid., p. 130.

28. Ibid., p. 103.

29. Ibid., p. 109.

30. Ibid., pp. 147–148.

31. Vincenti, "Chronology of Events," p. 322.

32. Shapiro, *Perfection Salad,* p. 152.

33. Ibid., pp. 75–76.

34. Ibid., p. 76.

35. Ibid., p. 136.

36. Ruth Schwartz Cowan, *More Work for Mother: The Ironies of Household Technology from the Open Hearth to the Microwave* (New York: Basic Books, 1983), p. 73.

37. Shapiro, *Perfection Salad,* p. 161.

38. Quoted in Andrew Heinze, "Jewish Women and the Making of an American Home," in *The Gender and Consumer Culture Reader,* ed. Jennifer Scanlon (New York: New York University Press, 2000), p. 22.

39. Clarence E. Rainwater, *The Play Movement in the United States* (Chicago: University of Chicago Press, 1922), p. 52.

40. Henry S. Curtis, *The Play Movement and Its Significance* (New York: Macmillan, 1917), pp. 1–10.

41. Lawrence Cremin, *Transformation of the School: Progression in American Education, 1876–1957* (New York: Random House, 1961), p. 71.

42. Paul C. Violas, *The Training of the Urban Working Class: A History of Twentieth Century American Education* (Skokie, IL: Rand McNally, 1978), pp. 67–92.

43. Sadie American, "The Movement for Vacation Schools," *American Journal of Sociology* (November 1898), pp. 310–312.

44. O. J. Milliken, "Chicago Vacation Schools," *American Journal of Sociology* (November 1898), pp. 291–295.

45. Cremin, *Transformation of the School,* p. 64.

46. Clarence Arthur Perry, *Wider Use of the School Plant* (New York: Russell Sage Foundation, 1910), pp. 3–4.

47. J. K. Paulding, "The Public School as a Center of Community Life," *Educational Review* (February 1898), p. 148; H. E. Scudder, "The Schoolhouse as a Centre," *Atlantic Monthly* (January 1896), pp. 103–109.

48. Clarence Arthur Perry, *The Social Centers of 1912–13* (New York: Russell Sage Foundation, 1920); and *School Center Gazette, 1919–1920* (New York: Russell Sage Foundation, 1920).

49. A. Gove, "Public Schoolhouses and Their Uses as Centers of Instruction and Recreation for the Community," *Education* (March 1897), pp. 407–411.

50. Edward J. Ward, *The Social Center* (New York: Appleton, 1913), p. 18.
51. Clarence Arthur Perry, *The School as a Factor in Neighborhood Development* (New York: Russell Sage Foundation, 1914).
52. T. Bowlker, "Woman's Home-Making Function Applied to the Municipality," *American City* 6 (1912), pp. 863–869.
53. David Tyack, *One Best System: A History of Urban Education* (Cambridge, MA: Harvard University Press, 1974), p. 230.
54. Ibid., p. 234.
55. W. E. B. Du Bois, "The Souls of Black Folk," in *Three Negro Classics,* ed. John Hope Franklin (New York: Avon Books, 1965), pp. 246–247.
56. Ibid., p. 373.
57. Ibid., p. 372.
58. James Anderson, *The Education of Blacks in the South, 1860–1935* (Chapel Hill: University of North Carolina Press, 1988), pp. 153–168.
59. Ibid., p. 153.
60. Ibid., p. 156.
61. Quoted in ibid., p. 156.
62. Ibid., p. 156.
63. Vanessa Siddle Walker, *Their Highest Potential: An African American School Community in the Segregated South* (Chapel Hill: University of North Carolina Press, 1996), p. 201.
64. Guadalupe San Miguel Jr., *"Let All of Them Take Heed": Mexican Americans and the Campaign for Educational Equality in Texas, 1910–1981* (Austin: University of Texas Press, 1987), p. 47.
65. Ibid., pp. 48–49.
66. Ibid., p. 50.
67. Gilbert Gonzalez, *Chicano Education in the Era of Segregation* (Philadelphia: Balch Institute Press, 1990), p. 21.
68. Ibid., p. 22.
69. Charles M. Wollenberg, *All Deliberate Speed: Segregation and Exclusion in California Schools, 1855–1975* (Berkeley: University of California Press, 1976), p. 111.
70. Ibid., p. 112.
71. Gonzalez, *Chicano Education,* p. 22.
72. David Montejano, *Anglos and Mexicans in the Making of Texas, 1836–1986* (Austin: University of Texas Press, 1987), pp. 230–231.
73. Gonzalez, *Chicano Education,* pp. 35–36.
74. Ibid., p. 41.
75. San Miguel, *"Let All of Them Take Heed,"* p. 33.
76. Gonzalez, *Chicano Education,* pp. 133–134.
77. Ibid., pp. 134–135.
78. Montejano, *Anglos and Mexicans,* p. 231.
79. Gonzalez, *Chicano Education,* p. 105.
80. Mario T. Garcia, *Mexican Americans: Leadership, Ideology, and Identity, 1930–1960* (New Haven: Yale University Press, 1989), pp. 25–62.
81. Ibid., p. 30.
82. Ibid.
83. Quoted by San Miguel in *"Let All of Them Take Heed,"* p. 72.
84. Ibid., pp. 76–78.
85. Ibid., pp. 79–80.

86. For a study of changes in the racial composition of textbooks, see Joel Spring, *Images of American Life: A History of Ideological Management in Schools, Movies, Radio, and Television* (Albany: State University of New York Press, 1992), pp. 205–214.

87. Wollenberg, *All Deliberate Speed,* p. 118.

88. Margaret Szasz, *Education and the American Indian: The Road to Self-Determination, 1928–1973* (Albuquerque: University of New Mexico Press, 1974), p. 19.

89. Quoted in ibid., p. 22.

90. Lewis Meriam, *The Problem of Indian Administration* (Baltimore: Johns Hopkins Press, 1928).

91. Ibid., p. 346.

92. Ibid.

93. Ibid., pp. 346–403.

94. See Szasz, *Education and the American Indian,* pp. 37–106; and Jon Reyhner and Jeanne Eder, *A History of Indian Education* (Billings: Eastern Montana College, 1989), pp. 102–109.

95. John Hawkins, "Politics, Education, and Language Policy: The Case of Japanese Language Schools in Hawaii," in *The Asian American Educational Experience,* ed. Don T. Nakanishi and Tina Yamano Nishida (New York: Routledge, 1995), p. 35.

96. Ibid., p. 35.

97. Ibid., p. 33.

98. Quoted in Sucheng Chan, *Asian Americans: An Interpretative History* (New York: Twayne Publishers, 1993), p. 114.

99. Quoted in ibid., p. 114.

100. Aida Negron De Montilla, *Americanization in Puerto Rico and the Public School System, 1900–1930* (Rio Piedras: Editorial Edil, 1971), p. 135.

101. Ibid., pp. 140, 170.

102. Ibid., pp. 172–173.

103. Ibid., p. 178.

104. Ibid., p. 180.

105. Ibid., pp. 260–261.

106. Ibid., p. 183.

107. Ibid., p. 181.

108. Ibid., p. 187.

109. Catherine Walsh, *Pedagogy and the Struggle for Voice: Issues of Language, Power, and Schooling for Puerto Ricans* (New York: Bergin & Garvey, 1991), p. 20.

110. Ibid., pp. 20–21.

111. Miriam Cohen, "Reconsidering Schools and the American Welfare State," *History of Education Quarterly* (Winter 2005), p. 521.

112. Ibid., p. 512.

113. See Spring, *Globalization of Education,* pp. 29–83.

9

Human Capital: High School, Junior High School, and Vocational Guidance and Education

By the twenty-first century, human capital goals for education dominated global discussions. Simply stated, *human capital* refers to the role of education in growing the economy and helping graduates find jobs. Today most of the world's policy leaders promote education as an economic solution for unemployment and improved living conditions. Students often consider schooling as the key to their economic future. Human capital education goals have often displaced in importance goals such as active citizenship and transmission of cultural knowledge.[1]

The human capital argument was present at the birth of American schools when Horace Mann claimed that public schooling would increase community wealth. This justification for public schooling became extremely important in the late nineteenth and early twentieth centuries with the advent of vocational education and vocational guidance and the development of the high school as a mass institution.

This chapter explores the early concepts surrounding the relationship between education and human capital economics:

- The evolution of the high school as a mass institution.
- The development of vocational education and vocational guidance.
- The birth of the junior high school.
- Pedagogies serving the new industrial system.
- The historical debate about whether human capital education placed schools in service to corporations.

THE HIGH SCHOOL

The high school was not a mass institution in the nineteenth century, but it did serve a broad spectrum of the population. David Labaree, in his history of Central High School of Philadelphia between 1838 and 1939, found that parental and student pressure on the school forced it to become an institution that provided credentials for getting a job. When the school opened, it was dedicated to providing a moral and civic education along with practical skills. Within a short time, however, pressure from students and parents and public leaders concerned with human capital development forced the school to focus on training for the job market.[2]

The increasing importance of the high school in the twentieth century is best reflected in the changing patterns of school attendance. In 1890 a total of 202,963 students attended 2,526 public high schools. Ten years later, in 1900, these figures had more than doubled—to 519,251 students in 6,005 public high schools. In 1912, the enrollment level reached 1,105,360. These dramatic increases continued; by 1920, 28 percent of American youths—or 2,200,389 students—between the ages of fourteen and seventeen were in high school. During the 1920s the high school truly became an institution serving the masses. By 1930, 47 percent of youths between the ages of fourteen and seventeen—or 4,399,422 students—were in high school, and during the Depression years of the 1930s the American high school began to serve the majority of youths. Enrollment increased to 6,545,991 in 1940, representing two-thirds of the population between the ages of fourteen and seventeen.[3]

The emphasis on education to serve economic goals shaped the development of the modern high school. By the late nineteenth century, high schools began to adopt a differentiated curriculum to serve different vocational aspirations. For those with vocational aspirations that required a college diploma, high schools began to provide a specific college preparatory curriculum. For those who wanted a high school education for employment immediately after graduation, a more general curriculum was offered. In addition, many high schools began to adopt vocational education programs.

The modern high school also embodied a greater concern with the social development of youth. In concrete terms, this meant the addition of high school activities such as clubs, student government, assemblies, organized athletics, and other social events. These social activities were also justified by their contribution to the workings of the economic system. Through these activities American youths were to learn how to cooperate in an industrial society based on large-scale corporations and unions.

The general legal status of high schools was uncertain until the *Kalamazoo* decision of 1874, which was interpreted as supporting the general development of the public high school. The case resulted from a Michigan law of 1859 authorizing school districts with more than one hundred children to establish high school departments if so mandated by the vote of the people. In *Charles E. Stuart and Others v. School District No. 1 of the Village of Kalamazoo and Others* (1874), the plaintiffs claimed that the high school in their area was illegal because a vote had never been taken and that no authority existed in the state to create free high schools through taxation levied on the people. In his written decision, Justice Thomas M. Cooley of the Michigan Supreme Court dismissed the issue of the public vote by noting many irregularities in municipal administration and by arguing that the public showed its approval through its support of the institution.[4]

Although the *Kalamazoo* decision laid the groundwork for the inclusion of high schools in the general interpretation of state constitutional provisions for free schooling, some confusion developed over the purposes of a high school education and the relationship between high schools and colleges. In 1892, at the beginning of the period of rapid expansion of the high school, the National Education Association formed the Committee of Ten on Secondary School Studies under the leadership of Harvard's president, Charles Eliot. The initial concern of the committee was to create uniform requirements for admission to colleges. Many high school educators found it difficult to organize a course of study when different colleges had different requirements for admission. Of course any decision about the organization of studies had to consider the general purposes of a high school education.

The Committee of Ten's final report established a general framework for discussion of the goals of secondary education. In many ways the committee report reflected the crossroad between an educational system designed to provide everyone with a common education and an educational system organized to provide everyone with a specific education based on a future social destination.

One of the major questions facing the Committee of Ten was whether different courses of study should be offered to students ending their education at the secondary level and those planning to go on to college. In other words, should preparation for life differ from preparation for college? This seemingly innocuous question had important implications for the role of education in a democratic society. Because more children of wealthy families tended to go to college than those of poor families, a difference in curriculum for college- and non-college-bound students had the potential of creating a class system of education.

The response of the Committee of Ten to this issue was to recommend against any differences in the courses of study for the two groups of students. Debate immediately following the issuance of the report in 1894 recognized the social implications of the decision against separate curricula for college- and non-college-bound high school students. For example, at the first official presentation of the report, Francis Parker stated, "One unanimous conclusion of all the conferences [that produced the report], a conclusion without a single dissenting voice, or vote, is worth all the cost and all the pains that were necessary to produce the report. That conclusion is that there should be no such thing as class education." He went on to argue that an attempt was under way to reduce city schools to charity schools and to provide the poor with only a partial education. In the context of rejecting a class-based education, Parker stated, "There is no reason why one child should study Latin and another be limited to the '3 R's.'"[5]

Central to discussions about the Committee of Ten report are concerns about differences between the rich and the poor. Some argued that the poor needed a practical education that would prepare them for the realities of their future lives; this suggestion could be considered a means of meeting individual needs and interests. Of course meeting those needs in this fashion limited the educational opportunities of the poor and gave the rich a superior education as measured by the social and cultural power it conferred.

A debate over the meaning of education in a democratic society was fundamental to the organization of the American high school. The most influential position taken on this issue was that of educators and civic leaders concerned with social efficiency.

A leading early twentieth-century educator, William Chandler Bagley, claimed in 1905 that "social efficiency is the standard by which the forces of education must select the experiences that are impressed upon the individual. Every subject of instruction, every item of knowledge, every form of reaction, every detail of habit, must be measured by this yardstick."[6]

The proponents of socially efficient education accepted the growth of large-scale organizations in a modern corporate society but felt that certain changes needed to occur to ensure efficient operation of the new economic system. It was argued that the new large-scale organizations required cooperation, not competition. What this meant for public schools was that students needed to be taught to work together. During the early part of the twentieth century, these ideas resulted in an emphasis in the schools on group activities, sharing, and working together.

Social efficiency doctrines stressed the importance of specialization and expertise in the new large-scale organizations. Specialization, it was reasoned, increased efficiency by allowing each person to concentrate on a single individual task. This was the model of the assembly line and modern bureaucracy, where individual tasks were coordinated through the organization. For educators, specialization meant education of the student for a particular occupation. Under the doctrines of social efficiency, the ideal was to socialize students for cooperation in large-scale organizations where each individual would be performing a specialized task.

Cooperation, specialization, and equal opportunity were the key concepts around which the modern high school was organized. Of course these doctrines of social efficiency ran counter to the traditional academic thrust of the high school.

The battle between the older academic concepts of the high school and the new doctrines of social efficiency was waged in the popular presses in the early part of the twentieth century. For instance, in 1912 the *Saturday Evening Post* published two articles opposing the academic tradition in the high school. One article, by William Mearns, carried the opinionated title "Our Medieval High Schools: Shall We Educate Children for the Twelfth or the Twentieth Century?" The author argued that "culture" had come to dominate the high school, which he stereotyped as an institution wherein "it is clean hands and a pure collar . . . it is knowledge of Hegelian philosophy; it is Greek; it is Latin; it is a five-foot shelf of books; it is twenty thousand a year; it is a sight of truth and a draught of wisdom; it is a frock coat and pearl gloves." In contrast to what he labeled the medieval concept of high schools, Mearns argued, the modern high school should become a democratic institution in which the only studies offered would provide for "efficient service to the community about it."[7]

The other *Saturday Evening Post* article, "The High School and the Boy," by William Lewis, argued that "the high school's largest service is the best possible training for economic efficiency, good citizenship, and full and complete living for all its pupils." The author thought this could best be accomplished by eliminating the dissection of literary masterpieces, providing a wide range of mathematics (but not algebra), and offering foreign languages only as electives. In a later book, *Democracy's High School,* Lewis called for an education "in citizenship and in right social thinking."[8]

The High School and Adolescent Psychology

Central to the high school becoming a mass institution were new theories about adolescents. Early theorists of adolescent psychology believed that it was the key period of development for teaching cooperation and social service required by modern society. The most influential psychologist in this area was G. Stanley Hall (1844–1924), founder of the child study movement in the 1890s and pioneer in the field of adolescent and developmental psychology.

In his classic work *Adolescence,* published in 1904, Hall stated, "The whole future of life depends on how the new powers [of adolescence] now given suddenly and in profusion are husbanded." According to Hall's theory of recapitulation, each stage of individual development parallels a stage of social evolution. Childhood, the years between four and eight, corresponds to a cultural epoch when hunting and fishing were the main activities of humanity. From eleven to twelve, according to Hall, the child recapitulates the life of savagery. During puberty, the new flood of passions develops the social person: "The social instincts undergo sudden unfoldment and the new life of love awakens."[9]

Hall's theories supported other contemporary beliefs that adolescent interests and abilities must be harnessed and directed to some socially useful function. This meant the establishment of institutions such as the high school to capture and channel the sexual and social drives of the adolescent. Hall argued that the utilization of adolescent drives should be the criterion by which institutions are evaluated. He believed that the proper socialization of adolescents is the panacea for most social problems: The "womb, cradle, nursery, home, family, relatives, school, church and state are only a series of larger cradles or placenta, as the soul . . . builds itself larger missions, the only test and virtue of which is their service in bringing the youth to ever fuller maturity."[10]

The image of adolescence projected by Hall's psychology and represented in the popular press of the time was of a romantic stage of life during which the developing sexual and social drives could lead the adolescent to either a life of decadence or a life of social service. The romantic and poetic impulses of youth, it was believed, could be captured and directed toward socially useful projects such as helping the poor, the community, or the nation. Boy Scouts, Girl Scouts, the YWCA, the YMCA, and other youth organizations were justified by their ability to channel the sexual and social drives of the teenager for the good of society. But when youths of the 1920s adopted the style of the Jazz Age, the popular press warned of the imminent collapse of civilization. In other words, youth represented either a promising future or a collapsing civilization.

The Comprehensive High School and the Cardinal Principles of Secondary Education

The National Education Association organized a commission in 1913 whose report eventually established the basic framework for the modern comprehensive high school. This group, the Commission on the Reorganization of Secondary Education, issued its final report in 1918 as the now famous *Cardinal Principles of Secondary Education.* The report, which reflected the strong influence of social efficiency rhetoric, attempted to shape the high school to meet the needs of the modern corporate state. Its final recommendation called for the creation of a comprehensive high school that would include a wide variety of curricula designed to meet the needs of different types of students. The comprehensive high school became the standard for secondary education for more than a half century.[11]

Unlike the report of the Committee of Ten, *Cardinal Principles of Secondary Education* called for a broad program of various courses of study: "Differentiation should be, in the broad sense of the term, vocational . . . such as agricultural, business, clerical, industrial, fine-arts, and household-arts curriculums." One of the major questions facing the commission was whether a differentiated curriculum should require the establishment of separate schools to teach the different curricula—for instance, separate academic and vocational schools.[12] The commission's answer to this question provided the framework for the organization of the comprehensive high school.

The commission argued for comprehensive schools in which all students would come together because this would aid "the pupil through a wide variety of contacts and experiences to obtain a basis for intelligent choice of his educational and vocational career" and would ensure the choice of a curriculum best suited to the student's need. According to the commission, specialized schools might introduce distracting influences, such as location, athletic teams, and friendships. These influences, rather than consideration of curriculum, might determine which school the student attended. The comprehensive high school, in the opinion of the commission, would eliminate those factors from consideration; everyone would attend the same school regardless of his or her choice of course of study.[13]

The commission also used the rhetoric of social efficiency to justify the comprehensive high school, which, the commission argued, allowed for what it called the "two components of democracy"—specialization and unification. The commission's report states, "The purpose of democracy is so to organize society that each member may develop his personality primarily through activities designed for the well-being of his fellow members and of society as a whole." The specialized and differentiated curriculum of the comprehensive high school was to train each student to perform a specific task that would benefit society. Within the context of this argument, democracy was viewed mainly as a means of social organization that would allow each individual to do what she or he is best able to do for the good of the social whole. Education was supposed to fit the individual into a social position that would enable him or her to make a maximum contribution to society. The report stated in bold type that "education in a democracy . . . should develop in each individual the knowledge, interests, ideals, habits, and powers whereby he will find his place and use that place to shape both himself and society toward ever nobler ends."[14]

According to the report, the second component of democracy, or social efficiency, is unification. This democratic ideal shaped the social organization of the modern high school. The report defined *unification* as that part of the ideal of democracy that brought people together and gave them "common ideas, common ideals, and common modes of thought, feeling, and action that made for cooperation, social cohesion, and social solidarity." Although educators in the nineteenth century stressed the importance of schooling in building social cohesion, their primary focus was on the early grades. *Cardinal Principles,* however, gave the major responsibility for socialization to the high school: "In this process the secondary school must play an important part because the elementary school with its immature pupils cannot alone develop the common knowledge, common ideals, and common interests essential to American democracy."[15]

The major problem in providing social cohesion was the fact that students pursued different courses of study. To compensate for the separation caused by the differentiated curriculum, the commission proposed three means of creating a sense of unity. The first, which was directed at the immigrant, emphasized the need for teaching the "mother tongue" and social studies. The other two were organizational techniques. One was "social mingling of pupils through the organization and administration of the school," and the other, directly related to this proposal, was "participation of pupils in common activities . . . such as athletic games, social activities, and the government of the school."[16]

High School Social Life: Cheerleaders and Assemblies

Thus the twentieth-century solution to building unification and cooperation through education was to provide extracurricular activities in the high school. The various elements of school life that were included in the term *extracurricular activities* were in existence long before the issuance of *Cardinal Principles,* but during the 1920s extracurricular activities developed into an educational cult. Courses in organizing extracurricular activities were offered in teacher training institutions, and textbooks and books of readings on the topic were published. In 1926 the *Twenty-Fifth Yearbook of the National Society for the Study of Education* was devoted to the topic. As in any educational movement, certain figures emerged as leaders. One in particular was Elbert K. Fretwell of Teachers College, who organized summer courses for school administrators on preparation of extracurricular programs. Between 1923 and 1927, Fretwell flooded *Teachers College Record* with long bibliographies of material on assemblies, clubs, student government, and homerooms.[17]

Student government was supposed to be the central feature of all extracurricular activities programs. The important place student government assumed in the public schools resulted from activities in the 1890s by New York City urban reform groups, who saw student government as a method of preparing the children of immigrants for participation in democratic government. In 1904 Richard Welling organized the National Self-Government Committee, which campaigned vigorously into the 1940s for student government in public schools and colleges. Before organizing the student government campaign, Welling claimed he realized that education was the key to civic reform. In 1903 he lamented that merely "telling the voters that their taxes were too high did not lead to action at the polls." The best method of encouraging political involvement, he decided, was to give citizens an opportunity to practice the intelligent use of political rights. Having reached this conclusion, he contacted Charles Eliot, then president of the National Education Association, and asked permission to address the organization's annual convention. Before the convention, he made a ringing appeal for student government as a means of curing corrupt government. He told gathered educators, "The new generation must be imbued with a new spirit of civic patriotism . . . you must teach the machinery of government by means of some form of applied civics."[18]

Student governments were instituted by American schools at a phenomenal rate, and by the middle of the twentieth century few high schools were without some form of student government. Throughout this course of development, no serious suggestion was ever made that students be given real power. The purpose of student government was to provide applied civics, not to run the school. William McAndrew, onetime superintendent of the New York City public schools, expressed a typical attitude. Writing in 1897 on a proposed student government plan, he stated, "I believe the plan of delegating any of the executive powers of that officer [principal] to those so irresponsible as students would be unwise."[19] There was general agreement, at least among educators during this period, that, as one writer stated, "any plan that gives pupils full control of the government of a school, a school city, or a school democracy, without the advice and aid of teachers will necessarily lead to an ignominious failure."[20]

The other organizations making up extracurricular activities were justified as contributing to the unification of the school and the preparation of students for participation in a cooperative democracy. In most plans, student governments or student associations were to work with the faculty in administering additional extracurricular activities, which usually included the student newspaper, clubs, athletics, and assemblies. One principal stated in 1917 that an organized program of this nature would "assist in making the spirit of democracy, 'all for each and each for all,' to pervade the school."[21]

The school newspaper was justified as a means of teaching both English and teamwork and of creating a spirit of unity within the school. Clubs in high school programs ranged across a variety of areas. Most high schools and academies in the nineteenth century had some social organizations—usually literary and debating societies—but in the twentieth century a much broader choice of club activities was offered and was justified with claims that the clubs would teach participation in cooperative activities. After the 1918 publication of *Cardinal Principles,* which suggested that one purpose of education was the development of meaningful leisure activities, the argument frequently appeared that clubs prepared students for worthy use of leisure time. For example, one article in 1921 on club activities stated, "A school's service to the future makers of America does not end with preparing them for working hours which occupy only a third of the day. It must also provide specifically for the worthy use of leisure."[22]

The argument was made that athletics could contribute to training for participation in a democratic community in two ways. First, as part of a general health program, it would ensure individual physical efficiency. In language common to human capital theories, *Cardinal Principles* stressed good health as a means of assuring the maximum development of human resources. Second, athletics taught the student how to cooperate and work with a team. This orientation was one reason for the rapid growth of football in the public schools. As a team game, football fostered the coordination and cooperation believed to be needed in a corporate organization. A Seattle high school principal told the National Education Association in 1915, "In the boy's mind, the football team is not only an aggregation of individuals organized to play, but a social instrument with common needs, working along common lines, and embodying a common purpose."[23]

According to *Cardinal Principles,* the activity that was most important in contributing to school unity was the assembly because it brought together students who were otherwise separated by grades, courses of studies, and ability groups. A statement in 1925 by an associate superintendent of schools in Pittsburgh, Pennsylvania, illustrates this point of view: "Students are divided into classes according to their academic advancement, further divided by their curricula. . . . Blocking the pathway to unity is an almost infinite variety of individual differences. The assembly is the one agency at hand capable of checking these tendencies."[24] Assemblies became one of the great events in American high schools. Books, programs, and articles with suggestions for auditorium exercises flooded the educational market. Band concerts, vocational talks, drama productions, class projects, and patriotic celebrations all became part of the public school paraphernalia. The importance of the assembly as school unifier continued through the 1920s. This is exemplified by the opening words of a book titled *Assemblies for Junior and Senior High Schools,* published in 1929: "Junior and senior high schools daily accept the challenge to prepare students for life in a democracy. . . . Specialized organization and complex activities necessitate unification through athletics, the school newspaper, and the assembly. Because of its frequency and provision for universal participation, the assembly may be considered the foremost integrating factor."[25]

The desire to create a cooperative and unified spirit was one of the major factors in the organization of the comprehensive high school. *The Fifth Yearbook of the Department of Secondary-School Principals,* published in 1921, states with regard to extracurricular activities, "What we wish the state to be the school must be. The character of our citizens is determined by the character of our pupils and the development of character in this broadest sense must be the goal of education."[26]

The comprehensive high school became a mixture of planned social activities and a variety of curricula, all of which were attempts to prepare a new generation for a society based on large organizations and occupational specialization. In this context, the development of human capital meant selection and training for a specialized task and socialization for a society based on cooperation.

VOCATIONAL EDUCATION

Vocational education was considered necessary for the United States to compete against other economic powers. Vocational education made the development of human capital through training an important part of the educational system.

Vocational guidance became the institutional mechanism for matching students and educational programs with the needs of the labor market. Together, vocational education and vocational guidance assumed the function of promoting industrial efficiency through the proper selection and training of labor power. Early junior high schools experimented with ideas about vocational guidance and preparation for the corporate world and thus contributed to the development of the comprehensive high school.

Historian Harvey Kantor argues that vocational education never fully succeeded in training workers for industrial occupations. What vocational education did accomplish was to make preparation for jobs the major function of American high schools. In addition, it predisposed educators and other public leaders to think of education as a cure for economic problems. This thinking about the role of public schools has persisted into the twenty-first century.[27]

The early development of vocational education has often been associated with the manual training movement. In 1880 Calvin Woodward founded the Manual Training School at Washington University in St. Louis. The idea of manual training was not to teach a trade but to provide the student with manual activities that would complement a liberal education. In most cases, the emphasis in manual training was on metalworking, woodworking, and drafting.

Before 1900, little support existed for public education that would train students for specific occupations. A major factor in changing attitudes about specific job training was concern about the position of the United States in world markets relative to other industrialized countries, such as Germany. This concern was made explicit in a series of reports in the early twentieth century urging the development of vocational education. The 1905 report of the Committee on Industrial Education of the National Association of Manufacturers states, "Technical and trade education for youth is a national necessity, and the . . . nation must train its youth in the arts of production and distribution." Germany was both feared for its activities in world markets and admired for its educational system, which included vocational and trade schools. For many, copying the German vocational system of education was necessary for improving America's position in international trade. For example, the 1905 report states, "The German technical and trade schools are at once the admiration and fear of all countries. In the world's race for commercial supremacy we must copy and improve upon the German method of education."[28]

In its 1912 report, the Committee on Industrial Education directly related concerns about developing human capital to concerns about global competition. The report argued that two types of capital exist in the world. One type includes land, machinery, and money, and "the other kind is human capital—the character, brains and muscle of the people. . . . This capital we have not developed; we have overlooked the whole question of its complete and efficient development." The failure to develop this human capital, according to the report, was leading to great industrial waste. The report warns, "We should act at once because of the stress of foreign competition. We are twenty-five years behind most of the nations that we recognize as competitors. We must come nearer to the level of international competition."[29]

The 1914 report of the Commission on National Aid to Vocational Education was the most important document in the early vocational education movement.

Established by the U.S. Congress, the commission issued recommendations that were incorporated into the 1917 Smith-Hughes Act. The report opens with a general plea for vocational education as a means of reducing waste in the use of human resources. It also argues that vocational education is justified from a purely educational point of view because it meets the individual needs of students; provides equal opportunity for all to prepare for their lifework; develops a better teaching process—learning by doing; and introduces the idea of utility into education. The report also claims that vocational education would reduce the discontent of workers: "Industrial and social unrest is due in large measure to a lack of a system of practical education fitting workers for their calling."[30]

The report of this congressional commission elaborates on the necessity for vocational education as a means of developing human capital through addressing problems in natural resources and the traditional dependence of American industry on foreign labor. The report argues that as America's natural resources were being depleted, foreign countries were finding new sources of supply. "We cannot continue to draw indefinitely on Europe for cheap labor, nor will cheap labor in the immediate future meet the urgent need in American industry for the more intelligent service necessary if we are to satisfy the rising demand for a better product from our domestic as well as our foreign markets." Vocational education was advocated as an important answer to the economic problems facing the United States.[31]

Like other reports of this period, that of the Commission on National Aid to Vocational Education claims that vocational education would meet the individual needs of students. In making this claim, the report gives a particular meaning to the term *equality of opportunity*. The report states,

> 1. Vocational Training Is Needed to Democratize the Education of the Country: (a) By recognizing different tastes and abilities and by giving an equal opportunity to all to prepare for their life work.[32]

During the common school period in the nineteenth century, equality of opportunity meant giving everyone the same education so that everyone could compete on equal terms in the labor market. In the context of the commission's report, equality of opportunity meant giving students different types of education based on individuals' future occupations. This change in meaning had important implications for the general organization of the educational system and was one of the major shifts in educational ideology to take place between the nineteenth and twentieth centuries.

The commission's report resulted in the passage of the Smith-Hughes Act. This legislation contained a very narrow definition of vocational education, which, according to Marvin Lazerson and W. Norton Grubb in their introduction to their *American Education and Vocationalism: A Documentary History, 1870–1970,* resulted in "strengthening and legitimizing the evolving dual system of education." The legislation defined vocational education as dealing with specific occupational skills. The alternative, according to Lazerson and Grubb, was a broad concept of vocational education that would have prepared the individual for a wide variety of occupations and made individuals competent to change their skills to keep up with changes in technology. The Smith-Hughes Act reinforced a dual system of education—a differentiated curriculum—by clearly separating vocational training from academic training and providing federal money to accomplish that task.[33]

The legislation established a federal board for vocational education, whose tasks were to advise local communities and states, administer vocational education funds, and publish research. Federal expenditures in 1917–1918 represented 27 percent of money spent nationally on vocational education—in 1925–1926, 24 percent. The Smith-Hughes legislation did not result in rapid growth in the number of students in full-time vocational education courses. In 1912–1913, 6.9 percent of high school students were in vocational programs; in 1924, the figure was only 6.7 percent.[34]

The campaign for vocational education led to more general consequences for American schooling. This campaign reinforced arguments for elective courses and differentiation of the curriculum. More important, according to Krug, it contributed "to a widespread bias against the so-called academic side of school work, particularly for the alleged 'masses.' This bias flowed from the attempt to promote industrial education by disparaging the work of what were referred to as the 'literary' schools."[35] By distinguishing between the "abstract-minded" and the "concrete-minded," the vocational education movement opened the door for a class-based education, which assumed that the majority of the children of workers would be best served by vocational programs.

Vocational Guidance

Vocational guidance was the other important aspect of selection and training of students based on the development of human capital. Its purpose was to reduce inefficiency in the distribution of human resources. Vocational guidance developed in a number of cities during the early twentieth century. The movement was inspired by the drive for industrial efficiency and, like other movements in education, contained utopian hopes for the general reform of the social system.

Eli Weaver, the pioneer of vocational guidance in New York City, envisioned the establishment of a central government vocational bureau that would function as a commodity exchange market. He made this proposal after organizing, between 1906 and 1910, committees of teachers in the New York high schools to work with students in planning the students' careers. The function of the central bureau would be to determine the types of training and character needed in available occupations. The bureau would also survey the labor market to identify labor shortages and surpluses. This information would be used to encourage or discourage training in particular occupations, depending on the needs of the labor market. Within the schools, vocational guidance and educational programs would be based on information supplied by the bureau. Also, the bureau would place high school graduates in appropriate occupations. Weaver claimed that the guidance agency would "facilitate the exchange of labor between the workers and employers as the exchange of other commodities is now assisted through the standardizing operations of other exchanges."[36]

There was a tendency in the early stages of the guidance movement to view students as raw material for the industrial machine and to assume the responsibility for shaping good industrial character. For instance, as reported in 1913, as part of the guidance program at the DeKalb Township High School in Illinois, the principal would quote business maxims such as "It is none of my business what you do at night, but if dissipation affects what you do the next day, and you do half as much as I demand, you will last half as long as you hoped." Frank Parsons, founder of the first vocational bureau in Boston in 1908 and often called the "father of vocational guidance," would use an interview and a self-analysis sheet to determine what personality adjustments would be necessary for his clients. During an interview, Parsons would make his own character appraisal by watching the manners and habits of his subject. This appraisal would be followed by a take-home questionnaire. The instructions on the questionnaire told the client, "Look in the glass. Watch yourself. Get your friends to . . . tell you confidentially what they think of your appearance, manners, voice. . . . Get your family and friends to help you recognize your defects." Following these instructions, the individual would answer questions ranging from issues of self-reliance and industriousness to queries such as "Do you wear your fingernails in mourning and your linen overtime?"[37]

The role of the vocational guidance counselor, as it emerged from these more general social goals, was part labor specialist, part educator, and part psychologist. As labor specialist, the guidance counselor needed to understand the job market and its requirements. At the founding meeting of the Vocational Educational Association in 1913, Frederick G. Bonser of Teachers College demanded that a professional education be developed that would train the vocational counselor to know the "relationship between present and probable supply and demand, the relative wages, and the changes in methods, devices, and organization affecting the workers." Bonser emphasized the importance of studying "the physical and mental requirements of occupations."[38]

As psychologist, the early guidance counselor used a variety of tests to determine occupational abilities. The earliest were developed by Harvard psychologist Hugo Munsterberg, who pioneered vocational aptitude testing when he designed tests to determine which Boston streetcar motormen would be least likely to have accidents. In historical terms, Munsterberg believed he was bringing together two major movements in American life: scientific management and vocational guidance.[39]

In the schools, vocational guidance was to help students select a course of study to match their vocational interests and abilities. The Grand Rapids Central High School in Michigan became an early model for vocational guidance. The first meeting of the Vocational Guidance Association in 1913 was held in Grand Rapids, and the principal of the school, Jesse B. Davis, was elected the first secretary of the association. The following year he was elected its president. Davis believed that the major function of education was to guide students into their proper place in the corporate structure and socialize them for that structure through the social life of the school. The social life of Central High School was organized into a pyramid of activities. At the base of the pyramid were clubs, athletics, and student government; then in ascending order were a Boys and Girls Leadership Club, a student council, an advisory council, and, at the top, the principal. Davis believed that this school organization reflected the realities of an organized industrial system. He compared his position as principal to that of a general manager: "The ideals upon which honest living and sound business stand, are the ideals of the public schools."[40]

Typical of the developing role of the counselor was the one suggested by Meyer Bloomfield, Frank Parsons's successor as director of the Boston Vocation Bureau. In an article in Charles Johnston's 1914 anthology *The Modern High School,* Bloomfield states that the "vocational guidance movement has . . . made clear one of the most important and generally neglected services which a school can render, and that is educational guidance."[41] Educational guidance was defined as helping students select educational programs that matched their interests, abilities, and future occupations. Within this framework, the curriculum was to be subservient to the occupational goals of the students. Ideally the school counselor would match a student to an occupation and then to a course of study that would prepare the student for his or her vocation.

JUNIOR HIGH SCHOOL

One of the main arguments for the establishment of the first junior high schools was that they would facilitate the vocational guidance of students and the differentiation of the curriculum. As Edward Krug states in *The Shaping of the American High School,* the junior high school "put forward as advantageous features . . . the advancement of practical subjects, the provision for early differentiation, and the fostering of socialized aims."[42] In 1910 differentiation of the curriculum was one of the major features of the first junior high school to receive national attention. Superintendent Frank Bunker of the Berkeley, California, school system wrote in support of his nationally publicized three-year intermediate school, "To force all children in the seventh and eighth grades . . . to take the same work is clearly wrong."[43]

Within the new junior high schools, guidance personnel were to have the role of helping seventh- and eighth-grade students to choose a course of study. A report on the Rochester, New York, junior high schools stated that they provided "vocational counselors, teachers with shortened teaching programs, [who] confer with pupils and visit homes to consult with parents."[44] In other school systems, the principal often functioned as counselor. For instance, the Los Angeles school system opened its first junior high in 1911; in this school, pupils chose, with the aid of the principal, among six courses of study.

Another response to the guidance problem was to institute the advisory, or homeroom, period. This special period was eventually utilized as both a center for social activity in the school and a part of the guidance program. One highly publicized example was the Ben Blewett Junior High School in St. Louis.

Beginning in the seventh grade, each child at the Ben Blewett School spent 150 to 200 hours a year in advisory periods. In the seventh-grade advisory periods, the student chose a future career. In the eighth grade each student was pro-grammed into one of three different courses of study, depending on vocational choice. Principal Philip Cox, who organized the school in 1917, stated that a guiding principle was the "responsibility [of the school] to each child as an individual, and to society, whose agent it is for leading the children as individu-als and as groups toward the goal of social efficiency."[45]

In the same way that arguments were made for developing unity and coopera-tion in the comprehensive high school, it was argued that socialization was an important goal of the junior high school. One enthusiastic supporter of the junior high school idea wrote in the May 1919 issue of *Educational Review* that a new spirit would pervade the junior high school: "This spirit will be the spirit of cooperation, the spirit of service and of sacrifice for the common good." As in the comprehensive high school, the vehicle for the new social spirit was to be extra-curricular activities. A 1922 survey of the nine years of development of New York junior high schools showed 387 clubs and 68 other after-school activities in opera-tion. The clubs ranged from 83 centering around physical training to 31 devoted to history projects.[46]

One of the major debates about the junior high school was the degree of dif-ferentiation that should be undertaken with early adolescents. This was one of the issues considered by the Commission on the Reorganization of Secondary Educa-tion in *Cardinal Principles*. The commission concluded that the junior high school years should be a period of vocational exploration and prevocational counseling and that differentiation based on vocational choice should be delayed until high school. In general, this became the accepted pattern for junior high education in the 1920s.

The wedding of vocational guidance and socialization in the junior high school provided the complete educational program for the development of human capital. Differentiation would prepare the student for a particular place in society, and socialization would teach the student to cooperate and work for the good of the entire organization. One example of this combination was evident at the Ben Blewett Junior High School. Its principal claimed that teachers could differ with him on anything except "the two fundamental principles for which the school stands." The first principle was a differentiated curriculum, and the second was that "the school cannot be a preparation for adult social life except as it reproduces within itself situations typical of social life."[47]

ADAPTING THE CLASSROOM TO THE WORKPLACE: LESSON PLANS

With the focus on educating for the workplace came new theories of instruction and classroom organization. The idea that teachers should have a formal lesson plan resulted from the Herbartian movement, which was active in the United

States in the 1880s and 1890s. The movement originated in the work of German psychologist Johann Herbart (1776–1841). The major contribution of the Herbartian movement was the class lesson plan suitable for any type of class size or organization. Undoubtedly the lesson plan became a fixture of American education because it allowed bureaucratic control over the teacher. It became a means by which the school principal or supervisor could quickly check on teacher activity. Also, as it developed, the lesson plan reflected a conceptualization of education that emphasized order and planning. To a certain extent, it fit the requirements of large classes with fixed environments.

Herbartians believed in more than just lesson plans; but in the final analysis, the public school classroom reduced Herbartian ideas to a concern with detailed planning of classroom practices. Charles De Garmo, a leading American exponent of Herbart, argued in a book published in 1895 that Herbart added an essential ingredient to the pedagogy of Johann Pestalozzi. According to De Garmo, Herbart accepted Pestalozzian ideas of learning through the senses and with objects but thought that Pestalozzian pedagogy lacked a clear idea of how knowledge is assimilated into the mind. In the chapter "What Pestalozzi Left for Herbart to Do," De Garmo states that the Pestalozzian method "does not show how mental assimilation can best take place, or how the resulting acquisition can be made most efficiently to influence the emotional and volitional side of our nature. Perception is . . . the first stage in cognition, but its equally important correlative is apperception, or mental assimilation."[48]

According to the Herbartians, the best method of instruction is to present material that is related to a previous interest of the student. Therefore, it is important to coordinate subject matter properly and to organize lessons based on the stages of development of student interests. For instance, Herbart argued that the natural interests of the child dictate the teaching of Greek before the teaching of Latin.

The Herbartian lesson plan follows five steps: (1) preparation, (2) presentation, (3) comparison and abstraction, (4) generalization or definition, and (5) application. Preparation involves reminding students of previous knowledge and interests that relate to the material being presented. Presentation is organized so that the material is related to previous interests and knowledge. Comparison and abstraction show the relationships between the new material and things already known by the students. Generalization attempts to make up a single definition that expresses the central idea of the lesson. Application applies the generalization to other experiences.

Willard Elsbree states, "Without question, these five simply stated steps exercised more influence on teaching practice in America between 1890 and 1905 than all other psychological discoveries and philosophical creations combined."[49] Although the Herbartian lesson plan underwent significant change over time, the idea of a formally organized daily lesson became a fixed feature of American education. An educational environment of large classes and bolted-down desks was not antithetical to the lesson plan. Daily lesson plans also suited an environment based on hierarchical control, order, and discipline.

ADAPTING THE CLASSROOM TO THE WORKPLACE: PROGRESSIVISM

In contrast to required lesson plans, the progressive educational theories of John Dewey (1859–1952) had a hard time becoming part of standard classroom instruction. When Dewey was organizing his famous Laboratory School at the University of Chicago in 1896, one problem he encountered was finding tables suitable for the work of groups of children, in place of individual desks designed to be permanently fixed to the floor. In practice, Dewey's methods emphasized student interests, student activity, group work, and cooperation—methods premised on the idea that the school had to serve a new social function in helping students adjust to an urban and industrial society.

When Dewey founded the Laboratory School, he wanted to develop methods that would demonstrate to the student the social value of knowledge and the interdependence of society. One method Dewey hoped would achieve these objectives was the development of social imagination through cooperative group activities. Dewey defined *social imagination* as "the habit of mentally constructing some actual scene of human interaction, and of consulting that for instruction as to what to do." One of his early educational experiments took place in the 1890s in a high school ethics class. Dewey wanted the students to view ethics in relation to real problems as opposed to abstract principles. Dewey presented the students with an actual case of human misery and asked them to use social imagination to work out the problem of charity. Social imagination is the ability to relate isolated ideas to the actual conditions that have given them their original meaning. Dewey argued that this method aided a student in forming "the habit of realizing for himself and in himself the nature of the practical situations in which he will find himself placed."[50]

This method of teaching ethics is based on another important principle. Dewey believed that ideas, values, and social institutions originate in the material circumstances of human life. He rejected the notion that they are of divine origin or reflect some type of ideal. One problem, he thought, is that a belief in ideal forms causes civilization to become trapped by ideas and institutions that are no longer practical. According to Dewey, ideas, values, and institutions should change as the needs of society change. The term *pragmatism,* which is often associated with this school of philosophy, means in its simplest form that humans should adopt those ideas, values, and institutions that best *work* in a particular social situation.

One can understand why many religious groups in the twentieth century reacted negatively to Dewey's ideas. Most religious groups believe that human action should be guided by the word of God and that legitimate values are of divine origin, whereas Dewey's philosophy relies on the ability of individuals to interpret their own experience instead of relying on the word of God.

Dewey believed it was unnecessary for students to become aware of the relationship between knowledge and social experience and to be given an opportunity to act on ideas. It was his conviction that the product of social imagination is merely information until acted on. When acted on, it becomes judgment. "The child," Dewey stated, "cannot get power of judgment excepting as he is continually exercised in forming and testing judgment." Therefore, as Dewey saw it, the school must avoid teaching abstract ideas; rather, it must provide actual conditions out of which ideas grow, and the child must be given an opportunity within the school to test moral and social judgments. In other words, according to Dewey, the school had to become a community of real social relationships.[51]

An often quoted statement by Dewey is that the school is a community with a real social life. Dewey wanted to utilize this community and make it a part of the learning process. He believed that the learning process should be part of an active solution to a social problem because this provides the best basis for helping the student to see the social value of knowledge. For instance, counting was introduced at the Laboratory School by having nursery school children set the table for the midmorning snack. The children quickly learned to count by matching the number of utensils to the number of students.

Dewey, like others of his generation, believed that modern urban industrial life was not providing the social context for teaching children habits of order, industry, and cooperation. He hoped students would learn such habits while working in the school community. In 1899 Dewey explored these issues in "The School and Society," a series of lectures given in response to criticism of the work at the Laboratory School. In the lectures, he stressed that the march of industrialism had destroyed a form of household and community life that had given the child "training in habits of order and of industry, and in the idea of responsibility, of obligation to do something, to produce something, in the world." In the past, he argued, these habits had been learned because most occupations centered around the household. Dewey reminded his audience in industrial Chicago that "those of us who are here today need go back only one, two, or at most three generations to find a time when the household was practically the center . . . [of] all the typical forms of industrial occupation."[52]

It was Dewey's contention that at one time the child experienced and participated in the total industrial process of the community. From these community experiences, the child learned moral habits, industry, and social cooperation. "But it is useless to bemoan the departure of the good old days of children's modesty, reverence, and implicit obedience," Dewey stated. The problem was to retain the advantages of the present and at the same time introduce "into the school something representing the other side of life—occupations which exact personal responsibilities and which train the child in relation to the physical realities of life."[53]

The work that went on in the Laboratory School was designed to create social interaction among pupils that would foster efficient learning and good social habits. The activity of the younger members of the school centered around household occupations. Work directed toward a common productive end, Dewey believed, created an atmosphere of community. Children between the ages of four and five were given the responsibility of preparing their own midmorning meals. They discussed their home life and were led to explore marketing, mail service, and other related occupations. The children played at making a dry-goods store that provided them with the opportunity to develop habits of industry, responsibility, and social cooperation. As a requirement of completing their projects, they also learned to read, write, and do arithmetic.

As the children progressed, they were led to ever-widening circles of activity. At age six, the children were introduced to farm activities. They built a farmhouse and barn of blocks and explored the problems of climate and farm production. At age seven, they began to study the historical development of civilization—a theme that persisted throughout the rest of their stay at the Dewey school. Activity was always associated with their studies; for example, the children began their study of history by investigating occupations and engaging in activities such as weaving and building smelters.

The study of history at the Laboratory School reflected Dewey's ideas about social imagination and community. Children were to develop social imagination by learning to relate ideas, inventions, and institutions to the social conditions that gave birth to them. This process was also supposed to make the pupil aware of interdependence within society: "A society is a number of people held together because they are working along common lines, in a common spirit, and with references to common ends."[54] Dewey felt that a community had existed in America's past because individuals had been aware of the total industrial process, and this awareness joined people into a community through a sense of working together. Dewey believed that modern urban industrial society was destroying this sense of community and common goals and that the school had to actively foster their growth. The function of social imagination, learned in the cooperative work of the school, was to help students relate their work to the total industrial process and to become aware of sharing common social purposes.

Facing his audience of critics in industrial Chicago in 1899, Dewey stated, "How many of the employed are today mere appendages to the machines which they operate! This . . . is certainly due in large part to the fact that the worker has had no opportunity to develop his imagination and his sympathetic insight as to the social and scientific values found in his work."[55] In 1902 Dewey argued before the National Education Association that the school should be the center around which a genuine community life is maintained in urban America: "It must interpret to [the worker] the intellectual and social meaning of the work in which he is engaged: that is, must reveal its relations to the life and work of the world."[56]

As other educators translated Dewey's ideas into classroom practice, many of his concerns about social imagination and the historical roots of occupations were lost. For many, Dewey stood for group activity, learning by doing, relating material to the interests of the child, and doing projects. Statements by Dewey such as "the true center of correlation on the school subjects is . . . the child's own social activities" were used to justify a variety of group and social activities within the school. Often these methods placed an emphasis on group conformity that went beyond anything Dewey intended. For instance, Dewey believed that motives and choices grow out of social situations; he did not believe, as many other educators were to argue, that individual motives and goals should conform to the wishes of the group. Dewey wanted to free individual action, not submerge it in the mediocre standard of group consensus.

In 1906 Colin Scott, one popularizer of group activity in the classroom, organized the Social Education Association. The reason Scott wanted to organize classrooms into working groups is because that is how modern society is organized, and thus he considered working groups the most efficient form of social organization. He argued that the traditional classroom atmosphere ran counter to modern social organization and that the classroom should initiate group projects as preparation for entering a society of cooperative groups.

Through the Social Education Association, Scott promoted the use of self-organized group activity in the classroom as a means of preparing students for life in a cooperative society. The association's charter states, "The fundamental purpose of education should be to prepare the child for a useful life of social service as an active and creative member of the social organism." Scott's principle of self-organized group activity was to allow children to choose their own goals, organize their own groups, and organize their own work.[57]

Scott relates an example of this method. Students were asked, "If you had time given to you for something that you enjoy doing, and that you think worthwhile, what should you choose to do?" Three boys immediately decided on printing. They formed a printing group and began publishing material for the class. In other examples given by Scott, history classes were divided into the Senate and the House of Representatives, and some students chose to be government printers and studied history as a series of legislative bills and debates.[58]

With the spread of Dewey's work and the activities of the Social Education Association, the idea of socialized classroom activity became popular. Articles in educational journals and books on group classroom activities appeared in large numbers. The topics ranged from socializing arithmetic drills to teaching cooking with self-organized groups. Following the lead of education professors like Michael V. O'Shea at the University of Wisconsin and Irving King at the University of Iowa, courses in social education began to be offered in teacher training programs.

At Teachers College, Columbia University, William Heard Kilpatrick used his classes in educational theory to teach a form of group learning called the "project method." His article on the method was first printed in 1918 and became so popular and widely used that it went through seven printings by 1922. The heart of the project method is what Kilpatrick called the "socially purposeful act"—an activity directed toward a socially useful end. As an example, Kilpatrick cited the situation of a girl making a dress. The act of making a dress could be considered a project if the girl were motivated by a social purpose and if she actually planned and made the dress. According to Kilpatrick, the purposeful act is the basic unit of the worthy life and democracy: "A man who habitually so regulates his life with reference to worthy social aims meets at once the demands for practical efficiency and of moral responsibility. Such a one presents the ideal of democratic citizenship." Within the classroom, children were prepared for a purposeful life by pursuing projects that grew out of social situations.[59]

Kilpatrick's project method also reflects the tendency in many social education proposals of the 1920s to stress social conformity. He considered development of moral character to be one of the important results of the project method, and he defined moral character as "the disposition to determine one's conduct and attitudes with reference to the welfare of the group." In the classroom, the inculcation of this disposition was a function of group acceptance or rejection: "There are few satisfactions so gratifying and few annoyances so distressing as the approval and disapproval of our comrades. . . . When the teacher merely coerces and the other pupils side with their comrade . . . conformity may be but outward. But when all concerned take part in deciding what is just . . . conformity is not merely outward." According to Kilpatrick, moral character is developed when the individual is conditioned always to respond to the desires of the group.[60]

The project method, group activity, socialized learning, child-centered education, and the educating of social imagination were ideas that received a wide audience in the educational community. In many ways, these methods of instruction seemed suitable for preparing students for a world of highly organized living in cities and corporations. Undoubtedly, most teachers trained in the first half of the twentieth century received some exposure to these methods. The actual use of the methods depended on the teacher, the school district, the number of students in a class, and the environment of the classroom.

ADAPTING THE CLASSROOM TO THE WORKPLACE: STIMULUS–RESPONSE

More popular than progressivism were the teaching methods advocated by William James and Edward Thorndike. James (1842–1910), a leading Harvard philosopher and psychologist, condensed his two-volume work, *Principles of Psychology* (1890), into a one-volume text for teachers. This condensation was published in 1899 under the title *Talks to Teachers on Psychology: And to Students on Some of Life's Ideals.* Thorndike (1874–1949) studied under James at Harvard and incorporated many of James's ideas into his own work. Thorndike can be considered the "father of educational psychology." His major work, *Educational Psychology,* published in 1913, set the tone in education for several decades.

Both James and Thorndike were associated with the development of stimulus–response, or behavioral, concepts of learning. In James's classic example of learning, in the opening section of *Principles of Psychology,* a baby is pictured reaching for a candle flame, a reflex action caused by the stimulation of the fire. The baby's fingers are burned, and it learns not to reach for the flame. James contends that in any future stimulation by the fire of a candle, the baby's nervous system would respond with memories of pain, inhibiting the original grasping reflex and causing the hand to be withdrawn.[61]

For James, this simple learning situation initiates the development of habits in the baby. James considered the building of habits to be the most important function of education because through controlled development of habit, social order could be maintained:

> Habit is thus the enormous fly-wheel of society, its most precious conservative agent. It alone is what keeps us all within bounds of ordinance, and saves the children of fortune from the envious uprisings of the poor. It alone prevents the hardest and most repulsive walks of life from being deserted by those brought up to tread therein.[62]

James extended the concept of habit into the thought process. As he envisioned it, the mind contains a steady stream of consciousness; and when confronted with a choice, the individual selects an action out of that stream of thought. Of course the individual is conditioned to attend to particular ideas in the stream of consciousness in particular situations. James believed that choices are determined by previous stimulus–response learning. This reasoning about human action was problematic for James because it seems to deny free will. If all actions and choices are determined by previous learning, then there is no free will and no individual responsibility for one's actions. This issue has been a central problem in behaviorism since the time of James's original study. James argued his way out of the dilemma by claiming that individuals have the power to make the effort to attend to particular things in the stream of consciousness.

Although James never advocated specific classroom practices, his psychological theories suggest that correct habits can be built through exercise and drill. Edward Thorndike made these two classroom practices part of his pedagogical theory when he translated stimulus–response learning into what he called "connectionism." Connectionism refers to the connection, or relationship, between stimulus and response. Thorndike argued that all changes in the human intellect are the result of certain fundamental laws that affect these connections.

What Thorndike called "fundamental laws of change" became his basic methods of instruction. In general, they are mechanical methods that had been traditional classroom practices. In some ways, Thorndike simply justified the traditional by making it sound scientific. For instance, his first fundamental law, the Law of Exercise, states that "other things being equal, the oftener or more emphatically a given response is connected with a certain situation, the more likely it is to be made to that situation in the future." He gives as an example a child responding "six" to the question "How many are four and two?" Supposedly, if the child repeats the answer to the question enough times, the question and the answer will be permanently connected in the mind. Thorndike states this law more briefly: "Other things being equal, exercise strengthens the bond between situation and response."[63]

Thorndike's second law of learning, the Law of Effect, states, "The greater the satisfyingness of the state of affairs which accompanies or follows a given response to a certain situation, the more likely that response is to be made to that situation in the future." For instance, in the example of the child responding "six" to the question "How many are four and two?" the correct answer would be strengthened if the child were rewarded with candy or a smile.[64]

Thorndike viewed teaching as a science concerned with the control of human behavior: "Using psychological terms, the art of teaching may be defined as the art of giving and withholding stimuli with the result of producing and preventing certain responses." The power of the teacher was in his or her control of the stimuli. Thorndike divided stimuli into two categories: "under direct control" and "under indirect control." Stimuli under direct control include love and tact—shown by gestures, facial expressions, and speech. Stimuli under indirect control are the physical conditions of the school and classroom.[65]

Thorndike's dream was to turn all teaching into a scientific profession in which all educators would be guided by the scientific method and spirit. As scientific professionals, educators would be concerned with controlling the learning of students and with scientific measurement of results. In Thorndike's world, the scientifically constructed test is at the heart of the educational process: "Testing the results of teaching and study is for the teacher what verification of theories is to the scientist. . . . It is the chief means of fitting teaching to the previous experience and individual capacities of pupils."[66]

Like Dewey, Thorndike had a social vision that was directly related to the educational methods he advocated. At the center of his social vision was the concept of tests and measurement. He believed that the ideal social organization is one in which people are scientifically selected for their social roles through testing. According to Thorndike, human classification through tests and measurement would produce a more efficient society by matching individual talents with social needs. This theory made psychologists and schools the major determiners of the distribution of human resources.

Thorndike's social ideals had important implications for the meaning of democracy and equality of opportunity. Measurement was central in Thorndike's social philosophy, based on his role in the development of intelligence tests.

Thorndike believed that intelligence is determined by nature and that it can be measured by tests. He defined intelligence as the number of connections the mind can make between stimuli and responses: A "person whose intellect is greater or higher or better than that of another person differs from him in the last analysis in having, not a new sort of physiological process, but simply a larger number of connections of the ordinary sort." This definition of intelligence allows for measurement of the number of connections and, consequently, for the quantification of intelligence.[67]

The idea that intelligence is primarily a product of nature, as opposed to environment, had major implications for social policy. Thorndike stood squarely on the nature side of the nature–nurture debate. Regarding measurement of intelligence, he states, "What is essential to the hypothesis is that by original nature, men differ in respect of the number of connections or associations with ideas which they can form, so that despite identical outside environments, some of them would have many more than others."[68] Psychologists who believed that nature is the primary determiner of intelligence also believed that intelligence can be inherited. These beliefs usually led to the conclusion that racial differences exist regarding intelligence. For instance, a common belief of the period was that Northern Europeans had naturally superior intelligence compared to Southern Europeans.

The classroom environment of bolted-down desks and large numbers of students was more conducive to Thorndike's stimulus–response, drill, reward, and measurement methods of instruction than to the types of group activity and socialized forms of instruction advocated by the social educators. One can easily imagine that a teacher trained in both traditions, when faced with a controlled and structured classroom environment, would tend to adopt Thorndike's scientific methods. One also can imagine that, under these conditions, many teachers accepted the doctrines of classroom control preached by William Chandler Bagley in his popular book *Classroom Management*.

CLASSROOM MANAGEMENT AS PREPARATION FOR FACTORY LIFE

Classroom Management became a standard teacher training text during the first quarter of the century and was reprinted thirty times between 1907 and 1927. Bagley believed that the primary role of the school is to build good industrial habits of the type needed on the assembly line. Bagley's ideal teacher was one who would "rigidly 'hew to the line' in all of those initial stages of habit building," and in his ideal school everything was reduced to rigid routine. Bagley stated that the expert observer could immediately gauge the efficiency of the teacher by "the manner in which lines pass to and from the room."[69]

Because Bagley could find no arguments against pupils keeping step while walking, he advocated the Lancasterian method of lockstep marches. He also insisted that students be given drills in packing their desks in a certain order, in going to assigned places at the blackboard, in leaving the room, and in marching through the cloakroom to collect coats. To reduce the problem of children interrupting class activities, he stated that "regular habits should be speedily established with regard to the bodily functions." He recommended that lines of children pass through the lavatories at recess time before they are allowed on the playground. Bagley urged teachers to train their students to give physical attention on command: "In general, the command, Attention! should be stimulus for the habitual adjustment of the body in a certain definite posture." He recommended as the ideal posture "head erect, eyes turned toward the teacher, hands or arms folded (preferably the former), feet flat on the floor, instant cessation of all . . . school work or activity."[70]

Many teachers faced with large classes and wanting to maintain order probably followed Bagley's recommendations. As the most popular system of classroom management, it complemented Thorndike's instructional methods more than those of the social educators. But what teachers actually did in their classrooms demonstrated a great deal of variation. In his analysis of classroom activity in the New York schools between 1920 and 1940, Larry Cuban found that in elementary schools most group instruction (41 percent) was a mix of teacher- and student-centered instruction. Strictly teacher-centered instruction occurred 27 percent of the time, and student-centered instruction occurred 32 percent of the time. Cuban found similar variation of proportions for classroom activities and high school instruction. He found more student-centered instruction during this period in Denver than in New York, whereas patterns in Washington, DC, were closer to those in New York.

Cuban's general conclusion about teaching during this period is that teachers used a variety of methods depending on the conditions they encountered and their own personal philosophies. The problem was that many of these approaches to instruction contradicted one another. It was difficult to reconcile the doctrines of John Dewey with those of Edward Thorndike, for example, or the demands for efficiency with those for child-centered education. Cuban argues that teachers were beset with contradictory "impulses to be efficient, scientific, child-centered, and authoritative," and the result was that "teachers constructed patchwork compromises to contain these competing, often contradictory, impulses but (and here I can only speculate) at a cost of leaving within many a vague uneasiness over the aims of teaching, classroom discipline, and relations with students that seldom [went] away."[71]

HISTORICAL INTEPRETATIONS: PUBLIC BENEFIT OR CORPORATE GREED?

Whether the expanded role of the school, the changes in classroom practices, and the development of the comprehensive high school, of vocational education, and of vocational guidance reflected corporate greed or public demands is widely debated by historians. At one end of the spectrum, historians have described the major educational changes occurring in the late nineteenth and early twentieth centuries as simply responses to the problems caused by the collapse of traditional institutions and the influx of immigrants unfamiliar with American democratic ways of living. At the other end of the scale, the argument has been made that the schools were brought under the control of the new corporate elite to serve its social and economic interests. In the middle of this debate has been the claim that immigrants and workers helped to define their own educational future through rational economic choices.

One early interpretation of this period is that given by Ellwood Cubberley. In *Public Education in the United States: A Study and Interpretation of American Educational History,* first published in 1919, Cubberley reflected the attitudes of many educators about social and economic conditions in the late nineteenth and early twentieth centuries and the thinking of some educational reformers of that period. His interpretation was that the schools had to change to meet the threat posed to democratic institutions by immigrants from Southern and Eastern Europe and to instill the social values lost with the passing of small-town rural life.

Cubberley portrayed the immigrants from Southern and Eastern Europe as being politically, socially, and educationally backward in comparison with earlier immigrants from Northern and Western Europe. He stated that these newer immigrants were "largely illiterate, docile, often lacking in initiative, and almost wholly without the Anglo-Saxon conceptions of righteousness, liberty, law, order, public decency, and government, [and] their coming has served to dilute tremendously our national stock and to weaken and corrupt our political life." He included in this category Italians immigrating after 1870; Poles, Bohemians, Hungarians, Slovaks, and Austrians arriving after 1880; and Jews, Russians, Japanese, Koreans, and residents of the Balkans. According to Cubberley, these immigrant groups were a threat to the American way of life.[72]

Cubberley argued that in the past the assimilation of immigrant groups was easier because most (except the Germans) spoke English, had common values, and were free "of a priesthood bent on holding nationalities together for religious ends." The assimilation of newer groups was retarded because of their large numbers, their settlement in urban areas, and various language and religious differences. Cubberley argued that these conditions made it necessary for the schools consciously to institute Americanization programs "to so assimilate the foreign-born that they come to have our conceptions of law and order and government, and come to act in harmony with the spirit and purpose of our American national ideals."[73]

After detailing the technological and industrial changes after the Civil War and the growth of urbanization in America, Cubberley maintained that the influence of the home and church were seriously weakened, and consequently traditional values of courtesy, respect, obedience, and honesty were not so widely taught to children as in the past. In addition, the homogeneous community of the American past was dissolving, so that it no longer exercised restraint over individual actions; and the nature of employment had changed to meet the growing requirements of specialization in the factory system.

Cubberley argued that, against the background of these changes, the school changed to meet the needs of society: "As modern city-life conditions have come more and more to surround both boys and girls, depriving them of the training and education which earlier farm and village life once gave, the school has been called to take upon itself the task of giving training in those industrial experiences and social activities which once formed so important a part of the education of American youths." Also, he claimed, the growth of divisions among social classes as a result of industrialization required the schools to build a new social consciousness and unity.[74]

From this perspective, Cubberley's interpretation of the educational changes of the late nineteenth and early twentieth centuries is that the school changed simply to solve social and economic problems. Within this framework, the school is seen as a mere captive of social conditions. There was little or no discussion by Cubberley of the school as a political institution shaped by the competition of various interest groups in society.

Lawrence Cremin, in his 1961 landmark study *The Transformation of the School: Progressivism in American Education, 1876–1957,* used the same interpretative framework, but without the attitude of Anglo-Saxon superiority found in Cubberley's description of the new immigrants. Cremin placed all major educational changes of the late nineteenth and the twentieth centuries under the label "progressivism" and stated that this movement began as "a many-sided effort to use the schools to improve the lives of individuals." Cremin listed as elements in this "many-sided effort" the expansion of the social functions of the school "to include direct concern for health, vocation, and the quality of family and community life"; the use of principles of psychology and the social sciences in classroom instruction; and the attempt to have instruction meet the needs of "different kinds and classes of children."[75]

Like Cubberley, Cremin did not deal with political conflicts or with the issue of whose interests were being served by the changes in educational institutions. His basic assumption was that the school was a benign institution and that most educational changes were the result of attempts to improve the quality of life for all people.

Unlike Cubberley, however, Cremin presented a broader view of the educational community's reaction to the new immigration. He identified one school of thought, which he associated with Cubberley, as believing that Americanization meant Anglicization. Cremin argued that others believed that the promise of national unity was in the creation of a new nationality that would result from a melting together of the old and new immigrants. Still another group believed that cultural pluralism was possible, allowing ethnic identity to be maintained in the framework of shared American values. Cremin also provided an in-depth and scholarly interpretation of the school's response to industrialization and urbanization.

Many scholars have opposed the view that most educational change in the late nineteenth and early twentieth centuries was primarily a product of altruism. One set of interpretations argues that the political and administrative structure of education changed to ensure elite and corporate control of the educational system and to produce cooperative and docile workers. Another set of interpretations portrays the educational change of the period as a result of the dynamic interplay between the demands of industry and the demands of workers. This interpretative framework makes historical change a product of conflict—not the manipulation of passive workers by powerful business leaders.

The earliest historical study to span both interpretative frameworks was Merle Curti's *Social Ideas of American Educators*. Curti contended that the majority of educational changes that occurred at that time were designed to serve the interests of the owners of industrial enterprises. For instance, he argued that vocational education and manual training were attempts to control and counteract radicalism among American workers: "An increasing number of educators advocated manual training and industrial education as the best specific means of counteracting radicalism on the part of the working masses." According to Curti, vocational education, the differentiated curriculum of the comprehensive high school, and other educational reforms were designed specifically to improve the industrial efficiency of America for competition in world markets. Even the values of cooperation and interdependence that were to be taught in the classroom were considered by Curti to be attempts to deny the inevitable conflict between labor and capital. Curti maintained that the values of most leading educators were economically conservative: "Hardly an annual meeting of the National Education Association was concluded without an appeal on the part of educators for the help of the teacher in quelling strikes and checking the spread of socialism and anarchism." The educators who were developing moral training for the schools, he stated, "turned . . . increasingly to the social sciences as means by which schools might inculcate respect for law and order, and suspicion for the doctrines of socialism and anarchism."[76]

Another school of historical interpretation places this era's educational changes in the broader conceptual framework of the rise of the corporate liberal state. Clarence Karier, Paul Violas, and Joel Spring's *Roots of Crisis: American Education in the Twentieth Century,* Joel Spring's *Education and the Rise of the Corporate State,* and Clarence Karier's *Shaping the American Educational State* advanced the idea that schools in the late nineteenth and early twentieth centuries were shaped as instruments of the corporate liberal state for maintaining social

© *Corbis*

control. Karier stated that some believed that the corporate liberal state "could be used as a positive vehicle to reconcile the competing interest of capital, labor and the public welfare. They further surmised that such conflicting interest could be reconciled by effectively rationalizing and stabilizing an ever expanding economy of production and consumption of goods and services."[77] In other words, the government was to intervene in the economy and social system to maintain balance and rational order. The public schools were seen as an important instrument used by the government to aid in the rationalization and minimization of conflict by selecting and training students for their future positions in the economy and by imbuing the population with a sense of cooperation and national spirit.

According to this interpretation, the corporate liberal state was operated by expert managers using scientific methods, which in the case of the public schools meant psychologists armed with tests to measure intelligence, abilities, and interests. Within this interpretative context, the expanded social functions of the school, the socialized classroom with its emphasis on cooperation, vocational education, vocational guidance, testing, and a differentiated curriculum were all instruments to provide rationality and order in society.

This group of historians emphasized the concept of social control—a concept born during the late nineteenth and early twentieth centuries and used by the architects of corporate liberalism to justify their actions. This idea was most clearly stated by sociologist Edward Ross in a series of articles that appeared in the *American Journal of Sociology* between 1896 and 1898. In these articles, Ross defined *social control* as the means of maintaining social order, and he divided the means of control into external and internal forms. External forms of control involve direct confrontation between individuals and the police or government. Internal forms of control, which Ross considered more democratic and to be most relied upon, involve psychic control—control of the conscience of individuals. In America's past, Ross argued, internal forms of control were established through the community, family, and church. The problem for the future, he maintained, was that these traditional instruments of internal control were collapsing with the growth of industrialization and urbanization.

Ross suggested that these traditional instruments of social control be replaced with new forms, such as mass media, propaganda, and education, and he argued that reliance on education as a means of control was becoming characteristic of American society as the school began to take the place of the church and family: "The ebb of religion is only half a fact. The other half is the high tide of education. While the priest is leaving the civil service, the schoolmaster is coming in. As the state shakes itself loose from the church, it reaches out for the school."[78]

Ross believed that modern civilization was learning this important lesson. He argued that the advantage of the school over the home as a means of control was in the fact that a public official was substituted for a parent: "Copy the child will, and the advantage of giving him his teacher instead of his father to imitate, is that the former is a picked person, while the latter is not." In the school, the child learned "the habit of obedience to an external law which is given by a good school discipline." In rather interesting language, Ross referred to education in the context of social control as collecting "little plastic lumps of human dough from private households and shap[ing] them on the social kneadingboard."[79]

In summary, those who argue within the framework of the corporate liberal state interpret educational changes in the late nineteenth and early twentieth centuries as an attempt to scientifically engineer a specialized and cooperative society. According to these educational historians, the major problem in this effort is that science and claims of objective social engineering were only masks for values that were racist and designed to control the majority of people. In contrast, some argue that controllers of the liberal corporate state were merely trying to engineer a society that would protect their interests and that educators, the schools, social science, psychologists, and other engineers of the human mind were merely servants of power.

A variation on the theme of the corporate liberal state was used by David Tyack in his well-written, scholarly study *The One Best System: A History of American Urban Education.* An important element in Tyack's history is the development of modern urban educational bureaucracies and power structures. Like Merle Curti, Tyack concluded that education was controlled by business and corporate elites, and like Karier, Violas, and Spring, he believed that an alliance existed between the new corporate leaders and the intellectuals who served as their instruments of power. Regarding the campaign from 1890 to 1920 to reform urban education, Tyack stated, "At that time an interlocking directorate of urban elites—largely business and professional men, university presidents and professors, and some 'progressive' superintendents—joined forces to centralize the control of schools."[80]

Using the corporate model developed by the historians of the corporate liberal state, Tyack argued that the administration of schools during this period was patterned after that of the modern corporation and factory. He called these centralizers of organizational control and power "administrative progressives," in contradistinction to the political progressives who had organized the corporate liberal state.

Another approach to interpreting history is to consider social change as a product of interaction between different social groups. William Reese's *Power and the Promise of School Reform: Grassroots Movements during the Progressive Era* stressed that many of the changes in the social functions of schools in the late nineteenth and early twentieth centuries were a product of local groups putting pressure on the business leaders and professionals who were gaining control of local school systems. His study focused on the history of three communities: Milwaukee, Wisconsin; Toledo, Ohio; and Rochester, New York. Reese portrayed within these communities a combination of parents' associations, women's organizations, labor unions, and other groups struggling to have the schools meet the needs of the local community. Out of this struggle came the use of the schoolhouse as a social center, the establishment of playgrounds, the provision of health facilities in schools, and the creation of summer schools.

The important issue raised by Reese is whether or not school reform was imposed on a passive population. Reese's research certainly disproved this interpretation. But the arguments regarding the use of these reforms as instruments of social control by a dominant elite are also valid. Reese recognized that these different groups fought for the control of schools and of the school reform movement. He summarized this situation in the following words:

> To a banker on the Milwaukee board of education in 1910, school organization represented business ethics, and teachers were hired to instill proper values into incipient workers. To members of middle-class women's organizations, however, schools were humanitarian institutions that sponsored free breakfasts for the hungry and safe playgrounds for guttersnipes. Political radicals and progressive trade unionists, on the other hand, often saw schools as evolving democratic forms that nevertheless required vigilance and continual protection from the serpentine arms of manufacturers and capitalists.[81]

Reese's interpretation provides a method of interpreting the politics of education in the twentieth century. Within this interpretative framework, the school is seen by a variety of opposing groups as an institution that can serve their particular purposes. By the twenty-first century, one could see this particular theme in the struggles over educational policy taking place between the Democratic and Republican parties.[82]

With regard to the early twentieth century, there would appear to be some contradiction between the idea of elites using school reform as an instrument of social control and more populist groups supporting similar reform to benefit the working class. These seemingly contradictory interpretations can be resolved by the argument that the haves and have-nots shared a similar vision of the best organization for society.

CONCLUSION: THE MEANING OF EQUALITY OF OPPORTUNITY

In the twentieth century, one of the dominant themes in education was equality of opportunity. The differentiated curricula of the junior and senior high schools, together with vocational guidance, were to provide equal opportunity from the perspective of improving human capital. Within this context, equality of opportunity took on special and complex meanings. First, equal opportunity was considered good for society because it increased industrial efficiency by matching individual talents to specific occupational requirements. Everyone was to be given an equal chance to rise or fall on the social ladder according to individual abilities. This meant everyone would be given an equal chance to run the social race—not that everyone would have equal income or social status. Second, equal opportunity was considered good for the individual because it allowed a person to find the best place in the economic system in which to develop personal interests and abilities.

A major change occurred between the nineteenth and twentieth centuries in the school's role in providing equal opportunity. In the early days of the common school movement, education was to provide equal opportunity by giving everyone a common or equal education, after which the social race would begin, with everyone competing for places in the social and economic structure. In the twentieth century, the provision for equal opportunity was made part of the school system through vocational guidance and a differentiated curriculum. No longer did students receive an equal, or common, education; rather, they received different educations based on individual differences. The race for social positions was to be a function no longer of the marketplace but of the scientific selection process in the school.

Notes

1. For a history of the globalization of human capital educational goals, see Joel Spring, *Pedagogies of Globalization: The Rise of the Educational Security State* (Mahwah, NJ: Lawrence Erlbaum, 2006).
2. David F. Labaree, *The Making of an American High School: The Credentials Market and the Central High School of Philadelphia, 1838–1939* (New Haven: Yale University Press, 1988).
3. Edward Krug, *The Shaping of the American High School, vol. 1, 1880–1920* (New York: Harper & Row, 1964), pp. 169–170, 284; and *The Shaping of the American High School, vol. 2, 1920–1941* (Madison: University of Wisconsin Press, 1972), pp. 42, 218–219.
4. Edward Krug, *Salient Dates in American Education: 1635–1964* (New York: Harper & Row, 1966), pp. 91–95.
5. Quoted in Krug, *Shaping, vol. 1,* p. 68.
6. Quoted in ibid., pp. 274–275.
7. Quoted in ibid., p. 280.
8. Quoted in ibid., p. 281.
9. G. Stanley Hall, *Adolescence, vol. 1* (Englewood Cliffs, NJ: Prentice Hall, 1904), p. xv; and G. Stanley Hall, "Childhood and Adolescence," in *Health, Growth, and Heredity,* ed. Charles Strickland and Charles Burgess (New York: Teachers College Press, 1965), p. 108.

10. G. Stanley Hall, *Adolescence, vol. 2* (Englewood Cliffs, NJ: Prentice Hall, 1904), p. 125.
11. Commission on the Reorganization of Secondary Education, National Education Association, *Cardinal Principles of Secondary Education,* Bureau of Education Bulletin (Washington, DC: U.S. Government Printing Office, 1918). The remainder of the discussion of *Cardinal Principles,* the comprehensive high school, and extracurricular activities is taken from Joel Spring, *Education and the Rise of the Corporate State* (Boston: Beacon Press, 1972), pp. 108–125.
12. Commission on the Reorganization of Secondary Education, *Cardinal Principles,* p. 109.
13. Ibid., pp. 109–110.
14. Ibid., p. 110.
15. Ibid.
16. Ibid., p. 111.
17. For instance, Elbert K. Fretwell, "Extra-Curricular Activities of Secondary Schools," *Teachers College Record* (January 1923; January 1924; May 1926; June 1926; June 1927).
18. Richard Welling, *As the Twig Is Bent* (New York: Putnam, 1942), p. 91.
19. William A. McAndrew, *School Review* (September 1897), pp. 456–460.
20. Walter L. Phillips, "Pupil Co-operation in Self-Government," *Education* (April 1902), p. 543.
21. Edward Rynearson, "Supervised Student Activities in the School Program," *First Yearbook, National Association of Secondary School Principals* (Cicero, IL: National Association of Secondary School Principals, 1917), pp. 47–50.
22. Mary A. Sheehan, "Clubs—A Regular Social Activity," *High School Journal* (October 1921), pp. 132–135, reprinted in Joseph Roemer and Charles F. Allen eds., *Readings in Extra-Curricular Activities* (New York: Teachers College Press, 1929), p. 304.
23. V. K. Froula, "Extra-Curricular Activities: Their Relation to the Curricular Work of the School," *National Education Association Proceedings* (1915) (Washington, DC: National Education Association, 1915), pp. 738–739.
24. Charles R. Foster, *Extra-Curricular Activities in the High School* (Richmond, VA: Johnson Publishing Company, 1925), pp. 108–109.
25. Eileen H. Galvin and M. Eugenia Walker, *Assemblies for Junior and Senior High Schools* (New York: Professional & Technical Press, 1929), p. 1.
26. Francis H. J. Paul, "The Growth of Character through Participation in Extra-Curricular Activities," *The Fifth Yearbook of the Department of Secondary-School Principals* (Cicero, IL: National Association of Secondary School Principals, 1921), vol. 2, pp. 54–60.
27. Harvey R. Kantor, *Learning to Earn: School, Work, and Vocational Reform in California, 1880–1930* (Madison: University of Wisconsin Press, 1988).
28. National Association of Manufacturers, "Reports of the Committee on Industrial Education (1905, 1912)," ibid., p. 91.
29. Ibid., pp. 92–96.
30. U.S. House of Representatives, "Report of Activities of the Commission on National Aid to Vocational Education," 63rd Cong., 2nd sess. (1914), ibid., pp. 116–132.
31. Ibid.
32. Ibid.
33. Marvin Lazerson and W. Norton Grubb, *American Education and Vocationalism: A Documentary History, 1870–1970* (New York: Teachers College Press, 1974), pp. 30–31.
34. Ibid.

35. Krug, *Shaping, vol. 1,* pp. 243–244.
36. Eli W. Weaver, *Wage-Earning Occupations of Boys and Girls* (New York: Student's Aid Committee of the High School Teachers' Assoc., 1912). The remainder of the discussion of the history of vocational guidance and the junior high school is taken from Spring, *Education and the Rise of the Corporate State,* pp. 91–108.
37. Frank Parsons, *Choosing a Vocation* (Boston: Houghton Mifflin, 1909), pp. 32–44.
38. Frederick G. Bonser, "Necessity of Professional Training for Vocational Counseling," in *Vocational Guidance: Papers Presented at the Organization Meeting of the Vocational Association, Grand Rapids, MI, October 21–24, 1913,* in *U.S. Bureau of Education Bulletin,* no. 14 (1914), p. 38.
39. Hugo Munsterberg, *Psychology and Industrial Efficiency* (Cambridge, MA: Harvard University Press, 1913), pp. 36–55.
40. Jesse B. Davis, *Vocational and Moral Guidance* (Boston: Ginn and Company, 1914), pp. 46–123.
41. Meyer Bloomfield, "Vocational Guidance in the High School," in Charles H. Johnston, *The Modern High School* (New York: Scribner's Son, 1914), p. 612.
42. Krug, *Shaping, Vol. I,* pp. 327.
43. Quoted in Ibid., p. 328.
44. Quoted in *Report of the Committee to Make a Survey of the Junior High Schools of the City of New York* (New York: New York City Department of Education, 1924), p. 236.
45. Philip Cox, "The Ben Blewett Junior High School: An Experiment in Democracy," *School Review* (May 1919), pp. 345–359.
46. Thomas W. Gosling, "Educational Reconstruction in the Junior High School," *Educational Review* (May 1919), pp. 384–385.
47. Cox, "Ben Blewett Junior High School," p. 346.
48. Charles De Garmo, *Herbart and the Herbartians* (New York: Scribner, 1895), p. 7.
49. Willard Elsbree, *The American Teacher: Evolution of a Profession in a Democracy* (New York: American Book Company, 1939), p. 407.
50. John Dewey, "Teaching Ethics in the High School," *Educational Review* (November 1893), p. 316.
51. John Dewey, "Ethical Principles Underlying Education," *The Third Yearbook of the National Herbart Society* (Chicago: National Herbartian Society, 1897), p. 31.
52. John Dewey, "The School and Society," in *Dewey on Education: Selections,* ed. Martin Dworkin (New York: Teachers College Press, 1959), p. 36.
53. Ibid., p. 37.
54. Ibid., p. 39.
55. Ibid., p. 46.
56. John Dewey, "The School as Social Center," *National Education Association Proceedings* (1902) (Washington, DC: National Education Association, 1902), p. 381.
57. "Social Education Association," leaflet included in bound edition of *Social Education Quarterly vol. 1* (1906).
58. Colin A. Scott, *Social Education* (Boston: Ginn, 1908), pp. 102–146.
59. William Heard Kilpatrick, *The Project Method* (New York: Teachers College Press, 1918), p. 6.
60. Ibid., p. 14.
61. William James, *Principles of Psychology, vol. 2* (1890; reprint, New York: Dover, 1950), pp. 24–26.
62. Ibid., p. 121.

63. Edward Thorndike, "Education, a First Book," in *Psychology and the Science of Education: Selected Writings of Edward L. Thorndike,* ed. Geraldine Joncich (New York: Teachers College Press, 1962), p. 79.
64. Ibid.
65. Edward Thorndike, "The Principles of Teaching Based on Psychology," ibid., pp. 60–61.
66. Ibid., pp. 65–66.
67. Edward Thorndike, "The Measurement of Intelligence," ibid., p. 104.
68. Ibid., pp. 105–106.
69. William Chandler Bagley, *Classroom Management* (New York: Macmillan, 1925), pp. 18–40.
70. Ibid.
71. Larry Cuban, *How Teachers Taught: Constancy and Change in American Classrooms, 1890–1980* (White Plains, NY: Longman, 1984), pp. 103–104.
72. Ellwood Cubberley, *Public Education in the United States: A Study and Interpretation of American Educational History* (Boston: Houghton Mifflin, 1934), pp. 485–486.
73. Ibid., pp. 488–489.
74. Ibid., pp. 502–504.
75. Lawrence Cremin, *The Transformation of the School: Progressivism in American Education, 1876–1957* (New York: Vintage Books, 1961), pp. viii–ix.
76. Merle Curti, *The Social Ideas of American Educators* (Paterson, NJ: Pageant Books, 1959), pp. 218–222.
77. Clarence Karier, *Shaping the American Educational State, 1900 to Present* (New York: Free Press, 1975), p. xix.
78. Edward A. Ross, *Social Control* (New York: Macmillan, 1906), p. 175.
79. Ibid., p. 168.
80. David Tyack, *The One Best System: A History of American Urban Education* (Cambridge, MA: Harvard University Press, 1974), p. 7.
81. William J. Reese, *Power and the Promise of School Reform: Grassroots Movements during the Progressive Era* (Boston: Routledge & Kegan Paul, 1986), p. xx.
82. I use this interpretative framework in Joel Spring, *Conflict of Interests: The Politics of American Education* (White Plains, NY: Longman, 1988).

10

Scientific School Management: Testing, Immigrants, and Experts

By the twenty-first century the vision of a scientifically managed educational system resulted in extensive use of standardized tests, standardized curricula, teacher's merit pay based on student test scores, and extensive data collection at state and federal levels of government. The attempt to scientifically manage the educational system began in the early twentieth century with the emergence of professionally trained school administrators, university-based educational researchers, and the development of standardized tests.

The push for scientific educational management resulted in educational administrators wanting greater control of the schools with less public involvement and a diminished governing role for boards of education. "Keep the schools out of politics!" became the war cry of the new professional administrators.

Within the schools, psychologists and professional administrators joined hands to preach a new version of equal opportunity. No longer were the schools to play a passive role in providing equal opportunity by simply providing an equal education and letting social position be determined by competition in the marketplace. The new breed of scientific managers distrusted the free interaction of the marketplace because uncontrollable factors such as family wealth or poverty could cause a mismatch between individual abilities and occupational requirements. The free marketplace was considered both unfair and inefficient in the distribution of human resources.

The new school leaders hoped to replace the alleged unfairness and inefficiency inherent in free-market competition with the supposedly scientific objectivity and fairness of the scientifically managed public school. Instead of leaving social selection to the uncertainties of the marketplace, school administrators hoped that social selection—the provision of equal opportunity—would become a function of scientific management and measurement in educational institutions. The new tools for providing equal opportunity were the junior and comprehensive high schools, with their differentiated curricula, and the new tests being developed within the expanding field of psychology.

Universities were the source of the new elite of professional managers and social scientists and the citadel of hope for the scientific understanding and management of society. By the end of the nineteenth century, colleges and universities began to change from institutions that simply conferred a liberal education and prepared students for the professions into institutions that were to be both centers for the creation of new knowledge through research, and training grounds for the scientific management of society. Spurred by the increasing importance of science and the model of the German university, American higher education underwent a major transformation with the creation of graduate education and the new vision of the social role of the college and university.

This chapter will focus on the following issues involving scientifically managed schools:

- Meritocracy and the schools' role in providing equal opportunity.
- Reducing public control of schools.
- Professionalization of education administrators.
- The development of standardized testing, particularly intelligence testing.
- Restricting immigration based on test scores.
- The development of special education classes.
- Eugenics: increasing the intelligence of the population.
- The university as a source of new scientific managers.

SCIENTIFICALLY MANAGED SCHOOLS: MERITOCRACY AND REDUCING PUBLIC CONTROL

Meritocracy is a concept of society based on the idea that each individual's social and occupational position is determined by individual merit, not political or economic influence. Scientific management of both human capital and organizations is a central idea in the meritocracy concept. For the schools, meritocracy was both a social goal and a method of internal organization. To achieve meritocracy as a social goal, the schools were to create a society based on merit by objectively selecting and preparing students for their ideal places in the social order. As a method of internal organization, meritocracy meant creating an administrative structure in which the positions held by professionals depended on their training and abilities as opposed to their political influence and power.

The attempt to create a meritocracy in the organization of the schools was concurrent with the establishment of small school boards. In fact, several related changes in the administrative and political structure of American schools occurred at the same time as the concept of meritocracy gained prominence. Of major importance was the establishment of small school boards and the resultant increase in the number of duties and, consequently, the power of school administrators. As this occurred, school administrators adopted techniques of scientific business management.

Three important sets of ideas were used to justify these political and administrative changes:

- The first was the concept that the school should be kept out of politics and managed by trained experts.

MERITOCRACY, SCHOOLS, AND THE LABOR MARKET TIME LINE

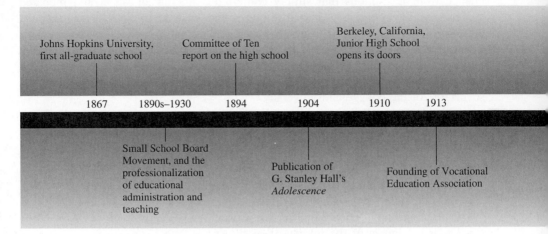

- The second set of ideas centered on the concept of democratic elitism and was used to justify the creation of small school boards. What is meant here by *elitism* is control of the schools by local civic elites composed primarily of people who exercise power over local public policy without, in most cases, holding offices in government.[1]
- The third set of ideas dealt with the proper relationship between the school board and the school administration.

The reduction in size of school boards and the accompanying decline in public control of schools was one factor contributing to increasing administrative power. As school boards declined in power and ability to function in the schools, their traditional activities were passed on to the school administration. Also, the growth in size of school districts, particularly urban ones, required more administration and coordination. In turn, school administrators welcomed these changes because they increased their power, status, and income. School administrators championed ideas such as keeping the schools out of politics and maintaining clear lines between the functions of the school board and those of the administration. Administrators willingly adopted the principles of scientific management because it gave them status comparable to that of members of the business community.

The close relationship between local elites and school administrators became an important factor in the politics of education in the twentieth century. This relationship can be traced in the history of early school board reforms. One historical study of these changes is Joseph M. Cronin's *Control of Urban Schools: Perspectives on the Power of Educational Reformers*. Cronin argues that the major concern of reformers in urban schools in the 1890s was to reduce the power of local ward bosses, whose influence encompassed the appointment of teachers and members of the board of education. Within the context of this argument, the influence of ward bosses was a threat to the power of middle- and upper-class reformers.[2]

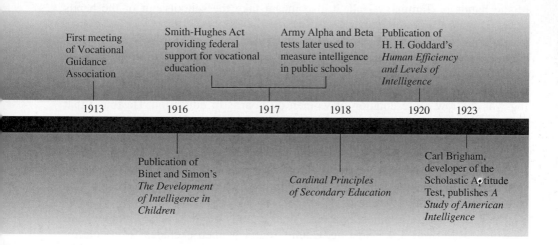

The way to destroy the influence of ward bosses over urban schools was to centralize control, reduce the size of school boards, and make elections nonpartisan and at large. Middle- and upper-class reformers also hoped that the social composition of boards of education would change by eliminating the participation of workers and small-business people. In other words, these changes were intended to ensure the power of the groups campaigning for them.

For example, a pamphlet published by the Voter's League of Pittsburgh for the 1911 fall election deplored the fact that school boards contained only a small number of "men prominent throughout the city in business life . . . in professional occupations . . . holding positions as managers, secretaries, auditors, superintendents and foremen." The pamphlet argued that a person's occupation was a strong indication of her or his qualifications for the school board: "Employment as ordinary laborer and in the lowest class of mill work would naturally lead to the conclusion that such men did not have sufficient education or business training to act as school directors." Included on the list of those the reform group thought should not be on school boards were "small shopkeepers, clerks, workmen at any trades, who by lack of educational advantages and business training, could not, no matter how honest, be expected to administer properly the affairs of an educational system."[3]

Sol Cohen shows in *Progressives and Urban School Reform* how reform movements in New York City combined destruction of ward control of the schools with anti-Catholic sentiments. In the 1894 New York mayoral election, a reform mayor was elected who fought for centralization of control and removal of schools from the power of the politicians. Under the traditional New York ward system, the mayor appointed twenty-one commissioners of common schools, and they in turn appointed five trustees for each ward. The ward trustees appointed all teachers and janitors, nominated principals and vice principals, and furnished school supplies. This system provided opportunity for graft, but it also required the trustee to be sensitive to local needs and desires. As Cohen states, "The reformers' battle cry, 'Take the schools out of politics,' not only meant take the schools out of the hands of Tammany Hall, it also meant take the schools out of the hands of the Roman Catholic Church."[4]

In 1916 Scott Nearing, a professor of economics at the University of Pennsylvania, wrote to the superintendents of 131 school systems in cities with populations over 40,000 (according to the 1910 census) to get information about the social composition of their boards of education. One important discovery by Nearing was the low representation of women on boards of education. He found that in large cities (with populations over 500,000), 12 percent of board members were women. In cities with populations of 100,000 to 500,000, 8 percent were women, and in cities of under 100,000, 5 percent were women. In general, Nearing found that 75 percent of all board members from reporting cities were professionals or businesspeople and that businesspeople composed more than 50 percent of the total number of board members.[5]

In 1927 George Counts published a similar study of 1,654 school boards, half of which were rural. Like Nearing, Counts found women excluded from control; only 10.2 percent of board members were women, and they were mainly on urban school boards. He found that urban school boards were dominated by proprietors, professionals, and business executives and that farmers were in the majority on rural school boards. One cause of this situation, Counts noted, was the argument that developed in the twentieth century that it was necessary for professionals and business leaders to control school boards.[6]

PROFESSIONALIZING EDUCATIONAL ADMINISTRATION

Accompanying the rise of elite school boards was the introduction of modern business techniques into the management of the schools. The earliest study of this phenomenon, one that is critical of this direction in twentieth-century American education, is Raymond E. Callahan's *Education and the Cult of Efficiency.* Callahan portrays the school administrator in the early twentieth century as capitulating to a businessperson mentality because of both public pressure and the rewards that could be gained by adopting a status equal to that of members of the business community. He suggests that school administrators abandoned the scholarly role of educational philosopher and curriculum leader for that of school administrator as businessperson.[7] Although more recent studies suggest that school administrators had traditionally viewed their role in business terms,[8] all agree that school administration became professionalized around concepts of scientific management borrowed from the business community.

Scientific management, or "Taylorism," exploded on the American scene in the early part of the twentieth century under the leadership of time-and-motion-study pioneer Frederick W. Taylor. Taylor believed that the basic problems of American industry stemmed from unsystematic organization and control of work. He argued that scientific study could determine the proper method of doing every job. The problem in the past, he maintained, was that workers in factories and business organizations had been allowed to follow their own decisions or rules of thumb for the completion of a task. Scientific management promised to replace the unsystematic actions of workers with a planned and controlled work environment.

One principle of Taylorism that had important consequences for the organization of schools is hierarchical organization, with management directing the actions of workers. In Taylor's words, in the past, "almost all of the work and the greater part of the responsibility were thrown upon the men."[9] Under Taylorism, management assumed more duties by reducing workers' responsibilities and need for decision making. An organization was envisioned in which decisions would be made at the top, based on scientific studies, and would flow to the bottom.

Taylorism complemented the social efficiency thinking of educators because it mandated that workers be scientifically selected and trained for their particular jobs and that cooperation between management and workers occur "so as to insure all of the work being done in accordance with principles of the science which has been developed." The principles of hierarchical management, scientific study and control of the elements in the organization, selection and training of individuals for places within the organization, and cost-effectiveness became the focus for the professionalization of public school administration. Public school leaders jumped on the scientific management bandwagon with a vengeance. For instance, well-known efficiency expert Harrington Emerson was asked to speak at the 1911 meeting of the High School Teachers Association of New York City on the topic "Efficiency in the High Schools through the Application of the Principles of Scientific Management." After telling his audience that it needed to have high ideals, good counsel, discipline, and common sense, he presented the practical side of the administrative efficiency movement. He stated that the most important element in practical methods or principles was standardization: planning, standard records, standard conditions, standardized operations, standard instructions, and standard schedules.[10]

Across the country, school administrators applied themselves to their newly acquired roles by trying to establish uniform procedures and lines of control. Standardization became the magic word. Administrators were preoccupied with standardizing student forms, evaluations of teachers and students, attendance records, personnel records, and hiring procedures. Cost-effectiveness also became an important part of this process as administrators worried about cost in the classroom, in the ordering of supplies, in the purchase of insurance, in building maintenance, and in office management. For many superintendents, the dollar became the major educational criterion. For instance, Frank Spaulding, a nationally renowned superintendent of the period, conducted studies of the economic value of different parts of the curriculum. Using a complex and vague formula, Spaulding reported in 1920 on the comparative worth of high school subjects. He argued that educational administrators needed to determine the cost and educational value of the subjects taught so that scientific decisions could be made about the cost-efficiency of the curriculum. For example, he determined "that 5.9 pupil-recitations in Greek are of the same value as 23.8 pupil-recitations in French; that 12 pupil-recitations in science are equivalent in value to 19.2 pupil-recitations in

English." Based on these calculations and a concern with cost-effectiveness, Spaulding argued that "when the obligations of the present year expire, we ought to purchase no more Greek instruction at the rate of 5.9 pupil-recitations for a dollar. The price must go down, or we shall invest in something else."[11]

Business values affected thinking about both administration and the value of education. Between 1900 and 1924, school administration rapidly professionalized around these values of cost-effectiveness and scientific management. An important factor in professionalization was specialized training, and one measure of this factor was the increase in the number of graduate courses in educational administration. In 1910, when principles of scientific management began to sweep the nation, Columbia University's Teachers College conferred thirteen graduate degrees in administration and supervision out of a total of seventy-three. In 1916, the institution granted 316 graduate degrees, of which 95 were in administration and supervision. By 1924, not only had the number of degrees jumped to 939, but 390 of these were in administration and supervision.[12]

More revealing is the actual content of the education of professional administrators. One content analysis of textbooks in educational administration conducted in the early 1930s (which means that the texts analyzed had been written in the 1920s or earlier) found "over four-fifths of eight thousand pages are devoted to the purely executive, organizational, and legal aspects of administration." These texts lacked critical analysis of educational problems, educational philosophy, or educational issues in a social context. The focus of training for school administrators was not scholarship and learning but principles of management.[13]

A shared belief developed among the community of educational administrators that their major concern should be management. A survey of professors of administration and superintendents of city schools conducted in the early 1930s found that school finance was considered the most important topic in a school administrator's education, followed in descending order by business administration, organization and administration of supervision, organization and supervision of the curriculum, administration of teaching personnel, public relations and publicity, and organization of schools and the school system. The list continued through issues of school housing, school law, and school records, without any mention of instruction or discussion of broader concerns about the role of education in society, the nature of learning, or issues in educational policy.[14]

A survey of doctoral dissertations on educational administration written between 1910 and 1933 reveals the major topics of research to be the following: 55 dissertations out of 290 were on fiscal administration, followed by business administration (34), pupil personnel (29), personnel management (29), and legal provisions (24). The remainder of the dissertation topics ranged from buildings and equipment to educational organization. Many of them dealt with topics such as "school plumbing, the school janitor, fire insurance and the cafeteria."[15]

The professionalization of educational administration around principles of scientific management, cost-effectiveness, and a business mentality did not escape criticism. Jesse Newlon, a school administrator and president of the National Education Association, warned his colleagues at the association's 1925 meeting of the danger of superintendents' functioning only as business managers. Callahan states, "[Newlon] told his audience of administrators that they must be 'students of the social sciences, of all that is included in the fields of history, sociology, economics, psychology, political science. . . .' The educational leader, [Newlon] said, 'must be a reader and a student.' "[16]

In his history of the professionalization of educational administration, Callahan bemoans the fact that educational administration took the route of business rather than that of scholarship. From another perspective, in *The One Best System: A History of American Urban Education,* David Tyack labels this new breed of school executive as "administrative progressives" who "(1) were a movement with identifiable actors and coalitions; (2) had a common ideology and platform; and (3) gained substantive power over urban education."[17]

Tyack stresses that an interlocking set of interests, values, and purposes existed among civic elites, reform groups, and the new breed of administrative progressives. From Tyack's perspective, the actions of this informal network shaped the modern school system. Therefore, educational reform took place from the top down.

Within Tyack's framework, it is logical that the new form of school board dominated by civic elites appointed administrators who reflected their business values and interests. Of course, it cannot be determined whether the administrative progressives adopted these values in response to the civic elites or, given the spirit of the period, whether they actually had a common culture. Whatever the reason, between 1890 and the Depression years of the 1930s, business dominated control of the schools, and business values dominated management of the schools. Tyack states, "Educational administrators drew elaborate comparisons between the roles of business leaders and superintendents." He gives as an example Professor Franklin Bobbit of the University of Chicago, who in 1916 contrasted a manufacturing company of 1,200 people with a school system of similar size. After comparing citizens to stockholders and superintendents to corporate managers, Bobbit concluded, "When it is asserted that educational management must in its general outlines be different from good business management, it can be shown from such a parallel study that there is absolutely no validity to the contention." Bobbit's comparison was used verbatim by the U.S. commissioner of education.[18]

An almost symbiotic relationship developed between the new breed of school administrators and the elite school boards. The smaller school boards required increased administrative assistance and welcomed a sharing of business values. In turn, the administrative progressives depended on elite school boards for their appointments as school superintendents. For instance, in Cincinnati a system of mutual support was established between the Citizens School Committee (the organization of civic leaders that had gained control of school board elections) and the superintendent. In the 1921 school board election, Superintendent Ralph Condon actively campaigned for the candidates of the Citizens School Committee. When, at the September 26, 1921, board meeting, a resolution was introduced condemning his actions, Condon responded, "I want to repeat . . . that it was my duty . . . to advocate election of candidates who represented the nonpartisan control of education, for, to my mind, there is no greater issue involved in the administration of education than this: Keep the schools out of politics; keep politics out of the schools." In this context, keeping the schools out of politics simply meant keeping the schools within the control of the local civic elite.[19]

With the professionalization and increase in duties of educational administrators and the decrease in functions of boards of education, clear definitions of proper roles developed. In the rhetoric of the times, school boards were to establish general education policies, and administrators were to administer those policies without interference from the boards. In part, self-interest and self-protection prompted school administrators to support these clear distinctions in roles. They wanted freedom from the school board and the resultant increase in power.

The concerns of the new educational administrators and elite school boards matched the general educational rhetoric about social efficiency and the development of human capital. In one sense, the administrative progressives became the new social engineers, organizing and directing a school system that would produce measured and standardized workers for the labor market, much as factories standardized products. The business attitudes and cost-consciousness of the school administrators pleased the businesspeople who dominated the boards of education. These professionals and businesspeople were happy to relinquish functions to an administration that promised to provide more education at less expense and to graduate students who would meet the occupational requirements of American business. Of course this was not the entire story—other political forces also played a role in shaping American schools.

MEASUREMENT, DEMOCRACY, AND THE SUPERIORITY OF ANGLO-AMERICANS

"Great will be our good fortune," wrote Robert Yerkes, head of the U.S. Army psychology team, "if the lesson in human engineering which the war has taught is carried over directly and effectively into our civil institutions and activities." The decisive point in the development of the science of measurement was World War I and the organization of the modern American army. Psychologists involved in constructing intelligence tests for the classification of army personnel, which later became models for tests used in the public schools, considered the army the ideal form of modern social organization because it embodied what was considered the proper classification of labor power. Expressing great hope for the future, Yerkes stated, "Before the war mental engineering was a dream; today it exists and its effective development is amply assured."[20]

One reason for the popularity of the new intelligence tests among some Americans was that they seemed to confirm the racial superiority of the English and Germans. Also, they seemed to confirm to Anglo-Americans that Native Americans and African Americans were inferior races. Using the results of intelligence tests, many Anglo-Americans protested not only the immigration of nonwhite peoples but also the immigration of Southern and Eastern Europeans. Whereas the "Founding Fathers" wanted to restrict immigration to whites, the new cry among Anglo-Americans was to restrict the immigration of whites from Southern and Eastern Europe.

The vision of a society in which scientific measurement would be used for organizing society and racial classification raised basic questions about the meaning of democracy. The fundamental problem for social scientists was to resolve the conflict between a belief that only those of high intelligence should rule and the concept of a democratic society in which people with low intelligence are allowed to vote. In addition, during the post–World War I period, most psychologists believed that intelligence is inherited and can be controlled through selective breeding. For some, this meant that eugenics and the elimination of defective forms of intelligence were the major hopes for the improvement of civilization.

For many psychologists, the concept that intelligence is inherited also meant that intelligence levels vary among different ethnic groups. A major result of the army tests developed during World War I was allegedly proof that ethnic groups from Southern and Eastern Europe had lower levels of intelligence than those from Northern Europe. This finding led many psychologists to argue that the new wave of immigration from Southern and Eastern Europe was reducing the general level of intelligence of the American people. These findings played a major role in the passage of legislation restricting immigration into the United States.

Psychologists saw the schools as playing a major role in the realization of a society in which intelligence would rule and students would be scientifically selected and educated for their proper places in the social organism. It was hoped that testing in the schools would enable schools to fulfill the dream of providing fair and objective equality of opportunity through scientific selection. Tests were considered the key to a socially efficient society.

Henry Herbert Goddard captured this vision in a lecture given in 1920: "[It] is not so much a question of the absolute numbers of persons of high and low intelligence as it is whether each grade of intelligence is assigned a part, in the whole organization, that is within its capacity." Goddard went on to suggest that humans could learn from the busy bee how to achieve "the perfect organization of the hive." "Perhaps," he stated, "it would be wiser for us to emulate the bee's social organization more and his supposed industry less."[21]

The most significant analysis of the implications of this testing was made by historian Clarence Karier in *Shaping the American Educational State: 1900 to the Present*. Karier's book is both an analysis of the movement and an anthology of original articles. Karier argued that the use of intelligence testing as a means of establishing a meritocracy became another method of justifying social class differences and racial discrimination. Now the wealth of the rich could be justified on the grounds of innate levels of intelligence. Indeed, psychologists at the time argued that the rich deserved their wealth because they were more intelligent than the poor. In Karier's words, "The hierarchical social class system was effectively maintained then as it is today, not so much by the sheer force of power and violence, but by the ideological beliefs of people within the system." One method of getting people to accept their position in society was to convince them that the particular position they held reflected their individual merit. Measurement of intelligence was one method of convincing a person of his or her particular social worth. Karier stated, "There is, perhaps, no stronger social class stabilizer, if not tranquilizer, within a hierarchically ordered social class system than the belief, on the part of the lower class, that their place in life is really not arbitrarily determined by privilege, status, wealth and power, but is a consequence of merit, fairly derived."[22]

The army intelligence tests were developed by a team of psychologists who met at Henry Herbert Goddard's Vineland Institute in New Jersey. Goddard founded the Vineland Institute in the late 1880s as a training school for the feeble-minded. He later translated and introduced into the United States the writings and intelligence tests of French psychologist Alfred Binet, who, at the request of the French minister of public instruction, had developed tests to separate mentally retarded children from normal children. Binet's intelligence test became a model for the development of intelligence tests in the United States.

In the 1890s Goddard argued that many social problems of urban and indus-trial society would be solved through classification of intelligence and institution-alization of individuals with lower levels of intelligence. He believed that the major problem in modern society was that people of lower intelligence, who were suitable for agricultural and rural societies, had migrated to urban areas, where they were unable to deal with the complexities of living. He contended that this situation was responsible for the increase in urban crime. For Goddard, the social importance of intelligence testing was its ability to identify persons of lower intel-ligence before they committed crimes and were institutionalized.

As was mentioned previously, lurking behind the early discussions of intelli-gence were assumptions about the relative intelligence of different ethnic groups and social classes. Because the definition of the term *intelligence* was often vague, psychologists tended to build their personal prejudices into tests. For instance, underlying Binet's test was a definition of intelligence that was both vague and relative. On the one hand, Binet defined native intelligence as "judgment, other-wise called good sense, practical sense, initiative, the faculty of adapting one's self to circumstances"; on the other hand, he claimed that intelligence is relative to the individual's social situation. Thus "an attorney's son who is reduced by his intel-ligence to the condition of a menial employee is a moron . . . likewise a peasant, normal in ordinary surroundings of the fields, may be considered a moron in the city." While admitting that important differences in language ability between social classes might affect test results, he stated that social class differences added valid-ity to the test: "That this difference exists one might suspect, because our personal investigations, as well as those of many others, have demonstrated that children of the poorer class are shorter, weigh less, have smaller heads and slighter mus-cular force, than a child of the upper class; they less often reach the high school; they are more often behind in their studies."[23]

Early test writers never distinguished between native intelligence and charac-ter. For example, Goddard argued that the scores achieved on intelligence tests indicated how well an individual could control his or her emotions; in other words, level of intelligence indicated type of character—the wise person is also the good person. Edward L. Thorndike went so far as to suggest that ability to do well on tests gives evidence of justice and compassion. He purposely tried to make his intelligence tests difficult and long, so they would demonstrate the "ability to stick to a long and, at the end, somewhat distasteful task." A report from one institution of higher learning using the Thorndike test in the early 1920s states, "Two or three students fainted under the three-hour strain, and the faculty became indignant at this alleged imposition of hardship."[24]

The team of psychologists gathered at Vineland in 1917 had little time to debate the meaning of the word *intelligence.* Working with amazing speed, the group completed its work by June 10 and, after trying out the tests in army camps, sent a copy of the examiner's guide to the printer on July 7. Two forms of the test were developed—the Alpha, for literate soldiers, and the Beta, for illiterate soldiers. By the end of World War I, the tests had been given to 1,726,966 members of the army.

After the 1918 armistice, the government flooded the market with unused test booklets, which educators immediately utilized. Guy M. Whipple, a leading psychologist at that time, reported in 1922 that the army Alpha test was most widely used in colleges both because it was the first test constructed by a team of well-known psychologists to be tried on large numbers of men in the army and because "the test blanks were procurable for several months after the armistice at prices far below [those at which] other tests could be produced."[25]

The results of the army tests raised some important questions in the minds of psychologists about immigration and the functioning of democracy. Analysis of the tests yielded the startling conclusion that the average mental age of Americans was thirteen. This finding caused Goddard to ask, in a book published shortly after World War I bearing the suggestive title *Human Efficiency and Levels of Intelligence,* "What about democracy, can we hope to have a successful democracy where the average mentality is thirteen?" According to Goddard, the ideal would be for the top 4 percent of the population in intelligence to rule the other 96 percent. The problem, however, was the masses' lack of confidence in those with higher intelligence. In Goddard's words, "Here is the root of our social troubles and here is found the explanation of everything from local labor troubles to Bolshevism. Intelligence has made the fundamental error of assuming that it alone is sufficient to inspire confidence."[26]

According to Goddard, once confidence was established, those with little intelligence would elect those with a great deal of intelligence: "Intelligence can only inspire confidence when it is appreciated. And how can unintelligence comprehend intelligence?" Goddard then argued that although the morons and imbeciles at the Vineland Training School did not elect the superintendent, "they would do so if given a chance because they know that the one purpose of that group of officials is to make the children happy."[27]

Goddard argued that those with intelligence must devote themselves to the welfare of the masses. In his words, "Whenever the four million choose to devote their superior intelligence to understanding the lower mental levels and to the problem of the comfort and happiness of the other ninety-six million, they will be elected the rulers of the realm and then will come perfect government—Aristocracy in Democracy."[28] This vision of the ideal meritocracy—rulership by an aristocracy of intelligence—was Goddard's solution to reconciling a belief in a meritocracy based on intelligence with the concept of democracy.

Building the confidence of the masses in those with intelligence is an important element in maintaining a meritocratic society of experts. Building this type of confidence was also a self-serving endeavor for psychologists, because it required that people respect the ability of psychologists to manage human resources. Thorndike captured the spirit of this reasoning in a 1920 article in *Harper's,* "The Psychology of the Half-Educated Man." Thorndike portrayed the "half-educated" person as one with just enough knowledge to think he or she can act independently of the expert. In Thorndike's words, "Such a man is likely to try (and fail) to understand the specialist instead of obeying him. He does not 'know his place' intellectually."[29]

For Thorndike, the person who tries to act independently of expert opinion is a public danger and at the mercy of clever charlatans. The rural society of the past, Thorndike reasoned, could rely on the common sense of individuals; but modern complex society depends on the rule of experts: "Wherever there is the expert . . . should we not let him be our guide? Should we not, in fact, let him do our thinking for us in that field?"

Out of this discussion of the half-educated person emerged a startling description of the educated person. "The educated man," Thorndike proclaimed, "should know when not to think, and where to buy the thinking he needs." This is another important element in reconciling meritocracy with democracy: The masses must be made confident so they will elect the most intelligent, and they must be educated not to think but to buy the thinking they need. In such a society, the role of the school is to select individuals for their places in the meritocracy and to provide an education that prepares individuals to live in a society ruled by merit and intelligence.

As a tool for racial classification, the testing movement seemed to confirm the beliefs of the "Founding Fathers" in the racial superiority of Anglo-Americans. Following in the tradition of the Naturalization Act of 1790, these new scientific racial classifications heralded a new era in restrictive immigration. The study that seemed to confirm traditional racial theories was Carl Brigham's *A Study of American Intelligence,* published in 1923. Although Brigham later disavowed the racist conclusions of his study, in the mid-1920s he developed the Scholastic Aptitude Test (SAT), which was destined to dominate the field of college entrance examinations. Brigham divided the ethnic stock of America into Nordic, Alpine, Mediterranean, and Negro categories. Nordic stock originated in countries such as Sweden, Norway, and England; Alpine stock came from countries such as Romania, Austria, and Hungary; and Mediterranean stock came from areas such as Italy, Greece, and Spain. According to Brigham's analysis of the Alpha and Beta tests, Nordic groups were intellectually superior to Alpine and Mediterranean groups, Alpines were superior to Mediterraneans, and Mediterraneans were superior to Negroes.[30]

Brigham was concerned that the intermixture of these ethnic groups would cause a decline in the general level of American intelligence: "We must now frankly admit the undesirable results which would ensue from a cross between the Nordic in this country with the Alpine Slav, with the degenerated hybrid Mediterranean, or with the Negro, or from the promiscuous intermingling of all four types." After examining immigration patterns in the nineteenth and twentieth centuries, he warned, "According to all evidence available, then, American intelligence is declining, and [this decline] will proceed with an accelerating rate as the racial admixture becomes more and more extensive." The only hope for stopping this downward spiral of American intelligence, he maintained, was restrictive and highly selective immigration laws and "the prevention of the continued propagation of defective strains in the present population."

Thus, as the use of tests spread through the schools, separating students into different curriculum groups, the tests also reinforced ethnic and social class differences. For educators who adhered to the arguments of the psychologists, it appeared natural to channel children from lower economic and social groups into vocational education and those from upper social groups into college preparatory courses. In fact, the allegedly scientific nature of the tests gave an air of objectivity to ethnic and social class bias.

The widespread adoption of intelligence tests in the 1920s created a major debate over whether nature or nurture exerted the greatest influence on level of intelligence. An important defense of nature was given by Lewis M. Terman (1877–1956), an original member of the army team of psychologists who had gained fame for his revision of the original Binet test, which is now known as the Stanford-Binet test. Terman also developed the intelligence quotient (IQ) scale, which assigns normal intelligence a value of 100. Terman accepted the existence of ethnic differences in intelligence, and in an article in *World's Work* in 1922 he claimed that "the immigrants who have recently come to us in such large numbers from southern and southeastern Europe are distinctly inferior mentally to the Nordic and Alpine strains we received from Scandinavia, Germany, Great Britain, and France."[31]

The major educational debates about nature versus nurture occurred within the National Society for the Study of Education. In the society's 1928 yearbook, Terman considered the importance of this debate in relation to the future goals of education: "If the differences found are due in the main to controllable factors of environment and training, then theoretically, at least, they can be wiped out by appropriate educational procedures—procedures which it would then become our duty to provide."[32] However, the majority of studies reported in the yearbook reached the opposite conclusion; they found that the number of days of attendance, amount spent on education, and preschool education were less important factors in predicting achievement than was measured native intelligence.

Faced with what he considered to be overwhelming evidence for the dominant role of native intelligence, Terman did not reject the importance of schooling but argued that emphasis should be placed on nonacademic goals. He argued that even though intelligence test scores were not influenced by schooling, mass education should not be rejected, nor should it be concluded "that we might as well discard our alphabet, nail up our schools, and retreat to the jungle." For Terman, the question was not whether the school should be abandoned but what form education should take. He thought that the studies of the relationship among schooling and intelligence and educational achievement suggested that schools placed too much emphasis on mastery of subjects because mastery depends not on length of schooling, cost, or other factors but on a factor that is independent of schooling: intelligence. He argued that the school, viewed in this context, should "place more emphasis than we now do upon the ethical and social ends of education, and care more than we now do about making the school a wholesome place to live."[33]

Ironically, at the same time that measurement people were giving the school a central role in the distribution of human resources, they were also promulgating a doctrine of native intelligence that undercut the ameliorative role of the school. What this means is that the early measurement movement reinforced social class and ethnic differences by claiming they reflected differences in intelligence; but at the same time it discounted the role of the school in doing anything about these differences. In the eyes of the leaders of the measurement movement, the role of the school was to build correct social attitudes, select individuals for their places in society, and educate them for those places. For Terman, Thorndike, Goddard, and others, improvement in the population could be achieved only through sterilization, restrictive immigration, and selective breeding.

CLOSING THE DOOR TO IMMIGRANTS: THE 1924 IMMIGRATION ACT

Since the 1890s nativists had wanted to restrict immigration from Southern and Eastern Europe. Brigham's book on American intelligence added another justification. The right of Congress to restrict and control of immigration was supported by a series of U.S. Supreme Court rulings in 1892. One ruling proclaimed,

> It is an accepted maxim of international law, that every sovereign nation has the power, as inherent in sovereignty, and essential to self-preservation, to forbid the entrance of foreigners with its dominions, or to admit them only in such cases and up on such conditions as it may see fit to prescribe.[34]

This ruling was followed by another declaring that deportation was not a punishment.[35]

From the 1890s to the passage of the 1924 Immigration Act, members of Congress tried to restrict the new immigration from Southern and Eastern Europe. One restriction voted into law by Congress but vetoed by President Grover Cleveland in 1897 was a literacy test for immigrants. In proposing the legislation, U.S. representative Henry Cabot Lodge of Massachusetts proclaimed, "This measure, if adopted, will exclude a large portion of the present immigration, and with few exceptions will tell exclusively on the most undesirable portions of immigration alone."[36] Although President Cleveland vetoed the bill as an unsuitable device to screen immigrants, he did say that some form of restriction was needed because of the "necessity of protecting our population against degeneration and saving our national peace and quiet from imported turbulence and disorder."[37] Those wanting to restrict immigration hoped for a return to a mythical homogeneous nation dominated by Anglo-Saxons. In the 1920s André Siegfried in *America Comes of Age* stated, "The essential characteristic of the postwar period in the United States is the nervous reaction of the original American stock against an insidious subjection by foreign blood."[38]

The final solution was the 1924 Immigration Act, which imposed immigration quotas based on nationalities. This legislation dominated immigration policy until the 1960s. The effect, as shown in Table 8.1 in Chapter 8, was to dramatically reduce immigration, particularly the new immigration from Southern and Eastern Europe. The 1924 legislation used two methods to restrict immigration. The first was simply to limit the total number of yearly immigrants. The second method, which reflected the negative feelings of some Americans toward immigrants from Southern and Eastern Europe and Asia, imposed percentages of particular nationalities that would be allowed in each year. These percentages were determined by the percentage of any foreign-born nationality in the United States according to the 1910 census. The actual number of immigrants of any nationality would be limited to 5 percent of the foreign-born nationals in the United States in 1910.

According to immigration historian Roger Daniels, the result of the 1924 legislation was "a quota of about six hundred thousand slots per year for Europe, the bulk of which would go to British, Germans and Scandinavians."[39] The effect on public schools was to end most Americanization programs and to shift educational policy away from concerns about teaching non-English-speaking students. Concerns about immigrant education would return to the nation's classrooms after the immigration door was reopened in the 1960s.

"BACKWARD" CHILDREN AND SPECIAL CLASSROOMS

In *From "Backwardness" to "At-Risk:" Childhood Learning Difficulties and the Contradictions of School Reform,* Barry Franklin chronicles the history of the inclusion in schools of children with learning, behavioral, emotional, and physical disabilities.[40] Franklin argues that in the late nineteenth and early twentieth centuries urban and industrial changes increased the number of children attending schools, including those labeled as "backward." As a general welfare institution, the school tried to accommodate those considered backward and those with physical disabilities. Providence, Rhode Island, was credited with opening in 1896 the first special class for backward children. Other schools and classes were created around the country for children who were classified as deaf, blind, and suffering from orthopedic handicaps.[41]

In "Bureaucratic Order and Special Children: Urban Schools, 1890s–1940s," Joseph Tropea argued that compulsory education laws resulted in school administrators having to accommodate children with disabilities and those with behavior problems. For instance, before the passage of compulsory education laws in Pennsylvania and Maryland, neither Philadelphia nor Baltimore had special classes for "exceptional children," but after passage of these laws in Pennsylvania in 1897 and in Maryland in 1902, both cities instituted special classes. It should be noted that teachers resisted the enforcement of the laws because it meant they would have to deal with problem children. Tropea quotes the superintendent of the Baltimore schools after passage of the 1902 law: "When the school attendance law goes into operation in January, some special provision will need to be made for . . . boys who are unmanageable in the regular schools."[42] Since the concern was with maintaining classroom order, the majority of students placed in these special classes were male. In Tropea's words, "Compulsory attendance laws did not eliminate exclusionary practices; they merely changed the form of exclusion to in-school segregation."[43]

School leaders emphasized the importance of classification and segregation of children with learning and physical disabilities. For instance, in 1920 New York School Superintendent William L. Ettinger stated, "The proper classification and segregation of such children was . . . desirable, not only from a humanitarian, but also economic standpoint."[44] According to Franklin, "School reformers promoted these programs to minimize the financial costs associated with educating difficult to teach children as well as the educational burdens their presence in regular classrooms brought to teachers and students alike. At the same time, however, they supported these classes to supposedly help the handicapped."[45] By the end of the twentieth century, the segregation of students with disabilities would become a major issue.

During the 1920s, special classes began to assume a broader range of labels. For instance, in 1922 Baltimore had special classes for "Open Air," "Crippled," "Deaf," "Subnormal," and "Disciplinary." Enrollment in "Subnormal" classes in the Baltimore schools expanded rapidly from 56 students in 1921 to 1,179 students in 1925. After 1925, enrollments in "Disciplinary" and "Subnormal" classes declined and were balanced by increased enrollments in new classes called "Vocational," "Prevocational," and "Mentally Handicapped." Mentally and physically handicapped students remained excluded from regular classrooms until the 1970s, when lobbying by groups representing the interests of the handicapped, plus federal legislation, forced schools to mainstream handicapped children into regular classes. Tropea summarizes his study: "Since rules of law [compulsory attendance laws] and classroom order appeared incompatible, administrators had to mediate between legislative mandates and expectations of teaching authority. The conflict between compliance with the law and satisfaction of teachers' concerns for order was resolved through the special classroom."[46]

EUGENICS AND THE AGE OF STERILIZATION

For some people living in the first half of the twentieth century there was a logical connection between a belief in inherited intelligence and a program of eugenics or controlled human breeding. What better way, they thought, to improve the level of intelligence of the American population than by making it impossible for those with low levels of intelligence to have children. In 1909 California began a program of sterilization of those classified as "mentally impaired or mentally ill." Those institutionalized as "mentally impaired or mentally ill" were often sterilized before being discharged. Although sterilization laws were passed in twenty-nine other states, California led the way in the actual numbers of required sterilizations.[47]

In a 1926 article, "The Eugenical Sterilization of the Feebleminded," Harry Laughlin provided the major rationale for sterilization programs.[48] Laughlin formulated a model sterilization law that was used by Nazi Germany in 1933 for creating its sterilization laws and served as framework for laws enacted by several of the thirty states that engaged in sterilization. He worked for the Carnegie Institute from 1910 to 1940 as superintendent and director of the Eugenics Record Office of the Department of Genetics and served as the eugenics expert for the Committee on Immigration and Naturalization, U.S. House of Representatives.[49]

Laughlin argued that the state had two major responsibilities regarding those with "defective mentality," with the first being to care for those who were unable to care for themselves and consequently might become a "menace to the state." The second responsibility was sterilization: "Secondly, it [the government] should seek, so far as possible, to reduce to the minimum the production of the feeble-minded."[50] The problem, from Laughlin's perspective, was not those who were institutionalized but those who are released or who are borderline "mentally defective." "So long as a feeble-minded person is sexually capable of reproduction," he argued, "and is not protected by segregation in a modern institution, such an individual is a potential parent of more inadequates."[51] Although institutionalization keeps inmates from breeding, he contended, it is expensive. Far less expensive for future generations was reducing the numbers that needed to be institutionalized by implementing sterilization laws.

The welfare of the nation, Laughlin declared, depended on eugenic policies that utilized sterilization. He called on all social welfare agencies to recognize the importance of eugenics: "Only those persons best endowed with superior mental, physical, and temperamental hereditary qualities should be permitted to reproduce, and thus to serve as seed-stock for the next generation."[52]

The eugenics movement would eventually disappear as a result of the public reaction to Nazi attempts in the 1930s and 1940s to create a "super race" through eugenics and sterilization programs. But there was still a lingering desire to find a means of sorting the population through a system of tests. After the defeat of the Nazis and the end of World War II this desire found expression, as discussed in Chapter 13, in the founding of the Educational Testing Service and the almost universal use by American colleges of the Scholastic Aptitude Test.

THE UNIVERSITY AND MERITOCRACY

In the minds of those who envisioned a scientifically managed society, the university was at the pinnacle. The role of graduate schools in the evolving world of public education was to provide the research and educate the leaders for the scientific management of school systems. In the twentieth century, schools of education were expanded to include graduate studies and educational research in addition to teacher training programs. These new graduate schools of education became centers of professional control.

Although German and English universities were important models for the development of American higher education, the university in America became a unique institution devoted to a concept of service. This concept of social service is part of the general ideology of placing the expert in charge and of service to society. In an article published in 1906, Lyman Abbot, a clergyman and editor of *Outlook* magazine, explored this role of the American university. Abbot argued that English universities emphasized culture and the education of aristocrats, whereas German universities focused on scholarship and the education of scholars. American universities emphasized service to society and education for a life of social service.[53]

The idea of the institution of higher education as a center of expert service for society represented a sharp break with traditional goals. Colleges in the nineteenth century focused on liberal education as provider of the discipline and furniture of the mind. By the end of the nineteenth century, the role of higher education had shifted dramatically to that of servicing the needs of the corporate state. Several important events occurred as these changes evolved in the goals of higher education. First, the passage of the Morrill Land Grant Act of 1862 was the beginning of federal government involvement supporting a broad social role for higher education. Second, large numbers of American students went to Germany in the latter half of the nineteenth century and returned with the idea of organizing graduate schools patterned after German universities. Third, modern industry began to depend on research to maintain a competitive edge in the marketplace. Over time, industry and government increasingly used universities as centers for research and development.

In the twentieth century, this new role for higher education generated a persistent tension between the earlier concept of providing a liberal education and the emerging concept of servicing industrial and government needs and conducting research. In addition, the concept of academic freedom, which allowed escape from the narrow and restrictive thought of the nineteenth-century college, came into conflict with the new emphasis on service to society.

The 1862 Morrill Act establishing land grant colleges was the culmination of many years of work by reformers in higher education to achieve a greater service orientation in institutions of higher education. Henry Tappan (1805–1881), foremost among these early reformers as a critic of *The Yale Report* and as president of the University of Michigan between 1852 and 1863, tried to give new direction to higher education. In his 1852 inaugural address at Michigan, he embraced the model of the German university and proclaimed the university to be a major center for the creation and expansion of national wealth: "In demanding the highest institutions of learning, . . . [we are] creating not only, important and indispensable commodities in trade, but providing also, the very springs of all industry and trade, of all civilization and human improvement, of all national wealth, power and greatness."[54]

Tappan argued that the university's pursuit of science would lay the groundwork for the future prosperity of business and industry. As he told his audience, "A people aiming at large increases of wealth by agriculture, manufactures, and commerce, of all others should aim to found and foster the noblest institutions of learning. . . . They of all others require men of science." He said a university should encompass all areas of knowledge, including knowledge of the objective world and knowledge about oneself. Following what he called the "Prussian model," Tappan proposed the establishment of a scientific course of study that would parallel the classical curriculum. Tappan tried to convince his audience that he was not discrediting classical learning by proposing a scientific course of study, but was attempting to provide an education suited to differing individual interests and tastes. He argued that the classical and the scientific curricula were equally good and equally responsive to a student's needs, and, in an example indicating the direction in which he wanted the university to move, he stated, "A farmer may find Chemistry very closely connected with his calling but what can he do with Latin and Greek and the higher mathematics?"[55]

The Morrill Act was passed against a backdrop of arguments that the role of higher education was to provide an education suited to one's place in life and that science played an important role in industrial and agricultural advancement. The sponsor of the legislation was Representative Justin Morrill of Vermont, who had first tried to get federal aid for higher education in 1859. Along with Tappan, many other national leaders had been calling for more practical forms of higher education similar to that proposed in the Morrill Act. Of particular importance was Jonathan Baldwin Turner's 1851 plan for an industrial university, eventually endorsed by the Illinois state legislature. Turner divided society into two classes and argued that traditional liberal education served the interests of the upper class but not those of the industrial class. He wanted a university to be established with a dual curriculum to serve both classes. He warned that a system of higher education that served only one class created the possibility "that they should form a ruling caste or class by themselves, and wield their power more or less for their own exclusive interests and the interests of their friends."[56]

The Morrill Act of 1862 dealt specifically with the issue of educating the industrial classes. The legislation stated that the money derived from lands granted under the act would be used "to teach such branches of learning as are related to agriculture and the mechanic arts, in such manner as the legislatures of the States may respectively prescribe, in order to promote the liberal and practical education of the industrial classes in the several pursuits and professions in life." The Morrill Act gave to each state 30,000 acres of public land per each senator and representative the state sent to Congress. Because the Civil War was in progress at the time, the teaching of military tactics was included in the legislation. The major effect of the legislation was to create, after the war, a rapid expansion of higher education designed to aid the agricultural and industrial sectors.

The emphasis on providing higher education to serve the agricultural and industrial sectors was only one aspect of the changes occurring in higher education. The other major changes resulted from the influence of the German universities and their emphasis on science, research, and academic freedom. The authors of *The Yale Report* of 1828 did not incorporate into their document any goals related to higher education as producer of new knowledge, but the universities by the latter part of the nineteenth century had become centers of research aimed at discovering new knowledge to improve society and the economic system.

In the latter half of the nineteenth century, many outstanding American students made pilgrimages to study at German universities. Before 1850, roughly 200 American students had made the trip, but after the Civil War the numbers increased rapidly, and during the decade of the 1880s almost 2,000 made the journey. Many of these students earned their doctorates in Germany and returned to hold important positions in universities.

They returned with ideas about the importance of science and research. In Germany, and later in the United States, scholars began to apply scientific methods of research to every field of knowledge, including economics, history, and theology. German research began to take on the characteristics of specialization, objectivity, and the use of heavily documented evidence. The German concept of science emphasized the pursuit of truth for its own sake, not merely for utilitarian purposes. Although this concept of research did take hold in the United States, it was often in conflict with demands for research to produce useful products. This tension has continued into the twenty-first century—in science and in other fields of research.

The idea of the university as a center for research in the pursuit of truth changed the concept of teaching. In the American college of the nineteenth century, teaching involved students learning traditional forms of knowledge, often by recitation or through the explication of texts. In the German universities, these methods were replaced with lectures on the results of research. In addition, the research seminar and laboratory were used to train students to conduct research under the supervision of a professor.

The German idea of the university became the model for the American graduate school. Specialized learning, the research seminar, and an emphasis on research became hallmarks of the graduate school concept. These changes in higher education gave new meaning to the role and status of the college professor. No longer did professors simply educate the future generation; now they were experts producing new knowledge and often serving as consultants to business, industry, government, and educational institutions.

With its new sense of social importance, the American professorate became dissatisfied with traditional methods of college governance, which placed strictures on the actions of faculty in and out of the classroom. Of major importance in justifying increased freedom of and control by the faculties was the German concept of academic freedom. German academics believed that the pursuit of truth required absolute freedom of inquiry, so that any avenue of investigation could be followed. In Germany, academic freedom included the concepts of *Lernfreiheit* and *Lehrfreiheit*.

Lernfreiheit refers to the right of German students to determine their field of studies, follow any sequence of courses, govern their own private lives, and assume primary responsibility for final examinations. This concept of academic freedom for the student found little support in American higher education, except for the freedom of choice through an elective system. On the other hand, *Lehrfreiheit* became an important part of academic life in the United States. Based on the idea that the pursuit of truth requires freedom to conduct research, the ideal of *Lehrfreiheit* gave university professors freedom to lecture and report on their research as well as to conduct any type of research. In Germany, freedom of teaching and inquiry became a distinctive feature of the academic profession, one not shared with other members of society. In fact, a distinction was made between freedom within the university and freedom outside the university. Within the university, the academic profession was expected to make bold statements about society and about academic research.

In the United States, the concept of academic freedom underwent considerable modification, in part because American institutions of higher learning were governed by boards of trustees that often represented important economic and political interests outside the universities. At the time, these boards of trustees prevented the independence of the faculty. What evolved in the United States was a concept of academic freedom in which professors were not expected, as they were in Germany, to attempt to win students to their point of view. In Germany, academic freedom included the idea that faculty members had the freedom to teach whatever they wanted and the right to persuade students to accept their personal opinions and interpretations of a field of knowledge. For the American professorate, the tradition that developed was one of objectively presenting a variety of points of view on a controversial topic and refraining from commenting on issues outside the professor's area of expertise.

Ideas about academic freedom and the new role of the university were introduced into older American institutions. For instance, in his 1869 inaugural address as president of Harvard University, Charles Eliot, who later headed the Committee of Ten and served as president of the National Education Association, told his audience, "A university must be indigenous; it must be rich; and above all, it must be free. The winnowing breeze of freedom must blow through all its chambers. It takes a hurricane to blow wheat away. An atmosphere of intellectual freedom is the native air of literature and science." While recognizing the importance of freedom in the university, Eliot prescribed faculty actions befitting the particular notion of academic freedom that evolved in the United States. "It is not the function of the teacher," Eliot stated in his inaugural address, "to settle philosophical and political controversies for the pupil, or even to recommend to him any one set of opinions as better than any other. Exposition, not imposition, of opinions is the professor's part."[57]

A factor that restrained academic freedom in the United States was the underwriting of new American universities by industrial barons. During the latter half of the nineteenth century, the model of the German university found its home in these newly established schools. In 1865 Ezra Cornell, having earned a fortune in the telegraph business and public lands, endowed Cornell University, which was to serve the industrial classes and be a model research institution. In 1867 Johns Hopkins, who had gained a considerable fortune through commerce, endowed Johns Hopkins University. The primary purpose of this university was to function as a graduate school. New England industrialist Jonas Clark's endowment of Clark University in 1887 allowed G. Stanley Hall to turn it into a major center for graduate studies. A railroad empire provided the money for Leland Stanford to found Stanford University in 1885, and oil money allowed John D. Rockefeller to establish the University of Chicago in 1890. The Armour Institute was funded by the meatpacking industry, and the Carnegie Institute by the steel industry.

These are only a few of the major institutions of higher learning that were backed by large-scale corporate wealth and that adapted the German model of the university to research in service to industry and government. In the words of David Noble in *America by Design: Science, Technology, and the Rise of Corporate Capitalism,* "The growing need within industries for scientific research, and the drive toward cooperation with educational institutions to secure it, paralleled the development of research within the universities." Noble argued that these new universities, like the public schools, were given the task of educating individuals to meet the needs of the industrial system: "While the primary mission of the university within the industrial system was the 'efficient production of human material' according to 'industrial specifications'—which made not only the building of universities, but education itself an industry—the role of universities as centers of research for industry was also a vital one." Within the context of Noble's argument, the "efficient production of human material" referred to the education of scientists, managers, and engineers and the training of economists, psychologists, and sociologists to aid in industrial production.[58]

An inevitable tension developed between the interests of corporate wealth that came to dominate American higher education and the increasing independence and prestige of the American professorate. In the late nineteenth and early twentieth centuries, many professors were threatened because of their political views. For example, in 1894 Richard Ely, director of the University of Wisconsin School of Economics, Politics and History, was accused by the Board of Regents of believing in strikes and boycotts. Ely was charged with threatening to boycott a local firm in support of an employee strike and with expressing the same pro-union sentiments in his writings. The regents eventually exonerated Professor Ely and issued what has been called the "Wisconsin Magna Charta," which contains the famous lines "Whatever may be the limitations which trammel inquiry elsewhere we believe the great State University of Wisconsin should ever encourage that continual and fearless sifting and winnowing by which alone the truth can be found."[59]

At Stanford University, Professor Edward Ross, educated in Ely's seminars at the University of Wisconsin, defended socialist Eugene V. Debs and wrote, in favor of free silver, a pamphlet that was used by the Democratic Party. Mrs. Leland Stanford was upset by Ross's actions and wrote a letter to the president of Stanford complaining that Ross was playing "into the hands of the lowest and vilest elements of socialism."[60] In May 1900 Ross spoke at a meeting of organized labor to protest immigration of Chinese labor. This action struck home for the Stanfords because Chinese labor had been widely used in their railroad empire. Again Mrs. Stanford reacted and this time forced Ross's resignation. Ross defended himself in his resignation letter, declaring, "I had no choice but to go straight ahead. The scientist's business is to know some things clear to the bottom, and if he hides what he knows, he loses his virtue."[61] Ross expressed the moral imperative of academic freedom—the constant quest for truth regardless of the difficulties. Of course, this quest was sometimes hindered by self-interested trustees and by faculty members interested in personal security and gain.

Ross's resignation led to an investigation by the American Economic Association. This action established a precedent for the protection of academic freedom that eventually led to the organization of the American Association of University

Professors (AAUP) in 1915. As in previous defenses of academic freedom, the AAUP rested its case for academic freedom on the requirements of science. Of course, underlying the argument that freedom is necessary for research was a defense of the new independent status of the American professorate as a leader of technological, scientific, and social change.

In this atmosphere of research, science, and the new role of universities, graduate schools of education blossomed. Several factors complicated the development of colleges and departments of education in American universities. First, a tradition existed of training elementary school teachers in two-year normal schools. Second, the standards for admission to normal schools were low—in most cases not even a high school diploma was required. Finally, many secondary school teachers who were educated at colleges had not received any professional training.

In the late 1800s, several factors began to change this nineteenth-century pattern of teacher training. First, the requirements for admission to normal schools were tightened. In 1895, 14 percent of a sample of fifty-one normal schools required a high school diploma for admission. By 1905, the percentage had increased to 22 percent. The Department of Normal Schools of the National Education Association passed a resolution in 1908 in favor of requiring a high school diploma for admission to normal schools. By the 1930s, most normal schools required a high school diploma.

Second, the four-year teachers college began to replace the normal school. It was argued that the two-year normal school course did not provide the teacher with a broad enough liberal education. This transition occurred rapidly during the 1920s. In 1920, there were 137 state normal schools and 46 teachers colleges in the United States. By 1933, the number of normal schools had decreased to 30 and the number of teachers colleges had increased to 146.

Last, as part of the more general trend toward establishing graduate schools, colleges and universities began to add departments and colleges of education. The first permanent chair of education in the United States was established at the University of Iowa in 1873, and the University of Iowa created the College of Normal Instruction in 1878. The University of Michigan opened the Department of the Science and Art of Teaching in 1879; in 1881, the Department of Pedagogy was opened at the University of Wisconsin; in 1887, Teachers College at Columbia University was founded. By 1899, departments or chairs of education had been established at 244 American universities.

Working in the midst of these changes in the organization of professional training in education and as a professor of education at Stanford University, Ellwood Cubberley viewed the rapidly proliferating graduate schools of education as producers of and leaders in the new scientific study of education. Writing about the first quarter of the twentieth century, he stated, "Within this period of time entirely new means of attacking educational problems have been developed through the application of statistical procedures, the use of standardized tests, and the devising of scales for the measurement of the intelligence of school children." He argued that the development of the scientific study of education allowed for the evaluation of educational results in quantitative terms.[62] Like their colleagues in other divisions of the university, faculties in graduate schools of education tried to increase their status by conducting research and applying the scientific method to problems in education. As noted earlier, graduate schools of education enhanced the status of practitioners by conferring graduate degrees. In turn, graduate students in education, seeking improved employment by gaining advanced degrees, created an avalanche of often useless educational research.

Although graduate schools of education became important for conferring status in the world of the public schools, they often struggled for status among other university disciplines. Theodore Sizer and Arthur Powell argued that the low status of the education faculty on university campuses was a result of the type of recruiting that occurred when education faculties rapidly expanded in the early part of the twentieth century. They contend that most of the positions were filled by people who had received basic training through their work in the field of education. Thus colleges of education were staffed with former school administrators and teachers who primarily taught and wrote about their personal experiences. In most cases, the study of education was not grounded in theory but instead reflected the professors' individual experiences. Sizer and Powell painted an uncomplimentary picture of the professor of education as he or she emerged in the early twentieth century: a "gentle, unintellectual, saccharine, and well-meaning . . . bumbling doctor of undiagnosable ills, harmless if morosely defensive. He is either a mechanic . . . or he is the flatulent promoter of irrelevant trivia."[63]

Even though graduate schools of education struggled for status on university campuses, their power was soon felt in the education world. In *Managers of Virtue: Public School Leadership in America, 1820–1980,* David Tyack and Elisabeth Hansot depicted the leading professors in the new graduate schools as important members of what they called the "educational trust." They argued that the alliance of these faculty members with school administrators, elite school boards, and big business produced the major changes in education during the early twentieth century.

A major source of power for some of these faculty members and graduate schools derived from the education and placement of school administrators. On a national level, the most powerful faculties were at Teachers College at Columbia University, the University of Chicago, and Stanford University. Tyack and Hansot described the leading faculty in school administration at these institutions as the "placement barons." Citing Robert Rose's 1969 dissertation, "Career Sponsorship in the School Superintendency," they reported that George Strayer, Paul Mort, and Nicolaus Engelhardt at Teachers College established an "old boys' network"—that is, faculty members were known to board members and other school administrators around the country. They quoted one of Rose's informants as saying, "All of them had the knack of conveying the feeling that they were definitely aware of you as a person, had an affinity for you, and were concerned with being helpful to you in your future career.. . . They took pride in talking about 'their boys.'" The power of the "placement barons" at Teachers College was reflected in the 1939 roster of the American Association of School Administrators; Tyack and

Hansot reported that according to this roster, "287 superintendents held Teachers College M.A.'s and 32 had doctorates, a far greater proportion than that represented by any other university."[64]

Tyack and Hansot also reported that at the University of Chicago, Professor William C. Reavis's endorsement of students prompted students to establish a Reavis Club. In California, Ellwood Cubberley, the educational historian whose more traditional historical interpretations have been cited in this text, endorsed and was a mentor to most of the administrators in California in the early twentieth century. Cubberley was often referred to as "Dad Cubberley" and reportedly was admired and emulated throughout the state.

While Teachers College, Stanford, and the University of Chicago were powerful on a national level, many state universities came to dominate local areas. According to Tyack and Hansot, at institutions such as Ohio State University, for instance, professors of administration knew most school superintendents by their first names and exerted influence over boards of education in the region. Many faculty members at these "local" institutions had been trained at "national" institutions; this created an informal national alliance of educational faculties.

In addition to their power to recommend school administrators and influence their opinions, important faculty members earned a great deal of money by consulting with local school districts. The magic words of the new progressive administrators were *research* and *study,* and for university people this meant extra income. Tyack and Hansot quoted a comment made by one graduate of Teachers College: "Once when Strayer and Engelhardt came out [from] a meeting . . . they expressed disappointment that they were not getting some consulting work in this state. I told them I couldn't see why I shouldn't be making that money as well as they."[65]

CONCLUSION

Graduate schools of education were one important link in the educational power structure that came to dominate public schools in the early part of the twentieth century. In their quest to create a well-ordered, scientifically managed society, they joined hands with the new breed of school administrators using business management techniques, with elite school board members, with faculties in graduate schools of education, and with experts in measurement.

There was a close relationship between the increasing role of schools in the labor market, on one hand, and the ideology of meritocracy and the role of standardized testing, on the other. The standardized testing movement was an essential part of the development of vocational guidance. Vocational guidance was central to the evolution of the comprehensive high school, vocational education, tracking, and ability grouping. The twentieth-century concept of equal opportunity through schooling was born in the context of strengthening the role of the schools in determining the future occupations of citizens.

Notes

1. David Kirby, T. Robert Harris, and Robert Crain, *Political Strategies in Northern School Desegregation* (Lexington, MA: Lexington Books, 1973), p. 116.
2. Joseph M. Cronin, *The Control of Urban Schools: Perspectives on the Power of Educational Reformers* (New York: Free Press, 1973).
3. Quoted in Samuel P. Hays, "The Politics of Reform in Municipal Government in the Progressive Era," *Pacific Northwest Quarterly* (October 1961), p. 163.
4. Sol Cohen, *Progressives and Urban School Reform* (New York: Teachers College Press, 1964), pp. 16–55.
5. Scott Nearing, "Who's Who in Our Boards of Education?" *School and Society* 5 (January 20, 1917), pp. 89–90.
6. George S. Counts, *The Social Composition of Boards of Education: A Study in the Social Control of Public Education* (Chicago: University of Chicago Press, 1927).
7. Raymond E. Callahan, *Education and the Cult of Efficiency* (Chicago: University of Chicago Press, 1962).
8. See, for example, Barbara Berman, "Business Efficiency, American Schooling and the Public School Superintendency: A Reconsideration of the Callahan Thesis," *History of Education Quarterly* (Fall 1983), pp. 297–319.
9. Quoted in Callahan, *Cult of Efficiency,* p. 27.
10. Ibid., pp. 27, 55–57.
11. Quoted in ibid., p. 73.
12. Ibid., p. 214.
13. Ibid., p. 200.
14. Ibid., p. 201.
15. Ibid., p. 202.
16. Ibid., p. 203.
17. David Tyack, *The One Best System: A History of American Urban Education* (Cambridge, MA: Harvard University Press, 1974), p. 128.
18. Ibid., p. 144.
19. *Cincinnati Board of Education Proceedings,* (Cincinnati: Cincinnati Public Schools, 1921), September 26, 1921, pp. 5–7.
20. Quoted in Joel Spring, "Psychologists and the War: The Meaning of Intelligence in the Alpha and Beta Tests," *History of Education Quarterly* (Spring 1972), p. 3.
21. Henry Herbert Goddard, *Human Efficiency and Levels of Intelligence* (Princeton, NJ: Princeton University Press, 1920), pp. 35, 62.
22. Clarence J. Karier, ed., *Shaping the American Educational State: 1900 to the Present* (New York: Free Press, 1975), p. 138.
23. Alfred Binet and Theodore Simon, *The Development of Intelligence in Children* (Baltimore: Williams and Wilkins, 1916), p. 318.
24. Guy M. Whipple, "Intelligence Tests in Colleges and Universities," *National Society for the Study of Education Yearbook,* vol. 21 (1922), p. 260.
25. Ibid., p. 254.
26. Henry Herbert Goddard, "Human Efficiency," in Karier, *Shaping the American Educational State,* pp. 165–170.
27. Ibid.
28. Ibid.
29. Edward L. Thorndike, "The Psychology of the Half-Educated Man," in Karier, *Shaping the American Educational State,* pp. 238–244.

30. Carl C. Brigham, *A Study of American Intelligence* (Germantown, NY: Periodicals Service Co., 1923), pp. 207–215.
31. Lewis M. Terman, "Were We Born That Way?" ibid., pp. 197–207.
32. Quoted in Edgar Gumbert and Joel Spring, *The Superschool and the Superstate* (New York: Wiley, 1974), p. 101.
33. Ibid., pp. 104–105.
34. Aristide R. Zolberg, *A Nation by Design: Immigration Policy in the Fashioning of America* (Cambridge: Harvard University Press, 2006), p. 225.
35. Ibid., pp. 225–226.
36. Quoted in ibid., p. 226.
37. Quoted in ibid., p. 227.
38. Quoted in ibid., p. 244.
39. Roger Daniels, *Coming to America: A History of Immigration and Ethnicity in American Life,* 2nd ed. (New York: Perennial, 2002), p. 280.
40. Barry M. Franklin, *From "Backwardness" to "At-Risk:" Childhood Learning Difficulties and the Contradictions of School Reform* (Albany: State University of New York Press, 1994).
41. Ibid., pp. 6–7.
42. Joseph L. Tropea, "Bureaucratic Order and Special Children: Urban Schools, 1890s–1940s," *History of Education Quarterly* 27, no. 1 (Spring 1987), p. 32.
43. Ibid., p. 34.
44. Quoted by Franklin, *From "Backwardness,"* p. 6.
45. Ibid., p. 7.
46. Tropea, "Bureaucratic Order," p. 52.
47. Karen Keely, "Sexuality and Storytelling: Literary Representations of the 'Feebleminded' in the Age of Sterilization," in *Mental Retardation in America: A Historical Reader,* eds. Steven Noll and James W. Trent (New York: New York University Press, 2004), pp. 210–211.
48. Harry Laughlin, "The Eugenical Sterilization of the Feebleminded," in Noll and Trent, *Mental Retardation in America,* pp. 225–231.
49. "About the Contributors," in Noll and Trent, *Mental Retardation in America,* p. 502.
50. Laughlin, "Eugenical Sterilization," p. 225.
51. Ibid., p. 227.
52. Ibid., p. 228.
53. Frederick Rudolph, *The American College and University* (New York: Knopf, 1962), pp. 356–357.
54. Henry Philip Tappan, "Inaugural Discourse," in *The Colleges and the Public, 1787–1862,* ed. Theodore Rawson Crane (New York: Teachers College Press, 1963), p. 150.
55. Ibid., p. 165.
56. Jonathan Baldwin Turner, "Plan for an Industrial University for the State of Illinois (1851)," in Crane, *Colleges and the Public,* pp. 172–190.
57. Quoted in Walter Metzger, *Academic Freedom in the Age of the University* (New York: Columbia University Press, 1955), p. 126.
58. David F. Noble, *America by Design: Science, Technology, and the Rise of Corporate Capitalism* (New York: Knopf, 1977), pp. 131, 147.
59. Quoted in Metzger, *Academic Freedom,* p. 153.
60. Ibid., pp. 164–165.

61. Edward Ross, "Statement Regarding Forced Resignation from Stanford University, November 13, 1900," in Karier, *Shaping the American Educational State,* pp. 25–28.
62. Ellwood Cubberley, *Public Education in the United States: A Study and Interpretation of American Educational History* (Boston: Houghton Mifflin, 1934), p. 689.
63. Arthur G. Powell and Theodore Sizer, "Changing Conception of the Professor of Education," in *To Be a Phoenix: The Education Professorate,* ed. James Cornelius (Bloomington, IN: Phi Delta Kappa, 1969), p. 61.
64. David Tyack and Elisabeth Hansot, *Managers of Virtue: Public School Leadership in America, 1820–1980* (New York: Basic Books, 1982), pp. 140–142.
65. Quoted in ibid., p. 143.

11

The Politics of Knowledge:
Teachers' Unions,
the American Legion,
and the American Way

In the early twentieth century, the major participants in the politics of education and knowledge were school boards, teachers' unions, state governments, business, and special interest groups such as the American Legion and the National Association of Manufacturers. Concern with ideological management of knowledge permeated society. After World War I, the American Legion joined with the National Education Association in an effort to weed out so-called radical ideas from public schools. Under the banner of "100% Americanism," the American Legion campaigned against what it called subversive teachers and radical ideas in the curriculum. In the 1930s, the National Association of Manufacturers launched the "American Way" campaign through schools and other organizations to try to create an automatic association in the public mind between democracy and capitalism.

The struggles over ideological management unfolded as educational politics became increasingly complex. The professionalization of educational administration and changes in the election of school boards contributed to the development of teachers' unions. In turn, there was increasing conflict between teachers' unions, administrators, and school boards. Members of the labor movement who believed the schools taught conservative economic doctrines wanted to push a more liberal agenda for the public schools. During the 1930s, those arguing for a more liberal school agenda were joined by educators wanting the schools to play a role in the "social reconstruction" of society.

This chapter will focus on the political struggle between teachers and administrators and over the ideas taught in public schools, including

- The birth of the American Federation of Teachers.
- The conservative influence of the National Education Association.
- The Great Depression and business–school relations.
- Using schools to stop the spread of radical ideas.
- The "American Way of Life": business and schools.
- Propaganda and school textbooks.

TEACHERS VERSUS ADMINISTRATORS: THE AMERICAN FEDERATION OF TEACHERS

By the late nineteenth century, low wages, lack of retirement funds, and the scientific management plans of administrative progressives caused some teachers to seek aid through mutual organization. Low salaries and a lack of retirement funds were persistent problems throughout the nineteenth century. In many ways, because of the number of women who entered teaching after the Civil War, these problems were directly related to other feminist issues of the period. Viewed from this perspective, the early attempts to organize teachers can be considered primarily a women's movement.

The scientific management reforms of administrative progressives contributed to an increased sense of powerlessness among many teachers. Scientific management institutionalized and provided justification for the traditional educational harem of female schoolteachers ruled by male administrators. Within the hierarchical structure of the new corporate model, teachers were at the bottom of the chain of command. Orders flowed from the top of the administrative structure. Teachers became objects of scientific management, having no power or organizational means of directly influencing educational policy. This was one reason teachers began to organize—to gain influence over educational policy, in addition to seeking better wages and better working conditions.

An excellent study of the development of teachers' organizations is Wayne Urban's *Why Teachers Organized.* Urban argues that teachers organized for two major reasons: to improve wages and working conditions and to secure seniority. In Urban's words, "First, teachers organized to pursue material improvements, salaries, pensions, tenure, and other benefits and policies which helped raise teaching in the cities to the status of a career for women who practiced it." In other words, the struggle for increased economic benefits made it possible for women to consider teaching a lifelong career, not just an interim occupation before marriage. In addition, Urban states, "Through the pursuit of salary scales and other policies, teachers sought to institutionalize experience, or seniority, as the criterion of success in teaching."[1]

Urban uses the history of teachers' organizations in Atlanta, Chicago, and New York to support his interpretation. Although these cities differ in size and location, the teachers' organizations in each shared similar goals and concerns. One common theme was resistance to administrative reforms. This was particularly true in the Chicago Teachers Federation and the teachers' associations organized in New York City. These organizations resisted not only scientific management but also the centralization of power in small school boards, which they considered elitist and anti-immigrant. Consequently, teachers' organizations in these cities struggled against both administrative progressives and urban elites. The resistance to elite takeover of the schools was an important factor in causing some teachers to associate with organized labor in what was viewed as a common struggle against corporate managers and control by the rich.

From Urban's perspective, these conflicts resulted in differing interpretations of the meaning of professionalism: "Teachers sought to preserve their existing employment conditions and therefore labeled attacks on them 'unprofessional,' while administrative reformers labeled their innovations attempts to 'professional-ize' the teaching force."[2] Thus for some teachers the word *professional* meant greater teacher control of educational policy, and for administrators it meant improving the quality of the teaching force through scientific management. Administrators thought teachers were acting in an unprofessional manner if they resisted administrative control.

Most teachers' associations in the early part of the twentieth century, in contrast to those in New York and Chicago, tended to be politically conservative and did not join the organized labor movement. An example was the Atlanta Public School Teacher's Association (APSTA), which was formed in 1905. This organization, Urban argues, was more typical of most teachers' associations: "The Atlanta teach-ers' reluctance to formally affiliate with labor and their hesitancy to link their own salary battles to political reforms like women's suffrage were representative of the caution which characterized teachers' associations in most cities."[3]

The goals adopted by the APSTA when it was organized remained consistent throughout its first fifteen years of existence: improving salaries and working conditions, generally promoting teachers' rights and interests, and providing a means of social contact for teachers. According to Urban, "From 1905 to 1919, the association devoted itself to pursuing higher salaries."[4]

Clearly unlike the Chicago and New York teachers' associations, the APSTA avoided taking positions on educational policy issues and forming alliances with organized labor. The organization even avoided involvement in educational policy issues such as promotion of students and grading policies. But the association responded rapidly to issues involving wages. For instance, in 1915 the Atlanta board of education adopted a merit system of pay in response to pressure exerted by the APSTA.

The fight in Atlanta over merit pay illustrates the conservative nature of many reforms resulting from the work of administrative progressives. In this case, merit pay was a means of reducing the payroll by $15,000. The savings would come from the anticipated reduction in the salaries of high-seniority teachers considered undeserving of merit increases. To battle against merit pay, the teachers' associa-tion became directly involved in school board elections in 1918 and proposed a slate of school board candidates who opposed the policies of the dominant elite. In 1919, in an attempt to strengthen its general political power, the APSTA joined the American Federation of Teachers (AFT).

Atlanta demonstrates the tensions that developed among teachers, school board members, and school administrators. In this case, the arguments of scientific management through merit pay clearly worked in the interests of those concerned with keeping down the costs of public education. To conservative interests, merit provided a "scientific" means of justifying reductions in teachers' salaries. For school administrators, merit pay strengthened their positions within the educa-tional system by giving them more control over teachers and expanding their range of activity. This situation led naturally to a sharp division of interests between school administrators and teachers, and between teachers and the local power elite.

The lack of a radical political ideology distinguished the APSTA and most other teachers' associations from those in New York and Chicago. Although the APSTA recognized the differences between members' own economic interests and those of the administrators and power elite, it did not conclude that these differences reflected a more general difference between the economic interests of capital and labor. Organized labor, in contrast, did articulate its position that the goals of scientific management would turn the worker into a well-controlled, poorly paid employee. From the perspective of organized labor, the differences between teachers and school boards reflected the more general differences between the interests of the worker and the capitalist. Organized labor believed that elite school boards and school administrators wanted to deny children of workers a quality public school education and would do so through the device of reducing costs.

The Chicago Federation of Teachers (CFT) was a militant and radical union. Organized by Margaret Haley and Catherine Goggin in 1897, this organization was the forerunner of the American Federation of Teachers, established in 1916. The CFT allied itself with organized labor because it believed that workers and teachers shared a set of interests. The ideological position taken by the CFT is important because the efforts of this group were primarily responsible for the formation of the AFT. Also, the political battles of the CFT clearly illustrate the differing economic interests of those who supported and those who rejected the reforms of administrative progressives.

An excellent study of the CFT is Julia Wrigley's *Class Politics and Public Schools: Chicago, 1900–1950.* Wrigley portrays a sweeping battle in which organized labor and teachers were on one side and conservative business interests and school administrators on the other. The struggle she depicts involved issues of educational policy in addition to those of wages and working conditions. According to Wrigley, these differences were linked to the opposed interests of capital and labor.

In part, the more radical position of the CFT is explained by its association in 1902 with the Chicago Federation of Labor (CFL). It is impossible to know whether the CFT would have independently maintained a radical perspective. Certainly its linkage of educational issues with more general political and economic problems made the CFT the most radical teachers' organization in the United States in the early twentieth century. The motivation for the CFT to join the CFL in 1902 was a letter from the president of the CFL that declared, "The time has come for the workingmen of Chicago to take a stand for their children's sake, and demand justice for the teachers and the children so that both may not be crushed by the power of corporate greed."[5] When the CFT aligned itself with the CFL, it told the many teachers who hesitated to take such a bold step that the children of working-class people were more interested in education than was any other group in Chicago. In political terms, the leadership of the CFT saw workers as representing the largest group of organized voters concerned with schooling.

From this perspective, affiliation with organized labor meant increased political power for teachers. Later this theme was stressed by the teachers' union as the reason for its superiority over the National Education Association (NEA).

Even with fewer members than nonaffiliated organizations, labor-affiliated teachers' associations claimed they were in a better bargaining position because they were backed by the money and large membership of organized labor.

Concerns about gaining political power and winning the allegiance of a large block of organized voters spurred the CFT to link its efforts to the women's suffrage movement. Margaret Haley's description of Catherine Goggin, cofounder with Haley of the CFT, captures the spirit of the relationship between the teachers' unions and the women's suffrage movement: "[Goggin] brought home to the teachers in her unique, forceful way the revelation of their disadvantage as nonvoters. I remember the effect it had on the audience of teachers when she said, 'Why shouldn't the City Council give our money to the firemen and policemen? Haven't they got votes?' There was no doubt but that this incident converted many a teacher to the cause of woman's suffrage."[6]

CFT activism in opposition to scientific management resulted in the appointment by the Chicago board of education of Ella Flagg Young as superintendent of schools in 1909. Young was one of the first women in the United States to hold the position of superintendent in a large city. She believed in democratic control of the schools and had excellent rapport with the CFT. It can be argued that her appointment was an attempt to decrease militancy among teachers. In fact, however, after her appointment, she established teachers' councils as a method of increasing teachers' participation in and control of the educational system.[7]

Young's perspective on the nature of teachers' organizations is historically important. At first she worried about the affiliation of teachers with organized labor and the general militancy of the CFT, but she claimed these reservations were removed with the unfolding of teacher militancy. At the 1916 convention of the NEA, President of the Chicago Board of Education Jacob Loeb delivered a speech attacking the CFT, to which Young replied, "I was not large enough in the beginning to see, I had not the insight to see, that these women were realizing that they had not the freedom, the power, which people should have who are to train the minds of the children." As for the CFT's affiliation with organized labor, Young said she at first thought it was a mistake but later accepted it because it increased the political power of teachers. She argued before the convention, "They [the teachers] found that in order to get anything done they must have voting power behind them. And they found that people, the men, in their own station and rank in life, the college-bred men, were not ready to do anything for them; therefore they were compelled to go in with those who had felt the oppression and the grind of the power of riches." Young concluded her speech by arguing that the cause of disagreements between the teachers and the board of education was "class antagonism."[8]

Young's speech reflects the atmosphere and the language in use during the first decades of the 1900s. In the latter part of the twentieth century, it became unusual for educational leaders to refer to class antagonisms and the power of the rich. In fact, since the 1970s, teachers' unions have tended to adopt a much more conservative approach to social and political issues.

The American Federation of Teachers (AFT) was formed in 1916 at a meeting in Gary, Indiana, of three Chicago teachers' organizations—the CFT, the Chicago

Federation of Men Teachers, and the Chicago Federation of Women High School Teachers. The membership quickly expanded to include locals from Indiana, New York, Pennsylvania, and Washington, DC. The American Federation of Labor (AFL) quickly welcomed the AFT into its membership. At the presentation ceremony accepting the AFT into the AFL, Samuel Gompers, president of the AFL, welcomed the new union with the hope that it "may bring light and hope in the lives of American educators, and give and receive mutual sympathy and support which can be properly exerted for the betterment of all who toil and give service— Aye, for all humanity."[9]

Until the 1970s, the AFT was considered the radical alternative to the National Education Association (NEA). Certainly the CFT exemplified the more radical wing of the teachers' movement. Whether radical, like the CFT, or more conservative, like the APSTA, all groups involved in the movement to organize teachers shared certain themes. Wages and working conditions were central to the concerns of teachers. Throughout the nineteenth century, low wages had discouraged long-term employment in teaching. The reforms instituted by progressive administrators and school boards had not included increasing teacher salaries as a central focus of concern. In fact, many school boards wanted to keep down the cost of education and thus opposed salary increases. Certainly these economic conditions contributed to a feeling among teachers that they needed to organize for increased wages. In addition, teachers opposed both the attempts of administrators to gain greater control and the administrative use of the principles of scientific management.

The movement to establish teachers' organizations added a new dimension to the politics of education in the twentieth century. It created an organizational forum for the expression of tension generated by the reforms of administrative progressives and the continuing problems of low teacher salaries. These new organizations created a political struggle both within the educational establishment and against conservative groups wanting to maintain low teacher salaries and impose a conservative ideology in the schools. The importance of teachers' unions in the politics of education increased in the 1960s, when the unions accepted the use of strikes, and the NEA became a militant teachers' organization.

THE RISE OF THE NATIONAL EDUCATION ASSOCIATION

The National Education Association was formed in 1857 by ten state teachers' organizations with the common objective of upgrading the teaching profession. By the 1890s the NEA had become the major leader in formulating educational policies and the center of development of educational policy. The original name of the group, National Teachers' Association, was changed in 1870 to National Education Association. Although the professed goal of the organization was to improve teaching, teachers had a difficult time gaining power within the organization. Nothing better exemplifies the early attitudes of the NEA than the fact that women were excluded during the first year of the organization's existence.

By the 1870s the NEA had developed into an umbrella organization with four policy-making divisions named after their particular areas of concern—Normal Schools, Higher Education, Superintendence, and Elementary Education. As the NEA evolved, more divisions were added to encompass most areas in education. From about 1890 to the 1950s, general educational policy was formulated through formal and informal contacts within these divisions. In the 1950s the federal government began to assume the leadership role in national educational policy.

Particularly within the NEA's Department of Superintendence, powerful cliques formed and became part of what David Tyack calls the "educational trust." Their contacts within the NEA and other organizations allowed administrative progressives to spread their reforms—which, as was discussed earlier, were from the top down.

In the early twentieth century, attempts were made within the organization to get the leadership of the NEA to concentrate on teacher welfare issues. Margaret Haley, who had helped to organize the CFT, was a leader in this attempt. As David Tyack and Elisabeth Hansot state in *Managers of Virtue: Public School Leadership in America, 1820–1980,* "Margaret Haley was the main leader among those female militants who challenged the male old guard in the NEA and sought to force them to attend to the concerns of the women teachers who made up the vast majority of the profession." According to Tyack and Hansot, the first signs of Haley's militancy appeared at the 1901 NEA convention, at the conclusion of William T. Harris's remarks on the flourishing condition of public education and the advisability of the rich giving money to the schools. Haley jumped up and attacked the idea of big business support, arguing that low teacher salaries were the important issue. Harris responded with words reflecting the sexism within the organization and the elitist mentality of its leaders: "Pay no attention to what that teacher down there has said, for I take it she is a grade teacher, just out of her school room at the end of the year, worn out, tired, and hysterical. . . . It was a mistake to hold NEA meetings at this time of year . . . and if there are any more hysterical outbursts, after this I shall insist that these meetings be held at some other time of the year."[10]

Haley envisioned an organization controlled by and operated for the benefit of teachers. She argued that her opponents wanted central control by a small group that was part of a "conspiracy to make a despotism of our entire school system."[11] Greater control by teachers could be achieved only through a reorganization to distribute increased power to the rank-and-file teacher, but the actual reorganization resulted in decreased teacher power. Improvements brought about by teacher activism were the establishment of the Department of Classroom Teachers within the NEA in 1912 and greater attention by the leadership to teacher welfare issues.

By 1917 the NEA had become large enough to warrant hiring its first full-time secretary and moving its headquarters to Washington, DC. The NEA's leaders believed that this move would strengthen relations with the federal government and would increase membership. The decision to work with the federal government was the first step in forging close ties between the NEA and educational bureaucrats in the government. As part of the war effort and the NEA's desire to work with the federal government, the NEA established the Commission on the

National Emergency to publicize the NEA's war work in the schools and to develop new ideas about the role of government in education. A few of the commission's ideas became realities several decades later. Federal aid to education is one important and highly debated idea that emerged from the commission. Another proposal called for the creation of a separate department of education in the federal government.

The drive during World War I to increase NEA membership not only was successful but, ironically, contributed to the demise of teacher power in the NEA. Between 1917 and 1920, NEA membership increased from 8,000 to 50,000. In the campaign to bring in more members, the NEA leadership organized discussions of a national program for improving teacher salaries and gaining greater support for the schools and called for greater participation by teachers in the administration of the schools. The massive increase in membership led to a reorganization that virtually eliminated teacher power in the NEA for the next five decades.

Prior to its reorganization, NEA conventions were conducted like town meetings; each member in attendance was allowed one vote. Thus teachers in the city in which the NEA held its convention could attend en masse and cast more votes than the sum of those cast by delegates from other cities. For instance, at the 1918 and 1919 NEA conventions, attendance by local teachers was large enough to defeat plans for reorganization.

The leadership of the NEA proposed a representative form of governance under which each state association would elect delegates to the convention. The plan was to limit voting rights to these elected delegates. Although the leadership argued that more orderly meetings would result, activist teachers did not accept this argument because they felt the reorganization was a threat to teacher power within the NEA. This threat was a reality. In *Why Teachers Organized*, Wayne Urban demonstrates the effect of reorganization on teacher power. He cites as an example the 167 voting delegates from Illinois in the 1920s; of these, 135 were "county and city superintendents, college presidents and professors, or elementary- and high-school principals." Of the remaining delegates, only fourteen were elementary school teachers.[12]

Until the 1920 convention, activist teachers were able to defeat reorganization plans by packing the convention with local teachers. These efforts were defeated in 1920, when the convention was held in Salt Lake City, Utah. In a conservative state like Utah, teachers listened to their administrators and bowed to authority. At the convention, teachers voted in town meeting style to eliminate that voting format in favor of voting by delegates. In addition, state superintendents and NEA state officers were made ex officio delegates. Consequently the NEA became an organization dominated by administrators, with little power given to teachers.

Urban argues that the takeover of the NEA by administrators was part of the general increase in school administrators' power during the 1920s. He concludes, "The defeat of teachers' power in the NEA was one case among many where teachers lost to the new educational executives. The consequence of reorganization was a large-membership, administrator-dominated NEA which retained that character until the early 1970s."[13]

The NEA continued as a powerful force in the development of educational policy until the rise of federal government power in the 1950s. In the 1950s, when the public schools came under attack and professional educators were blamed for the anti-intellectual state of the schools, the NEA was considered a major source of the problem. And of course the 1920 reorganization only increased the tension existing between teachers and administrators. This tension was not eased until the 1960s and 1970s, when the NEA was reorganized into a militant teachers' union.

THE POLITICAL CHANGES OF THE DEPRESSION YEARS

The economic depression of the 1930s caused several major political shifts in the educational world. First, the economic crisis began to split the alliances among local school administrators, local school boards, and local elites. Many school administrators and school boards wanted to maintain educational programs in the face of demands by other local leaders to reduce educational spending. Second, the economic pressures of the Depression caused some leading educators to advocate use of the schools to bring about a radical transformation of society. This created the image that radicals were taking over the schools, which contributed to right-wing arguments in the 1940s and 1950s that public schools had come under the influence of communism. Last, the federal government introduced new programs to solve the problem of youth unemployment. This expanded the role of the federal government in education and set the stage for later intervention in the 1940s and 1950s. In addition, government involvement created tension between professional educators and the federal government over each group's role in control of youth.

Jeffrey Mirel's prize-winning essay "The Politics of Educational Retrenchment in Detroit, 1929–1935" is an excellent study of educational politics during the Depression. According to Mirel's study, the Detroit school board resisted demands by the conservative business and financial community to reduce educational spending. Obviously school administrators supported the position of the school board. What is interesting about this situation is that school board membership was drawn from the same elite group that was demanding reductions in spending.

Mirel points out that the Depression hit the Detroit public schools after a decade of growth and reform. The city's educational program had been expanded to include junior high schools, vocational education, and manual training. Reforms in the administration of the schools paralleled those in other school systems around the country. In addition, the Detroit school system became heavily indebted for construction of new school buildings to accommodate an increasing student population. Between 1920 and 1930, the student population of the school system increased from 122,690 to 250,994, and the number of administrators and teachers increased from 3,750 to 7,525. In 1916 the school board had been reorganized to reduce its membership from twenty-one members elected by ward to seven members elected at large. In Mirel's words, "Where the old Board had had a sizable number of clerks and tradesmen, the new Board was composed entirely of important businessmen, professionals, and, in the case of Laura Osborn, the wife of a prominent attorney."[14]

When the Depression hit Detroit, school revenues plummeted from $17,885,000 in 1930–1931 to $12,875,000 in 1932–1933. Furthermore, the student population increased, and debts continued from the school-building boom of the 1920s. Faced with these conditions, members of the business and financial community began to call for reductions in teacher salaries and educational programs. The school board accepted the idea of salary reductions but resisted cutbacks in educational programs.

A major demand by the business community was to eliminate "fads and frills" in the schools. In particular, vocational education and kindergarten were singled out as areas that could be eliminated. The board's resistance to these cuts indicates a dedication by board members to the use of the schools to improve the workings of the economic system. In Mirel's words, "Recent scholarship has specifically identified kindergartens, manual training, home economics and athletics as programs designed to shape proper roles and attitudes for future workers and managers. The Detroit school board's [action] to save programs and cut salaries is consistent with that model."[15] The split between school board members and the business community indicates an emerging division at the time between those wanting to solve the problems of the Depression by reducing government spending and those wanting to use the government to protect the economic system.

Other factors complicated these political divisions. On issues other than those involving money, the school board and the business community remained in agreement. On one hand, the school board joined the business community in resisting demands by Communist groups to hold weekend rallies in the schools. On the other hand, labor groups and socialists supported the school board's resistance to program cuts. This did not mean that the school board and the socialists had a common ideology, but that both groups were interested, for different reasons, in protecting social institutions.

David Tyack, Robert Lowe, and Elisabeth Hansot, in *Public Schools in Hard Times: The Great Depression and Recent Years,* stressed the tensions that arose between school people and the business community during the Depression. They argued that as the Depression worsened and the public became more critical of business interests, "school leaders attacked their former allies. In part, their new-found hostility stemmed from a common belief that industrial and commercial leaders were spearheading a campaign to cut school taxes." The educational retrenchment proposals of the U.S. Chamber of Commerce exemplify the growing tension between the business community and public educators. In 1932 all members of the U.S. Chamber of Commerce received letters from the manager of the organization's finance committee asking for consideration of a range of possible educational cutbacks in their communities. This letter proposed retrenchment through "the elimination of evening classes and kindergartens, the shortening of the school day, an increase in the size of classes, and the imposition of tuition for high school attendance."[16]

Responding to calls for retrenchment by the U.S. Chamber of Commerce and other business organizations, in 1933 the NEA established the Joint Commission on the Emergency in Education (JCEE). The JCEE and many school administrators believed public relations was the key to fighting retrenchment. The JCEE used the public relations model as a two-pronged attempt to unite all educators in resisting attempts at retrenchment and to provide publicity to persuade the public to support the schools. The superintendent of the Pasadena, California, public schools commented about the onset of the Depression, "The immediate response of the friends of public education was to turn to the public relations agent, the professional public opinion builder, the fashion setter in a desperate and dramatic appeal to rebuild the faith of the American people in public education and to restore the support of public education."[17]

In their quest for better public relations, the JCEE and Phi Delta Kappa, the honorary education fraternity, analyzed public criticisms of the schools as reported in the popular press. They found the top five criticisms to be as follows: "soft pedagogy, lack of contact with life, overemphasis on vocations, severe discipline and overwork, and neglect of character."[18] These findings were distributed as a mimeographed booklet, "Evaluating the School Program," for the purpose of responding to proposals for cutbacks made by the U.S. Chamber of Commerce.

The arguments between the JCEE and the U.S. Chamber of Commerce illustrate the tensions occurring at the national level between professional educators and the business community. As relations grew more strained, more members of the education community began to issue radical critiques of the economic system and to propose using the school as a means of social reconstruction. Although the average local school administrator was not very influenced by these more radical arguments, the business community did express concern that radical educators were taking over the schools. The emerging educational philosophy of social reconstructionism contributed to the collapse of relations between professional educators and the business community.

Social reconstruction was born in a speech, "Dare Progressive Education Be Progressive?" given by George Counts at the 1932 annual meeting of the Progressive Education Association. A version of the speech was later distributed under the title "Dare the School Build a New Social Order?" In his speech, Counts attacked the organization of capitalism as being "cruel and inhuman" and "wasteful and inefficient." He argued that concepts of competition and rugged individualism had become outmoded with the development of science and technology and called for a new economic system that would free people from poverty.[19]

During the 1920s Counts had criticized business control of boards of education. According to Counts, a major requirement of using the schools to build a new social order was to find a group of leaders whose interests focused on the needs of society and its children. He proposed that teachers assume leadership of the reconstruction of society because their primary allegiance was to children, not to private economic interests. In Counts's vision, teachers would lead children down the path of social reconstruction by openly admitting that all teaching was indoctrination. Once this was out in the open, the teacher could rationally select which principles would be indoctrinated into the child.

Counts recognized that teachers would need to choose between indoctrinating children into a conservative or a progressive economic philosophy and that doing so would require teachers to "combine education with political statesmanship." In *The Progressive Educator and the Depression: The Radical Years,* C. A. Bowers quotes Counts's statement: "I am not over sanguine, but a society lacking leadership as our does, might even accept the guidance of teachers." Counts went on to exhort teachers to reach for power: "If democracy is to survive, it must seek a new economic foundation . . . natural resources and all important forms of capital will have to be collectively owned."[20]

Members of the NEA quickly picked up the challenge of using the schools to build a new social order. At the 1932 convention in Atlantic City, New Jersey, the NEA Committee on Social-Economic Goals for America issued a report in which direct reference is made to the importance of Counts's "Dare the School Build a New Social Order?" The report, which urges the NEA to assume leadership in constructing the new social order, states, "The NEA is saying, and I hope saying more or less militantly, that a social order can be built in which a social collapse such as the present one will be impossible."[21] The committee's resolution was accepted without major debate by the convention. Although the NEA never assumed militant and radical leadership during the 1930s, the very act of approving the report indicated growing militancy among educators and the association's split from the business community. A journal called *The Social Frontier,* founded in 1934, eventually became the focal point of social reconstructionist writings. Three major themes emerged from the journal's editorial writing: (1) Capitalism has failed to fully use science and technology for the benefit of humanity. (2) In the capitalistic system, the profit motive has a negative effect on individual morality. (3) The current economic order in the United States creates economic insecurity for large groups of people.[22]

It would be difficult to measure the impact of the social reconstructionist movement on American education. The actual number of subscribers to *Social Frontier* was only 3,751, and in fact during the Depression years the public schools never did assume a leadership role in the rebuilding of society. Nonetheless, the social reconstructionist movement contributed to the image that educational leaders were among the more liberal elements in society. This image only helped to widen the gap between the community of professional educators and the business community.

Federal government involvement in education created another arena of political struggle. One important factor in this struggle was President Franklin D. Roosevelt's dislike and distrust of professional educators. The antagonism between the federal government and professional educators continued through the 1950s. Adding to the conflict was the NEA's demand for federal money without federal control. One important consequence of this political friction was that, except for its funding of a few programs, the federal government gave little aid to the public schools.

For the most part, federal attention was directed to the problem of youth and youth unemployment. Two of the most important programs to emerge from this concern were the National Youth Administration (NYA) and the Civilian

Conservation Corps (CCC), which will be discussed later in this section. Both programs were products of general anxiety about the effect on youths of the Depression. This anxiety can be understood by examining the romantic concept of youth that developed in the twentieth century. Early in the twentieth century, thinking about youth concentrated on the relationship between sexual drives and socialization. Many educators during this period argued that institutions such as the high school needed to direct the sexual and social drives of youths to social service.

During the 1920s, youths were increasingly displaced from the labor market and attended school in greater numbers. This, plus all the previously mentioned factors, contributed to the development of a unique cultural style that came to be known as the Jazz Age or Flapper Era. New forms of dress, music, dance, codes of conduct, and technology emerged. The flapper, jazz, modern dance, a new morality, and the automobile all became part of youth culture. Youth fads of the 1920s centered on consuming new products of technology. The automobile provided a form of mobility that had never before existed.

Those concerned with the youth problem often traced the supposed decline of morality, as well as youth's free spirit and rebellion against authority, to the automobile. Lengthy articles and discussions about the automobile and morality appeared in popular magazines. In 1926 the headmaster of the Lawrence School lamented the maelstrom his students would be entering. When he was eighteen, he said, life had been less difficult because there had been no "prohibition," "ubiquitous automobile," "cheap theater," "absence of parental control," and "emancipation of womanhood."[23]

Many Americans agreed during the 1920s that youth was being led down the path to hell—a place or condition of hedonistic pleasure and liberated sexuality. In 1926 *Forum* magazine published two articles by members of the younger generation under the title "Has Youth Deteriorated?" The affirmative response to this question in one article reflected concern that unrepressed sexuality might lead to chaotic and uncivilized disorder. Young people, one of the youthful authors stated, "rush in an impetuous, juvenile stampede, not knowing what lies ahead. They have hurled aside all conventions; accepted standards are 'nil.' . . . 'Liberate the Libido' has become, through them, our national motto." To the author of the negative response, it was important that "beauty and idealism, the two eternal heritages of Youth, are still alive. It is a generation which is constituting the leaven in the rapid development of a new and saner morality." Both articles referred to youth as "us" and stressed that the central concern of youth appeared to be sexual standards. As one of the young writers stated,

> This tremendous interest in the younger generation is nothing more or less than a preoccupation with the nature of that generation's sex life. What people really want to know about us, if they are honest enough to admit it, is whether or not we are perverted, whether we are loose, whether we are what they call immoral; and their curiosity has never been completely satisfied.[24]

When *Literary Digest* conducted a national survey on the younger generation in 1922, it found an overriding concern with the decline of sexual morality. The survey questioned high school principals, college presidents and deans, editors of college newspapers, and editors of religious weeklies across the country. The editor of *Moody Bible Institute Monthly* responded to the survey with a declaration that in both manners and morals, society "is undergoing not a revolution, but a devolution. That is to say, I am not so impressed by its suddenness or totalness as by its steady, uninterrupted degeneration." From a college newspaper editor at the University of Pennsylvania came the opinion that "the modern dance has done much to break down standards of morals." Describing life on his campus, the editor complained, "To the girl of to-day petting parties, cigarette-smoking, and in many cases drinking, are accepted as ordinary parts of existence. . . . She dresses in the lightest and most flimsy of fabrics. Her dancing is often of the most passionate nature." A respondent from the Phi Kappa Psi House at Northwestern University in Evanston, Illinois, summed up the general mood of the survey: "One outstanding reflection on the young set today is the reckless pursuit of pleasure."[25]

To those who believed that social order depends on properly directing social and sexual instincts, the new morality of the 1920s directly threatened the foundations of civilization. However, the frivolous style of life associated with youth in the 1920s came to an abrupt end when the Depression struck. Unemployed youths now became a central issue. Like other marginal groups—such as blacks—youths were the last hired and first fired. Lacking the seasoned skills of older workers, young people found it increasingly difficult to obtain jobs during a time of high unemployment. According to the 1940 census, by the end of the Depression, 35 percent of the unemployed were under age twenty-five, whereas only 22 percent of the total employable population fell within that age range.

In 1935, in response to the crises of the Depression, the American Council on Education established the American Youth Commission to investigate the problems of youth in America. In 1937 the chairman of the council offered the following picture: Defining youths as individuals between the ages of sixteen and twenty-four, he describes the mythical town of Youngsville, which had a population of 200 youths. Within this town, 76 youths had regular jobs, 40 attended school or college, 5 attended school part-time, 28 were married women, and 51 were out of work and out of school. Half of those out of work received federal aid. Youngsville was also experiencing a major decline in personal health. According to the statistics of the Youth Commission, one out of four young people in America at the time had syphilis or gonorrhea, and 5 percent were, would be, or had been in an asylum. Added to these problems was the highest crime rate in the country.[26]

One striking characteristic of youths during the Depression was their reported lack of idealism and rebelliousness. Unlike in the past, marginality in the 1930s was accompanied not by affluence but by a desire for economic security. When Howard Bell of the American Youth Commission surveyed the young people of Maryland in the 1930s as a representative sample of all American youth, he found that 57.7 percent of the youths surveyed named lack of economic security as the major problem for young people in America. Concerns about economic security were accompanied by a realization that youth was a special group in society. Bell found "that only one-fourth of the youth believed that there was no youth problem."[27]

A second important condition affecting youths during the Depression was the cultural and social climate of the period. *McCall's* magazine assigned Maxine Davis to travel around the country and report on the state of youth. Traveling for four months and covering ten thousand miles through the cities and along the back roads of America, she produced not only articles but also a book in which she labeled the youth of the Depression the "lost generation." Among the "lost generation," she reported, "we never found revolt. We found nothing but a meek acceptance of the fate meted out to them, and belief in a benign future based on nothing but wishful thinking." The major problem among the lost generation was lack of economic security. The collective nature of the lost generation, Davis argued, was a product of the psychopathic period in which these young people had grown up:

> Boys and girls who came of voting age in 1935 were born in 1914. Their earliest memories are of mob murder and war hysteria; their next, the cynical reaction to war's sentimentality and war's futility. Their adolescence was divided between the crass materialism of the jazz 1920s and the shock of economic collapse. In effect, they went to high school in limousines; in college, they washed dishes.[28]

In the context of these attitudes about youth, the federal government launched the National Youth Administration (NYA) and the Civilian Conservation Corps (CCC). Of the two programs, the CCC was more important in terms of future developments because it became a model for youth corps programs. The major goal of the NYA, which was started in 1935, was to relieve youth unemployment by providing economic incentives for returning to school. In a crass way, the schools were considered to be custodial institutions that could take the pressure off unemployment rates. During the first year of its existence, the program provided six dollars a month for high school students, fifteen dollars a month for college students whose parents were on relief, and other financial aid to older youths who were out of school. In addition, institutions were asked to develop special work projects for students receiving NYA aid. Many institutions organized beautification and landscaping projects.

The first CCC camp opened in 1933 amid great hopes that outdoor group living would solve unemployment problems and implant a spirit of democratic cooperation among the participants, who lived a semimilitary life with reveilles, inspections, and physical training. Some of the leaders of the CCC came from the army and the Forest Service. These leaders believed that a productive adult could be created through hard work, clean living, and discipline. Educators in the camps played a subordinate role to both the camp administrators and the camp's organizational goals.

Participants in the CCC would usually rise at 6 a.m. After breakfast and perhaps physical exercise, they would work at planting trees, building bridges, clearing trails, fighting fires, and other types of forestry activities. At the end of the day, members of the CCC could take classes. Attendance at the courses was voluntary, and the subject matter was determined by the participants. In general, the courses were devoted to remedial training, vocational education, or general instruction.

In *The Shaping of the American High School: 1920–1941,* Edward Krug argued that the CCC set the stage for a battle between professional educators and members of the federal government over who should control American youth. Although there was no winner of this battle, the consequence was increased strain between the federal government and the educational community. According to Krug, the cause of the problem was that since World War I, educators had placed hopes in the development of a total youth program. The CCC had the potential to be such a program, but it was under the control of the federal government, not the educational establishment. In Krug's words,

> It seemed to educators at this point that the country was ready for the total youth program envisioned since the end of the War. Now, with victory in their grasp, the ideologues of social efficiency faced the loss of all this to the extraschool agencies of the New Deal.[29]

The war of educators against the NYA and the CCC was highlighted by the publication of *The Civilian Conservation Corps, the National Youth Administration and the Public Schools* by the Educational Policies Commission in 1941, after the beginning of World War II. The Educational Policies Commission had been organized in 1932 by the Department of Superintendence of the NEA and the Commission on the Social Studies in the Schools. The book recommended that during periods of unemployment, the federal government provide money for public works but not for the purpose of training, and also that federal funds be used under state and local control. The report argued that the CCC and the NYA should be abolished as soon as emergency defense work was completed and all their functions were transferred to state and local governments. The book criticized the federal programs for high costs per enrollee in comparison with the cost of educating a public school student.

Although this book represented a declaration of total war against the New Deal programs, World War II was responsible for their actual demise. Congress, in a desire to eliminate nonwar spending, eliminated appropriations for the CCC in 1942 and the NYA in 1943. In a sad way the war solved the problem of unemployed youths, but the CCC model would remain for years in legislators' minds. Even during the war, government officials searched for some form of total youth program similar to the CCC.

THE POLITICS OF IDEOLOGICAL MANAGEMENT: THE AMERICAN LEGION

Beginning in the 1920s, there was an effort by organizations, parents, and politicians to control the exposure of children to what were considered subversive and immoral ideas. The American Legion, focusing attention on public schools, played a major role in attempting to purge what was considered the Communist menace. The American Legion was organized in 1919 in the wake of World War I. Its organizers were U.S. Army officers who feared that members of the U.S. military forces in Europe were being exposed to radical political ideas, and worried about

reports from the United States of the increasing spread of bolshevism. The organizational structure of the American Legion maximized opportunities for influencing both local and national education policy. Policy making was centralized, while
membership was attached to local American Legion posts. An organizational goal
of the American Legion was to present a united front.[30] Within this organizational
structure, its National Americanism Commission dictated the Legion's Americanism campaign to local posts. The resolution passed at the Legion's first convention
in 1919 calling for the creation of the commission stated, "The establishment of
a National Americanism Commission of the American Legion [is] to realize in
the United States the basic ideal of this Legion of 100% Americanism through
the planning, establishment and conduct of a continuous, constructive educational
system." The resolution listed the following goals in the promotion of "100%
Americanism":

- Combat all anti-American tendencies, activities and propaganda.
- Work for the education of immigrants, prospective American citizens, and alien
  residents in the principles of Americanism.
- Inculcate the ideals of Americanism in the citizen population, particularly the
  basic American principle that the interests of all the people are above those of
  any special interest or any so-called class or section of the people.
- Spread throughout the people of the nation information as to the real nature
  and principles of American government.
- Foster the teaching of Americanism in all schools.[31]

The campaign for "100% Americanism" reinforced a traditional goal of using
government schools for building patriotism. Most governments of the world, in
varying degrees, use national educational systems for this purpose. Normally the
goal is to create a love of country or government. This is accomplished by having
schoolchildren sing patriotic songs, recite a loyalty pledge or pledge of allegiance,
study a highly patriotic form of the nation's history, participate in nationalistic
ceremonies, and study the national literature. For some governments, the ideal is
to instill in citizens such a strong love of their country that they are willing to
die in war for its preservation.

As part of its Americanism campaign, local American Legion members were
urged to help weed out subversives from local school systems. The 1921 Legion
convention passed a resolution calling for state laws to cancel certificates of teachers "found guilty of disloyalty to the government." In addition, Legion members
were asked to volunteer to local school boards the names of subversive teachers.
In 1919 the National Americanism Commission warned, "We have those who
believe that the red, white and blue presided over by the eagle shall be replaced
by the red flag with the black vulture of disloyalty and international unrest perched
upon its staff. Through the schools and through the churches the radicals are now
seeking to put across their policies."[32]

American Legion pressure on the public schools continued through the 1930s.
In 1934 Edward Hayes, national commander of the American Legion, told the
delegates at the National Education Association (NEA) convention, "I pledge to
you the tireless and loyal support of our 11,003 posts of the American Legion,

in making of our schools the guardians of good citizenship." The secretary of the NEA, J. W. Crabtree, responded to this pledge with a declaration of pride about "cementing the relationship" between the two organizations and declared, "The members of the Legion, if need be, will fight as hard to save the schools as they did to save a world."[33]

During the 1930s, the American Legion continued to advocate the firing of "disloyal" teachers. To that end, it supported requiring loyalty oaths of all teachers. The Legion considered any opposition to loyalty oaths to be the work of "subversive" elements in American society. In 1933 the National Americanism Commission reported that eight states had passed legislation requiring loyalty oaths of teachers. Other reports showed that by 1935, twenty states required loyalty oaths of teachers.[34] After World War II, the American Legion joined many other patriotic organizations in attempts to weed subversion from schools. Suspected teachers and administrators were fired, and patriotic groups purged textbooks of anything that sounded like liberalism or communism.

SELLING THE "AMERICAN WAY" IN SCHOOLS AND ON BILLBOARDS

Launched in 1936, the "American Way" public relations campaign was designed to counter the growth of radical and antibusiness attitudes. Business's efforts to introject particular economic ideas into school curricula paralleled the Americanism campaign of the American Legion. The National Association of Manufacturers (NAM) spearheaded business's public relations efforts. A 1936 internal NAM memo contended that public opinion was not based on rational discourse. The memo stated, "Public sentiment is everything—with it nothing can fail; without it nothing can succeed. . . . Right now Joe Doakes—the average man—is a highly confused individual."[35] The memo went on to argue that Joe Doakes should be resold the advantages of a competitive economy. The next year, the NAM began a national campaign, placing billboards in every U.S. community over 2,500 declaring either "World's Highest Standard of Living—There's no way like the American Way" or "World's Highest Wages—There's no way like the American Way."[36] An early American Way advertisement captured the meaning of the campaign:

WHAT IS YOUR AMERICA ALL ABOUT?
Our American plan of living is simple.
Its ideal—that works—is the greatest good for the greatest number.
You . . . are part owner of the United States, Inc. . . .
Our American plan of living is pleasant.
Our American plan of living is the world's envy.
No nation, or group lives as well as we do.[37]

Also in 1937, the National Industrial Council, the newly formed public relations arm of the NAM, issued a diagram for a "Suggested Community Program to Create Better Understanding of Local Industry." The diagram depicted a local public relations committee composed of manufacturers, merchants, civic clubs, churches, bar associations, and educators. Conspicuously absent from this committee were labor union representatives. According to the diagram, the local committee was hiring a publicity director to spread the pro-business message.

The diagram clearly connected the segments of the community to be used for controlling public opinion. This schema corresponded to what Edward Bernays, founder of the public relations profession, called "the wires which control the public mind."[38] The diagram showed "wires" leading from the publicity director to schools, newspapers, radio, civic speakers, clubs, open house meetings for workers in factories, and theaters. These wires to the public mind, Bernays had suggested, resulted in "regimenting the public mind."[39]

Already feeling the influence of local American Legion officials, the NAM suggested that publicity directors introduce pro-business ideas into schools through the medium of printed materials for school libraries and classrooms, by sparking an interest in studying local industries, and by using movies and slides. In 1937 Lewis H. Brown, president of Johns-Manville Corporation, declared, "We must with moving pictures and other educational material carry into the schools of the generation of tomorrow an interesting story of the part that science and industry have played in creating a more abundant life for those who are fortunate to live in this great country of ours."[40] He warned that teachers knew more about Karl Marx than about the inner workings of local factories.

By the time the NAM focused on schools, the public relations profession had adopted a number of techniques for controlling public opinion. Visualizations and symbols were considered a method for galvanizing public opinion without generating debate. The use of trusted leaders was a means of building public confidence for an idea or product. For example, Bernays recommended that bacon be sold by having a physician testify to its health benefits. Also, Bernays argued that a public relations campaign should be directed toward a person's desires and emotions rather than reason. A symbol could be used to evoke positive emotions.

To avoid public debate, public relations relied on emotional rather than rational persuasion. The billboards that the NAM placed in practically every community in the United States offered only slogans. True to the principles of visualization and appealing to emotions, the billboards proclaiming "World's Highest Standard of Living" showed a happy white family of four riding in a car. Seen through the car's front windshield was a smiling, clean-shaven father wearing a suit and tie, sitting next to his grinning wife. In the rear seat were equally happy children. Hanging out the window was a white dog. Next to the car was the slogan "There's no way like the American Way." The NAM billboards proclaiming "World's Highest Wages" showed an aproned white mother standing in a doorway and looking out at her clean-shaven husband, who was dressed in a suit, tie, and hat and was tossing their blond-haired daughter into the air.[41] There were no suggestions as to why the "American Way" provided the "World's Highest Standard of Living" and the "World's Highest Wages."

In the schools, the National Association of Manufacturers conducted a public relations campaign to establish in the public mind the "inter-relation" and "inseparability" of free enterprise and democracy. On the surface, these two ideas were distinct: Free enterprise was an economic doctrine, and democracy was a political principle. Many European countries, however, practiced varying forms of democratic socialism; a democratic government might have a socialized economy. And a totalitarian government might allow free enterprise. Believing that emotions rather than reason shaped public opinion, in 1939 the NAM public relations committee announced that its goal was to "link free enterprise in the public consciousness with free speech, free press and free religion as integral parts of democracy."[42]

Eager to create positive opinions of American business and establish in the public mind a connection between free enterprise and democracy, corporations and the NAM flooded classrooms with printed material and movies. The NAM distributed to schools a series of booklets titled *You and Industry,* which were designed to evoke in the reader positive feelings about the American industrial system. In 1937 the NAM began distributing to 70,000 schools a newsweekly, *Young America,* that contained articles such as "The Business of America's People Is Selling," "Building Better Americans," and "Your Local Bank."[43] A ten-minute film, *America Marching On,* was distributed to schools with the message "America marching upward and onward to higher standards of living, greater income for her people, and more leisure to enjoy the good things of life as the greatest industrial system the world has ever seen began to develop."[44]

Propaganda and Free Speech in the Schools

As the NAM was targeting its public relations campaign at schools, some educators were telling students that propaganda was not a problem in a democratic society because of the freedom to debate different subjects. Unlike the public relations professionals, these educators were operating on the assumption that the U.S. public was able and willing to engage in rational political discourse. In the early 1930s, educators expressed interest in protecting free speech as they worried about the increasing role of propaganda in forming public opinion. "The present age might well be called the age of propaganda," wrote the Commission on Character Education for the 1932 yearbook, *Character Education,* published by the Department of Superintendence of the NEA. "With the development of the press, the cinema, and the radio, instruments have been forged through which ideas, attitudes, and philosophies may be quickly impressed upon vast populations," noted the commission. "And in every society there are powerful minority groups struggling for the control of these instruments and bent on conserving or grasping special privileges of all kinds."[45]

Concerned about citizen education, the Educational Policies Commission conducted a survey of school instruction between September 1939 and January 1940. The Educational Policies Commission was a joint venture started in 1935 by the NEA and the American Association of School Administrators to improve education for democratic citizenship. The survey, *Learning the Ways of Democracy: A Case Book in Civic Education,* provided snapshots of the actual ideas and values that many sampled American high schools were trying to disseminate to students at the outbreak of World War II. The survey found that high schools emphasized the study of public opinion as protection against the propaganda of totalitarian governments.

The commission found that many social studies classes were investigating issues related to public relations methods and government propaganda. For instance, a ninth-grade unit on public opinion in the Cleveland public schools focused on free speech and the censorship of newspapers, radio, and movies. Students studied "The Struggle for Personal and Political Liberty."[46] Twelfth-grade classes in Rochester, New York, discussed "What serious questions exist in American democracy today concerning public opinion?" In reference to the repressive measures used during the Red scare of the 1920s, students were asked, "What is a 'red scare'? Look up the Lusk Laws 1921 in New York State."[47] A study guide for the eighth grade in Schenectady, New York, stressed the importance of using actual concrete information in forming opinions. According to the guide, "in a democracy where free speech and free press are so highly prized, this is very important." The guide called for a study of newspapers, magazines, books, radio, and motion pictures as agencies "which aid in opinion expression and formation."[48]

Study guides included sections dealing with threats to freedom of speech. The high school study guide for Rochester, New York, contained a unit that listed the following topics:

- Current threats to civil and political liberty.
- Academic freedom and discussion of public problems in the classroom.
- Extension of procedures of scientific thought to public and personal problems.[49]

Commission members were pleased by the discussion of controversial issues and wrote, "Freedom of discussion of controversial subjects is more than a right. . . . If citizens do not have this right, they are unable to make intelligent decisions, and control passes into the hands of those individuals who are adroit enough to attain positions of power and influence."[50]

While the free speech issues were debated in classrooms, the American Legion continued to work with the NEA to weed out so-called subversives from schools. At its 1935 annual convention, the American Legion passed a resolution against "the advocacy in America of Nazism, Fascism, Communism, or any other isms that are contrary to the fundamental principles of democracy, as established under the Constitution of the United States." Local branches of the Legion's National Americanism Commission were ordered to give close attention to possible "subversive" activities in their communities.[51]

The Legion continued advocating the firing of "disloyal" teachers and demanded that teachers take loyalty oaths. In the same year, Congress passed an appropriations bill containing a rider forbidding the payment of salary to any teacher spreading Communist doctrines. The rider kicked off a storm of protest lasting until 1937, when President Roosevelt got the act repealed.[52]

Textbook Censorship and the American Way

Important textbook series came under attack for supposedly containing ideas that did not support the American Way. Foremost among these was Harold Rugg's social studies textbook series. Augustin Rudd, who campaigned to get Harold Rugg's textbooks off the market, blamed the supposed deterioration of public schools and their infiltration by subversives on progressive education. In 1940 Rudd was made chairperson of the newly organized Guardians of American Education. The organization's goal was to defeat "left-wing . . . educational leadership . . . [which is trying to replace] our American way of life . . . [with] a 'new social order' based on the principles of collectivism and socialism."[53] Particularly distressing to Rudd were statements in the social reconstructionist journal *The Social Frontier* calling for economic planning and presenting society as a collective organization. Rudd objected to a lead editorial that argued, "For the American people the age of individualism in economy is closing and the age of collectivism is opening. Here is the central and dominating reality in the present epoch." To Rudd and other members of patriotic organizations, social reconstructionism was a subversive plot to undermine American capitalism. Rudd was particularly upset by an April 1935 issue of *The Social Frontier* that proclaimed, "The end of free enterprise as a principle of economic and social organization adequate to this country is at hand."[54]

In sharp contrast to NAM's public relations efforts, Harold Rugg's social studies series emphasized collective action and planning. In the 1920s the series began as pamphlets that integrated the teaching of history, economics, and sociology to junior high school students. Between 1927 and 1931, Rugg pulled together the pamphlets into six 600-page books for senior and junior high school students. Published by Ginn and Company from 1933 through 1936, the series was expanded to include grades 3 through 6. At the peak of its popularity, in 1938, the series sold 289,000 copies. Rugg estimated that during the 1930s, the books were used in over five thousand schools by several million schoolchildren. After public attacks on the books, annual sales plummeted to 21,000 copies.[55]

A series goal was educating children to assume intelligent control of their institutions and environment. The books did not advocate communism or socialism, but they did argue that intelligence should be applied to planning the economy and operating public institutions. U.S. history was presented as the transformation of an individualistic agrarian society to a collective industrial society. Rugg's message was that modern urban and industrial society required cooperative planning. In the modern world, corporations, factories, public institutions, and urban living all depended on cooperative behavior. In addition, the complexity of modern life required cooperative planning to achieve economic and social goals.

Rugg's ninth-grade textbook, *Citizenship and Civic Affairs,* claimed the "American Spirit" evolved from individualism to cooperation.[56] Rejecting the premise that free enterprise and Americanism were synonymous, Rugg's series brought on the wrath of patriotic organizations and individuals. A typical reaction was the words of a middle-aged woman at a 1940s public hearing on the textbook series: "I am here, not thinking that I was going to be at all, but I am and I want to say just a few words. Righteousness, good government, good homes and God— most of all, Christ—is on trial today." Even though she admitted not reading any of the Rugg books, she proclaimed, "You can't take the youth of our land and give them this awful stuff and have them come out safe and sound for God and Righteousness." At another meeting, according to Rugg, a youth of twenty leaped into the air waving his arms and shouting, "If you let these books go in and if what I've heard is true, it'll damn the souls of the men, women and children of our state."[57]

The business community's reaction to Rugg's books was orchestrated by B. C. Forbes, financial writer and founder of *Forbes Magazine,* through editorials distributed nationally in Hearst-owned newspapers. In a 1939 article, Forbes called Rugg's books "viciously un-American . . . [Rugg] distorts facts to convince the oncoming generation that America's private-enterprise system is wholly inferior and nefarious." In words that must have made the textbook industry shudder, Forbes wrote, "I plan to insist that this anti-American educator's textbooks be cast out. . . . I would not want my own children contaminated by conversion to Communism."[58] In his syndicated Hearst newspaper column Forbes asked this question every week during the war years: "Are too many educators poisoning the minds of the younger generation with prejudiced, distorted, unfair teachings regarding the American system of economy and dazzling them with overly-rosy pictures of conditions in totalitarian countries?"[59]

Rugg and Advertising

Lessons on evaluating advertising were a unique feature of Rugg's books. The advertising industry was concerned because the lessons prepared public opinion to be skeptical of advertising claims. The Advertising Federation of America, the public relations arm of the industry, distributed pamphlets titled "Facts You Should Know about Anti-Advertising Propaganda in School Textbooks." The pamphlets criticized the Rugg books for turning students against advertising.

Both the Rugg books and the reaction of the Advertising Federation of America typified the consumerist concerns of the 1930s. During the Depression years, consumer organizations tried to educate the public about false advertising claims and shoddy consumer products. Highlighting the anti-advertising crusade was the 1931 publication of *Ballyhoo* magazine featuring satirical comments on ads and advertising, including the Ten Commandments of Advertising: "10. Thou shalt covet thy neighbor's car and his radio and his silverware and his refrigerator."[60] This surprisingly successful magazine was followed by books criticizing the wastefulness of American consumerism, including F. J. Schlink's *100,000,000 Guinea Pigs* (1933) and James Rorty's *Our Master's Voice* (1934).[61] In 1929 the Consumer Research organization was founded, which in the early 1930s spawned the establishment of the Consumers Union.

It was in this anti-advertising climate that the Advertising Federation of America worried about the Rugg books. In 1939 the federation declared that critics of advertising were "those who prefer collectivism and regimentation by political

POLITICS OF EDUCATION AND KNOWLEDGE TIME LINE

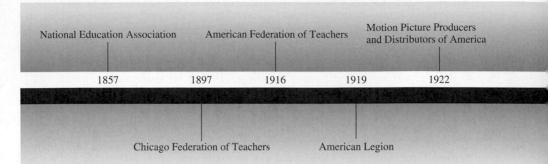

force."[62] The Advertising Federation claimed that communism was the basis for anti-advertising attitudes and the development of the Consumers Union. During this period, the House Committee on Un-American Activities held hearings that linked consumer rights efforts to communism. The Consumers Union survived by focusing on product testing and publishing *Consumer Reports* magazine.[63]

The Advertising Federation's anti-Rugg pamphlet objected to an opening section in Rugg's series on advertising because it bred distrust of widely advertised products. The section opened with the following story:

> Two men were discussing the merits of a nationally advertised brand of oil.
>
> "I know it must be good," said one. "A million dollars' worth of it is sold each year. You see advertisements of that oil everywhere."
>
> The other shook his head. "I don't care how much of it is sold," he said. "I left a drop of it on a copper plate overnight and the drop turned green. It is corrosive and I don't dare to use it on my machine."[64]

In April 1940 the president of the Advertising Federation sent to major advertisers a letter that opened, "Advertised products are untrustworthy! That is the lesson taught to the children in 4,200 school systems by a social science textbook of Professor Harold Rugg of Teachers College, Columbia University."[65] The American Legion joined ranks with the Advertising Federation in a 1940 pamphlet by O. K. Armstrong, originally published in the *American Legion Magazine,* titled "Treason in the Textbooks." In the pamphlet, a cartoon depicts Rugg as a devil putting colored glasses over children's eyes. The caption on the picture stated, "The 'Frontier Thinkers' are trying to sell our youth the idea that the American way of life has failed." The Legion article and pamphlet also listed several other books and *Scholastic Magazine* as being subversive.[66]

As head of the Guardians of American Education, Augustin Rudd believed Rugg's textbooks would undermine American institutions. Formed in 1940, the Guardians of American Education wanted to preserve American traditions. The association urged parents, "Examine your child's textbooks, Demand to see the teacher's guides . . . Look for subversive material in . . . books or courses." Regarding Rugg's series, Rudd wrote, "He [Rugg] was one of the principal

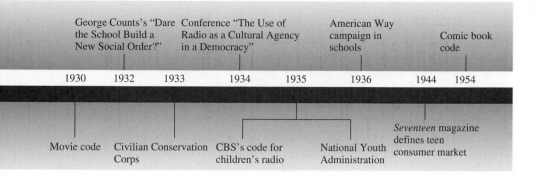

George Counts's "Dare the School Build a New Social Order?" | Conference "The Use of Radio as a Cultural Agency in a Democracy" | American Way campaign in schools | Comic book code

1930   1932   1933   1934   1935   1936   1944   1954

Movie code   Civilian Conservation Corps   CBS's code for children's radio   National Youth Administration   *Seventeen* magazine defines teen consumer market

architects of the ideological structure known as the 'new social order.' From his faculty position at Columbia University Teachers College," Rudd stated, "[Rugg's] propaganda and doctrines were spread throughout the United States. He also exercised a strong influence . . . through his Teachers' Guides, which interpreted his economic, political and social philosophies to thousands of classroom teachers using his social science courses."[67]

There was a dramatic reaction to these public criticisms. In September 1940 *Time* magazine reported that members of the Binghamton, New York, school board called for public burning of Rugg's textbooks. The article reported,

> But last fortnight Rugg book burnings began to blaze afresh in the small-town, American Legion belt. In rapid succession the school boards of Mountain Lakes and Wayne Township, N. J., banished Rugg texts that had been used by their pupils nearly ten years. Explained Wayne Township's Board Member Ronald Gall: "In my opinion, the books are un-American but not anti-American."[68]

Particularly dramatic were events in Bradner, Ohio, where the community divided over the issue of "teaching communism" in the schools. According to a Cleveland newspaper account of the events, "The rural Red hunt . . . has resulted in: explosion of a dynamite charge and the burning of a fiery cross in front of the home of . . . [the] school board president." The explosions and cross burning were accompanied by the spectacle of school board members shoving books into the school furnace.[69]

Rugg's publishers, Ginn and Company, sent him on a national tour to defend the series. At a public hearing in Philadelphia, a participant pointed his finger at Rugg and shouted, "There sits the ringmaster of the fifth columnists in America financed by the Russian government. I want you people to look at him."[70] Rugg felt frustrated at public meetings by the open admission by critics that they had never read any of his books. Person after person at these hearings, Rugg wrote, would begin their statements with the phrase "I haven't read the books, but. . . ." The phrase would be followed with comments such as "He's from Columbia, and that's enough"; "I have heard of the author, and no good about him"; and "my brother says the schools and colleges are filled with Communists."[71]

CONCLUSION

The demise of the Rugg books demonstrated the power of public relations campaigns to associate in the public mind anything critical of the U.S. economic and political system with un-Americanism and communism. Similar to the automatic association between democracy and free enterprise achieved by the NAM, public relations efforts resulted in part of the public instinctively associating progressive education with un-Americanism, communism, and socialism. This pattern of public opinion continued after World War II as anticommunism became a standard for evaluating school textbooks and curricula. The activities of the American Legion and the National Association of Manufacturers set the stage for struggles over the ideas to be taught in public schools that would continue into the twenty-first century.

Notes

1. Wayne Urban, *Why Teachers Organized* (Detroit: Wayne State University Press, 1982), p. 22.
2. Ibid., p. 41.
3. Ibid., p. 45.
4. Ibid., p. 53.
5. Quoted in Julia Wrigley, *Class Politics and Public Schools: Chicago, 1900–1950* (New Brunswick, NJ: Rutgers University Press, 1982), p. 34.
6. Quoted in ibid., pp. 34–35.
7. Ibid., p. 124.
8. Quoted in ibid., p. 127.
9. Quoted in William Edward Eaton, *The American Federation of Teachers, 1916–1961* (Carbondale: Southern Illinois University Press, 1975), p. 17.
10. Quoted in David Tyack and Elisabeth Hansot, *Managers of Virtue: Public School Leadership in America, 1820–1980* (New York: Basic Books, 1982), pp. 186–187.
11. Quoted in ibid., p. 186.
12. Urban, *Why Teachers Organized,* p. 127.
13. Ibid., p. 133.
14. Jeffrey Mirel, "The Politics of Educational Retrenchment in Detroit, 1929–1935," *History of Education Quarterly* 24 (Fall 1984), p. 325.
15. Ibid., p. 350.
16. David Tyack, Robert Lowe, and Elisabeth Hansot, *Public Schools in Hard Times: The Great Depression and Recent Years* (Cambridge, MA: Harvard University Press, 1984), pp. 22, 58.
17. Quoted in ibid., p. 74.
18. Quoted in ibid., p. 75.
19. C. A. Bowers, *The Progressive Educator and the Depression: The Radical Years* (New York: Random House, 1969), p. 15.
20. Quoted in ibid., p. 19.
21. Quoted in ibid., p. 23.
22. Ibid., p. 24.
23. Quoted in Mather A. Abbott, "The New Generation," *Nation* (December 8, 1926), p. 587.

24. Anne Temple, "Reaping the Whirlwind," *Forum* 74 (July 1926), pp. 21–26; and Regina Malone, "The Fabulous Monster," *Forum* 74 (July 1926), pp. 26–30.
25. "The Case against the Younger Generation," *Literary Digest* (June 17, 1922), pp. 40–51.
26. "Outlook for Youth in America: Report on Panel Discussion," *Progressive Education* 14 (December 1937), p. 595.
27. Howard Bell, *Youth Tell Their Story* (Washington, DC: American Council on Education, 1938).
28. Maxine Davis, *The Lost Generation* (New York: Macmillan, 1936), p. 4.
29. Edward A. Krug, *The Shaping of the American High School 1920–1941,* vol. 2 (Madison: University of Wisconsin Press, 1972), p. 325.
30. William Gellerman, *The American Legion as Educator* (New York: Teachers College Press, 1938), pp. 20–39.
31. Quoted in ibid., p. 68.
32. Quoted in ibid., pp. 90–91.
33. Ibid., pp. 225–227.
34. Ibid., p. 122; and Harold Hyman, *To Try Men's Souls: Loyalty Tests in American History* (Berkeley: University of California Press, 1959), pp. 323–326.
35. Stuart Ewen, *PR! A Social History of Spin* (New York: Basic Books, 1996), p. 203.
36. Ibid., pp. 322–323.
37. Quoted in ibid., p. 304.
38. Ibid., p. 167.
39. Ibid., p. 163.
40. Ibid., pp. 297–298.
41. Photos of billboards shown in Ewen, *PR!,* p. 323.
42. Ibid., p. 306.
43. Ibid., p. 314.
44. Ibid., p. 315.
45. Commission on Character Education, *Tenth Yearbook, Character Education* (Washington, DC: Department of Superintendence of the National Education Association, 1932), p. 15.
46. Educational Policies Commission, *Learning the Ways of Democracy: A Case Book of Civic Education* (Washington, DC: NEA, 1940), pp. 63–64.
47. Ibid., p. 65.
48. Ibid., p. 109.
49. Ibid., p. 110.
50. Ibid., p. 171.
51. Gellerman, *American Legion,* p. 93.
52. Ibid., p. 122; Hyman, *To Try Men's Souls,* pp. 323–324; and Krug, *Shaping,* pp. 231–232.
53. As quoted in Mary Anne Raywid, *The Ax-Grinders: Critics of Our Public Schools* (New York: Macmillan, 1963), p. 51.
54. Augustin G. Rudd, *Bending the Twig: The Revolution in Education and Its Effect on Our Children* (New York: New York Chapter of Sons of the American Revolution, 1957), pp. 26–27.
55. Harold Rugg, *That Men May Understand: An American in the Long Armistice* (New York: Doubleday, Dome, 1941), pp. 36–44.
56. Reprinted in ibid., pp. 54–69.
57. Ibid., pp. 10–11.
58. Ibid., p. 25.

59. Ibid., pp. 29–30.
60. Quoted by Stephen Fox, *The Mirror Makers: A History of American Advertising and Its Creators* (Urbana: University of Illinois Press, 1997), p. 123.
61. Ibid., pp. 123–124.
62. Quoted by Gary Cross, *An All-Consuming Century: Why Commercialism Won in Modern America* (New York: Columbia University Press, 2000), p. 135.
63. Ibid., p. 135.
64. Rudd, *Bending the Twig,* p. 85.
65. "Advertising Groups Pursuing Professor Rugg's Books," *Publishers Weekly* 138 (September 28, 1940), pp. 1322–1323.
66. Ibid., p. 1323.
67. Rudd, *Bending the Twig,* p. 65.
68. "Book Burnings: Rugg Texts," *Time* 36 (September 9, 1940), pp. 64–65.
69. Rugg, *Bending the Twig,* p. 3.
70. Ibid., p. 4.
71. Ibid., p. 12.

12

Schools, Media, and Popular Culture: Influencing the Minds of Children and Teenagers

In the twentieth century, educators felt threatened by the advent of movies, radio, television, and comic books. Would media and popular culture become more influential than schools over the minds of children and youth? What should be the relationship between schools and media? Movies were the first media to raise this problem among educators, followed by radio and television.

This chapter will focus on

- Censorship and movies as a form of public education.
- Educators and the movie industry.
- Schools against radio in the struggle over control of national culture.
- Children's radio and the birth of the superhero.
- Controlling the content of comic books.
- High school and teenage consumer markets.
- Changing images of children and youth.

CENSORSHIP OF MOVIES AS A FORM OF PUBLIC EDUCATION

Reflecting the concern of educators about the influence of movies, Will Hays, president of the newly formed Motion Picture Producers and Distributors of America (MPPDA), spoke at the 1922 annual meeting of the National Education Association. Hays stated his organization's commitment to the goals of "establishing and maintaining the highest possible moral and artistic standards in motion picture production, and developing the educational as well as the entertainment value and the general usefulness of the motion picture." Hays concluded the speech with the promise, "We accept the challenge in the righteous demand of the American mother that the entertainment and amusement of . . . youth shall be worthy of their value as a potent factor in the country's future."[1]

Hays's appearance before the NEA illustrates the complex combination of political pressures and interrelationships between educators and the entertainment world that has affected the content of movies, radio, television, and public schools. One reason the MPPDA was formed was to counter demands for increased government censorship of movies. In its public relations campaign against government censorship, the MPPDA considered it essential to win the NEA—the largest and most influential educational organization—to its side.[2]

Hays devoted part of his speech to warning educators about the evils of government censorship of movies. He told the delegates to the convention, "I am against political censorship, of course, because political censorship will not do what is hoped for it in the last analysis." What Hays offered the educators as an alternative to political censorship was censorship by the industry at the point of production. In his words, "But there is one place and one place only where the evils can be eliminated . . . and that is at the point where and when pictures are made." Hays promised his audience, "Right is right and wrong is wrong, and men know right from wrong. The corrections can be made, real evil can and must be kept out, the highest standards of art, taste, and morals can be achieved, and it is primarily the duty of the producers to do it."[3]

By the 1930s, a combination of pressures from religious organizations, fear of government censorship and antitrust action, and the desire to attract middle-class families to movie houses resulted in the MPPDA enforcing a self-regulatory code that shaped the moral, social, and political content of American films. The values contained in the movie code were close to those being taught in American schools. Youngsters during this period might attend school during weekday hours and attend movies at night and on weekends. Whether sitting in rows in schoolrooms or in movie houses, children received a consciously constructed vision of the workings of the world.

The debate over movie censorship centered on the question of whether mass media in the twentieth century should be controlled to avoid negative influences on audiences or to teach audiences moral and political lessons. For those advocating *government* censorship of movies, the primary concern was the removal of objectionable material from films. Those advocating *self-censorship* tended to argue that the content of films should be controlled to teach social lessons. For economic reasons, the movie industry favored self-censorship and self-regulation. Government censorship created economic problems because films had to be edited after production to meet the requirements of local and state censorship. The movie industry's commitment to self-censorship led to an acceptance of the idea that films should consciously teach moral and political lessons.

Defenders of government censorship stressed the obligation of government to maintain social order and compared censorship to other government controls over the distribution of ideas—controls such as public schools. Ellis Oberholtzer, secretary of the Pennsylvania State Board of Motion Picture Censors, wrote in 1921 in comparing state censorship to public schools,

> The efforts which are made to convert the unlikeliest of young human beings at school into useful citizens are many. From the care of their teeth and the public feeding of them when they are hungry up to the old purely educational processes developed to the nth degree, our social efficiency has been tried and proved. . . . I for one fail to see, therefore, how by any fair system of reasoning we can be held to be without some duty to inquire into the course of the film man with his 15,000 or more picture houses set in every nook and corner of the land at the door of each inhabitant.

Oberholtzer placed censorship into the general category of government responsibility for the actions of citizens: "The misbehavior of this citizen [the one influenced by movies]," Oberholtzer concluded, "is not beyond our concern."[4]

The advocates of self-regulation, as opposed to government censorship, explicitly argued that self-regulation should ensure that movie audiences were taught moral and social lessons. They criticized government censorship because it merely removed negative scenes without controlling the general theme of a film. One of the earliest arguments for self-censorship was given by John Collier, a cofounder of the privately operated National Board of Review or, as it was sometimes called, the National Board of Censorship.

John Collier presented the guiding philosophy of the National Board of Review in a series of magazine articles in *Survey*. As Collier explained, the board's censorship code emphasized the importance of movies teaching moral lessons. These censors wanted movies to be uplifting by teaching the public moral lessons in a manner similar to that used by schools. The organization's code stressed the importance of movies depicting good winning out over evil. The code states, "The results of the crime [as shown in movies] should be in the long run disastrous to the criminal so that the impression is that crime will inevitably find one out. The result (punishment) should always take a reasonable proportion of the film." In addition, emphasis was to be given to the role of government in maintaining a moral society. "As a general rule," the code argues, "it is preferable to have retribution come through the hands of authorized officers of the law, rather than through revenge or other unlawful or extra-legal means." Of course the board expressed a great deal of interest in the portrayal of sexual relationships. The board's standards would "not allow the extended display of personal allurements, the exposure of alleged physical charms and passionate, protracted embraces," and it would "also disapprove the showing of men turning lightly from woman to woman, or women turning lightly from man to man in intimate sexual relationships."[5]

Following Collier's line of reasoning, the major defense of voluntary self-censorship was that movies were an art form that had the responsibility to teach the public moral and social lessons. Because it was in the economic interest of the movie industry to support self-censorship, this argument became the standard defense of the industry against government censorship. To justify its self-censorship code, the MPPDA used the argument that films were a form of social art. When the National Board of Review was undermined with the passage of a New York State law requiring the licensing of movies in 1921, the MPPDA assumed leadership in advocating self-censorship.[6]

The concentration of the industry in the MPPDA made it possible for the Hays Office, as it was called, to exercise a "dictatorship of virtue" over the content of American films. The exercise of this power occurred when movies were becoming a major part of the leisure activities for most Americans. Money spent on movies was the largest portion of the recreation budget for the average American family during the 1920s. Large cities averaged one movie seat for every five to seven people in the population. Also, the composition of movie audiences had changed. In 1912 only 25 percent of the movie audiences were clerical workers and 5 percent were from the business classes, but during the 1920s the audiences changed from being mainly working class and immigrant to including the middle class.[7]

EDUCATORS AND THE MOVIES

Will Hays first appeared before the National Education Association in July 1922, only one month after the forming of the Public Relations Committee and six months after he accepted the leadership of the MPPDA. His pledge to accept the challenge "of the American mother" for worthy entertainment for American youth was given to an audience that had mixed feelings about the educational value of movies. On one hand, many educators considered movie houses major competition to schools for control of children's minds. On the other hand, educators recognized the importance of using movies for instruction. As the relationship between the movie industry and the educational establishment evolved in the 1920s and 1930s, the two groups found ways to serve each other's needs. The movie industry welcomed educators' claim that schools could improve movies through the education of future audiences, because such education would provide another argument against government censorship. This claim led to the establishment of movie appreciation courses in high schools. Besides providing an argument against government censorship, these courses benefitted the movie industry by creating an audience for certain types of movies. In addition, the movie industry used educators for public relations and for the sale of classroom films. Educators benefitted by financial support from the movie industry, the development of classroom films, and justification of the importance of the school in educating movie audiences.

The ambivalent attitudes of educators toward the movie industry were evident in early discussions about educational films. Alfred Saunders, the manager of the education department of Colonial Picture Corporation, spoke in 1914 to the NEA on "Motion Pictures as an Aid to Education." As one of the first representatives of the movie industry to speak to the NEA, Saunders was concerned primarily with selling films to public schools. After his review of available movie projectors and films suitable for schools and a claim that "every school that is equipped with a projecting machine may cover the cost of it by allowing the parents to attend exhibitions in the evening," a discussion erupted among the gathered educators about the values of movies.[8]

Educators complained, as they later would about radio and television, that movies were in competition with the schools for children's minds. In the NEA discussion in 1914, Peter Olesen, superintendent of schools from Cloquet, Minnesota, stated, "In less than twenty years, the motion picture business has secured a hold on the minds of people which is almost equal to that of the school and the daily press." Olesen warned that movies might be having a stronger hold on the mind of the child than the schools: "I believe that one reason why it is hard to interest some children in school today is that their minds have been filled and their imagination thrilled with too vivid motion pictures, and, when these children come to school, they are disappointed because the teacher cannot make the subject as interesting as a motion-picture show."[9]

The educators' fears about the effect of movies on children were reinforced in the 1920s and 1930s by an extensive set of research monographs called the Payne studies, which are considered by the early MPPDA historian Raymond Moley to be one of the major contributing factors to the final enforcement of the movie code.[10] The Payne studies were organized in 1928 under the leadership of W. W. Charters, director of the Bureau of Educational Research at Ohio State University. The idea for the studies came from Reverend William Short, organizer of the Motion Picture Research Council in 1927 and a longtime critic of the movies. In 1928 he brought together a group of educators, psychologists, and sociologists to discuss possible research studies on the effect of movies on children. After the meeting, Short received financial support from a private foundation, the Payne Fund, for creation of a Committee on Educational Research and for a series of research studies.[11] Twelve research studies were completed under the sponsorship of the Payne Fund. The studies were done by a formidable array of social scientists and educators and published in a series of volumes by the Macmillan Company.[12] In addition, Charters published a final summary volume in 1933. A popular summary of the studies was written under the auspices of the Payne Fund by Henry James Forman and published in 1935 under the title *Our Movie Made Children.* The popularity of Forman's book was reflected in the fact that it was reprinted seven times between 1933 and 1935.[13]

Touching on parental fears, one of the Payne studies concluded that movies had a detrimental effect on the health of children by disturbing sleep patterns. In cooperation with the Bureau of Juvenile Research in Columbus, Ohio, researchers wired the beds of children in a state institution to measure the amount of movement during sleep. The children were divided into different groups to measure the effect of movies and other conditions on restlessness during sleep. One group of children was made to drink coffee at 8:30 p.m. Another group underwent sleep deprivation, being kept up until midnight and then awakened early in the morning, until complaints by the matrons of the institution ended this part of the experiment. Another group of children was taken to the movies before going to bed. The research findings concluded that movie attendance caused as much disturbance during sleep as drinking two cups of coffee at 8:30 p.m. On the basis of this study, Charters warned, "Thus it appears that movies selected unwisely and indulged in intemperately will have a detrimental effect upon the health of children."[14]

Charters described the sleep studies as one link in a chain of negative effects of movies on children. The other links involved the content and attitudes of

movies. Researchers found that movies significantly affected the conduct and attitudes of children. One study compared the behavior of children who attended
movies four to five times a week with those from similar economic and social
backgrounds who went to movies twice a month. It was found that those who
attended more frequently had lower deportment grades in school, did more poorly
on school subjects, and were rated lower in reputation by their teachers. A study
of children living in congested areas of New York City arrived at a similar conclusion about the effects of movies on behavior.

Another Payne study focused on the effect of movies on the emotional
responses of children. In this experiment, children seated in the balcony and rear
seats of a movie theater in Columbus, Ohio, were wired to galvanometers. These
devices measured their responses to scenes depicting dangerous situations and
containing sexual material. The study found that scenes of danger created the
greatest reaction in nine-year-olds, the degree of reaction declining with age, and
that, not surprisingly, teenagers had a greater reaction to sex scenes than young
children did. The reaction to scenes of danger was considered to cause unnecessary fright in young children, and the reaction to sex scenes was considered
unhealthy for teenagers.

Adding to the concern about the emotional reaction of teenagers to movies was
the important study by Herbert Blumer, associate professor of sociology at the
University of Chicago, using the autobiographies of 1,800 college and high school
students, office workers, and factory workers. This study was important from two
standpoints. First, it demonstrated the important role of movies in bringing about
the sexual revolution of the twentieth century. Second, it added significantly to fears
that movies were having a detrimental effect on the population. Blumer asked his
1,800 participants to keep journals discussing the effects of movies on their lives.
One of the major conclusions Blumer reached after reading the journals was the
important role of movies in teaching lovemaking. Blumer wrote, "They [the jour-
nals] force upon one the realization that motion pictures provide, as many
have termed it, 'liberal education in the art of loving.'"[15] Typical of the journal
entries was that of a male college sophomore who recounted, "She would make me
go with her to see [a movie] . . . and then when we returned home she made me
make love to her as she had seen the other two on the screen." Another college
male wrote, "The technique of making love to a girl received considerable of my
attention, and it was directly through the movies that I learned to kiss a girl on her
ears, neck, and cheeks, as well as on the mouth." The journal of one female high
school sophomore was typical of other journals by girls of her age: "I have learned
quite a bit about lovemaking from the movies."[16] In addition to teaching teenagers
about lovemaking, Blumer concluded that movies were taking over the fantasy
world of youth. He claimed that 66 percent of 458 journals written by high school
students provided evidence that movies were linked to daydreaming.

In general, the Payne studies presented a negative portrait of the effects of
movies on children. Movies were said to disturb children's sleep patterns, heighten
emotional feelings, influence social attitudes, cause daydreaming, teach lovemaking, and flood the mind with ideas and facts that were retained over long periods.

In addition, movie attendance was linked to poor grades, misbehavior in school, and juvenile delinquency.

Of particular importance in heightening public concern about the effects of movies was the supposed link between movie attendance and delinquency. Henry Forman presented this argument in graphic detail in his popularized version of the Payne studies. Forman wrote, "A number of adolescent and youthful criminals give circumstantial accounts of their path to, and arrival at, criminality, and, rightly or wrongly, but very positively, they blame the movies for their downfall." Forman stated that girl inmates in an institution for sex delinquents attributed "to the movies a leading place in stimulating cravings for an easy life, for luxury, for cabarets, road-houses and wild parties, for having men make love to them and, ultimately, for their particular delinquency." Citing one of the Payne studies, Forman stated, "[in] a high-delinquency area and a region where most of the youth is of foreign-born parentage, the movie enters into innumerable patterns of their lives and constitutes, in effect, an institution of informal education, socially uncontrolled and wholly unsupervised." Forman wanted to impress the reader with the evils of the movie house. Quoting the words of one Dr. Wesley Mitchell, Forman expressed the sentiment, "Motion pictures are one of the most powerful influences in the 'making of mind' at the present time. They affect great masses of people during the impressionable years of childhood and youth."[17]

A major recommendation of the Payne studies was the creation of movie appreciation courses in public schools. In fact, a volume written for the Payne series by Edgar Dale, research associate at the Bureau of Educational Research of Ohio State University, was *How to Appreciate Motion Pictures: A Manual of Motion-Picture Criticism Prepared for High-School Students.*[18] In preparing this manual, Dale worked with members of the National Council of Teachers of English and with William Lewin, chairman of the council's Committee on Photoplay Appreciation.[19] In 1934 the National Council of Teachers of English published Lewin's manual for the teaching of movie appreciation in high schools.[20] In addition, Dale received help from Paramount Studios and the MPPDA.

The Committee on Photoplay Appreciation chaired by William Lewin gathered statistics on adolescent movie selection and attendance and conducted an experiment—involving sixty-eight groups of students in sixteen states and the District of Columbia—comparing students receiving instruction in movie appreciation with those receiving no instruction. The study claimed that movie appreciation classes caused children and youth to select movies that had a positive effect on their conduct. Only 14 percent of the students who did not receive movie appreciation courses could name movies that affected their conduct, whereas 26 percent of those taking movie appreciation courses could name movies that affected their conduct. Although the percentage of those whose conduct was affected by movies was relatively low, the committee used the figures to demonstrate the importance of movie appreciation training. As examples of the important influence of movies on conduct, the committee quoted an eleventh-grade girl in Memphis: "After seeing [the movie] *Sign of the Cross,* I went to church on a weeknight." In reference to the same movie, a twelfth-grade girl in Los Angeles wrote, "It made me glad I was a

Christian: it made me stronger in my faith; it made me hold to my religion." Regarding the movie *Twenty Years in Sing Sing,* an eleventh-grade boy in Newark wrote, "It took away my tendency, more or less, from crime." And a boy in St. Cloud, Minnesota, stated about the same film, "It influenced me to be careful of my actions, as it is difficult to escape the arm of the law."[21]

Certainly the movie industry must have been pleased that the National Council of Teachers of English was advocating movie attendance as part of the general education of youth and was motivating students to attend more movies. Rather than movie attendance being viewed in a negative light, it was being presented by the council as an extension of the work of the school. In the general conclusion of Lewin's study, an eleventh-grade student was quoted: "Before this experiment [the movie appreciation course], I went to movies just to kill time; movies weren't even a favorite hobby of mine. I didn't realize that there could be both educational and enjoyable pictures. . . . I've learned to select the better pictures. I think now I'll go to more pictures and appreciate them more."[22]

The Committee on Photoplay Appreciation concluded that movie appreciation courses combined with movie attendance had a positive effect on the character and education of students. In the words of the committee, "Class instruction excels in developing appreciation of high ideals of character in screen portrayals, the greatest gain being in appreciation of honesty, with large gains registered also for bravery, devotion, and self-sacrifice. . . . Movie influence on instructed pupils . . . is generally in the direction of higher ideals."[23] As will be discussed in the next section, uplifting the ideals of the movie viewer was precisely the goal of the movie code adopted by the MPPDA in the 1930s.

In a finding that must have pleased the movie industry, the National Council of Teachers of English concluded that movie attendance increased the reading of books used in writing screenplays. This conclusion provided justification for cooperation between the National Council of Teachers of English and the MPPDA in the writing and distribution of study guides to the public schools. In 1933, after the experiment of the Committee on Photoplay Appreciation, the council established a central reviewing committee for films, which during that year produced study guides for the films *Emperor Jones, Little Women,* and *Alice in Wonderland.* In 1934 the work was transferred from the National Council of Teachers of English to the National Education Association's Department of Secondary Education. In 1934 and 1935 study guides were distributed to public schools for *Great Expectations, Treasure Island, Little Women, David Copperfield, Dog of Flanders,* and *Les Misérables.*[24]

The movie industry and, supposedly, public school teachers were ecstatic about the distribution of these guides. For the movie industry it meant increased attendance at particular movies, free publicity, and good public relations. By 1937 study guides and information about movies were being sent to teachers of English, history, geography, and the sciences, to be used for directing students to see movies that illustrated material used in classroom instruction. It was estimated that by 1937, three million students were receiving instruction in movie appreciation.

An example of the importance of study guides to the motion picture industry was outlined in an article in the May 16, 1936, *Motion Picture Herald* about the marketing of *Romeo and Juliet.* According to the article, the MPPDA directed its marketing campaign to sixteen national social, community, and educational groups with an estimated membership of 36,211,395. Based on an average admission of twenty-five cents, it was estimated that the potential admission gross of this group was about nine million dollars. As part of the campaign, the Department of Secondary Education of the National Education Association prepared a study guide that was expected to be used in every high school English class in the United States. In describing the relationship between the movie industry and the schools in the marketing of films, the article stated, "Half a million copies of this study guide will be made available for use as text material in schools and to be taken home to be read by all the family. All of this has a definite relation to the box office potentialities." In addition to the study guides, exhibits about the movie were shown in a school, library, or museum in fifty major cities in the United States. According to the *Motion Picture Herald,* these efforts made the film the number one box office success for September 1936 and one of the top ten box office successes in 1937 and 1938.[25]

These developments in the relationship between the movie industry and educators were reviewed by Will Hays when he appeared before the annual meeting of the NEA in 1939, seventeen years after his initial appearance.[26] In his speech, Hays recognized the similar responsibilities of educators and movie producers in the distribution of ideas in society. "That educators and motion picture producers have certain specialized and mutual interests in the motion picture as a purveyor of ideas and motivator of activities," Hays told the convention, "even the layman has come to realize." Hays described the importance of the movie code for making films educational and morally uplifting. In Hays's words, the code required "that [in films] crime, wrong doing, evil, or sin shall not be made attractive; that correct standards of life shall be presented; that law, natural or human, shall not be ridiculed, or sympathy created for its violation."[27] The standards of this code, Hays maintained, made it possible to bring together the worlds of the movies and the schools as purveyors of ideas.

THE PRODUCTION CODE: MOVIES AS EDUCATORS

Intense economic pressures placed on the movie industry by religious organizations, particularly the Catholic Church, by educators, and by other concerned groups resulted in the enforcement of the production code Hays proudly referred to in his 1939 speech before the NEA. Like other proposals for self-censorship, the production code was designed to shape movies so they taught audiences moral, political, and social lessons. With the enforcement of the code in the 1930s, the movie industry joined the schools as an institution that consciously attempted to form the public mind.[28]

The 1930 movie code stressed the importance of the social role of entertainment and art; it stated that entertainment can be morally uplifting or morally degrading.[29] As examples, the code described baseball and golf as being morally uplifting and cockfighting and bullfighting as being degrading. In the words of the code, "Correct entertainment raises the whole standard of the nation. Wrong entertainment lowers the whole living conditions and moral ideas of a race." A similar argument was used regarding the social role of art. Significantly, the code called movies "the art of the multitudes." As with entertainment, the code stressed that art can be morally uplifting or degrading. The code mentioned great painting and music as examples of morally uplifting art and indecent books and unclean paintings as examples of degenerate art.

The 1930 code gave as its first general principle, "No picture shall be produced which will lower the moral standards of those who see it. Hence the sympathy of the audience shall never be thrown to the side of crime, wrong-doing, evil or sin." Envisioned in the first general principle of the 1930 code was a moral world where good always triumphed over evil and good people were always justly rewarded. It was a movie-made world where cowboys in white hats always beat the bandits in black hats. The code stated that movies must avoid scenes that might make evil attractive to audiences. A problem would arise, according to the code, when "evil is made to appear attractive or alluring and good is made to appear unattractive." Distinguishing between sympathy for a crime or sin as opposed to sympathy for the plight of a sinner, the code warned against the sympathy of the audience being "thrown on the side of crime, wrong-doing, evil, sin."

In support of the creation of a moral universe in movies where a triumphal good holds sway over a hated evil, the second general principle of the 1930 code stated, "Correct standards of life, subject only to the requirements of drama and entertainment, shall be presented." While the code gave no specific definition of "correct standards of life," it stated that the plots and characters in movies should develop the right ideals and moral standards. This was to be accomplished by movies giving audiences a moral model for living. In the words of the code, "If motion pictures consistently hold up for admiration high types of characters and present stories that will affect lives for the better, they can become the most powerful natural force for the improvement of mankind."

The third general principle of the 1930 code protected the image of laws and governments. This principle stated, "Law, natural or human, shall not be ridiculed, nor shall sympathy be created for its violation." Natural laws were defined by the code as the principles of justice dictated by a person's conscience. With regard to human law, the code specified that audience support should always be developed for government laws. The code warned against movies that were sympathetic to the commission of a crime as opposed to favoring the law. In addition, the code stated, "The courts of the land should not be presented as unjust." Although individual court officials might be portrayed in movies as unjust, the code warned, "the court system of the country must not suffer as a result of this presentation."

In summary, fears of government censorship, a desire to maintain good public relations and attract families to movies, complaints by educators about the effect of movies on children and youth, and pressures from religious organizations forced the movie industry to adopt a censorship code that shaped the moral, social, and political content of movies. After 1934, movie audiences were presented with a moral world where good always won out over evil, collective action resulted in mob violence, and good triumphed because of individual action. Regarding political action, audiences saw a world where government was benign and the good citizen did not try to change basic political processes but reformed government by getting rid of corrupt politicians. In addition, at least until the propaganda films of World War II, movies presented an uncritical and superficial view of the nations of the world.

SHOULD COMMERCIAL RADIO OR EDUCATORS DETERMINE NATIONAL CULTURE?

"British vs. American Radio Slant, Debate Theme in 40,000 Schools" headlined a front-page story in 1933 in *Variety,* the theatrical trade weekly. The pro-industry weekly reported that radio circles believed the selection of the theme for high school debates around the country was part of an "anti-radio" propaganda campaign against the American system of broadcasting. (*Variety* used "anti-radio" to describe opponents of commercial radio.) This campaign was being waged by educators, religious groups, and nonprofit organizations that wanted the federal government to license more educational and nonprofit radio stations. The central issue in the high school debate was whether radio should be privately owned and financially supported by advertising or, like the British system, operated by the government and supported by some form of taxation. With the profits of advertising determining the content of programming, these educators worried that commercial radio might be destroying American national culture. With an estimated one hundred persons expected at each debate, the major radio networks feared that a possible four million people might hear the question discussed. "Many, perhaps most, of these people," *Variety* lamented, "have been unaware of the existence of the question."[30]

In the 1930s commercial radio networks operated under constant fear that government action might take away their domination of the airwaves. They were particularly concerned about educators who were angry about the loss of radio licenses as a result of government favoritism toward commercial radio. As a result of government actions, there was a dramatic decline in educational radio stations. The National Advisory Council on Radio in Education determined that between 1921 and 1936 there were 202 licenses granted by the government to educational organizations. As of January 1, 1937, only 38 licenses were held by educational institutions.[31]

The first major network, the National Broadcasting Corporation (NBC), was organized in 1926 under the combined ownership of the Radio Corporation of America, General Electric, and the Westinghouse Corporation. American Telephone and Telegraph backed out of participation when an agreement was signed that NBC would continue to use its own telephone wires as its broadcast network. Until 1943 NBC operated a "red network" and a "blue network." Under government pressure, it sold the blue network, which became the American Broadcasting Company (ABC). The Columbia Broadcasting System (CBS) was formed in 1928 under the leadership of William Paley, with Paramount-Publix, the movie giant, holding a 49 percent partnership. Providing some competition with these broadcasting giants, the Mutual Broadcasting System was formed in 1934.[32]

Commercial networks were nervous about the national high school debate theme because a vocal coalition of educators, religious organizations, and other interested groups were demanding that 25 percent of the broadcasting licenses be given to nonprofit institutions. Leading this movement was the National Committee on Education by Radio. Formed in 1930 and funded by the Payne Foundation, the committee had representatives from nine major national educational organizations, including the National Education Association, the National Catholic Association, the American Council on Education, the National Association of State Universities, and the National Council of State Superintendents.[33]

Like the advocates of self-censorship of movies, who wanted entertainment to be a vehicle for moral and civil lessons, the members of the National Committee on Education by Radio were concerned primarily about radio programming serving as an instrument for building a national culture. When they met in May 1934 in the midst of efforts to get Congress to grant 25 percent of broadcast licenses to nonprofit stations, the committee selected as its topic "The Use of Radio as a Cultural Agency in a Democracy." At the meeting, John H. Mac-Cracken, associate director of the American Council of Education, argued that radio would never have an important role in ordinary classroom instruction. Instead, he argued, the phonograph record was a more flexible means of conveying a lesson requiring dramatization of the human voice.[34] In general, the conference members believed that the most important educational role for radio was to build a national culture outside of school and to provide adult education.

The general tenor of the conference was reflected in the question posed for the first morning session: "A National Culture—By-Product or Objective of National Planning?" The topic was first discussed by Jerome Davis, a member of the executive committee of the American Sociological Society and a faculty member of the Yale Divinity School. After reviewing the rise of commercial radio and the decline of educational radio, Davis argued that radio of the 1930s was distributing negative cultural values through advertising. "Children," Davis told the gathered educators, "are told that when they drink Cocomalt they are cooperating with Buck Rogers and heroine Wilma. . . . I am not questioning the quality of Cocomalt, but the outrageous ethics and educational effects of this advertising on the child mind." Davis argued that if it were possible to plan programs "for the younger generation on an educational instead of a profit basis, the dramatic adventures of historical figures in American life—those who have really contributed something to the welfare of the nation and the world—could be told." Davis lashed out against programming driven by profits and the quality of music and programs on commercial radio, and he concluded with a demand that commercial radio be required to devote at least 20 percent of its programming to educational programs.[35]

Joy Elmer Morgan, editor of the *Journal of the National Education Association,* chair of the National Committee on Education by Radio, and later president of the NEA, echoed Davis's sentiments when warning the audience, "You will discover that the advertising agency is taking the place of the mother, the father, the teacher, the pastor, the priest, in determining the attitudes of children."[36]

Morgan made a sweeping attack on the effects of radio and movies on American culture. Based on a pursuit of profits, these two media, Morgan argued, were spreading a form of entertainment that was the negation of culture and positive values. In fact, Morgan maintained, the only things keeping the country going were the culture and values from the period prior to the advent of these forms of mass entertainment. In Morgan's words, "America today is operating on a momentum which was acquired in the days before radio. It is operating on a momentum which the people acquired before the motion picture began teaching crime and gambling and the cheap and flippant attitude toward the verities of life." Speaking as editor of the *NEA Journal,* Morgan worried about what would happen to the United States when the generation being raised in the age of commercial media reached adulthood. The problem, as Morgan saw it, was the pursuit of profits by movies and radio determining national culture. "No one knows what will happen," Morgan told the sympathetic audience, "when this country comes into the hands of those who have been exposed to the propaganda of the money changers and to the debasing material which they have broadcast into the lives of the people."[37]

When answering the session's question of whether culture was a by-product or an objective of national planning, Morgan discussed the differences between public schooling as a creator of mass culture, and commercial radio and movies. She listed three requirements for building a culture: (1) freedom of speech, (2) the idea of progress, and (3) planning. Freedom of thought, Morgan argued, provided the opportunity for creation of new ideas in science and in social and political thought. Without advances in these areas, culture remained static.

Reflecting the belief that public schools were in competition with commercial radio and movies for the determination of national culture, Morgan related the idea of progress to the development of the common school system in the United States. She argued that it had been Horace Mann's belief in the possibility of progress through human improvability that had led to his crusade for common schools. And it was the common school of the 1890s, Morgan claimed, that had made possible the rapid advances in American civilization in the 1890s and early twentieth century. In Morgan's words, "The first great development of the common school came during the 1890s and when that generation which was in the schools in the '90s came onto the scene of action, America had a period of the most rapid advance which has ever been known in any civilization."[38]

Morgan also related planning to the development of the common school. From her perspective, planning, accompanied by freedom of thought and a belief in progress, made possible the advance of civilization. "The common school," Morgan stated, ". . . is an example of far-sighted planning. It does not expect to make a profit today or at the end of the month or even at the end of the year."[39] The common school exists to serve society, and therefore its use can be planned.

Within this conceptualization of the development of culture, public schools advance culture, whereas movies and radio destroy culture. Morgan argued that radio and movies hindered the advancement of civilization because profits took precedence over freedom of thought, the idea of progress, and socially meaningful planning. Morgan's answer for making radio an important contributor to the advancement of culture was to eliminate private ownership of broadcasting, to have listeners' interests determine program content, and to promote the cultural use of radio over commercial uses. In addition, Morgan argued, children needed to be protected against commercial exploitation. "We should look upon the effort to go over the heads of parents, the church, and the school, to the child mind with something of the horror that we would look at the poisoning of a spring or well."[40]

The afternoon session tackled the question "On Whom Rests the Responsibility for the Cultural Use of Radio?" It was followed the next morning by reports from various committees discussing the questions posed on the first day of the conference. Of particular interest in this follow-up discussion were the comments of William G. Carr, research director of the National Education Association, regarding the similar problems posed by movies and radio. Carr called for studies of the effects of radio that would be similar to those of the Payne studies of movies. Carr stated, "We have in radio a problem somewhat similar to that of the motion pictures. Both are growing privately owned businesses with great possibilities for constructive or destructive educational effects." A set of findings on the effect of radio, he believed, would arouse public interest.

The last session on the afternoon of the second day was devoted to discussing the adoption of the "Report of Committee on Fundamental Principles Which Should Underlie American Radio Policy." The report contained a summary of the opinions regarding national radio policy held by representatives from the major educational organizations attending the conference. The report, like discussions of self-censorship in the movie industry, stressed the importance of using radio as a means of social control. In fact, it stressed the importance of conscious control for this purpose. The opening to the final report of the conference states, "Radio broadcasting—this great, new agency—should be so guided and controlled as to insure to this nation the greatest possible social values." And, the report went on, "The social welfare of the nation should be the conscious, decisive, primary objective, not merely a possible by-product incidental to the greatest net returns to advertisers and broadcasters."

To achieve this conscious control of the social values promoted by radio, the report recommended that listeners' needs and desires take precedence over commercial interests; that minority groups gain access to radio; that the "impressionable, defenseless minds of children and youth must be protected against insidious, degenerative influences"; and that controversial issues and America's best culture be broadcast over radio. With regard to the issue of ownership, the report made a general statement: "The government should cease incurring expense for the protection of channels for the benefit of private monopoly without insuring commendable programs satisfactory to citizen listeners."

In response, broadcasters launched a campaign to prove that commercial radio brought educational programs to the American home. The most articulate defense came from CBS president William Paley in an address titled "Radio as a Cultural Force." Commercial radio was democratic, Paley asserted, because it was based on listener selection. In this situation, arguments for democracy were used to defend a broadcasting system that was controlled primarily by two networks and whose content was influenced by government officials, corporate needs, and the bias of advertisers. Paley stated, "We cannot assuredly, calmly broadcast programs we think people ought to listen to, if they know what is good for them; and then go on happily unconcerned as to whether they listen or not."[41]

Paley also attacked the format of educational radio as being undemocratic and based on aristocratic assumptions. Quoting from an article he had written for the *Annals of the American Academy of Political and Social Science,* he argued that the common school system had created independent and critical thinkers. Paley stated that American democratic education prepared citizens for direct application of the humanities and arts as opposed to the aristocratic concept of learning for learning's sake. In his words, "Experience has taught us that one of the quickest ways to bore the American audience is to deal with art for art's sake, or to deify culture and education because they are worthy gods."[42]

The Federal Communications Commission (FCC) sided with the radio industry and reported to Congress that commercial radio was providing adequate educational programming. What was needed, the commission argued, was cooperation between broadcasters and the educational community. For this purpose the commission created the Federal Radio Education Committee, which became another platform for the debate over the role of education in the American broadcasting system.

Obviously the creation of the Federal Radio Education Committee as an alternative to the 25 percent allotment plan was favored by the broadcasting industry but not by the members of the Committee for Education by Radio. The goal of the Federal Radio Education Committee was to establish cooperation between educators and commercial broadcasters and to support studies of the educational use of radio. This action created no threat to the broadcasting industry and, in fact, provided a means for commercial broadcasters to prove that they were serving the public interest. Educators gained federal assistance in the development of education by radio, but they lost at this time in their efforts to create an educational network. Public broadcasting was eventually to be realized with the passage of the Public Broadcasting Act of 1967.

CREATING THE SUPERHERO FOR CHILDREN'S RADIO

In December 1934 Thomas Rishworth, the director of radio station KSIP in St. Paul, Minnesota, made the mistake of challenging the local Parent-Teacher Association (PTA) to stop its "glib" criticism of children's radio programs and offer constructive advice. He said that he was tired of hearing the Minnesota PTA complain that radio broadcasts were disturbing children with blood-and-gore tales, causing them to toss and turn in their sleep, and making them miss meals when their favorite programs were being aired.[43]

One week later, representatives of the PTA and Boy Scouts and other community members met with Rishworth to discuss the problems of children's radio.

Besides the previously mentioned complaints, John Donahue, a probation officer in St. Paul, stood up at the meeting and warned that radio programs like "Jack Armstrong" were causing law-breaking tendencies among the community's children through their portrayal of likable villains.[44]

Contrary to Rishworth's original intentions, the meeting ended with a call for boycotts of advertisers of children's programs and strict censorship of radio listening by parents. Even the trade newspaper *Variety* was caught by surprise by the outcome of the meeting. *Variety* tended to take the side of the networks. Its original article about the topic gave the impression that Rishworth would easily be able to handle the critics of children's radio. After the critics announced a boycott of advertisers, *Variety,* in an article titled "Air Reformers after Coin," claimed that the real goal of critics in St. Paul was to make money in the radio business. Without naming the group, the newspaper stated that one of the groups represented at the meeting with Rishworth was trying to peddle its own scripts to commercial sponsors.[45]

The interaction between Rishworth and the local PTA exemplified the protests against children's radio that were occurring across the country. Complaints about children's radio began to appear in popular magazines in the early 1930s. Typical of these articles was a 1933 editorial in *Parents Magazine* written in response to the many complaints received in its offices about children's programs. The editorial was accompanied by a cartoon depicting a frightened young girl sitting on the floor next to a radio spewing forth the words "Scram! Don't Shoot! Kidnapped! They're Going to Kill Me! Help! Murder! Bang! Bang! Kill Him! Police!" The editorial stated that the majority of complaints it received were about the high pitch of fear and emotional excitement radio caused in young children. The editor urged parents to write to sponsors to protest the quality of children's programs.[46]

Parental protests were voiced through local PTAs and women's clubs. For example, in February 1933 the Central Council of the PTA of Rochester, New York, issued a public statement that, according to *Variety,* declared "the crime ideas [in radio programs] harmful to moral fibre of children and the bloodcurdling situations tend to excite youngsters in a manner to interfere with their sleep." The PTA sent protests to local stations with hints of a boycott of advertisers.[47] A few months later the California PTA issued a list of "bad" radio programs and called for unofficial censorship of programs broadcast between 5 p.m. and 8 p.m., which were considered the prime hours for children to listen to radio. The California PTA expressed its concern about "all programs emphasizing killing, robbing, impossible or dangerous situations."[48]

The actions of PTA groups began to have some effect on network broadcasting. In February 1933 NBC announced that in response to mounting mass complaints that children were trying to mimic the action of criminals appearing on radio programs, it would begin to "blue-pencil" radio scripts that had criminal themes.[49] Advertisers began to show concern. *Variety* announced in August 1933, "Commercials are yielding to the agitation of PTA associations." The advertising agency for Jell-O was supposedly leading the way by shifting from sponsorship of horror programs to a radio version of *The Wizard of Oz.* Members of other advertising agencies expressed surprise that the protests hadn't started sooner and believed that horror on radio was overdone.[50]

The other major organization protesting the content of children's radio was the National Council of Women, composed of twenty-eight national women's organizations. The head of the council's Women's National Radio Committee, Mrs. Harold V. Milligan, laced her attack against children's radio with strong feminist language. In a 1935 letter to *Variety,* she described her committee as the first coordinated effort by women to register their complaints against radio, which, in her words, was "man-made" and "man-regulated."[51] The following year, at a national radio conference, she declared, "Women vote, and they have influence on public opinion, yet big business does very little to indicate its willingness to earn the respect of millions of women who are serious about the one problem—children's programs on the radio."[52]

Like the PTA, the Women's National Radio Committee was concerned about the blood and gore in children's programming. In addition, the organization was concerned about the effects of advertising. In describing the growth of women's interest in radio, Milligan stated, "there sprang into being . . . a consciousness on the part of women that radio was a guest in the American home. . . . [We] were grateful for the stimulating experience . . . but we were dubious of the growing tendencies of the American advertiser to inflict programs that we did not think were worthy of our children's attention." To capture the child's attention, she argued, the advertiser believed that it had to make programs highly stimulating. Also, she complained, advertisers were exploiting children as consumers.[53]

Modeling themselves after the movie industry, the radio networks reacted to these pressures by trying to include complaining organizations in a public relations campaign. The fact that the radio industry was borrowing methods from Will Hays's Motion Picture Producers and Distributors Association was boldly stated in a headline in *Variety:* "Radio Wants Clubwoman Good Will: Offer Transmitters to Gals with Messages—Will Hays Started It." The article dealt with CBS Chicago affiliate WBBM offering free airtime to local women's clubs, the Daughters of the American Revolution (DAR), and the PTA. The *Variety* article stated, "Following the plan laid down by Will H. Hays of the picture industry in organizing public opinion, stations are giving attention to the problem of building up goodwill."[54]

By 1935 the FCC began to respond to the complaints of the PTAs and women's clubs. On April 3, 1935, *Variety* announced, "Deluged with bleats from educators and parents, Commish [FCC] is agreed that if broadcasters do not move on their own to cook up more satisfactory entertainment for children the government must apply the whip." The FCC admitted that under its "anti-censorship" clause it could not directly control the content of children's radio, but it could threaten stations with the possibility of taking away licenses by stringently applying the public service requirement and by rigidly enforcing technical rules. In addition to feeling pressure from public groups, the FCC was receiving pressure from the White House and Congress to do something about "goosepimple kid shows." In the words of *Variety,* "Kids' programs of blood-and-thunder type appear doomed under new drive."[55]

In response to increasing political pressure, CBS announced in May 1935 a self-censorship code designed to "clean up" broadcasting.[56] NBC reacted to the announcement of CBS's code by claiming it had adopted a similar code in 1934.[57] But NBC did not pull together its broadcast standards into a single booklet for public distribution until 1939. Before 1939 NBC claimed that its broadcast standards were stated in personal letters to advertisers.[58]

The CBS code dealt directly with the two major complaints about American broadcasting: advertising and children's radio. Of central importance to the future of children's radio programs was the emphasis in the code on creating moral and social heroes to guide youth. The code was premised on the notion of the importance of hero worship in a child's life. Radio programs such as *Superman, The Lone Ranger,* and *Tom Mix* exemplified this type of hero-based children's drama. Like the movie code, CBS's code emphasized the importance of not teaching children antisocial behavior by presenting criminals and crime in a positive light. In addition, the code reflected the complaints of women's clubs about the quality of advertising on children's programs.

The section about children's programs began with a discussion of the varieties of viewpoints among parents and authorities as to which programs were suitable for children and the attempt by commercial sponsors to provide appropriate programs. But even with these considerations, the code argued, it was necessary to eliminate instances of poor judgment. The code disclaimed any attempt by CBS to be "arbiter of what is proper for children to hear."[59] But, the code states, CBS "does have an editorial responsibility to the community, in the interpretation of public wish and sentiment, which cannot be waived."[60] Using this justification, the code provided the following list of themes and dramatic treatments that would not be allowed on children's programs:

- The exalting, as modern heroes, of gangsters, criminals, and racketeers will not be allowed.
- Disrespect for either parental or other proper authority must not be glorified or encouraged.
- Cruelty, greed, and selfishness must not be presented as worthy motivations.
- Programs that arouse harmful nervous reactions in the child must not be presented.
- Conceit, smugness, or an unwarranted sense of superiority over others less fortunate may not be presented.
- Recklessness and abandon must not be falsely identified with a healthy spirit of adventure.
- Unfair exploitation of others for personal gain must not be made praiseworthy.
- Dishonesty and deceit are not to be made appealing or attractive to the child.[61]

After stating those prohibitions, the code presented an argument for centering children's radio around hero worship. The code argued that radio programs for children of elementary school age should provide entertainment of a moral nature. The code noted that children's literature provided "heroes worthy of the child's ready impulse to hero worship, and of his imitative urge to pattern himself after the hero model." Literature of this nature, the code noted, "succeeds in inspiring the child to socially useful and laudable ideals such as generosity, industry, kindness and respect for authority . . . it serves, in effect, as a useful adjunct to that education which the growing and impressionable child is absorbing during every moment of its waking day."[62]

As mentioned, NBC claimed it had been using a similar code since 1934 and in 1939 officially released its code. NBC censorship of children's programs actually began in 1933, when the network announced that listeners' complaints about the effects of crime shows on youth were causing it to "blue-pencil" scripts with crime themes. Officials at NBC expressed concern that letters indicated children were trying to mimic criminals and crime situations.[63]

Like the CBS code, NBC's code linked self-censorship to protection of markets. The code argued that enforcing self-censorship would avoid the broadcast of anything that "might in any way divert part of an audience from one network or station to another." The first section of NBC's code banned from the network advertisements dealing with speculative finances, personal hygiene, weight-reducing agents, fortune-tellers, professions, cemeteries, alcoholic beverages, and firearms. The second section of the code was devoted to children's programs and the last section to general standards that would govern all programs.[64]

The NBC code stressed that all children's programs should stress law and order, adult authority, good morals, and clean living. As in the CBS code, heroes were to play a function in shaping children's morality. The code stated, "The hero or heroine and other sympathetic characters must be portrayed as intelligent and morally courageous . . . and disrespect for law must be avoided as traits in any character that may be presented in the light of a hero to the child listener." In addition, the code stated that programs' themes should emphasize mutual respect, fair play, and honorable behavior. Adventure stories were singled out because of their potential to upset children emotionally. Prohibited from adventure programs were torture, horror, superstition, kidnapping, "morbid suspense," and extreme violence.

Children's programs were also to be covered by eleven "basic program standards" that were to be applied to all NBC programs. Three of these standards dealt with items that might offend religious groups, such as irreverent reference to God, material offensive to religious views, and sacrilegious material. Included in the standard regarding material offensive to religious groups was a ban on statements offensive to racial groups. The standards also discouraged the introduction of murder and suicide into programs and prohibited descriptions of "antisocial" practices and insobriety. One standard reserved the use of "flash" to special news programs, and another warned against false statements. Except in factual news statements, there were to be no references to people featured in criminal and sensational news stories. And reflecting broadcasting's concern about offending important people, one standard read, "Figures of national prominence as well as the peoples of all nations shall be presented with fairness and consideration."[65]

CONTROLLING THE INFLUENCE OF COMIC BOOKS

Appearing in large numbers on magazine racks in the 1930s, comic books were filled with violence and sexuality, and educators and parents became concerned about their growing influence. One critic went so far as to call comic books "the marijuana of the nursery." These criticisms eventually led to the comic book industry adopting a self-censorship code similar to the early movie and radio codes. By 1940 there were 150 comic book titles generating an annual revenue of $20 million. By 1950 there were 300 comic book titles, with annual revenues of $41 million. Between 1950 and 1953 the number of titles jumped to over 650, and revenues leaped to $90 million a year.[66] The parallels between industry regulation of comic books and codes covering the movies and broadcasting were pointed out in a 1954 article in *Christian Century:* "Like movie magnates and radio station operators before them, 24 of the 27 leading publishers of these often lurid picture-pulps [comic books] are trying to still cries for censorship by promising to censor themselves."[67]

What set off the disputes about this new form of children's literature was the appearance of crime and horror comics between 1945 and 1954. Unlike television executives, comic book publishers defended the use of crime and gore. In 1954, when the Senate subcommittee on juvenile delinquency opened hearings on comic books, Senator Estes Kefauver confronted William Gaines, president of the Entertaining Comics Group, with a cover of one of his company's comic books, *Shock Suspense Stories,* depicting an ax-wielding man holding the severed head of a blonde woman. Gaines responded by saying that the cover would be in bad taste only if the head were held "a little high so the neck would show with the blood dripping from it." Kefauver shot back, "You've got blood dripping from the mouth."[68]

Horror and crime comic books of the early 1950s depicted criminal acts, maimed and tortured individuals, and suggestive sexual scenes. At the New York City hearings of the Senate subcommittee on juvenile delinquency, a variety of comic books were introduced to illustrate possible harmful effects on children. In one example, "Bottoms Up" from *Story Comics,* an alcoholic father was responsible for the accidental death of his son while obtaining liquor from a bootlegger. The mother is shown taking revenge in the final four panels of the story by proceeding to kill and hack her spouse to pieces with an ax. The first panel shows her swinging the ax and burying its blade in her husband's skull. Blood spurts from the open wound, and the husband is shown with an expression of agony. She then cuts his body into smaller pieces and disposes of it by placing the various pieces in the bottles of liquor her husband had purchased. She then returns the liquor to the bootlegger and obtains a refund. Another example provided by the subcommittee was from "Frisco Mary" from *Ace Comics.* One scene in this story showed Mary standing over a police officer pouring machine-gun bullets into his back while other gang members urge her to stop shooting and flee. In "With Knife in Hand" from *Atlas Comics,* a young surgeon ruins his career by being forced by the spendthrift habits of his wife to treat criminals. In the final scenes of this story, a criminal brings in his wounded girlfriend to be treated by the doctor. The doctor discovers that the girlfriend is his own wife. The next panel shows the doctor committing suicide by plunging a scalpel into his own abdomen. His wife, gasping for help, dies on the operating table for lack of medical attention. The last scene shows her staring into space, arms dangling over the sides of the operating table. The doctor is sprawled on the floor, his hand still clutching the knife handle protruding from his bloody abdomen. There is a leer on his face, and he is winking at the reader, displaying satisfaction at having wrought revenge upon his unfaithful spouse. One comic book was described as ending with the victim "lying dead on the bed with a gaping hole in his chest, a rib protruding, blood flowing over the bed onto the floor, his face fixed in a death mask as he stares at the reader."[69]

Following the pattern of movies and broadcasting, the comic book industry adopted a pro-family code. Wanting to avoid continued community protest and the threat of censorship laws, comic book publishers organized to create and impose their own standards. Their first attempt was the 1948 formation of the Association of Comics Magazine Publishers and its adoption of a six-point code. A seal was to be attached to comic books to indicate conformity to the code. As in other codes, there was an emphasis on issues involving sex, crime, language, the family, and attacks on religious and racial groups. This early code proved ineffective; only twelve of the thirty-four major publishers of comic books belonged to the comic book association. In response to increased pressure from government and private organizations, a new organization, Comics Magazine Association of America, was formed in 1954 with a membership of twenty-eight of the then thirty-one major publishers of comic books. This association appointed New York City magistrate Charles Murphy to enforce a comic book code. The words *horror* and *terror* were not allowed in titles. Crime comics were to be screened to exclude certain methods of committing crimes. No sympathy was to be given to criminals, and nothing should "create disrespect for established authority." In addition, the code banned "profanity, obscenity, smut, vulgarity, ridicule of racial or religious groups."[70]

In keeping with the belief that the sanctity of the family was necessary for protection of the American way of life and against juvenile delinquency, the code ensured protection of the "sanctity of marriage" and the "value of the home." In addition, "divorce was not to be shown as desirable."[71] Beginning in 1955, a seal was placed on the front of comics as proof that these values were being protected. It was estimated that the code was enforced on 75 percent of the estimated sixty million comic books published each month in the United States.[72] Dell Comics, one of the three publishers that did not belong to the Comics Magazine Association of America and publisher of approximately 20 percent of the comic books in the United States, did not join the association because it already had its own code of ethics. In any case, Dell primarily published comics based on adventure stories and Walt Disney characters. It was known in the trade as having a "wholesome approach." One of the other nonmembers was Classics Illustrated, which adapted classic novels, such as Charles Dickens's *Oliver Twist,* to a comic book format. William Gaines, the originator of horror comics and another nonmember, announced that he would cease publishing all horror and terror magazines. Thus comic books joined in the media chorus protecting the American way of life.[73]

EDUCATING CHILDREN AS CONSUMERS

Educators' and parents' fears that commercialized media would exploit children and youth became a reality as advertising began to target these markets. In the early twentieth century, children were targeted through magazines. In 1904 the advertising manager of the *Atlantic Monthly* wrote that the "farsighted advertiser" begins with the female child so that the brand name follows her "to school, thrusts its self upon her as she travels, and all unconsciously engraves its self upon her memory." The result is that when the child grows up and goes on her first shopping trip as a wife, "She orders Pears' Soap, White Label Soup, Pearline, Walter Baker's Cocoa, and Knox's Gelatine, because she knows and remembers the names, and does not realize that she has chosen in every instance an article made familiar to her, perhaps, by advertising only."[74]

Advertising competitions were a popular technique for interesting children in brand names. In 1911 Colgate toothpaste launched in a children's magazine a contest that offered monetary prizes for writing the best ad copy. The ads instructed participants, "Just imagine that you're writing a short letter to one of your schoolmates telling how important it is to take proper care of the teeth and how [Colgate] Ribbon Dental Cream is not only the best cleanser but besides is so delicious in flavor that its use is a real treat. . . . And remember, the more you believe it the easier it will be to write it and the better the advertisement."[75]

In a 1904 ad in *McClure's* magazine, an eight-year-old boy sits on the floor surrounded by opened magazines. Looking at this mother, he tells her, "Mamma, you know magazines are very useful. They tell you what you want, and where to get it."[76] Early ads used cartoon figures that were marketed to children as dolls. Through these dolls, which also were sources of revenue, children gained brand loyalty. In the early twentieth century, Jell-O ads used cute little Kewpie figures that were nude infant shapes with pointed hairdos that performed tasks beyond their years. Kewpies appeared on Jell-O packages and Jell-O recipe books. One early recipe book showed a little girl pouring hot water into a container of Jell-O while one Kewpie pointed at the Jell-O box and another held up a Jell-O mold. Campbell Soup ads used Campbell Kids' characters in a similar fashion. Both Kewpies and the Campbell Kids were marketed as dolls for children's play.[77]

It was the business genius of Walt Disney's brother Roy that led to product spin-offs of media characters. The Disney Corporation's first product spin-off was Mickey Mouse. Walt Disney created the Mickey Mouse character in 1928 and in the same year produced three animated Mickey Mouse cartoons, including the sound cartoon *Steamboat Willie*.[78] After the opening of *Steamboat Willie,* Walt Disney recalled, "Right after Mickey Mouse hit, I was in New York and we needed money. A fellow kept hanging around the hotel with three hundred dollars cash waving at me, and I finally signed a deal to put Mickey Mouse on these big cheap [writing] tablet type things. It was the first deal ever signed."[79] Roy Disney decided to copyright the Mickey Mouse character and sell products using Mickey's characters and those of other Disney cartoon figures. In 1930 Roy began a campaign to adorn products with these figures and signed a contract with George Borgfeldt to make toys and other objects using Mickey and Minnie Mouse.[80] The marketing of these products was tied to Disney movies, syndicated newspaper comic strips, and newly formed Mickey Mouse Clubs. Roy Disney explained the company's merchandising techniques:

> Mickey Mouse [newspaper cartoon strip] is now being handled . . . through King Features syndicate, who are rapidly placing the strip in many leading newspapers. . . . Borgfeldt & Co. New York have taken the world rights to manufacture toys and novelties. . . . Villa Moret, Inc. . . . are publishing the Mickey Mouse song, used in the pictures. . . . Also in connection with our pictures we have launched a campaign for the formation of Mickey Mouse Clubs in theaters where the cartoons are shown. . . . The idea is meeting with astonishing success.[81]

In 1932 the Disney brothers realized that there was a two-way relationship between the promotion of Disney movies and the earnings from merchandise bearing Disney logos. Walt was contacted by an advertising man who convinced him that the Mickey character could be promoted through merchandising. The Disney brothers agreed, and a first spin-off was the now famous collector's item, the Mickey Mouse watch. Lionel Toys, which was having difficulty selling model trains during the Depression, joined the promotion effort. Regarding Lionel Toys, Walt recalled, "During the Depression, it was just bad for the toy business. They made this little windup Mickey Mouse that ran around a track. It was a big item. It sold everywhere."[82]

With the advent of television, Mickey Mouse Clubs became an important part of marketing strategy for movies, products, and theme parks. On October 3, 1955, shortly after the opening of the Disneyland theme park, *The Mickey Mouse Club* children's TV program premiered on ABC. The most famous merchandise sold through the show was a cap with mouse ears. Children around the country would don their mouse-ear caps to sing the program's opening song, which began, "M-I-C-K-E-Y M-O-U-S-E, Mickey Mouse." *The Mickey Mouse Club* program proved a bonanza for other Disney products. Constantly plugged through the first programs were Disneyland and two recent Disney movies—*20,000 Leagues under the Sea* and *Lady and the Tramp*. It was believed that both were box office successes because of the plugs they received on the TV program.[83]

In the same year as the premier of *The Mickey Mouse Club,* Disney launched another TV series—*Disneyland.* The first ninety-minute show was devoted to the Disneyland theme park. This marked the beginning of the TV infomercial, an entire program devoted to information about a product. Many subsequent programs were about Disney movies, including one about the making of *20,000 Leagues under the Sea.* A program devoted to Davy Crockett tied a Disney movie to Disneyland and a variety of product spin-offs. Davy Crockett was linked to the Disneyland attraction Frontierland. In addition, Disney studios released the movie *Davy Crockett, King of the Wild Frontier.* The movie's theme song proved a hit among children, and Disney licensed products bearing Crockett's name—coonskin hats, soaps, lamps, dolls, and a host of other children's products.[84]

Before Disneyland opened on July 17, 1955, it had received publicity through Disney's TV infomercial and *The Mickey Mouse Club.* Every child who donned the mouse-ear cap or wore Crockett's coonskin hat knew about Disneyland. Its success spawned a new generation of theme parks designed to organize and sell leisure activities to families. Walt Disney designed his first park to attract middle-class families. While riding around the Disneyland construction site, Walt Disney commented to his biographer Bob Thomas, "Disneyland isn't designed just for children. . . . I believe the right kind of entertainment can appeal to all persons, young or old. I want Disneyland to be a place where parents can bring their children—or come by themselves and still have a good time."[85] On another occasion, Disney commented,

> We gotta charge people to get in. If we don't, we'll get all kinds of drunks and molesters; they'll be grabbing girls in the dark. You'll get a better class of people if you charge them to enter. . . . One of the things I hated about carnivals and piers was all the crap that was everywhere. You're stepping on chewing gum and ice cream cones. I think people want clean amusement parks.[86]

THE CREATION OF TEENAGE MARKETS

"Civic consumerism" was Kelly Schrum's description of the editorial message for teenagers in *Seventeen* magazine in the late 1940s and early 1950s.[87] Scrum defined "civic consumerism" as "combining one's democratic role as active citizen with one's duty as a responsible and active consumer."[88] During the late 1940s and 1950s, she argued, "Voting and democracy, as well as pride in America and the right to buy goods, were common themes through this period, a reflection of both lingering war rhetoric and the beginning of the Cold War."[89] Corresponding to earlier concerns with controlling adolescent sexuality through high school activities, advertisers hoped to channel teenage sexuality into consumerism. Ads for girls displayed clothing and other products that would enhance their dating potential. Boys directed their consumer sexuality at cars with the hope that a hot car or "hot rod," a term with interesting sexual overtones, would result in a hot date.

The post–World War II era witnessed the appearance of the affluent high school student. The 1930s teenage culture, spawned by the mass institutionalization of youth in high school, lacked spending power. Between 1900 and 1940, the percentage in high school of those between fourteen and seventeen years old increased from 11 to 80 percent.[90] After World War II, spending patterns changed. The publication of *Seventeen* magazine, with its slogan "Teena means business," symbolized the change. Teenage girls, like their mothers, were a primary target for marketers. The word *teenager,* according to Kelly Schrum, was invented by marketers. At first marketers experimented with *teenster* and *Petiteen;* then *teenager* was popularized during the 1940s to mean a group defined by high school attendance. In a crass commercial effort, *Seventeen* magazine advertised the potential teenage market with slogans such as "When is a girl worth $11,690,499?"[91] Sounding like an allusion to prostitution, the slogan referred to the amount of money spent on teenage ads.

Was a national teenage culture a result of advertising? Advertising certainly provided national models for white teenagers to emulate. Black, Native American, and Mexican Americans youth were not subjects of these early ad campaigns. One can imagine teenagers fantasizing about themselves looking like the youths in national ads. The ads provided models of dress and lifestyles. Also, they carried messages about teenage sexuality.

A 1950s Seven-Up ad played on the concept of "going steady." A 1950s dating ritual of teenagers, going steady was similar to a pre-engagement rite. The boy gave the girl an ankle bracelet, a varsity jacket, or some other consumer adornment to indicate that they would date only each other or, in the language of the times, were "going steady." Violation of the going-steady agreement could result in a pseudo-divorce. The going-steady process mirrored the marriage and divorce practices of adults. In the Seven-Up ad, a neatly dressed white teenage couple holding Seven-Up bottles stands next to a jukebox. The ad headline proclaims, "It's great to 'go steady' with this COOL, CLEAN, TASTE!" Playing again on the theme of the couple's relationship, the text of the ad declares, "Here's the drink that's fun to be with—it has such a *sparkling personality* . . . For a really 'cool' date . . . make yours 7-Up."[92]

Other ads played directly to female sexuality. A 1945 *Seventeen* perfume ad embodied sexuality in the brand name, illustration, and text. The ad for Vigny's Beau Catcher perfume showed a young girl in a windblown and revealing skirt holding a string wrapped around a "Beau Catcher Date Book." Two other strings were tied to the product icon and to a bottle of perfume. The ad's text read, "Vigny's Beau Catcher Perfume fills your date book. It's the saucy scent that won't take 'no' for an answer."[93]

A national white teenage culture was created through the common high school experience and national advertising. *Seventeen* magazine sold advertising on the basis that teenagers shared a common public mind. Magazine copy claimed, "Teena is a copycat—what a break for you. . . . She and her teen-mates speak the same language . . . wear the same clothes . . . use the same brand of lipstick."[94] The magazine included in its proclamation of a national teenage market a message that youths were responsible citizens. In other words, teenagers were responsible consumer citizens.

Adolescent sexuality was central to teen ads and public concerns. Ironically, the high school heightened teenage sexuality by putting boys and girls within close proximity of each other. Advertising added to this concentrated sexuality by playing on themes of dating and relationships. *Seventeen* tried to balance this blatant sexuality with advice that discouraged heavy necking and petting. It also stressed the importance of political involvement, patriotism, and maintaining knowledge of current events. Scrum concluded that the general message was for teenage girls to practice civic consumerism.

Of course advertising placed sexuality at the center of teenage life by following its long tradition of playing to feelings of personal inadequacy. Like adult women in the 1920s, teenagers were confronted with the possibility of being dateless because of body odors, bad breath, and unfashionable hairstyles and clothing. The purchase of deodorants, mouthwashes, cosmetics, hair products, and fashionable clothing promised the necessary sexual appeal.

CHILDREN AND YOUTH FROM THE 1950S TO THE TWENTY-FIRST CENTURY

The growth of a teenage consumer market after World War II was part of a general trend to provide most children and teenagers (referring to the age group attending high school) with what Steven Mintz has called a "protected childhood" where the family focuses on ensuring that children have a carefree life with proper nutrition, shelter, health care, and schooling.[95] Until the early part of the twentieth century, street children and working children, particularly in factories and mines, did not receive a protected childhood. The Civil War ended the plight of enslaved children, but poverty following the war forced many to work. The expansion of the high school during the Depression began to give most teenagers the status of protected childhood.

The 1950s ushered in the golden era of protected children and teenagers. In *Huck's Raft: A History of American Childhood,* Steven Mintz warns that it is easy to think of the 1950s as an ideal world for children and teenagers. However, a third of postwar children lived in families near or below the poverty line and, as discussed previously in this chapter, there were major concerns about juvenile delinquency.[96] What made the 1950s a golden period for most American children and teenagers was a stable divorce rate, a low number of women in the workforce, a high birthrate, increased family income, and the development of child-centered suburbs. The low number of women in the workforce was, according to Mintz, out of line with historical trends. Except for privileged households, most women worked in the nineteenth and early twentieth centuries on farms, as domestic help, and in factories, businesses, and stores. After the 1970s a decline in family incomes along with the women's movement resulted in women returning to the labor market. As Mintz stated, "Economics was a driving force behind changing family patterns. During the 1970s, in a period of prolonged inflation and economic stagnation the maintenance of a middle-class standard of living required mothers to work and limit births."[97]

The social conditions of the 1950s created the image of a child-centered society with stay-at-home mothers focusing their attention on child rearing. The most popular child-rearing book of the period was Benjamin Spock's *The Common Sense Book of Baby and Child Care,* which urged mothers to abandon rigid child-rearing practices of the past and follow their instincts. Parents worried about having healthy and happy children who would become well-adjusted adults. Consequently there was a focus on the psychological conditions of childhood, with one 1947 book, *Modern Women: The Lost Sex,* warning that "the spawning ground for most neurosis in Western civilization is the home. The basis for it is childhood."[98] There was also an emphasis on teaching gender distinctions.

Child-rearing experts warned about boys becoming "sissies" and the possible emergence of masculine traits among girls.[99]

The golden era of protected childhood and teenagers of the 1950s spawned what Mintz calls the "youthquake" of the 1960s. The high birthrates of the 1950s caused the unprecedented expansion of the number of teenagers and youths of college age in the 1960s. In addition, during the 1960s divorce rates doubled, and the number of couples living together outside marriage increased sixfold. Women began to reenter the workforce, particularly those who had been stay-at-home mothers in the 1950s. Popular books began to criticize the permissive child-rearing practices of the 1950s for creating a generation of promiscuous and defiant youths. Magazine articles appeared warning of a generation of youths who were spoiled and soft. Images of protesting youths in civil rights marches and anti–Vietnam War demonstrations filled the media. The stress on gender differences in the 1950s gave way to an emphasis on gender equity.[100]

Many parents of the 1970s, according to Mintz, changed their concept of childhood from "protected" to "prepared" as birthrates declined, more women returned to the workforce, and divorce rates climbed. Rather than trying to protect childhood innocence, parents now wanted children to be prepared for the dangers of promiscuous sex, drugs, and alcohol abuse. There was public support for drug and sex education programs. In addition, the increased number of single-parent families led to a valuing of independence and resourcefulness among children who might have to let themselves into the house after school, call their mothers, and prepare their own meals.

The concern about "prepared" childhood ushered in an era of attempts at greater institutional control, particularly in schools. The call for increased testing and standardization of the school curriculum, as discussed in Chapter 15, reflected public anxiety that school requirements needed to be tightened to control student behavior. By the 1980s, children and youths were to be prepared as workers for the global economy. No longer was childhood viewed as an innocent and carefree time. Now it was a period of life surrounded with dangers that children needed to be prepared to fight off while being prepared for the job market. This image of prepared childhood was carried into the twenty-first century and was symbolized by the title of the 2001 legislation "No Child Left Behind" (discussed in Chapter 15). No Child Left Behind focused schools on preparing children and teenagers for the labor market. Preparation replaced protection and innocence as even children in kindergarten were educated to be global workers.[101]

CONCLUSION

Although the content of media came under increasing control because of complaints by educators and parents, advertising flourished. The result was the education of children and teenagers as future consumers. Combined with the "American Way" campaign discussed in Chapter 11, commercialized media were teaching children and teenagers to become consumer citizens. In some minds, democracy was slowly becoming equated with the freedom to consume products.

Notes

1. Will Hays, "Improvement of Moving Pictures," *Annual Proceedings of the National Education Association,* vol. 60 (Washington, DC: National Education Association, 1922), pp. 252–257.
2. An analysis of the public relations campaign can be found in a report by the Department of Research and Education, Federal Council of the Churches of Christ in America, *The Public Relations of the Motion Picture Industry* (New York: Federal Council of Churches, 1931).
3. Ibid., p. 255. A history of the development of the MPPDA can be found in Raymond Moley, *The Hays Office* (Indianapolis: Bobbs Merrill, 1945). For surveys of state and municipal censorship boards, see Thomas Leary and J. Roger Noall, "Note: Entertainment: Public Pressures and the Law—Official and Unofficial Control of the Content and Distribution of Motion Pictures and Magazines," *Harvard Law Review* 71 (1957), pp. 326–367; and Richard Randall, *Censorship of the Movies: The Social and Political Control of a Mass Medium* (Madison: University of Wisconsin Press, 1965), pp. 15–18, 88–89.
4. Ellis Oberholtzer, "What Are the 'Movies' Making of Our Children?" *World's Work* 4 (January 1921), pp. 249–263. Also see Lary May, *Screening Out the Past: The Birth of Mass Culture and the Motion Picture Industry* (New York: Oxford University Press, 1980), pp. 53–55.
5. John Collier, "Censorship and the National Board," *Survey* 35 (October 1915), pp. 9–14.
6. Randall, *Censorship of the Movies,* p. 16.
7. May, *Screening Out the Past,* pp. 164–165, 169–177.
8. Alfred H. Saunders, "Motion Pictures as an Aid to Education," *Annual Proceedings of the National Education Association,* vol. 52 (Ann Arbor: National Education Association, 1914), pp. 743–745.
9. "Discussion," ibid., p. 747.
10. Moley, *Hays Office,* pp. 77–78.
11. See W. W. Charters, "Chairman's Preface," in *Motion Pictures and Youth: A Summary* (New York: Macmillan, 1933), pp. v–vii.
12. The following is a list of authors and research titles sponsored by the Payne Fund. Many of the researchers were famous within their disciplines, which added to the prestige of the studies: (1) P. W. Holaday, Indianapolis Public Schools, and George Stoddard, Director, Iowa Child Welfare Research Station, "Getting Ideas from the Movies"; (2) Ruth C. Peterson and L. L. Thurstone, Department of Psychology, University of Chicago, "Motion Pictures and the Social Attitudes of Children"; (3) Frank Shuttleworth and Mark May, Institute of Human Relations, Yale University, "The Social Conduct and Attitudes of Movie Fans"; (4) W. S. Dysinger and Christian Ruckmick, Department of Psychology, State University of Iowa, "The Emotional Responses of Children to the Motion Picture Situation"; (5) Charles Peters, Professor of Education, Pennsylvania State College, "Motion Pictures and Standards of Morality"; (6) Samuel Renshaw, Vernon L. Miller, and Dorothy Marquis, Department of Psychology, Ohio State University, "Children's Sleep"; (7) Herbert Blumer, Department of Sociology, University of Chicago, "Movies and Conduct"; (8) Edgar Dale, Research Associate, Bureau of Educational Research, Ohio State University, "The Content of Motion Pictures"; (9) Edgar Dale, "Children's Attendance at Motion Pictures"; (10) Herbert Blumer and Philip Hauser, Department of Sociology, University of Chicago, "Movies, Delinquency, and Crime"; (11) Paul Cressey and Frederick

Thrasher, New York University, "Boys, Movies, and City Streets"; (12) Edgar Dale, "How to Appreciate Motion Pictures."

13. Henry James Forman, *Our Movie Made Children* (New York: Macmillan, 1935).
14. Charters, "Chairman's Preface," p. viii.
15. Herbert Blumer, *Movies and Conduct* (New York: Macmillan, 1933), p. 50.
16. Ibid., pp. 45–49.
17. Forman, *Our Movie Made Children,* pp. 280–282.
18. Edgar Dale, *How to Appreciate Motion Pictures: A Manual of Motion-Picture Criticism Prepared for High-School Students* (New York: Macmillan, 1933).
19. Ibid., p. vii.
20. William Lewin, *Photoplay Appreciation in American High Schools* (New York: Appleton-Century, 1934).
21. Ibid., pp. 30–33.
22. Ibid., p. 51.
23. Ibid., pp. 94–95.
24. Moley, *Hays Office,* pp. 148–149.
25. The article is quoted in ibid., pp. 151–153.
26. Will H. Hays, "The Motion Picture in Education," *Annual Proceedings of the National Education Association,* vol. 127 (Washington, DC: National Education Association, 1939), pp. 80–86.
27. Ibid., p. 80.
28. Moley, *Hays Office,* pp. 57–58. Also see Martin Quigley, *Decency in Motion Pictures* (New York: Macmillan, 1937).
29. Reprints of movie codes can be found in Moley, *Hays Office,* pp. 240–248; and in *The Movies in Our Midst,* ed. Gerald Mast (Chicago: University of Chicago Press, 1982), pp. 321–333.
30. "British vs. American Radio Slant, Debate Theme in 40,000 Schools," *Variety* 111, no. 12 (August 29, 1933), p. 1. Also see Philip T. Rosen, *The Modern Stentors: Radio Broadcasters and the Federal Government, 1920–1934* (Westport, CT: Greenwood Press, 1980), pp. 128–133; and Erik Barnouw, *A Tower of Babel: A History of Broadcasting in the United States to 1933* (New York: Oxford University Press, 1966), pp. 172–179.
31. S. E. Frost, *Education's Own Stations: The History of Broadcast Licenses Issued to Educational Institutions* (Chicago: University of Chicago Press, 1937), pp. 1–5.
32. Ibid.
33. The other members were the National University Extension Association, the Jesuit Educational Association, the Association of Land Grant Colleges and Universities, and the Association of College and University Broadcasting Stations.
34. Tracy F. Tyler, ed., *Radio as a Cultural Agency: Proceedings of a National Conference on the Use of Radio as a Cultural Agency in a Democracy* (Washington, DC: National Committee on Education by Radio, 1934), p. 125.
35. Ibid., pp. 3–10.
36. Joy Elmer Morgan, "A National Culture—By-Product or Objective of National Planning?" ibid., p. 29.
37. Ibid., p. 30.
38. Ibid., p. 27.
39. Ibid., p. 30.
40. Ibid., p. 32.
41. William Paley, "Radio as a Cultural Force: These notes on the economic and social philosophy of America's radio industry, as represented by the policies and practices

of the Columbia Broadcasting System, Inc., were embodied in a talk on October 17, 1934, before the Federal Communications Commission, in its inquiry into proposals to allot fixed percentages of the nation's radio facilities to noncommercial broadcasting," *CBS Reference Library,* New York City, pp. 8–9.

42. Ibid., p. 13.
43. *Variety* 117, no. 1 (December 18, 1934), p. 34.
44. "St. Paul Meet on Kid Programs Calls Radio Villains Likable; Suggest Boycott, Probation," *Variety* 117, no. 2 (December 25, 1934), p. 29.
45. "Air Reformers after Coin," *Variety* 117, no. 7 (January 29, 1935), pp. 1, 66.
46. Clara Savage Littledale, "Better Radio Programs for Children," *Parents Magazine* 18, no. 13 (May 8, 1933), p. 1.
47. "Boycott MDSE in Air Protest?" *Variety* 109, no. 12 (February 28, 1933), p. 47.
48. "Cal. Teachers List 'Bad' Programs," *Variety* 110, no. 8 (May 2, 1933), p. 34.
49. "Squawks Force NBC Move for Less Horror," *Variety* 109, no. 12 (February 26, 1933), p. 45.
50. "Now Agree Too Much Horror for Kids, Junior Programs Turning to Fantasy," *Variety* 111, no. 8 (August 1, 1933), p. 41.
51. "Women's Radio Committee Clarifies," *Variety* 118, no. 10 (May 22, 1935), p.36.
52. "Mrs. Harold Milligan," in *Educational Broadcasting 1937,* ed. C. S. Marsh (Chicago: University of Chicago Press, 1938), p. 259.
53. Ibid., pp. 258–259.
54. "Radio Wants Clubwoman Good Will: Offer Transmitters to Gals with Messages— Will Hays Started It," *Variety* 112, no. 6 (October 17, 1933), p. 37.
55. "Dime Novel Air Stuff Out: Protests Chafe FCC into Action," *Variety* 118, no. 3 (April 3, 1935), pp. 1, 58.
56. "Summary of CBS Policies Relating to Program Material and Advertising Copy," prepared by CBS Research Department, October 1940, *CBS Reference Library,* New York City.
57. "NBC Slant on CBS Policy," ibid., p. 37.
58. "Sponsor Rights Defined," *Variety* 134, no. 4 (April 5, 1939), p. 23.
59. "Statement by William S. Paley over the Columbia Network, Tuesday, May 14, 1935," *CBS Reference Library,* New York City, p. 2.
60. "New Policies: A Statement to the Public, to Advertisers and to Advertising Agencies," May 15, 1935, *CBS Reference Library,* New York City, p. 4.
61. Ibid., p. 5.
62. Ibid., p. 6.
63. "Squawks Force NBC Move," p. 45.
64. "NBC's Tentative Program Code," *Variety* 134, no. 4 (April 5, 1934), p. 24.
65. Ibid.
66. *Comic Books and Juvenile Delinquency: A Part of the Investigation of Juvenile Delinquency in the United States: Interim Report of the Subcommittee to Investigate Juvenile Delinquency to the Committee on the Judiciary Pursuant to S. Res. 89 and S. Res. 190* (Washington, DC: U.S. Government Printing Office, 1955), p. 3.
67. "Comic Book Publishers Promise Reforms," *Christian Century* 71 (November 10, 1954), p. 1357.
68. "Senate Sub-Committee Holds Hearings on 'Comics,'" *Publishers Weekly* 165 (May 1, 1954), p. 1903.
69. *Comic Books and Juvenile Delinquency,* pp. 8–9.

70. "Purified Comics," *Newsweek* 32 (July 12, 1948), p. 56; "Better Than Censorship," *Christian Century* 65 (July 28, 1948), p. 750; and *Comic Books and Juvenile Delinquency,* p. 31.

71. "Comics' Publishers Institute Code, Appoint 'Czar,'" *Publishers Weekly* 166 (September 25, 1954), p. 1386; "Progress in Comic Book Cleanup," *America* (October 30, 1954), pp. 1–14; and "Code for Comics," *Time* (November 8, 1954), p. 60.

72. "First 'Seal of Approval' Comics out This Month," *Publishers Weekly* 167 (January 15, 1955), p. 211.

73. "Comics' Publishers Institute Code," p. 1386; and "Correspondence: Comic-Book Code," *America* (November 13, 1954), p. 196.

74. Quoted by Ellen Gruber Harvey, *The Adman in the Parlor: Magazines and the Gendering of Consumer Culture, 1880s to 1910s* (New York: Oxford University Press, 1996), p. 54.

75. Ad reproduced in ibid., p. 63.

76. Ad reproduced in ibid., p. 56.

77. Susan Strasser, *Satisfaction Guaranteed: The Making of the American Mass Market* (Washington, DC: Smithsonian Institution Press, 1989), pp. 115–119.

78. For a chronological list of Walt Disney films see Leonard Mosley, *Disney's World* (Lanham, MD: Scarborough House, 1990), pp. 309–315.

79. Quoted in Bob Thomas, *Building a Company: Roy O. Disney and the Creation of an Entertainment Empire* (New York: Hyperion, 1998), pp. 67–68.

80. Ibid., p. 68.

81. Quoted in ibid., p. 69.

82. Quoted in ibid., p. 70.

83. Ibid., p. 198.

84. Ibid., pp. 187–188, 198.

85. Bob Thomas, *An American Original: Walt Disney* (New York: Disney Editions, 1994), p. 11.

86. Thomas, *Building a Company,* p. 197.

87. Kelly Schrum, "Teena Means Business: Teenage Girls' Culture and 'Seventeen Magazine,' 1944–1950," in *Delinquents and Debutantes: Twentieth-Century American Girls' Cultures* (New York: New York University Press, 1998), p. 149.

88. Ibid., p. 149.

89. Ibid., p. 156.

90. Ibid., p. 136.

91. Ad reproduced in ibid., p. 143.

92. Ad reproduced in Juliann Sivulka, *Soap, Sex, and Cigarettes: A Cultural History of American Advertising* (Belmont, CA: Wadsworth, 1998), p. 262.

93. Reproduced in Schrum, "Teena Means Business," p. 148.

94. Ibid., p. 142.

95. Steven Mintz, *Huck's Raft: A History of American Childhood* (Cambridge: Harvard University Press, 2004), pp. 75–77.

96. Ibid., pp. 275–276.

97. Ibid., p. 342.

98. As quoted in ibid., p. 280.

99. Ibid., p. 281.

100. Ibid., pp. 310–334.

101. Ibid., pp. 355–384.

13

American Schools and Global Politics: The Cold War and Poverty

After World War II, global events, particularly the Cold War between the United States and the Soviet Union, directly affected American schools. As a result of the Cold War, the federal government became more involved in controlling the schools to meet national goals. In the 1960s federal education policies expanded to an attempt to end poverty through funding of education programs such as Head Start and compensatory education programs. A belief that preschool education was a key to ending poverty led to the creation of the television program *Sesame Street.*

The Cold War between the United States and the Soviet Union spawned demands for more academic courses in the schools and a greater emphasis on science and mathematics as a means of winning the weapons race with the Soviet Union. It also resulted in the expansion of college attendance as returning World War II veterans used federal money from the GI Bill to attend college. Concern with the schools' role in the Cold War was behind the federal government's decisions to continue the military draft into peacetime as a means of controlling human resources, to establish the National Science Foundation (NSF), and to pass the National Defense Education Act (NDEA). These actions affected the curriculum of the schools and the educational choices made by students.

During the 1960s, when civil rights and poverty were national concerns, the federal government made education part of a national campaign against poverty. Like common school reforms of the nineteenth century, the federal government's War on Poverty of the 1960s attempted to eliminate poverty through special educational programs. In addition, civil rights legislation gave the federal government the responsibility to ensure that schools were not committing discriminatory actions against minority groups.

The expansion of the federal government's role in education took place in a climate of strong public reaction against the schools. This negative reaction came from several sources. Immediately following World War II, members of the radical right charged that the schools had been infiltrated by Communists. Right-wing groups demanded the removal of anti-American literature from the schools and the dismissal of left-leaning teachers. At the same time, those committed to victory for the United States in its technological race with the Soviet Union accused the public schools of being anti-intelligent and charged that professional educators had led the schools to ruin.

This chapter will discuss

- Youth unemployment: universal military service and the GI Bill.
- Establishment of the National Science Foundation.
- Military deferments to channel youth into college.
- Sorting youth: the Scholastic Aptitude Test and the Educational Testing Service.
- Cold War: anticommunism in schools.
- The War on Poverty of the 1960s.
- *Sesame Street.*

YOUTH UNEMPLOYMENT: UNIVERSAL MILITARY SERVICE AND THE GI BILL

During World War II, President Franklin D. Roosevelt wanted to solve the youth problem and maintain world peace by requiring universal military training for all males. This concept of a year of service had existed since World War I and had been one reason for the formation of the CCC during the Depression. In June 1945 the congressional Select Committee on Postwar Military Policy proposed a training plan that would "be universal and democratic, applicable to rich and poor alike, and with a minimum of exceptions." After Roosevelt's death in 1945, President Harry S. Truman quickly seized the banner of universal military training and proposed one year of training for all American young men. Truman believed that universal training would be a panacea for many of America's problems. He told a joint session of Congress that a plan of this type would provide national security and "raise the physical standard of the Nation's manpower, . . . lower its illiteracy rate, and . . . develop in our young men the ideals of responsible American citizenship."[1]

Congress, which was hoping to solve any unemployment problems by providing funds for returning members of the military to attend school, expressed little enthusiasm. Congress passed the Servicemen's Readjustment Act of 1944 (commonly known as the GI Bill of Rights) with provisions for educational benefits. Under the terms of the legislation, veterans would receive support for tuition, books, and living expenses. The legislation had a major impact on college enrollment. In 1945, 1,013,000 veterans attended college, doubling the existing college population. In the seven years in which benefits were provided, 7.8 million veterans received some form of postsecondary education.

Although the GI Bill solved part of the problem of youth unemployment, calls for universal service continued until the early 1950s, when the Korean War provided a final impetus for serious consideration of universal training. The drama that led to passage of the Universal Military Training and Service Act of 1951— legislation that directly affected the lives of young American men for the next two decades—began on the morning of January 10, 1951. The issue was balancing

THE COLD WAR AND CIVIL RIGHTS TIME LINE

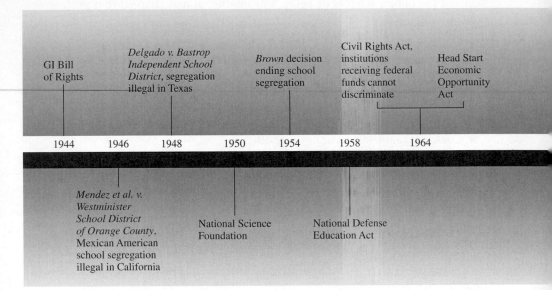

security needs—for more engineers and scientists—with military needs. The agenda included debate of the concept that universal military service could be used to channel and control the distribution of human resources.

The National Science Foundation and Science Instruction

The National Science Foundation was established both to attract more students to science and engineering courses and to fund basic research. Two proponents of a federally funded National Science Foundation (NSF), Vannevar Bush and James B. Conant, also supported universal training. Bush and Conant worked together on scientific research for the federal government during World War II and were architects of the government's scientific policies during and after the war. In 1944 President Roosevelt asked Vannevar Bush to prepare a plan for continued government involvement in research after the war. Bush responded with an enthusiasm that reflected his own belief that science was the panacea for the world's problems.

In 1945 Bush issued his reply to the president in a report with the glowing and hopeful title *Science—The Endless Frontier.*[2] Bush argued that continuation of basic scientific research was essential for maintaining full employment, world leadership, national security, and national health. The keys to increasing scientific capital were, first, ensuring that large numbers of men and women received scientific training and, second, supporting basic scientific research in colleges, universities, and research institutes. This could be accomplished, Bush felt, through the establishment of a National Science Foundation that would become a focal point for planning and supporting a workforce of scientists.

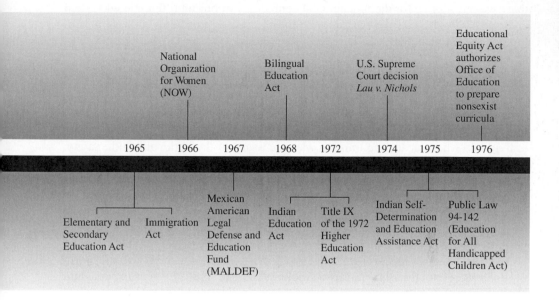

Besides funding basic research, Bush envisioned the National Science Foundation working to improve science education in the public schools and establishing a system of undergraduate and graduate fellowships for training and scientific research. Bush believed that improvement of science teaching in high schools was imperative if latent talent in science was to be properly developed. He viewed as a great danger the prospect of high school science teachers failing to awaken interest or provide adequate instruction.

James B. Conant, then president of Harvard University and the first chairman of the board of the NSF, supported universal military training and the channeling of human resources into science and engineering. Conant was an important figure in discussions of channeling human resources because of his leadership role in science and his later study of the American high school. His support of universal military training and the channeling of human resources provided the basic framework for his discussions about the American high school.

Conant's ideas on the channeling of human resources were given before a congressional hearing in 1947, when he was asked to testify in favor of legislation supporting the establishment of the NSF. He told the committee that his primary concern was to secure provisions for granting scholarships and fellowships: "It is men that count. And today we do not have the scientific manpower requisite for the job that lies ahead."[3]

Conant emphasized these ideas in a speech to a 1947 meeting of the American Association of School Administrators titled "The Dilemma of American Education." The dilemma, as Conant described it, was similar to the dilemma facing those considering universal military training: How do you make treatment equal but at the same time make provision for channeling superior human resources into needed occupations? Conant never resolved the dilemma, but he did suggest that "we pay a price for the fundamental democracy of our undifferentiated system of public schools. . . . [I]f we are wise the price need not be as high as it is at the present moment."[4]

Universal Military Training and the Channeling of Youth for Global Warfare

The 1951 amendments to the Universal Training and Service Act provided for control and channeling of human resources by authorizing the president to defer individuals whose academic training was necessary to the national health, safety, or security interests. College students could be deferred by receiving a certain score on the national Selective Service College Qualification Test or by maintaining a certain class rank. Ultimate power over the system was placed into the hands of local draft boards, and restriction of presidential power was ensured by specifically exempting draft boards from the obligation to defer students solely on the basis of federally established criteria.

The 1951 amendments to the Selective Service Act established the major form of government youth policy in effect in the 1950s and 1960s. Young males could choose either to remain in school or to serve in the armed forces. Complaints about the inequalities inherent in the system began within a year after the passage of the amendments. Obviously the system favored those who were able to attend universities and colleges, which often meant that the poor went into the military while the middle class and the rich attended college.

Administrators of colleges and universities were pleased with the selective service amendments because they guaranteed an increasing student population. In fact, by the late 1960s, when the selective service system was abandoned, the number of college graduates had increased to the point of flooding the labor market. The result was educational inflation—that is, a decline in the economic value of a college degree in the labor market. As a system of controlling human resources, selective service failed because it was based on the erroneous assumption that channeling talent into higher education would increase economic growth.

Both Conant and Bush were satisfied with the selective service legislation because it promised to channel more youth into science and engineering, but they also feared that public schools were not academically advanced enough to meet the challenge of the Cold War. In part, the NSF was designed to provide some impetus for public schools to emphasize science and mathematics, but it did not answer all concerns about the academic quality of American schools. Consequently Conant and Bush joined the chorus of voices raising doubts about the academic quality of American schools. Two major groups led public criticism of the school system. One group, the radical right, linked the alleged decline of academic standards to Communist infiltration of American education. The other group, primarily from the academic community, claimed that professional educators were anti-intellectual and that scholars should have the major influence over the public school curriculum.

THE SCHOLASTIC APTITUDE TEST (SAT) AND THE EDUCATIONAL TESTING SERVICE

The Big Test: The Secret History of the American Meritocracy is what Nicholas Lemann called his history of the Educational Testing Service (ETS) and the increased importance of standardized testing in determining the status and income of Americans.[5] As I discussed in Chapter 10, many psychologists and educators in the early twentieth century were enamored with the idea of finding the perfect test to determine a person's place in the labor market. One of those was Carl Brigham, whose book *A Study of American Intelligence* (1923) influenced the 1924 law restricting immigration and who in the 1920s developed the Scholastic Aptitude Test (SAT).[6] The Scholastic Aptitude Test became the mainstay of the Educational Testing Service's efforts to sort students for placement in colleges and universities.

The 1947 founding of ETS brought together two major tests used for college selection: the College Entrance Examination Board (CEEB) and the SAT. The CEEB test was created near the end of the nineteenth century as a subject-matter-oriented examination for college entrance. During the 1930s James Conant became an advocate for the SAT. In 1937 he urged that both the CEEB and SAT be used to determine college admissions before a meeting of the Educational Records Bureau. In part, Conant's interest in the merger reflected his commitment to the ideal of the school as a social sorting institution.[7]

During World War II Conant's efforts received support from Henry Chauncey, an assistant dean at Harvard. Chauncey became the ETS's first president. In the last days of World War II Chauncey mused in his diary about plans for America's future: "There will undoubtedly in the near future be a greater emphasis on taking a census of our human resources in terms of capacities for different kinds of employment . . . This project requires . . . men of vision in the field of testing, vocational guidance, government, economics, education."[8]

Chauncey hoped that the ETS would fulfill his dream by developing a series of multiple-choice mental tests that would determine everyone's place in society. Though the ETS never developed a full range of mental tests to classify the American population, the SAT became a central gatekeeper for dividing the population between those considered capable of going to college and those considered incapable. As income became more tightly related to years of education, the SAT served the function of dividing the population by income and status. Regarding the founding of ETS, Lemann stated, "Chauncey's wishes and Conant's both came true: the United States did embark on the world's largest-scale program of mental testing, and one consequence of this (though not the only one) was the establishment of a new national elite."[9]

The founding of ETS ushered in a new age of meritocracy based on testing. The SAT was justified as providing everyone an equal opportunity to receive a college education if the test was passed. The SAT was not strictly speaking an IQ test, but was supposed to predict success in college. However, the SAT tested mental skills in contrast to academic knowledge. Lemann called the SAT a descendent of

IQ-standardized tests. He considered the phenomenon of standardized testing, which gained greater importance in the twenty-first century as the driving force in American schooling, a result of an interrelated set of historical ideas:

- The desire of the founders of the nation, particularly Thomas Jefferson, to use schooling to identify a national governing elite.
- The desire in the early twentieth century to make standardized testing central to governing society.
- The eugenics movement, which while being discredited by German Nazism, fostered the idea that in a complex society the most intelligent members would rise to the top.
- The claims of early twentieth-century promoters of IQ testing that these tests could identify those who should enter the national elite.[10]

Lemann concluded, "The Educational Testing Service's tests for admission to college and graduate school have the essential effect of restricting study in the premier universities, and membership in the professions, to people who score well on IQ tests."[11] The result of the founding of ETS, according to Lemann, was a recomposition of America's governing elite.

THE COLD WAR AND PURGING THE SCHOOLS OF COMMUNISTS

After World War II, the American Legion continued its quest to purge from the schools—and from movies, radio, and television—any ideas that could possibly be linked to communism. With the growing fears generated by the Cold War, many organizations joined the efforts being made by the American Legion. In 1951 the executive secretary of the NEA's National Commission for the Defense of Democracy through Education reported in a slightly hysterical tone that the number of "attacks" on public schooling had increased rapidly since the closing days of World War II. According to the commission's survey, the pace of "attack" was so swift that more than twice as many attacks occurred in the three-year period after 1948 as in the three-year period before 1948. The phraseology and reaction of educators often made them appear to be warriors doing battle with an enemy that was storming the walls of the public schools. Words like *attack, counterattack,* and *siege* were hurled around when they described the plight of the professional educator. The executive secretary of the National Commission for the Defense of Democracy through Education, in reporting the increasing criticism of the schools, exemplified the battle mentality. He stressed that the "attacking groups are not as dangerous as they seem. . . . But we all need to be alarmed as were the Minute Men by Paul Revere in 1775." He went on to call the educational troops together with this plea: "If, like the Minute Men, we are ready to carry out individual responsibilities of intelligent group planning, professional unity, organized action, and friendly contact with our allies, we will be as successful in defending our cause as were the gallant men at Concord."[12]

The forced resignation in 1950 of School Superintendent Willard Goslin of Pasadena, California, probably left other school administrators in a state of apprehension about their own jobs. Goslin was a national figure in professional education circles, having served in 1948 as president of the American Association of School Administrators. In 1949, when Goslin proposed a tax increase, members of the local community mounted an attack charging that the schools had fallen under the control of communism. This charge, plus the publicity it aroused, forced Goslin's resignation.

The anti-Communist campaign directed at Superintendent Goslin was based on pamphlets distributed by the National Council for American Education, headed by Allen Zoll—one of many national organizations focusing attention on subversion in the schools. Other organizations of this type included the American Coalition of Patriotic Societies, the American Council of Christian Laymen, the Anti-Communist League of America, the California Anti-Communist League, the Christian Nationalist Crusade, Defenders of American Education, the Daughters of the American Revolution, and the Sons of the American Revolution.

Zoll organized the National Council for American Education in 1948. He reportedly began his crusade with the "Michigan statement": "We form hell-raising groups to find out what is being taught in the schools, and then we raise hell about it." Pasadena, of course, was not the only community influenced by Zoll's pamphlets. In 1951 *Saturday Review of Literature* devoted a large section of its education issue to school controversies around the country. In Denver Zoll's pamphlets, including one titled *The Commies Are after Your Kids,* supposedly provided a good deal of ammunition for local citizen groups. In Englewood, New Jersey, and Port Washington, New York, Zoll's writings reportedly exerted a significant influence. In Pasadena the Zoll pamphlet that attracted attention was *Progressive Education Increases Juvenile Delinquency,* which stated that "so-called progressive education, shot through as it is with the blight of Pragmatism, has had a very deleterious effect upon the original character of American education."[13]

The textbook industry was also being charged with Communist infiltration. In 1949 Lucille Cardin Crain began issuing a quarterly newsletter, the *Educational Reviewer,* that had as its goal the weeding out of subversive material from public school textbooks. Her first target was a popular high school text, *American Government,* by Frank Abbott Magruder. She claimed that Magruder's view of democracy led "straight from Rousseau, through Marx, to totalitarianism" and that the book gave a favorable view of the workings of the government of the Soviet Union. Convinced that the text was designed to undermine the free enterprise system, she gave wide circulation to her critique of the book. Her arguments eventually reached the ears of national radio commentator Fulton Lewis Jr., who used portions of Crain's analysis on a coast-to-coast broadcast and added a scare statement: "That's the book that has been in use in high schools all over the nation, possibly by your youngster."[14]

Other groups joined in the work of the *Educational Reviewer,* including Allen Zoll's National Council for American Education, the Daughters of the American Revolution, the Sons of the American Revolution, and the Guardians of American Education. These groups published their own lists of subversive books and other texts. Throughout the country during the 1950s and 1960s, community members armed with one of these lists would demand that certain subversive books be removed from library shelves and from the curricula of the schools. Suggestions were even made that textbook writers be required to take a loyalty oath. These actions alarmed the textbook industry, and in 1953 an official statement of the American Textbook Publishers Institute warned against a loyalty oath for authors because it would lower the quality of textbook authorship and material. The institute claimed that the highly individualistic and competitive system in the textbook industry provided adequate safeguards against "the deliberate introduction of harmful or subversive material." To curb local attacks, it recommended that states establish public agencies to monitor complaints about textbooks.

AMERICAN SCHOOLS: WEAKEST LINK TO GLOBAL VICTORY?

Since the 1950s American schools have been blamed for America's poor position in global military and economic competition. In the 1980s they would be blamed for American global economic problems, whereas in the 1950s the focus was on military competition with Soviet Union.

In the 1950s university scholars complained about the poor quality of American schools. Criticism of public schools was led by historian Arthur Bestor. In 1952, at the annual meeting of the American Historical Association, he delivered a paper titled "Anti-Intellectualism in the Schools: A Challenge to Scholars." As part of his presentation, Bestor submitted a series of proposals based on a detailed resolution he had drafted and circulated among scholarly friends for their approval and signatures. By the time of the meeting, he had collected 695 signatures. Of the signatories, 199 were historians, 93 were English professors, 86 were in the biological sciences, 77 were in mathematics, and the others came from a variety of other academic fields. The preamble of the resolution expressed alarm at the "serious danger to American intellectual life arising from anti-intellectual tendencies" and the "anti-intellectualism conceptions of education among important groups of school administrators and educational theorists." The actual resolutions proposed a close working relationship between the scholarly community and professional educators.

What prompted Bestor to prepare his resolution was the life adjustment education movement, which was launched in 1945 at a conference sponsored by the Vocational Education Division of the U.S. Office of Education. At this meeting, a well-known leader of vocational education, Dr. Charles Prosser, introduced the following resolution: "The vocational school of a community will be able better to prepare 20 percent of the youth of secondary school age for entrance upon desirable skilled occupations; and . . . the high school will continue to prepare another 20 percent for entrance to college." The question in Prosser's mind was what to do with the other 60 percent. He gave the following answer in his resolution: "We do not believe that the remaining 60 percent of our youth of secondary school age will receive the life adjustment education they need . . . unless . . . the administrators of public education with the assistance of vocational education leaders formulate a similar program for this group."[15]

Bestor's anger was sparked by copies of the life adjustment education materials distributed by the Illinois Secondary School Curriculum Program. He quickly recognized and criticized the methods used by educators to sell life adjustment curricula to the public. In his criticisms of the public schools, Bestor quoted from the Illinois materials: "Given the American tradition of the local lay control of public education, it is both necessary and desirable that a community (patrons, pupils, teachers) consensus be engineered in understanding support of the necessary changes before they are made."[16] Bestor responded, "We approach here the real meaning of what educationists euphemistically describe as 'democracy in education.' It is the democracy of the 'engineered consensus.'" He concluded that control of the educational system was not in public hands but in the hands of professional educators or, as he referred to them, "educationists."[17]

Life adjustment education also convinced Bestor that professional educators were responsible for the anti-intellectual quality of American schools. He noted, for example, that in one of the Illinois documents, "Problems of High School Youth," an overwhelming proportion of problems cited dealt with what he called "trivia" and that no mention was made of mathematics, science, history, or foreign languages. In the list of fifty-five "Problems of High School Youth," he cited as trivia such items as "the problem of improving one's personal appearance"; "the problem of selecting a family dentist"; "the problem of developing one or more 'making things,' 'making it go,' or 'tinkering' hobbies"; and "the problem of developing and maintaining wholesome boy–girl relationships."[18]

Bestor wanted public schools to reject the traditional emphasis on socialization and the social sorting function of schooling. From his perspective, curricula should be organized around traditional subject matter disciplines. In the schools, he argued, "The important books must be read. . . . Fundamental problems must be studied, not merely talked about."[19] This would occur in a climate where the basic scientific and scholarly disciplines were presented as systematic ways of thinking, with each discipline organized around a structure and methodology of its own. The disciplines to be studied would include mathematics, science, history, English, and foreign languages.

Bestor rejected the notion of a differentiated course of study based on the future social destination of the individual. He accepted the existence of differences in intellectual ability among students but argued, in reference to students of lower mental ability, "Most of them, I believe, can be brought at a slower pace along the same route."[20] Elimination of the emphasis on socialization and the sorting of human resources in the schools, Bestor felt, could curb the tide of anti-intellectualism in society by creating a new respect in the student and in the home for knowledge and cultural achievement.

In 1952 the American Historical Association was unable to reach a consensus on Bestor's proposal. In its place was substituted a weakly worded resolution supporting Bestor's basic concerns and calling for further study of the possibility of working with other learned societies. Undeterred by the setback, Bestor searched for another means of implementing his ideas. In 1956 he helped to organize the Council for Basic Education and became its first president. Shortly after the founding of this group, Mortimer Smith became its executive director and the major force behind the operations of the organization.

Within a short time after Bestor's initial criticism, a chorus of other voices joined in condemning the schools and their control by professional educators. Alan Lynd's *Quackery in the Public Schools,* published in 1953, criticized the anti-intellectual quality of college and university courses in teacher education. He blamed this situation on control of higher education by professional educators.

Smith made his views known nationally in two publications: *And Madly Teach: A Layman Looks at Public School Education* (1949) and *The Diminished Mind: A Study of Planned Mediocrity in Our Public Schools* (1954). Smith, like his colleagues, charged the schools with anti-intellectualism and domination by the professional educator, but he gave greater emphasis to the idea that the schools were undemocratic. Bestor had complained that a differentiated curriculum was undemocratic because it did not allow schools to prepare students equally for participation in the world. Smith thought that a differentiated curriculum worked against the functioning of a democratic society because it resulted in inequality of individual educational development.

The most widely heard of the critics in the 1950s was Vice Admiral Hyman G. Rickover, often called the "father of America's nuclear navy." He carried his message of the dismal failure of American schools to such meetings as the one held by the Society of Business Magazine Editors in 1956, the Westinghouse Science Talent Search Award Ceremony in 1957, the Engineering Society of Detroit in 1957, and the Harvard Club of New York in 1958, and finally into a best-selling book, *Education and Freedom.* Admiral Rickover's basic message asserted that the United States was losing the technological and military race with the Soviet Union because America's public schools were failing to identify and adequately educate talented youth as future scientists and engineers. In an interview conducted by news commentator Edward R. Murrow, Rickover stated that education "is even more important than atomic power in the navy, for if our people are not properly educated in accordance with the terrific requirements of this rapidly spiraling scientific and industrial civilization, we are bound to go down. The Russians apparently have recognized this." Like other critics of the time, Rickover blamed professional educators for creating an anti-intellectual atmosphere in the schools and claimed that the schools were the weakest link in America's overall defense strategy.[21]

These attacks on the public schools provided the background for the most significant educational legislation of the 1950s. Throughout the late 1940s and 1950s, educators had been seeking some form of federal legislation to help build schools and pay teacher salaries. Local schools were seriously pressed for space and money to educate the many children born in the baby boom period after World War II. National political leaders failed to respond to these requests; they neither passed nor approved legislation for federal aid to local school districts.

On October 4, 1957, resistance to federal aid to education disappeared. The Soviet Union launched *Sputnik I.* That the Soviet Union was the first in space indicated to many Americans that America was losing the technological and military race. Of course the public schools were blamed for the lag in technological development, and voices were lifted to demand a greater stress on mathematics and science.

GLOBAL IMPERATIVES: THE NATIONAL DEFENSE EDUCATION ACT

In 1958, responding to *Sputnik I* and public outcries about conditions in the schools, Congress passed the National Defense Education Act (NDEA). The name of the legislation defined its goals. Before the legislation was passed and immediately after the launching of *Sputnik I,* President Dwight D. Eisenhower outlined the relationship between education and Cold War strategy and set the stage for passage of the legislation. In Oklahoma City on November 13, 1957, Eisenhower gave a speech pointing out that the Soviet Union had converted itself in only forty years from a nation of peasants to an industrial nation that had accomplished major technological achievements and established a rigorous educational system. He went on to warn, "When such competence in things material is at the service of leaders who have so little regard for things human, and who command the power of an empire, there is danger ahead for free men everywhere."

Eisenhower argued that the United States must meet the Soviet threat on its own terms by outmatching the Soviet Union in military power, technological advancement, and specialized research and education. Essential to a program of national defense was increased military research, which would be directed toward the production of intercontinental ballistic missiles. Eisenhower tried to assure the nation that it was well on the way to developing adequate missile power. "Young people now in college," he emphasized, "must be equipped to live in the age of intercontinental ballistic missiles." Specifically, Eisenhower called for a system of nationwide testing of high school students and a system of incentives to persuade students with high ability to pursue scientific or professional studies. He urged a program to stimulate quality teaching in mathematics and science and fellowships to increase the number of teachers.[22]

On January 27, 1958, Eisenhower delivered a special message to Congress outlining his program of education for national defense. The first item on his list of recommendations was a fivefold increase in appropriations for the educational activities of the NSF. Second, he called for reducing the waste of national talent by providing grants to states for improved testing programs and guidance and counseling services. This recommendation eventually became Title V of the 1958 NDEA. Title V appropriated $15 million for each of four succeeding fiscal years for guidance, counseling, testing, and identification of able students. All these programs were considered essential for controlling and developing human resources for the Cold War.

Third, Eisenhower recommended federal funds to improve the teaching of science and mathematics through the hiring of additional science teachers and the purchase of equipment and materials. This became Title III of the NDEA, which appropriated $70 million for each of the next four fiscal years to be used for equipment and materials and for the expansion and improvement of supervisory services in the public schools in science, mathematics, and modern foreign languages. Eisenhower's fourth recommendation was for a graduate fellowship program to prepare more students for college teaching careers. This became Title IV of the NDEA and resulted in the National Defense Fellowship program.

The issue of foreign languages and their relationship to national security was the subject of Eisenhower's fifth recommendation. Eisenhower argued, "Knowledge of foreign languages is particularly important today in the light of America's responsibilities of leadership in the free world. And yet the American people generally are deficient in foreign languages, particularly those of the emerging nations in Asia, Africa, and the Near East."[23] The foreign language sections of the NDEA were clearly seen as provisions to strengthen America's competition with the Soviet Union for influence over the developing nations of the world.

The categorical nature of aid given under the NDEA reflected the government's negative feelings toward professional educators and its decision to take responsibility for establishing educational policies that would serve other national policies, such as defense. At the hearings on the NDEA, the head of the NEA defended the schools and requested that money be appropriated for general use by local schools. Scientists and other officials, however, gave strong testimony against general aid to the public schools, given the fact that professional educators had the power to determine the use of the funds. These critics of the schools and educators wanted the federal government to specify the categories under which the money could be used; this limitation was written into the NDEA. As a consequence, the NDEA became a means by which the federal government could control local educational policy simply by offering money for the establishment of specified educational programs. Local educators did not have to accept the federal money, but few refused because financial conditions in most school districts made them eager for the funds.

Cold War concerns also got the federal government involved in developing new curricula, particularly in the areas of mathematics and science. Money flowing from the NSF was used to develop curriculum materials and to train teachers. The most dramatic development in this area was the "new mathematics," as it was called in the early 1960s. The new mathematics was based on the idea of teaching students basic mathematical concepts such as set theory and functions. When it swept the nation, many parents found themselves unable to understand or to help their children with the material.

In summary, a major effect of the Cold War on educational policies was to link the youth issue to selective service and to push the federal government into a leadership role in educational policies. Mounting criticism of the schools, which had begun during the Depression years, created a major split between professional educators and the public. This split widened in the 1960s, when the schools were accused of being racist. Another major consequence of the Cold War was an emphasis on the idea that schooling is the key to the development of human resources and the distribution of human resources in the labor market. This continued to be an important theme through the 1980s.

SCHOOLS AND THE WAR ON POVERTY

The federal government's War on Poverty during the 1960s was reminiscent of the beliefs of nineteenth-century common school reformers that education could reduce social class divisions and eliminate poverty. In some ways President Lyndon Johnson can be considered a twentieth-century version of Horace Mann. But the difference between nineteenth-century reformers and twentieth-century leaders was the latters' belief that schools should develop and sort human resources. By the 1960s it was commonly believed that discrimination and poverty were the two basic problems preventing the use of schools as a means of discovering and classifying talent for service to the national economy and national defense. Within this framework, school integration and the elimination of poverty were necessary to ensure unbiased development and selection of human talent.

Congress's response to the issue of poverty was passage of the Economic Opportunity Act of 1964 (EOA) and the Elementary and Secondary Education Act of 1965 (ESEA). Two of the most important EOA programs were the Job Corps and Head Start. Head Start was established to provide an opportunity for children of the poor to enter the social sorting process of education on equal terms with children from more affluent backgrounds. The ESEA contained major provisions for improving educational programs for children from low-income families.

The War on Poverty encompassed three major areas of concern: unemployed and delinquent youths; disadvantaged students for whom education did not provide equal opportunity; and the cycle, or circle, of poverty. The concept of a circle of poverty gained popularity with the publication of Gunnar Myrdal's *American Dilemma.* This 1940 study described poverty among poor blacks as a set of interdependent causal factors. For instance, a poor education restricts employment opportunities, which causes a low standard of living and consequently leads to poor medical care, diet, housing, and education for the next generation. This model of poverty suggests that one can begin at any point in the set of causal relationships and move around the circle of poverty.

Myrdal's model captured the imagination of the Kennedy administration in the early 1960s. A story was told that the idea for launching a massive federal program against unemployment and poverty came directly from President Kennedy in 1962, when he told Walter Heller, chairman of the Council of Economic Advisers, to gather all the statistics on poverty. At the time, Kennedy requested copies of Michael Harrington's recently published *The Other America: Poverty in the United States.* By 1963 President Kennedy had decided to launch a War on Poverty that would attack the social structure that caused poverty.

Michael Harrington's book influenced the final report on poverty written by the Council of Economic Advisers and presented to Congress as the basic program for the EOA. Harrington believed that insulation of the poor from the rest of America was dividing the nation into two cultures. Within the circle of poverty, the poor get sick more often because of unhealthful living conditions in slums and inadequate nutrition. Inadequate medical care causes their illnesses to last longer, resulting in lost wages and work. Because of lost wages, the poor cannot afford adequate housing, education, and medical care. Harrington argued that there is a much richer way of describing this circle—as a culture. The vicious circle of poverty has created its own cultural patterns. Its family structure is different from that of the rest of society—it has more homes without fathers, early pregnancy, different attitudes toward sex, and less marriage. Millions of children of the poor, Harrington claimed, do not know affection or stability. The culture of poverty is also defined by the actions of other institutions in society. For instance, there is a marked difference between how the police treat the poor and how they treat the middle class.

Of significance for modern times, Harrington argued, is the fact that the culture of poverty is beginning to perpetuate itself under the pressures of modern technology. As technology increases, so do educational requirements for occupations. As technological progress sweeps through the rest of society, the poor are increasingly left behind, and it becomes more difficult for them to move up in the social structure. Poverty is passed on from generation to generation because of the increasing difficulty poor children face in receiving adequate education and job training. The price of more complex technology is the growing existence of a culture that cannot participate in its benefits.

An attack on the culture of poverty became a central focus of the Kennedy administration. In October 1963 Walter Heller began to draw together various plans for an invasion of the culture of poverty. Heller sent government agencies a memorandum requesting plans that would help avoid entrapment in the culture of poverty and would provide a means of escape. In November 1963, while responses to the memorandum were being reviewed, President Kennedy was assassinated. Almost immediately President Johnson announced his intention of supporting the program and directed Heller to complete his task. In January 1964 Heller's report was included in the annual report of the Council of Economic Advisers as "The Problem of Poverty in America."

The report strongly emphasized the role of education in uprooting the culture of poverty. Certainly social scientists such as Myrdal and Harrington considered education to be a link in the circle of poverty, but the Heller report placed education in the central role of the battle strategy: "Equality of opportunity is the American dream, and universal education our noblest pledge to realize it. But, for the children of the poor, education is a handicap race; many are too ill motivated at home to learn at school." The report claimed that poverty is directly linked to education: "The chief reason for low rates of pay is low productivity, which in turn can reflect lack of education or training, physical and mental disability, or poor motivation." This argument places the responsibility for low incomes directly on the shoulders of wage earners, not on the economic system. "The importance of education," the report continues, "as a factor in poverty is suggested by the fact that families headed by persons with no more than 8 years of education have an incidence rate of 37 percent."[24]

The Heller report underlined the importance of education in the War on Poverty when it claimed, "The severely handicapping influence of lack of education is clear. The incidence of poverty drops as educational attainments rise for non-whites as well as white families at all ages." One section of the report, labeled "The Vicious Circle," began with the straightforward statement "Poverty breeds poverty." The report defined the role of education in this circle: "It is difficult for children to find and follow avenues leading out of poverty in environments where education is deprecated and hope is smothered."

The major strategy the report advocated was the use of education to end poverty. It flatly stated, "Universal education has been perhaps the greatest single force contributing both to social mobility and to general economic growth." In addition, the report argued, if the children of poor families were given skills and motivation, they would not grow up to be poor adults. The current problem, the report maintained, was that many young people were condemned to inadequate schools and instruction, and many school systems concentrated their efforts on children from higher-income groups. Effective education for children at the bottom of the economic ladder would require special methods and greater expenses: "The school must play a larger role in the development of poor youngsters if they are to have, in fact, 'equal opportunity.'" In language pointing toward the eventual plans for Head Start, the report continued, "This often means that schooling must start on a pre-school basis and include a broad range of more intensive services." In addition, the report urged the development of a Youth Conservation Corps, adult education programs, day care centers for working mothers, improved health programs, and increased assistance to the aged. In sum, the Heller report outlined a total package designed to uproot and destroy the environment and culture of poverty.

President Johnson accepted the argument that the problem of poverty in the 1960s was different from that of the Depression. He wrote about his meeting with Heller, "The most significant aspects of this new poverty, once the spotlight of attention was thrown on it, were the dismaying nature of its stubborn entrenchment and total entrapment of its victims from one generation to the next." Johnson announced plans for the War on Poverty in his State of the Union message to Congress on January 8, 1964. He told Congress it was its responsibility to replace despair with opportunity and declared, "This administration today, here and now, declares unconditional war on poverty in America." He also told Congress and the American people that the chief weapons of the battle would be better schools, better health, better homes, and better training and job opportunities. This would be a battle to help Americans escape squalor, misery, and unemployment.[25]

The War on Poverty began with the signing of the EOA on August 20, 1964. Part A of Title I of the EOA established the Job Corps—a unique combination of approaches to the youth problem. First, it attacked unemployment among youths by providing urban and rural residential training centers. This program was modeled on the CCC of the 1930s, in which residents devoted their time to conserving and managing natural resources. Parts B and C of Title I provided programs for work training and work-study. In both programs, youths were to learn skills while working on a government project.

Head Start and the Origins of No Child Left Behind

Head Start and Title I were legislative parts of the War on Poverty that would last in the twenty-first century, with Title I in 2001 being renamed in No Child Left Behind. Head Start was developed under Title II of EOA legislation, which provided for community action programs. It was the first and probably the most popular of the national community action programs. The Economic Opportunity Act of 1964 made no specific mention of the education of younger children as a component of the War on Poverty. One reason for this was that the highly explosive issues of race and church–state relationships had in the past hindered the passage of federal education bills. A congressional amendment to establish a preschool program had been attached to the original EOA but was withdrawn when assurances were given that the Office of Economic Opportunity would support the program. In January 1965 President Johnson announced the decision to fund a preschool program named Head Start under the antipoverty program. In February Sargent Shriver, head of the Office of Economic Opportunity, announced that the program would be launched during the summer of 1965. The response to the announcement was immediate and enthusiastic, and during the first summer 560,000 children entered the Head Start program.

The ESEA was signed by President Johnson on April 11, 1965, in the one-room schoolhouse near Stonewall, Texas, where his own education had begun. For the occasion, his first schoolteacher was flown in from retirement in California to stand at his side. The most important section of the ESEA was Title I, which provided funds for improved educational programs for children designated as educationally deprived. Title I, later amended and renamed No Child Left Behind, specifically states, "The Congress hereby declares it to be the policy of the United States to provide financial assistance . . . to expand and improve . . . educational programs by various means . . . which contribute particularly to meeting the special educational needs of educationally deprived children."[26]

In essence, Title I was the major educational component of the War on Poverty. At the opening congressional hearings on the bill, Secretary of Health, Education, and Welfare Anthony J. Celebrezze and Commissioner of Education Francis Keppel provided the president's justification and rationale for special educational assistance to the educationally deprived. In his opening statement to the committee, Celebrezze quoted President Johnson's statement, "Just as ignorance breeds poverty, poverty all too often breeds ignorance in the next generation." Celebrezze went on to claim, "The President's program . . . is designed to break this cycle which has been running on from generation to generation in this most affluent period of our history." He stated that a clear link exists between high educational and high economic attainment.[27]

Commissioner Keppel's statement also drew on the rhetoric and arguments that had come to characterize the government's approach to the problem of poverty. But in this case, as in the report of the Council of Economic Advisers, education was viewed as the major element to be attacked in the cycle of poverty. Keppel told the committee, "Archimedes . . . told us many centuries ago, 'Give me a lever long enough and a fulcrum strong enough and I can move the world.' Today, at last, we have a prospect of a lever long enough and supported strongly enough to do something for our children of poverty." The lever, of course, was education, and the fulcrum was federal financial assistance.[28]

Other sections of the legislation covered a variety of special purposes, which in many cases were included to ensure passage of Title I. Title II provided financial assistance for school library resources, textbooks, and other instructional materials. A primary reason for including Title II was to win support from private school interests because they would be eligible for the aid. Furthermore, Keppel supported Title II during the congressional hearings with statistics showing that the quality of the school library was strongly associated with student performance.

Title III provided funds for the establishment of supplementary educational centers to promote local educational innovations. Educators who helped President Johnson draft the legislation hoped this could be one method for stimulating creativity in local school systems. Title IV provided money for educational research and for the establishment of research and development centers. Title IV was included because the drafters of the legislation believed it would receive minimal legislative support if it were submitted as a separate bill. In a sense, the concept of research and development in education rode in on the coattails of Title I.

Funds for strengthening state departments of education were designated under Title V. The purpose of providing these funds was to allay fears about federal control of education. One interesting result of federal support of education under the ESEA was the increased power this gave to state departments of education in relation to local school districts.

In general, the ESEA followed the tradition of federal involvement in education that had been evolving since World War II. The basic thread was planning for the use of human resources in the national economy. In the 1950s, under pressure from the technological and scientific race with the Soviet Union, emphasis had been placed on channeling talented youth into higher education. In the early 1960s the emphasis shifted to providing equal opportunity as a means of utilizing the poor as human resources. President Johnson, who had chaired the Senate hearings on selective service in the early 1950s, clearly reiterated this in his message to Congress that accompanied the proposals for the ESEA: "Nothing matters more to the future of our country; not our military preparedness, for armed might is worthless if we lack the brainpower to build a world of peace; not our productive economy, for we cannot sustain growth without trained manpower."[29]

However, unlike the human resource policies of the 1950s, the approach of the 1960s was essentially to wage war on a culture. Within the theoretical framework of the War on Poverty, the social and economic system that had created poverty and allowed it to continue was not considered the problem; the problem was the culture of the poor. Indeed, the overall strategy was to integrate the poor into the existing social and economic system. Very simply, this can be called blaming the victim—placing the full responsibility for poverty on the shoulders of the poor. They—not the economic system that had produced poverty—were expected to change.

SESAME STREET AND EDUCATIONAL TELEVISION

Debates about the content of movies, radio, and television continued after World War II. During World War II the federal government made a concerted attempt to shape the content of radio and movies for the war effort. Immediately following the war, public schools, movies, and broadcasting were affected by the Red scare, and suspected Communists were purged. These agencies for the dissemination of ideas to the public were "cleansed" to meet the requirements of the Cold War. By the 1960s less attention was paid to movies as television became a dominant media form. As with radio, the ideas and values distributed to the public by television were influenced by both the government and advocacy groups.[30]

As they did with movies, educators complained about the negative effects of television on children's learning. This criticism received public support in the 1960s from the head of the FCC, Newton Minow. In a speech at the 1961 meeting of the National Association of Broadcasters, Minow declared that television was a vast "wasteland." He opened the speech with praise for the potential of television and a denial that he intended to use government powers to censor broadcasting. After soothing his audience with these words, Minow launched his attack. He invited the broadcasters to sit with their eyes glued to their television sets from the time stations went on the air until the stations signed off. "I can assure that you will observe," he told them in words that were to be echoed around the country, "a vast wasteland." This wasteland is, he stated, "a procession of game shows, violence, audience participation shows, formula comedies about totally unbelievable families, blood and thunder, mayhem, violence, sadism, murder, Western bad men, Western good men, private eyes, gangsters, more violence, screaming, cajoling, and offending. And most of all, boredom. True, you will see a few things you will enjoy. But they will be very, very few."[31]

Minow's speech sparked the interest of many Americans and eventually culminated in the forming of the Carnegie Commission on Educational Television. In 1967 President Lyndon Johnson accepted the recommendations of the Carnegie Commission. A major recommendation, eventually approved by Congress, was for the creation of the Corporation for Public Broadcasting. To a certain extent, the legislation envisioned commercial television producing programs for low culture and public television producing programs for high culture. Also, the legislation reflected the concerns of educators in the 1930s about the effect of broadcasting on national culture.[32]

The Carnegie Commission's recommendations for children's television included the use of television as a means of social reform. The commission's proposal for children's programming contained two revolutionary ideas about the educational use of television. First was the idea that television could be used as an informal means of education. This proposal harkened back to the debates during the early days of movies when it was proposed that censorship be used to turn entertainment movies into a form of public education. In the words of the Carnegie Commission, "Important as this can be for adults, the informal educational potential of Public Television is greatest of all for children."[33]

Second, the commission proposed that television should focus on preparing preschool children for formal education. This proposal was very much in line with the development in the 1960s of Head Start programs, which were to prepare "disadvantaged" children for kindergarten or the first grade. Under this proposal, television would informally educate preschool children as well as focus on the education of the "disadvantaged." "Public Television programs," the report states, "should give great attention to the informal educational needs of preschool children, particularly to interest and help children whose intellectual and cultural preparation might otherwise be less than adequate."[34]

The proposal was based on an idea gaining increasing popularity in the 1960s that preschool education significantly improved the achievement of children in school and that it could break the cycle of poverty. At a dinner party in March 1966, one of the supervisors of the Carnegie Corporation's grants, Lloyd Morrisett, proposed the idea of television as a form of preschool education to television producer Joan Cooney. Funded by the corporation, in October 1966 Cooney completed a feasibility study of the use of television to educate preschool children.[35]

Lloyd Morrisett hoped television could solve the problem of the slow spread of kindergarten and nursery schools around the United States. Believing that preschool education was important for the cognitive development of children, he worried that preschools "would slowly, if at all, reach many of the children who needed them, particularly underprivileged children for whom preschool facilities might not be available." The answer to this problem, he felt, was in the ability of television to reach large numbers of children.[36]

As Morrisett conceptualized the project, television should become one partner in the general education of children. Within this framework, television was the third educator along with the family and the school. "The real answer to problems of early education," Morrisett wrote, "is for the total culture of childhood, including television as an important element, to work in harmony with the family and later the school."[37]

Again a proposal of the Carnegie Corporation received federal money. During the two years between the feasibility study and the establishment of the Children's Television Workshop, 48.8 percent of the $8 million spent on the project came from federal sources. The majority of the federal money came through the U.S. Office of Education. The importance of the informal relationship between the government and foundations is illustrated by a story told in Ellen Condliffe Lagemann's history of the Carnegie Corporation. Lagemann describes a trip by Joan Cooney, now an employee of the corporation, and Barbara Finberg, a corporation program officer concentrating on early childhood education, to Washington to see the U.S. commissioner of education. According to Lagemann, Commissioner

Harold Howe II was "well acquainted with many people at the Carnegie Corporation, including Morrisett . . . [and he was] quickly interested in the idea of a children's series. 'Let's do it,' Cooney remembered him saying at the end of their meeting."[38] Commissioner Howe became a major proponent of preschool education through television. In 1968 the Children's Television Workshop was organized, and on November 10, 1969, the first production of *Sesame Street* was broadcast.

The organization of the Children's Television Workshop required cooperation between educators and television producers. As Joan Cooney described the process, the informal network of the Carnegie Corporation was used to select an educational adviser for the workshop. Cooney had met many academics selected by the corporation while doing the feasibility study. In addition, Lloyd Morrisett, in Cooney's words, "through his position at Carnegie, knew personally most of the leading people in the field of educational psychology." As their first choice, they decided to ask Gerald Lesser, Bigelow Professor of Education and Developmental Psychology at Harvard, to be their chief adviser and chairman of the board of advisers.[39]

Lesser was the guiding hand in the development of the educational goals for the first major production of the Children's Television Workshop, *Sesame Street*. Lesser rejected the attitude held by many educators that education could solve most of the world's problems. He wrote, "Educators cannot remedy the injustices to minorities in our society or create new life styles or new communities to replace deteriorating ones. Yet they sometimes act as if they think they can."[40] The belief that education could have only a limited role in social reform tempered the original focus on helping children of the poor.

While Lesser saw a limited role for education in social reform, he did believe that something drastic had to be done about the educational problems in the United States. Writing about the "fifty billion dollars" that was spent on a "massive educational superstructure which holds captive over fifty million children," he complained, "[that] we are failing to educate our children, either disastrously or to a degree no worse than the failures of other social and political institutions, is almost beyond dispute."[41]

Lesser believed that television could be a means of rescuing the entire educational system. In fact, he argued that television had certain ingredients that made it somewhat superior to the public schools. Public schooling, he maintained, depended on control of the student by others, public humiliation, and the continuous threat of failure. Television learning contained none of these elements. In front of the television, Lesser argued, the child learns without fear of a public or teacher, there is no threat of humiliation, and the child can control the learning process by the flip of a switch. Consequently Lesser believed that television was an ideal educator. It was nonpunitive, and it provided a shelter from the emotional stresses of society. "We may regret the conditions in our society that make sanctuaries necessary and must guard against a child's permanent retreat into them," Lesser wrote, "but sanctuaries are needed, and television is one of the few shelters children have."[42]

Also, Lesser believed television was a superior educator because it could be entertaining. He argued that traditional thinkers separated the idea of entertainment and education. In fact, many believed that entertainment would contaminate education. Lesser referred to this as a "lunatic" view of education. Like the early censors who wanted entertainment movies to be educational, Lesser believed that television would be an ideal vehicle for educating through entertainment.[43]

Besides lauding the potential educational value of television, Lesser was impressed by the statistics on television viewing. Using calculations made in 1967, Lesser estimated that in homes with preschool children the television was on fifty-four hours per week and that, on average, a high school graduate had spent 12,000 hours in school and 15,000 hours watching television. In fact, a high school graduate had spent more time watching television than was spent at any other activity.[44]

Given all of those factors, Lesser believed that television could be the savior of the entire educational system while at the same time he doubted the ability of education to cause massive social reform. Consequently he felt the Children's Television Workshop should not limit its focus to the education of children of the poor. In part, the desire for success influenced the decision to create a program for all children. In Lesser's words, "To succeed, a national television series must attract as large a national audience as possible, including children from all social classes and cultural groups and from all geographic regions."[45]

Producing a program for all children caused a dilemma regarding the desire to reduce the educational gap between the children of the rich and the poor. Obviously the attempt to reach all children restricted the ability of a program to narrow the gap. In fact, as Lesser admitted, the program could increase the gap. Lesser wrote, "We hoped that poor children would learn as much and that the gap would not be widened, despite the fact that almost all comparisons of educational progress show middle-class children proceeding more rapidly."[46] The solution offered to this dilemma was to make the series appealing to children of the poor and to encourage viewing in poor families. Therefore, while *Sesame Street* was supposed to appeal to a national audience, concerns with educating the children of the poor directly influenced the overall goals of the program. Even though Lesser felt negatively about public schooling, he argued that the only realistic goal was to emphasize an education that would prepare children to enter school. This decision tied the program directly to the needs of formal schooling.

Because of his negative feelings about formal schooling, Lesser added a somewhat cynical note to how the program could prepare children. "Since one major premise was the preparation of disadvantaged children for school," Lesser argued, "the most useful ammunition we could give the child was the ability to 'read' the teacher, to pick up the small covert clues in the teacher's behavior that would allow him to guess what the teacher wants to hear."[47] Therefore, from Lesser's perspective, *Sesame Street* could help children by teaching them the implicit rules of schooling so that the child could conform to the behavioral expectations of teachers. Lesser's cynical proposal was overruled by the staff of the Children's Television Workshop.

The emphasis on preparation for school and concerns about children of the poor determined the basic shape of *Sesame Street*. The staff decided that poor parents wanted their children to achieve in the basic subjects of reading, writing, and arithmetic. The major complaint of these parents, the staff felt, was the failure of the school to teach these subjects. Therefore, the staff concluded that the program should focus on preparation for learning these subjects in school.

According to Lesser, teaching the alphabet was the most controversial decision regarding preparation for school. This decision created "howls of repugnance . . . over . . . use of the new technology to teach what appears to be an arbitrary and useless skill."[48] But, it was argued, the alphabet was essential for early reading. What television could accomplish, in the framework of Lesser's belief that learning can be entertaining, was to make memorization of the alphabet a form of entertainment.

During its early years, *Sesame Street* did score a major success in reaching children of the poor. During the first broadcast year, it was estimated that almost 50 percent of the potential preschool audience watched the program, including children in day care and other prekindergarten programs serving children of the poor. It was found that the program was watched by 91 percent of the at-home children in the low-income Bedford-Stuyvesant and Harlem sections of New York City. Eighty-eight percent of low-income families interviewed in Chicago tuned their sets to *Sesame Street.*[49]

One reason for the success of the program was the campaign, particularly in low-income urban areas, to create awareness of the program. *Sesame Street* clubs were established; people went door-to-door to alert families to the program; a *Sesame Street* magazine was distributed; and announcements were made through libraries, schools, and community organizations. In Chicago 120 mothers in low-income areas conducted *Sesame Street* viewing sessions. A similar project was conducted in the Mexican American section of Los Angeles. The Children's Television Workshop ran a Neighborhood Youth Corps Project that involved adolescents from poor families in teaching preschool children. Of course the project focused on the viewing of *Sesame Street.* During the first broadcast year, 240 adolescents worked in viewing centers with 1,500 children. The following year the numbers increased to 1,200 adolescents helping 15,000 children of the poor in thirteen different cities. By 1972 there were 10,000 tutors helping 100,000 preschool children in viewing centers.[50]

In a broader framework, the publicity campaign helped to legitimize television as the third educator that could be considered equal to the role of formal schooling and the family. The *Sesame Street* concept was different from instructional television designed for the classroom. Now education moved into the home in the format of an entertainment program. In addition, it truly nationalized the educational process. From coast to coast, children were watching the same program. The program created a mass culture among preschool children.

The use of television as a third educator seemed to contradict the charges that television viewing was a passive and mind-numbing experience. Lesser argued that a great deal of learning takes place through modeling. According to Lesser, children do not need to interact to learn; they can model themselves after television characters. In fact, modeling fit Lesser's concept of a nonpunitive form of education. "The child," Lesser wrote, "imitates the model without being induced or compelled to do so. . . . By watching televised models, children learn both socially desirable and undesirable behaviors."[51] Television, Lesser argued, can provide models that show what behaviors are possible and what consequences might result from an action.

In addition to modeling behavior, Lesser believed television could create myths to guide children's actions. In this context, television was supposed to educate the public in the same manner as movies censored by the 1930 code. In Lesser's words, television could provide "a vision of the world as it might be." These myths were to be created by the presentation of what Lesser called "simple goodness." He believed that children did not learn from preaching. Considering television's role in presenting life's tensions and deprivations, Lesser reasoned, "Surely it can create others [myths] that help them toward a more humane vision of life."[52]

The argument for creating myths made ideological management dependent on creating unrealistic images of goodness. As in previous movie and broadcasting codes, good had to win out over evil. This reasoning spilled over into decisions about portraying normal urban life on *Sesame Street*. In the end, the decision was made to present urban life as "a vision of the world as it might be" and not in its reality.

Lesser believed that little could be gained by showing the child living in an urban ghetto the harsh realities of life. As planning of the program evolved, there was a drift toward presenting the sweeter side of life. In giving only the positive side of life, the staff realized that they might be accused of presenting a sugar-coated world.[53]

The decision to present a distorted view of urban living is exemplified by Lesser's description of a program designed to show children how an urban bus driver and passengers act on a trip around the city. "Now, we all know that a bus driver is often not our best example of someone who is courteous and civil," Lesser wrote. "But on *Sesame Street's* bus trip, the driver responds to his passengers' hello's and thank-you's, tells a child who cannot locate his money, 'That's all right you can pay me tomorrow,' and upon seeing a young woman running after his bus just as it has left the curb, actually stops to let her on."[54]

This depiction of an urban bus trip was a major misrepresentation of most urban transportation systems. In fact, Lesser himself referred to it as an "outrageous misrepresentation." But he justified the decision as presenting a model of behavior that would guide children to a better world. In justifying the presentation of an urban transportation system in this idealized fashion, Lesser stated, "We wanted to show the child what the world is like when people treat each other with decency and consideration. Our act of faith . . . was that young children will learn such attitudes if we take the trouble to show them some examples, even if we stretch familiar reality a bit in order to do so."[55]

The desire to create positive myths and to help children of the poor influenced the decision to present strong male identification figures. The staff reasoned that poor children lacked positive male role models and that public schooling was dominated by female role models. Therefore, they decided to "show men on *Sesame Street* in warm, nurturing relationships with young children." The result was an attack on the program for the lack of strong female characters. Newspaper columnist Ellen Goodman complained, "The females that do live on *Sesame Street* can be divided into three groups: teacher, simp, and mother. . . . Oh yes, a cow." As time went on, the program introduced positive female roles. But the early emphasis was on strong male roles.[56]

Sesame Street was harmoniously integrated. Of course this presentation sugar-coated the harsh realities of racial conflict in American society. Lesser noted that one of the charges made against the program was that it taught "minority-group children to accept quietly middle-class America's corrupt demands to subjugate themselves." Multiracial groups worked and played harmoniously on *Sesame Street* while whites and African Americans clashed on the streets.[57]

The production of *Sesame Street* opened the door to a new era in public education and to the influence of national educational policy on the world of television. *Sesame Street* extended organized education to the out-of-school student while joining the government's War on Poverty. This new era in television was highlighted by the Children's Television Workshop production of *The Electric Company* and *3-2-1 Contact.*

Edward Palmer, the director of research for the Children's Television Workshop, called *The Electric Company* and *3-2-1 Contact* "home-and-school hybrids." Like *Sesame Street,* they were expected to attract out-of-school viewers. In addition, they could be viewed in school. Consequently, these programs brought together the worlds of home television viewing and formal classroom instruction. Also, like *Sesame Street,* the programs reflected federal educational policy. Or in the words of Palmer, "Both series further illustrate how television can be tied to needs of children in which our whole society has a stake."[58]

The production of *The Electric Company* was directly tied to the Nixon administration's concern with the teaching of basic skills. Its first broadcast in 1971 was intended to reach seven- to ten-year-olds who might be having difficulty reading. It was also used in first-grade classrooms as an introduction to reading. It was estimated that half the viewers were in school settings and the other half in out-of-school settings. After one year, 34 percent of the nation's elementary schools were using the program. Using closed-circuit television systems, some elementary schools made the program available to teachers throughout the school day. Nixon's commissioner of education, Sidney Marland, called *Sesame Street* and *The Electric Company* "the best educational investment ever made."[59]

3-2-1 Contact was directly related to the career education goals of the Nixon administration, which believed it would reduce campus unrest and solve labor market problems by relating all academic subjects to career education. In addition, there was continuing pressure to educate more scientists and technical workers. As Palmer indicates, the program was a direct reflection of these national policy objectives. Palmer wrote, "The series was created in the late 1970s because the U.S. had fallen behind as a nation in preparing large enough numbers of children well enough to fill the demand for specialists in science and technology in the workplace." The program was designed to attract children to science and technology before they entered the ninth and tenth grades.[60]

The Children's Television Workshop continued the pattern of trying to shape public morality by presenting the world as harmonious and good. Like the movie and broadcasting codes of the 1930s, programs such as *Sesame Street* created a tension between the projected image of the world and reality. On one hand, this tension might have created a cynical feeling about these images of morality, which might have led to a rejection of these forms of projected morality. On the other hand, these images might actually have provided a standard for what the world should be like.

Therefore, the creation of the Corporation for Public Broadcasting and the Children's Television Workshop added a new dimension to ideological management in the United States. Corporations, foundations, educators, and government officials joined hands to make television an instrument of federal educational policies and a molder of high culture. Along with the family and the school, public television, by instructing out-of-school children, became the third educational institution. While commercial television was given influence over mass culture, public television assumed the leadership of high culture.

CONCLUSION

After World II, ideological management in schools extended into the areas of military defense and the War on Poverty. Public schools were enlisted in an international Cold War, resulting in the purging of so-called subversive teachers and ideas and the organizing of the curriculum to provide school graduates who would contribute to the strengthening of U.S. military technology. Reflecting the initial concerns of Horace Mann in using schools to eliminate poverty, the federal government enlisted the schools and television in a War on Poverty. Given the increasing political nature of education and struggles over the cultural content of schooling, the War on Poverty would inevitably be challenged by those waving Noah Webster's banner proclaiming that schools should create cultural unity and by those wanting to reduce the welfare role of the government and schools.

Notes

1. President's Advisory Commission on Universal Training, "Staff Study: Universal Military Training in the United States: A Brief Historical Summary," in *A Program for National Security: Report of the President's Advisory Commission on Universal Training* (Washington, DC: U.S. Government Printing Office, 1947), pp. 401–406.
2. Vannevar Bush, *Science—The Endless Frontier: A Report to the President* (Washington, DC: U.S. Government Printing Office, 1945).
3. U.S. Congress, Senate Committee on Interstate and Foreign Commerce, *Hearings before the Committee on Interstate and Foreign Commerce,* 80th Cong., 1st sess., March 6–7, 1947 (Washington, DC: U.S. Government Printing Office, 1947), p. 147.
4. Ibid., pp. 155–157.
5. Nicholas Lemann, *The Big Test: The Secret History of the American Meritocracy* (New York: Farrar, Straus and Giroux, 2000).
6. See Chapter 10 of this book.
7. Joe Spring, *The Sorting Machine Revisited: National Educational Policy since 1945* (New York: Longman, 1989), pp. 27–28.

8. Quoted in Lemann, p. 4.
9. Ibid., p. 6.
10. Ibid., pp. 343–344.
11. Ibid, p. 344.
12. Richard Barnes Kennan, "No Ivory Tower for You," *NEA Journal* 40 (May 1951), pp. 317–318.
13. Quoted in David Hulburd, *This Happened in Pasadena* (New York: Macmillan, 1951), pp. 90–91.
14. Quoted in Jack Nelson and Gene Roberts Jr., *The Censors and the Schools* (Boston: Little, Brown, 1963), pp. 40–53.
15. Quoted in Franklin R. Zeran, "Life Adjustment in Action, 1944–1952," in *Life—Adjustment Education in Action,* ed. Franklin R. Zeran (New York: Chartwell House, 1953), p. 86.
16. Arthur Bestor, *Educational Wastelands* (Urbana: University of Illinois Press, 1953), p. 86.
17. Ibid., pp. 36–38.
18. Ibid.
19. Ibid.
20. Ibid.
21. Quoted in Edward R. Murrow, foreword to Hyman G. Rickover, *Education and Freedom* (New York: Dutton, 1959), pp. 5–7.
22. Dwight D. Eisenhower, "Our Future Security," in U.S. Congress, Senate Committee on Labor and Public Welfare, *Science and Education for National Defense: Hearings before the Committee on Labor and Public Welfare,* 85th Cong., 2nd sess., 1958 (Washington, DC: U.S. Government Printing Office, 1958), pp. 1357–1359.
23. Dwight D. Eisenhower, "Message from the President of the United States Transmitting Recommendations Relative to Our Educational System," ibid., pp. 239–262.
24. "The Problem of Poverty in America," in *The Annual Report of the Council of Economic Advisers* (Washington, DC: U.S. Government Printing Office, 1964). Also see Maris A. Vinovskis, *The Birth of Head Start* (Chicago: University of Chicago Press, 2005).
25. Lyndon B. Johnson, "The State of the Union Message to Congress, 8 January 1964," in *A Time for Action: A Selection from the Speeches and Writings of Lyndon B. Johnson* (New York: Atheneum, 1964), pp. 164–179.
26. "Elementary and Secondary Education Act of 1965, Public Law 89-10," reprinted in Stephen Bailey and Edith Mosher, *ESEA: The Office of Education Administers a Law* (Syracuse, NY: Syracuse University Press, 1968), pp. 235–266. Also see Lawrence J. McAndrews, *The Era of Education: The Presidents and the Schools, 1965–2001* (Urbana: University of Illinois Press, 2006), pp. 7–51, 89–118, for a legislative history of the ESEA and the struggle over aid to religious schools, particularly Catholic schools.
27. U.S. Congress, House Committee on Education and Labor, *Aid to Elementary and Secondary Education: Hearings before the General Subcommittee on Education of the Committee on Education and Labor,* 89th Cong., 1st sess., 1965 (Washington, DC: U.S. Government Printing Office, 1965), pp. 63–82.
28. Ibid., pp. 82–113.
29. Ibid., p. 63.
30. For a study of the role of the federal government in coordinating movies and radio for the war effort, see Allan M. Winkler, *The Politics of Propaganda: The Office of War Information 1942–1945* (New Haven: Yale University Press, 1978). For a study

of the effect of the Cold War on the movie industry, see Larry Ceplair and Steven Englund, *The Inquisition in Hollywood: Politics in the Film Community, 1930–1960* (Berkeley: University of California Press, 1979). The Red scare in the broadcasting industry was discussed by Erik Barnouw in *The Golden Web: A History of Broadcasting in the United States, 1933–1953* (New York: Oxford University Press, 1968), pp. 253–305. Kathryn Montgomery's *Target Prime Time: Advocacy Groups and the Struggle over Entertainment Television* (New York: Oxford University Press, 1989) provides a history and analysis of the effect of advocacy groups on the ideological content of entertainment television.

31. As quoted in James L. Baughman, *Television's Guardians: The FCC and the Politics of Programming, 1958–1967* (Knoxville: University of Tennessee Press, 1985), p. 61.
32. See Joel Spring, *Images of American Life: A History of Ideological Management in Schools, Movies, Radio, and Television* (Albany: State University of New York Press, 1992), pp. 231–251.
33. Ibid., p. 95.
34. Ibid.
35. Ellen Condliffe Lagemann, *The Politics of Knowledge: The Carnegie Corporation Philanthropy, and Public Policy* (Middleton, CT: Wesleyan University Press, 1989), p. 232.
36. Lloyd Morrisett, "Introduction," in Gerald S. Lesser, *Children and Television: Lessons from "Sesame Street"* (New York: Vintage, 1975), p. xxi.
37. Ibid., p. xxvi.
38. Lagemann, *The Politics of Knowledge,* p. 233.
39. Joan Cooney, "Foreword," in Lesser, *Children and Television,* p. xvii.
40. Lesser, *Children and Television,* p. 7.
41. Ibid., pp. 8–9.
42. Ibid., p. 23.
43. Ibid., pp. 89–90.
44. Ibid., p. 19.
45. Ibid., p. 80.
46. Ibid., pp. 80–81.
47. Ibid., p. 60.
48. Ibid., p. 47.
49. Ibid., p. 204.
50. Ibid., pp. 208–211.
51. Ibid., pp. 24–25.
52. Ibid., pp. 254–255.
53. Ibid., p. 95.
54. Ibid.
55. Ibid.
56. Ibid., p. 199.
57. Ibid., p. 200.
58. Edward L. Palmer, *Television and America's Children: A Crisis of Neglect* (New York: Oxford University Press, 1988), p. 103.
59. Ibid., p. 104.
60. Ibid., pp. 106–108.

14

The Fruits of Globalization: Civil Rights, Global Migration, and Multicultural Education

Symbolic of the continuing global integration of world societies and education systems was the 1945 founding of the United Nations and its 1948 Universal Declaration of Human Rights, which declared in Article 26, "Everyone has the right to education."[1] This declaration of the right to education was followed in 1960 by the United Nations Convention against Discrimination in Education, which stated that people should not be deprived of an education or limited to an inferior education. The convention defined educational discrimination as "any distinction, exclusion, limitation or preference . . . based on race, color, sex, language, religion, political or other opinion, national or social origin, [and] economic condition or birth."[2]

In the context of the global movement to extend rights to all people previously discriminated against, groups in the United States pushed for an end to school segregation and equal educational opportunities. This included women, students with disabilities, and African, Native, Asian, and Hispanic/Latino Americans.

The American civil rights movement combined with increasing global migration to the United States after passage of the 1965 Immigration Act opened a new chapter in the educational culture wars. Many people wanted schools to protect their cultures and non-English languages. This resulted in struggles over the language and culture of instruction. The global context for the push to protect languages and cultures can be found in the 1960 Convention against Discrimination in Education:

> It is essential to recognize the right of members of national minorities to carry on their own educational activities, including maintenance of schools and, depending on the educational policy of each State, the use or the teaching of their own language.[3]

In the United States the attempt to protect minority languages led to conflict between advocates of bilingual instruction and those demanding English only. Eventually this issue would find its way into the 2001 federal No Child Left Behind legislation.

This chapter will examine the American school experience in this global civil rights context by discussing the effect on schools of

- The civil rights movement and school desegregation.
- The struggle for equal educational opportunity by African, Native, Asian, and Hispanic/Latino Americans.
- Bilingual education.
- The Immigration Act of 1965 and the new American population.
- Multicultural education.
- Equal educational opportunity for women.
- Textbooks and equal educational opportunity.

ENDING SCHOOL SEGREGATION OF NATIONAL MINORITIES

Globally, the end of World War II marked the beginning of international recognition of the problem of discrimination in education against national minorities and women. The United Nations 1960 Convention against Discrimination in Education attests to this global concern. In the United States struggles against educational discrimination began before World War II. A major effort occurred to end segregation of national minorities in public schools. A key organization in these efforts was the National Association for the Advancement of Colored People (NAACP).

The issue of segregation of national minorities was finally decided by the U.S. Supreme Court in 1954 in *Brown v. Board of Education of Topeka*. The decision did not bring immediate results because of resistance to court-ordered desegregation. The frustration caused by the slow pace of school integration and the continuation of other forms of discrimination contributed to the growth of a massive civil rights movement in the late 1950s and early 1960s. National political leaders responded to the civil rights movement by enacting strong civil rights legislation.

The key legal issue in the 1954 *Brown* decision was the interpretation of the Fourteenth Amendment to the U.S. Constitution. This constitutional amendment was ratified in 1868, shortly after the Civil War. One of its purposes was to extend

AFRICAN AMERICAN CIVIL RIGHTS EDUCATION TIME LINE

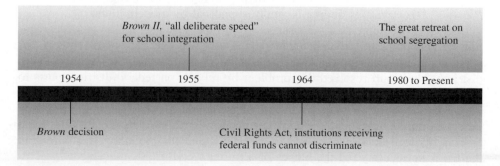

the basic guarantees of the Bill of Rights into the areas under state and local government control. The most important and controversial section of the Fourteenth Amendment states, "No State shall make or enforce any law which shall abridge the privileges or immunities of citizens . . . nor . . . deprive any person of life, liberty, or property, without due process of law, nor deny to any person within its jurisdiction the equal protection of the laws."

The overturning of the "separate but equal" doctrine and a broader application of the Fourteenth Amendment came in 1954 in the historic and controversial Supreme Court decision *Brown v. Board of Education of Topeka. Brown* was one of five school segregation suits to reach the Supreme Court in 1953; the five cases were heard in alphabetical order. The *Brown* case began in 1951, when Oliver Brown and twelve other parents represented by NAACP lawyers brought suit to void a Kansas law that permitted but did not require local school segregation. In this case, Oliver Brown's daughter was denied the right to attend a white elementary school within five blocks of her home and was forced to cross railroad tracks and travel twenty-one blocks to attend an all-black school. The federal district court in Kansas ruled against Oliver Brown, using the argument that the segregated schools named in the suit were substantially equal and thus fell within the "separate but equal" doctrine.

In preparing its brief for the Supreme Court, the NAACP defined two important objectives: (1) to show that the climate of the times required an end to segregation laws and (2) to show that the "separate but equal" doctrine contained a contradiction in terms—that is, that separate facilities were inherently unequal. To prove that separate facilities were inherently unequal, the NAACP presented new findings from the social sciences. These findings provided the basis for overturning the "separate but equal" doctrine. Opponents of the decision complained that the Supreme Court was making decisions using nonlegal arguments based on social science research. Throughout the South, it was widely believed that the Court was being persuaded by Communist-oriented social scientists. Billboards appeared next to highways demanding the impeachment of Chief Justice Earl Warren for subverting the Constitution.

The Supreme Court argued in the *Brown* decision, "In the field of public education the doctrine of 'separate but equal' has no place. Separate educational facilities are inherently unequal." To support this argument, the Supreme Court wrote one of the most controversial single sentences ever to appear in a Court decision: "Whatever may have been the extent of psychological knowledge at the time of *Plessy v. Ferguson,* this finding is amply supported by modern authority."[4]

In 1955 the Supreme Court issued its enforcement decree for the desegregation of schools. One problem facing the Court was the lack of machinery for supervising and ensuring the desegregation of vast numbers of segregated school districts. The Court resolved this problem by relying on federal district courts to determine equitable principles for desegregation. Federal judges were often part of the social fabric of their local communities and resisted attempts at speedy desegregation. Consequently integration occurred at a slow pace until additional civil rights legislation was passed in the 1960s and the mounting frustrations in the black community fed the flames of a militant civil rights movement.[5]

African American students return to Clinton High School, Clinton, Tennessee. African American students are shown arriving at Clinton High School as white students line school steps. After the African American students entered the building, a U.S. marshall proclaimed from the steps that a federal court injunction against interfering with integration at the school applied to all residents of Clinton and Anderson counties.
© *Brown Brothers*

The evolution of the mass media in the 1950s was an important factor in the civil rights movement because it became possible to turn local problems into national issues. Thus, even though presidents had traditionally shown a great deal of deference to the important white southern political structure, the emergence of the mass media as a powerful force allowed both the federal government and civil rights groups to put unprecedented pressure on southern political leaders, forcing them to comply with national civil rights legislation. In fact, enforcement of the Supreme Court school desegregation ruling depended in large part on civil rights groups making effective use of television. In one sense, the struggle that took place was a struggle between public images. Concern over America's international image grew as pictures of racial injustice flashed around the world, and the president's public image was often threatened when examples of racial injustice were shown to millions of television viewers who asked, What is our president doing about this situation?

The most dramatic technique used by civil rights groups was nonviolent confrontation. The massive nonviolent demonstrations by blacks and whites were met by cursing southern law enforcement units using an array of cattle prods, clubs, and fire hoses. These scenes were broadcast on television around the world. The Congress on Racial Equality (CORE), the Student Nonviolent Coordinating Committee (SNCC), and the Southern Christian Leadership Conference (SCLC), led by the Reverend Martin Luther King Jr., forced the passage of national civil rights legislation.

THE REVEREND DR. MARTIN LUTHER KING JR.

The introduction of nonviolent confrontation into the civil rights movement came from the Christian student movement of the 1930s, which, under the leadership of the Fellowship for Reconciliation, was committed to use of the Gandhian technique of *satyagraha* (nonviolent direct action) in solving racial and industrial problems in the United States. CORE, a major player in the civil rights movement, was organized at the University of Chicago in 1942. The two basic doctrines of the early CORE movement were commitment to racial integration and the use of Christian nonviolent techniques.

CORE did not rise to national prominence until the late 1950s, when another Christian leader, Dr. Martin Luther King Jr., made nonviolent confrontation the central drama of the civil rights movement. King was born in 1929 in Atlanta, Georgia, into a family of Baptist ministers. His maternal grandfather founded the Ebenezer Baptist Church in Atlanta, and his father made the church into one of the largest and most prestigious Baptist churches in the area. In 1944 King entered Atlanta's Morehouse College, where he was influenced by Henry David Thoreau's *Essay on Civil Disobedience.* He later wrote about the essay, "Fascinated by the idea of refusing to cooperate with an evil system, I was so deeply moved that I reread the work several times. This was my first intellectual contact with the theory of non-violent resistance."[6]

In 1948 King entered Crozier Theological Seminary in Chester, Pennsylvania, where he became acquainted with pacifism through a lecture by A. J. Muste. King wrote that at the time he considered Muste's pacifist doctrine impractical in a world confronted by the armies of totalitarian nations.

Also of importance to King's intellectual development was his exposure to the social gospel philosophy of Walter Rauschenbusch, a philosophy that actively involved the church in social reform as a means of creating a kingdom of God on earth. Although he rejected the optimistic elements in the social gospel, King argued that any concern with the souls of humans required a concern with social and economic conditions.

King also studied the lectures and works of Mohandas K. Gandhi. The Indian leader's work convinced King that the Christian doctrine of love could be a force for social change. King wrote, "Gandhi was probably the first person in history to lift the love ethic of Jesus above mere interaction between individuals to a powerful and effective social force on a large scale." Like the early members of CORE, King became convinced that nonviolent resistance "was the only morally and practically sound method open to oppressed people in their struggle for freedom."[7]

The incident that launched Martin Luther King's civil rights activities and provided scope for his Gandhian form of the social gospel occurred on December 1, 1955. On that date Rosa Parks, who had worked a regular day as a seamstress in one of the leading department stores in Montgomery, Alabama, boarded a bus and took the first seat behind the section reserved for whites. Later during the journey home, several white passengers boarded the bus. The driver ordered Rosa Parks and three other black passengers to stand so the white passengers could have seats. Rosa Parks refused and was arrested. The black ministers in the community quickly organized in response to this incident, and on December 5 the Montgomery bus boycott began.

The bus boycott lasted for over a year. It ended on December 21, 1956, when, after the Supreme Court decision against segregation on buses, the Montgomery transit system was officially integrated. King emerged from the struggle a national hero among dominated groups. In 1957 he organized the Southern Christian Leadership Conference (SCLC), which became a central organization in the civil rights struggle.

After SCLC was formed, boycotts and nonviolent demonstrations began to occur throughout the South. On May 17, 1957, Martin Luther King gave his first nationwide address in Washington, DC. He told his audience, "Give us the ballot and we will quietly, lawfully, and nonviolently, without rancor or bitterness, implement the May 17, 1954, decision of the Supreme Court." For King, meaningful school desegregation depended on the power of the black voter.

As civil rights demonstrations increased in intensity, national leaders began to work for federal legislation. In 1957 and 1960 two ineffective forms of civil rights legislation were passed by Congress. The most important civil rights legislation was not enacted until 1964, when violence in Birmingham, Alabama, and a mass march on Washington forced a response from the federal government. The civil rights movement made Birmingham and its director of safety, Eugene "Bull" Connor, symbols of the oppression of black people in the United States. President John F. Kennedy was quoted as saying, "Our judgment of Bull Connor should not be too harsh. After all, in his way, he has done a good deal for civil rights legislation this year."[8] The March on Washington symbolized to Congress and the American people the growing strength of the civil rights movement and provided the stage for television coverage of speeches by civil rights leaders.

The result of these activities was the Civil Rights Act of 1964. Under eleven different titles, the power of federal regulations was extended in the areas of voting rights, public accommodations, education, and employment. Titles IV and VI of the legislation were intended to end school segregation and provide authority for implementing the *Brown* decision.

Title VI, the most important section, established the precedent for using disbursement of government money as a means of controlling educational policies. Originally President Kennedy merely proposed a requirement that institutions receiving federal funds must end discriminatory practices. In its final form, Title VI required withholding of federal funds from institutions that did not comply with its mandates. It states that no person, on the basis of race, color, or national origin, can be excluded from or denied the benefits of any program receiving federal financial assistance, and it requires all federal agencies to establish guide-lines to implement this policy. Refusal by institutions or projects to follow these guidelines will result in the "termination of or refusal to grant or to continue assistance under such program or activity."

The power of Title VI rests in its ability to withhold federal money from financially pressed school systems. This became a more crucial issue after the 1965 passage of the Elementary and Secondary Education Act. The rate of deseg-regation was more rapid after the 1964 Civil Rights Act than before, but abundant evidence by the end of the 1960s showed that segregated education continued in the South. School desegregation moved at an even slower pace in the North. Originally it was believed that the *Brown* decision would affect only those states whose laws required segregated education. However, by the late 1960s the courts began to rule that the *Brown* decision applied to all schools in the country, if it could be proved that segregation was the result of intentional actions by school boards or school administrators.

NATIVE AMERICANS AND INDIGENOUS EDUCATIONAL RIGHTS

Globally, indigenous peoples, including Native Americans, suffered from the effects of colonialism. The United Nations estimates that there are 370 million indigenous peoples existing around the globe in areas of the South Pacific, Asia, Europe, and, of course, including the numerous indigenous nations of Africa and North and South America. Indigenous peoples are identified by a number of characteristics, including long-term occupancy of the land, tribal organization, and subsistence-oriented production. Indigenous groups have a social and cultural identity distinct from dominant national societies.[9]

In recognition of the global exploitation and subjugation of indigenous peo-ples, the United Nations approved the 2007 Declaration on the Rights of Indigenous

NATIVE AMERICAN CIVIL RIGHTS EDUCATION TIME LINE

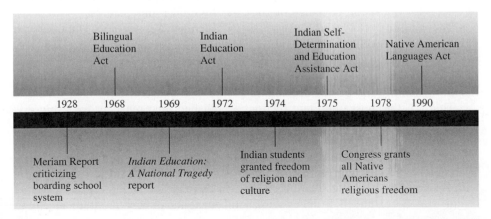

Peoples. This declaration of rights included the right to control the education of their children. The reader will recall that since colonization of North America efforts were made to use schools to change or destroy indigenous cultures. The Declaration of the Rights of Indigenous Peoples was intended to restore control of schooling to native peoples; it states the following:

- Indigenous peoples have the right to establish and control their educational systems and institutions providing education in their own languages, in a manner appropriate to their cultural methods of teaching and learning.
- Indigenous individuals, particularly children, have the right to all levels and forms of education of the state without discrimination.
- States shall, in conjunction with indigenous peoples, take effective measures, in order for indigenous individuals, particularly children, including those living outside their communities, to have access, when possible, to an education in their own culture and provided in their own language.[10]

In the United States Native Americans also attempted to gain control of the education of their children and restore their cultural heritage and languages. Native Americans shared a common interest with Mexican Americans and Puerto Rican Americans in supporting bilingual and multicultural education.

During the 1940s and 1950s, federal Native American policy was directed at termination of tribes and reservations. The leader of the termination policy, Senator Arthur V. Watkins of Utah, declared in 1957, "I see the following words emblazoned in letters of fire above the heads of the Indians—THESE PEOPLE SHALL BE FREE!"[11] Freedom in this case meant freedom from federal supervision and control. It also meant the end of official tribal status.

Termination policies attempted to break up tribal relations by relocating Native Americans to urban areas. Relocation to urban areas was similar to the nineteenth-century federal policy that sent Native Americans to Indian Territory and reservations. But in this case Native Americans were to be "civilized" by being dispersed throughout the general population.

Termination efforts met stiff resistance from Native American and white civil rights activists. In 1961, 450 Native American delegates from ninety tribes attended the American Indian Chicago Conference at the University of Chicago. The delegates issued a *Declaration of Indian Purpose* calling for the end of termination policies. In the end, termination policies resulted in about 3 percent of the Native American tribes being terminated, including the Menominee of Wisconsin and the Klamath Indians of Oregon.[12]

While resisting termination policies, Native Americans began to demand greater self-determination. This was reflected in policy changes in the Bureau of Indian Affairs after the election of John F. Kennedy in 1960. Condemning the termination policies of the 1950s, the Kennedy administration advocated Native American participation in decisions regarding federal policies. Kennedy's secretary of the interior, Stewart Udall, appointed a Task Force on Indian Affairs, which, in its 1961 report, states, "to insure the success of our endeavor we must solicit the collaboration of those whom we hope to benefit—the Indians themselves . . . equal citizenship, maximum self-sufficiency, and full participation in American life."[13]

One result of the drive for self-determination was the creation, in 1966, of the Rough Rock Demonstration School. Established on a Navajo reservation in Arizona, the school was a joint effort of the Office of Economic Opportunity and the Bureau of Indian Affairs. A major goal of the demonstration school was for Navajo parents to control the education of their children and participate in all aspects of their schooling.[14]

Besides tribal control, one important feature of the Rough Rock Demonstration School was the attempt to preserve the Navajo language and culture. In contrast to the deculturalization efforts of the nineteenth and early twentieth centuries, the goal of learning both Navajo and English was presented as a means of preparing children to "fend successfully in both cultures and see the Navajo way as part of a universal system of values."[15]

The struggle for self-determination was aided by the development of a Pan-Indian movement in the United States. The Pan-Indian movement was based on the assumption that Native American tribes shared a common set of values and interests. Similar to the role played by CORE, the SNCC, and the SCLC among African Americans, Pan-Indian organizations, such as the American Indian Movement (AIM) and the Indians of All Tribes, led demonstrations demanding self-determination. In 1969 members of the Indians of All Tribes seized Alcatraz Island in San Francisco Bay as a means of calling attention to the plight of Native Americans and demanded that the island, which Native Americans had originally allowed the federal government to use (Native Americans did not recognize the concept of private ownership of land) for twenty-four dollars' worth of beads, be made a Native American cultural and education center. In 1972 AIM organized a march on Washington, DC called the Trail of Broken Treaties. Members of the march seized the Bureau of Indian Affairs and at the entrance hung a large sign declaring it the American Indian Embassy.[16]

Native American Education: A National Tragedy

Throughout the 1960s and 1970s, federal administrators gave support to Native American demands for self-determination. During his election campaign in 1968, Richard M. Nixon declared, "The right of self-determination of the Indian people will be respected and their participation in planning their own destiny will actively be encouraged."[17]

It was in this climate of civil rights activism and political support for Native American self-determination that the U.S. Senate Committee on Labor and Public Welfare issued in 1969 the report *Indian Education: A National Tragedy—A National Challenge.* The report opened with a statement condemning previous educational policies of the federal government: "A careful review of the historical literature reveals that the dominant policy of the Federal Government toward the American Indian has been one of forced assimilation . . . [because of] a desire to divest the Indian of his land."[18]

After a lengthy review of the failure of past educational policies, the report's first recommendation was "maximum participation and control by Indians in establishing Indian education programs."[19] In its second recommendation, the report called for maximum Native American participation in the development of educational programs in federal schools and local public schools. These educational programs were to include early childhood education, vocational education, work-study, and adult literacy education. Of special importance was the recommendation to create bilingual and bicultural education programs.

Native American demands for bilingual and bicultural education were aided by the passage of Title VII of the Elementary and Secondary Education Act of 1968 or, as it was also called, the Bilingual Education Act. This was, as I will explain later in this chapter, a product of political activism by Mexican American groups. Native Americans used funds provided under this legislation to support bilingual programs in Native American languages and English. For instance, the Bilingual Education Act provided support for bilingual programs in Navajo and English at the previously mentioned Rough Rock Demonstration School.[20]

The congressional debates resulting from the criticism leveled at Native American education in the report *Indian Education: A National Tragedy—A National Challenge* eventually culminated in the passage of the Indian Education Act in 1972. The declared policy of the legislation was to provide financial assistance to local schools to develop programs to meet the "special" educational needs of Native American students. In addition, the legislation created a federal Office of Indian Education.[21]

In 1974 the Bureau of Indian Affairs issued a set of procedures for protecting student rights and due process. In contrast to the brutal dictatorial treatment of Native American students in the boarding schools of the late nineteenth and early twentieth centuries, each Native American student was extended the right "to make his or her own decisions where applicable." And in striking contrast to earlier deculturalization policies, Native American students were granted "the right to freedom of religion and culture."[22]

The most important piece of legislation supporting self-determination was the 1975 Indian Self-Determination and Education Assistance Act, which gave tribes the power to contract with the federal government to run their own education and health programs. The legislation opened with the declaration that it was "an Act to provide maximum Indian participation in the Government and education of Indian people; to provide for the full participation of Indian tribes in programs and services conducted by the federal government."[23] The Indian Self-Determination and Education Assistance Act strengthened Native American participation in the control of education programs. The legislation provided that, in a local school district receiving funds for the education of Native American students that did not have a school board having a majority of Native Americans, the district had to establish a separate local committee composed of parents of Native American students in the school. This committee was given authority over any Native American education programs contracted with the federal government.

The principles embodied in the Indian Self-Determination and Education Assistance Act were expanded upon in 1988 with the passage of the Tribally Controlled Schools Act. In addition to the right to operate schools under federal contract as provided in the 1975 legislation, the Tribally Controlled Schools Act provided outright grants to tribes to support the operation of their own schools.[24]

Efforts to protect Native American culture were strengthened with the passage in 1978 of a congressional resolution on Native American religious freedom. Remember that missionaries and federal policies from the seventeenth to the early twentieth centuries attempted to eradicate Native American religions and replace them with Christianity. The resolution recognized these earlier attempts to abridge Native American rights to religious freedom, stating, "Henceforth it shall be the policy of the United States to protect and preserve for American Indians their inherent right of freedom to believe, express and exercise traditional religions . . . and the freedom to worship through ceremonial and traditional rites."[25]

In addition to protecting religion, the federal government committed itself to promoting traditional languages with the passage of the Native American Languages Act of 1990. This act commits the federal government to "preserve, protect, and promote the rights and freedom of Native Americans to use, practice, and develop Native American languages."[26]

There is, of course, an ironic twist to federal legislation designed to promote self-determination and preservation of Native American languages, religions, and cultures when placed against the backdrop of history. The Five Civilized Tribes in Indian Territory were operating their own tribal governments and school systems in the nineteenth century. The Cherokees were conducting bilingual education programs and protecting their cultural and religious traditions. These forms of self-determination and protection of languages and cultures ended when Indian Territory was dissolved in 1907. Also, the tribes placed onto reservations in the nineteenth century were subjected to policies consciously designed to destroy their cultures, languages, and religions. Therefore, the federal legislation of the 1970s and 1980s, which were designed to reverse these policies, required many tribes to discover and resurrect languages and traditions that the federal government had already partially destroyed.

ASIAN AMERICANS: EDUCATING THE "MODEL MINORITY"

The global migration of peoples from Asia to the United States increased with the passage of the 1965 Immigration Act (discussed later in this chapter). As Asians' immigration rates increased, their image changed from "yellow peril" to "model minority."

Several authors have suggested that this public image emerged in the 1950s and 1960s as part of the white backlash to the militancy of the black civil rights movement. Faced with the anger of black Americans demanding equal rights and economic opportunity, some European Americans began pointing their fingers at the Asian community and argued that they were successful in achieving the American dream without contentious demonstrations and accusations of prejudice and discrimination. "If," these European Americans seemed to say, "the black population acted like the Asian population, they could achieve economic success without criticizing the white population."

In a sharp break with the previous public image of Asian American students as "deviants" and a "yellow peril," the model minority image presented the Asian American as possessing the "ideal" public school personality traits of obedience, punctuality, neatness, self-discipline, and high achievement motivation. Historian Bob Suzuki has argued that portrayals of the model minority image often neglect the historical evolution of the Asian American community. For instance, the early Chinese immigrants were hardly docile and were often described as being a "worldly, rebellious, and emotional lot."[27] Interestingly, Suzuki argued that the current school traits associated with the model minority image are a result of the assimilation process of the U.S. school system. Suzuki concluded, "The personality traits exhibited by Asian Americans are the result of a socialization process in which the schools play a major role through their selective reinforcement of certain cultural behavior patterns and inculcation of others that are deemed 'appropriate' for lower-echelon white-collar wage workers."[28]

Historian Robert Lee identified as typical of this new public image a story appearing in a December 1966 issue of *U.S. News and World Report* titled "Success Story of One Minority in the US." The article contended, "At a time when it is being proposed that hundreds of billions be spent on uplifting Negroes and other minorities, the nation's 300,000 Chinese Americans are moving ahead on their own with no help from anyone else."[29] Lee argued that popular theories about ethnicity and cultural assimilation of the 1950s and 1960s helped popularize the model minority image. Popular ethnicity theorists envisioned a color-blind society where achievement would be determined by individual competition. This approach, which avoided analysis of racism or the role of racism in U.S. history, simply called for the elimination of personal prejudice and racism without any government intervention in the economy or private institutions. In the context of these arguments, education and schooling would be the key to creating a color-blind society based on individual competition. In Lee's words, to ethnicity theorists and politicians "who sought both to develop the Negro and to contain black demands for the systematic and structural dismantling of racial discrimination, the representation of Asian-American communities as self-contained, safe, and politically acquiescent became a powerful example of the success of the American creed in resolving the problems of race."[30]

Ki-Taek Chun argued that the model minority image reached its peak with the publication of Harry Kitano's *Japanese Americans: The Evolution of a Subculture* (1969) and William Peterson's *Japanese Americans: Oppression and Success* (1971).[31] Both of these books linked schooling to what the authors considered the remarkable success of Japanese Americans. Peterson claimed that Japanese Americans were better off than any other group in U.S. society, including native-born whites. In an indirect criticism of the black community, Peterson contended that unlike other oppressed minorities, Japanese Americans "have realized this remarkable progress by their own almost unaided effort."[32] Kitano presented a success story marked by high educational levels and income. Thus Chun found that by the early 1970s the claim of Asian American success in education and work was believed by most U.S. social scientists.[33]

Statistics provided evidence of Asian American success in education but not economically. In 1970, prior to large-scale immigration from other parts of Asia, the educational attainment of Chinese, Japanese, and Filipino Americans was higher than or about equal to that of the white population. The median number of years of schooling for white males was 12.1, while the medians for Chinese, Japanese, and Filipino Americans were 12.5, 12.6, and 11.9 respectively. However, economic achievement did not match educational achievement. The median white male annual income in 1970 was $6,772, which was less than the Japanese American average of $7,471. However, the incomes for Chinese American males ($5,124) and Filipino American males ($4,921) were considerably below those of white males.[34]

Critics of the model minority image claimed it was used to cover up the continuing racism in U.S. society. The disparity between educational achievement and income highlighted how education could be used to achieve the American dream in schooling but not in the workplace. Bob Suzuki argued, "Although they have attained high levels of education, the upward mobility of Asian Americans has been limited by the effects of racism and most of them have been channeled into lower-echelon white-collar jobs having little or no decision-making authority, low mobility and low public contact."[35]

I would argue that the model minority image created in the 1960s and 1970s might have distorted the image European Americans had of Asian immigrants arriving from Southeast Asia, particularly the Hmong and Cambodians. Assuming that these Asian immigrants would live up to the model minority image, European American educators might have neglected the real educational problems confronting these populations. For instance, the children of some Cambodian immigrants, despite the model minority image, were easily recruited during the 1980s and 1990s into existing violent youth gangs in the Los Angeles area. One reason was the continuation of racist attitudes toward Asian Americans. Describing his school experience in Stockton, California, in the 1980s, Sokunthy Pho complained, "I hated my parents for bringing me and my sisters . . . to America because we were always being picked on by the white kids at our school. . . . They spat at us, sneaked behind us and kicked us. . . . We didn't respond. . . . Instead, we kept quiet and walked home with tears running down our brown cheeks."[36]

Asian Americans: Language and the Continued Struggle for Equal Educational Opportunity

School problems for Asian Americans continued despite popular media extolling the virtues of the model Asian American student. The continuing struggle against educational discrimination was dramatized by events surrounding the historic 1974 U.S. Supreme Court decision *Lau v. Nichols*. The decision guaranteed equal educational opportunity to non-English-speaking students by requiring public schools to provide special assistance to help these students learn English so they could participate equally in the educational process. In the words of the U.S. Supreme Court, "there is no equality of treatment merely by providing students with the same facilities, textbooks, teachers, and curriculum; for students who do not understand English are effectively foreclosed from any meaningful education."[37]

The problem presented in the *Lau* case was a classic example of the indirect forms of discrimination in the U.S. school system. Because English is the reigning language of the system, students not speaking English or with limited English ability cannot fully participate in classroom activities or instruction. Without some special help in learning English, limited-English-speaking immigrants and some native-born citizens, such as Native Americans and Mexican Americans, are deprived of equal educational opportunity.

The *Lau* case originated in concerns by Chinese American parents about the difficulties faced by their children in the San Francisco school system. In the 1960s and early 1970s, the Chinese American community complained to the school district that the language problems faced by their children were contributing, despite the model minority public image, to school failure and juvenile delinquency. Even a report issued by the San Francisco school system in 1969 admitted, "When these (Chinese-speaking) youngsters are placed in grade levels according to their ages and are expected to compete with their English-speaking peers, they are frustrated by their inability to understand the regular work."[38] Stressing the language problem, a persistent issue for Asian American immigrant children, the 1969 school report concluded, "For these children, the lack of English means poor performance in school. The secondary student is almost inevitably *doomed to be a dropout and another unemployable in the ghetto* [emphasis added]."[39] This concern certainly didn't match the Asian American success stories touted in the press.

Despite recognizing the problem, school authorities did little to alleviate it. In 1970 only one-fourth of the limited-English-speaking Chinese American students in the San Francisco school system were receiving help. The statistics were worse for Chinese-speaking students. A 1970 investigation conducted by the federal district court in San Francisco found that 2,856 Chinese-speaking students needed help in learning English. However, more than 62 percent or 1,790 of these students were receiving no special instruction. For the other 38 percent, help was provided primarily through once-a-day 40-minute English-as-a-second-language (ESL) instruction. Students were removed from their regular classes to receive ESL instruction. According to L. Ling-Chi Wang, this approach to language instruction was called "once-a-day ESL bitter pill."[40] Wang wrote that after the ESL class, students "were required to attend regular classes taught only in English and compete helplessly and hopelessly with their English-speaking peers in all subject areas."[41]

Angered by the neglect of their children's educational problems, the families of Kinney Kinmon Lau and twelve other Chinese American students in 1970 sued in federal district court, asking that the San Francisco school system provide special English classes taught by bilingual teachers. The school district objected to the demand and claimed that receiving help in learning the English language was not a legal right. The district court agreed with the school district and argued that limited-English-speaking and non-English-speaking students were receiving equal educational opportunity because they were receiving the same education as all students in the district.

After the district court ruling, the case hinged on the question of whether students are entitled to special instruction as part of the right to equal educational opportunity. The case was appealed to the U.S. Court of Appeals for the Ninth Circuit. The appeals court agreed with the school district that the legal responsibility of the school district extended "no further than to provide them with the same facilities, textbooks, teachers and curriculum as is provided to other children in the district."[42]

In 1974 the U.S. Supreme Court overturned the decisions of the lower courts and argued that sometimes equal educational opportunity requires special programs for students. In language that would have a profound impact on the education of all limited-English-speaking and non-English-speaking students, the Supreme Court maintained, "There is no equality of treatment merely by providing students with the same facilities, textbooks, teachers, and curriculum; for students who do not understand English are effectively foreclosed from any meaningful education."[43]

The *Lau* decision did not end the educational problems faced by the Chinese American community in San Francisco. Led by the Chinese for Affirmative Action, the local community had to struggle with the school district to implement the *Lau* decision. This struggle was part of a larger effort by the Asian American community to protect their civil rights.

HISPANIC/LATINO AMERICANS

As it did for Asian immigrants, the 1965 Immigration Act increased migration from Central and South America and the Caribbean to the United States. The struggles of Mexican Americans and Puerto Rican Americans increased the opportunities for Hispanic/Latino immigrants arriving after the 1960s. Like African Americans, Mexican Americans turned to the courts to seek redress for their grievances. In Ontario, California, in 1945, Mexican American parents demanded that the school board grant all requests for transfer out of the segregated schools. When the board refused this request, Gonzalo Mendez and William Guzman brought suit for violation of the Fourteenth Amendment to the Constitution. The school board responded to this suit by claiming that segregation was not based on race or national origins but on the necessity of providing special instruction.

HISPANIC/LATINO CIVIL RIGHTS EDUCATION TIME LINE

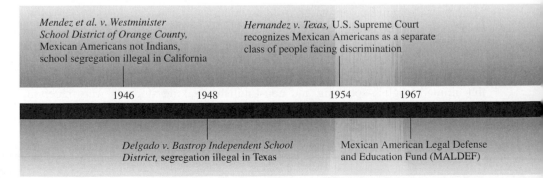

Mendez et al. v. Westminister School District of Orange County, Mexican Americans not Indians, school segregation illegal in California

Hernandez v. Texas, U.S. Supreme Court recognizes Mexican Americans as a separate class of people facing discrimination

1946   1948   1954   1967

Delgado v. Bastrop Independent School District, segregation illegal in Texas

Mexican American Legal Defense and Education Fund (MALDEF)

In 1946 a U.S. district court ruled in *Mendez et al. v. Westminster School District of Orange County* that Mexicans were not Indians as claimed under the 1935 California law. The judge argued that the only possible argument for segregation was the special educational needs of Mexican American children. These needs centered around the issue of learning English. Completely reversing the educational justification for segregation, the judge argued that "evidence clearly shows that Spanish-speaking children are retarded in learning English by lack of exposure to its use by segregation."[44] Therefore, the court ruled that segregation was illegal because it was not required by state law and because there was no valid educational justification for segregation.[45]

Heartened by the *Mendez* decision, the League of United Latin American Citizens (LULAC), the Mexican American equivalent of the NAACP, forged ahead in its legal attack on segregation in Texas. With support from LULAC, a group of parents in 1948 brought suit against the Bastrop Independent School District, charging that local school authorities had no legal right to segregate children of Mexican descent and that this segregation was solely because the children were of Mexican descent. In *Delgado v. Bastrop Independent School District,* the court ruled that segregating Mexican American children was illegal and discriminatory. The ruling required that the local school district end all segregation. The court did give local school districts the right to separate some children in the first grade only if scientific tests showed that they needed special instruction in English and the separation took place on the same campus.[46]

In general, LULAC members were pleased with the decision. The one point they were dissatisfied with was the provision for the separation of children in the first grade. This allowed local schools to practice what was referred to in the latter part of the twentieth century as "second-generation segregation"—the practice of using educational justifications for segregating children within a single school building. In fact, many local Texas school districts did use the proviso for that purpose.[47]

Although the *Mendez* and *Delgado* decisions held out the promise of ending segregation of Mexican Americans, local school districts used many tactics to avoid integration, including manipulation of school district lines, choice plans, and different forms of second-generation segregation. For instance, the California State Department of Education reported in 1966 that 57 percent of the children

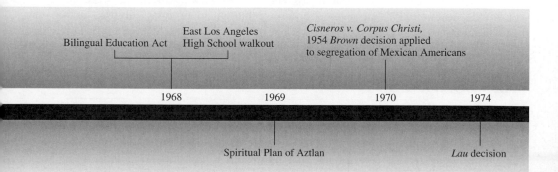

Bilingual Education Act	East Los Angeles High School walkout	Cisneros v. Corpus Christi, 1954 Brown decision applied to segregation of Mexican Americans
1968	1969	1970	1974
	Spiritual Plan of Aztlan		Lau decision

with Spanish surnames were still attending schools that were predominantly Mexican American. In 1973 a civil rights activist, John Caughey, estimated that two-thirds of the Mexican American children in Los Angeles attended segregated schools. In *All Deliberate Speed: Segregation and Exclusion in California Schools, 1855–1975,* Charles Wollenberg estimated that in California by 1973 more Mexican and Mexican American children attended segregated schools than in 1947.[48]

The continuation of de facto forms of segregation resulted in the formation in 1967 of the Mexican American Legal Defense and Education Fund (MALDEF). Initially MALDEF worked on cases dealing with students who were punished for participating in civil rights activities. In 1968 MALDEF focused its attention on the inequitable funding of school districts in Texas that primarily served Mexican Americans. Not only were Mexican American children facing de facto segregation, but the schools they were attending were also receiving less funding than schools attended by Anglos.[49]

The case brought by MALDEF, *Rodriguez v. San Antonio Independent School District,* had major implications for financing of schools across the country. In the case, a group of Mexican American parents brought a class action suit against the state of Texas for the inequitable funding of school districts. In 1971 a federal district court ruled that the Texas school finance system was unconstitutional. In its decision, the federal district court applied—as the U.S. Supreme Court had in the 1954 school desegregation case—the equal protection clause of the Fourteenth Amendment. The unequal financing of school districts was considered a denial of equal opportunity for Mexican American children to receive an education. The U.S. Supreme Court overturned the decision on March 12, 1973, with the argument that school finance was not a constitutional issue. This Supreme Court decision meant that all school finance cases would have to be dealt with in state courts. Since 1973 numerous cases involving unequal financing of public schools have been argued in state courts.[50]

In 1970 in the MALDEF case *Cisneros v. Corpus Christi Independent School District,* Mexican Americans were officially recognized by the federal courts as an identifiable dominated group in the public schools. A central issue in the case was whether the 1954 school desegregation decision could be applied to Mexican Americans. The original *Brown* decision had dealt specifically with African Americans who were segregated by state and local laws. In his final decision, Judge Owen Cox ruled that African Americans and Mexican Americans were segregated in the Corpus Christi school system law and that Mexican Americans were an identifiable dominated group because of their language, culture, religion, and Spanish surnames.[51]

BILINGUAL EDUCATION: THE CULTURE WARS CONTINUED

As previously mentioned, the 1960 Convention against Discrimination in Education barred discrimination based on the language of the student. In addition, the convention declared it a right for national minorities to conduct schools in their own languages and cultural traditions. In the United States, Spanish-speaking cultures were concerned about preserving their languages.

During the 1960s Mexican Americans began to demonstrate for the use of Spanish in schools and for the teaching of Mexican American history and culture. In 1968 Mexican American students boycotted four East Los Angeles high schools, demanding bilingual programs, courses in Mexican American history and culture, and the serving of Mexican food in the school cafeterias. In addition, the students demanded the hiring of more Spanish-speaking teachers and the firing of teachers who appeared to be anti–Mexican American.[52]

The school boycotts in Los Angeles attracted the attention of the newly formed La Raza Unida. La Raza Unida was formed in 1967 when a group of Mexican Americans boycotted federal hearings on the conditions of Mexican Americans and started their own conference. At the conference, La Raza Unida took a militant stand on the protection of the rights of Mexican Americans and the preservation of their culture and language. A statement drafted at the first conference proclaimed, "The time of subjugation, exploitation, and abuse of human rights of La Raza in the United States is hereby ended forever."[53]

La Raza Unida's statement on the preservation of culture and language reflected the growing mood in the Mexican American community that public schools needed to pay more attention to dominated cultures and languages. The statement drafted at the first conference affirmed "the greatness of our heritage, our history, our language, our traditions, our contributions to humanity and our culture."[54]

Politicians responded to Mexican American and Puerto Rican demands for the presentation of Spanish in the schools. Liberal Democratic Senator Ralph Yarborough of Texas, believing that he would lose the 1970 election to a wealthy and conservative Democrat, decided that Hispanic support was crucial to his coalition of African Americans, Mexican Americans, and poor whites. In an effort to win Hispanic support, Yarborough, after being appointed to a special subcommittee on bilingual education of the Senate Committee on Labor and Public Welfare, launched a series of hearings in major Hispanic communities.[55] The testimony at these hearings came primarily from representatives of the Mexican American and Puerto Rican communities, not educational experts or linguistic theorists. The hearings concluded in East Harlem, with Senator Edward Kennedy and Bronx borough president Herman Badillo decrying the fact that there were no Puerto Rican principals and only a few Puerto Rican teachers in the New York City school system.[56]

Yarborough supported bilingual legislation that focused on students whose "mother tongue is Spanish." The legislation included programs to impart knowledge of and pride about Hispanic culture and language and to bring descendants of Mexicans and Puerto Ricans into the teaching profession. The legislation was clearly designed to win political support from the Hispanic community in Texas. Yarborough's efforts resulted in the passage of the previously mentioned Bilingual Education Act of 1968.

Native Americans, along with Mexican Americans and Puerto Ricans, welcomed the idea of bilingual education. The legislation promised that their cultures and languages would be preserved by the public schools. Bilingual education, as it was conceived of in Hispanic and Native American communities, involved teaching both English and Spanish or a Native American language. Some of the Civilized Tribes in Indian Territory used bilingual methods in their schools. In addition, bilingual education existed at differing periods in Mexican American and Puerto Rican schools. The goal was, and is, to teach students to be fluent in two languages. In addition, Mexican Americans, Puerto Ricans, and Native Americans consider bilingual education to be part of a general effort to transmit their cultural traditions to students.

By the 1980s, the two major U.S. political parties were divided over bilingual education. Traditionally, organized ethnic groups, including Mexican Americans and Puerto Ricans, were a strong force in the Democratic Party. In contrast, bilingual education became a major target of attack during the Republican administrations of the 1980s and 1990s. In fact, some members of the Republican Party joined a movement opposing bilingual education and supporting the adoption of English as the official language of the United States. The movement to make English the official language was led by an organization, U.S. English, founded in 1983 by S. I. Hayakawa, a former Republican senator.

In 1986, in reaction to the Reagan administration, the National Association of Bilingual Education increased its political activities and intensified its public relations efforts. In reference to S. I. Hayakawa and U.S. English, Gene T. Chavez, the president of the association, warned that "those who think this country can only tolerate one language" were motivated more by political than by educational concerns. At the same meeting, the incoming president of the organization, Chicago school administrator Jose Gonzalez, attacked the Reagan administration and the Department of Education for entering an "unholy alliance" with right-wing groups opposing bilingual education—groups such as U.S. English, Save Our Schools, and the Heritage Foundation.[57]

Within the Reagan administration, Secretary of Education William Bennett attempted to reduce support for bilingual education by appointing opponents of it to the government's National Advisory and Coordinating Council on Bilingual Education. The new appointees expressed a preference for immersing non-English-speaking children in the English language rather than teaching them in a bilingual context. In addition, the new appointees favored giving more power to local officials to determine programs. Of course such a policy would undercut the power the Hispanic community had gained by working with the federal government. Originally Hispanics had turned to the federal government for assistance because they lacked power in local politics.[58]

One of Bennett's appointees to the National Advisory and Coordinating Council on Bilingual Education, Rosalie Pedalino Porter, director of the Bilingual and English as a Second Language programs in Newton, Massachusetts, wrote a book about the controversy with the descriptive title *Forked Tongue: The Politics of Bilingual Education*. For Porter, the politics of bilingual education involved both political struggle within the educational establishment and the broader issue of cultural politics. Like other Bennett appointees, Porter rejected bilingual education that is also bicultural. She believed that language training should be geared toward providing students with the language tools necessary for equal opportunity within the mainstream economy. But unlike the more conservative of Bennett's appointees, she did not support attempts to make English the official language of the United States.

Porter's conclusions regarding bilingualism reflected her broader views on cultural politics. She argued against bilingualism that is also bicultural because it segregates dominated communities with the least power. In her words, "The critical question is whether education policies that further the cultural identity of dominated groups at the same time enable dominated children to acquire the knowledge and skills to attain social and economic equality."[59]

Porter opposed the efforts of U.S. English because its efforts are provocative and based on anti-immigrant attitudes and threaten special programs for language minority groups. She quoted a statement by Richard Rodriguez as representing her position on attempts to enact an amendment to the Constitution making English the official language:

> What bothers me most about defenders of English comes down to a matter of tone. Too shrill. Too hostile. Too frightened. They seem to want to settle the issue of America's language, once and for all. But America must risk uncertainty if it is to remain true to its immigrant character. . . . We must remind the immigrant that there is an America already here. But we must never forget that we are an immigrant country, open to change.[60]

Despite opposition from civil rights organizations and professional organizations—including the National Association of Bilingual Education, the National Council of Teachers of English, the Linguistics Society of America, and the Modern Language Association—efforts to make English the official language continued at the state and national levels. In 1923 Nebraska made English the official state language, followed by Illinois in 1969. In 1978 Hawaii made English and Hawaiian the official state languages. Indicative of the concerns of the 1980s, between 1984 and 1988 fourteen other states made English their official state language.[61]

The major target of those supporting English as the official language is the ballot. Extensions to the 1965 Voting Rights Act granted citizens the right to voting information in their native languages. In communities where 5 percent or more of the population speak languages other than English, voting material must be provided in those languages. Supporters of English-language amendments argue that voters should be fluent in English and that naturalization procedures require a test given in English. Therefore, from their standpoint, ballots and election materials should be kept in English. Opponents argue that election materials should be presented in native languages so that all groups will be on an equal footing with those who are fluent in English.

Besides the issue of political power, language is considered a cultural issue by Mexican Americans, Puerto Ricans, and Native Americans. A person's cultural perspective is directly related to attitudes regarding making English the official language. This connection is exemplified by Humberto Garza's comment regarding a requirement that Los Altos, California, city employees speak only English on the job: "Those council people from Los Altos should be made to understand that they are advocating their law in occupied Mexico [referring to the U.S. conquest of Mexican territory, including California]. . . . They should move back to England or learn how to speak the language of Native Americans."[62]

THE IMMIGRATION ACT OF 1965 AND THE NEW AMERICAN POPULATION

Similar to the reaction to global migration in the late nineteenth and early twentieth centuries, debates over the education of foreign-born children occurred after passage of the 1965 Immigration Act. Although Americanization programs in schools were dominant from 1890 to 1930, the new immigration after 1965 sparked educational debates about multiculturalism and language policies. The new wave of immigration to the United States occurred while Native Americans, Mexican Americans, Puerto Ricans, and African Americans were demanding a place for their cultures in the public school curriculum.

Why might some Americans of European descent feel threatened by the new immigration resulting from the 1965 legislation? Consider the dramatic change in immigration shown in Table 14.1, with the percentage immigrating from Europe declining from 90 percent (1861–1900) and 85 percent (1900–1920) to 13.7 percent in 1998. The decline in European immigration, as shown in Table 14.1, was supplanted by increased immigration from Asia and North America (including Mexico). For instance, only 6 percent of the total immigration between 1900 and 1920 was from North America (including Mexico) as compared to 38.3 percent in 1998. Similar changes occurred for Asian immigration, with 4 percent of the total immigration between 1900 to 1920 as compared to 33.3 percent in 1998.

Besides experiencing changes in immigration patterns, Americans living between 1930 and 1970 had grown used to a relatively small foreign-born population. This was a result of the quota system imposed by the 1924 Immigration Act. As indicated in Table 14.2, the percentage of foreign born as part of the total population declined from 14.7 percent (1890) and 11.6 percent (1930) to

TABLE 14.1 Immigrants to the United States by Region, 1861–1920, 1998 (Percentages)

Region	1861–1900	1900–1920	1998
Europe	90%	85%	13.7%
North America (includes Mexico)	7	6	38.3
Asia	2	4	33.3
South America	–	4	6.9
Other	1	1	7.8

Source: Adapted from Roger Daniels, *Coming to America: A History of Immigration and Ethnicity in American Life,* 2nd ed. (New York: Perennial, 2002), Tables 6.1 and 17.3, pp. 122, 415.

TABLE 14.2 Foreign-Born Population of the United States: 1890, 1930, 1970, and 2002

Year	Total Population of the United States (Numbers in Thousands)	Foreign born (Numbers in Thousands)	Percentage of Foreign Born in U.S. Population
1890	62.6	9.2	14.7%
1930	122.8	14.2	11.
1970	203.2	9.6	4.7
2002	282.2	32.5	11.5

Source: Adapted from Dianne Schmidley and J. Gregory Robinson, "Measuring the Foreign-Born Population in the United States with the Current Population Survey: 1994–2002," *Population Division Working Paper No. 73* (Washington, DC: Population Division, U.S. Bureau of the Census, 2003), Table 3A, p. 14.

4.7 percent in 1970. This 1970 figure changed dramatically after the 1965 immigration legislation began to be felt. By 2002, as shown in Table 14.2, the percentage of the U.S. population that was foreign born increased to 11.5, which was almost the same percentage as in 1890. As shown in Table 14.3, the major sources of the new immigration were Mexico (19.9 percent), China and Hong Kong (6.4 percent), India (5.5 percent), the Philippines (5.2 percent), the former Soviet Union (4.6 percent), and the Dominican Republic (3.1 percent).

MULTICULTURAL EDUCATION AND THE CULTURE WARS

Global migration sparked debates about multicultural education throughout the world.[63] The new immigration plus the continuing cultural concerns of previously dominated groups resulted in a discussion about the possibility of multicultural education in U.S. public schools. In many ways this could be branded a radical movement because of previous cultural and immigrant programs, such as the Americanization programs in the early twentieth centuries and the historic attempts at deculturalization of minority cultures. Opponents of multiculturalism argued that the public schools should emphasize a single culture—traditional Anglo-American culture. In contrast to the late nineteenth and early twentieth centuries, when immigrants from Southern and Eastern Europe were greeted with Americanization programs designed for deculturalization and the implanting of Anglo-American values, the new immigrants were swept up into the debate over multiculturalism initiated by the civil rights movement.

Influenced by the civil rights movement, the 1965 Immigration Act eliminated the blatantly racist and ethnocentric aspects of the 1924 Immigration Act. The results of the U.S. Army Alpha and Beta examinations administered during World War I contributed to the belief in the superior intelligence of northern Europeans. To protect the existing racial composition of the United States, the 1924 Immigration

TABLE 14.3 The Top Regions and Countries of Immigrants to the United States, 1998

Region	Rank	Numbers	Percentage of Total Immigration for 1998
North America (includes Mexico)	1	252,996	38.3%
Asia	2	219,696	33.3
Europe	3	90,793	13.7
South America	4	45,394	6.9
Africa	5	40,660	6.2
Countries	Rank	Numbers	Percentage of Total Immigration for 1998
Mexico	1	131,575	19.9%
China and Hong Kong	2	42,159	6.4
India	3	36,482	5.5
Philippines	4	34,466	5.2
Former Soviet Union	5	30,163	4.6
Dominican Republic	6	20,387	3.1

Source: Adapted from Roger Daniels, *Coming to America: A History of Immigration and Ethnicity in American Life,* 2nd ed. (New York: Perennial, 2002), Table 17.3, p. 415.

Act established annual quotas for immigration from individual countries based on the percentage of each national group in the total U.S. population in 1920. The openly stated purpose of the legislation was to limit immigration of nonwhite populations. Immigration to the United States sharply declined after 1924. After passage of the 1965 Immigration Act, immigration rapidly increased, and by 1980 the top five sources of immigration were Mexico, Vietnam, the Philippines, Korea, and China/Taiwan.[64]

By the 1990s, as a result of the civil rights movement and the new immigration, the debate about multicultural education ranged from concerns with empowering oppressed people to creating national unity by teaching common cultural values. Originally leaders of the multicultural movement in the 1960s and 1980s, such as James Banks, Christine Sleeter, and Carl Grant, were concerned with empowering oppressed people by integrating the history and culture of dominated groups into public school curricula and textbooks. In general, they wanted to reduce prejudice, eliminate sexism, and equalize educational opportunities.[65]

It was argued that the integration of different histories and culture into the curriculum would empower members of dominated and oppressed immigrant cultures by providing an understanding of the methods of cultural domination and by helping to build self-esteem. For instance, the study of African American, Native American, Puerto Rican, and Mexican American history would serve the dual purpose of building self-esteem and fostering empowerment. In addition, the empowerment of women and people with disabilities would involve, in part, the inclusion of their histories and stories in textbooks and in the curriculum.

The study of a variety of cultures had an important influence on textbooks and classroom instruction in the United States. The cultural studies movement resulted in the integration into the curriculum of content that deals with dominated and immigrant cultures, women, and people with disabilities.

Many multicultural educators felt that simple integration of cultural studies into textbooks and the curriculum was not enough. Multicultural educator James Banks worried that many school districts consider content integration as the primary goal of multicultural education. He states, "The widespread belief that content integration constitutes the whole of multicultural education might . . . [cause] many teachers of subjects such as mathematics and science to view multicultural education as an endeavor primarily for social studies and language arts teachers."[66]

Banks proposed that multicultural education be considered a basic part of a student's general education, which means that all students should become bilingual and study different cultural perspectives. In addition, multiculturalism should pervade the curriculum, including the general life of the school—bulletin boards, lunchrooms, and assemblies. In other words, all teachers and subjects should reflect a multicultural perspective.

In opposition to simply integrating the history and culture of dominated groups into the curriculum, some African American leaders, such as Molefi Asante, demanded ethnocentric schools that would focus on the history and culture of a specific group and teach from a particular cultural perspective.[67] Although Afrocentric schools gained the greatest attention, some Native Americans, Puerto Ricans, and Mexican Americans organized similar schools. The movement for ethnocentric schools, unlike the original movement for multicultural education, did not include concerns with gender, prejudice, and disabilities.

The most popular of the ethnocentric schools associated with dominated cultures were Afrocentric. In the 1990s public school districts in Miami, Baltimore, Detroit, Milwaukee, and New York created or considered plans for Afrocentric schools.[68] Advocates of Afrocentric education argued that they can improve a student's sense of self-worth, help students relate to the curriculum, and help students understand the causes of cultural domination.

An important concept in the argument for ethnocentric schools is cultural perspective. For instance, because African American culture evolved in the context of slavery and later forms of segregation and racism, there developed a distrust and suspicion about the white Anglo-American Protestant tradition. Consequently the Afrocentrist turned to other traditions. As one of the leading Afrocentrists, Molefi Asante, argued, "Afrocentrism directs us to . . . meditate on the power of our ancestors. . . . Afrocentricity is the belief in the centrality of Africans in postmodern history."[69]

Teaching from an Afrocentric, Native American–centered, Mexican American–centered, or Puerto Rican–centered perspective creates a view of the world different from that of a white Anglo-American Protestant culture. In fact, according to Asante, moving away from a white Anglo-American Protestant–centered curriculum will completely change a student's view of the world. Asante wrote about

this new perspective, "A new consciousness invades our behavior and consequently with Afrocentricity you see the movies differently, you see other people
differently, you read books differently, you see politicians differently; in fact,
nothing is as it was before your consciousness."[70]

Supporting ethnocentric education, Jawanza Kunjufu argued that the inherent
racism of white-dominated institutions hindered the education of African Americans. In his words, "We must develop programs and organizations to protect and
develop African American boys because a conspiracy exists to destroy African
American boys. The motive of the conspiracy is racism, specifically European
American male supremacy."[71] He proposed an educational program that would
prepare African American boys to understand their oppression and to be able to
have a career. An important part of his proposal was to present strong African
American male role models to young black boys so they could break through the
conspiracy. Similar arguments can be presented for Native American–, Puerto
Rican–, and Mexican American–centered educational programs.

During the 1980s and 1990s, there was sharp reaction against multicultural
education and the ethnocentric education advocated by dominated groups.[72] Protectors of Anglo-American culture, such as Arthur Schlesinger Jr., argued that
students should be united around a set of core values derived from white Anglo-
American Protestant traditions.[73] Schlesinger, the author of many U.S. history
books, argued that the institutions and culture of the United States are primarily
the product of English and European values and that these core values should
be the source of national unity. In his words, "The language of the new nation,
its laws, its institutions, its political ideas, its literature, its customs, its precepts,
its prayers, primarily derived from Britain."[74] Historically, Schlesinger argued,
the culture of the United States was unified by the common use of the English
language and core values derived from this white Anglo-American Protestant
tradition. These core values, he stated, include mutual respect, individual rights,
tolerance of differences, and individual participation in government.[75]

Like Schlesinger, Thomas Sobol, New York commissioner of education, stated
his approval of a curriculum that unites different cultural groups around common
values. Sobol stated, "The democratic ideals and values to which we still aspire . . .
the rule of law, freedom of speech, minority rights, tolerance of dissent, respect for
individuals, and more—derive from British political and legal traditions."[76]

In California, State Superintendent of Education Bill Honig defended a new
social studies curriculum by an appeal to the teaching of core values. Honig stated
in 1991, "This country has been able to celebrate pluralism but keep some sense
of the collective that holds us together. . . . Democracy has certain core ideas—
freedom of speech, law, procedural rights, the way we deal with each other."[77]

Schlesinger, Sobol, and Honig recognized that U.S. history contains many
examples of the violation of these principles by federal and state governments. They
recognized that at various times in history, federal and state governments supported
slavery, committed genocide against Native Americans, and denied equal rights and
opportunities to many ethnic groups. But, they argued, core values provided the
impetus for correcting these wrongs. The abolition of slavery, the extension of political rights to women, and the civil rights campaigns by African Americans, Mexican
Americans, Native Americans, Puerto Ricans, and Asian Americans reflect these

core values. These civil rights movements, according to Schlesinger, were based on the core values of the white Anglo-Saxon Protestant tradition.[78]

Given this perspective, it is hardly surprising that those calling for the teaching of core values would object to the forms of ethnocentric education, particularly Afrocentric education, advocated by dominated groups. Schlesinger attacked Afrocentric education for distorting the importance of Africa in the development of Western traditions and in the development of African American culture. Because of the variety of African cultures from which African Americans are descended, Schlesinger argued, it is hard to identify a common African heritage for African Americans. In addition, many African cultures are more oppressive than the white Anglo-American Protestant culture, as proved by the fact that slavery continued in Africa for many years after it was abolished in the United States.[79]

In addition, Schlesinger rejected the idea of teaching history for the purpose of building a sense of self-worth among children. In his words, "The deeper reason for the Afrocentric campaign lies in the theory that the purpose of history in the schools is essentially therapeutic: to build a sense of self-worth among minority children."[80] With regard to the teaching of the history of Africa, Schlesinger rejected the direct connection between African heritage and African American culture and dismissed the practice with this statement: "There is little evidence, however, that such invention of tradition is much more than a pastime of a few angry, ambitious, and perhaps despairing zealots and hustlers."[81]

The culture wars of the late twentieth century reflected the centuries-old effort to make English and Anglo-American Protestant culture the unifying language and culture of the United States. A sense of racial and cultural superiority was brought to North America by English colonists and emerged during cultural wars throughout U.S. history. The attempt to make Anglo-American culture the dominant culture of the United States came from that sense of superiority—which was challenged by the civil rights movement and the new immigration.

SCHOOLS AND THE INTERNATIONAL WOMEN'S MOVEMENT

The struggle for equal educational opportunities for women was a global movement after World War II as exemplified by the 1979 United Nations' Convention of the Elimination of all Forms of Discrimination against Women. Article 10 of the Convention calls for taking "all appropriate measures to eliminate discrimination against women in order to ensure to them equal rights with men in the field of education." Article 10 includes the following goals to achieve equal educational opportunity for women:

- Access to the same curricula, the same examinations, teaching staff with qualifications of the same standard, and school premises and equipment of the same quality.
- The elimination of any stereotyped concept of the roles of men and women at all levels and in all forms of education.
- The same opportunities to participate actively in sports and physical education.[82]

The goals of the international Convention of the Elimination of all Forms of Discrimination against Women reflected those of the women's movement in the United States, which had a long history dating back to the eighteenth century. However, white women in the United States did not gain full citizenship rights until the ratification of the Nineteenth Amendment on August 18, 1920. This amendment gave women the right to vote.

In the 1960s women began to focus on discrimination in schools. Equal educational opportunity for women was high on the agenda of the National Organization for Women (NOW) when it organized in 1966. The founding document of the organization declared, "There is no civil rights movement to speak for women as there has been for Negroes and other victims of discrimination. The National Organization for Women must therefore begin to speak."[83] During its first years of activism, NOW focused on

- Eliminating discriminatory quotas against women in college and professional school admissions.
- Urging parents, counselors, and teachers to encourage women to pursue higher education and professional education.
- Eliminating discriminatory practices against women in the awarding of fellowships and loans.
- Investigating the problem of female school dropouts.

NOW's activities and those of other women's organizations turned to legal action with the passage of Title IX of the 1972 Higher Education Act. Title IX provided for gender equality in employment in educational institutions and for gender equality in educational programs. The legislation applied to all educational institutions, including preschools, elementary and secondary schools, vocational and professional schools, and public and private undergraduate and graduate institutions. A 1983 U.S. Supreme Court decision, *Grove City College v. Bell,* restricted Title IX in its application to specific educational programs within institutions. In the 1987 Civil Rights Restoration Act, Congress overturned the Court's decision and amended Title IX to include all activities of an educational institution receiving federal aid.

Armed with Title IX, NOW and other women's organizations placed pressure on local school systems and colleges to ensure equal treatment of women in vocational education, athletic programs, textbooks and the curriculum, testing, and college admissions. Here is a brief chronological list of achievements in providing equal educational opportunity for women:

1972—Legal action was taken against school systems with segregated courses in home economics and industrial arts.

1974—Women's studies: With backing from NOW, more than one thousand women's studies departments were created on college campuses.

1975—Federal regulations were set forth to end sex discrimination in athletics.

1976—Lawsuits were filed regarding female participation in athletics and gender-biased hiring in school administration.

1976—The Educational Equity Act authorized the Office of Education to prepare "non-sexist curricula and non-discriminatory vocational and career counseling, sports education, and other programs designed to achieve equity for all students regardless of sex."

1983—The last all-male school in the Ivy League, Columbia University, became coeducational.

1986—The FairTest was organized to counter gender bias in high-stakes tests.

1996—Virginia Military Institute and the Citadel became coeducational.

By 1996 NOW and other women's organizations could claim the following accomplishments:

- The number of female medical school graduates increased from 8.4 percent in 1969 to 34.5 percent in 1990.
- The percentage of doctoral and professional degrees awarded to women increased from 14.4 percent in 1971 to 36.8 percent in 1991.
- Most discrimination in vocational programs ended. Female participation in high school athletics increased from 7 percent in 1972 to 37 percent in 1992 and in college athletics from 15.6 percent in 1972 to 34.8 percent in 1993.

CHILDREN WITH SPECIAL NEEDS

Similar to other struggles for equal educational opportunity, equal rights for children with disabilities became a global cause after World War II. Article 23 of the 1989 Convention of the Rights of the Child states, "State Parties recognize that a mentally or physically disabled child should enjoy a full and decent life, in conditions which ensure dignity, promote self-reliance and facilitate the child's active participation in the community."[84]

Parents of handicapped children and children needing special education had for years complained about segregation and the lack of services for their children. The political movement for federal aid to help handicapped students followed a path similar to that of the struggles over segregation. First, finding themselves unable to change educational institutions by pressuring local and state governments, organized groups interested in improving educational opportunities for the handicapped turned to the courts. This was the path taken in the late 1960s by the Pennsylvania Association for Retarded Children (PARC).

PARC was one of many associations organized in the 1950s to aid handicapped and retarded citizens. These organizations were concerned with state laws that excluded retarded and handicapped citizens from educational institutions because these citizens were considered uneducable and untrainable. State organizations like PARC and the National Association for Retarded Children campaigned to eliminate these laws and to demonstrate the educability of all children. But as the civil rights movement discovered throughout the century, local and state officials were resistant to change, and relief had to be sought from the judicial system.

In *Pennsylvania Association for Retarded Children (PARC) v. Commonwealth of Pennsylvania,* a case that was as important to the handicapped rights movement as the *Brown* decision was to the civil rights movement, PARC objected to conditions in the Pennhurst State School and Hospital. In framing the case, lawyers for PARC focused on the legal right to an education for handicapped and retarded children. Working with the Council for Exceptional Children (CEC), the major federal lobbyist for handicapped children, PARC overwhelmed the court with evidence of the educability of handicapped and retarded children. The state withdrew its case, and the court enjoined the state from excluding mentally retarded children from a public education and required that every mentally retarded child be allowed access to an education. The *PARC* case prompted lobbying groups representing the handicapped to file thirty-six cases against state governments. The CEC prepared model legislation and lobbied for its passage at the state and federal levels.[85]

One political problem facing advocates of federal aid for children with special needs was the possibility of excessive federal control resulting from attempts to define an appropriate education for each handicapped or retarded child. In fact, to do so would have raised the specter of federal control of local education and alienated many members of Congress. The resolution of this political problem, as it appeared in 1975 in Public Law 94-142 (the Education for All Handicapped Children Act), was the requirement that an individual educational plan (IEP) be developed for each child jointly by the local educational agency and the child's parents or guardians. This gave the child or the parents the right to negotiate with the local school system about the type of services to be delivered.

The IEP was considered to be a brilliant political strategy. In their study of the legalization of special education, David Neal and David Kirp called the IEP "an ingenious device in terms of political acceptability":

> It avoids attempting to mandate specific services; it recognizes the rights of recipients, empowers them, and involves them in the process; it avoids treading on the professional discretion of teachers and potentially enhances their influence over placement decisions; it provides a means of holding local administrators accountable while paying some deference to the belief that the federal government should not interfere too much with local autonomy in education; and it appeals to local school officials by fixing the upper limit of the liabilities with respect to the child.[86]

The gains made by women and by children with special needs highlight the power and inclusiveness of the civil rights movement. A broad range of groups who felt excluded from equal participation in education joined a common struggle in the streets, in school systems, in the courts, in state legislatures, and in the halls of Congress. Also, the civil rights movement illustrates the power people have to change social and political conditions if they are willing to organize and join in a common struggle.

THE COLORING OF TEXTBOOK TOWN

Publishing is now a global industry marketing textbooks to schools around the world. To a great extent textbooks determine the ideological message schools send to students. To market books in the United States, publishers had to remain sensitive to civil rights issues. Of course the required use of any textbook is problematic because usually some group will object to its part of its content. Textbooks also pose a problem for the right to freedom of thought for children when they are given to children as supposed "truth." The 1989 Convention of the Rights of the Child protects the freedom of thought of children without specifying how will it be achieved in schools. Article 14 of the Convention asserts, "State Parties shall respect the right of the child to freedom of thought, conscience, and religion."[87]

In the United States the civil rights movement put textbooks on trial for their racial images and their potential to shape student thought. A 1964 California State Department of Education report on "The Negro in American History Textbooks" declared that "[Ralph Ellison's novel, *Invisible Man*] demonstrates whites frequently do not 'see' Negroes. But Negroes are Americans. . . . They need to be 'seen' in textbooks."[88] The report was issued by a distinguished panel of University of California historians headed by Kenneth Stampp. The panel had been organized in 1963 by the Berkeley, California, chapter of the Congress on Racial Equality (CORE) to analyze American history textbooks adopted for use in grades 5 and 8 and two textbooks used in the state's high schools. The panel's report was important because the California State Board of Education selected textbooks that were adopted by local state school systems. Given the large number of sales involved, the textbook industry was very attuned to the desires of the California State Board of Education. The State Board of Education distributed the report to interested groups, including textbook publishers, and in 1966 it played an important role in the deliberations of the U.S. House of Representatives' investigation of the treatment of minority groups in textbooks; the House reprinted the report in its proceedings.[89] Intensifying discussions about racial images in textbooks was the news that New York City's African American elementary school students were drawing white faces when asked to complete self-portraits.[90]

CORE's panel of academic historians found almost total neglect of African American history. One textbook failed to mention African Americans. One did not refer to slavery during the colonial period. Others did not discuss African Americans after the Civil War. The report complained, "The greatest defect in the textbooks we have examined is the virtual omission of the Negro."[91] The panel criticized the unrealistic treatment of the relationships between whites and African Americans. When discussed at all in the textbooks, interracial contacts were portrayed as harmonious. The history of racial violence was seldom mentioned in textbooks. "In their blandness and amoral optimism," the panel's analysis concluded, "these books deny the obvious deprivations suffered by Negroes. In several places they go further, implying approval for the repression of Negroes or patronizing them as being unqualified for life in a free society."[92] The report recommended full treatment of African American history. The historians on the panel suggested that books begin with the early importation and treatment of slaves and conclude with the recent history of the civil rights movement. And, the report urged, "Gains that have been made should be described realistically and not as an ode to the inevitable justice and progress of the democratic system."[93]

The National Association for the Advancement of Colored People (NAACP) and the editors of *Ebony* magazine were also concerned about textbooks. Since the NAACP's demonstrations against the movie *Birth of a Nation* in 1915, the organization had paid vigilant attention to public images of African Americans. In 1966 the organization issued a guide to integrated textbooks that stated, "In the crucial effort to guarantee to all our children, white and black, a curriculum that makes sense in a multi-racial society, such a listing is long overdue."[94] The senior editor of *Ebony,* Lerone Bennett, after five years of studying textbooks, concluded, "The use of textbooks filled with half-truths, evasions and distortions is disastrous to both white and black Americans . . . [and] white oriented textbooks tend to inoculate white Americans with the virus of racism." Bennett called on the federal government to provide the resources and power to solve the textbook problem.[95]

Bennett warned, in testimony before the 1966 House subcommittee investigating textbooks' racial and cultural content, that "segregated textbooks . . . are as dangerous to the internal peace of America as segregated schools and residential areas." In fact, he argued that if all schools and neighborhoods were immediately integrated without integrating textbooks, then all schools and neighborhoods would soon become segregated again. Bennett found it ironic that the largest race riots had occurred in Chicago, which was originally founded by African American Jean Baptiste Pointe Du Sable. "And it seems to me," he declared, "that a solution to our current crisis depends to a great extent on the opening of our minds and our textbooks to all the Du Sables and the excluded range of American life and culture that they personified."[96]

Publishers expressed their concerns about racial integration of textbooks through their trade association, the American Textbook Publishers Institute (ATPI), which represented 110 publishers of textbooks and other educational materials. The organization scheduled a 1965 joint conference with the Urban League to determine "the needs of the Negro child and the kinds of materials which would help him relate to the total American society."[97] The executive director of the National Urban League, Whitney Young Jr., told the meeting, "You publishers want the respect of generations born and generations yet unborn. We live together as brothers, or we die together as fools." Another member of the Urban League, Edwin Berry, insisted that publishers do more than just integrate textbooks with pictures of differing ethnic groups. They should also, he argued, provide a realistic view of society by including "tall people, short people, fat and slim people, people with glasses, balding men and pregnant women."[98]

Meeting in 1965 with the Great Cities Research Council, the ATPI agreed to collect urban—by this time *urban* was a code word for poor and nonwhite students—educational materials in cooperation with the United States Office of Education. The ATPI organized itself as a clearinghouse for new research on urban education. To further aid the objectives of publishers, the joint conference arranged visits by teams of publishers to meet with educators in member school systems. Also, before congressional investigators, ATPI's McCaffrey described how publishers were being pressured by local school systems to produce multiracial textbooks: "I think 2 or 3 years ago a number of principal cities in the country passed resolutions in their boards of education that it was the policy of these cities to purchase only books that had a fair representation of minorities."[99]

Publishers claimed federal money made it possible to produce multiracial texts. Robert W. Locke, a senior vice president of McGraw-Hill, told the House subcommittee, "Purchases of new textbooks and other instructional materials have risen sharply this year because of ESEA, and part of the gap has been closed between what should be done for schoolchildren and what is being done." In fact, Locke indicated that federal money was the most important element in the expansion of the textbook publishing industry in the early 1960s; he told the subcommittee, "My guess is that something like 30 or 40 percent of our increase in sales this year at the elementary and secondary level will be a result of . . . [federal] funds."[100] Publishers sought more federal funds when ATPI and Scott, Foresman's president, Darrel Peterson, told the House subcommittee, "I would like to offer strong endorsement for the Government's efforts to improve the quantity and quality of educational materials available to students in our schools. . . . These Federal investments in libraries and instructional materials in general are eminently worthwhile."[101]

Responding to federal actions, McGraw-Hill published texts depicting multiethnic urban settings. In 1965 the company issued the Skyline reading series for grades 2 through 4; it contained stories about people living in multiethnic cities. For example, one story, "The Hidden Lookout," was about Rosita's search for a place of her own in a city with millions of people. Eventually she builds a box house on an apartment roof. The Skyline series was only one of several related series published by McGraw-Hill in 1965. It also published that year the series Americans All, with specific titles "The American Negro," "Our Oriental Americans," "Our Citizens from the Caribbean," and "Latin Americans of the Southwest." In 1965 the company published a high school textbook focusing on civil liberties, *Heritage of Liberty.*[102]

Some publishers were accused of shady practices—namely publishing special editions for the southern market. For example, Harcourt, Brace & World issued some textbook editions that were free of multiracial pictures. In 1965 southern states approved sight-unseen new editions of the company's elementary school grammar and composition texts. Southern school districts complained about books containing illustrations of white and African American children playing together. Harcourt vice president Cameron S. Moseley explained to the House subcommittee, "There was an unofficial, implied threat to cancel all our contracts." Consequently the company printed a special edition that "de-integrated" the illustrations by showing only white children.[103]

In a similar situation, Scott, Foresman in 1965 published three new multiethnic series in reading, health, and social studies. "These books," company president Peterson stated, "which are multiethnic in character, present all kinds of children in natural situations and, where appropriate, contribute to the positive imagery of the diversified composition of American society."[104] However, Scott, Foresman continued printing its 1962 all-white edition of the reading series. When questioned about the all-white series, Peterson claimed that the company was not producing a series just for the South because both series were being sold throughout the country. All school districts in the country had a choice between the multiethnic and all-white versions. The increased cost of publishing two editions, he explained, was balanced by the bigger volume of business.[105]

Illustrations were the major difference between the all-white and the multi-ethnic editions. In describing his company's new urban social studies program, Ross Sackett, the executive vice president of Holt, Rinehart & Winston, emphasized that "dramatic photographs capture the interaction between individuals and groups in an actual multicultural, multiracial community."[106] Publishers described books by the number of multiracial illustrations. For example, Craig Senft, president of Silver Burdett, proudly described a new first-grade textbook, *Families and Their Needs,* as identifying "facts that determine just how the needs of families from a variety of physical environments and cultures are met. It so happens that of the 54 photographs illustrating some aspect of American families, 18 show minority group families or individuals." He emphasized, "We intentionally chose photographs that included minority groups to show as many ethnic and socioeconomic strains as were needed to portray the differences that give our society its variety and richness."[107]

The process of adding African Americans to pictures was sometimes referred to as giving textbook characters a "sunburn." There were several techniques involved in this process. One created "integrated" drawings by using different mechanical color separations or simply two colors. Simple black-and-white line drawings showed ethnically vague features that could be filled in by the reader's imagination. Photographs of integrated groups were frequently used in popular settings such as stores, playgrounds, neighborhood streets, and homes. Relying on changes in illustrations, textbook publishers could claim integration of a wide variety of texts, including those in science and mathematics. McGraw-Hill's representative Locke considered his company's elementary school science program Experiences in Science integrated because, in his words to the House subcommittee, "we have taken great care to include minority-group children in the illustrations."[108] He also included an arithmetic filmstrip because its frames included both white and nonwhite groups.

In the new Textbook Town, multiracial images resided in a world of social harmony. In textbook scenes, African Americans and whites worked and played together despite continued discrimination and racial violence in society. No longer invisible in textbooks, African Americans were catapulted to a world of equality and racial harmony. Integrated textbook stories also conveyed a message of racial harmony. While illustrations were the easiest and most popular method for publishers to integrate textbooks, multiracial and multiethnic stories were placed in readers. "Galumph," the opening story of Houghton Mifflin's second-grade reader, was about a cat who divided its time between an African American child, an Italian baker, a Hispanic girl, and a sick white child. Another story, "Traffic Policeman," was about a white child cooperating with an African American policeman. And "A Penny for a Jack Rabbit" was an unlikely tale—given the racial tension and housing discrimination in the society at that time—of suburban African American and white children playing together at a party.[109]

The setting and population of Textbook Town changed without disturbing the basic message of harmony and happiness. Political pressures and government funding added an urban dimension and a multiracial and multiethnic population to Textbook Town. Textbook Town now included apartment buildings as well as suburban bungalows, where happy groups of multiracial children played together.

History textbooks contained sections about slavery and the civil rights movement. But an integrated Textbook Town still seemed out of touch with the reality of racial violence and discrimination.

LIBERATING THE TEXTBOOK TOWN
HOUSEWIFE FOR MORE CONSUMPTION

As the color and setting changed in Textbook Town, images of women in text-books changed from being dependent housewives to portraying personal freedom outside the home. In its 1966 founding statement, the National Organization for Women (NOW) emphasized that public schools were "the key to effective partici-pation in today's economy . . . [and they should educate each woman] to her full potential of human ability."[110] Besides changes in public school textbooks that depicted women in a variety of occupations, schools encouraged women's sports and gender-integrated vocational courses. Media responded with movies and tele-vision programs depicting women as professionals and workers, and as both inde-pendent singles and divorcees. The public images found in the 1950s Textbook Town became a thing of the past.

New feminist images were used by the advertising industry. Maidenform bra ads showing political buttons on women's chests resulted in double-digit sales increases. The buttons proclaimed "No Means No," "My Body My Choice," and "Right to Life." The accompanying ad headline read, "Isn't it great when a woman's mind gets as much support as her body."[111] Nike increased its sales to women by 40 percent in the 1990s with ads designed to make women feel empowered.[112] In contrast to 1920s ads that promised women weight reduction by smoking, Virginia Slims's cigarette ads of the 1970s declared, "You've come a long way, baby!"[113]

Products originally marketed with dependent and submissive female images were now targeted to independent women. For instance, a 1988 ad for Revlon's Charlie perfume showed the backs of a woman and a man, both dressed in busi-ness clothes and carrying briefcases. The woman's hand was shown patting the man's buttock, and the caption read, "She's Very Charlie."[114] In the 1930s Tampax pioneered independent women's ads by showing a woman diving off a swimming board; the caption read, "In 1936, Tampax invented a little something for women who had things to do."[115] In 1990 Tampax ads associated the product with female political activism as represented by environmentalism. One ad featured a line in the Helen Reddy song "I Am Woman": "I am woman, hear me roar, in numbers too big to ignore." The ad opened with World War II newsreel clips of the Wom-en's Air Force, then moved to a 1990s scene emphasizing that Tampax was bio-degradable. In it a young woman romped in a field of green as a voice-over proclaimed, "We thought you'd feel good knowing that more women trust their bodies to the tampon that's very, very kind to the earth."[116]

The 1950s housewife was reborn in the 1990s as *Good Housekeeping* maga-zine's "New Traditionalist," described as a "reaffirmation of family values unmatched in recent history."[117] The ad language supporting the concept empha-sized the ever-present word *choice*. Regarding the issue of work versus staying home, Carl Casselman, creative director of Jordan, McGrath, Case & Taylor, said, "We're saying they have a choice."[118] Supposedly the Yankelovich market research firm discovered the New Traditionalist and described it as a combination of family values of the 1940s and 1950s and personal choice values of the 1960s and 1970s.[119] In ads, personal choice meant consumer choice.

The real meaning of the new educational feminism for advertising and consumerism was exemplified by Parker Pen's 1974 TV ad "Finishing School." Listed by Bernice Kanner as one of the top 100 TV ads, the ad opened in a British finishing school where obviously wealthy students were being prepared for a final lesson on "how to spend Daddy's lovely money." The teacher commanded, "Checkbooks open, girls. Pens at the ready." When a student pulled out an unacceptable pen, the teacher warned her that she shouldn't shop with a poor-quality pen. The teacher gave the girl a Parker Pen in white rolled gold and declared that it was easy to write a check while shopping with "a pen with style, a pen with élan. A Parker lady in white rolled gold. Words just seem to roll from its tip. Signatures just flow with a flourish. Now, then, altogether girls."[120] In this manner, the educational reforms promising greater independence for women merged in the advertising world with the consumer market.

CONCLUSION: THE COLD WAR
AND CIVIL RIGHTS

Since the first arrival of English colonists in the seventeenth century, debates about schooling have included discussions of culture, race, and gender. The civil rights movement of the 1950s and 1960s continued these earlier controversies with an increasingly global flavor. In the 1950s and 1960s civil rights struggles took place at the same time that the Cold War was generating a stream of educational policies designed to use schools to strengthen national defense. The civil rights movement contributed to the expansion of the federal role in education along with the launching of the War on Poverty programs described in Chapter 13.

Notes

1. "Universal Declaration of Human Rights" in *Basic Documents on Human Rights: Third Edition,* ed. Ian Brownlie (New York: Oxford University Press, 1992), p. 26.
2. "Convention against Discrimination in Education, 1960," ibid., p. 319.
3. Ibid., p.321.
4. *Brown et al. v. Board of Education of Topeka et al.* (1954), reprinted in Albert P. Blaustein and Clarence C. Ferguson Jr., *Desegregation and the Law* (New Brunswick, NJ: Rutgers University Press, 1957), pp. 273–282.
5. "The Effects of Segregation and the Consequences of Desegregation: A Social Science Statement," appendix to Appellants' Brief filed in the *School Segregation Cases* in the Supreme Court of the United States, October term, 1952, in *The Afro-Americans: Selected Documents,* eds. John Bracey, August Meier, and Elliott Rudwick (Boston: Allyn & Bacon, 1972), pp. 661–671.

6. Martin Luther King Jr., *Stride toward Freedom: The Montgomery Story* (New York: Harper & Row, 1958), p. 91.
7. Ibid., pp. 94–97.
8. Quoted by David Lewis, *King: A Critical Biography* (New York: Praeger, 1970), p. 171.
9. UN News Service, "United Nations Adopts Declaration on Rights of Indigenous Peoples." Retrieved on September 14, 2007, from http//www.un.org/news/printnews. asp?nid=23794.
10. United Nations General Assembly, *Report of the Human Rights Council: United Nations Declaration on the Rights of Indigenous Peoples, Article 14* (New York: United Nations, 2007), p. 6.
11. Quoted by Francis Paul Prucha, *The Indians in American Society: From Revolutionary War to the Present* (Berkeley: University of California Press, 1985), p. 70.
12. Ibid., pp. 72–75.
13. Quoted in ibid., p. 74.
14. Jon Reyhner and Jeanne Eder, *A History of Indian Education* (Billings: Eastern Montana College, 1989), pp. 125–126.
15. Ibid., p. 126.
16. Prucha, *Indians in American Society,* p. 82.
17. Quoted in ibid., p. 83.
18. Senate Committee on Labor and Public Welfare, *Indian Education: A National Tragedy—A National Challenge,* 91st Cong., 1st sess. (Washington, DC: U.S. Government Printing Office, 1969), p. 9.
19. Ibid., p. 106.
20. Reyhner and Eder, *History of Indian Education,* pp. 132–135.
21. "Indian Education Act, June 23, 1972," in *Documents of United States Indian Policy,* ed. Francis Paul Prucha (Lincoln: University of Nebraska Press, 1990), pp. 263–264.
22. "Student Rights and Due Process Procedures, October 11, 1974," ibid., p. 271.
23. "Indian Self-Determination and Education Assistance Act, January 4, 1975," ibid., p. 274.
24. "Tribally Controlled Schools Act of 1988," ibid., pp. 314–315.
25. "American Indian Religious Freedom, August 11, 1978," ibid., pp. 288–289.
26. Quoted in Reyhner and Eder, *History of Indian Education,* p. 128.
27. Bob H. Suzuki, "Education and the Socialization of Asian Americans: A Revisionist Analysis of the 'Model Minority' Thesis," in *The Asian American Educational Experience,* eds. Don T. Nakanishi and Tina Yamano Nishida (New York: Routledge, 1995), p. 12.
28. Ibid.
29. Robert G. Lee, *Orientals: Asian Americans in Popular Culture* (Philadelphia: Temple University Press, 1999).
30. Ibid., p. 160.
31. Harry Kitano, *Japanese Americans: The Evolution of a Subculture* (Englewood Cliffs, NJ: Prentice Hall, 1969); and William Peterson, *Japanese Americans: Oppression and Success* (New York: Random House, 1971).
32. Quoted by Ki-Taek Chun, "The Myth of Asian American Success and Its Educational Ramifications," in Nakanishi and Nishida, *Asian American Educational Experience,* p. 97.
33. Ibid., p. 98.
34. Suzuki, "Education and Socialization," p. 123.
35. Ibid.

36. Quoted in Joel Spring, *Intersections of Culture: Multicultural Education in the United States and the Global Economy* (New York: McGraw-Hill, 2000), p. 56.
37. Quoted in L. Ling-Chi Wang, "*Lau v. Nichols:* History of a Struggle for Equal and Quality Education," in Nakanishi and Nishida, *Asian American Educational Experience,* p. 58.
38. Quoted in ibid., p. 60.
39. Ibid.
40. Ibid., p. 59.
41. Ibid.
42. Quoted in ibid., p. 60.
43. Quoted in ibid., p. 61.
44. Reyhner and Eder, *History of Indian Education,* p. 128.
45. Ibid., pp. 127–129. Also see Gilbert G. Gonzalez, *Chicano Education in the Era of Segregation* (Philadelphia: Balch Institute Press, 1990), pp. 147–156.
46. Guadalupe San Miguel Jr., *"Let All of Them Take Heed": Mexican Americans and the Campaign for Educational Equality in Texas, 1910–1981* (Austin: University of Texas Press, 1987), pp. 123–124.
47. Ibid., p. 125.
48. Charles Wollenberg, *All Deliberate Speed: Segregation and Exclusion in California Schools, 1855–1975* (Berkeley: University of California Press, 1976), p. 134.
49. San Miguel, *"Let All of Them Take Heed,"* pp. 169–173.
50. Ibid., pp. 173–174.
51. Ibid., pp. 177–179.
52. Wollenberg, *All Deliberate Speed,* pp. 134–135.
53. San Miguel, *"Let All of Them Take Heed,"* p. 168.
54. Ibid.
55. Hugh Davis Graham, *Uncertain Triumph: Federal Educational Policy in the Kennedy and Johnson Years* (Chapel Hill: University of North Carolina Press, 1984), p. 155.
56. Ibid., p. 156.
57. James Crawford, "Bilingual Educators Seeking Strategies to Counter Attacks," *Education Week* 5, no. 28 (April 9, 1986), pp. 1, 9.
58. James Crawford, "Administration Panel Praises Bennett's Bilingual-Education Stance," *Education Week* 5, no. 28 (April 9, 1986), p. 9.
59. Rosalie Pedalino Porter, *Forked Tongue: The Politics of Bilingual Education* (New York: Basic Books, 1990), p. 188.
60. Quoted in ibid., pp. 219–220.
61. Ibid., pp. 210–211.
62. Quoted in ibid., p. 216.
63. See Joel Spring, *Globalization of Education: An Introduction* (New York: Routledge, 2009), pp. 177–200.
64. David Reimers, *Still the Golden Door: The Third World Comes to America* (New York: Columbia University Press, 1985).
65. See James Banks, "Multicultural Education: Historical Development, Dimensions, and Practice," *Review of Research in Education,* vol. 19, ed. Linda Darling-Hammond (Washington, DC: American Educational Research Association, 1993), pp. 3–50; and Sonia Nieto, *Affirming Diversity: The Sociopolitical Context of Multicultural Education* (White Plains, NY: Longman, 1992).
66. Banks, "Multicultural Education," p. 5.
67. For instance, see Molefi Kete Asante, *Afrocentricity* (Trenton, NJ: Africa World Press, 1988).

68. Kevin Brown, "Do African American Males Need Race and Gender Segregated Education? An Educator's Perspective and a Legal Perspective," in *The New Politics of Race and Gender,* ed. Catherine Marshall (Washington, DC: Falmer Press, 1993), p. 107.

69. Asante, *Afrocentricity,* pp. 4–5.

70. Ibid., p. 7.

71. Jawanza Kunjufu, *Countering the Conspiracy to Destroy Black Boys* (Chicago: African American Images, 1985), p. 32.

72. A good case study of this reaction in California and Texas is Catherine Cornbleth and Detter Waugh's *The Great Speckled Bird: Multicultural Politics and Education Policy Making* (New York: St. Martin's Press, 1995).

73. See Arthur M. Schlesinger Jr., *The Disuniting of America* (Knoxville, TN: Whittle Direct Books, 1991).

74. Ibid., p. 8.

75. Ibid., p. 80.

76. Thomas Sobol, "Revising the New York State Social Studies Curriculum," *Teachers College Record* 95, no. 1 (Winter 1993), p. 266.

77. Caroline B. Cody, Arthur Woodward, and David L. Elliot, "Race, Ideology and the Battle over the Curriculum," in Marshall, *New Politics of Race and Gender,* p. 55.

78. Schlesinger, *Disuniting of America,* p. 15.

79. Ibid., pp. 40–55.

80. Ibid., p. 43.

81. Ibid., p. 47.

82. "Convention of the Elimination of All Forms of Discrimination against Women" in *Basic Documents on Human Rights,* pp. 173–174.

83. "Feminist Chronicles," http://www.now.org: NOW's official account of its struggle for equal opportunity and equal educational opportunity for women.

84. "Convention of the Rights of the Child, 1989" in *Basic Documents on Human Rights,* p. 190.

85. David Neal and David Kirp, "The Allure of Legalization Reconsidered: The Case of Special Education," in *School Days, Rule Days: The Legalization and Regulation of Education,* eds. David Kirp and Donald Jensen (Philadelphia: Falmer Press, 1986), pp. 346–348.

86. Ibid., pp. 349–350.

87. "Convention of the Rights of the Child," in *Basic Documents on Human Rights,* ed. Ian Brownlie (Oxford: Oxford University Press, 1992), p. 187.

88. *The Negro in American History Textbooks: A Report of a Study of the Treatment of Negroes in American History Textbooks Used in Grades Five and Eight and in the High Schools of California's Public Schools* (Sacramento: California State Department of Education, 1964), p. 2.

89. "The Negro in American History Textbooks," reprinted in *Hearings before the Ad Hoc Subcommittee on De Facto School Segregation* of the Committee on Education and Labor, House of Representatives, 89th Cong., 2nd Sess., on Books for Schools and the Treatment of Minorities, August 23, 24, 30, 31, and September 1, 1966 (Washington, DC: U.S. Government Printing Office, 1966).

90. Erik Barnouw, *The Golden Web: A History of Broadcasting in the United States, 1933–1953* (New York: Oxford University Press, 1968), p. 297.

91. "The Negro in American History Textbooks," p. 770.

92. Ibid., pp. 770–771.

93. Ibid., p. 772.

94. Roy Wilkins, *Books for Schools and Treatment of Minorities: Introduction* (Washington, DC: National Association for the Advancement of Colored People, 1966), p. 1.
95. "Statement of Lerone Bennett," *Hearings before the Ad Hoc Subcommittee,* pp. 214–215.
96. Ibid., pp. 213–214.
97. "Statement of Austin J. McCaffrey, Executive Director, American Textbook Publishers Institute," ibid., p. 107.
98. Joel Roth, "Dick and Jane Make Some New Friends," *Book Production Industry* (June 1965), reprinted in *Hearings before the Ad Hoc Subcommittee,* p. 816.
99. "Statement of Austin J. McCaffrey," *Hearings before the Ad Hoc Subcommittee,* p. 114.
100. "Statement of Robert W. Locke, Senior Vice President, McGraw-Hill Book Co., Accompanied by Dr. Richard Smith, Senior Editor, Text-Film Division, McGraw-Hill Book Co.," *Hearings before the Ad Hoc Subcommittee,* p. 191.
101. "Statement of Darrel E. Peterson, President, Scott, Foresman & Co.," ibid., pp. 122–123.
102. "Integrating the Texts," *Newsweek,* March 7, 1966, reprinted in *Hearings before the Ad Hoc Subcommittee,* pp. 826–827.
103. A. Kent MacDougall, "Integrated Books-School Texts Stressing Negroes' Role in United States Arouse the South's Pre-Primers Show Mixed Scenes, Some Publishers Turn out Special Editions for Dixie," *The Wall Street Journal,* March 24, 1966, reprinted in *Hearings before the Ad Hoc Subcommittee,* p. 804.
104. "Statement of Darrel E. Peterson," *Hearings before the Ad Hoc Subcommittee,* p. 122.
105. Ibid., pp. 124–125.
106. "Statement of Ross Sackett, Executive Vice President, Holt, Rinehart & Winston, Inc.," *Hearings before the Ad Hoc Subcommittee,* pp. 217–273.
107. "Statement of Craig T. Senft, President, Silver Burdett Co., a Division of General Learning Corporation," ibid., pp. 115–117.
108. "Statement of Robert W. Locke," ibid., p. 191.
109. "Statement of G. M. Fenollosa, Vice President and Director, Houghton Mifflin Co., Boston, Mass.," *Hearings before the Ad Hoc Subcommittee,* p. 129.
110. "National Organization for Women's 1966 Statement of Purpose" (adopted at the Organizing Conference in Washington, DC, October 29, 1966), http://www.now.org.
111. Leslie Savan, *The Sponsored Life: Ads, TV, and American Culture* (Philadelphia: Temple University Press, 1994), p. 225.
112. Ibid., pp. 226–227.
113. Juliann Sivulka, *Soap, Sex, and Cigarettes: A Cultural History of American Advertising* (Belmont, CA: Wadsworth, 1998), p. 303.
114. Reproduced in ibid., p. 374.
115. Reproduced in Savan, *Sponsored Life,* p. 205.
116. Ibid., p. 205.
117. Ibid., p. 198.
118. Ibid., p. 198.
119. Ibid., p. 199.
120. Bernice Kanner, *The 100 Best TV Commercials . . . and Why They Worked* (New York: Random House, 1999), p. 41.

15

Globalizing the American School: From Nixon to Obama

The goals of American schooling became focused on global economic competition with the federal government's 1983 report *A Nation at Risk,* which blamed schools for weakness in America's ability to compete in global markets. The report opened with this alarming language: "Our nation is at risk. Our once unchallenged preeminence in commerce, industry, science and technological innovation is being overtaken by competitors throughout the world."[1] Dramatically claiming that the poor quality of U.S. schools threatened the future of the nation, the report stated, "If an unfriendly foreign power had attempted to impose on America the mediocre educational performance that exists today, we might well have viewed it as an act of war."[2] The report urged reform of the educational system: "If only to keep and improve on the slim competitive edge we still retain in world markets, we must rededicate ourselves to the reform of the educational system for the benefit of all."[3]

Concern about the role of schools in global economic competition continued into the administration of President Barack Obama. His 2008 campaign platform emphasized the relationship between schools and global economic goals. The 2008 Democratic platform stated under a section titled "A World Class Education for Every Child,"

> In the 21st century, where the most valuable skill is knowledge, countries that out-educate us today will out-compete us tomorrow. In the platform hearings, Americans made it clear that it is morally and economically unacceptable that our high schoolers continue to score lower on math and science tests than most other students in the world and continue to drop out at higher rates than their peers in other industrialized nations.[4]

The globalizing of American educational goals took place with an increasing cultural divide over education between the Republican and Democratic parties. However, this cultural divide between the parties was tempered by their mutual support of the educational goal of improving U.S. competitive advantages in global economic markets.

Both political parties supported testing, charter schools, and state curriculum standards while disagreeing on cultural issues. This cultural divide emerged from the 1960s as a result of U.S. Supreme Court rulings regarding school prayer and Bible reading, continued civil rights protests, and demonstrations against the Vietnam War. By the 2008 presidential election certain educational values were associated with each political party.

By 2009 Republicans were associated in the public mind with the following cultural values in schools:

- The teaching of traditional American values and patriotism.
- Protection of religious rights in schools.
- English-only classroom instruction.
- Character education as a means of ending poverty.
- Abstinence sex education.

In contrast, Democrats became associated with the following:

- Multicultural education.
- Bilingual education.
- Ending poverty through universal preschool education and equal education opportunity.
- Instruction in family planning.

In discussing the recent history of American schools, including the Obama administration, I will address the following topics:

- School prayer and Bible reading.
- The Nixon years: career education and busing.
- The growing importance of standardized testing and accountability.
- The development of school choice and charter schools.
- Educating for a consumer economy.
- The No Child Left Behind federal legislation.
- Obama, human capital, and preschools.
- The rise and fall of environmental education.

EDUCATION INTO THE TWENTY-FIRST CENTURY

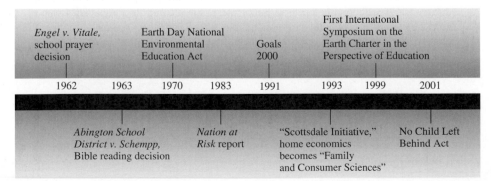

SCHOOL PRAYER AND BIBLE READING

The event that coalesced some Christian groups concerned with religious values in public schools was the 1962 U.S. Supreme Court decision in *Engel v. Vitale.* This court decision banned the official use of prayer in public schools. Since the founding of common schools in the early nineteenth century, many public schools had opened with prayer and a reading from the Protestant Bible. The 1962 decision denied the right of a public school system to conduct prayer services within school buildings during regular school hours. The case originated in New York when a local school system was granted the right by the New York Board of Regents to have a brief prayer said in each class at the beginning of the school day. The prayer, considered to be denominationally neutral, read, "Almighty God, we acknowledge our dependence upon Thee, and we beg Thy blessings upon us, our parents, our teachers and our country." The New York courts allowed local school systems to use this prayer.

When the U.S. Supreme Court ruled on the case, one of its major objections to the prayer was that a government official had written it. This violated the First Amendment—that is, it put the government directly in the business of establishing religion. The Court reviewed the early history of the United States, the struggle for religious freedom, and the ending of government support of churches. The writing of a school prayer, the Court argued, ran counter to the long tradition of separation of church and state.[5]

Given the purpose of common schools to protect a Protestant Anglo-American culture, the complaints of the religious right that the Supreme Court had undermined the moral and spiritual purposes of public schools were historically correct. The immediate reaction from the religious right to the school prayer decision was to claim that the U.S. Supreme Court had removed God from the schools. Adding to the fury of the response of the religious right was the 1963 U.S. Supreme Court decision in *Abington School District v. Schempp.* The issue in this case was a Pennsylvania law that permitted the reading of ten verses from the Bible at the opening of each public school day. Again the U.S. Supreme Court ruled that this violated the prohibition against linking church and state. Religious texts could be read, the Court argued, as part of an academic course such as literature or history.

For some Christians, potential solutions were the creation of a separate religious school system or the passage of a constitutional amendment allowing prayer in public schools. In the 1980s and 1990s Presidents Ronald Reagan and George H. W. Bush gained political support from the so-called religious right by supporting passage of a school prayer amendment to the U.S. Constitution and supporting legislation that would allow a choice, at public expense, between public and private schools.

Eventually, as I discuss later, this issue achieved some resolution with the 2001 signing of No Child Left Behind, which protects the religious freedom of students and teachers in its school prayer section. However, there was continued concern among some groups about the loss of religious values in schools, particularly after there were complaints about the "under God" phrase in the pledge of allegiance. The emotional feeling of those associated with what became known as the religious right or conservative Christian movement is expressed in a poem I received by e-mail from an anonymous source in 2009. The poem is inaccurate because students and teachers can still pray in clubs and other situations, and the pledge is still said throughout the country. Although it is inaccurate, the poem expresses one side of the cultural divide that exists over schools:

New School Prayer

Now I
sit me down in school
Where praying is
against the rule
For this great
nation under God
Finds mention of
Him very odd.
If
Scripture now the class recites,
It violates
the Bill of Rights.
And anytime my
head I bow
Becomes a Federal
matter now.
Our hair
can be purple, orange or green,
That's no
offense; it's a freedom scene.
The law is
specific, the law is precise.
Prayers
spoken aloud are a serious vice.
For
praying in a public hall
Might offend
someone with no faith at all.
In silence alone
we must meditate,
God's name is
prohibited by the state.
We're
allowed to cuss and dress like freaks,
And pierce our
noses, tongues and cheeks.
They've outlawed
guns, but FIRST the Bible.
To quote the Good
Book makes me liable.
We can

elect a pregnant Senior Queen,
And the "unwed
daddy," our Senior King.
It's
"inappropriate" to teach right from wrong,
We're
taught that such "judgments" do not belong.
We can
get our condoms and birth controls,
Study witchcraft,
vampires and totem poles.
But the Ten
Commandments are
not allowed,
No word of
God must reach this
crowd.
It's
scary here I must confess,
When chaos
reigns the school's a mess.
So, Lord, this
silent plea I make:
Should I be shot;
My soul please take!
Amen
If you
aren't ashamed to do this,
Please pass this
on.
Jesus
said,
"If
you are ashamed of me,
I will be
ashamed of you before my Father."
Not
ashamed. Pass this on.

THE NIXON YEARS: CAREER EDUCATION AND BUSING

The 1968 election of President Richard Nixon resulted in closer alignment of the schools with labor market needs and growing support of Republicans from white voters who disapproved of involuntary busing to achieve racial integration of schools. Besides the issue of school prayer and Bible reading, some Republican conservatives were distressed by the demands of African Americans, Native

Americans, and Mexican Americans for inclusion of their histories and cultures in the school curriculum, desegregation of schools, and turmoil on school campuses. Conservatives demanded an end to bilingual and multicultural education courses and restoration of an emphasis on Protestant Anglo-American culture.

In addition, there was a conservative reaction to student demonstrations that erupted on college and high school campuses in the late 1960s. The demonstrations occurred mainly in reaction to the Vietnam War and in support of the civil rights movement. As the demonstrations escalated, students began to question many institutions and values of American life. Demands were made for greater freedom of expression and more equality in the distribution of wealth. Universities and public schools were attacked as institutions of oppression and racism. Alternative schools began to appear in both private and public educational systems.

Richard Nixon was elected president on a ticket promising to solve the problem of the Vietnam War and restore law and order to American campuses. Restoring law and order was an important part of Nixon's presidential campaigns in 1968 and 1972. Part of Nixon's plan to restore law and order to campuses was career education. In 1971 and 1972 Sidney Marland Jr., Nixon's commissioner of education, began to earmark discretionary funds provided by Congress to the Office of Education for the development of career education projects. Marland's method of using discretionary funds turned career education into a reform movement originating at the top of the political structure of education. By 1972–1973, Marland was able to announce that in the first year of this program, 750,000 young people had participated.

Marland believed that career education was the answer to student rebellion, delinquency, and unemployment. In his first annual report to Congress, in 1971, he argued that disenchantment among youth existed because education did not lead to career opportunities. According to Marland, the villain was general education programs that lacked specific goals and were not linked to the job market. Marland argued that education should be meaningful; by *meaningful* he meant "related to a career objective." He stated, "When we use the word 'meaningful,' we imply a strong obligation that our young people complete the first 12 grades in such a fashion that they are ready either to enter into some form of higher education or to proceed immediately into satisfying and appropriate employment." This, of course, was a restatement of the traditional goal of the comprehensive high school; but Marland considered the primary weakness of the comprehensive high school to be its general education programs, which were not directly related to entry into either the job market or higher education. "The emergence of the comprehensive high school, properly defined and implemented, carries the ultimate solution."[6]

Marland believed that students and schools were in a state of turmoil because the schools had not achieved the goal of sorting students for the labor market. In his first report to Congress, he stated, "We must eliminate anything in our curriculum that is unresponsive to either of these goals [higher education and employment], particularly the high school anachronism called 'the general curriculum,' a false compromise between college preparatory curriculum and realistic career development."[7] For Marland, all elements of school life needed to be justified by their contribution to career development. In the words of Marland's associate commissioner, "The fundamental conception of career education is that all educational experiences, curriculum, instruction, and counseling should be geared to preparing each individual for a life of economic independence, personal fulfillment, and an appreciation for the dignity of work."[8] This meant a complete alignment between the job market and the public schools. Marland believed career education offered one solution "to some of our more serious social and economic problems, including high unemployment and the attendant problems of disaffection and drug excess among the young."[9]

Career education was unique in its attempt to make vocational guidance a part of the school academic program and to begin the program in the early grades. During the elementary and junior high school years, career education was to acquaint students with the world of work and the varieties of occupations by relating work and jobs to the subject matter of the curriculum. After study and preparation for an occupational choice in these early grades, the high school student was to begin preparing for entry into either an occupation or higher education. Advocates of career education also believed that higher education should be organized around this model. The real hope for higher education, Marland believed, was the community college. He argued that the community college should be viewed not as merely a "large anteroom for the four-year institutions"[10] but as a unique institution of higher learning whose developing philosophy was based on the concept of career education. Close ties with local businesses would make it possible for the community college to gear its programs to the needs of the labor market.

In addition to supporting career education, the Republican Party stressed its opposition to involuntary busing of students to end school segregation. President Nixon submitted legislation to Congress to end court-ordered busing. The 1972 Republican platform reminded the public, "Months ago President Nixon sent Congress a two-part comprehensive proposal on school busing. The first is the Student Transportation Moratorium Act of 1972—legislation to halt immediately all further court-ordered busing and give Congress time to devise permanent new arrangements for assuring desegregated, quality education."[11] The Republican platform declared, "We are irrevocably opposed to busing for racial balance. Such busing fails its stated objective—improved learning opportunities—while it achieves results no one wants—division within communities and hostility between classes and races. *We regard it as unnecessary, counter-productive and wrong* [author's emphasis]."[12]

In contrast, Democrats held open the option of involuntary school busing to end school segregation. Democrats would lose part of their white voters to Republicans, particularly in southern states, over this issue. Democrats supported busing as one option to achieve integration. The 1972 Democratic platform declared,

> We support the goal of desegregation as a means to achieve equal access to quality education for all our children. There are many ways to desegregate schools: School attendance lines may be redrawn; schools may be paired; larger physical facilities may be built to serve larger, more diverse enrollments; magnet schools or educational parks may be used.
>
> *Transportation of students is another tool to accomplish desegregation. It must continue to be available according to Supreme Court decisions to eliminate legally imposed segregation and improve the quality of education for all children* [author's emphasis].[13]

The Nixon administration's promotion of career education committed the schools to educating students for jobs. "Go to school to get a job" would become the major justification for supporting the school system. In addition, the issue of school busing increased the growing cultural divide between political parties and segments of the American population.

ACCOUNTABILITY AND STANDARDIZED TESTING

By the time of the Obama administration in the twenty-first century, accountability and standardized testing dominated the educational system. The concept of accountability developed during a debate over who should control public schools.

Similar to administrative progressives in the early twentieth century who argued for control by experts, the proponents of accountability considered education an arena for professional decision making. Control by experts was an important theme of the book that sparked the accountability movement. Leon Lessinger's *Every Kid a Winner: Accountability in Education* considered the community control movement a threat to the quality of education.[14] Lessinger used the model of the hospital to attack the concept of democratic control. He argued that in a hospital, patients and the community in general do not and should not participate directly in decisions regarding medical treatment or surgery because these areas of decision making require expert knowledge and training. For Lessinger, the idea of democratic control in surgery was ludicrous and dangerous to the patient. In his opinion, users of medical services might complain, but decisions about how to deal with the complaint should remain in the hands of medical experts.

Lessinger felt that this model applies to education. Modern schooling, he maintained, is based on professional knowledge gained through research and study. The average member of the community does not have the training necessary to make correct educational decisions. Like the hospital clientele, the community has the right to complain but does not have the right or the knowledge to make decisions regarding the resolution of complaints. Only the educational expert should be entrusted with decision-making power.

Even with his reliance on experts, Lessinger recognized that in a democratic society schools must be responsive to the public. He felt this responsiveness could be achieved by the schools reporting their accomplishments and failures to the public. This public accounting of the results of schooling was the heart of the accountability movement. Lessinger envisioned the creation of a national educational accounting firm operated by educational engineers who would measure educational results by achievement tests and report the results to the public. He assumed these results would give the public expert data that could be used to express approval or criticism of school system accomplishments.

As the accountability movement spread in the early 1970s, states and local communities began to require schools to annually publish standardized test scores. The use of test scores to measure school success kept power in the hands of educational experts. In the schools, students found themselves taking an increasing number of achievement tests to satisfy the requirements of accountability. One result was that testing, or measurement, was restored to a central place in the educational process. Accompanying this rebirth of interest in standardized testing was an increasing emphasis on behaviorism and on teaching with specific behavioral objectives.

The accountability movement's emphasis on testing and instruction according to specific behavioral objectives fit the pattern of traditional approaches to classroom instruction. While these practices for reform of American schools were being advocated, a more progressive approach to classroom organization, called the "open classroom," was also being pushed. The differences between these approaches to instruction highlight the continuing debate about instruction. In addition, as I will discuss later in this chapter, the creation of standardized achievement tests became a central feature of national educational policy in the early 1990s.

GLOBAL EDUCATIONAL GOALS: NATIONAL STANDARDS, CHOICE, AND SAVAGE INEQUALITIES

It was during the Reagan years from 1980 to 1988 that American schools were committed to the goal of improving the nation's ability to compete in world markets by educating a globally competitive workforce. In addition, during the Reagan administration the cultural divide increased. President Ronald Reagan appealed to religious and political conservatives by supporting school prayer, educational choice, and a restoration of moral values in the public schools. Also, he promised to limit federal involvement in education. And reacting to the culture wars, he tried to stem the tide of federal support for bilingual education. The actual educational program offered by the Republican Party in 1980 and 1984 included abolishing the Department of Education, amending the Constitution to allow prayer in public schools, and providing choice of public and private schools through tuition tax credits.

During the 1980 and 1984 presidential elections, each political party appealed to a particular educational constituency. The Democrats appealed to the two major teachers' unions, members of dominated cultures, and liberals favoring increased federal aid to local schools. Republicans appealed to the religious right and conservatives. These clear differences between the two parties meant that education was a national issue with clearly defined national constituencies.

One of the high points in the Reagan administration was the issuance, in 1983, of a report, *A Nation at Risk,* which blamed public schools for America's difficulties in competing with Japan and West Germany in world markets. The allegedly poor academic quality of American public schools was seen as the cause of productivity rates lower than those of Japan and West Germany, as well as of the declining U.S. lead in technological development. A similar argument had been used earlier in the twentieth century to justify federal aid to vocational education. At that time, the major international competitor was Germany, and the American school system was compared unfavorably with the German school system. The difference between the earlier plea for vocational education and the reform proposals in *A Nation at Risk* is that the latter did not call for increased federal aid. *A Nation at Risk* exhorted states and local communities to increase academic standards, improve the quality of teachers, and reform the curriculum.

A Nation at Risk put the Reagan administration into an interesting political situation. On one hand, blaming the public schools for international economic problems appealed to members of the Republican constituency who were highly critical of the workings of schools. On the other hand, the report could not call for federal intervention to aid the schools because of Republican promises to decrease federal involvement in education. Finally, the Reagan administration placed the issue of schooling on a national political agenda by linking it to national trade problems. In other words, the net effect of Republican actions was to ensure that education would remain a national issue.

A major strategy of the Republican administration was to increase the role of states in education as the federal role declined. The role of state governments in education had increased with federal legislation in the 1960s. Most federal money was channeled through state departments of education, and funds were provided to increase the administrative staff at the state level. Thus the actions of the Reagan administration reinforced existing trends in the distribution of political power. As power over education shifted back and forth between state and federal agencies, the power of local school boards over education declined.

Republicans also advocated closer ties between big business and public schools. An example of this argument was the 1983 report of the Task Force on Education for Economic Growth, *Action for Excellence.* The report called for closer relationships between American business and the schools. The introduction to the report states, "We believe especially that businesses, in their role as employers, should be much more deeply involved in the process of setting goals for education in America and in helping our schools to reach those goals." One of the "action recommendations" of the report states, "Business leaders should establish partnerships with schools." And in bold type in the section titled "Education and Growth," the report proclaims, "If the business community gets more involved in both the design and the delivery of education, we are going to become more competitive as an economy." The call for greater participation of the business community in establishing the goals of public schools was couched in the traditional language of the promise of American schooling. Like the proclamations of school reformers and public leaders in the nineteenth century, the report labeled education as a panacea for society's ills: "It is the thesis of this report that our future success as a nation—our national defense, our social stability and well-being and our national prosperity—will depend on our ability to improve education and training for millions of individual citizens."[15]

With the election of President George H. W. Bush in 1988, the contribution of public schools to the economy and business continued to be emphasized. Receiving support from the religious right, Bush also advocated school prayer and some form of educational choice. With regard to the economic goals of education, Bush, on April 18, 1991, unveiled Goals 2000—plans for achieving national education goals by the year 2000. Similar to the rhetoric of the Reagan administration, these plans were presented as necessary for improving the ability of U.S. companies to compete in international markets. Administration officials admitted that the plans were also designed to ward off criticism during the 1992 election campaign that Bush had no domestic agenda.[16]

The Bush administration proposed creating voluntary "American Achievement Tests" for grades 4, 8, and 12. The tests would cover five core subjects, and students would be measured by "world-class standards." To accomplish this goal, the Bush administration, in cooperation with Congress and the National Governors Association, created the National Council on Education Standards and Testing (NCEST).

The election of President Bill Clinton in 1992 did not substantially change the direction of educational policies. Clinton did not try to appeal to the religious right by promising school prayer and financial support of choice between public and private schools, but he did support Bush's Goals 2000 program. On March 31, 1994, Clinton signed the Goals 2000 Educate America Act. The legislation was the culmination of proposals Bush had initiated five years earlier when Clinton was governor of Arkansas.[17] At the time, Clinton, as governor of Arkansas, and his future secretary of education, Richard Riley, former governor of South Carolina, were active in formulating the educational goals of the National Governors Association. Those goals eventually became part of the Goals 2000 Educate America Act,[18] which again linked education to the needs of big business by emphasizing the importance of educating workers for competition in international trade. For the Clinton administration, the Goals 2000 Educate America Act was one part of a plan for lifelong learning. The plan included funding of preschool and adult education. Clinton's preschool efforts focused on increased funding for Head Start programs. Another part of the program focused on training the workforce to meet new economic demands.[19] Influenced by his secretary of labor, Robert Reich, President Clinton gave particular attention to improving the skills of the general workforce. Also, Clinton believed the children of the poor required a greater opportunity to receive a quality education and attend college.

In summary, the major contribution of the Reagan, Bush, and Clinton administrations was the creation of closer ties between the needs of business and the public schools. The task of schooling was defined as improving American competitiveness in world markets and a preparation for work. In many ways it could be argued that this period represented the triumph of the social efficiency and human capital arguments of the early twentieth century.

THE END OF THE COMMON SCHOOL: CHOICE, PRIVATIZATION, AND CHARTER SCHOOLS

Choice, privatization, charter schools, and multicultural education put the final nail in the coffin of the common school. Choice, privatization of schools, and charter schools were promoted as a key to improving education and America's competitive advantage in world markets. During the Reagan, Bush, and Clinton administrations religious conservatives' support of school choice began to attract a wide audience ranging from liberals to profit-making educational corporations. The basic idea of choice runs counter to the common school ideal of having all children receive a common education that inculcates a common culture and common moral and political values.

There were important differences in choice plans. One plan, often supported by the religious right, was providing public support for the choice between public and private schools. The other plan limited choice to schools within a school district or to schools throughout the state. In 1990 the choice idea was supported by the findings of two political scientists, John Chubb and Terry Moe. In their book *Politics, Markets and America's Schools,* they argued that a major hindrance to student achievement is the existence of large bureaucracies that impose their will on local schools. Their criticism of the educational bureaucracy reflected conservative complaints since the 1930s. Chubb and Moe maintained that bureaucracies work against the basic requirements of effective school organizations by imposing goals, structures, and requirements. Bureaucracies, according to Chubb and Moe, do not allow principals and teachers to exercise their professional expertise and judgment but, instead, deny them the flexibility they need to work effectively together to ensure student achievement. Chubb and Moe concluded that schools controlled by competition in a free market have less bureaucracy and, consequently, promote student achievement.[20]

Choice plans were also supported by liberals concerned about the education of children from low-income homes. According to many liberals, public schools had failed these students. In response to this argument, the Wisconsin state legislature in 1990 passed a bill allowing students whose parents' income was less than 75 percent of the poverty level established by the federal government to choose a nonsectarian, private school. Wisconsin governor Tommy Thompson argued, "Choice gives poor students the ability to select the best school that they possibly can. The plan allows for choice and competition, and I believe competition will make both the public and private schools that much stronger."[21]

In the 1990s, in response to pressures from the religious right, conservatives, and liberals, state and local school boards adopted choice plans. Minnesota was one of eight states in 1992 allowing choice between public schools. The other states were Arkansas, Idaho, Iowa, Nebraska, Ohio, Utah, and Washington. In the fall of 1992, the New York City Board of Education, one of the largest school systems in the country, unanimously adopted a plan that would allow parents to choose any public school in the system.[22]

In addition to choice plans, privatization and charter schools contributed to the demise of the common school. Are charter schools a spin-off of the privatization movement? Privatization involves private companies operating public schools. "Governors William Weld of Massachusetts and Ruddy Roemer of Colorado," wrote *New York* magazine reporter James Traub, "contacted [Benno] Schmidt in the fall 1992 to say that they would like to find a way to bring Edison into the public schools in their states. Both states went on to pass 'charter school' laws that permit states and school systems to award contracts to . . . private contractors."[23]

Charter schools eventually received strong support in 2009 from President Obama's administration. Charter school legislation enables the development of privatized schools. A private company, a group of teachers, or parents can petition a local school board or state agency to establish a public school or create a special program in an existing public school. Once the charter school is approved, it operates in a semi-autonomous fashion and receives public funds for its support. The basic goal is to create public schools that can act with a certain degree of independence from local and state educational bureaucracies. It is hoped that, freed from bureaucratic control, charter schools will develop and maintain unique and innovative alternatives to traditional public schools.

By 1994 eight states—California, Colorado, Georgia, Massachusetts, Michigan, Minnesota, New Mexico, and Wisconsin—had charter school laws, and fourteen other state legislatures were considering charter school bills. The bills in these various states differed markedly in their definitions of *charter school*. Some states limited conversion to charter schools to existing public schools. Some gave primary responsibility for the creation of charter schools to local school boards. In Massachusetts, local boards were bypassed.[24]

The creation of choice plans, the coming of privatization, and the development of charter schools reflected the general breakdown of the common school ideal of unifying the nation around Protestant Anglo-American culture. Ironically, political and religious conservatives supported these new educational movements because they believed that U.S. Supreme Court rulings on school prayer and Bible reading, and the rise of multicultural education, had shattered the dominance of Protestant Anglo-American culture in public schools. Choice, privatization, and charter schools held out the promise to conservatives and the religious right of allowing the creation of schools that would reflect their traditional values. Of course, these same educational innovations allowed dominant cultures to send their children to schools reflecting their cultural backgrounds. In contrast, liberals could jump on the bandwagon of choice, privatization, and charter schools because of the possibility of having public schools serve the interests of children from low-income groups.

EDUCATING FOR THE CONSUMER ECONOMY

The global economy of the twentieth and twenty-first centuries was a consumer economy dependent on constant purchasing and manufacturing of consumer items. Store chains and brand names became globalized. Travelers around the world

The Reverend Graham H. Walworth, rector of Trinity Episcopal Church in the Long Island community of Northport, looks at the sign he posted on his outdoor bulletin board protesting the Supreme Court's decision banning prayer in New York public schools.
© *Bettmann/Corbis*

could now shop in the same franchised stores and buy the same brands in any country. Fast-food chains spread from America around the world.

As schools geared up to educate workers for the global economy, they became sites for training future consumers. Equality of opportunity now meant equal opportunity to consume. Schools trained future consumers by becoming willing sites for commercial advertising and converting traditional home economics courses into consumer sciences courses. In addition, commercial enterprises such as fast-food chains invaded the school curriculum. Alex Molnar, author of the best-selling book *Giving Kids the Business: The Commercialization of America's Schools* and head of the University of Wisconsin's Center for the Analysis of Commercialism in Education, detailed the extremes that companies, such as Coca-Cola and PepsiCo, use to advertise and sell their products in schools.[25] On September 14, 2000, the U.S. General Accounting Office released a report on the commercialization of U.S. schools. The report stated,

> In-school marketing has become a growing industry. Some marketing professionals are increasingly targeting children in schools, companies are becoming known for their success in negotiating contracts between school districts and beverage companies, and both educators and corporate managers are attending conferences to learn how to increase revenue from in-school marketing for their schools and companies.[26]

The General Accounting Office found the following:

- About 25 percent of the nation's middle schools and high schools were showing Channel One, a broadcast of news features and commercials.
- Two hundred school districts signed exclusive contracts with soft-drink companies to sell their beverages in schools.
- Students using computers in classrooms were being offered incentives to enter personal data—names, addresses, information about personal habits—which was then sold to advertisers.[27]

Other examples abound, including, as I discuss later, the involvement of the fast-food industry in education. In *Education and Commercialization: Raising Awareness and Making Wise Decisions,* Lynn Schrum provided other instances of advertising in schools:

- Eli Lilly representatives discussed Prozac with high school students in Washington, DC.
- Procter & Gamble sponsored oral hygiene classes in elementary school in return for distributing samples of Crest.
- The National Soft Drink Association provided a poster titled "Soft Drinks and Nutrition."
- The M&M candy company declared the nutritional value in its products.
- McGraw-Hill's math book, *Mathematics: Applications and Connections,* used by sixth-, seventh-, and eighth-grade students in at least sixteen states, inserted products such as Barbie dolls, Big Macs, and Oreo cookies into math problems. For example, "Will is saving his allowance to buy a pair of Nike shoes that cost $68.25. If Will earns $3.25 per week, how many weeks will Will need to save?"[28]

Symbolizing the change to educating for a consumer economy was the new emphasis in home economics on consumer services. In 1993, while floating candles in a hotel pool to symbolize the new spirit of home economics, home economics leaders adopted the "Scottsdale Initiative" and changed the field's name to "Family and Consumer Sciences." The term *consumer* in the new name "was viewed not as a subject matter or content area but as recognition that individuals are both family members and consumers."[29] The Scottsdale Initiative officially recognized students as consumers to be trained for future consumption. Translated into middle and high school family and consumer sciences courses, the outcome goal for students was "Functioning effectively as providers and consumers of goods and services."[30] Besides being a site for advertising and marketing, schools were now engaged in the specific task of teaching consumerism and careers in consumer industries.

The historic role of home economics courses was transformed from teaching women to be scientific producers of food and clothing in the home to preparation for almost complete reliance on consumer products and for work in the food and textile industries. Of course home economics courses had always taught how to be a good shopper through household management of the budget. What was different was the abandonment of home production for complete reliance on product consumption. Despite this change, some patterns remained the same. For instance, fashion shows and learning to shop wisely for ready-to-wear clothes were regular features of 1920s home economics courses. In the 1990s this instruction continued under the title "Apparel Shopping on the Web."[31]

In 1995 the professional organization for middle and secondary school teachers, the Home Economics Education Association, changed its name to "Family and Consumer Sciences Education Association." The newly named organization issued national standards for family and consumer sciences courses.[32] In the early twentieth century, home economics courses focused on teaching cooking, sewing, and household management to girls. The new national standards were directed at teaching both girls and boys career, family, and consumer roles. Cooking classes were replaced with the study of "careers in food production and services" and "careers in food science, dietetics, and nutrition." In the early days, the goals of cooking classes for young women were to Americanize immigrants, reform home diets, and turn housewives into scientific workers. The new standards were geared to training workers to work in industries that produced processed and packaged foods. Unlike early sewing instruction, the new standards were strictly geared to careers in the ready-to-wear and related industries or, in the words of the national standards, "careers in textiles and apparels." Whereas early home economics courses sometimes focused on family leisure activities, the new standards focused on commodified forms of leisure by introducing students to "careers in hospitality, tourism, and recreation." And household management became a study of "careers in housing, interiors, and furnishings."[33]

Under the national standard for "Consumer and Family Resources" the goal was "Demonstrate management of individual and family resources including food, clothing, shelter, health care, recreation, and transportation."[34] This goal simply means learning to budget for the purchase of these items through reasonable use of consumer credit.

The commitment of the new Family and Consumer Sciences to consumerism was highlighted in the national standards' goal: "Analyze interrelationship between the economic system and consumer actions."[35] It suggested that the economy should be examined from the standpoint of consumer actions, such as consumer confidence and spending. For instance, students would learn why retailers and economists worry about holiday purchases, future consumer spending, and measures of consumer confidence. This view of the economy supported public attitudes that measure the success of a Christmas season by the amount of consumer spending.

The national standards also reinforced the importance of consumerism in students' minds by informing them of "careers in consumer services." The term *consumer services* suggests activities directly supporting a consumer-based economy. Students were to "Demonstrate skills needed for product development, testing, and presentation."[36] Also under "consumer services" was "developing a long-term financial management plan." Reflecting the critical edge in family and consumer sciences courses, "consumer services" also included analyzing "consumer advocacy" and "resource consumption for conservation and waste management practices."

Fast-food franchises continued the development of the American cuisine started in the 1890s when home economists embraced Jell-O and packaged and prepared foods and attempted to standardize American tastes in school cafeterias and hospital kitchens. Most franchises were born in the 1950s when the automobile and suburban living created a mobile population looking for a quick meal. To a certain extent, fast food realized home economist Ellen Richard's dream of community kitchens and convenience food that freed women from cooking.

Fast food's involvement in education was a logical outgrowth of efforts by fast-food restaurants, similar to those of Disney, to project an impression of being friendly and clean places for children and families to eat. Also, educational involvement served as a public relations method to create a positive community image. Beginning shortly before the opening of Disneyland, themed fast-food designs and logos identified establishments to passing motorists to attract children and families. For instance, McDonald's, founded in 1953, changed the "M" representing the name McDonald's into the golden arches symbol now recognized around the world. In 1960 a Washington, DC, McDonald's restaurant sponsored the children's television program *Bozo's Circus,* and Bozo appeared at the restaurant, attracting large crowds. When the television program was canceled, an ad agency created a new clown called Ronald McDonald.[37] Adding to the kid-friendly image created by Ronald McDonald was the introduction of indoor play areas for children. With its own line of children's videos, McDonald's wedded advertising and entertainment in one video starring Ronald McDonald, *The Wacky Adventures of Ronald McDonald.*[38] In the early twenty-first century, it was estimated that at least once a month 90 percent of U.S. children between the ages of three and nine visited a McDonald's restaurant.[39]

McDonald's rival Burger King was founded in Daytona, Florida, in 1953 by Keith Cramer after he visited and studied the newly opened McDonald's in California.[40] Like McDonald's, Burger King used themed architecture including playgrounds. Also, Burger King exploited media connections. A 2002 marketing agreement with DreamWorks film studio let Burger King distribute Virtual Vision Scopes for the studio's showing of *Spirit: Stallion of the Cimarron.* In another media connection, Burger King had an agreement with the Nickelodeon TV network to cooperate in reviewing and showing television videos submitted by children.[41]

Burger King surpassed McDonald's educational and community efforts by operating Burger King Academies and was involved in welfare reform. Jumping on the charter school bandwagon, Burger King, in cooperation with Communities in Schools Inc. (CIS), opened twenty-four CIS/Burger King Academies across the nation for students facing problems of "poor school attendance, illiteracy, teen pregnancy, drug and alcohol abuse, school violence, and lack of self-esteem."[42] Bearing the appellation "Burger King Scholars," needy students could attend college or postsecondary vocational schools with scholarships from the Burger King/ Lahore Foundation's North American Scholarship Program, which in 2001 provided $1,082,000 in awards.[43]

The global corporation most involved in education was YUM Brands, which over the years acquired Taco Bell, A&W, KFC, Long John Silver's, and Pizza Hut. When YUM Brands acquired A&W and Long John Silver's in 2002, the company proudly announced, "The acquisition allows us to accelerate our multibranding strategy and . . . to be expanded international leaders . . . in chicken, pizza, Mexican and seafood." The company's motto was this: "Our passion is to put YUM on our customer's faces all over the world."[44] YUM Brands became a leader in the construction and operation of themed environments.

Three of the five YUM franchises—Taco Bell, Pizza Hut, and KFC—were directly involved in educational activities. In 1999 for the first time, all three were linked to a media event when they gained exclusive rights as global restaurant partners for *Star Wars Episode I*.[45] Taco Bell's educational projects overshadowed those of McDonald's. Taco Bell began in the same year and in the same town as McDonald's when Glen Bell opened a Bell Taco stand in San Bernardino, California. Bell developed a assembly line method for making tacos.[46] More recently, as sponsor of the Discovery Science Center in Santa Ana, California, Taco Bell provided science programs geared to California State Science Content Standards. One program was "Dynamic Earth"; another was "Astronomy—Avoiding Misconceptions." Both programs were made in cooperation with NASA and were provided free to teachers. Also free were science exhibits and a 3D (three-dimensional) theater with science shows. In cooperation with the Bank of America, the Discovery Center provided a free open house to teachers along with free field trips for students.[47] Taco Bell Foundation, in partnership with Boys and Girls Clubs of America, operated TEENSupreme programs throughout the United States and on U.S. military installations abroad. According to an official Taco Bell statement, the programs were "designed to develop leadership skills, values, and a voice among our nation's youth to prepare them to become successful adults and productive leaders." To build public awareness of its sponsorship of TEENSupreme, Taco Bell provided in-store canisters so patrons could donate to support the program.[48]

In 1988 President Reagan awarded Pizza Hut president Art Gunter a Private Initiative Citation for Pizza Hut's national reading incentive program, "Book It!"[49] The first Pizza Hut restaurant opened in 1958 in Wichita, Kansas, and the first Pizza Hut franchise opened in Topeka the following year. In 1965 Pizza Hut's first TV commercial featured the musical jingle "Putt-Putt to Pizza Hut." In 1967 the company gained global recognition for baking the world's largest pizza (6 feet in diameter). In 1975 it promoted itself through product placement in the movie *The Bad News Bears.*[50] In 1982 it linked itself to the movie *ET* by distributing ET glasses at its franchises.

Pizza Hut's "Book It!" program began in 1984 with an enrollment of 200,000 elementary school students across the nation. By the 1998–1999 school year, 22 million children in 895,000 classrooms were enrolled. The program served as a public relations project and as an advertising gimmick and indirectly sold extra pizzas to parents of student winners. (Remember that advertisers in the early twentieth century had suggested that it is important to implant brand names in children to establish adult preferences.) Children who achieved monthly reading goals were rewarded with a Personal Pan Pizza and a button from the manager of the local Pizza Hut restaurant. Achieving six monthly goals earned a child an All-Star Medallion at a local Pizza Hut restaurant. In 1998 the "Book It! Beginners Program" started for preschool and kindergarten students with a monthly Personal Pan Pizza award. In 1999 this beginners program was active in 20,000 kindergarten classrooms and day care centers around the country.[51]

YUM Brands' Kentucky Fried Chicken (KFC) franchises focused on early childhood education. The original KFC started in 1930 when Harland Sanders began cooking and serving food at his service station in Corbin, Kentucky. Developing his Kentucky fried chicken recipe using a "secret blend" of herbs and spices, he moved from his service station to a restaurant across the street. In 1935 Kentucky's governor Ruby Laffoon officially named Harland Sanders a "Kentucky Colonel" for his contribution to the state's cuisine.[52]

KFC entered education in a big way via the day care business for infants and preschool children. On August 4, 2001, the first Colonel's Kids Child Care Center opened in Columbus Junction, Iowa. The center initially offered for children from two weeks to twelve years old services ranging from infant care, day care, crisis care, and before- and after-school care, to summer recreational programs.[53] The name of the program was "The Colonel's Kids Charity." A promotion piece for the program asked this question: "Did you know more than 29 million children have no place to go while their parents work?"[54] KFC then defined the child care crisis in the following words:

> There is a child care crisis in the U.S. Every state reports shortages in child care. Consider this:
>
> - Nearly two-thirds of parents (65 percent) juggle multiple child care arrangements.
> - More than 15 million people work during nontraditional hours and are in need of child care.
> - Nine out of ten adults agree that finding affordable quality child care is difficult for most American families.

As they spread around the world, fast-food chains contributed, along with the new home economics focused on family and consumer sciences, to education of the global consumer citizen. Coupled with an emphasis on education for the global labor market, schools were now to educate worker–consumer citizens.

EDUCATION FOR GLOBAL WORK AND CONSUMPTION

Sparked by concerns of religious conservatives and about America's place in the global economy, Congress reauthorized in 2001, with support from both Democrats and Republicans, Title I of the 1965 Elementary and Secondary Education Act (ESEA) as the now famous law called No Child Left Behind. Essentially, among other things, this legislation nationalized federal accountability standards for the purpose of educating global workers. In addition, the legislation addressed conservative religious issues including school prayer, family planning, and homosexuality.

As discussed in Chapter 13, the goal of the 1965 legislation was to eliminate poverty in the United States by providing compensatory education programs. The programs under the 1965 legislation were designed to serve, in the language of the 1960s, "culturally disadvantaged" students. These programs were to achieve equal educational opportunity for all students.

No Child Left Behind dramatically changed the coverage of the 1965 legislation from a specified group of students needing help to all students in all public schools. All public school students were required to conform to federal requirements. In other words, legislation that was originally intended for only a select number of students now became a law affecting all students. This represented a major change in the governance of public schools.

To provide equal educational opportunity, the law required states to establish uniform standards and tests for all public schools. To ensure that children were not trapped in schools considered to be failing because of student test scores, the law required failing schools to improve; and if these schools were unable to improve, they were to be completely restructured. While the failing schools were being improved, students were given the option of choosing another public school and special services such as tutoring.

Essentially the legislation created a nationalized school system. Some semblance of local control was maintained by states being able to determine the content of the federally mandated requirement that they establish standards and tests for all public schools. However, state control was compromised by the requirement that every other year a sample of fourth and eighth graders in each state would be required to take national tests administered by the National Assessment of Educational Progress. The results of these national tests would be compared to the tests created by each state. In other words, the National Assessment of Educational Progress tests would have a determining effect on the construction of states' tests. The legislation mandated a schedule, target populations, and reporting procedures for high-stakes testing and academic standards. By 2002–2003, states were required to provide annual report cards containing student achievement scores and test scores by school district. Each school district was required to provide districtwide scores and school-by-school scores. In the same year, school districts were to begin biennial assessments using the National Assessment of Educational Progress tests for fourth- and eighth-grade reading and mathematics. By 2005–2006, each state was required to have academic standards in mathematics, reading or language arts, and science for all public elementary and secondary school children. Also in 2005–2006, all states were required to administer annual statewide tests in reading and mathematics for grades 3 through 8. By 2007–2008, states were required to implement science tests once during elementary, middle, and high school.[55]

With regard to cultural and language issues, No Child Left Behind favored a monolingual and monocultural society as opposed to a multilingual and pluralistic society. The legislation erased the efforts by Native Americans, Mexican Americans, and Puerto Ricans to institute bilingual education in public schools. The efforts to create multicultural school systems were defeated as the new law mandated standardized tests and state standards to regulate the school curriculum to ensure that a single culture would dominate the schools.

In 2001 President George W. Bush and a majority of Congress opposed bilingual education and endorsed the principle that the primary objective of U.S. schools should be teaching English without any major support for preserving minority languages. Reflecting the ongoing culture wars, No Child Left Behind placed the federal government's support on the side of English acquisition, not bilingual education. The part of the legislation titled "English Language Acquisition, Language Enhancement, and Academic Act" changed the name of the federal government's Office of Bilingual Education to Office of English Language Acquisition, Language Enhancement, and Academic Achievement for Limited English Proficient; its shortened name was simply Office of English Language Acquisition. The director of bilingual education and minority language affairs became the director of English language acquisition.

Limited exceptions to the stress on English acquisition were provided for Native Americans and Puerto Ricans. While recognizing programs designed to maintain Native American languages and Spanish, the law mandated that the major thrust of these programs was to be English proficiency. The legislation declared that programs authorized under this part that served Native American (including Native American Pacific Islander) children and children in the Commonwealth of Puerto Rico would include programs ". . . designed for Native American children learning and studying Native American languages and children of limited Spanish proficiency, except that an outcome of programs serving such children *shall be increased English proficiency among such children* [emphasis added]."[56]

The testing requirements of the No Child Left Behind Act conformed to the goal of producing workers to compete in a global economy that was first expressed in the 1983 report *A Nation at Risk.* President George W. Bush provided a global context for his sweeping educational changes, as represented in No Child Left Behind. On the opening page of a 2006 U.S. Department of Education publication with the descriptive title *Answering the Challenge of a Changing World: Strengthening Education for the 21st Century,* President Bush stated,

> We need to encourage children to take more math and science, and to make sure those courses are rigorous enough to compete with other nations. . . . If we ensure that America's children succeed in life, they will ensure that America succeeds in the world. [57]

Was No Child Left Behind a fulfillment of the American educational dream? It certainly embodied some historical ideas associated with the American school,

© *Jason Reed/Reuters/Corbis*

including creating a common culture, providing equal opportunity in the labor market, ensuring that all students would have equal educational opportunity, using standardized testing to control the educational system, treating students as human capital, providing choice and a free market in education, and using education to ensure that America would be a leader in global economic competition.

No Child Left Behind and Religious Conservatives

As part of the compromise between Republicans and Democrats regarding No Child Left Behind, many issues dear to religious conservatives could be found in the legislation. The No Child Left Behind legislation's "Section 9524: School Prayer" commanded,

> The Secretary [U.S. Secretary of Education] shall provide and revise guidance, not later than September 1, 2002, and of every second year thereafter, to State educational agencies, local educational agencies, and the public on *constitutionally protected prayer* in public elementary schools and secondary schools, including making the guidance available on the Internet.[58]

This section of No Child Left Behind was the result of efforts to counter the previously discussed ruling of the U.S. Supreme Court banning official prayers in schools. In 1994, after failing to add an amendment to the U.S. Constitution allowing official prayers in schools, the leading political lobby for conservative Christians, the Christian Coalition, supported an amendment for religious freedom in schools. Leaders of the Christian Coalition hoped that a religious freedom amendment would protect the rights of students to express their religious beliefs in the classroom. In 1996, reflecting what became a compromise position about school prayer, Haley Barbour, chairman of the National Republican Committee, stated that the Republican Party supported the "right to voluntary prayer in schools . . . whether through a constitutional amendment or through legislation, or a combination of both."[59] Unable to achieve an amendment to the U.S. Constitution, religious conservatives saw No Child Left Behind as an opportunity to protect religious freedom. The school prayer section of No Child Left Behind mandated the protection of religious freedom in public schools. The legislation required the U.S. Secretary of Education to issue guidance for protecting constitutionally approved prayer. Dated February 7, 2003, the U.S. Department of Education guide reminded local education agencies that they must report that their schools have "no policy that prevents, or otherwise denies participation in, constitutionally protected prayer in public schools as set forth in this guidance."[60] The guidelines stated,

> Although the Constitution forbids public school officials from directing or favoring prayer, students do not "shed their constitutional rights to freedom of speech or expression at the schoolhouse gate," and the Supreme Court has made clear that "private religious speech, far from being a First Amendment orphan, is as fully protected under the Free Speech Clause as secular private expression." Moreover, not all religious speech that takes place in the public schools or at school-sponsored events is governmental speech. For example, "nothing in the Constitution . . . prohibits any public school student from voluntarily praying at any time before, during, or after the school day," and students may pray with fellow students during the school day on the same terms and conditions that they may engage in other conversation or speech. Likewise, local school authorities possess substantial discretion to impose rules of order and pedagogical restrictions on student activities, but they may not structure or administer such rules to discriminate against student prayer or religious speech.[61]

The 2008 Republican platform restated the No Child Left Behind support of religious freedom in public schools: "We will energetically assert the right of students to engage in voluntary prayer in schools and to have equal access to school facilities for religious purposes."[62]

Religious concerns about homosexuality, pornography, and birth control also appeared in No Child Left Behind. The "Boy Scouts of America Equal Access Act" section of the legislation was in response to a decision in the 1990s by the Boy Scouts to deny membership to homosexuals. In 2000 the U.S. Supreme Court ruled in *Boy Scouts of America v. Dale* that the Boy Scouts were a private association and had the right to set standards for membership and leadership. As a result, school districts across the country banned the Boy Scouts from using school facilities because they discriminated against homosexuals. In the "Boy Scouts of America Equal Access Act" of No Child Left Behind, public schools receiving funds under the legislation were prohibited from denying Boy Scouts use of school facilities. The legislation stated, "Notwithstanding any other provision of law, no public elementary school, public secondary school, local educational agency, or State educational agency that has a designated open forum or a limited public forum and that receives funds made available through the Department shall deny equal access or a fair opportunity to meet to, or discriminate against, any group officially affiliated with the Boy Scouts of America."[63]

Religious conservatives were also concerned about pornography on the World Wide Web and television. In its effort to remove pornography (cyberporn) from the World Wide Web, the Christian Coalition sought the aid of Democrats after Massachusetts Democratic Representative Edward Markey introduced a bill requiring television manufacturers to install "v-chips" to allow parents to block programs with too much violence.[64] Working with a group of Democrats and Republicans, the Christian Coalition claimed major responsibility for writing the 1995 Telecommunications Act requiring censorship of cyberporn and v-chips. The work on the telecommunications bill demonstrated that the Christian Coalition could influence both political parties. Ralph Reed argued that the relationship between evangelical Christians and the Republican Party was strategic. "The two are not one and the same," he stated. "Indeed, the partnership between the profamily movement and the GOP is less a romance than a shotgun wedding."[65]

No Child Left Behind included these concerns in "Title II—Preparing, Training and Recruiting High Quality Teachers and Principals." Title II required schools to have "a policy of Internet safety for minors . . . that protects against access through such computers to visual depictions that are—(i) obscene; (ii) child pornography; or (iii) harmful to minors."[66]

No Child Left Behind also contained prohibitions against using any money granted by the legislation to promote birth control or homosexuality. Section 9526: General Prohibitions specifically stated, "None of the funds authorized under this Act shall be used . . . to develop or distribute materials, or operate programs or courses of instruction directed at youth, that are designed to promote or encourage sexual activity, whether homosexual or heterosexual."[67] Also, funds could not be used "to distribute or to aid in the distribution by any organization of *legally* obscene materials to minors on school grounds [author's emphasis]."[68] In addition, No Child Left Behind promoted abstinence education and banned teaching about birth control by prohibiting funds for "sex education or HIV-prevention education in schools unless that instruction is age appropriate and includes the health benefits of abstinence; or . . . to operate a program of contraceptive distribution in schools."[69]

THE 2008 ELECTION: GLOBAL ECONOMY AND CULTURAL DIVIDE

During the 2008 presidential election, both Democratic candidate Barack Obama and Republican John McCain supported No Child Left Behind to increase America's competitive abilities in the global economy. However, the cultural divide over education between the two political parties continued.

Since the 1980s, Democrats kept repeating their support of education for competition in the global economy. When Democratic President Bill Clinton ran in 1992, the Democratic platform declared, "A competitive American economy requires the global market's best educated, best trained, most flexible work force."[70] Education and the global economy continued as a theme in President Clinton's 1996 reelection: "Today's Democratic Party knows that education is the key to opportunity. In the new global economy, it is more important than ever before. Today, education is the fault line that separates those who will prosper from those who cannot."[71] The 2004 Democratic platform stressed the following points:

- Today, our people compete with workers on every continent. Information flows across oceans.
- High-wage jobs are more dependent than ever on high-level skills.
- Now, as never before, education is the key to opportunity, essential to a strong America.

As mentioned at the beginning of this chapter, during the 2008 campaign President Obama continued to use the rhetoric of education for global competition. The 2008 Democratic platform declared, "Americans made it clear that it is morally and economically unacceptable that our high schoolers continue to score lower on math and science tests than most other students in the world and continue to drop out at higher rates than their peers in other industrialized nations."[72]

Regarding the goals of postsecondary institutions, the platform stated, "We believe that our universities, community colleges, and other institutions of higher learning must foster among their graduates the skills needed to enhance economic competitiveness. We will work with institutions of higher learning to produce highly skilled graduates in science, technology, engineering, and math disciplines who will become innovative workers prepared for the 21st century economy."[73]

The themes of education for a global economy with an emphasis on science and math were stressed by President Obama in his book *The Audacity of Hope: Thoughts on Reclaiming the American Dream.*[74] In advocating government action that would make higher education affordable to Americans, he stated, "In a knowledge-based economy where eight of the nine fast-growing occupations of this decade require scientific or technological skills, most workers are going to need some form of higher education to fill the jobs of the future."[75]

What about the traditional Democratic concern with equal educational opportunity and ending poverty through education? Obviously educating for employment in the global economy might be one way of ending poverty. The 2008 Democrat platform identifies this historic concern in a section titled "Poverty," which declares, "Working together, we can cut poverty in half within ten years. *We will provide all our children a world-class education, from early childhood through college* [author's emphasis]."[76]

In *Audacity of Hope,* President Obama supported universal preschool education because it would have the highest impact on school achievement. He claimed that "we already have hard evidence of reforms that work . . . early childhood education."[77] After being elected in 2008 and before his inauguration as president, he promised to work for a $10 billion federal investment in preschool education. When his transition team was asked if the existing financial problems would force President Obama to cut back on his promised investment in early childhood education, Jen Psaki, a spokeswoman for the his transition team, said, "We simply cannot afford to sideline key priorities like education."[78]

Human capital theories have always had a role in the Democratic Party's support of preschool education. Head Start, the first major federal investment in preschool education, occurred when human capital theories were being used to justify federal investment in education as a means of ending poverty. When President Obama took on the cause of funding preschool education, including Head Start and Early Head Start, he was working within a Democratic legacy dating back to the 1960s. After being elected, President Obama made these remarks referring to preschool studies and linking them to the math and science skills needed for the global economy:

> Studies show that children in early childhood education programs are more likely to score higher in reading and math, more likely to graduate from high school and attend college, more likely to hold a job, and more likely to earn more in that job. For every dollar we invest in these programs, we get nearly $10 back in reduced welfare rolls, fewer health care costs, and less crime. That's why the American Recovery and Reinvestment Act that I signed into law invests $5 billion in growing Early Head Start and Head Start, expanding access to quality child care for 150,000 more children from working families, and doing more for children with special needs. And that's why we are going to offer 55,000 first-time parents regular visits from trained nurses to help make sure their children are healthy and prepare them for school and for life.[79]

President Obama's opponent, Senator John McCain, shared a concern with education making Americans more competitive in the global economy. The 2008 Republican platform echoed Democratic global education goals in titling its education section "Education Means a More Competitive America."[80] The necessity of education for global competition was captured in the opening lines of the platform's education section: "Education is a parental right, a state and local responsibility, and a national strategic interest. Maintaining America's preeminence requires a world-class system of education, with high standards, in which all students can reach their potential."[81]

The 2008 election mirrored the cultural divide between Republicans and Democrats. Unlike the 2008 Democratic platform, the 2008 Republican platform balanced the plea for improved education for global competition with a stress on protecting traditional American values. The 2008 Republican platform contended, "Education is essential to competitiveness, but it is more than just training for the workforce of the future."[82] Why is schooling more than just job training? The 2008 Republican platform stated, "It is through education that we ensure the transmission of a culture, a set of values we hold in common. It has prepared generations for responsible citizenship in a free society, and it must continue to do so."[83] The 2008 Republican platform promised, "Our party is committed to restoring the civic mission of schools envisioned by the founders of the American public school system. Civic education, both in the classroom and through service learning, should be a cornerstone of American public education and should be central to future school reform efforts."[84]

Also, the 2008 Republican platform affirmed its commitment to the English-only movement and its opposition to bilingual education: "To ensure that all students will have access to the mainstream of American life, we support the English First approach and oppose divisive programs that limit students' future potential. All students must be literate in English, our common language, to participate in the promise of America."[85]

The 2008 Republican platform restated the No Child Left Behind support of religious freedom in public schools: "We will energetically assert the right of students to engage in voluntary prayer in schools and to have equal access to school facilities for religious purposes."[86]

There was also the issue of civil rights for homosexuals, which were strongly objected to by religious conservatives. Republicans reacted swiftly when gay and lesbian marriage became an issue in the early twenty-first century. The 2004 Republican platform called for a constitutional amendment that would outlaw gay and lesbian marriages: "We strongly support President Bush's call for a constitutional amendment that fully protects marriage . . . We believe, and the social science confirms, that the well-being of children is best accomplished in the environment of the home, nurtured by their mother and father and anchored by the bonds of marriage."[87] The 2008 Republican platform included a section called "Preserving Traditional Marriage," which opened, "Because our children's future is best preserved within the traditional understanding of marriage, we call for a constitutional amendment that fully protects marriage as a union of a man and a woman . . . In the absence of a national amendment, we support the right of the people of the various states to affirm traditional marriage through state initiatives."[88]

Republicans continued their support of abstinence sex education and their opposition to school instruction about birth control. The 2008 Republican platform stated,

> We renew our call for replacing "family planning" programs for teens with increased funding for abstinence education, which teaches abstinence until marriage as the responsible and expected standard of behavior. Abstinence from sexual activity is the only protection that is 100 percent effective against out-of-wedlock pregnancies and sexually transmitted diseases, including HIV/AIDS when transmitted sexually. We oppose school-based clinics that provide referrals, counseling, and related services for abortion and contraception.[89]

Discussions of education for global competition and differences in cultural values would continue to dominate education discussions while global concern about the environment was neglected by both parties' education platforms. Essentially, education was to support a global consumer society without focusing on its environmental consequences.

GLOBAL CRISIS AND THE DEMISE OF ENVIRONMENTAL EDUCATION

Although the Republican and Democratic agendas in 2008 focused on education for the global economy, there was no mention by any political party leaders of education to prepare students to deal with the world crisis of global warming and resulting climate change. In the 2008 election, the platforms of both major political parties addressed concerns about the environmental crisis but never mentioned environmental education. At the time of this writing there is a historical mystery, which may eventually be explained, of how environmental education disappeared from discussions of national education policies.

National environmental education policies can be traced back to the beginning of the celebration of Earth Day. Launched on April 22, 1970, by U.S. Senator Gaylord Nelson, Earth Day focused on concerns about industrial pollution, global warming, and destruction of water and air quality. According to the Earth Day Network, "Earth Day 1970 achieved a rare political alignment, enlisting support from Republicans and Democrats, rich and poor. . . . The first Earth Day led to the creation of the United States Environmental Protection Agency and the passage of the Clean Air, Clean Water, and Endangered Species acts."[90] Protection of the environment was proclaimed necessary for the protection of human life or, in the words of the Earth Day Network, for "the common good."[91] The annual celebration of Earth Day every April 22 is a "collective expression of public will to create a sustainable society."

Sparked by the Earth Day celebration, Congress passed the National Environmental Education Act. Limited in scope and underfunded, the legislation reflected a radical change in perspective about the relationship of humans to the environment. The act created an Office of Environmental Education within the U.S. Department of Health, Education and Welfare. The Office of Environmental Education distributed curricula, lesson plans, and teacher guides and influenced the inclusion of environmental issues in science textbooks. In the 1980s President Reagan's administration withdrew support from the Office of Environmental Education, causing a decline in its activities. A new National Environmental Education Act was passed in 1990, but little federal money was provided, and local school activities were limited to celebrations of Earth Day and Arbor Day. Interest in environmental education declined again at the turn of the century with the election of President George W. Bush. Nevertheless, despite little federal and state support, environmental issues continued to appear in science and social studies textbooks, and environmentally conscious teachers and students continued to be interested and concerned.[92]

What has been called the "greatest landmark in the history of attempting to define the term 'environmental education'" occurred in 1970 at a joint meeting

© *Creatas/PunchStock*

of IUCN/UNESCO on "Environmental Education in the School Curriculum," held in Carson City, Nevada.[93] The meeting issued what is now called the classic definition of environmental education:

> Environmental education is the process of recognizing values and clarifying concepts in order to develop skills and attitudes necessary to understand and appreciate the inter-relatedness among man, his culture and his biophysical surroundings. Environmental education also entails practice in decision-making and self-formulation of behavior about issues concerning environmental quality.[94]

The current trend in U.S. environmental education is represented by the writings of Chet Bowers and David Orr. Bowers and Orr criticized educational goals based on economic growth. According to Bowers, these ideas are rooted in the Western idea of industrial progress, which considers economic growth and technological development the key to advancing the interests of the human species. Bowers and Orr agreed that most current educational debates assume the same goals and differ only about the best means of achieving them. In discussing these debates, Orr wrote that all sides "agree on the basic aims and purposes of education, which are to equip our nation with a 'world-class' labor force, first, to compete more favorably in the global economy, second, to provide everyone with the means for maximum upward mobility."[95] The industrial ideal, Orr argued, has turned all levels of schooling into knowledge factories and has corrupted universities through a "marriage between the academy and the worlds of power and commerce."[96] Bowers agreed with this assessment of current educational debates and asserted that even so-called educational radicals share the same "cultural assumptions . . . with the elites they criticize."[97] Chet Bowers identified the assumptions of the industrial paradigm as "viewing change as progressive in nature, intelligence and creativity as attributes of the autonomous individual, science and technology as the source of empowerment, and the commodification of all areas as the highest expression of human development."[98]

Orr saw the industrial paradigm as part of the hidden curriculum of modern schooling. He argued, "We will have to challenge the hubris buried in the hidden curriculum that says that human domination of nature is good; that the growth of economy is natural; that all knowledge, regardless of its consequences, is equally valuable; and that material progress is our right."[99] Another part of the hidden curriculum, according to Orr, teaches that technological development is a good thing and that it defines the meaning of progress. Orr stated, "True believers [in technology] describe progress to mean not human, political, or cultural improvement but a mindless, uncontrollable, technological juggernaut erasing ecologies and cultures as it moves through history."[100] The question that must be asked, he argued, is whether or not technology is improving human well-being.

Both educators agreed that the industrial paradigm causes social injustice rather than providing a just social and economic system. Their arguments were based on the internal problems within the industrial paradigm and on the destructiveness of that paradigm to the biosphere. For instance, the industrial paradigm promises that schooling will provide equal opportunity for all people to achieve wealth. Bowers asserted, "Educational institutions perpetuate the further creation of wealth at the top rather than nurturing at the grassroots level both material and social forms of wealth."[101] The primary result of the present paradigm governing educational discussions is to ensure that rich people within nations get richer and that rich nations increase their total wealth in relation to poorer nations.

The industrial paradigm fosters social injustice by ignoring the limited availability of natural resources and the potential industrial destruction of the biosphere. These two factors guarantee that the distribution of consumer wealth will be limited in the biosphere. Wealth in the industrial paradigm is measured by the consumption of products. In claiming to provide equal opportunity, schools are promising an equal opportunity to consume. Bowers noted that most often missing from lists "of educational goals are skills and knowledge needed for leading less commodified lives."[102] The result is a process of schooling that implants an acceptance of the industrial paradigm in each student and misguides students into thinking that everyone on the planet will eventually have an equal opportunity to consume.

But the rejection of the industrial paradigm also questions the global economy for which students are being educated. Is this the reason for neglect of environmental education in major national education policies? Were schools viewed by national political leaders as sources for workers and consumers but not as sources for environmental activists? Was this the blind spot in national education policies in the early twenty-first century?

CONCLUSION: FROM HORACE MANN TO BARACK OBAMA

By the time of the Obama administration, the American school was dedicated to the economic goal of educating workers to compete in the global economy. How was this different from the past? When Horace Mann led the common school in the 1830s and 1840s, he emphasized the goal of reducing class warfare by providing through schools equal opportunity to compete in the labor market. Also, Mann hoped to create a common social and political culture to stabilize the nation. With urbanization and massive immigration at the end of the nineteenth century, the schools expanded their role in providing equal opportunity through vocational education, vocational counseling, tracking students into separate curricula, and standardized testing. Efforts to create a common social and political culture expanded the schools as a welfare agency by turning schools into social centers, Americanizing diets in the school cafeteria, instituting Americanization programs, and developing a common school spirit through extracurricular activities. This common school spirit was supposed to be carried into the national arena. In addition to these functions, concerns about the welfare of the student and community led to the introduction of kindergartens, playgrounds, school nurses and health facilities, school showers, and after-school student and adult activities.

From the 1920s through the 1950s, the major cultural issue for schools was the threat of political radicalism. During this period, schools were purged of teachers and textbooks that some thought threatened the American way of life; and schools tried to create in student minds an image of the American way of life that included an inseparable relationship between capitalism and democracy, while neglecting to mention the existence of social democracies. Part of the American way of life was educating, as it was called in the 1950s, the consumer–citizen.

From the 1930s into the 1960s, equal opportunity through schooling was linked to national manpower needs. In the 1930s the problem was youth unemployment, which led to federal government intervention to keep youths out of the labor market through public works projects. After World War II, concerns about unemployment among veterans led to the passage of the GI Bill. In addition, the Selective Service Act was designed to channel national manpower into occupations needed to win the Cold War. The founding of the Educational Testing Service and its national college entrance exam, the Scholastic Aptitude Test (SAT), marked the modern age of testing students as a means of sorting national manpower.

Horace Mann promised that the common school and equal opportunity would end poverty. However, racial and economic school segregation made it impossible to provide equal opportunity through schooling. Horace Mann's quest for economic justice reverberated through the 1960s War on Poverty and its resulting federal programs and legislation, such as Head Start and the compensatory education programs supported by the Elementary and Secondary Education Act. The War on Poverty occurred while the idea of a common culture seemed be abandoned for multicultural and bilingual education.

The No Child Left Behind Act of 2001 set the agenda for equality of educational opportunity and creating a national culture. No Child Left Behind was passed against a background of concern about U.S. competition in global markets. Equal opportunity was important because it would give America a competitive advantage but ensure that the talents of students were matched to employment requirements.

Equal opportunity was to be achieved under No Child Left Behind through nationalizing the school system by requiring each state to adopt uniform curriculum standards and to measure student achievement with standardized testing. Under this legislation equal educational opportunity meant that every student in a state would be taught the same curriculum and tested with the same standardized tests. In other words, *equality* was translated into equal exposure to a uniform curriculum and uniform tests.

What about the issue of the common school promoting a national culture? Under No Child Left Behind, the culture taught in schools would be the culture embodied in state curriculum standards and testing. In other words, all students would be exposed to the same cultural instruction, thus contributing to development of a national culture.

The Obama administration supported the concept of equality and culture embodied in No Child Left Behind. In 2009 the Obama administration added another element to nationalizing the school system when President Obama's economic stimulus package required a national data system to record student test scores and to track student progress through the educational system. The data system would supposedly identify good teachers and college training programs. U.S. Secretary of Education Arne Duncan explained what he considered to be the importance of this data system:

> We need comprehensive data systems that do three things. One, track students throughout their educational trajectory. Secondly, track students back to teachers so we can really shine a spotlight on those teachers that are doing a phenomenal job of driving student achievement. And third, track teachers back to their schools of education so . . . over time we'll really understand which schools of education are adding value with their graduates.[103]

The proposal for national data collection would seem to link the Obama administration to efforts at scientific management of schools and students originating in the early twentieth century. What was lacking in this earlier time were computers that could process national education data. In the twenty-first century this was no longer the case. The Obama administration seemed to have a technocratic view of the educational system and seemed to believe that it could be engineered. This implied a view that schools would now be, among other things, data collection centers with students being reduced to statistical data.

Notes

1. National Commission on Excellence in Education, *A Nation at Risk: The Imperatives for Educational Reform* (Washington, DC: Department of Education, 1983), p. 5.
2. Ibid., p. 5.
3. Ibid., p. 5.
4. Democratic National Convention Committee, "Report of the Platform Committee: Renewing America's Promise." Presented to the 2008 Democratic National Convention on August 13, 2008, p. 18. Retrieved from the American Presidency Project Document Archive at http://www.presidency.ucsb.edu/papers_pdf/78283.pdf on November 13, 2008.
5. See Louis Fischer et al., *Teachers and the Law* (White Plains, NY: Longman, 1990).
6. "Quoting Marland," *American Education* 7 (January–February 1971), p. 4.
7. Sidney P. Marland Jr., "The Condition of Education in the Nation," *American Education* 7 (April 1971), p. 4.
8. Quoted in Robert M. Worthington, "A Home-Community Based Career Education Model," *Educational Leadership* 30 (December 1972), p. 213.
9. Sidney P. Marland Jr., "The School's Role in Career Development," *Educational Leadership* 30 (December 1972), pp. 203–205.
10. Sidney P. Marland Jr., "Career Education and the Two-Year Colleges," *American Education* 8 (March 1972), p. 11.
11. Republican Party Platform of 1972 (August 21, 1972), p. 14. Retrieved from the American Presidency Project Document Archive at http://www.presidency.ucsb.edu/ws/index.php?pid=25842 on January 5, 2009.
12. Ibid, p. 14.
13. Democratic Party Platform of 1972: New Directions: 1972–76 (July 10, 1972), p. 48. Retrieved from the American Presidency Project Document Archive at http://www.presidency.ucsb.edu/ws/?pid=29605 on January 5, 2009.
14. Leon Lessinger, *Every Kid a Winner: Accountability in Education* (New York: Simon & Schuster, 1970).

15. Task Force on Education for Economic Growth, *Action for Excellence* (Denver: Education Commission of the States, 1983), pp. 3, 6–7, 18.

16. John E. Yang, "Bush Unveils Education Plan: States, Communities Would Play Major Role in Proposed Innovations," Compuserve Executive News Services, *Washington Post* (April 19, 1991).

17. "Text of Statement on Education Goals Adopted by Governors," *Education Week* (March 7, 1990), p. 16.

18. Mark Pitsch, "Stage Set for Senate Showdown on Goals 2000," *Education Week* (March 30, 1994), p. 16.

19. Ibid.

20. John E. Chubb and Terry Moe, *Politics, Markets and America's Schools* (Washington, DC: Brookings Institution, 1990).

21. Amy Wells, "Milwaukee Parents Get More Choice on Schools," *The New York Times* (March 28, 1990), p. B9.

22. Lynn Olsen, "A Matter of Choice: Minn. Puts 'Charter Schools' Idea to Test," *Education Week* (November 25, 1992), pp. 1, 10; Lynn Olsen, "Claims for Choice Exceed Evidence, Carnegie Reports," *Education Week* (October 28, 1992), pp. 1, 12; and Lynn Olsen, "Open-Enrollment Survey Finds Modest Effects in Minn.," *Education Week* (November 4, 1992), p. 5.

23. James Traub, "Has Benno Schmidt Learned His Lesson?" *New York* (October 31, 1994), pp. 51–59.

24. Ibid.

24. Lynn Olsen, "Varied Laws Raise a Question: What Is a Charter School?" *Education Week* (January 19, 1994), p. 14.

25. Alex Molnar, *Giving Kids the Business: The Commercialization of America's Schools* (Boulder: Westview Press, 1996).

26. Constance L. Hays, "New Report Examines Commercialism in U.S. Schools," *New York Times on the Web* (September 14, 2000).

27. Ibid.

28. Lynne Schrum, *Education and Commercialization: Raising Awareness and Making Decisions* (Athens: University of Georgia, College of Education, 2002), p. 5.

29. Coby B. Simerly, Penny A. Ralston, Lydia Harriman, and Barbara Taylor, "The Scottsdale Initiative: Positioning the Progression for the Twenty-First Century," in *Themes in Family and Consumer Sciences: A Book of Readings, 2001,* vol. 2, eds. Coby B. Simerly, Sharon Y. Nickols, and Jan M. Shane (Alexandria, VA: American Association of Family and Consumer Sciences, 2001), p. 15.

30. "Our Mission," http://www.cwu.edu/~fandcs/fcsea.

31. Marilyn R. DeLong, "Apparel Shopping on the Web," in Simerly et al., *Themes in Family and Consumer Sciences,* pp. 109–113.

32. "About FCSEA," http://www.cwu.edu/~fandcs/fcsea.

33. "National Standards for Family and Consumer Sciences Education," http://www.isbe.net/secondaryed/FCS/fcs.htm.

34. Ibid.

35. Ibid.

36. Ibid.

37. Eric Schlosser, *Fast Food Nation: The Dark Side of the All-American Meal* (New York: Houghton Mifflin Company, 2001), p. 41.

38. Ibid., p. 48.

39. Ibid., p. 47.

40. Schlosser, p. 22.

41. "Burger King Big Kids," http://www.burgerking.com.
42. "BK Academies," http:www.burgerking.com.
43. "BK Scholars," http://www.burgerking.com.
44. "Welcome to YUM!," http://www.yum.com/home.asp.
45. "The Pizza Hut Story," http://www.pizzahut.com, p. 6.
46. "Taco Bell History," http://www.tacobell.com.
47. "Discovery Science Center," http://www.discoverycube.org.
48. "TEEN SUPREME," http://www.teensupreme.org/main.html.
49. "Pizza Hut Story," p. 4.
50. Ibid., p. 3.
51. "Pizza Hut News: Facts about Book It! and Book It! Beginners," http://www.pizzahut.com.
52. "About KFC: The Story of Colonel Harland Sanders," http://www.kfc.com.
53. "Nation's First Colonel's Kids Child Care Center Opens August 4, 2001!" http://www.colonelskids.com.
54. "Colonel's Kids Charity—The Child Care Issue," http://www.colonelskids.com.
55. Public Law 107–110, 107th Congress, Jan. 8, 2002 [H.R. 1], "No Child Left Behind Act of 2001" (Washington, DC: U.S. Government Printing Office, 2002). For a political history of No Child Left Behind, see Patrick J. McGuin, *No Child Left Behind and the Transformation of Federal Education Policy, 1965–2005* (Lawrence: University of Kansas Press, 2006).
56. Ibid.
57. U.S. Department of Education, *Answering the Challenge of a Changing World: Strengthening Education for the 21st Century* (Washington, DC: U.S. Department of Education, 2006), p. 1.
58. "No Child Left Behind Act of 2001," pp. 556–557.
59. Haley Barbour, *Agenda for America: A Republican Direction for the Future* (Washington, DC: Regnery, 1996), p. 159.
60. U.S. Department of Education, "Guidance on Constitutionally Protected Prayer in Public Elementary and Secondary Schools (February 7, 2003)." Retrieved from http://www.ed.gov/policy/gen/guid/religionandschools/prayer_guidance.html on March 7, 2003.
61. Ibid.
62. Republican Party Platform of 2008, p. 44–45. Retrieved from the American Presidency Project Document Archive at http://www.presidency.ucsb.edu/papers_pdf/78545.pdf on February 10, 2009.
63. "No Child Left Behind Act of 2001," p. 557.
64. Ralph Reed, *Active Faith: How Christians Are Changing the Soul of American Politics* (New York: Free Press, 1996), pp. 229–231.
65. Ibid., p. 234.
66. "No Child Left Behind Act of 2001," p. 262.
67. Ibid., p. 558.
68. Ibid., p. 558.
69. Ibid., p. 558.
70. Democratic Party Platform of 1992: A New Covenant with the American People (July 13, 1992), p. 5. Retrieved from the American Presidency Project Document Archive at http://www.presidency.ucsb.edu/ws/index.php?pid=pid29610 on January 5, 2009.
71. Democratic Party Platform of 1996: Today's Democratic Party: Meeting America's Challenges, Protecting America's Values (August 26, 1996), p. 5. Retrieved from the American Presidency Project Document Archive at http://www.presidency.ucsb.edu/ws/print.php?pid=29612 on January 8, 2009.

72. Democratic National Convention Committee, "Report of the Platform Committee: Renewing America's Promise," Presented to the 2008 Democratic National Convention August 13, 2008, p. 18. Retrieved from the American Presidency Project Document Archive http://www.presidency.ucsb.edu/papers_pdf/78283.pdf on November 13, 2008.
73. Ibid., p. 20.
74. Barack Obama, *The Audacity of Hope: Thoughts on Reclaiming the American Dream* (New York: Vintage Books, 2006).
75. Ibid., p. 194.
76. Democratic Party Platform of 2008 . . . , p. 15.
77. Obama, *Audacity of Hope,* p. 191.
78. Sam Dillon, "Obama's $10 Billion Promise Stirs Hope in Early Education (December 17, 2008). Retrieved from http://www.nytimes.com on December 17, 2008.
79. "Remarks by the President to the Hispanic Chamber of Commerce on a Complete and Competitive American Education (March 10, 2009)." Retrieved from http://www.whitehouse.gov/the_press_office/Remarks-of-the-President-to-the-Hispanic-Chamber-of-Commerce/ on March 10, 2009.
80. Republican Party Platform of 2008, p. 43.
81. Ibid., p. 43.
82. Republican Party Platform of 2008, p. 43.
83. Ibid.
84. Ibid.
85. Ibid., p. 44.
86. Ibid., pp. 44–45.
87. Republican Party Platform of 2004. Retrieved from http://www.presidency.ucsb.edu/ws/index.php?pid=25850 on March 1, 2009
88. Republican Platform of 2008, p. 53.
89. Ibid., p. 45.
90. "How It All Began," http://www.earthday.net/about/history.stm.
91. "Earth Day—Making a Difference," http://www.earthday.net/about/difference.stm.
92. John F. Disinger, "The United States of America," in *Environmental Education in the Twenty-First Century: Theory, Practice, Progress and Promise,* ed. Joy Palmer (New York: Routledge, 1998), pp. 225–227.
93. Joy A. Palmer, *Environmental Education in the Twenty-First Century* (London: Routledge, 1998), p. 6.
94. Ibid., p. 7.
95. David W. Orr, *Earth in Mind: On Education, Environment, and the Human Prospect* (Washington, DC: Island Press, 1994), p. 26.
96. Ibid., p. 29.
97. C. A. Bowers, *Educating for Eco-Justice and Community* (Athens: University of Georgia Press, 2001), p. 17.
98. C. A. Bowers, "Changing the Dominant Cultural Perspective in Education," in *Ecological Education in Action,* eds. Gregory A. Smith and Dilafruz R. Williams (Albany: State University of New York Press, 1999), p. 162.
99. Orr, *Earth in Mind,* p. 32.
100. Ibid., p. 33.
101. Bowers, *Educating for Eco-Justice,* p. 13.
102. Ibid., p. 13.
103. "Duncan Underlines Top Federal Education Priorities," *Education Week* (April 1, 2009), p. 21.

Index

Information in figures and tables is indicated with *f* and *t*.